THE
LIVES
OF
JOHN LENNON

Books by Albert Goldman

Wagner on Music and Drama
(co-editor with Everett Sprinchorn)

The Mine and the Mint:
Sources for the Writings of Thomas De Quincey

Freakshow

Ladies and Gentlemen—LENNY BRUCE!!!

Carnival in Rio

Grass Roots: Marijuana in America Today

Disco

Elvis

The Lives of John Lennon

THE
LIVES
OF
JOHN LENNON

ALBERT GOLDMAN

WILLIAM MORROW AND COMPANY, INC.
NEW YORK

Grateful acknowledgment is made to the authors, publishers, and other copyright holders for permission to reprint previously published materials from:

THE BEATLES by Hunter Davies. Copyright © 1969 by Hunter Davies. Reprinted by permission of Curtis Brown Associates, Ltd.

THE PLAYBOY INTERVIEWS WITH JOHN LENNON & YOKO ONO by David Sheff. Copyright © 1981 by Playboy Press. Reprinted by permission of The Berkley Publishing Group.

YOU DON'T HAVE TO SAY YOU LOVE ME by Simon Napier-Bell. Copyright © 1982 by New English Library. Reprinted by permission of Simon Napier-Bell.

COME TOGETHER: JOHN LENNON IN HIS TIME by John Wiener. Copyright © 1984. Reprinted by permission of Random House, Inc.

LOVING JOHN by May Pang and Henry Edwards. Copyright © 1983 by Warner Books, Inc. Reprinted by permission of Warner Books, Inc.

JOHN LENNON IN MY LIFE
Copyright © 1983 by Pete Shotton and Nicholas Schaffner
Reprinted with permission of Stein and Day Publishers

DAKOTA DAYS by John Green. Copyright © 1983 by St. Martin's Press, Inc. Reprinted by permission of St. Martin's Press, Inc.

JOHN LENNON, 1940–1980 by Ray Connolly. Copyright © 1981 by Fontana Books. Reprinted by permission of A. D. Peters & Co., Ltd.

UP AND DOWN WITH THE ROLLING STONES by Tony Sanchez. Copyright © 1979 by William Morrow & Company, Inc. Reprinted by permission of Writers House, Inc.

JOHN LENNON: FOR THE RECORD by Peter McCabe and Robert D. Schonfeld. Copyright © 1984 by Peter McCabe and Robert D. Schonfeld. Reprinted by permission of Bantam Books. All rights reserved.

THE CONTINUUM CONCEPT by Jean Liedloff. Copyright © 1986 by Addison-Wesley Publishing Co. Inc. Reprinted by permission of Jean Liedloff.

Library of Congress Cataloging-in-Publication Data

Goldman, Albert Harry, 1927–
The lives of John Lennon.

Bibliography: p.
Includes index.
1. Lennon, John, 1940–   . 2. Rock musicians—
England—Biography.   I. Title.
ML420.L38G6   1988   784.5′4′00924 [B]   88-8986
ISBN 0-688-04721-1

Printed in the United States of America

First Edition

1 2 3 4 5 6 7 8 9 10

BOOK DESIGN BY M 'N O PRODUCTION SERVICES, INC.

FOR MAX PALEVSKY

CONTENTS

Contents

WAKE-UP TASTE

Like a Zen arrow flying through the night, Kit Carter comes winging up Central Park West in the predawn darkness of a December morning in 1979. When he reaches the intersection with 72nd Street, he glances up at the Dakota, glimmering dimly in the light of a solitary streetlamp, like a ghostly German castle. Darting across the street to the iron portcullis guarding the tunnel-like carriage entrance, he gives the night bell a short, sharp jab. Shuffling restlessly in the chill wind off the park, he waits for the doorman to emerge from the wood-and-glass windbreak surrounding the building's recessed entrance. As soon as the gate lock is snapped, Kit slips through and bounds up the steps to the concierge's office, where he exchanges a perfunctory nod with the night man before plunging into the maze of passageways that leads to the tall oak door of Studio One, the office of Yoko Ono.

Lightly he raps. Instantly he is answered by the metallic snap of the dead bolt. As the towering wooden leaf swings open, there stands little Yoko, her face masked by black wraparound shades. While Kit notes how ill she looks—and that she's dressed in the same black shirt and jeans that she's worn all week—she reaches up like a cat and snatches out of his hand a packet of tinfoil. Ducking into her private bathroom, she slams the door and turns on the faucets full blast. As Kit removes his shoes, preparatory to entering the back office, he hears above the rush of water a series of loud snorts, followed by the hideous noise of retching.

Yoko's retreat is sumptuous and eerie. Concealed lights shine up from the thick white carpet, casting shadows on the cloud-bedecked ceiling and reflections on the smoked-glass mirrors that rise from the waist-high oak wainscoting. An immense Egyptian revival desk stands catercorner to the shaded windows on the courtyard, its gleaming mahogany sides inlaid with large ivory reliefs of the ibis-headed Thoth, god of scribes, and the winged disk-and-cobra symbol of the sun.

11

Yoko's commanding seat is an exact replica of the throne found in King Tutankhamen's tomb.

As Kit sinks into the creamy white leather couch, he stares at the objects that give the room its magical air: the gray little skull between the two white Princess phones, the Egyptian baby's gold breastplate, the bronze snake slithering along the crossbar of the coffee table by Giacometti. This is the sixth week since he began making these deliveries, but he still thinks about the first time

He had been so frightened that he had brought the heroin in a hollowed-out book wrapped in brown paper. Yoko he found sitting behind the accountant Richie DePalma's desk in the outer office, talking on the phone in Japanese. For five long minutes she continued to jabber away, as unconcerned as if she were holding a delivery boy from the pharmacy. Finally, she hung up and said nonchalantly: "Oh, hi! You're Kit!" Extending her hand, she took his package, dismissing him without another word or look. Later he learned that she had been intensely curious about him, but it was her practice in such situations to feign indifference.

Initially, he made his deliveries once or twice a week. The night before he would pick up the stuff from a 57th Street jeweler, who was the connection. At first a gram of H cost $500, but as soon as Yoko started running up her habit, the price increased. Now Kit is paying $750 for that same little gram, which means that Yoko has got herself a $5,000-a-week habit. A street junkie could score that much smack for a quarter of what Yoko is paying, but she doesn't care. Why should she? John Lennon is a rich man.

By the time Yoko rejoins Kit, she's walking like La Sonnambula, trying to appear cool and casual, but betrayed by the faint traces of white powder about her nostrils. She's bearing, as usual, a tray with two turquoise cups in which Lipton's teabags are steeping. Kit was puzzled at first by Yoko's insistence on serving tea every time he made a drop. Then he realized that a highborn Japanese lady can't score her wake-up taste like a common junkie. She has to save face by masking the sordid transaction with a gracious ceremony.

"How are you today?" inquires Yoko politely, as if she were laying eyes on Kit for the first time that morning. "I can see you're miserable," she continues before he can answer. She lights and puffs once on a brown Nat Sherman, before waving it from her mouth with a theatrical gesture. "We're all miserable!" she intones in her drowsy, singsong voice, adding, as if offering the clincher, "*I'm* miserable!" Then, without a trace of irony, she quotes Woody Allen as if he were Confucius: "There are two states in which we live—miserable and horrible." A long silence signals that the topic is closed.

As Yoko and Kit take their tea, the plant lights, controlled by an unpredictable timer, suddenly brighten. Instinctively Kit flinches, expecting to hear a tough voice bark, *"Freeze! This is a bust!"*

Once the demands of Oriental decorum have been satisfied, Yoko rises deliberately and sleepwalks to her massive desk, banging it in passing with her hip. She opens a drawer and removes her antique bag. Snapping its top, she hauls out a huge wad of $100 bills. Counting off eight mint-fresh notes, she hands them wordlessly to Kit. (He always receives a $50 tip.) Before he can turn to leave, Yoko seats herself upon her throne. Fixing him with an imperious look cast through her dark Porsche goggles, she warns, "John must never know."

John Lennon comes to consciousness before dawn in a pool of light cast by two spots above the polished dark wood of his church-pew headboard. These lights are never extinguished because John has a horror of waking in a dark bedroom. Darkness to him is death. The first thing he looks for with his feeble eyes are the fuzzy red reflections in the big oval mirror above his bed. These smudges assure him that his life-support system is working, for night and day he lives buffered by its soothing sounds and flickering images, like a patient in a quiet room.

So faintly does the rhythm of the day beat in this secluded chamber that only John's internal clock can wake him. No sounds from the streets below penetrate the enormously thick walls of this century-old building, whose floors are packed with tons of soil from the excavation of Central Park. Daylight is barred by the dark wooden shutters and clumsily hung fabric that seal the big window looking down seven stories to 72nd Street and across the park to the towers of midtown Manhattan. As shadowy as an attic, the room is filled with lumber: an old wicker chair, an Art Deco vanity, cardboard cartons, stacks of discarded newspapers and magazines, an upright piano with its lid closed. Even the futuristic red guitar suspended above the bed testifies dustily to desuetude. If it were not for the sighing sounds of the speakers over John's head and the colored flickering of the two big TV sets at his feet, this dark chamber with its narrow spill of artificial light could be a tomb.

Lennon has confined himself to this room for the past three years. Save for summer holidays in Japan, he rarely leaves his queen-size bed, to which he clings like a sailor aboard a life raft. Much of the time he sleeps, perhaps half the day, in two- to four-hour spells. The balance of the day he spends sitting in the lotus position, his head enveloped in a cloud of tobacco or marijuana smoke, reading, meditating, or listening to tapes, including self-hypnosis cassettes with titles like *I Love My Body* or *There's No Need to Be Angry*. Sometimes he makes an entry in his log, a *New Yorker* diary with a cartoon on every page, which he may redraw or retitle. Everything he prizes most—his drugs, his manuscripts, girlie mags, his British harmonica—he keeps at the foot of the bed in a little domed chest blazoned LIVERPOOL. His raft is rigged with excellent communications gear, all the controls lying convenient to his right hand in a white Formica cabinet. With an endless supply of books and cassettes, records and videotapes, he has everything he requires for journeys that take him not only to the ends of the earth but back through the roll call of civilizations and forward through space into the world of the future.

Though he is lying in the bosom of his family, John could not be much more removed from them even if he spent his life out on the road. The only times he sees them are for an hour or two in the morning and during supper and a little thereafter, when Daddy, as he likes to call himself, watches TV with his little boy, Sean. All the rest of the day Lennon is back here in his room, alone and silent.

Lennon's only companions aboard his raft are his three cats, Sasha, Misha, and Charo, owl-faced, yellow-eyed, black-haired Persians. When he makes out his list of chores every morning, the needs of the cats stand first. If one of them appears to be missing, John will sound an alarm on the intercom to the kitchen, and the maids will start scouring the halls, even knocking on the neighbors' doors. Though averse to any kind of physical effort, John loves to cut into tiny morsels the cats' prime beef and costly liver and to groom their gleaming coats with his array of combs, brushes, and clippers. The other members of the household dislike these animals because they foul the rooms with their hair and excrement, but John insists that his pets be treated as if they lived in ancient Egypt.

To satisfy his need to play a part in the family's life, John has cast himself in the role of "househusband." He and Yoko have exchanged sexual stereotypes, with her becoming the breadwinner and he the bread baker. Yoko has sustained her part with grim determination, spending her whole life pent up in her office. John's role is largely fantasy. He did try his hand once at baking bread, but what he really wanted to pop out of the oven was a tray of hash brownies. Given his druthers, John would pig out on junk food—Burger King Whoppers; gooey, tangy slices of pizza; huge, one-pound Hershey bars. But what he's done for most of his adult life is starve himself to perfection. Far from being a bread baker or even a hearty eater, John Lennon is a hunger artist.

The onset of his anorexia can be traced back to the year 1965, when some fool described him in print as the "fat Beatle." That phrase struck such a blow to his fragile ego that the wound has never healed. Now, at thirty-nine, his supreme goal in life is to recover the body image he presented at nineteen. Volumes could be filled with the history of his punishing diets, dangerous fasts, and self-lacerating attacks of guilt over that extra cup of coffee or slice of toast. He's forever reading the kind of book that admonishes: "Success is ours when we can smilingly make a meal off ten carefully counted beans flavored with slices of preserved radish." An instinctive ascetic, John can deny the flesh anything but coffee and cigarettes. His addiction to these legal substances has cost him far more worry than his habitual use of virtually every drug listed in Schedule I. Nowadays, to be sure, he has relented a bit in his war on food. He will take a couple of bites of fish or chicken with his brown rice and boiled vegetables. But he still runs a string around his waist every morning on arising, and if he sins by eating something forbidden, he will duck into the bathroom and stick a finger down his throat.

As he slips out of bed now to perform his yoga limbering exercises, he displays the bag-of-bones body of an Indian fakir. His arms are clay pipe stems, not just skinny but so devoid of muscle that when he picks up a hollow-bodied guitar, he complains of its weight. You could pour a cup of water into the hollows of his collarbones. His once-shapely legs resemble the stalks of wading birds. He's pale, naturally, because he never goes out in the sun, but what is strange about his skin is the way it glows. This unnatural sheen is produced by bathing a dozen times a day and washing his face and hands twice as often.

He shrinks from contact with either flesh or fabric, rarely wearing clothing, apart from a pair of backless slippers. If he spies a few of his wife's long, coarse black hairs on the pure white carpeting that covers the entire flat, he will summon the maid to remove the offensive threads. Sometimes in Yoko's presence, he will tilt up his nose, sniff delicately, and then, registering an expression of disgust on his face, turn and leave the room. As a rule he avoids touching anyone. If in a rare access of parental affection he takes Sean on his knee, John will make sure to seat the child facing away from him so that the boy will not have the opportunity to plant a wet, smacky kiss on his father's face.

As John ducks into his surgically clean bathroom, whose big old-fashioned tub only he is permitted to scrub, the image he presents to the mirror is startling. No wonder that on those infrequent occasions when he slips out the side of the building and walks down 72nd Street to buy a paper, nobody ever recognizes him. John Lennon no longer resembles himself. His trademark granny glasses have long since disappeared, replaced by ordinary plastic specs with blue-tinted lenses to shield his weak, hooded eyes, so sensitive to light that he complains of the glare from the tiny bulbs on the Christmas tree. The famous Lennon nose is still prominent, but it has caved in so badly along the sides that it resembles now the proboscis of a strange bird. The rest of his face is concealed by an ugly, scraggly, untrimmed beard and a wispy mustache. His hair has grown so long that he wears it in a ponytail that he secures with a barrette embellished by a tiny Barbie or Ken doll. John claims that he resembles Prince Myshkin in *The Idiot*, the Christ-like epileptic hero who screams so violently when he throws a fit that his would-be assassin drops his knife and flees in terror. In truth, Lennon looks less like a prince than an old beachcomber.

As soon as John has satisfied himself that he is perfectly clean, he clacks through the curtain of white beads, made by the ancient Tairona Indians of Colombia, that Yoko purchased for $65,000 to guard the bedroom against the intrusion of evil spirits. Turning a corner, he opens the door that leads from his room into the long, tunnel-like central corridor. Striding along with his jerky, pigeon-toed gait, he passes a series of lofty white chambers that offer panoramic views of Central Park: past the White Room, furnished with white overstuffed furniture and the white piano from *Imagine;* past the Pyramid Room, filled with Egyptian antiquities, including a gilded sarcophagus containing a 3,000-year-old mummy; past the Black Room, with its ebony-finished furnishings, where John was quarantined for six months after *l'affaire Pang;* past the Library, which offers an amusing confrontation between Yoko's black lacquer Shinto altar and John's collection of girlie mags and pornographic books; past the Playroom, facing the rear courtyard, whose ambiance is signaled by yards of butcher paper affixed to the hallway walls, bearing the exuberant crayon and watercolor daubings of Sean and his playmates, until at last he reaches the northernmost room, the Nursery, where Sean (if he has not crept into bed with Daddy) will still be sound asleep in the arms of his nanny, Yoko having spent the night in her office, calling overseas or catnapping on her mink-upholstered Napoleonic camp bed.

Turning sharply to the left, John flips on the tracklights of the kitchen, illuminating a space as large as a loft, divided into separate areas for work and recreation: first, a home entertainment center, stacked with the latest audio-visual gear and stocked with thousands of LPs massed on fifteen-foot shelves; then a lounge, with a pair of sofas facing across a cocktail table and a desk set against the opposite wall for Yoko beside a door that opens upon a full bath; and finally, the kitchen proper, lined along both sides with appliances and white Formica counters and shelves. Filling the kettle and settling it on the hooded restaurant range, John struggles to catch the pilot light, a trick he has never quite mastered. As the water heats, he examines carefully the open shelves, searching for foods that are on his index expurgatorius, which includes the vast majority of things that people eat. If he discovers a substance that is forbidden, he will hurl it into the garbage can with a snarled curse. The cook is always complaining that when she reaches for an ingredient, she can never be sure that she will find it.

When his tea is ready, John settles himself at the butcher-block table set before the big arched window that overlooks the central courtyard. Taking his ease in a yellow cushioned canvas-backed director's chair, he luxuriates in the serenity of the hour before dawn. Breakfast is his favorite meal and he celebrates it ritually by eating invariably the same foods: Nabisco shredded wheat and honey bran biscuits smeared with Hain's orange marmalade. Though violently opposed to sugar (which gives you *"the sugar blues,"* according to a book he lays on people like a religious tract), John consumes marmalade by the case. The same irrationality appeared for years in his even more immoderate consumption of tea. He drank nothing but Red Zinger under the illusion that it contained no caffeine. When he learned that this hippie favorite did contain the dread stimulant, he switched to a staid English brand—but he didn't stop drinking twenty to thirty cups of tea or coffee a day.

Once his small appetite has been sated and a filter-tipped Gitane is fuming between his long, tobacco-stained fingers, he takes a felt-tip pen and a slip of paper out of the table drawer. Printing laboriously in block letters, he makes up his daily list of personal needs. Because he spends his life in bed, John can fulfill his desires only through an agent, someone who goes out into the world to do his bidding. His morning list may run to ten or twelve items, ranging from a TV channel that isn't coming through clearly to a new book he wants to read to a staple that's running low, like Meow Mix. Some of the items are accompanied by stinging comments, signaling John's displeasure with the way this order was filled last time. When he's finished, he puts his note on the counter for his assistant, Fred Seaman.

The Seaman family has been associated with Yoko Ono for nearly thirty years. Fred's uncle Norman Seaman, a small-time concert promoter, was Yoko's first manager, back in 1960, when she was just starting out as a performance artist; Norman's wife, Helen, is Sean's nanny. (In the Lennon family constellation, Norman and Helen sustain the roles of Sean's grandparents.) Young Fred, blond and handsome, the son of an American concert pianist and a German woman, was educated alternately in Europe and the United States. Fresh out of City College, where he took a degree in journalism, he has been working for John almost a year, plying back and forth between his desk in Studio One and the bedroom or driving about the city in a green Mercedes station wagon, performing his chores. Only once in all this time has Fred had a long face-to-face encounter with his employer—when Lennon delivered a strange, self-revealing monologue from midnight to dawn in an empty mansion in Palm Beach.

Having gotten into the mood to do a bit of writing, John decides next to leave a note for Yoko. Seating himself at her desk, he rolls a sheet of paper into the typewriter, which he operates hunt-and-hit style. He's very unhappy these days at the way Yoko ignores him, always saying she's busy. It's gotten so bad that he has to make an appointment with a member of her staff just to speak with her on the phone, nor is he allowed to enter her private office if she's on the phone, as she is day and night. So he has taken to writing her little notes designed to prod her sense of guilt gently without provoking her. After all, he can't very well complain that she works twenty hours a day when it was *he* who dumped the full responsibility for their family and fortune in her lap, giving her a power of attorney and making her his proxy in any and every matter of business. If he wants to live without a care, he must pay the price. Hence, his rather pathetic tone, conveyed by the heading: WHEN TO IGNORE WHAT YOUR HUSBAND SAYS.

The message is simply a list of all those moments in the day when he feels that Yoko is neglecting him: (1) when he awakens; (2) before he has coffee; (3) after he has coffee; (4) early in the morning or late in the afternoon; (5) during the evening TV shows; (6) when he's just had a smoke—in short, all the time. After signing off DADDY IN/SIGHT THE BEDROOM, he rolls the paper out of the machine and picks up his pen to sketch his trademark signature.

Embellishing the long line of his nose with two little loops for glasses, he touches in the mouth and beard before crowning his head with big loops of hair, working into the whorls on the left the letter *W* and in those on the right the letters *ill*. *Will* is the title of a best seller by G. Gordon Liddy that John has been much taken with lately, especially those parts in which Liddy explains how he learned to control his violent temper and how he earned the respect of his fellow prisoners by holding a burning match under his palm without flinching.

When John finishes his caricature, he glances over his shoulder at the kitchen window and discovers that the opposite wing is starting to catch the pink light of dawn. On that signal he rises abruptly and stalks up the long corridor to his dim and unchanging bedroom.

Apartment 72 remains quiet until the arrival, around eight, of Myoko and Uda-San, little women with bold peasant faces. As they begin their daily chores, doing the laundry or making miso soup, Yoko walks through the apartment's rear door, which bears a brass plate reading: "Nutopian Embassy." Instantly she begins issuing orders in Japanese. Just as she seats herself at her desk and picks up the phone, the four-year-old Sean comes hurtling into the room with his nanny in hot pursuit.

A most attractive child, Sean does not resemble in the least his fa-

mous father. He has a distinctly Eurasian appearance, with a full face
and faintly olive complexion. Nor does he favor Yoko. His short,
straight nose, rosebud mouth, and burnished chestnut brown hair
make him look like a changeling, which is why when John gets angry
he will say that Sean is not his son.

A nature boy, Sean has been reared since birth completely free of all
the restraints and demands normally imposed on children. Never
weaned or toilet-trained, he runs around at the age of four wearing
diapers and sucking on a bottle that has already begun to rot his teeth
and give him a lisp. If he wants to smear the white walls with paint or
slam a pizza onto the new bedspread or urinate all over the back seat of
the limousine, he will never meet with a check or reproof from the
servants or his mother, who maintains an unnatural calm in the face of
his feral antics. Yoko prides herself, in fact, on treating children as
equals, just as she habitually treats adults as children.

John regards his son with characteristic ambivalence, delighting in
the boy's precocious creativity but turning on him ferociously if he does
anything to disturb Daddy's peace of mind. Nor is he completely averse
to disciplining Sean. When a mother complained to John that Sean had
bitten her little girl, he seized his son's arm and bit him. Such actions
might intimidate some children—and Sean is wary of his father—but
unlike his half-brother, Julian, who is frozen with fear in John's presence, Sean never abandons his efforts to woo his crotchety dad. Often
he will crawl up to John like a pussycat because Sean is smart enough
to recognize that John's favorites are his cats.

Shortly after nine the back door buzzer sounds. After squinting
through the peephole, Yoko opens up, and in flows a great tide of
normal life. Marlene Hair, Yoko's only close friend and confidante, arrives every morning at this hour, shepherding her two pale-skinned,
Celtic-looking children: Caitlin, age four, and Sam, age nine. No
sooner are the kids through the door than they start screaming and
dancing about Sean, who is like a brother to them because they not
only play with him every day but often sleep with him at night, either
in this house or their own. Instantly Helen Seaman, a robust woman in
her early sixties, rushes forward and herds the children off to the adjacent Playroom. Then she retires for some welcome rest and privacy to
her small flat over the gate to the building.

"Marn the Barn," as John calls Marnie Hair, is a very important
figure in the emotional economy of the Lennons, though she hasn't an
inkling of her real role in this eccentric household. Like everything of
importance in the life of Yoko Ono, Marnie is the fulfillment of an
oracular prophecy. A year after Sean was born, Yoko's tarot reader,
John Green, predicted that a woman would be found living on Yoko's

block who had borne a son on the same day and in the same place as Yoko. This woman was destined to become Yoko's soul mate. Soon after the prediction, Masako, Sean's original nanny, reported that she had encountered a woman wheeling a baby the age of Sean who lived just a few doors away. Marnie was promptly invited to tea, and her psychic data collected and examined.

John Green's prophecy required some adjustment to fit the facts. Caitlin was born in the same year as Sean but eight months earlier; Sam, however, though five years older, was born on 9 October, the most important date in the Lennons' calendar because it is the birthday of both John and Sean. So by melding the two Hair children into one magical body and then telling Marnie a little white lie—that Yoko had lain in at Lenox Hill Hospital (Sean was actually delivered at New York Hospital)—the prophecy was fulfilled.

But the real meaning of the Lennons' relationship with Marnie Hair turns on the crucial figure in their marriage: the Missing Mother. As John and Yoko learned through primal therapy, their basic problems— as well as their basic affinity—arose from the fact that they both were deprived of the mothering they craved as children. For John the solution to this problem was to make Yoko his mother, an identification he proclaims every time he addresses her as "Mother" or "Mommy," especially when he speaks to her in baby talk. Yoko, for her part, sought to resolve her problem by assiduously denying any possible identification with her mother; hence her lifelong insistence that she has neither the desire nor the ability to be a mother. Marnie, by contrast, is the ideal mother.

At first glance a careworn and rumpled housewife, endowed with strong Irish features, an earnest, thoughtful expression, and a sturdy body with broad shoulders and a big bust, Marnie has only to put her head on her hand and stare you straight in the eye and you begin to feel affection and gratitude toward her. Her mere presence has a reassuring and strengthening effect. Though she has a string of degrees in English and linguistics, as well as an expired commission as a captain in the United States Army, her consuming passion is children, which doubtless has a lot to do with the fact that she was an orphan. Yoko Ono, whose greatest gift is her capacity for making use of people, must have quickly realized that Marnie offered the ultimate solution to the burdensome problem of rearing Sean.

The boy had an excellent nanny, of course, but a nanny is simply an employee, a woman who executes the orders of her mistress. What Yoko evidently desired for Sean was a woman who could be entrusted often with the full responsibility for the child, including that of making those difficult decisions demanded at moments of crisis, such as a sudden illness or injury. In fact, what Yoko appears to have been yearning for was a bountiful maternal breast to which she could attach Sean so that he would be filled with love, abundance, and security. So Marnie was encouraged to spread her wings over Sean, to treat him as one with her children, allowing him to share a bed every night with Caitlin, and watching over him every day as the children play.

The clearest evidence of Marnie's role as the Missing Mother is the fact that no sooner does she appear than the hermit of the back bedroom pops out of his den and makes his second demarche of the morning down the long corridor to the kitchen. John's abrupt entrance on the apartment's stage is a lot more daring than were his entrances as a Beatle. He arrives before his audience of middle-aged ladies totally starkers! Without a thought for whom he may meet, male or female, friend or stranger, the great Lennon walks in *au naturel,* raw as a clam on the half shell—and puts the kettle on for tea.

Nobody is ever embarrassed by these naked tiffins because John is the emperor who wears no clothes. He can sit naked by the hour with his feet up on the butcher-block table and his dick lying in his lap like a sleeping pet and produce no stir. Sexually speaking, John is off the air.

The arrival of Lennon is the signal for the women to break up their tête-à-tête in the lounge and shift to the kitchen table, where John has ensconced himself with a mug of tea in one hand and in the other a filter-tip Gitane. This is one of his favorite moments of the day: the Naked Professor's Lecture. Marn the Barn is the perfect pupil, just back, in fact, from her latest semester of postgraduate work in Colorado. John is no less perfect as the teacher because he can hold forth from one end of the day to the other and wind up stronger than when he started. His own ideas exhilarate him, but he requires an attentive and sympathetic listener to nerve him up for a close encounter with his own mind.

Today's topic? It will be that great contemporary theme—assassination. Make no mistake. John Lennon is not interested in the matter from a political standpoint. What intrigues John about the famous killings is the *conspiratorial* angle. When Marnie asks him, for example, "What's the real story of the murder of Martin Luther King?" John explodes: "Who the hell cares who murdered that nigger! What matters is the *system!*" His obsession with the shadowy world of murderous governments, hired gunmen, and brainwashed fall guys makes him crass about their victims. At the same time it makes him sympathetic toward the killers, whom he views as the true victims. He sees James Earl Ray as a guy who was framed. The Ray hearings fascinated Lennon; some days he would haul Marnie down to the other end of the kitchen and make her view the proceedings with him. *"Look at him!"* Lennon would yell. "It's obvious! He doesn't have to ask for a glass of water or take a leak. He's *drugged!"*

Conspiracy theories are but the outer husk of Lennon's obsession with these terrible crimes. Catch him on a good morning, and he'll go much deeper. At his best John Lennon is a seer, a blind Tiresias staring at the TV screen of the modern world. What he "sees" is not the image on the tube but its echo in his mind. Instead of being fascinated by the sight of a man taking a bullet, the stock action of every adventure film, John is obsessed with how it feels to be on the receiving end of that slug. Last year he got a marvelous opportunity to satisfy his curiosity, when Norman Seaman was shot in front of Carnegie Hall.

The old man was driving down Seventh Avenue and making the turn into 57th Street, when the driver behind him, impatient with Seaman's slowness, gunned his car forward and cut Norman off. Both men emerged from their vehicles to exchange angry words. In the midst of their argument, a woman got out of the front car. Pointing a pistol at Norman, she shot him point-blank. Then she and her companion vanished down 57th Street. The only clue to the crime, never solved, was the bullet—of a type commonly used by the police.

By a miracle, Norman Seaman survived. As soon as he was discharged from Roosevelt Hospital, he was summoned to John's presence. Lennon peppered Seaman with questions. Can you see the bullet emerging from the gun? How does it feel when the slug rips into your body? What goes through your mind when you realize that you've been hit and you may be dying? Having absorbed all this firsthand information, the Naked Professor was better prepared for his favorite theme. Now his mornings are often given to describing in mordant detail the sensations of being shot. Sometimes he makes gallows jokes or broods over the meaning of this act, which he describes as a contemporary form of crucifixion, with lead bullets taking the place of iron nails.

Death and dying, even crucifixion, are hardly new topics for John Lennon. He's been obsessed with such matters all his life. Many's the time he feared he was about to die during his days as a Beatle, in a burning plane or at the hands of his crazy fans or as the target of some religious fanatic in the Deep South. Lennon's ultimate solution to the whole problem of human mortality was to embrace the doctrine of reincarnation. Karma is the key to life, he insists, but to be born again with the best of karma, you have to die right—solid and centered and confronting your doom. John wants to die standing there like a saint, like Jesus, confronting his assassin with a soul sublimely at peace.

When he holds forth on this alarming theme, John displays absolutely no emotion. He will say, for example, "I'm not afraid of dying. It's just like getting out of one car and into another." Marnie, however, divines the fear that underlies this unnatural display of sangfroid. She becomes troubled and demands: "Why are you so interested in death?" Or she'll scold him, describing his obsession as "morbid." Inevitably she winds up by exhorting him: "Do something for yourself! Go out running!"

Instantly John will be on the defensive. "I can do what I want!" he'll protest like a sullen child. "I can say what I want. I don't have to answer to anybody. I'm *me. I'm John Lennon!*" He's been saying that ever since he was a little boy and would go from one passenger to another aboard the buses in Liverpool repeating that same phrase, "I'm John Lennon!," as if he were surprised that people didn't recognize him.

The moment Marnie sees that she has upset John, she locks her lips and returns to her customary role, sitting across the table, her eyes fixed on John as he stares off into space, talking as if he were broadcasting. As Marnie listens to the lecture, her gaze wanders to Yoko, sitting at the end of the table, her face impassive, her hands folded across her belly. Feeling still the effects of her wake-up taste, she's disposed to nod out. Yet behind her expressionless mask, an imp of mischief is alert and active.

As John drones on, Marnie sees Yoko reach out slyly to nudge John's tea mug or his ashtray beyond his reach. When he extends his hand to grasp the mug or flick off the ash from his cigarette, he finds himself seizing air or soiling the tabletop. Some mornings, when Marnie and Yoko are sitting in the lounge drinking tea and talking, Yoko will suddenly raise her head as she catches the sound of John's footsteps thudding down the hallway. Quick as a cat, she jumps up and darts over to the cat box, where she seizes a little turd that she plants in John's path. When the master of the house makes his big entrance, he puts his foot squarely in cat shit.

There are those mornings, however, when Yoko is a bit too slow and John catches her in the act! Then there's hell to pay. John seizes Yoko by her great mop of hair and hauls her, screaming and scratching, to the stove, where he threatens to set her hair afire! That's why there's never a match in this kitchen. Sometimes, when Marnie arrives in the morning, she looks down and discovers that the whole floor is strewn with Yoko's torn-out hairs.

Though Marnie spends a lot of time listening to Lennon hold forth, she much prefers those times, perhaps two or three mornings a week, when John proposes that they join the children in the Playroom. Equipped like a playground with a jungle gym, slide, climbing rope, trampoline, and pile of big building blocks, the room is also equipped with a kiddie jukebox and a menagerie of giant stuffed animals. Though this big chamber is lit by only one overhead bulb, the ceiling shows to good effect because it has been painted with a comic-book mural featuring John as Superman, Yoko as Wonder Woman, and Sean as Captain Marvel, the family of heroes surrounded by a retinue of animals from the Magic Kingdom.

The room also contains an old upright at which John seats himself as he prepares to give the kids a lesson in songwriting. "Give me a word!" he urges, intending to demonstrate how easy it is to make anything into music.

One of the kids shouts, "Toe!"

"That's a good word," John replies. Then he demands, "What's the sound that goes with 'toe'?" Singing "Do, re, mi!" he drops back to "do," banging it out on the piano repeatedly while singing, "Do . . . toe . . . do! Good!"

Now they need another word, a word that goes with "toe."

"Nail!" yells another kid.

"Toenail!" echoes John, who's now beginning to get interested in the game—just as the kids are starting to lose interest and drift. As John demands more words and more sounds to make their new song, he begins to realize that the kids aren't with him anymore. When one of them laughs at the wrong moment, his temper suddenly flashes forth. Leaping to his feet, John slams down the lid on the piano, nearly catching one of the kids' fingers. Angrily he turns to Marnie and barks, "I can't fuckin' believe what a short attention span these kids have! How can you teach these rug rats anything?" With that he stomps out of the room and up the hall to his lair.

When John gets back atop his bed, he seats himself in the lotus position and yanks the little drawer out of his flat traveler's desk. Seizing a Thai stick—five inches off the top of a potent plant bound with white thread to a sliver of bamboo—he crumbles the grass without even unwinding it and rolls it into a huge bomber. As he drags the spicy smoke deep into his lungs, he picks up a letter he wrote the other day to his aunt Mimi, the woman who reared him in Liverpool.

After all these years they are still locked in the same quarrels over the same issues that divided them when John was a rebellious teenager. What galls John is that even now, when he is universally regarded as a genius, his goddamned aunt won't give him credit for having achieved a thing. She still criticizes him and condemns him as if he were a naughty child. "I do believe in ME . . . who the hell else is there?" he writes defiantly, as if he had to defend his very existence from this old lady, whom he hasn't laid eyes on in ten years.

The books strewn across Lennon's quilt testify to how hard he's working still to break the shackles of his childhood. Tossing aside the letter to Mimi, which he'll never mail, he picks up the book that has meant the most to him since Arthur Janov's *The Primal Scream*. *The Continuum Concept* argues that the solution to the problems of neurotic dependency lies in adopting the child-rearing technique of primitive peoples, whose women strap their children to their bodies and go about their work with the children sustained at every moment in their experience of their new lives by continuous physical contact with their mothers. This idea appeals enormously to John, who has always felt that his mother abandoned him. That was the theme of his most haunting and harrowing record, "Mother," a psychodrama that exposed the anguish at his core.

Commencing with the tolling of funereal church bells, old and faded as the world they symbolize, the track dollies in on a piano and a voice. The piano utters but one chord at a time, allowing the notes to decay and fade with the melancholy resonance of an empty room. The voice is just as bleak and dreary, like a prisoner in a dungeon or a lunatic in an attic. Though the voice cries in protest, there is no passion in its note. It sounds more like a man repeating an *idée fixe* or reciting a verse from a psychotic nursery rhyme.

Suddenly, though, the voice changes. A terrifying uprush of emotion, like a hysteric's fit, comes bursting out. Lennon screams first for his mother, then for his father. Then he just screams and screams! But his screams aren't the open-throated hollering of a gospel singer or the abandoned shrieking of the horror movie. His screams are so strangled that they sound like retching. John Lennon is struggling to throw up his past. But no matter how hard he heaves, he can't get it out of his system.

FRED AND GINGER

The air-raid sirens had just begun to wail, around 6:30 on the night of 9 October 1940, when Mimi Smith got through to the Liverpool Maternity Hospital. For the past twenty-four hours she had been calling the hospital constantly, seeking news of her favorite sister's condition. By now Julia Lennon had been in labor for thirty hours, and the doctors were preparing to do a caesarian section. "I kept on ringing and ringing," related Mimi. "I was very keyed up. Finally, they told me it was a boy. I dropped everything and just ran out of the house.

"It was the night of the land mine raids. As I ran to the hospital [two miles distant], I could hear the sirens going off. But there was nothing going to stop me from being there—not even Hitler! I kept thinking: 'It's a boy!' You can't understand how excited I was. We all were! It was such a novelty to have a boy in the family. It was something we all longed for. When I got to the hospital, I couldn't take my eyes off him. He was such a beautiful baby. Even the nurses remarked so. He was born with blond hair, and I remember he weighed seven and a half pounds. Just the right weight! Not too big and not too small. I knew the moment I first set eyes on John that he was going to be something special."

Mimi wasn't permitted to gaze long at this coveted infant. A nurse in a long white apron and voluminous headdress strode into the room, took the baby out of Julia's arms and tucked it under the bed for safekeeping. Then she ordered Mimi to go down into the cellar or leave the hospital immediately. Mimi ran all the way home through the uproar of the air raid to bring the good news to her parents. Bursting into the house, she cried: "Mother! He's beautiful!"

Pop Stanley, Mimi's father, a salty old sea dog, growled: "He'd *have* to be better than any other."

When Julia Lennon gave birth to John, she was twenty-seven, but she behaved like a kid. Frolicsome, funny, full of mischief, she was also a

26

notorious flirt. With her long auburn hair done up in a glowing halo, her shapely legs flashing from under short skirts on high-heeled pumps, and with one of those faces that belong to the theater—high, broad cheekbones, boldly arched brows, and heavily rouged lips—she turned many a man's head. Offers of marriage had come raining down on her, often from men with good prospects, but no one could come between her and her favorite playmate, a young ship's steward—Freddie Lennon.

Freddie was Julia's Fred Astaire, just as she was his Ginger Rogers. Neat and nimble, with a fine Irish tenor voice and a "perfect profile," as even the disapproving Mimi conceded, Freddie sought to live in real life the same way his famous namesake cavorted on the silver screen. Who else would have behaved as Freddie did the first time he met Julia?

"I was sitting in Sefton Park with a mate who was showing me how to pick up girls," Freddie told Hunter Davies. "I'd bought myself a cigarette holder and a bowler hat. I felt that really would impress them. There was this little waif that we had an eye on. [Julia and Freddie were both about sixteen.] As I walked past her, she said, 'You look silly.' I said, 'You look lovely!' and I sat down beside her. It was all innocent. I didn't know anything. She said if I was going to sit beside her, I had to take that silly hat off. So I did. I threw it in the lake!" That gesture delighted Julia, who liked nothing better than to snap her fingers in the face of propriety.

Acting like a charming song and dance man was natural to Freddie because he had grown up enthralled by the image of his dead father, Jack Lennon, a pioneering British minstrel who had toured the United States back in the Nineties with Andrew Roberton's Kentucky Minstrels. When Freddie was at sea, working on the glamorous old liners of the Thirties, he would sometimes black his face and do a letter-perfect imitation of the great Al Jolson down on bended knee singing "Mammy." Indeed, what The Lennons—Jack, Freddie, and John—represented collectively was a whole century of English entertainers smitten by the magic of the black man's mojo.

Jack Lennon died when Freddie was seven—roughly the same age at which John lost Freddie and Sean lost John—leaving his son to be reared by the Blue Coat Hospital, Liverpool's foremost charitable institution. Freddie was proud to wear the traditional costume, blue tailcoat and silver-buttoned smallcoat with white bands at the neck and high-crowned hat, but what he really yearned for was the stage. At the first opportunity he ran away from the orphanage and joined Will Murray's Gang, a popular children's troupe. Dragged back and punished by the beadle, he was compelled to remain at his lessons until he was fifteen, receiving despite himself an excellent education. But he was haunted all his life by the thought that he had missed his calling. The first time he saw his famous son perform, at a Christmas pantomime in London, poor Freddie broke down and cried. Pointing at the stage, he sobbed: "That's where I should have been!"

Freddie's substitute for the stage was acting stagy. For a whole decade he played off Julia Stanley, laughing and singing, but never becoming physically intimate because they were an "act," more like best mates than lovers. He might have gone on in his juvenile style even longer if Julia had not proposed to him. Her unconventional proposition was prompted by a demand from her father that she either marry or cease keeping company with her unsuitable suitor. Pop Stanley reckoned his threat would end this foolish affair; instead, it inspired the audacious Julia to suggest to Freddie that they live together—an idea that shocked the young steward. "Me, I'd been brought up in orphanage," he explained. "I said we had to put up the banns and get married properly. She said, 'I bet you won't!' So I did—just for a joke. It was all a big laugh, getting married."

The preparations for this frivolous union had to be made in secret because neither family would have approved the match. The Stanleys looked down on Freddie because he was merely a ship's waiter; whereas Old Stanley was a real mariner, a man who had learned his craft of sailmaker before steam had conquered the seven seas. The Lennons, for their part, held a low opinion of Julia because they saw her as a frivolous little flirt.

When Freddie arrived at the Adelphi Hotel on his wedding morning, 3 December 1938, he was broke because he hadn't worked in months. Stepping across the street to a military tailor's shop, where the most responsible member of the family, his older brother, Sydney, labored in the cellar under glaring lights, Freddie disclosed his predicament. Sydney made a last-ditch effort to dissuade his kid brother; then he agreed to spend his lunch hour standing witness, along with another man named Edwards. Sydney was also good for a loan of one pound.

Julia arrived at the Bolton Street Registry Office, behind the hotel, just before it closed, accompanied by a couple of girls who worked with her as usherettes at the Trocadero Cinema. The clerk read the familiar service from the Book of Common Prayer, and the couple exchanged vows. Sydney stood lunch and drinks at a nearby pub. Afterward Julia and Freddie went off to the movies, which was the full extent of their honeymoon. That night, when bride and groom returned to their respective families, Julia was still a virgin.

Mimi recollected bitterly how Julia broke the news: "She just walked in and said, 'There! I've married him!' She threw the certificate on the table. We all knew nothing good would come of it, but there was no telling her. I don't think she ever thought about the consequences. That was typical of her."

Several days later Freddie Lennon shipped out on a cruise of the Mediterranean. When he returned, Pop Stanley, faced with the alternatives of accepting the marriage or losing his favorite daughter, suggested that Freddie should move in with the Stanleys. They had only recently left their old house in Toxteth to occupy a new home at 9 Newcastle Road in the Penny Lane district. Though this little row house, with its bay window thrust against the sidewalk, appears mean to the eye, it was a big step up from the ruinous neighborhood later notorious as Liverpool 8. Not only was the family's new home located in a desirable district, but it was provided with those prized amenities, an indoor toilet and a tiny backyard. It was in this house, in January 1940, during the lull in the hostilities called the Phony War that John Lennon was conceived.

By the time Julia had come to term, the Phony War had become the Battle of Britain. The Luftwaffe was bombing Liverpool night after night, setting the docks afire and causing much damage in the residential neighborhoods. When the sirens sounded, Julia and her family would retreat to a bomb shelter made by laying a concrete slab over a narrow alley behind the house.

Surrounded by a family who doted on the baby, Julia began to feel deserted as, first, her mother died; then Mimi went off to live with her husband, after his discharge from the army. Freddie was never home, being at the forefront of the war as one of thousands of brave merchant seamen who risked their lives running the U-boat blockade. Mimi, quick to respond to her sister's predicament, suggested that Julia move into a cottage owned by Mimi's husband and located near her house at 120A Allerton Road in the suburban village of Woolton.

The moment Julia left home, her whole life changed. Night after night she went out dancing in the village, whose pubs were full of men in uniform, drinking, singing, and raising the roof in that reckless spirit typical of wartime. Never a drinker, she began to tipple, though at first two sherries would send her into a fit of giggling. Because she couldn't afford a baby-sitter—and couldn't ask Mimi to watch John while his mother went off pub crawling—Julia fell into the habit of slipping out after John had fallen asleep, leaving him alone.

A pampered child, accustomed to being closely watched, John would awake in the dark and discover not only that he was unattended but that the house was empty. Alarmed, he would imagine a ghost or a goblin standing next to his bed. Crying out in terror, he would raise such a racket that sometimes the neighbors would be obliged to investigate.

When Freddie came back from sea, he learned about Julia's nightly escapades and reprimanded her. She retaliated by pouring a cup of scalding hot tea over his head. Enraged, Freddie slapped Julia's face—the only time he ever hit her—making her nose bleed. Mimi, a former nurse, was summoned, and after she had stopped the bleeding, she gave her errant sister a sharp lecture on her improper conduct.

Julia returned to the parental house in Penny Lane in 1943, when her father left to live with his sister. Now she could arrange her evenings out much better, for by clubbing together with two other young mothers on the block, Dolly Hipshaw and Ann Stout, she could hire a baby-sitter who would watch all the children. Nothing improper ever occurred during these social evenings, until Freddie Lennon got into trouble.

The fateful cruise that sank the Lennons' marriage began on 14 July 1943, when Freddie sailed on the *Samothrace* bound for the Port of New York. Initially the problem was that Freddie, recently promoted to saloon steward (headwaiter), had allowed himself to be persuaded to sign on for this cruise at the lower rating of assistant steward; then he began to fear that he had jeopardized his promotion. After conferring with his former captain during a long layover in New York, he failed to report for the ship's next sailing, going off instead to plead his case with the British consul. The official proved completely unsympathetic: he ordered Freddie back to sea without his rating, and assigned him to the *Sammex,* which was sailing on 9 February 1944 for the Algerian port of Bône.

Soon Freddie discovered that the whole crew, save the captain and the "sparks," were involved in a black-market smuggling racket; yet it was not the smugglers but Freddie who was arrested when the ship made port in North Africa because the shore patrol found him drinking a bottle of beer that was not ship's issue. Sentenced to nine days in a hideous military prison, he found himself upon his release a long way from home.

The next six months of Freddie Lennon's life were full of dangerous adventure. He got involved in the local underground after its leader, a Dutchman named Hans, saved Freddie from a gang of Arabs in the Casbah. After making a couple of runs on a Dutch-manned ship carrying troops from North Africa to Naples, he secured passage on a vessel bound for England, arriving at Liverpool in November 1944, eighteen months after his departure.

Since his arrest at Bône, Freddie's pay—and consequently Julia's allotment—had been stopped, but until the final months of his absence he had kept her informed of his situation by writing long, chatty letters. In later years, however, when Mimi was obliged to explain to little John the disappearance of his father, she invented the story that Freddie had jumped ship and abandoned his family, a yarn that was picked up and disseminated irresponsibly by the press. This explanation masked the real story of the dissolution of the Lennons' marriage, which commenced when Freddie got home and discovered how his wife had been behaving in his absence.

In the spring of 1944 Julia Lennon had met a fair-haired Welsh soldier named Taffy Williams, attached to an antiaircraft unit billeted at Mossley Hill Barracks. Williams turned up one night at the British Legion club in the company of a good-looking man with a dark complexion and pencil-line mustache named John Dykins. Julia flirted gaily with the soldier; meantime, Dykins was chatting up Ann Stout. At the end of the evening Dolly went home alone, leaving her neighbors with their new men friends.

From that night on Julia and Taffy, Ann and Bobby (as Dykins was called) were a foursome, often accompanied by Dolly. Dykins proved a great party man. A wine steward at the Adelphi, he could procure rare treats, like cigarettes, fresh fruits, real chocolate, and scotch whiskey. Julia flourished in this pleasure-loving company. She was a good-time girl, and this was her natural way of living. For six months she was very happy, perhaps happier than at any time in her entire life. Then she found herself pregnant.

Taffy wasn't put off by the discovery. He wanted Julia to leave home and live with him. After all, she rarely saw her husband. Why shouldn't she exchange this absent man for someone with whom she could enjoy her life? It was a tempting offer, and chances are Julia would have gone off with Taffy but for the fact that he didn't want to take John. Julia's refusal to abandon her son corresponded with Taffy's transfer across the Mersey to the Wirral Peninsula. At that point the lovers parted company—and Freddie arrived home.

When Freddie saw his wife for the first time in a year and a half, she staggered him by announcing that she was carrying another man's child. She insisted, however, that the pregnancy was not her fault. Freddie's younger brother, Charles, home on leave from the Royal Artillery, witnessed what followed: "Alfred come to see me," he recalled. "He told me that he had come home and found her six weeks gone but not showing. She claimed that she was raped by a soldier. She gave a name. We went over to the Wirral where the soldier was stationed. I was able to enter his gun site and consult with his officer and take the soldier outside to talk to my brother. Freddie was not a violent man. Hasty-tempered but not violent. We are not a violent family. Freddie said: 'I believe you're havin' affairs with my wife, and she accuses you of rapin' her.' 'No such thing,' he said. 'It wasn't rape. It was consent. I been with her quite a while now, until I moved over the water to the West Derby area.' The soldier come back with us, but it was a wasted journey for him. He got the Order of the Boot from Julia [she laughed in his face and shouted, "Get out you bloody fool!"], even though she was carrying his child. My brother, Alfred, decided to take John to my other brother, Sydney, in Maghull [a village north of Liverpool]. Never at any time did he want Julia's sister, Mary [Mimi], to have control over John."

Mimi could do nothing with Sydney, who was her counterpart in the Lennon family, so she trained her attentions on Julia's pregnancy. First, Pop Stanley told Julia that he would not taint his house by harboring a bastard: either she must go—or the baby. When Julia agreed to give up the child, Mimi made the necessary arrangements. She went to a Salvation Army orphanage for girls close by her house, a weird-looking Tudor folly, rather like the ogre's castle in a fairy tale, called Strawberry Field (not Fields). The matron gave Mimi the name of a nursing home on North Mossley Hill Road, where Julia could lie in. When Freddie returned from his next trip, he went to the Elmswood Nursing Home and begged Julia to allow him to give the baby his name. She refused, saying, "I won't do it because someday you'll get angry and say, 'Look at the little bastard!'" Freddie turned next to Mimi, beseeching her to take the child. Mimi rejected the suggestion scornfully.

Julia named the baby, born 19 June 1945, Victoria, which chimed nicely with the triumphant conclusion of the war in Europe, and also with the patriotic middle name she had given John—Winston. "I remember her well," recalled Julia's sister Anne Cadwallader: "She was a beautiful baby, but we never knew who the father was. . . . One day a Salvation Army captain came and took the baby away. That was the last we saw of her." When Freddie appealed to the Army to inform him of the fate of the child, he was told that the policy was to provide no information to either the parents or the foster parents of an adopted child. The most the matron would reveal was that the adopting family was that of a Norwegian ship captain. Presumably John Lennon's half-sister was reared in Norway, but all efforts to trace her have failed.

Having rid herself of Victoria, Julia insisted that Freddie fetch back John from Sydney's house. Sydney protested vehemently, citing all the reasons why Freddie's reconciliation with his wife would not long continue and the dangers to the child if there were further quarrels and separations. Freddie would hear nothing of these objections. He was still persuaded that he could patch up his marriage, using John as mortar.

Sydney proved a true prophet. No sooner did John return to his mother's home than new complications arose in her life that led to further trouble. John Dykins had broken up by now with Ann Stout and had begun to court Julia. He offered her a much different life from that she had experienced with Freddie. Dykins made a good living and loved to live well. He was very attractive and experienced with women. Soon he was spending a lot of time at the house on Newcastle Road, where he ingratiated himself with Pop Stanley, who had come back to live with Julia.

There was only one difficulty with the new arrangement: John Lennon was extremely upset by the presence of this new man in his house. His anger and resentment betrayed itself by hostile behavior, particularly attacks on weaker children. In the afternoons, for example, it was Dolly Hipshaw's custom to invite John to her house to have his tea with her three young children, Pauline, Helen, and Carol, aged five, three and a half, and two and a half. Frequently, during the course of these meals, the five-year-old John would attack one of the girls and make her scream with fright. Since Julia never disciplined John, it fell to Dolly's lot to chastise the boy.

Matters grew worse when Pauline and John entered kindergarten in November 1945 at nearby Mosspits Infants' School. John would lie in wait until the little girl stepped out of her house. Then he would leap upon her from his hiding place. Pauline came to dread these ambushes so much that she refused to go to school. Again, Dolly had to discipline John. Eventually she concluded that he was "hard—very hard-going." This was also the finding of the Mosspits Infants' School, which expelled John Lennon for misbehavior in April 1946, when he was five and a half.

John's expulsion from kindergarten was closely connected with yet another series of highly disturbing incidents at home. On 26 March 1946 Freddie Lennon, straight off the *Dominion Monarch,* arrived at Newcastle Road, where he was confronted by Julia, John Dykins, and Pop Stanley, who informed his son-in-law that the rent book (the ledger signed by the landlord upon receipt of the rent) had been changed back from "Alfred Lennon" to "George Stanley." When a quarrel erupted over this issue, Dykins butted in and accused Freddie of beating Julia—an allusion to the incident of the hot tea. "I don't even know who you are!" exclaimed the outraged Freddie. Next moment the men came to blows, and the angry steward threw the natty waiter out of the house. While the quarrel was raging, John crept down from upstairs. He witnessed his father punching it out with his mother's lover—a scene he never forgot.

Julia took matters into her own hands now. Informing Freddie that she was going off to live with Dykins, she and Dolly started moving all the furniture into the house next door. Freddie, at his wits' end, rushed to his mother's home at 57 Copperfield Street and cried, "Mum! Julie is leavin' me!"

Mother Polly told him sternly, "Go back and stop in that house until she leaves, even if she leaves you sittin' on a chair."

So poor Freddie had to bear witness to his wife's packing and departure, even lending a helping hand with the heavy pieces. Mindful of his mother's word, he finally said: "Aren't you going to leave me so much as a chair?" Julia pointed scornfully to an old broken chair and told Freddie it was his to have and to hold.

After spending most of April trying to patch up his marriage, Freddie left for Southampton to sail as a night steward aboard the *Queen Mary*. No sooner was he out the door than Julia moved all the furniture back into the house. Her removal had been a ruse to convince Freddie that the marriage was at an end. No wonder that little John behaved so badly at school that he was expelled. In the past, when he was very upset, he had sometimes run away from home, making his way to Mimi's house on a tram that he recognized by its black leather seats—and sometimes winding up in the boondocks when he chose the wrong tram. (To the end of his life he could remember the smell of those leather seats.) Now he ran away again.

When Mimi opened the door and saw John standing there forlornly, her wrath against Julia rose up. "All she did was *have* you!" exclaimed Mimi—a line echoed many years later in "Mother."

No sooner did Mimi discover how matters stood at Newcastle Road than she put through an emergency call to the *Queen Mary*, which was at the point of sailing. Mimi told Freddie to come home immediately because John had run away. Next, she put John on the line. He said that he didn't like his new daddy and wanted Freddie to come home. Freddie promised that he would return as soon as he could get off the ship.

Good as his word, Freddie appeared at Mimi's house two weeks later, having sacrificed the best berth of his career. Mimi reported that she had enrolled John at Dovedale Infants' School in Penny Lane. She also announced that she had bought the boy a lot of new clothes and presented Freddie with the bill. Next morning, when Freddie sat down with his son, he asked to see his new things. John replied that he hadn't received any new clothes.

Freddie, convinced now that Mimi's interest was mercenary, asked John if he would like a holiday at Blackpool, the famous beach resort up the coast from Liverpool. John was thrilled by the idea. Mimi couldn't refuse to allow Freddie to take his boy on vacation. So Freddie took off with John, intending never to return!

For six weeks at Blackpool, John lived in a child's world of delight. He could watch the day-trippers, kerchiefs knotted about their heads, trousers rolled to their knees, stalking across the sands like wading birds. Doubtless he rode a donkey and stood atop the iron tower over the resort, gazing down at dusk on the dazzle of the Golden Mile. Alone at last with his sorely missed dad, John Lennon experienced all those pleasures that boys enjoy most keenly with their fathers. He also caught for the first time in his life the savor of a world of men.

Freddie was staying with an old shipmate, who was planning to emigrate to New Zealand. Impulsively Freddie decided to throw in his lot with this man. Emigration would give them all a fresh start, which was just what everybody craved after the war. For John this was wonderful news because he had always dreamed of going off to sea aboard a great white ship with his dad.

Little John's dream soon twisted into a nightmare. Julia turned up unexpectedly with Bobby Dykins. She told Freddie that now she was settled with her new man she wanted to take John back. Freddie explained that they were preparing to emigrate to New Zealand. He offered to take Julia with him. Julia started to put up a fight. Finally, Freddie said the boy should make his own decision. "I shouted to John," recollected Freddie. "He runs out and jumps on my knee, asking if she's coming back. That's obviously what he wanted. I said no, he had to decide whether to stay with me or go with her. He said me. Julia asked again, but John still said me. Julia went out the door and was about to go up the street when John ran after her. That was the last I saw or heard of him till I was told he'd become a Beatle."

Little John chose his mother, but what he got was his aunt. No sooner did Julia return with her son than she put him into the hands of her sister, who now became his foster mother. This final betrayal was enough to convince John, once and for all, that his mother did not love him. In fact, what he really believed was that nobody loved him because nobody wanted him. Freddie Lennon, who did love John, disappeared completely at this time. Overcome by despondency at the loss of his wife, whom he would continue to love for the next twenty years, Freddie betook himself to sea. Thus, at one stroke, John Lennon lost both mother and father.

If the reason for Freddie's disappearance from John's life at this time is clear, no less so is the reason for Julia's simultaneous disappearance. Having consented to her father's demand that she not expose John to the effects of an irregular household, Julia was obliged to hand the boy over to Mimi, who demanded, in turn, that Julia stay out of John's way, lest her appearances make Mimi's task even harder. Julia could have responded by divorcing Freddie and marrying Dykins, by whom she was soon to have two children, but she knew that Freddie would never consent to a divorce. So Julia remained to the end of her life Mrs. Alfred Lennon while presenting herself to the world as Mrs. John Dykins.

Freddie Lennon remained at sea almost continuously for eighteen months after the heart-wrenching scene at Blackpool. Finally, after a voyage to New Zealand, he returned to England the week before Christmas 1949, intent upon reclaiming John and carrying out his original plan to emigrate. Feeling the need to jack up his nerve before the anxiously anticipated showdown with Julia, Freddie got drunk with a shipmate in London. While sauntering down Oxford Street, he suddenly beheld in a shop window a beautiful red-haired mannequin that reminded him of his wife. Instantly he smashed the glass and seized the dummy, with which he was dancing madly when he was arrested by the police. Hauled before a stern judge, Freddie was given the choice of paying £250—a sum well in excess of a workingman's annual wage—or serving six months in prison. Unable to pay, Freddie was locked up in Wormwood Scrubs.

While in prison, he wrote Mimi to solicit her aid in recovering John. (He assumed, naturally, that the boy was living with his mother.) It was only when he received Mimi's scathing reply that he recognized the true state of affairs. Mimi, who had always viewed Freddie with contempt, regarded him now as a reprobate threatening her custody of John. Rearing up like the deadly orc in *Sinbad the Sailor,* she came swooping down on the hapless mariner, heaping scorn upon him for bringing "shame and scandal" upon his innocent family. To make sure that Freddie would not try again to reclaim John, she warned that if he sought to make contact with the boy, she would tell John that his father was a felon and a convict. That finished Freddie Lennon.

Imprisonment barred him from future service in the merchant navy, to which he had dedicated sixteen years of his life. No sooner was he released from prison than he learned of the death of his mother. Having lost wife, son, and mother, as well as being cut off from home and vocation, Freddie suffered most perhaps from being denied access to the sea, which, over the years, had replaced his early love of the stage. Now, at the age of thirty-two, he was a ruined man. Carrying his few private possessions in a battered suitcase, he took to traveling up and down the country, accepting whatever job he was offered in the catering trade, usually as a pot scrubber or pan scourer in a hotel kitchen.

By the time little John had settled into his aunt Mimi's home, he had suffered enough emotional trauma to cripple any but the strongest soul. He had been neglected, uprooted, passed from hand to hand, and finally compelled to make an impossible choice: either to give up his mother in order to retain his father or to relinquish his father in order to hold on to his mother, who, as it turned out, really didn't want him. After such a shattering barrage, it is not surprising that John developed that protective amnesia exhibited by soldiers who have been shell-shocked.

"I soon forgot my father," he recalled. "It was like he was dead. But I did see my mother now and again, and my feeling never died off for her. I often thought about her, though I never realized that she was living no more than five or ten [actually three] miles away. Mimi never told me. She said she was a long, long way away."

Julia did appear at Mendips occasionally, but her calls were not inspired by concern for her son. They were prompted by the perils of her own turbulent life. John recollected one such incident vividly: "My mother came to see us in a black coat with her face bleeding. She'd had some sort of accident. I couldn't face it. I thought, 'That's my mother in there, bleeding.' I went out in the garden. I loved her, but I didn't want to get involved. I suppose I was a moral coward. I wanted to hide all feelings." The "accident" was undoubtedly a beating by Bobby Dykins, a violent man when drunk. Julia had come to Mimi for succor. She was met by a blast of moral indignation that blew her out of the house. Leila Harvey, John's older cousin, was present that day. She remembered her embarrassment as she watched Mimi denounce Julia in front of John, thundering in the voice of a Jehovan judge: *"You are not fit to be this boy's mother!"*

MATRIARCHY'S CHILD

Once Mimi Smith became John Lennon's foster mother, she applied herself to this unwonted task with great zeal. "Never once in ten years did I cross that doorstep at night," she declared, contrasting herself implicitly with Julia, who, if the door were barred, would crawl out the window. John Lennon, for his part, always paid tribute to his aunt for providing him with all those things—a home, an education, the presence of concerned parental figures—of which he had been deprived by his parents' folly. At the same time John felt a deep resentment against Mimi, whom he blamed for driving him crazy by the way she brought him up. For despite her good intentions and prolonged self-sacrifice, Mimi Smith was not well suited to be a mother, much less the mother of a highly disturbed boy like John. More matron than mother, Mimi was a typical auntie type, who professed to love children but who wasn't very good with them because she had retained so little of the child within herself. Her own unhappy childhood provides the best explanation for her deficiencies as a parent.

The eldest of five daughters, Mimi was expected even as a little girl to play a responsible part in the rearing of her younger sisters. Having suffered from such a massive dose of motherhood when she was but a child, Mimi bridled at this prospect as an adult. Initially, however, she did not so much revolt against her destined role as give it another twist by becoming a nurse. At nineteen she left home to become a resident trainee at Woolton Convalescent Hospital, where for years she both lived and worked, rising gradually to the rank of nursing sister, or head nurse, in charge of a ward of mentally handicapped patients.

Nursing enabled Mimi to get free of her family without marrying, but it did not fulfill her true ambition, which was to live like a lady. She achieved this goal by becoming the private secretary of a wealthy man named Vickers, who owned a biscuit machinery factory in nearby Manchester. Mimi resided at the Vickers mansion in the picturesque Welsh town of Bettws-y-Coed in much the same style as a governess in a Victorian novel: being treated as a member of the family and accorded such privileges as sailing aboard her employer's yacht, which never put to sea but glided serenely in the Menai Strait between the island of Anglesea and the Welsh coast.

As for becoming a wife, Mimi never relished the prospect. "I had no intention of getting married," she explained, adding: "Mind you, I loved the company of men. But I didn't fancy being tied to a kitchen or a sink." So when the young man to whom she had been bespoken at an early age went off to Kenya, Mimi didn't pine for him. And when a good-looking young dairyman would arrive every morning at the hospital, driving a horse-drawn brown float filled with silver churns and dressed like a farmer in leggings and jodhpurs with a kerchief knotted about his neck, Mimi, a statuesque figure in her long blue gown, white bib apron, and nurse's veil, would respond coolly, perhaps with a certain hauteur, toward this countryman's cheery hello.

George Smith persisted in his attentions, however, and eventually he and Mimi drifted into one of those prolonged courtships typical of the Stanley sisters. Mimi recalled: "I used to phone him when I was hungry or stuck in town."

This one-sided relationship dragged on for more than a decade, until one night George forced the issue. Stopping on the street, he said: "Look here! I've had enough of you! Either marry me or nothing at all!"

Mimi retorted: "What are you shouting about? I will!"

Overjoyed, George picked her up and swung her about. Then, putting her down, he addressed her foursquare. "Shake hands," he demanded. "Farmers always shake hands on a bargain."

Mimi thrust out her hand and said firmly: "That's a bargain!"

They married on 15 September 1939, just twelve days after England declared war on Germany. George had been inspired to propose by the prospect of being called up. He must have wanted Mimi to have his pension in the event of his death. Mimi was thirty-three when she married, but she continued to live at home for the next three years, until George was discharged. Then they moved into Mendips, a seven-room semidetached house at 251 Menlove Avenue, in the middle-class suburb of Allerton. At that point, instead of having a child of her own, she adopted informally one of her sisters' sons.

The woman in whose hands John Lennon found himself now was in every respect the opposite of his mother, a fact that helps account for John's lifelong tendency to be of two minds about everything. Where Julia was gay and childish, given to laughing, singing, and playing with John in the bath, Mimi was cool and distant, deeply concerned for her little charge but not the kind to tolerate any nonsense. Where John's mother had been extremely flirtatious, actually bringing her lovers into the house and thereby arousing the boy's jealousy—another lifelong problem for John—Mimi and George lived like a staid middle-aged couple, who never exhibited any overt signs of affection, much less physical intimacy; in fact, John felt that Mimi was more concerned about her Persian cats than she was about her husband. The most apparent and pervasive difference in the two homes was one of atmosphere: Whereas Julia's house had been run helter-skelter, with no real concern for order and regularity, Mimi managed her large place the way a head nurse runs a ward. Indeed, it was precisely this insistence on discipline and routine, reinforced by quiet and seclusion, that Mimi was counting upon to stabilize John, whom she saw as a disturbed patient in need of careful nursing. Thanks to Sister Mimi, John Lennon grew up at Mendips like the sole inmate of a convalescent hospital for emotionally disturbed orphans.

The regimen that Mimi established was governed by two complementary goals. On the one hand, John was to be kept totally under control, and, on the other, he was to be accultured to a higher class. Hence, he was expressly forbidden to play with any children save those chosen by Mimi, while he was encouraged tacitly to play by himself, either in his room or, when the weather was fair, in his tree house in the back garden. Reading, writing, and painting, not rough-and-tumble games, were the activities most commended to the boy. To eradicate from his mind every trace of his working-class origins, Mimi denied him access to what she called picturedromes, the common resort of common children, his official ration of movies being but two pictures a year—the annual Disney offerings at Easter and Christmas. (Unofficially he would see the odd cowboy flick with his uncle George when that sympathetic soul could win his wife's permission.) Television was never permitted at Mendips, and trash like comic books was simply out of the question. John was given to read the *Just William* books, which concern the comic misadventures of an upper-middle-class boy in an affluent nowhere land back in the Twenties.

Thus it was in a relentlessly improving cultural atmosphere that John Lennon was reared, with his attentions focused on his treasured library card, his posh manner of speaking—he was taught to say "mater" and "pater"—and his studies, which were designed to fit him eventually to become the first boy in the family to achieve professional distinction. Mimi was seconded in all her pedagogic endeavors by her husband, who, though the son of a dairyman, had come from a family that had produced a number of teachers, including one eccentric brother who was on the staff of the Liverpool Institute. George Smith himself had aspired to be an architect and had won prizes for drawing and languages, but he had been expelled from school for kicking a ball after he was forbidden to do so. He had gone into his father's dairy business, but the farm was sold during the war after old Frankie Smith drowned himself in a scum-covered pond, the victim, it is said, of his wife's persecution.

After his discharge from the army, George had worked nights at an aircraft factory in Speke; then, when the war ended, he found himself without any employment. Always a great lover of the track, he was persuaded to open an illegal "book" that operated out of Mendips, but George lacked the quick wits and crooked character essential to such a business. After suffering heavy losses, which provoked violent quarrels with Mimi, he shut up shop and lapsed into a state of reluctant retirement in his mid-forties, his income reduced to the rents on some inherited cottages. At this point Mimi began taking in medical students, whom she provided with bed and board. The family's fortunes declined steadily thereafter, so much so that John was later to complain that as a growing boy he could never eat his fill, a frustration that may have laid the foundation for his later problems with diet.

George's business failure gave him a lot of spare time, some of which he employed in instructing young John. George taught the boy to read by putting him on his knee and pointing out to him the words in the Liverpool *Echo*. George also taught John to draw and paint in watercolors, thus launching him on his career as an artist. Neither George nor Mimi was musical, but music poured all day from the big radio-phonograph in the lounge, which John listened to by means of an extension speaker up in his little cabin-like room over the house entry. Here he loved to lie abed with his feet up the wall and his head cocked at an odd angle, reading the exotic adventure novels of H. Rider Haggard or the volumes that arrived regularly from Mimi's book club.

Though John was being carefully groomed to become a member of the middle class, Mimi and George were not socially acceptable in their middle-class community. Mrs. Fran Bushnell, who lived on the other side of the common wall that divided the double house, cited three reasons for the family's ostracism: (1) The Smiths were, no matter how genteel they appeared, working-class folk; (2) Mimi Smith was a distant and unfriendly person, who never once in ten years invited Mrs. Bushnell into Mendips, though the women often conversed over the garden wall; (3) George's bookmaking business had met with the disapprobation of his neighbors. These observations go a long way toward explaining John Lennon's lifelong social maladjustment.

Led to believe that he belonged to the middle class, he was condemned to discover in what must have been a whole series of confusing and embarrassing incidents the dismaying truth that he did not belong. The upshot was a lifelong rage not simply against the community that rejected him or even the middle class but against *all* society, including even its most bohemian and outlawed forms. As he remarked not long before his death, "You want to belong, but you *don't* want to belong because you *can't* belong."

The only social life at Mendips was that afforded by Mimi's sisters, Anne, Harriet, and Mary Elizabeth, and their children. Old Pop Stanley had spent most of his life at sea, with the result that his authority had devolved upon his wife, a beautiful and placid woman, content to see her powers usurped by her mother, a formidable old dame who spoke nothing but Welsh and ruled the house with an iron hand. Grandmother Mary Elizabeth was the hidden root of John Lennon's character (even though she died eight years before he was born) because she imprinted her personality upon her granddaughters—especially upon her namesake, John's Aunt Mimi—who then transmitted their impression of her character to their offspring.

The source of Grandmother Mary Elizabeth's authority is germane to Lennon's oddly religious nature, for the old lady was sustained by that absolute certainty about matters of right and wrong conferred by unquestioning belief in a creed. A lifelong member of the Welsh Chapel, a puritanical Methodist cult known for its zeal and stringency, the grandmother ran her daughter's household with Hebraic strictness. On the Sabbath, no child was allowed to disturb the peace by so much as bouncing a ball or opening a newspaper. So fiercely were the Stanley sisters whipped into line that even to this day, seventy years later, Anne will exclaim at the mere mention of her grandmother's name, "A holy terror!" Interestingly, virtually the same expression is habitually employed by Marnie Hair to describe how John would cow Sean and his playmates: "John could put the fear of God in you!" Indeed, he could—because at an early age he had been made to feel that fear himself.

So pronounced was the matriarchal character of John Lennon's family that in later life he described it as exclusively female: "Five women were my family—five strong, intelligent, beautiful women. One happened to be my mother." Exactly the same impression was conveyed by John's cousin Leila Harvey, M.D. "There were five sisters," she remarked, "who considered themselves one family." Each sister would take her turn acting as housemother. In the summer Elizabeth, the second oldest, called Mater by the children, would have all the bairns up to her house in Edinburgh or to her sheep croft in the Highlands. At Christmas and Easter it was the turn of Mimi at Allerton or of Harriet in nearby Woolton. Wherever the children stayed, they were always under the exclusive control of the women because, as Leila Harvey explained, "In our family women and children were important; men were somehow in the background." John Lennon put the same idea more strongly: "The men were just invisible in our family. I was always with the women. I always heard them talk about the men and talk about life. They always knew what was going on. The men never, never ever knew!"

The reason the men never "knew" was because they were shut out of their own families. "In our family," Leila observed, "men didn't have any say. They had to accept what the women decided." Needless to say, most of these men were weak, passive, and unsuccessful, like George Smith, content to accept the subservient role assigned them at home, where a couple of them were obliged to sleep apart from their wives. John's half-sister, Julia, summed up the whole matter with the humor characteristic of her mother. Asked if her family was matriarchal, she snapped, "Amazonian, more like! They all had their left [*sic*] tits cut off!"

JANUS LENNON

John Lennon's astrological sign was Libra, a perfect symbol for his dichotomous personality. Part passive introvert, part aggressive show-off, he characterized himself as one-half "monk" and one-half "performing flea." The monastic Lennon was a natural product of his claustral rearing at Mendips, confined to a strict regimen and encouraged to shun the outer world, concentrating upon intellectual activities. Thus, from an early age, he learned the price he must pay for protection. "I *saw* loneliness!" he exclaimed when he thought of those years in later life. Soon he saw even stranger sights, when his lonely and emotionally deprived existence began to spawn hallucinations.

By staring at his eyes in the mirror for as much as an hour at a time, he discovered that he could put himself into a trance. "I would find myself seeing these hallucinatory images of my face changing, and the eyes would get bigger and the room would vanish," Lennon told the Beatles' biographer Hunter Davies. This knack of stepping through the looking glass opened up to the boy a realm of visionary and spectral experience that he later sought to explore more fully through the use of hypnotic and psychotomimetic drugs.

One of the most important consequences of Lennon's visionary temper was that it made him fear that he was insane; yet, at the same time, his hallucinations made him swell with pride because they could be construed as the stigmata of genius. *"Am I crazy or am I a genius?"*—that was the question, early and late, for John Lennon. Once he had read about the fascinating Vincent van Gogh, Lennon was able to harmonize these conflicting views of himself in the idea of the "mad genius." It was in this spirit that he would warn Mimi when she threw out his verses or drawings that someday she would regret these acts of vandalism because she was destroying the work of a genius.

As no signs of genius or even of unusual talent appear in the childish pictures and writings that survived Mimi's housecleaning, we are obliged to add to the portrait of the boy Lennon a touch of megalomania, a trait that betrayed itself at first very subtly, as when he manifested surprise that he was not recognized by strangers on the bus, but that later became embarrassingly obvious when he proclaimed himself Jesus or declared that in his next reincarnation he would become the Messiah. For from the first John Lennon's afflictions were both inspired and assuaged by his grandiosity, a natural trait in a boy who had been fought over since birth like the Holy City.

Though the idea that he was the center of the universe laid the foundation for his later role as a superstar, the real basis of his future triumph lay in his peculiar sense of the *word*. Whatever fault may be found with Mimi Smith as a surrogate mother, she certainly can't be taxed with throttling John. The future hero of the oral culture was always a great talker, and his natural style of utterance owed an obvious debt to his aunt's distinctive delivery. That straight-from-the-shoulder idiom that produced in later years so much delight or consternation every time Lennon opened his mouth came from Mimi, who said simply: "I've always believed in speaking my mind." Mimi's characteristic tone—stern, haughty, morally indignant—was often to be heard in Lennon's speech, particularly after he had left the Beatles and set up as a pundit. But even in his teeny-pop years, the lyrics of his songs are notable for their directness and earnestness, so different from the feckless clichés of the typical pop song or the logorrhea of Bob Dylan, Lennon's principal rival.

When young John sought to step over the gap from the spoken to the written word, however, he stumbled badly. Imagine his teachers' dismay when they discovered that this bright boy, who exhibited a love of reading and employed an extensive vocabulary, could not learn to spell even the simplest words. Not only did he constantly reverse letters, but he displayed an unmistakable tendency to transform one word into another of similar sound. Thus, "funds" became "funs," and "chicken pox" came out "chicken pots." Only late in life did Lennon discover that the cause of these habitual mistakes (as well as his lifelong inability to spell) was dyslexia, a common neurological complaint. Depending on the part of the brain affected, the dyslexic has trouble figuring out the sounds of words from their appearance or, in the opposite case (which was Lennon's), picturing the word from its sound, as well as retaining its image after he has looked it up in the dictionary. Either way, there is the same tendency to invert sounds and letters, reaching its most extreme form in that bizarre affliction, mirror writing.

Normally a nuisance, dyslexia may actually have been of great benefit to John Lennon because he made such extensive use of inversion not only as a compositional device but as a means of covering his traces when he filched a phrase from another man's music. Indeed, there was nothing more characteristic of Lennon's mind than its tendency to reverse itself. In his music, he never settles in one key but continually bends his phrases this way or that so their direction can be construed in terms of alternate keys, a bit like musical puns. Likewise, he is given to drifting in and out of the modal, which can be construed as the opposite of the tonal. He was also fascinated by the sound of tape reversed, an effect he discovered accidentally one night when coming home stoned from the studio, he tried to play his latest song, the bagpipe-droning "Rain." The tape had been wound backward; so when it began to play, what came out of the speakers was not "Rain" but a weird yawing and jawing. Delighted with this Silly Putty symphony, John stuck some of it on the end of the record. From that day forth, the Beatles became the world's foremost tape inverts, a perversion that led ultimately to the "Paul is dead" mania.

Even more pronounced than the possible effects of dyslexia on Lennon's music was the way his lexic dysfunction appears to have affected his literary style. Just as his discovery of Elvis Presley's "Heartbreak Hotel" galvanized him at fifteen into becoming a rocker, so did his much earlier discovery of Lewis Carroll's "Jabberwocky" (in *Through the Looking-Glass*) launch John on the path that led eventually to his humorous writings and his surrealist songs. The trick of tongue that intrigued him most was what Carroll called "portmanteau words," words produced by thinking simultaneously of two associated terms, like "chuckle" and "snort," then telescoping them to make "chortle." Compare this illustration, supplied by Carroll, with John Lennon's most celebrated exchange with the press: Reporter—"Are you mods or rockers?" Lennon—"Neither, we're mockers." Eventually, Lennon became so adroit at telescoping words that he could pick up a book and translate it at sight into portmanteauese, which is how he composed "At the Dennis" from *In His Own Write,* a word-for-word paraphrase of a lesson in Professor Carlo Barone's *A Manual of Conversation English-Italian.* Viewed from this perspective, the culmination of Lennon's artistic development is "I Am the Walrus," in which he finally synthesized his musical puns with his verbal puns, thereby achieving the incantatory magic he had long admired in "Jabberwocky."

If dyslexia offered an advantage that outweighed its negative effects, the same cannot be said for myopia and astigmatism, which operated in precisely the opposite manner. Easily corrected complaints that need never have produced any problem more serious than a broken lens, these ocular defects were magnified by Lennon's phobic reaction to them, which magnified them into major disabilities that had a profound and destructive effect on his entire future life. Though he was not diagnosed as having defective eyesight until the age of eleven, John claimed after he had been in primal therapy that his eyes started going bad when his mother and father broke up, asserting: "I put it all into my eyes so I literally could not see what was going on." Psychologically, this makes sense; physiologically, it is nonsense. All the Lennons had bad eyes, just as they had long noses. What made trouble for John was not his eyes but his refusal to wear glasses, which he regarded as disfiguring and unmanly. Without glasses, John Lennon was legally blind. A juvenile Mr. Magoo, he saw the world as a mystifying blur, like a man gazing through a misted windshield. At the movies, for example, he would have to nag his companion to explain what was happening on the screen. On the street he might have to shinny up a signpost to discover his whereabouts. Once he ran his bike head-on into a parked car, escaping injury only by vaulting over the vehicle like a tumbler. In the long run, however, it was not the danger of accident that mattered so much as it was the effects of this self-inflicted blindness on Lennon's mental and emotional development.

Because the only things that John could see distinctly were those that lay under his nose—which he elevated instinctively to obtain a slightly clearer image (a mannerism that earned him the reputation for being stuck up!)—he drifted into the dangerous habit of ignoring everything he couldn't see. Thus, the lonely, self-involved boy sank even deeper into his solitude and solipsism. Even when he turned his gaze inward, however, he remained myopic because mental vision is patterned upon ocular vision—a fact that emerges clearly the moment you start studying the way Lennon wrote his songs.

His perspective as a composer was that of a man staring down the barrel of a microscope upon a tiny stage, where he assembles bits and pieces of sound and language. Relying almost exclusively on the most rudimentary particles—the one- or two-note chant, the drone, the brief motto—he operated with an ear that was as short-sighted as his eye. He complained to the producer George Martin, when the latter sought to introduce Lennon to *Daphnis and Chloe,* that he could not follow the piece because its melodies were "too long." How appropriate, therefore, that the most pervasive motif in all of Lennon's music should turn out to be the tritone theme of "Three Blind Mice," the germ of songs as different as "All You Need Is Love," "Instant Karma," and "My Mummy's Dead." He even employed this motto in the identifying jingle on his telephone-answering machine.

The performing-flea side of Lennon's personality was no less conspicuous than his introversion. In fact, the two seemingly disparate characters were at bottom closely connected, for the discomfort that John Lennon felt in virtually any social situation compelled him to seize control of the moment by making himself the sole focus of attention. But this strategy only further alienated him, as he found himself addressing the world across the gap between performer and audience.

His other strategy for dealing with others was to play the bully. As this behavior had gotten him kicked out of kindergarten, Mimi resolved, when she enrolled him in Dovedale Primary School in August 1946, to escort him to and from school daily to prevent his getting into scraps. John threw such a fit at this proposal that his aunt was obliged to back down; but she didn't abandon her design. "I'd let him get out of the house," she explained, "and then follow him to make sure he didn't get into mischief." Nor was her concern in the least exaggerated. In no time, John Lennon was notorious as the school bully. "We were all a little bit frightened of him," recalled a former pupil, adding: "The mothers had their eyes on him, as if to say: 'Keep away from that one!'" Significantly, the earliest moment at which John Lennon comes distinctly into focus as a personality is in a fight recollected by his closest boyhood friend, Pete Shotton.

A white-haired youngster of eight, a year younger than Lennon, Pete was crossing a bit of wasteland one day when John stepped out of ambush and threatened Shotton with a beating if he ever humiliated John again by addressing him by his detested nickname, Winnie. Pete took up the challenge immediately, and both boys went at it with clenched fists. John, older and tougher, soon had Shotton pinned to the ground, where he extracted from him the promise he was seeking. No sooner was Pete released, however, than he ran off a safe distance and screamed: *"Winnie! Winnie! Winnie!"*

John was enraged. With his face contorted by hate, he doubled up his fist and bawled: "I'll get you for that, Shotton!"

Pete hollered back: "Well, you're going to have to catch me first, then, won't you, Lennon?"

Each boy stood there glaring at the other, until Pete observed that John's expression was changing. "Very gradually," Pete recalled, "his face broke into an enormous grin." From that moment forth they were fast friends.

John's tight relationship with Pete established the pattern for all his future attachments, for as Shotton acutely observed: "Though I have yet to encounter a personality as strong and individualist as John's, he always had to have a partner." A partner was merely Lennon's minimal requirement for buttressing his fragile ego; he preferred to have a whole gang. As he recalled in later years, "I always had a group of three or four or five guys around me, who would play various roles in my life, supportive and subservient, me being the bully boy." These gangs were extremely important both in terms of Lennon's personal development and as prototypes of the Beatles. They were also typical of Liverpool youth culture, which was unique in its capacity to transform its fighting gangs into aggressive rock bands. The most important thing about Lennon's gangs was simply the fact that they were extensions of his own personality. He took great care to indoctrinate them with his beliefs, which, like those of any renegade, were founded on rejection of conventional authority. "Parents are not God," John would lecture his young henchmen, "because I don't live with mine."

For years John Lennon waged a guerrilla war against the adult world, eventually earning a very bad reputation in his placid middle-class neighborhood. He stuffed firecrackers in letter boxes, dashed about after dark ringing doorbells, blew up streetlamps with home-made bombs, filched records from shops, pulled down girls' panties in public, and, on one awesome occasion, ignited the Guy Fawkes bonfire a day early.

Almost invariably, Lennon's pranks turned on some cruel deceit. He would plant himself, for example, out on the road, lying prone with his bike beside him, like the victim of a hit-and-run driver. The first vehicle to come along would screech to a stop, its driver staring horrified at the inert, perhaps dead schoolboy. But by the time the driver got out of his machine and reached the spot where the boy lay, the victim had vanished into thin air.

Another of his favorite tricks entailed the use of the telephone, an instrument not yet taken for granted in provincial Liverpool. Imagine how Lennon's victim would feel when late at night his phone rang and he would find himself being addressed by a coarse voice, like that of a gangster in an American film. The voice would warn that the victim's house was being watched and that he was in serious trouble. On no account must he call the police!

John's favorite target for this prank was a high-school master named Dolson, who had suffered a nervous breakdown during the war. As soon as Lennon discovered this poor man's weakness, John was on him like a jackal. He would call Dolson after dark and, speaking in a hollow, menacing tone, demand, "The box! We want the box!" Next day at school John would study the master's face to determine whether the scare was having its intended effect. Dolson, who never knew when his phone might ring with another threatening message, soon began to betray signs of anxiety. John and his gang relished their success.

When the time came for John to be enrolled in high school, everyone in the family had urged Mimi to put the boy into the city's finest school, the Liverpool Institute; but she was highly alarmed by this idea because the Institute lay in the heart of Liverpool 8, a seedy bohemian district. So John was sent to a school just two miles from Mendips, in Calderstones, one of the city's finest residential districts.

In September 1952, just a month short of his twelfth birthday, clad still in short pants and schoolboy cap, John Lennon entered for the first time the imposing circular lobby of Quarry Bank Grammar

School, a public institution that closely resembled a prep school. A massive mock-Tudor mansion, built of brick and carved stone, paneled in splendid Victorian oak and inlay work, this classy British school stood at the opposite extreme from that classic rock 'n' roll setting, the big modern American high school. At Quarry Bank the boys wore black blazers and caps, gray sweaters and slacks, white shirts and black ties striped in maroon and gold, emblazoned with the school crest. Over their hearts they displayed the school emblem: a stag's head surmounted by four seashells and subscribed, *Ex hoc metallo Virtutem*— "Out of this rough metal, we forge excellence."

Though the pupils lived at home, they were organized, as in residence schools, into houses comprised of boys from particular districts and governed by housemasters. There were prefects to enforce discipline, and canings were administered by the black-gowned headmaster, who kept a record of every infraction in his punishment book. Academically Quarry Bank was a first-rate school, particularly strong in the humanities. Because it was so closely modeled on those citadels of privilege the ancient British public schools, it was highly appropriate that after it had produced a couple of socialist prime ministers, it should be dubbed by the press, the "Eton of the Labour Party."

John Lennon was a reluctant scholar, who had to be roused every morning by his aunt. After donning his detested school uniform, he would descend to the bright morning room and wolf down his breakfast. Strapping his books on the handlebars of his bike, he would pedal off along Menlove Avenue, pausing at the intersection with Vale Road, where he would meet Pete Shotton, the only boy from the neighborhood who had elected to attend Quarry Bank. Pupils were required to be at school by eight-thirty but Lennon made sure to arrive early so that he could spend some time showing off in front of the boys and girls who gathered every morning before the old gray mossy statues of the Four Seasons that mark the entrance to Calderstones Park. Here John would harangue his audience with a rap notable for its large number of academic words and locutions, like "pertaining to."

A witness to these sessions was Meg Dogherty, then Meg Drinkwater, who lived near Mendips and attended Calderstones, the girls' school adjacent to Quarry Bank. Meg described John's manner at thirteen as "arrogant, very arrogant and very self-assured." She also recalled his cruelty. "He was keen on discovering any cause for shame—a split home, your father away, your mother ill. If there was something that wasn't a hundred percent normal, he would go out of his way to find it out and play on it. Then he would get other people to rib you. A girl hadn't much of a chance in the face of this malicious fun." By the same token, Lennon was quick to change the conversation if he found the subject disturbing: "The minute parents were mentioned or you did anything as a family, like 'Mom and Dad took me to the cinema,' a barrier, a wall would come down. He would change the subject completely. Also he would never answer a question seriously. It was always a laugh and a joke."

John's cruelty was not confined to words; he would lash out instinctively at anyone who angered him. One day Meg came pedaling to school on a secondhand Dawes racing bike that she had been given for her birthday. As she pulled up at the Four Seasons, John was riding close behind her. The kids were so impressed by Meg's new machine that they ignored John. This made him so furious that he leaned over and gave Meg a vicious shove, sending her sprawling to the pavement. He fell off his own bike in the effort, but he managed to emit a mirthless laugh as he hit the ground. When Meg tells the story, she raises her skirt to show a scar on her left knee.

Extreme hostility coupled with extreme defensiveness characterizes the essential Lennon, early and late. These attitudes gripped John so powerfully that they bent him into a distinctive shape and gave him his characteristic gait. "He used to walk," recalled Pete Shotton, "all hunched up, his eyes and head down, like a scared rabbit driven into a corner but ready to lash out." Like most bullies, Lennon was frightened at heart. He sought to dominate through sheer aggression, especially by launching surprise attacks; but if he ran into someone bigger or braver, he would resort to psychological tactics, according to Shotton, "undermining them by abuse or sarcasm." If all else failed, Lennon would take to his heels. At school John and Pete were often caned by the headmaster, the notorious Ernie Taylor, but no matter how much Lennon was beaten, he never mended his ways. Instead, he adopted the attitude that he was beyond the pale, so what did it matter what he did or how much he was punished?

Aunt Mimi was very upset by the complaints that she received constantly from the school, actually feeling a chill every time the phone rang. Her own efforts to discipline John had long since failed. No matter how hard she came down on him, he seemed to win from her punishments the strength to commit new and greater outrages. George Smith, the man of the house, who might have been expected to correct John, spent his life screwed into a chair in the lounge, while Mimi ruled the roost. So with John and Mimi locked in combat and George withdrawn behind his newspaper, matters reached a crisis at Mendips in Lennon's thirteenth year.

The events of that explosive time impressed themselves so deeply on John's mind that he never forgot them. When he wrote Mimi in the last year of his life, he rehashed all his old grievances against her. What he resented most, interestingly, was her *bullying* him. He accused her of hurling cut-crystal ashtrays at him and urging the headmaster to give him "six of the best" because he was "too clever for his own good."

It appears clear from Mimi's treatment of Freddie that her principal weapon against men was shaming or humiliating them. Doubtless, she employed these same tactics against young John, but her efforts failed; hence the rage that impelled her to resort to violence. John, for his part, struggled to gain the upper hand by trying to shame Mimi, rubbing in the inconsistencies of her behavior or seizing upon anything else that would give him the upper hand. He had many legitimate grievances: Mimi did control him, spy on him, manipulate him, and deprive him of the pleasures that other children enjoyed freely. Hence, he had every reason to revolt, particularly at this moment when he was beginning to feel his burgeoning masculinity. But no matter how much he yearned to seize control of his life, at thirteen he still required a home and guardian.

Ironically, he found the ally he needed for his revolt against the matriarch, Mimi, in his mother, Julia.

KINKY HAVEN

No. 1 Blomfield Road, the home of the Dykins family, was not prepossessing. A box-like, semidetached council house, the first on a block of identical structures, the place looked neglected—lawns unmowed, garden gone to weed, puddle-ringed drains blocked. Once inside, however, the visitor would find himself in a warm and congenial atmosphere. A golden boxer would bound forward to nuzzle the stranger, the sound of "The Laughing Policeman," an archaic party record, would cackle from the massive old radio-phonograph, and, wherever the caller looked, his eye would be caught by trinkets and bric-a-brac. The most conspicuous feature of the lounge was a quilted bar, which boasted a tempting stock of good liquor.

No matter what the hour, Julia would be fully dressed and made up, her deep red hair ablaze about her head. Relieved of many domestic chores by Dykins, who was home all day and who liked to fetch in groceries, hang up clean curtains, or even bake a pie, Julia was free to indulge in her favorite pastimes, like sitting at the piano, which had a scrollwork grille backed by pleated colored silk, playing and singing songs from minstrel shows, music halls, and movies.

Julia's home was a haven for all the aggrieved children of the Stanley family. Leila remembered going there many times after a spat with her mother: "I'd go into the television room, and Judy would see that I wasn't feeling well, so she'd slip me a little apple. Soon as I was feeling better, I would go into the kitchen. An hour with her, you would just be in stitches. She was funny! She always did it. It came off the top of her head. If you went to Julia's house, the tears would be streaming down your face."

Pete Shotton recalled that the first time he was presented to John's mother, she sashayed up to him and exclaimed, "Ooh, what lovely slim hips you have!" As Pete reached out to shake hands, Julia began to stroke his hips, giggling all the while. When John confessed that they were playing hooky, Julia said gaily, "Don't worry about school. Don't worry about a thing! Everything's going to work out fine!"

John, who had a demeaning nickname for everyone, called his mother's common-law husband Twitchy, caricaturing his nervous habit of coughing and then putting his hand to his face, as if to assure himself that his nose was still in place. But actually, John got on well with John Dykins because he saw Twitchy as a soft touch. Whenever John and Pete would turn up, Dykins would lead them to the fishbowl where he kept his weekly tips and allow them one "lucky dip." He also bought John his first colored shirts and other items of apparel which Aunt Mimi did not approve of or could not afford. When John was old enough to be allowed a glass of beer, he and his stepfather grew much closer.

Handsome and well built, John Dykins had a slightly exotic air owing to his dark "Spanish" complexion and pencil-line movie-star mustache. (The Stanleys called him "Spiv," which connotes the slick black-market operator, implicitly a Jew.) He had a masterful bearing toward women that was just what Julia craved—and failed to find in Freddie. Despite his masculine qualities, however, Dykins was regarded by his next wife, Rona, as basically homosexual. She observed during three years of dating and three years of marriage that virtually all her husband's friends were gay.

A proficient worker, always in demand as wine steward or waiter in good hotels and gambling clubs, Dykins when not working was always drunk—so drunk that sometimes, when he drove home at night, he had to stop his car in the middle of the road to gather his wits. (He died after a car crash on 1 June 1966.) An impulsive spender, given to throwing his money around and showing everyone a good time, he was often so negligent that when he was out of town, Julia would have to go begging to the neighbors to get enough food for the family and enough coal to heat the house.

Usually Dykins doted on Julia and their two pretty daughters, Julie and Jacqueline, indulging all their whims. Sometimes, however, he would erupt violently in the middle of the night, attacking Julia physically and throwing her and the little girls out in the street. As they would stand there, shivering in the cold, Dykins would bellow: *"This is my house!"* Julia and her daughters would be obliged to trek across the Allerton Golf Course, flashlight in hand, to Mendips, where they could obtain shelter for the night. But wife beating was not uncommon in working-class Liverpool, and Julia was no longer of an age at which she could confidently anticipate finding another man. So she remained with Dykins, perhaps finding some perverse pleasure in his displays of violence, just as she would relish the pain from a cut in her flesh by rubbing salt in the wound.

Perhaps the most revealing feature of Jack Dykins's daily behavior was the manic style in which he sought a good time. He was a rounder, a restless, insatiable pleasure seeker, who, in a single night, would make the circuit of all the bars and clubs in his vicinity. His brother Leonard, a taxi driver, and his wife, Evelyn, recall being awakened many nights by a great banging at their door. Looking out the window, they would espy Jack standing below, flourishing a bottle. The moment he was admitted, he would pour each of them a drink and insist they throw it back. Then they had to get dressed and make the rounds, never pausing anywhere for longer than it took to order and down a single drink.

People who spent a lot of time with Jack and Julia, like the Leonard Dykinses, felt that the couple had a romantic relationship. Jack was both affectionate and considerate of Julia. A heavy smoker, whose satin tuxedo lapels often betrayed a dribble of white ash, he would never light a cigarette in Julia's company without lighting a second one for her. When Evelyn would ask her brother-in-law why he didn't marry Julia, he would reply: "Ev, there's somethin' about *not* being married— it brings you closer together." All the same, Jack and Julia comported themselves strictly as man and wife. Julia wore a wedding ring and was addressed invariably as Mrs. Dykins. Julia and Jacqueline never learned that their father and mother were not married until both parents were dead. In the Stanley family no one was supposed to know the truth about anything shameful.

John Dykins appears to have had a pronounced effect on John Lennon, which is not surprising, in view of the fact that John had no male role models, save for his uncle George, a weak and passive man. Virtually every one of Dykins's distinguishing traits, including the alcoholism, the wife beating, the closet homosexuality, and the spurts of compulsive partying, appeared subsequently in Lennon's behavior. Significantly, as soon as John made it big, he bought Twitchy a long white Riley sports car with a rumble seat.

If Julia and Twitchy offered John Lennon a temporary avenue of escape from those seven rooms of gloom on Menlove Avenue, another, even more enticing opening was afforded by Aunt Elizabeth. After the death of her first husband, Captain Charles M. Parkes, a naval architect and marine surveyor, she married in 1949 Robert Hugh Sutherland, an Edinburgh dental surgeon. Every summer until he was fifteen, John would be sent first to his aunt's town house at 15 Ormidale Terrace in Auld Reekie, and then on to the family's sheep croft at Sangobeg near Durness, on the northernmost coast of Scotland—a starkly beautiful region, redolent of Iceland and the Norsemen. The croft, an earth-hugging brick structure, was warmed by peat fires and illuminated by paraffin lamps.

Young John would go out exploring with his older cousins, Stanley Parkes and Leila Birch, hiking across miles of rocky hills or spongy peat and bog lands, always with a great mountain looming in the distance. They would stumble upon ruins that dated back to the Stone Age or engage in sports that belonged to the wilderness. John learned to cast a fly on a salmon river and to shoot with a twenty-two at rabbits, pheasant, and grouse. Everywhere he went, he heard the fascinating speech of the Highlanders, which he loved to mimic. On Sundays he would pore over the comics in the *Sunday Post,* a Scottish paper, where he made the acquaintance of cartoon characters like *The Broons* and *Oor Willie.* Scotland was an experience that John never forgot. Twenty years later he wrote his aunt that he remembered Scotland more fondly than he did England.

Scotland was such a tonic for Lennon that it's not surprising he should have received there the first intimations of his future vocation. One day he went out for a walk and lapsed into a trance: "I was kind of hallucinating," he recalled, "the ground starts going beneath you and the heather, and I could see this mountain in the distance. And this kind of *feeling* came over me: I thought, 'This is *something*! What is this? Ah, this is that one they're always talking about, the one that makes you paint or write because it's so overwhelming that you have to tell somebody . . . so you put it into poetry.'"

John was camping in Scotland when George Smith died on 5 June 1955 at the age of fifty-two. On the fatal day George got out of bed to go to the bathroom and began to vomit blood. Rushed to Sefton General Hospital, he died of a massive hemorrhage produced by cirrhosis of the liver. A couple of days later John was sent home by Mater without being told of his uncle's death. When he came bounding into the kitchen, asking for Uncle George, he found "Mimi crying over the carrots and her student lodgers trying to look sad." When Mimi told him the news, John withdrew into silence. "I went upstairs," he recalled; "then my cousin Leila arrived, and she came upstairs as well. We both had hysterics. We just laughed and laughed. I felt very guilty afterwards."

The death of Uncle George increased John's attachment to his alternate home at Blomfield Road, but what made his mother's house indispensable to him were his three new obsessions, all of which were anathema to Mimi: dressing like a Teddy Boy, screwing girls, and leading a skiffle band. The Teddy Boy identification was a natural for a lad as rebellious as Lennon. The Teds—who got their name from their uniform, the Edwardian lounge suit with long jacket and velvet collar (derived from young upperclass guards officers)—were working-class boys, who gave England its first taste of American-inspired juvenile delinquency.

The Year of the Teds was 1956. In September, when *Rock Around the Clock*, starring Bill Haley, opened in Britain, the Teds seized the occasion to celebrate their cult by ripping up movie theaters all over the country. This outburst of vandalism thrilled John Lennon. He felt a sudden affinity with the lower classes, but unlike the Teds, he didn't work in a factory where he could earn the money to tog out in a western gunslinger's jacket, drainpipe trousers, a bootstring tie (with a death's-head medallion), and crepe-soled brothel creepers or beetle crushers. The best a poor middle-class boy, attending the "Eton of the Labour Party," could do was cultivate a greasy quiff (pompadour) and sideboards (sideburns) and take in his wide trousers on his auntie's sewing machine. To wear the pants, he needed the cover provided by his mother's carefree house.

John's initiation into serious sex, as opposed to circle jerks and cinema balcony petting, was also something that demanded the concealment provided by Blomfield Road. Mimi not only had discovered the secret diary in which John recorded his sexual exploits but had cracked the code by which he had sought to conceal these wicked acts. After being so shamefully exposed, John recognized that there was no keeping anything to himself at home.

In later years, John was wont to say that he had been initiated into sex by an "older woman." Barbara Baker was no older than John Lennon, but she was certainly more experienced. She recalls first taking notice of John one Sunday afternoon when she was coming home from church school. She and another girl had taken shelter from a spring rainstorm in an alley. No sooner were they under cover than John and Pete came charging down the lane. When John spotted Barbara's long ponytail, he shouted: *"Oh, there's horseface! Horse's tail and horse's face!"* Barbara recognized John as the "little horror" who used to perch in a tree and shoot arrows at her as she walked home from school. Now she was surprised to see that he was smartly dressed in a white shirt, school tie, and blue blazer. A short conversation led to an invitation to walk about a few nights later.

Soon Barbara and John "went all the way." John's report to Pete was characteristically frank. "Well, Pete," he announced, "I've done it at last. I've had me first screw. I had a hell of a job getting inside Barb. It was like trying to get inside a mouse's earhole. Actually, I think, I'd rather have a wank."

But Barbara hunted John down. She "ought to have taken a tent for the number of times she was outside the house," reported Julie Dykins, "just watching the house, gardens, windows, and door." So practiced a hypocrite was the fifteen-year-old John that he actually asked his mother to go out and send Barbara away. When Julia confronted the girl, she ran off but was pursued and caught by Julie and Jacqueline, who were very curious about this mysterious business. Barbara asked the nine-year-old Julie to summon John without his mother's knowledge. When John got the message, he left the house with a great show of indifference, making it appear as though he were simply taking the air. What he didn't realize, poor blind lad, was that he was being shadowed by his sisters. They caught him lying in the grass, embracing Barbara passionately. John was so horrified at being discovered that he bought off the girls with a half crown. That night over tea Julia commiserated with John over his persecution at the hands of this terrible girl. John glared at Julie and gave her a smart kick under the table as a warning to keep her mouth shut.

Barbara Baker was a very sexy girl, with a body that would give a teenage boy the bends. John could enjoy his access to her without relinquishing his companionship with Pete, who had his own girl. Many times the two couples screwed in the same room or even in the same bed. The funniest such scene recounted by Shotton occurred one afternoon when the foursome were visiting the home of Pete's girlfriend. The moment the girl's mother left the parlor to make tea, John and Barbara started making out on the sofa, while Pete's girl pulled off her underpants and straddled Pete in a chair. At the height of their pleasure the young people were startled to hear a knock at the door. "Come in!" cried John, deftly zipping up his trousers.

The lady of the house fluttered inside, trilling: "Tea's ready!"

Pete was horrified but contrived somehow to avoid detection. John couldn't pass up the chance to torment his pal. Jumping up to assist the hostess, he pulled poor Pete out of his chair, where he had been trying desperately to shrink his protuberant member. "C'mon, Pete!" cried John. "What's the matter with you?"

John and Barbara were intensely involved during John's last year in high school and his first year in art college. Eventually Barbara met Julia, who received the girl in a friendly manner. Mimi was another matter. "She was so well dressed and well spoken," Barbara recalled. "I felt I better watch my P's and Q's with her." Everybody saw Mimi as stuck-up. "She always had to put on this image," said Barbara, adding: "I don't think she was popular." Mimi, for her part, found Barbara "very forward." As Barbara recognized, "I never got on with Mimi. I think she thought—and she was probably right—it was getting too hot. And we were too young."

"A very romantic boy, extremely romantic" is how Barbara Baker remembered John Lennon. "He wrote pages and pages of poetry to me. Love—absolute romance! 'Here,' he would say, 'I've written you a letter, a poem, read it! . . . When he took [art college] exams, he would put my name at the bottom of his picture. That way he felt sure he would pass."

The romance was stormy. In their second summer John and Barbara had a tremendous blowup. "I cooled off him," recollected Barbara, "and started going out with his best friend [as she called Bill Turner] behind his back. John went crazy. He nearly kicked a fence in that night. He was absolutely brokenhearted." After a few weeks Barbara decided, after all, that she preferred John. When she explained the situation to Bill, he, like a good mate, passed the word on to John, and the lovers were reconciled. What led to their final parting was the direct intervention of their families.

Barbara's mother was alarmed to see her daughter getting involved in an affair. She went to see Mimi. "Mimi and my mum had a conversation—and my father," recalled Barbara. "They sort of made us give it up. Made us split up." John continued to see Barbara on the sly for some time, but by the beginning of his second year in art college the romance was over. By that time John had a new steady, a girl who was much less "forward."

SUMMONS FROM ELVIS

Before he heard "Heartbreak Hotel," John Lennon was a Nowhere Boy. He was like those heroes in fairy tales who have been spirited away from court as infants and reared in the wilderness as utter naïfs. Only it wasn't from the intrigues of the wicked that Mimi had sequestered John but from the most familiar experiences of everyday life. Since anything that was "common," particularly the vulgar language and imagery of the mass media, was strictly forbidden at Mendips, even as late as 1956, when he was fifteen, John had only an inkling of that mass culture that was the lifeblood of his generation. The future media addict, media maven, and media master was an old-fashioned boy living in that print and picture book world that had been fading since the Twenties. Viewed against this dim background, the advent of Elvis Presley loomed like an atomic explosion.

"Heartbreak Hotel" spoke with stunning directness to the boy who "saw loneliness." Now he *heard* loneliness. It was coming at him from a strange creature thousands of miles away, but they were on the same wavelength. There was a direct heart-to-heart line of communication between rock's greatest stars because at heart they were the same human being. Both were lonely only children reared by overprotective matrons intent on binding them fast to home and mother for the rest of their lives. Both escaped from their throttling families by striking rebellious poses that made them generation heroes. At heart, though, both remained sad little blue boys, disposed to spend their lives in drugs and dreams, though sometimes roiled to passion they poured into their records. Hence, what "Heartbreak Hotel" did for John Lennon was give him a startling foreflash, a proleptic vision of his future life.

Significantly, this awesome feat of communication was achieved nonverbally. Though Elvis Presley and John Lennon spoke what was nominally the same language, John could not understand what Elvis was saying. Elvis was an American primitive, a bam-bam Caliban, passionate but unintelligble. That was the secret of his magical effect. Like that other great freak of the Fifties, Johnnie Ray, Elvis drove words and music over the line that separates language from action. Johnnie Ray didn't tell you about crying: he did it! Likewise, Elvis wasn't describing loneliness: he enacted it as an overwhelming tragedy, leading straight to the grave.

"Heartbreak Hotel" was not only a catalyst for Lennon but an initiation and an education. It beckoned to him in the tantalizing language of dreams. It also pointed him in his natural direction as an artist—toward the enactment of his deepest fears in a rock 'n' roll psychodrama. Never has a writer or performer received a more powerful and compelling summons to his profession.

Immediately John began itching to emulate his new hero. Spotting an ad for a secondhand guitar, "guaranteed not to break," in *Reveille,* he pestered both his mothers to buy him the instrument. Mimi was totally opposed to the idea and refused to do anything that might encourage this dangerous new obsession. Julia was of a different mind. She loved rock 'n' roll. In fact, she had picked up on the new music before her son, when the first big rock record, Bill Haley's "Rock Around the Clock," broke in Britain, back in September 1955. Every time this old jump tune came on the air, Julia would hop up and start jigging around her living room. She was also confident that she could teach John the guitar in the same way that her father had taught her the banjo. So she came up with the ten quid, and John received by mail a battered old Spanish guitar, about right for boxing oranges. Teaching John to play guitar as if it were banjo meant tuning the top five strings to G and allowing the bottom string to flop about uselessly. Right or wrong was all the same to John Lennon. He was intent now on learning his first tune: Fats Waller's "Ain't It a Shame."

In every account of Lennon ever published, the impression is created that the guitar was the first instrument that he owned or learned to play. This presumption is a vital part of the mistaken idea that John had no musical history prior to his infatuation with Elvis and hence that he was purely a product of rock 'n' roll. The fact is that John was given his first instrument as a child: a rudimentary accordion, upon which he learned to play the hits of the day: "Greensleeves," "Swedish Rhapsody," and "Moulin Rouge." Next, John took up the harmonica when a student lodger offered to give him an instrument if he could learn to play it. John mastered two tunes immediately and became so fond of harmonica playing that on a bus trip to Edinburgh he drove all the passengers crazy by playing relentlessly "The Happy Traveler." The bus driver, impressed by the boy's spirit, told him to come around next morning to the terminal, where he would give him a heavy professional-quality instrument. It was all those years of playing harp that enabled John to give the Beatles' first records their distinctive sound by bathing them in a blue wash of harmonica sonority. Actually, the harmonica suited John a lot better than the guitar because it offered him an instrumental voice that paralleled his singing voice.

If "Heartbreak Hotel" was not the beginning of Lennon's musical development, so learning to strum a guitar and sing a lot of late Fifties rockabilly and R&B songs didn't make John or his mates in the Beatles into Americans. Far too much emphasis has been laid on the Beatles' identification with American music and far too little on their basic alienation from American culture. The Beatles' primary achievement was to lift American pops off its foundations and transport it to England, where they transformed it into another music entirely. Obviously they could never have performed this astonishing feat if they had not been steeped to the lips in American music, but by the same token, they would not have revolutionized rock music if they had simply carried on like the Americans. What Elvis and rock 'n' roll did for John Lennon was give him something to shoot for. The gun and the ammunition were already in his hands, even if they were only a toy accordion and a heavy harmonica.

From the first, John's new obsession made trouble at Mendips. Aunt Mimi, annoyed by his constant guitar twanging and foot stamping, ordered him to practice inside the glass enclosure around the front door. "He leaned so long against the brick," she recalled, "I think he must have rubbed part of it off with his backside." A further problem arose when Mimi was forbidden to enter John's room, which became a chaos of discarded clothes, newspapers, and books. "If I opened the door, he'd say: 'Leave it, I'll tidy up.' He became a mess, almost overnight, and all because of Elvis Presley, I say. He had a poster of him in his bedroom, socks somewhere else, shirts flung on the floor." Mimi kept vowing loudly: "There's going to be a change in this house! We're going to have law and order!" But all they had was more Elvis, even after the lights went out. "John would listen to the Elvis songs on the radio [*The Jack Jackson Show* on Radio Luxembourg, whose weak, whistling signal was starting to come through at Liverpool]. He would take a radio to bed with him at night and listen under the covers, thinking I didn't know. But I didn't miss much, although you had to be sharp when John was around. He could get up to some tricks all right."

John's battered old Spanish guitar was not the sort of instrument that an Elvis Presley played. He started badgering Mimi to buy him a better guitar. Finally, she succumbed to his demands. "I thought I would teach him a lesson by getting him one. I thought that the novelty would wear off soon, and he would forget about it. So one Saturday we went down to Hessy's shop in Liverpool, and I bought him one there.

It cost me fourteen pounds, *fourteen pounds*! That was a lot of money in those days. I begrudged paying it on a guitar for him, but I thought that if it keeps him quiet, then there's no harm done. He would even stand in front of his bedroom mirror with the guitar pretending to be that man Elvis Presley."

Though the impact of Elvis on John's life was total, he was forced to recognize that there were better rock 'n' roll singers. At the same time that he discovered Elvis, he made an even more momentous discovery: Little Richard. The boy at whose home John heard Richard first was Mike Hill, who had a remarkable collection of American records, including all the great early R&B singers. Since Hill lived very near school and had a working mother, he was able to entertain John and his friends every day at lunch.

"This boy at school had been to Holland," recalled Lennon. "He said he'd got this record at home by somebody who was better than Elvis. Elvis was bigger than religion in my life. We used to go to this boy's house and listen to Elvis on 78s; we'd buy five Senior Service [cheap cigarettes] loose in this shop and some chips, and we'd go along. The new record was 'Long Tall Sally' [B-side:"Slippin' and Slidin'"]. When I heard it, it was so great I couldn't speak. You know how you are torn. I didn't want to leave Elvis. We all looked at each other, but I didn't want to say anything against Elvis, not even in my mind. How could they be happening in my life, *both* of them? And then someone said: 'It's a nigger singing.' I didn't know Negroes sang. So Elvis was white, and Little Richard was black. 'Thank you, God,' I said. There was a difference between them. But I thought about it for days at school, of the labels on the records. One was yellow [Little Richard] and one was blue, and I thought of the yellow against the blue."

This experience was the first augury of Lennon's later role as perhaps the foremost connoisseur of rock 'n' roll in England. Much of what the Beatles did in their early years was determined by their ability to spot the best things on the other side of the Atlantic and exploit them first. At this point, however, John was simply a fan with no hope of becoming a real rocker like Elvis, a fabulous creature who belonged to another world. As Pete Shotton remarked: "Even John did not aspire to sing, play guitar, or make a million dollars like Elvis. It would have seemed inconceivable to us that a boy of limited means from the provinces of England might emulate the *professional* achievements of a Bill Haley or an Elvis. To make real music, after all, one first had to have the money to buy expensive equipment and instruments—and these, moreover, presumably required years of tedious lessons and practice to master. Above all, rock and roll were—almost by definition—American."

The best a British boy could do, therefore, was follow the lead of

Lonnie Donegan, the inspiration for the skiffle craze and the real protoype of the Beatles because he was a very clever and resourceful young Englishman from the north who found a way to adapt American music to British taste and thereby spark a youthquake. A trad jazzman, Donegan was every bit as "professional" as Presley; in fact, he was a lot more professional, this son of a violinist in the National Scottish Orchestra, because he had a far greater command of music. He could cite chapter and verse for every move he made on the pop checkerboard.

Donegan's meat was black folk music, especially the records of the great Huddie Ledbetter, a real-life John Henry, who was such a beguiling singer and twelve-string guitar player that he sang his way out of prison after being locked up for murdering a man. Donegan's first and most famous hit was an emasculation of Ledbetter's recording of "Rock Island Line."

The secret of Donegan's success was precisely that of Presley before him and the Beatles after him: he made his old American black materials sound romantic and engaging to contemporary white kids. The train songs that became the staple of skiffle he performed in a light, fast, skimming or skiffling style. More than anything else, it was this light, speedy, horse-and-gig-across-the-range atmosphere that caught the kids' fancy. Even the name, "skiffle," was a clever bit of product identification, for the real skiffle, a kind of street-corner black jazz, was nothing like Donegan's style, which he appropriated from the western swing of Bob Wills and the Texas Playboys. The most remarkable thing about the music, however, was not its name, style, or content but the manner in which it was performed. Though Donegan used nothing but professional instruments, the practice sprang up of playing skiffle on homemade instruments, like the tea chest bass, fashioned out of a square wooden box and a broom handle, and the thimble-strummed washboard. Transformed into a game that any boy could pick up as easily as a yo-yo, skiffle erupted overnight into one of those manic fads characteristic of kiddie kulture.

As tens of thousands of British boys banded together, the entertainment industry responded with skiffle programs on radio and TV, skiffle contests in theaters, skiffle clubs in cities, and, of course, a profusion of skiffle records. Quick on the griddle and quick off, skiffle was simply the appetizer for the great feast of British rock 'n' roll, but it did demonstrate the enormous potential of the English youth market and the longing of thousands of kids to get into the act. The age of participatory culture was dawning.

Skiffle had an enduring effect on John Lennon and the other Beatles, as is apparent in the galloping western style they employed in some of their greatest hits, like "A Hard Day's Night," with its deeply twanging, Marlboro Man guitar break. Nearly as many Beatles songs owe their inspiration to country and western music as to rhythm and blues, although the latter was the style they most admired, for C&W presented none of the technical or ethnic obstacles of black music to these English boys; hence, it was always available as an easy fallback style, which also enjoyed the advantage of being ebullient and lighthearted, even downright funny. It is perhaps significant that Lennon's second big discovery after Elvis was that countrified rockabilly Carl Perkins, whom Lennon preferred to Elvis on "Blue Suede Shoes."

In March 1957 John Lennon, aged sixteen, formed his first band, a skiffle group that began with John as singer and guitarist, Pete Shotton on washboard, and Eric Griffiths, a studious-looking boy from Woolton, playing his new guitar à la Julia. As soon as John and Eric had gotten a couple of tunes down pat, they recruited Rod Davies, another local lad, who soon became Quarry Bank's head boy. Rod had just bought a secondhand Windsor World banjo. When he turned up for his first rehearsal at Eric's house, he confessed that he didn't know how to play. John and Eric taught him their system, which was to play everything in the key of C, using three chords: C, F, G7. Rod mastered the fingering, and the rehearsal commenced. As John sang, Eric would shout to Rod which chord to play. In a short time the clever Rod learned how to "busk."

Soon a couple more men were added to the band: Bill Smith of Childwall House on tea chest bass (he was soon "given the elbow" for missing rehearsals and replaced by Len Garry, from the Liverpool Institute) and Colin Hanton on drums. Hanton was the only member of the group who was not a grammar school boy, being an apprentice upholsterer who worked in a furniture factory in Speke and lived near Eric and Rod in Woolton. Hanton was a prized recruit since he owned a Broadway drum kit (bass drum, snare, side drum, and one cymbal), a rare because expensive instrument.

Because the band had adopted its uniform—black jeans and white shirt with bootlace tie—before it had a name, it chose a title to match its look, calling itself the Black Jacks and employing as its trademark a black tea chest embellished with silver musical notes and a treble clef, which Rod's father cut out of metallic paper. The change from the Black Jacks to the now-legendary Quarry Men was inspired simply by the fact that most of the boys attended Quarry Bank, whose school anthem traced the progress of the ideal pupil from a roughhewn lump of rock to a polished bit of masonry.

The repertory of the Quarry Men was the standard skiffle song bag, with a few eccentric additions. The boys did the obligatory hits of Lonnie Donegan—"Rock Island Line," "John Henry," "Don't You Rock Me, Daddyo"—plus the Vipers' "Maggie" (the traditional Liverpool song about a Lime Street whore) and Chazz McDevit and Nancy Whiskey's "Freight Train." A particular favorite was Burl Ives's "Worried Man's Blues," which the group took off a battered 78. Their only problem was that they couldn't crack the lyrics. But John Lennon, recognizing that the sound, not the words, was the important thing, felt free to replace any language he couldn't understand with verses of his own invention.

A typical example of his handiwork was his interpolation in the Del Vikings' hit "Come Go with Me." On the original record the lead takes off and sings: "Love, love me, darlin', Come and go with me, Please don't send me, 'way beyond the sea." The last phrase—so important for a Viking!—is virtually unintelligible, so Lennon consulted his sense of this raunchy American music, obviously conversant with criminality, and wrote: "Come, come, come, go with me, Down to the penitentiary"! With such hilarious patch-up jobs the lead singer of the Quarry Men commenced his career as the greatest lyricist of the Rock Age.

On 21 June 1957 John Lennon played his first professional engagement, at a daylong block party on Rosebury Street in the Dingle, a grid of two-up and two-down dollhouses sloping toward the Merseyside along narrow streets lined with lollipop trees. The occasion was a citywide celebration of the granting of Liverpool's charter by King John in the thirteenth century. Three blocks were roped off and festooned with bunting and Liverbirds. The roadway was lined like a carnival midway with refreshment and game booths and thronged by a cheery holiday crowd. The Quarry Men played twice on the back of a flatbed truck, working with acoustic guitars and a primitive PA system consisting of a mike and an old radio.

Lennon togged out for his debut in a plaid cowboy shirt open at the neck, with his hair in a rough approximation of Elvis's royal crown. The pictures of the band, the first ever taken of Lennon performing, show him twanging his guitar and singing into the mike with that snake-neck posture he never lost. According to Charles Roberts, who lived on the street, John acted "cocky, as if he knew he was good, winking at the girls as he played and showing a dry sense of humor." It was probably this show-off attitude that precipitated the abrupt and panicky end of the eight o'clock performance.

A couple of black boys from the neighboring ghetto on Hatherly Street showed up and made some threatening remarks about Lennon. Terrified of what he called the "nigger gang," John jumped off the truck and dashed with his band into the shelter of Charles Roberts's house. There Roberts's mother served the boys a salad and called for a policeman, who escorted the Quarry Men to a bus bound for Woolton. Two weeks later, on 6 July, the band played a similar engagement but one that ended in a meeting destined to influence the whole future course of pop music.

QUARRY ROCK

The annual St. Peter's Church garden fete in Woolton began with the crowning of a virginal rose queen, who advanced with her retinue through the village's narrow streets, lined with brown sandstone houses, until it reached the hill on which stood the somber old church. Nearby was a pleasure ground with lemonade and ice cream stalls, sideshows and a crude stage on which the children paraded in fancy dress and the brass band of the Cheshire Yeomanry performed.

Around six o'clock on the afternoon of 6 July 1957, Mimi Smith was taking tea in the refreshment tent when a strange, jangling noise sent all the kids scurrying toward the bandstand. Looking out to see what was afoot, Mimi was horrified to behold her John standing in front of the microphone, guitar in hand, a greasy forelock hanging in his squinty eyes and wearing a loud checkerboard shirt that fairly screamed "Teddy Boy!"

"John saw me standing there," recalled Mimi. "He started making up words about me in the song he was singing. 'Mimi's coming,' he sang, 'Oh, oh! Mimi's coming down the path.'" Mimi's ordeal was, fortunately, brief. After performing "Cumberland Gap," "Maggie May," and "Railroad Bill," the Quarry Men bowed and packed up their gear, which they carted back to the parish social hall, where they were slated to perform again that evening.

While they were setting up onstage, John's childhood playmate and neighbor Ivan Vaughan arrived, accompanied by a baby-faced, round-eyed young fellow wearing a white jacket with sparkles and flap pockets and the tightest of all possible black drainies. The lad was full of praise for the performance, though in fact, he had observed that John was playing his guitar incorrectly and faking the lyrics to "Come Go with Me." James Paul McCartney was obviously, even at the age of fifteen, a born diplomat. But what was really on his mind was finding an opportunity to demonstrate how much better he could play. Not troubled by shyness, he borrowed a guitar and went into his showpiece, Eddie

Cochran's "Twenty Flight Rock," a record well beyond the competence of the Quarry Men. Then Paul did "Be-Bop-a-Lula" correctly—in contrast with John's hokey rendering. Finally, this young "keenie" concluded his unsolicited audition with a shrieking imitation of Little Richard.

During his performance Paul noticed "this beery old man getting nearer and breathing down me neck as I was playing. 'What's this old drunk doing?' I thought. . . . It was John. He'd just had a few beers. He was [three months short of] sixteen and I was only fourteen [sic], so he was a big man. I showed him a few more chords he didn't know. Then I left. I felt I'd made a good impression."

John, despite his drunkenness, was impressed by Paul. "I half thought to myself, 'He's as good as me.' I'd been kingpin up to then. Now, I thought, 'If I take him on, what will happen?' It went through my head that I'd have to keep him in line if I let him join."

A couple of weeks later Pete Shotton ran into Paul, cycling along Menlove Road. After the usual exchange of greetings Shotton said, "By the way, I've been talking with John about it and—we thought maybe you'd like to join the group." A full minute elapsed while Paul pretended to consider the offer. Finally, Paul shrugged and replied, "Oh, all right." Then, without saying another word, he cycled off toward his home in Allerton.

The relationship so casually established was not one between peers. Not only would John soon be a college student while Paul remained in high school, but there were the great disparities created by experience, temperament, and the not insignificant fact that John had been reared a full rung higher than Paul on the all-important scale of British class structure. Paul's father was a salesperson on the Liverpool Cotton Exchange, who, after the collapse of the market in World War II, could never again make much of a living. When Jim McCartney retired in 1964 at the age of sixty-two, this hardworking man, who had begun his career at the age of fourteen, was earning only ten pounds a week.

But though Jim was not successful in business, he was a very good father to Paul—a man who put the rearing of his children at the top of his list of priorities. Jim was also a decisive influence on Paul's choice of careers, for in his youth Jim had led a local ragtime band, and so Paul grew up in a home where making music was an everyday activity. Paul's mother had been a very capable midwife, but she died of cancer in October 1956, leaving her husband to rear Paul, fourteen, and Michael, twelve. "What are we going to do without her money?" demanded the practical-minded Paul. Jim McCartney answered with an impressive display of self-discipline and self-sufficiency—precisely the traits that subsequently characterized his famous son.

The little family reallotted its tasks, the boys laying the fires and setting the table while their father did the cooking. At the same time they learned to practice the most stringent economy: Paul and Mike were forbidden to enter the house after school lest they bring along their schoolmates and eat up the family's carefully husbanded ration of eggs. Paul McCartney's parsimony as a middle-aged millionaire echoed his impecunious childhood, in which survival depended upon strictly enforced restraints.

The ultimate measure of Jim's success in rearing his boys was Paul's remarkably normal personality. In a business where freakishness and degeneracy are virtually the rule, Paul has spent his whole life without ever losing control or doing anything that could seriously jeopardize his astoundingly successful career. A firmly centered young man, he knew from his earliest years exactly what he wanted: "women, money, clothes." The best way to get those things, he recognized, was to leave school and go into the music business, where he has always kept his eye fixed fimly on the main chance.

Paul's normality, both in terms of personality and stance as an entertainer, set him on the opposite end of a teeterboard with John Lennon. Consider, for example, how each boy dealt with his anger, a crucial issue in any 'round-the-clock, high-stress relationship. When anything enraged John, he would either fly out of control or else sulk. Paul, by contrast, vented his spleen through sneak attacks. Speaking of his relations with his parents, he confessed, "If I ever got bashed for being bad, I would go into their bedroom when they went out and rip the lace curtains at the bottom—just a little bit!" This stab-in-the-dark strategy became crucial, one suspects, in the internal politics of the Beatles; in fact, Pete Shotton reports that no sooner did Paul join the band than John began doing things that so embarrassed him that he was impelled to offer apologies, an unheard-of act for the brash Lennon.

Though John was the boss of the band, Paul enjoyed from the first a crucial advantage: He was the group's foremost musician. When he joined the Quarry Men, he became John's tutor on guitar. The lessons were awkward because Paul was left-handed, which meant that the dyslexic Lennon learned the chords backward and then had to restore them to their normal positions by studying his hands in a mirror. The only professional instruction either boy received was from the skinny instruction manual of Bert Wheedon, Britain's original guitar man. Lennon claimed that by avoiding music lessons, the Beatles preserved the integrity of their imaginations, a trite and highly questionable idea that betrays his characteristic fear of being sucked into the normal world by absorbing its lessons. The truth was that the Beatles would have had far greater strength and freedom if they had known more about music. In any case, John wasn't speaking for Paul, who was an

instinctive pupil. If there had been a rock 'n' roll star resident in Liverpool, Paul would have been his closest disciple. When, for example, the
Beatles met Little Richard in 1962, Paul had hardly finished shaking
hands before he was demanding that his hero give him a lesson in that
high falsetto that was Richard's trademark. Paul wasn't afraid to learn.

Paul hadn't been in the Quarry Men for long before he started
pressing to have his mate from the Liverpool Institute, George Harrison, added to the roster. George was a year younger than Paul, thus
merely a boy when he met John Lennon, but Paul whetted John's curiosity by telling him that George was a better guitarist than either of
them—able to pick out actual solos instead of merely strumming!
When John, Paul, and Pete descended on George's little house in
Speke, a model working-class community, George was so much in awe
of these big boys, especially John—who didn't cut his hair and wore
pink shirts!—that the poor lad was struck dumb. Nevertheless, he got
off a flawless rendition of Bill Justis's "Raunchy," a typical Sun Records
rockabilly song.

Though George was not invited to join the band, because he was too
young to be taken seriously, he dogged John for a whole year, exhibiting the behavior of the born disciple, a role he has never outgrown.
"George used to follow me and Cynthia around," recalled John. "We
would come out of art school together and he'd be hovering around
the gate. Cyn and I would be going to a coffee shop or a movie, and
George would follow us down the street, about two hundred yards behind. Cyn would say, 'Who is this guy?' What's he want?' I'd say, 'He
just wants to hang out. Should we take him with us?' She'd say, 'OK,
let's take him to the bloody movies.'"

Of all the Beatles, George was the only one who was not deprived of
a parent at an early age. His father was, like Freddie Lennon, a head
steward aboard the old passenger liners, but he missed his family while
at sea and gave up the ships before the war to become a bus driver and
later a minor official of the transport workers' union. George's mother
was a very cheerful and supportive woman, who went out of her way to
sustain her son's ambitions because he was the youngest of her four
children and the shyest. She would sit up night after night, while
George painfully taught himself to play. Always lacking in flair as an
instrumentalist, George made up for his lack of confidence by sheer
doggedness. Eventually he would repeat the rigors of his apprenticeship to the guitar with the sitar.

"[George's parents] were very protective of him because they knew
he was vulnerable, a trusting, soft-natured person," explained Irene
Harrison, George's sister-in-law. The baby of his family, George became the baby of the Beatles, and just as he was always ready to do the
household chores, so he accommodated himself self-sacrificingly to the

ego-tripping demands of the big boys, John and Paul. In fact, the only manner in which George Harrison ever asserted himself forcefully, as either boy or man, was in his style of dress. George aspired to be a dandy.

At the height of his fame, George Harrison could still describe in minute detail his first smart gear: "I bought a white shirt with pleats down the front, black embroidery down the corners of the pleats, and a black waiter's waistcoat. It was double-breasted with drape lapels, and Paul had given it to me. (I think he got it from John, who got it from his stepfather, Mr. Dykins.) I also had one of our Harold's [George's brother] sport jackets dyed black, and you could still see the checkered design underneath. I wore black trousers made into drainpipes and those blue suede pointed shoes." It was Mimi Smith's loudly voiced disgust with both George Harrison's bizarre clothing and his broad scouse accent that finally inspired John to take his shadow into the band.

With two strivers of the order of Paul McCartney and George Harrison to support him, John Lennon should have led his band straight on to success. In fact, the group began to break up. One night at their regular gig at Wilson Hall, in a tough district near the airport, a fight broke out onstage between Pete Shotton and Colin Hanton. Pete claimed that Colin's drumming failed to coincide with John's leg movements in "I'm All Shook Up."

Hanton told Lennon: "It's him or me."

John told Pete: "Drums look better than washboards."

Pete was out—after John had broken the washboard over his head.

The Quarry Men disbanded early in 1959 after a gig at the Busman's Club in Prescott Road, a much plusher establishment than they were accustomed to play. The first set went well, but during intermission, the boys got drunk, leading to a disastrous second set. On the way home Colin got into a fight with Paul and decided to pack it in. Apart from a handful of dates later in the year, including a couple of amateur shows, that highly unprofessional night at the Busman's Club spelled tacet for the Quarry Men.

By this point in his life John Lennon had not made any decisive commitment to music. He was a full-time student at art college, where he was lucky to be, considering the mess he had made of his high school education. Back in the spring of 1957 he had taken the O-level (ordinary examinations) for the general certificate in education. He needed a passing grade of forty-five in four subjects to be invited to remain another two years at high school; then he could take the advanced examinations, which were prerequisites for admission to any major university. John failed *all* his O-levels—but generally by only a single point. The implication is that with just a little more effort, he would have passed some of the exams. (Paul McCartney, who was certainly no grind, scored six O-levels.) But John was so profoundly disaffected from the educational process that he could not spur himself to pass, even when his entire future was at stake. At this critical moment he went limp, allowing his fate to be determined by his aunt and the new headmaster, Mr. Pobjoy.

When Mimi received the bad news, she went to see the head, who received her in a calm, sympathetic, and professional manner, asking, "Well, Mrs. Smith, what are your thoughts about John's future? What do you think should be considered?" Mimi threw the question back in his face, demanding, "Well, what are *you* going to do? You've had him for five years. You should have his future all ready."

Mr. Pobjoy, who, at thirty-six, was perhaps the youngest headmaster in England, ignored the provocation he had been offered and said that as art was John's best subject, they should try to get him admitted to the Liverpool College of Art. Pobjoy proposed to write a letter recommending John and pointing out that his recent failure did not reflect his real ability, which was considerable. This was a generous offer, and Mimi seized on it. Art college was better than no college, and taking a job was something that never entered John's head. Even when it turned out that the arrangement would be costly for Mimi because she would have to pay John's first-year fees, he being ineligible for a grant, she agreed to deplete her scanty capital (George had left her only £2,000) to assure her nephew's education.

On the day of the interview at the art college Mimi was very busy. First, she supervised John's grooming, insisting that he wear a white shirt, a tie, an old suit of George's, and that he promise to be on his best behavior and *not chew gum*. Then she personally escorted him to the college. "I had to go down with him," she explained. "Otherwise, he would have probably skipped off and spent the bus fare money. I also wanted to make sure he found the place. You see, John hardly had any need to go to Liverpool." When they arrived at the handsome old building on Hope Street, John noted that the other applicants were all toting neatly arranged portfolios. He had his artwork done up in a sloppy parcel that made him feel self-conscious. All the same, the interview went off without mishap. John was admitted.

THE ARTIST AS A YOUNG PUNK

From his first day at the Liverpool College of Art, John Lennon was a pariah. He made a dreadful impression by appearing at registration clad in the preposterous regalia of a Teddy Boy. The girls in black stockings and duffel coats and the boys in the castoff clothes of the "Desert Rats" stared, smirked, and whispered behind their hands as they ogled this bizarre character attired in a pale blue Edwardian suit, bootlace tie, and brothel creepers. Holding his long nose in the air and squinting through his little almond-shaped eyes, he was the strangest-looking creature in the school. As Ann Mason, a classmate who proved the keenest of all Lennon watchers, remarked, "It must have taken a lot of courage to stand up to the ridicule."

Abandoning soon his Teddy Boy pose, Lennon—betraying already his lifelong obsession with costume and image—adopted next the somber uniform of a beatnik. Helen Anderson, his first girlfriend at college (today a successful fashion designer), recollected: "He wore gray worsted, dyed black, with eight-inch cuffs—so narrow you had to take off your shoes to put your foot through them. [She was recruited to narrow these drainies.] He wore a battle dress or leather jacket with a fur-lined collar, like a bomber jacket. He also had an overcoat, a crombie [Uncle George's], that came just below the knee, which he would wear with the collar up. With winklepickers [shoes so long and pointed that they suggested the implement for prizing the meat from periwinkles], the costume is complete." Not quite complete. Lacking are the heavy brown horn-rims that John was obliged to wear while working.

These large, thick spectacles provide the most telling feature of Ann Mason's powerful and penetrating portrait of Lennon, the single most revealing image of him ever projected. She took him unawares, sitting

73

hunched over, astraddle a straight-back chair, with his arms crossed in an *X*, as if he were seeking to protect his vitals, from breath to balls. His hands are tucked into his armpits, his features hatchet hard; his mouth is full of alum. The primary focus is upon the eyes, which are startling because they have vanished behind the glare of his lenses. Angry, hunched, and eyeless, Lennon's ominous black-clad image summons up some monstrous creature, like a man-size beetle.

The course of study upon which John embarked now was very demanding, especially for a student who had never developed any academic discipline. The first-year curriculum entailed "elementary perspective and geometrical drawing; an introduction to architecture; the study of basic natural forms; object drawing, anatomy and simple lettering, as well as life drawing." The students had to work from first light till dusk, trudging back and forth between classes through a warren of narrow passageways and oddly shaped rooms. Every time they changed floors, they trod a steep staircase wrapped about an exposed elevator shaft inside which the ancient lift rose and fell like a clock weight, measuring the passage of time in this claustrophobic workhouse.

The physical confinement of the college was matched by the clannishness of the student body, divided into cliques whose members had often known each other since high school. John resented these smugly self-involved klatches as much as he did the pressure of the work schedule. Instinctively he rebelled against the college, just as he had against Quarry Bank. By the end of his first year he was notorious as the most disruptive student in the school. He mocked the tutors, distracted the students, and sometimes brought the work of the class to a complete halt. His favorite arena for playing subversive pranks was the life class, held in a big attic room under a skylight, in whose cold glare posed a nude model atop a dais, warmed by an electric heater.

Picture the studio on a late afternoon in winter. Three dozen students stand before their easels in this old-fashioned chamber, with its pale green walls and plaster casts of classical statues. The tutor, Charles Burton, a small, tubby Welshman, walks about, making cutting comments as he examines the work. Finally, he leaves the room. As the class works on quietly, intently, totally absorbed in its task, a strange snuffling noise is heard from near the model's "throne." It is Lennon, who sounds as if he were suffering from catarrh. Again, the snuffling; only this time it sounds more like giggling. Suddenly the giggle swells into a maniacal *Goon Show* laugh. Lennon throws down his crayon and bounds up on the dais, landing in the astonished model's lap! As he whelps about in that comical posture, the whole class falls out, laughing and protesting in the same breath. The day's work is done.

Lennon's crazy antics soon attracted all the bad boys in the college—

the good-looking Tony Carricker; the huge Jeff Mohammed, half French, half Indian, who would come to school wearing a turban; Jeff Kane, skinny and red-haired, always falling victim to his own works (the plaster mask that nearly became a death mask, the metal construction from which he had to be freed by the fire brigade); the bearded Mickey Bidston, clad in a well-holed purple sweater; the professorial Alan Swedlow—and their girls: the red-nosed dark-haired Dorothy Courty, who was besotted with John, following him everywhere; Ann Mason, who was Jeff Mohammed's girl; Yvonne Shelton, who resembled the young Brigitte Bardot; and Carol Balfour, the best-looking girl in the school.

One of Lennon's favorite pastimes was to take his gang to the Pavilion in Lodge Lane, where twice a night, at seven and nine, the last surviving vaudeville acts performed. John enjoyed especially a dry, deadpan comedian named Rob Wilton, who specialized in working-class monologues. The whole point of his humor was to reduce the great events of the world to the mole-eyed perspective of the little guy. "The day war broke out," he would begin, speaking in an utterly flat and ordinary tone, "my missus said to me, 'What are you gonna do about it?'" That line killed Lennon. Next day the life class would be startled to hear a flat, ordinary, working-class voice declare out of nowhere: "The day war broke out . . ."

Another opportunity to escape the boring routine of the college was the lunchtime break. The Liverpool Institute, where Paul and George were students, adjoined the art college, so all three boys would bring their guitars to school and hold an impromptu session either on the little stage in the canteen or in Room 21, where they would draw a handful of listeners. John would do his impressions of the horn-rimmed Buddy Holly, his latest hero; Paul, his imitations of Little Richard; and the boys would harmonize a couple songs by the Everly Brothers, one of the greatest influences on the early Beatles. John liked to conclude his performance on a grotesque note by singing that genial old favorite, "When You're Smiling," in a cackling Goon voice.

After school and in the evenings, while the other students were sitting about in coffee bars, talking of Jean-Paul Sartre and Lawrence Durrell, Lennon would go out on the prowl. His favorite sidekick was Ian Sharp, a four-foot-ten sharpie, who worked as a compere (MC) and vocal impersonator. John liked to visit a shop near the entrance to the Mersey Tunnel that sold garish religious chromos and devotional objects. He would ask the sisters to fetch him something off a high shelf and then, when their backs were turned, filch a load of this stuff, which he found hysterically funny. Shoplifting had been one of his big thrills since he was a schoolboy in Penny Lane. Now he would go about at night with Jeff Mohammed, casing shops that they could burglarize.

John even dreamed of robbing a bank. But his favorite fantasy was that some great disaster had befallen the city, laying it open to pillage and rapine. In later years he conceded that had he become a professional crook, he would have spent much of his life in prison, because though his brain swarmed with criminal fancies, he was not street-smart. One night, he was dancing down the road, doing a takeoff on ballet dancers, when out of the shadows came two toughs who "nutted" (butted) Lennon and Sharp, nearly breaking their noses. Many a night, Sharpie, as John called him, felt himself going into a sweat as Lennon antagonized every man in a pub without the slightest awareness that he was begging for a beating. "You'll either wind up in jail or be a great success," prophesied Sharp, who recognized that his friend "lived on a knife-edge."

At the end of his first year at college, Lennon was advised that he would not be admitted to the painting department because his work did not measure up to the minimum requirements. His painting, according to Helen Anderson, was "violent, noisy, semifigurative work. It generally portrayed a Brigitte Bardot sitting in a very dark cocktail bar at night." Ian Sharp recalled an occasion when an instructor praised a clay figure that John had modeled. The moment the teacher turned his back, Lennon punched the statue into a shapeless lump.

Unhappy at school, John fared better at home. He spent every weekend and holidays at Blomfield Road, where he enjoyed his steadily reviving relationship with his mother. He was at the house on Tuesday, 15 July 1958, when Julia and Twitchy, who had probably been out late on the previous night, had one of their drunken fights. Julia went to see Mimi. Julie and Jackie, now eleven and nine, suspected something was in the wind when their mother didn't return by nightfall. Usually, when Julia had a blowup with Dykins, she would go to Harriet's cottage at Woolton. Going to Mimi could mean only one thing: Julia was getting permission to move herself and the children into Mendips, the only house that could accommodate them all.

The girls stayed up late, awaiting their mother's return. They were sitting at the head of the stairs when they saw a neighbor arrive, accompanied by a policeman. They could not catch what was said, but they were startled to hear their father cry out in pain and burst into tears. At that moment the little girls, fearing that something was terribly wrong, retreated to their room and eventually fell asleep.

Julia had intended to come home that night. She had left Mendips about nine-forty, after dark. Usually Mimi would have accompanied her sister to the bus stop, only a short distance from the house on the opposite side of Menlove Avenue. On this night Mimi excused herself because she was wearing her work clothes and did not feel comfortable about appearing ill-dressed in public. As the sisters were standing before the front gate, laughing and talking, one of John's neighborhood pals, Nigel Whalley, appeared. Discovering that John was not home, he left with Julia.

Menlove Avenue was divided in those days by a high hedge that had been planted atop the old trolley tracks. After bidding Nigel good-bye, Julia started across the road, disappearing as she made her way through the hedge. Not more than a minute later Nigel heard the sound of a car approaching at great speed, followed by a loud noise from the other side of the hedge. Turning toward the sound, he saw Julia's body fly up into the air. Dashing across the avenue, he found her lying on the roadway, inert. He turned and ran back to Mimi. "Oh, my God!" she cried, and ran off toward the spot. By the time she reached Julia, a number of people had gathered and an ambulance had been summoned. Julia was taken to Sefton General Hospital, but on the way she died.

Even years later, John recalled his mother's death with bitterness and rage: "We were sitting waiting for her to come home, Twitchy and me," he told Hunter Davies, "wondering why she was so late. The copper came to the door, to tell us about the accident. It was just like it's supposed to be, the way it is in the films—asking if I was her son and all that. Then he told us, and we both went white. It was the worst-ever thing that happened to me. We'd caught up so much, me and Julia, in just a few years. We could communicate. We got on. She was great. I thought 'Fuck it! Fuck it! Fuck it! That's really fucked everything! I've no responsibility to anyone now.' Twitchy took it worse than me. Then he said, 'Who's going to look after the kids?' And I hated him. Bloody selfishness! We got a taxi over to Sefton General, where she was lying dead. I didn't want to see her. I talked hysterically to the taxi driver all the way, just ranted on and on. . . . The taxi driver just grunted now and again. I refused to go in and see her. But Twitchy did. He broke down."

Dykins suffered one of those bouts of extravagant remorse and self-castigation typical of drunkards. He kept crying: "I'll never drink again!" He was so carried away by his grief that he never gave a thought to his daughters, who were home asleep. They got up the following morning and went off to school without the slightest awareness of the night's horrors.

After leaving the hospital, John returned to Mendips. Mrs. Bushnell, the next-door neighbor, was shocked to hear him out on the front porch playing his guitar. She couldn't comprehend that it was John's only consolation. There was no one to whom he could turn. Late at night he went down the road to Barbara Baker's house. He hadn't seen her since Mimi had forced him to break off the affair. Barbara walked with John into nearby Reynolds Park, trying to console him. Every time

John would start weeping, she would put her arms about him and cradle him. "We just stood there," she remembered, "crying our eyes out, the pair of us."

The funeral was held on Friday. Leila Harvey, who had been summoned by telegram from her summer job at a Butlins holiday camp, remembered that she could not accept the fact that "Judy" was dead. When the first shovelful of dirt was cast onto the coffin, she pictured her aunt back in her kitchen singing blithely. John was so devastated that all he could do at the funeral was lay his head numbly in Leila's lap.

Some months later John tried to contact his mother through a séance. He assembled some of his friends at Blomfield Road while Dykins was at work. "We sat 'round a circular table," Nigel Whalley recalled. "John switched the lights down low and spread the letter cards 'round the table. Then he began to rotate his hand 'round the top of the tumbler, and it started to move and spell out words. We sat there terrified, but he seemed quite calm, almost unmoved." John's stoic demeanor in public is also attested to by Pete Shotton, who ran into his friend in Woolton on the day after Julia's death. "Sorry about your mum," Pete mumbled.

"I know, Pete," John replied quietly. The subject was never opened again.

A coroner's inquest, held to determine the cause of death, established that the driver was a police officer who was late for duty and was driving without a license. A learner, not an experienced driver, he said that when he saw Julia in the middle of the road, he had hit his brake pedal, but it proved to be the accelerator. *"Murderer!"* shouted Mimi, making as if to thrash the man with her stick. There was nothing for it; the driver got off with a reprimand and a period of suspension from duty.

The effects of Julia's death on John were grave. Beneath his grief burned a terrible rage ignited by the recognition that once again he had been abandoned by his mother. John began to have dreams in which he crucified women or hacked them to pieces with an ax. He also began to drink heavily, with the result that for the next two years he was, as he put it, constantly "drunk or angry." Pete Shotton recalled boarding a bus bound for Woolton one evening and discovering John laid out across the back seats, unable to rise and making, most likely, his second or third trip of the night. Since John was living on a skimpy student grant, he had to cadge his drinks in the lowest dives by conning or badgering the customers. His bullying assumed now a very ugly cast. In one bar John habitually taunted a Jewish piano player named Reuben, disrupting his performance by shouting at him, *"Creepy Jewboy!"* or *"They should have stuck you in the ovens with the rest of 'em!"* Sometimes the poor musician was reduced to tears. As Shotton witnessed these scenes, he began to fear that John Lennon "seemed destined for skid row."

CYN AND STU

What John Lennon craved now was a soft, yielding, ultrafeminine girl who could soak up, like a sponge steeping in vinegar, the bitterness that was flooding his soul. The first such girl he found was Thelma Pickles, whom he met while registering for his second year at the college. A shy, sensitive-looking young woman with dark, thoughtful eyes and a slightly puckered mouth, disinclined to smile, Thelma was drawn to John the moment she met him by the force of his "magnetism." No sooner had they been introduced than she witnessed a scene that convinced her that John Lennon was a man of remarkable toughness. A girl breezed up to the registration table and called out to him: "Hey, John, I believe your mother was killed. Was it a police car?"

Thelma was shocked by such a show of callousness, but Lennon appeared to be completely unaffected. "Yeah, that's right," he drawled.

During the next few weeks Thelma and John ran into each other repeatedly. One day he offered to carry her art gear to the bus stop at Castle Street. Falling into an absorbing conversation, the pair sat down on the steps of the Victoria Monument. She asked him about his father. Once again John displayed the toughness about touchy matters that had so impressed Thelma. "He pissed off and left me as a baby," replied John nonchalantly.

Instinctively Thelma echoed: "So did mine!"

Thelma's father had abandoned her at the age of ten, and ever since she had brooded over her loss without talking about it because "in those days you never admitted you came from a broken home. You could never discuss it with anybody, and people like me, who kept the shame of it secret, developed terrific anxieties. It was such a relief to me when he said that."

Thelma's growing involvement with John was also based on the fact that having been deeply wounded as children, they both had developed a lot of hostility toward the world. "What I realized quickly," recalled Thelma, "was that he and I had an aggression towards life that stemmed entirely from our home lives. . . . We couldn't wait to grow up and tell everybody to get lost." This common attitude soon bonded John and Thelma.

They would drop into the student's favorite pub, Ye Cracke, and Thelma would watch, half shocked, half delighted, as John would make one sarcastic crack after another, getting more abusive with each fresh pint. If he encountered someone who was a bit "thick," he would cut him up with especial ferocity. His verbal dart games were as nothing, however, compared with his antics in the street. Liverpool was full of people who were deformed, crippled, retarded, or simply shrunken and enfeebled by age. John could not resist the temptation to treat these poor creatures like figures in a sick joke. Spotting a legless man being wheeled along, Lennon would greet the afflicted man with "How did you lose your legs? Chasing the wife?" Or he would overtake a cripple hobbling along the sidewalk, and after mimicking the man's lurching gait, John would pop up in front of him and start making faces at the cripple.

Lennon had no insight into this compulsion when young, but in later years he explained it by writing "Crippled Inside," which warns that if you're screwed up inside, it's going to show outside. Inside he had always felt "the pain of being a freak" but he had fought to maintain a normal appearance, which was why he resisted wearing glasses with such fanatical determination. He had also found a way of exorcising his terror of freaks by making fun of them, either through mimicking or by sketching them in his notebooks, which teemed with naked monsters, like a boulder-headed man set upon a spread of lizard feet or a skinny guy with his neck distended like an ostrich and his face squeezed into a bird's beak. By punching and pulling the human form divine into Silly Putty shapes, Lennon found relief for his tormented mind. Had he been born a decade earlier, he would have been completely at home in the world of sick humor, becoming perhaps an English Lenny Bruce, a comedian he adored. Having missed his ideal moment, Lennon was forced to cut against the grain of the lovey-dovey Sixties, spending his youth writing love songs for what he called the "meat market." Eventually, however, he gained the confidence to violate the taboos of his generation and returned to his mental monsters and hysterical fears, which he set to music no less primitive and grotesque.

Although Lennon exhibited no real talent for caricature, his drawings being merely a species of doodling, the caricaturist's mentality was apparent in almost everything he ever said or wrote. He was a man who functioned in terms of quick takes, penetrating perceptions, and exaggerated expressions. Nor was caricature the only visual art that contributed to his career as a songwriter. Actually, he made extensive use of all the techniques—collage, montage, ready-mades, abstraction, surrealism, and even automatic writing—fashionable in art college. Far from being out of his element in the school, he was actually receiving the ideal education of an English rock star. Pete Townshend, Keith Richard, Eric Burdon, Ronnie Wood—the list is long—were all art students. Not surprisingly, they all developed in roughly the same direction, by taking the raw material of American rock 'n' roll and subjecting it to the techniques that the British art schools had inherited from the prewar European avant-garde. In this manner, these subsequently famous graduates of Brit rock's favorite finishing schools became the first generation of musical Pop Artists.

John's relations with Thelma Pickles were not confined to hanging out. He was constantly struggling to get her into bed. They would stroll across Allerton Golf Course after dark and neck, but Thelma was terrified of becoming pregnant, as had five or six girls at the college that year alone. The impossibility of obtaining an abortion made sex a very anxious issue. Besides, Thelma was not really tempted because she found John devoid of romance. He called lovemaking a "five-mile run" and referred to girls who balked at the last moment as "edge-of-the-bed virgins." Thelma's friendship with John survived despite her repeated refusals to sleep with him because she proved an easy touch. John sought out such girls, having a name for them, as he did for everyone. He called them "spaniels."

Another spaniel was Cynthia Powell, a pretty, auburn-haired girl from Hoylake, a middle-class suburb on the Wirral Peninsula. Girls from this affluent district, with their twin-sweater sets, tweed skirts, permed hair, posh accents, and ladyfinger manners, were regarded by the college bohemians as hopelessly bourgeois. Cynthia was a fine specimen of the breed. Daughter of a traveling salesman for General Electric, who had died of cancer when she was seventeen, and of a very strong, determined mother, who looked rather like a bulldog, Cynthia was a timid soul. Her report cards read: "Very conscientious but lacks confidence." Though Cynthia was regarded as a good student, it was a sign of her low self-esteem that she chose as her special subject lettering.

In this class, made up for the most part of docile girls, content to spend their time calculating the proportions of this or that typeface, there was one totally incongruous character—John Lennon. After being kicked out of the painting department, Lennon had been drafted into lettering, with the idea that he might make an illustrator. When Cynthia saw this beatnik, dressed in black clothes that reeked of fish and chips, she had a perfectly normal reaction. "I felt," she recalled, "that I had nothing in common with this individual. He frightened me to death." John, for his part, was no more taken by Cyn, seeing her merely as an easy mark. Soon she discovered that after every class she was missing one of her favorite pencils or brushes.

Throughout the fall of John's second year at the college he and Cynthia had no closer contact than that provided by their twice-weekly classes. Then, one day at assembly, Cynthia found herself seated behind Lennon and his gang. Helen Anderson reached over to tidy John's greasy locks, and a pang shot through Cyn. Never before had she experienced this sensation. It took her quite a while to recognize that it was not disgust she had felt but jealousy. Her perplexity was natural because she had fallen in love with a man who was the opposite of everything she had been taught to admire. He was *her* opposite as well, embodying to an extreme degree every quality in which she was most lacking, from cocksureness and aggressiveness to ready wit and ability to command attention. Above all, John Lennon displayed a profound contempt for normal life and everything it entails. Yet there was an obvious link between Lennon and Cynthia. All her life she had been manipulated by her overbearing mother; now she had developed a passion for another masterful personality. The sole difference was that this one was male.

Though timid, Cynthia was not lacking in determination. Once she attached herself to an objective, she hung on to it for dear life. First, however, she had to find some way to make John notice her as a woman. Happily she was relieved of this embarrassing task when Jeff Mohammed told his friend at the Christmas dance that he should give Cyn a tumble because she was mad for him. When Lennon asked Cynthia to step out on the floor, she panicked. "I'm awfully sorry," she said in her plummy accent, "but I'm engaged to a fellow in Hoylake."

Lennon snapped: "I didn't ask you to marry me!" There, had he but known it, was where the shoe pinched. "Marrying" Lennon was precisely what she had in mind.

After the dance, John and Cyn went to Ye Cracke, where she had a few drinks and got tipsy. Seeing his chance, John invited her to a friend's flat nearby. Though this was the first time she had ever been alone with John, Cynthia surrendered to him immediately. "There was no question in my mind about whether or no we should make love," she recalled, explaining, "it all happened so naturally." Yet for a girl who had been reared as properly as Cynthia Powell and especially for one who was attending a college where every day young women suffered agonies over unwanted pregnancies, such heedless abandon appears remarkable. One thing is certain: Both Cynthia and John, each for his own reasons, was desperate for love. Once they struck a spark, their passions flamed up with astonishing force.

Psychodrama provides the best image for this ardent affair, with

Lennon the protagonist and Cynthia the supporting player. "I was hysterical," he confessed in later years. "I was neurotic, taking out all my frustrations on her." Cynthia submitted completely to John's demands and whims, but he always found some cause for jealousy—a stray glance, an innocent conversation, a misunderstood remark. Then he would go off into a towering rage. Cynthia was warned away from Lennon, but she believed that if she could just hold fast to him, he would change in time. She perceived, as did everyone who knew John well, that he had another side that was gentle and sweet, the little boy who had loved his mum—until she betrayed him.

Cynthia did everything else she could to hold Lennon's interest. When he raved about the mysterious glamour of Brigitte Bardot, as she appeared in *Heaven Fell That Night*—the shy and timid Cynthia sought to transform herself into the irresistible Bébé by bleaching her hair, wearing provocative clothes, and exhibiting, when she undressed in some filthy studio, the net stockings and black garter belt that inflamed John's imagination. Nothing helped. John Lennon remained, as Dezo Hoffmann, the Beatles' photographer, once remarked, "like a dog who has rabies—you never knew when he would jump up and bite you."

The flat to which John led Cyn that first night belonged to the most brilliant student in the college, Stuart Sutcliffe. A fair-haired, delicately featured boy, who bore a marked resemblance to the late Jimmy Dean, Stu first attracted Lennon's attention by his manner of dressing: skintight jeans, pink shirts, and boots with elastic gussets, worn with a fawn-colored corduroy jacket and a pair of sunglasses that he never removed, even at night. At the time Stu had a sparse beard and mustache and smoked cheroots to make himself appear older and more sophisticated. As a painter he exhibited astonishing virtuosity: his style ranged from that of the French Impressionists and English Pre-Raphaelites to Jackson Pollock, Nicholas de Stael and Lucian Freud. He was also steeped in the literature of the beats and strongly attracted by rock 'n' roll music, particularly Buddy Holly records, which played constantly while he painted.

At bottom, Stu was committed to living out the legend of the *poète maudit*, the foredoomed artist of genius, the myth that underlay the life of so many artists in the Fifties, from the jazzmen to the Action painters to the beat poets and novelists. Once when somebody told Stu that it was bad for his health to smoke sixty cigarettes a day, he replied, "I don't care. I might die in a year or two. You have to live hard and short."

Infatuated with rock 'n' roll, Stu found it wonderful that John Lennon should be the leader of a rock band. John, for his part, was taken by Stu's brilliance and energy, the way he togged out, and, above all, his success, for one of his paintings had been hung in the John Moores Exhibit, the British counterpart of the Venice Biennale. John Moores purchased this picture himself for the goodly sum of £65, which impressed Lennon enormously. Always a hero worshiper, John started following Stu about, according to the Liverpool poet Adrian Henri, "the way Prince Philip follows the queen."

Stu shared a pad with another art student, Rod Murray, at 3 Gambier Terrace, in the Hillary Mansions, a splendid row of late-Georgian houses overlooking St. James Cemetery and the rear of the immense Liverpool Cathedral. The flat was up a long flight of stairs and extended from the front of the house to the back. The rooms had high, molded ceilings, and the walls were painted three white and one brown, the chic decorator mannerism of the day.

Stu Sutcliffe's studio was at the back of the flat. Its sooty, coal-burning fireplace was packed with greasy fish-and-chip papers, and its furnishings consisted of a couple of broken chairs and tables, a ratty rug, and a tatty double mattress lying on the paint-spattered floor beneath a dirt-begrimed window. Stu had covered the walls with sketches of nudes and canvases so big that the little painter had virtually to leap up to touch their upper edges. The front room was shared by Rod Murray and Margaret "Diz" Dizley, but there were always other people crashing at the pad, like John Lennon, who slept in a coffin whose satin lining he liked better than bed sheets.

It was in this flat that Lennon was first brought to the attention of the national press. On Sunday, 24 July 1960, he and his mates were displayed by a reporter for *The People* as typical examples of what the paper slugged in giant type THE BEATNIK HORROR. The article was illustrated with a photograph of a group of young, roughly dressed men, hunkered down in a squalid pad. The writer's point was that "Most beatniks like dirt. They dress in filthy clothes. Their 'homes' are strewn with muck." Right in the middle of the muck, actually lying in it on the dirty floor, is John Lennon, not identified in the text but unmistakable in appearance.

John moved into Stu's flat at the beginning of 1960, during his third and last year of art school. By the age of nineteen his relationship with Mimi had taken a bizarre turn. Ian Sharp recollected spending a night at Menlove Avenue and being shocked by the way John treated his aunt. Constantly torturing her with manic put-ons, he would shout when she coughed in the night: "You've got TB and ten minutes to live!" When they left in the morning, John hollered through the window in the breakfast room, "Bye, Mimi!" But instead of leaving, he went back and shouted that same phrase again and again, jumping in and out of the bushes and holding out his hands like Al Jolson. He worked so hard to wind up the old lady that Sharp found the whole spectacle embarrassing to witness.

John would have left Mimi sooner if he had not been so dependent upon her financially. What emboldened him now was the decision he had made to become a professional musician. The timing of the act was determined by his imminent removal from the college rolls. He had failed the intermediate exam the previous summer; now he was on probation, thanks to the good offices of his tutor, Arthur Ballard, whom John spent a lot of time cultivating. But Ballard had not been able to persuade the staff to give Lennon another chance. So it was just a matter of time till John took the intermediate exam again, failed it again, and was kicked out of school. Hence, he decided to spend his last months under the college's aegis in organizing a band and cutting into the burgeoning Merseyside rock scene.

He was assured of the support of two key men: Paul McCartney and George Harrison. Paul was winding up his high school career that spring and had no desire to study further. George was planning to drop out of school and take a day job as an electrician's helper in a department store. The only problem was in recruiting the two missing players, the drummer and the bassist.

John invited Rod Murray and Stu Sutcliffe to join the band on bass. Rod said that he might give it a go if he could contrive to build a bass in the college woodworking shop. Stu was much more determined: He took the £65 he had gotten for his exhibition painting and went down to Hessy's, where he bought a splendid new Hohner bass. This impulsive act alarmed Stu's father, a Scottish ship's engineer, and his devoted and protective mother, Millie, who was tempted to cut off her son's allowance. When Stu informed the college that he was leaving, the faculty told him that he was mad to drop out when he had just become eligible to take his degree and embark on a professional career. Undeterred by the protests on every side, Sutcliffe set about making arrangements to learn his big and unwieldy instrument.

A local rocker, Dave May, bassist with Mark Peter and the Silhouettes, agreed to teach Stu a few tunes in exchange for the right to measure his instrument so that May could build a replica. The experienced hand taught the raw beginner the chords of Eddie Cochran's "C'mon Everybody." May found Stu "hopeless," but his judgment of Paul McCartney's abilities wasn't much more favorable.

Stuart Sutcliffe's first important contribution to the band was the name Beetles, the title of the other gang in Marlon Brando's motorcycle romance *The Wild One*. If it was natural that Stu, a great fan of Buddy Holly and the Crickets, should light on this insect name, it was just as natural that John Lennon, the habitual punster, should twist the

name around so that it echoed the "big beat" and "beats all." In this
manner the most famous rock band in history got the oddest name of
any band in its day.

Odder than the name was the failure of the billing to conform with
the universal practice of the day, which was to feature the star's name
above his backing group, as in Bill Haley and the Comets or Buddy
Holly and the Crickets. Though the Beatles experimented for years
with various names, only once, for a very short time in their dimmest
period, in 1959, did they sport a conventional monicker: Johnny and
the Moondogs. Never before or afterward did they feature their
leader. Why? Certainly not because John Lennon was such a great
team man; he was a solo personality and a loner all his life. Nor was it
because John was lacking in leadership qualities or indifferent to who
was boss. The truth is simply that for all his love of attention, Lennon
was too insecure to assert himself boldly as a star. He had to have a
partner or a gang; hence, he became the unfeatured leader of a star
group.

The germ of the Beatles, therefore, was not so much musical or
theatrical as it was psychological. The band sprang out of Lennon's
peculiar head. Hence, it was from the start totally different from any
other rock band in history and destined to develop along lines that
were unprecedented and never truly paralleled despite the fact that the
Beatles were the most imitated pop stars since Elvis. Perhaps the most
important implication of the Beatles' headless billing was that in seeking to buttress his frail but aggressive ego with a gang of onstage
henchmen, John Lennon had initiated a complicated chain reaction
that resulted eventually in his being swallowed up by his own creation,
which assigned to him the role of "Beatle John."

MERSEY BEAT

The Beatles embarked upon their fabulously successful career as bottom dogs. Unlike the glamorous Elvis, who achieved fame overnight, the boys from Liverpool had to spend years clawing their way to the top of the heap. At first, everything was against them. They were Englishmen trying to make it in an American entertainment idiom that was creatively alien even to most Americans because its roots were in the redneck South and the black ghetto. They were further handicapped by the fact that they came from Liverpool, which was famous for comedians and football players but had never counted for anything in the English music business. Not only had the Beatles never received any training, but they had not had much chance to observe real rock performers at first hand. When you get right down to it, about the only things the Beatles had in their favor initially were their intelligence and determination, as well as their innate buoyancy and playfulness. When things got bad, they would rally themselves by doing a routine they had picked up from a B movie about a Liverpool street gang.

"When we were all depressed," John recollected, "thinking that the group was going nowhere, this is a shitty deal, we're in a shitty dressing room, I would say, 'Where are we going, fellows?' And they would go, *'To the top, Johnny!'* in pseudo-American voices. And I would say, 'Where is that, fellows?' And they would say, *'To the toppermost of the poppermost!'* I would say, 'Right!' And we would all cheer up." During their first years the Beatles performed that ritual over and over as they soldiered through some of the shittiest deals and nastiest dressing rooms in the long and sordid history of the Big Beat.

The timing of the group's appearance could be construed, depending on how you view the matter, as very good or very bad. By the year 1960 rock 'n' roll was yesterday's story in Britain, just as it was in America. The departure of Elvis for the army and of Little Richard for the ministry had signaled the end of the first great era in the music's development and the onset of the Frankie Avalon, Ritchie Valens, Ricky

Nelson style of soft rock that was the inevitable commercial adultera-
tion of the real thing. The English had followed the trend slavishly
because Brit rock had aped the Yanks ever since it was spawned in the
coffee bars of Soho in the year of our Elvis 1956.

The stars of the English scene were for the most part copies of Presley, who, being a caricature himself, offered an irresistible target to any
copycat. Though these British imitators were laughably inferior to
their American prototype, they filled a crying need. For unlike the
United States, where Elvis was merely a symbol of triumph over the last
restraints upon the Permissive Generation, in Britain he spoke to a
more profound yearning: the desire to cast off the shackles of the op-
pressive caste system. To English working-class boys the Hillbilly Cat
was virtually a messianic figure because his legend proclaimed: "One
day a lorry driver and the next—the king!"

So great an inspiration, so abundant a source of life and joy could
not be simply contemplated from afar. Elvis had to be brought bodily
to Britain so that his idolators could commune with him in person. If
Elvis wouldn't come (and he never did, making him even more
mythical), he had to be replicated, knocked off, as garment makers do
with the latest fashions from abroad. How appropriate, therefore, that
the job of domesticating Elvis should have been done by a young man
in the retail clothing trade, Larry Parnes. Stagestruck himself and eager to get out of his family's business, Parnes stumbled upon the first
British rock star, a youthful merchant seaman named Tommy Hicks,
playing guitar and singing Bill Haley songs at the Two Is coffee bar in
Soho. Changing the seaman's name to Steele and giving him a bit of
promotion, Parnes struck a nerve that was set to vibrate. Overnight
Tommy Steele became the hottest new act in British show business.

At that point there was only one move for an experienced retailer:
reorder! Parnes quickly discovered another young talent, dubbing this
one Marty Wilde. Soon the young merchant extended his new rock line
further by adding such subsequently popular models as Billy Fury,
Johnny Gentle, Georgie Fame, and Dickie Fields, the "Sheik of Shake."
Within a few years Larry Parnes was as renowned in Great Britain as
Colonel Tom Parker in the United States.

It says a lot for the character of Liverpool that the northern metropolis never bought the Elvis clones. Even more remarkable, they rejected
Presley himself! The prototype of the Mersey rocker, Ted "Kingsize"
Taylor (six feet four, 280 pounds, identified often as the leader of the
first British rock 'n' roll band) put down Elvis in words strong enough
to blow out the Eternal Light above the old Shuck 'n' Jive King's tomb.
Looking back on the year 1956, when he first started playing rockabilly
professionally, Taylor recalled: "Elvis wasn't our scene. He was a bit
pouffy. He wasn't powerful enough for Liverpool people. We were

looking for what's now called 'heavy stuff.' Elvis was put up as a propaganda symbol to keep the blacks out." Taylor's sense of Elvis as a white substitute for the black hero who should have stood in his place is sound as far as it goes, but it doesn't explain how Taylor and the other Mersey rockers, even more "white" than Elvis, proposed to go about the task of playing "heavy stuff."

The problem they faced was by no means new, for Elvis Presley was simply the latest figure in that long tradition of whites taking off blacks that commences with the sentimental "coon songs" of Stephen Foster and the comic minstrelsy of "Jump Jim Crow." During the fifty years of white men working under cork that culminated in Al Jolson, all the ways in which the white performer could exploit the black song and dance tradition had been tried and tested. The result was plain to see. With the exception of a few cultural chameleons, who were good enough to "pass," the closer a white man came to authentic black music and dance, the more specious he appeared. Elvis confirmed this rule, once and for all. When he sang rockabilly, he was both brilliant and original, but when he started ripping off the black stars of his day, like Little Richard, Joe Turner, or even Willa Mae Thornton—whose original record of "Hound Dog" surpasses that of the King in every way—it soon became clear that the new thing was no substitute for the real thing. The Liverpudlians assumed, however, that because they were more virile than Elvis, they could succeed where he had failed. Plunging recklessly into the heart of darkness, they set out to master precisely that style of music most deeply imbued with the black essence.

Rhythm and blues in the late Fifties was not so much a style or genre as it was a crazy quilt, an often brilliant pastiche of every kind of black music from every era of black culture: gospel and blues, jazz and pops, minstrel show and Broadway musical. The product of a complete breakdown in all the taboos and traditions that had long kept these genres separate and distinct, the music was feverishly patched together without concern for anything but its impact on the black audience. One of the first tricks the English boys learned from their American models was this knack of combining things of radically different provenance to make a dazzling, almost surrealistic musical montage.

Initially, however, the Mersey rockers were intent simply upon capturing these enticing black sounds. Piracy was the enabling force of British rock, just as it had once been the greatest resource of the British Empire. The only difference was that now, instead of scheming to capture the gold and silver of the Spanish Main, these young English buccaneers sailed forth intent on ripping off the fabled riches of the Chitlin Circuit. Nor was theirs an easy task, for first there was the by no means simple problem of gaining access to their quarry. British radio offered little help because the airwaves were ruled still by the BBC, which was stuck back in the Forties in a time warp. Nor could the coveted discs be bought in a shop because most American race records were never issued in Britain. Ultimately, the Mersey rockers were driven to capitalize on the fact that they lived in the kingdom's second-greatest port.

Ted Taylor had an uncle who was an immigration officer and exciseman on the docks. Whenever the Cunard Yanks came ashore, they found this official on the lookout for the little vinyl nuggets that bore the logos of Specialty, Federal, King, Chess, or Atlantic. Once the records came to hand, the trick was to get them down fast and then perform them publicly before they could be released in the United Kingdom. This was an easy task in the Fifties, when the record companies were slow to pick up on the latest lick. In the Sixties the pace had to be forced to a mad dash because the British labels started catching on to the new taste. Kingsize Taylor, today a white-aproned butcher in Southport, laughs like a boy when he recollects how he knocked off Gary "U.S." Bonds's big hit "New Orleans," released in the United States in November 1960. "We rehearsed it for three days. Nobody could crack the words. Finally, we played the thing Thursday night. It was released on Friday!"

This exciting game had its good and bad sides. It was wonderful training for the ear, but it had an inhibiting effect on the Mersey rockers' creative abilities. "Nobody was writing gear," explained Taylor, "because you were playing a unique song. You couldn't hear it on the radio or buy it in the shop. So that was as good as writing your own material." But piracy condemned the Liverpool rockers to catching the coattails of American music instead of creating their own style.

The other problem faced by the Mersey rockers was not so susceptible of solution. This was the whole question of how they *heard* R&B. Supposedly an "international language," music is spoken everywhere with a different accent. Though now and again some clever lad, like Paul McCartney, might succeed in giving a near-perfect imitation of Little Richard, with his gospel frenzy, microtonal pitch distortions, and high, hollering voice, Paul's performance was just a stunt. Normally, Liverpool rockers sounded distinctly foreign to American ears. Their alienation was most apparent on the fundamental level of rhythm.

An American drummer learns from childhood that the stick has to hit the skin and come off again like a bouncing ball to give the beat that lilting ride that makes music swing or rock. A drummer like Ringo Starr, however, would bring down his stick like a gavel—clunk!—as if in hitting the drumhead he had said the last word on the matter. This flat-footed, thick-ankled style of drumming gave the Mersey beat as distinctive a character as the hypnotic rhythm of a black slum kid in Harlem or Rio. In each case, the beat was an expression of the culture that inspired it. Just as the black kids were the heirs of Africa, so the Liverpool kids were the scions of that Scotch-Irish culture symbolized by the Scotch snap, the Irish reel, and the ceremonial tattoos and marches of military show bands like the Black Watch. Military drumming was actually the background of most Mersey beaters, who learned their instruments in the drum and bugle corps of the Boys Brigade or the Boy Scouts.

Hence, in later years, the Beatles often strode along triumphantly as if stepping to the sound of a march or anthem. Likewise, they could move passably well to the slack and sloping times of country and western music or even run like breathless kids, as in "Help!" Only rarely, however, did they achieve the sexy, sensuous ball-and-sock-it power of even the most ordinary black R&B band. In fact, they fell so far short of that ideal that when Muhammad Ali got an earful of Ringo Starr, he gibed: "My dog plays better drums!"

One other trait distinguished the original Mersey rock from its roots (and from the later Mersey beat, which was inspired by the success of the Beatles). The Liverpudlians—and their later descendants in southern England, like the Who and the Stones—put a tough Teddy Boy accent on R&B. Many of the bands had started out being street-fighting gangs, and their male audiences were largely composed of surly, smoldering boys who were looking to find in rock 'n' roll the same violence that roiled in their own hearts.

If the beat scene along the Mersey differed from that along the Thames in terms of basic values—Little Richard as opposed to Elvis Presley's rhythm and blues as contrasted with rockabilly, a hard, tough urban sound as opposed to the naïveté and sentimentality of country and western—another fundamental difference between north and south lay in the all-important factor of money. Liverpool kids could not pay for entertainment at the same rates as their southern counterparts. So they made their own fun at home. Poverty more than anything else explains the rise of the basic institution of Mersey beat—the Liverpool dance hall. To appreciate how different was this local dance scene from what you would have found in any other part of Britain, you have to form first a mental picture of that great teenage meeting and mating ground, the ballroom.

Unlike the United States, where most ballrooms had shut down upon the demise of the big bands after World War II, in Britain these archaic establishments were preserved and consolidated into two great national chains: the Mecca Ballrooms and the Top Rank Dance Suites. The typical ballroom was located in a tarnished movie palace in the decaying inner city. The music was provided by a dance orchestra that alternated quicksteps and slow waltzes. Every half hour the revolving stage would turn, bringing a fresh band into play. The ballrooms were repressive and exclusionary. The Mecca chain barred as a matter of principle at one time or another groups as diverse as Teddy Boys, sailors, "coloreds," Jews, and the deaf and mute. Just to make sure that the runty and malnourished working-class boys did not get rowdy, there were posted at the door two hulking "stewards" or "ballroom attendants," actually tuxedo-clad bouncers with brass knuckles in their pockets.

There were Mecca and Rank establishments in Liverpool, just as there were in every other part of the kingdom. The difference was that they counted for nothing in the local youth culture. Liverpool kids did not conform to the national pattern. Instead of funneling into the inner city, to be hung on a meat rack, mulcted of their meager wages, and intimidated by bullies in smoking jackets, these young people remained on their own turf and created their own ad hoc dance halls. On a social night they would hop a "corpy" (a double-decker bus operated by the city corporation) and go to the local town hall, village hall, or church hall, where some part-time promoter had organized a dance. Here, on their home ground, among their neighbors and school chums, the kids were free to enjoy themselves as they pleased. They could dance to the music of their favorite bands instead of the old professional wheezes; they could wear the clothes they fancied; and they could cut the latest, hottest steps, as opposed to the chain ballrooms, which were posted prominently with signs reading NO JIVING.

What assured the success of the Liverpool system was its extreme economy. Admission was a quarter, and refreshments were confined to soft drinks and potato chips. A local beat band got seven or eight pounds a night, which meant that the promoter could hire several bands and offer continuous entertainment. (The bands, for their part, could hop from one gig to another, playing three dates in a single night!) The whole budget for a dance, including hall, PA system, ticket takers, bouncers, cleaners, and adverts, generally did not exceed fifty pounds.

As the popularity of Mersey beat mounted, more and more boys were inspired to have a go at playing in a rock band, and ever more tradesmen and hustlers were tempted to take a fling at staging a dance, for which more and more kids would turn out. Eventually the critical mass requisite for a real song and dance fad was achieved. Suddenly, Liverpool took off, like the tango-intoxicated Buenos Aires of the Twenties or the jazz-jumpin' Kansas City of the Thirties or the swingmatized New York of the Forties. At the height of the Mersey beat craze, inspired by the triumph of the Beatles, the city boasted 350 bands, scores of venues offering rock music every night, and even a rock newspaper, *Mersey Beat*. Ultimately whole rosters of rock bands would play all night in some vast old Victorian assembly hall that could accommodate thousands of people brought into the city by special buses and ferries—all this in a town where a few years earlier everything shut down at 10:00 P.M., when the last tram left Lime Street Station. Such a scene has never existed anywhere else in the thirty-year history of rock 'n' roll. Only in Liverpool—a city where there is nothing to restrain people because there is nothing to sustain them but their own spirits—could there have been' such an incredible rave-up.

Liverpool cannot be celebrated as the heavenly city of rock 'n' roll, however, without being stigmatized as the raging inferno of rock-inspired violence. Commencing with the first showing of *Rock Around the Clock,* the local street gangs took up rock music as their battlecry and chose the local dance halls as their battleground. Every week the Holly Road Boys, the Ferry Boys, the Park Gang, and a score of others would sally forth to defend their turf. Encountering rival gangs at the local dance, they would rub up against their adversaries until they struck sparks. Then rock 'n' roll would erupt in rock 'n' riot.

A perfect illustration of the warlike hostilities in the Liverpool dance halls is provided by the battle Allan Williams, the Beatles' first manager, witnessed one night at the Garston Baths, known in local parlance as the Blood Baths. The week preceding this punch-up, a gang called the Tigers had been barred from the baths because one of its members hurled a trash can through a window. When the next Saturday rolled around, the hall's bouncers, big, tough men wearing heavy leather gloves and wielding long batons, braced themselves for the return of the Tigers. The gang that appeared, however, was the Tank, so named because it fought in a phalanx. Far from provoking hostility, the Tankers appeared remarkably peaceful, paying for tickets without comment, dancing politely with the girls, and comporting themselves like model youth. The bouncers, lulled into a false sense of security, were totally unprepared when the Tigers launched a surprise attack, whooping through the entry armed with every weapon in the gang armory, from shivs and razors to bicycle chains and steel-tipped boots. As the bouncers turned bravely to confront their sudden foe, the Tank formed a phalanx and charged the guards from the rear. It was war to the death.

"I can still hear," recalled Williams, "the crunch of leather on bone as the boots went in, the sickening sound of the batons bouncing off skulls. I can still see the bright flashes of spurting blood. I saw one boy no bigger than a penny piece go for a bouncer with a knife. The bouncer swung his baton, and the boy went down, his face transformed into a mass of blood and splintered nose bone. He screamed as he lay there, thrashing about." Williams hastened out of the hall to reach his car. As he drove off, he caught a last glimpse of the boy being borne off by his comrades, stretched out upon a door, like a fallen soldier.

Allan Williams never had any use for the Beatles. "I wouldn't touch them with a barge pole!" he sneered after concluding his association with the world's most beloved entertainers. Seen through the bloodshot eyes of this Welsh plumber turned nightclub operator, a man who prided himself upon being a "professionally trained singer," the Beatles weren't even musicians; they were just a lot of lazy layabouts and yobbos, typical of the flotsam and jetsam of Liverpool 8. Williams would never have had any dealings with this lot were it not for his friendship with Stu Sutcliffe, a young man he admired as a true artist and idealist. In fact, the only gigs Williams thought suitable to the Beatles were those odd jobs always allotted to art students, like painting the ladies' loo in Williams's club, the Blue Angel, or making the floats for his Chelsea Arts Ball. Only after months of turning a deaf ear to their entreaties did the barrel-chested little promoter with the leonine head allow the boys to play—not for money but merely for refreshments—as the lull band at the Jacaranda.

The Jac—a coffee bar with plate-glass window and Formica cafeteria tables—resembled during the day, in Williams's words, "a stale, tired waiting room in a railway station." At night, its bleak, beat atmosphere was enlivened by the appearance of a West Indian steel band that tinkered on its drums in the murky basement, a favorite make-out place for the local guys and gals. On Monday night in their place would come the "Band with the Benzedrine Beat"—Cass and the Cassanovas, the most popular rock 'n' roll group in Liverpool. Known later as the Big Three, this legendary trio was driven by the crude but inspired drumming of a terrifying Teddy Boy with wolfish grin named Johnny Hutchison, the prototype of Ginger Baker.

Hutch's scorn for the Beatles, those "posers," as he saw them, is written all over his craggy face in a remarkable photograph of the early Beatles, humping their guitars and mimicking the footwork of Chuck Berry, while big Hutch in his windbreaker sits behind them, cool and contemptuous, gazing off to the side as he lays down the beat with confident authority. Casey Jones, the group's rhythm guitar, was no less scornful of these schoolboys turned rockers. He told them that their name was ridiculous, urged them to adopt a proper billing, like "Long John and the Silver Beatles." Lennon must have gagged at the idea of being tagged with the name of the one-legged pirate in *Treasure Island,* but for a few months the band advertised itself as the Silver Beatles.

Cilla Black, famous later as a pop star, often went to the Jac on Monday nights. "It cost a shilling to get in," she reported. "I'd pay to see Cass and the Cassanovas. Then on would come these Beatles as a fill-in group. They were scruffy and untidy. Paul McCartney played rhythm. He didn't put himself out about the strings on his guitar, and they'd keep breaking. I used to think one of us in the front row would get an eye knocked out. The Beatles hadn't much equipment. They'd borrow stuff from the Cassanovas. Anyway, I didn't dig the Beatles." With the fans talking like that, is it any wonder that Allan Williams regarded the Beatles doubtfully?

Persuaded finally by their relentless efforts at self-improvement, Williams sprang for group outfits. At Marks and Spencer, he bought them black crewneck sweaters, black jeans, and white-and-brown plimsolls (sneakers). Then, one day in May 1960, he told the boys that the great Larry Parnes was coming up to the Pool with his top star, Billy Fury, a local lad, to audition bands for a backup job. Every outstanding group in the area was on deck that day, sweating blood, because each regarded this job as the chance of a lifetime. Billy Fury was the latest Elvis clone. At this moment he stood at the peak of his career. Any player in his band stood to make the staggering sum of one hundred pounds a week! Plus a chance to break into the big time—and maybe go to America!

Of all the groups that played that day, the Beatles, aided by the powerful drumming of Big Hutch, made the best impression. Billy Fury turned to Larry Parnes finally and said: "This is the band I want. The Beatles will be marvelous!"

Parnes had only one objection: Stu Sutcliffe, who obviously couldn't play his instrument and sought to conceal the fact by turning away so that no one could see his fumbling fingers. When Mr. Big asked to hear the Beatles without their bass player, Williams turned to the band and asked in a wheedling tone: "Is it OK, boys?"

John Lennon replied in a voice like steel: "No, it's *not* OK." That blew the Beatles' big chance.

Billy Fury remarked shortly before his death in 1982: "I could see that if I took them on, there would be personality clashes. . . . Lennon was a troublemaker as far as I was concerned. I turned them down." Cass and the Cassanovas got the job.

Larry Parnes didn't forget the Beatles, however; a week later, when he needed a cheap backing for one of the hacks in his stable, a former carpenter named Johnny Gentle, he gave the Beatles the gig. The good-looking Gentle was at the peak of his modest career. He had put out a few records, his top chart position being twenty-eight with "Milk from a Coconut." At the box office he was worth about £100 a week (the equivalent of ten times as much today), of which he got £20, double the salary of a workingman. He spent a day or two teaching the

Beatles the six songs he did in his twenty-minute turn, mostly Ricky Nelson numbers. Then it was time to hit the road.

The tour embraced seven towns in the northeast of Scotland, of which the largest was Inverness, the capital of the Highlands. Transport was an old van into which were packed the Beatles, Johnny Gentle, and the driver, Jerry Scott, plus instruments, amps, personal effects, and drum kit. The routine was to take off at ten in the morn, after a generous breakfast, which was the Beatles' only assured meal of the day because it was part of the bed-and-board accommodation provided at his house by the Scottish promoter, Douglas McKenna, a sixty-year-old chicken farmer. When McKenna got an eye of the Beatles' outfits, which they wore for traveling as well as onstage, he called up Larry Parnes and raised hell about the band's scruffy appearance. Parnes wouldn't spend an extra farthing, so it fell to Johnny Gentle's lot to improve the Beatles' image. He noted that one of the boys had a black shirt. Gentle had a black shirt, too. "Well, we're halfway there," he decided. "If I go out and buy two black shirts, I'll let my shirt go to Paul; George has one; then, it only needs the bass player and John." At one pound fifty apiece, the band could be outfitted for three pounds.

They played generally in ballrooms, but they might land in a pungent exhibition hall that had just seen a cattle auction. Admission was five shillings, and the audience unspoiled. Local bands would play Scottish reels for the lads and lassies. Meantime, the big star from London would be wriggling into his tight breeches behind the buffet, where a woman would be serving tea and scones.

The Silver Beatles would come on first and do six songs, mostly hits by Little Richard. Then Johnny Gentle would appear in his DA and drape-shape sports clothes to do his Ricky Nelson numbers, like "Mary Lou" and "Poor Little Fool." The big hit of the tour was an old-fashioned jump song by Peggy Lee, "It's All Right, O.K., You Win." Gentle would shout, "It's all right!" and the Beatles would echo like a Forties swing band, "Ariiiight!" When the star's turn concluded, the boys would round off the show with six more tunes.

After the performance somebody might stand the band a drink. The Beatles had no money for beer because Larry Parnes was paying only five pounds a man—and nothing for Stu Sutcliffe. (The boys pooled their wages and cut Stu in for a full share.) What they craved most was not drink but food. Lennon, in particular, displayed a savage appetite. "He was an absolute gannet," says Tommy Moore, the band's new drummer. "He'd wolf down everything in his path in such an obnoxious and beastly way it would put me off my food just to watch him." Next to food, the boys were most interested in making out with girls.

Though even the mediocre Johnny Gentle regarded this tour with distaste, the Beatles were as enthusiastic as Boy Scouts on their first encampment. "The boys went out of their way to entertain me and amuse me and be good mates," recalled Gentle. "Pretty shrewd, when you think of it today. At the time I thought: 'That's the way they are.'" He found Lennon particularly spontaneous and amusing. "He was very keen to know how I got where I was," said Gentle. "He was envious." Gentle's advice to the Silver Beatles was to go to London, which he recognizes now "was all wrong, as it turned out."

Reckoning that the young John Lennon had a shrewd sense of the current pop scene, Gentle demonstrated for him his latest song, "I've Just Fallen for Someone," which he was about to record. Lennon said, "I don't care for the middle eight," and then improvised the words and music for a new bridge. (This was precisely the sort of thing that John did time and again in later years for Paul McCartney.) When the song was released as the B-side of a Johnny Gentle single on Parlophone in 1962, John Lennon received no credit for his contribution—but he had the pleasure of hearing eight bars of his music on a commercial record before the Beatles had cut one of their own songs.

The Scottish tour ran smoothly until Fraserburgh. Approaching the city after dark, Johnny Gentle came to a fork in the road and made a wrong turn. Next thing he knew, he was on a collision course with a "black box," a Ford Coronol. Both drivers assumed they had the right-of-way; they crashed head-on.

The Ford took a terrible bang, the steering wheel snapping off and hitting the old man driving the car in the face. The van jolted to a stop, but everything inside kept moving. John Lennon, who had been asleep in the front seat, did a forward somersault and landed under the dashboard. Miraculously, everybody came off scatheless save Tommy Moore, who caught a guitar case full in the mouth. Rushed to a local hospital by a passing motorist, Moore was informed that he had lost his front teeth and would have to be anesthetized while the doctors stitched up his face.

Johnny Gentle and the other Beatles drove on to the gig, where they found the local promoter impatiently awaiting them. When he learned about the accident, he was furious that it had cost him his drummer. "Why don't you go to the hospital and drag him out?" suggested Lennon, quick to tease a sorehead. One man's jest is another man's earnest. The promoter raced to the hospital, where he found the groggy Tommy Moore coming out of the anesthetic. Before the Beatles hit the stage, the drummer was back on the gig. Lennon screamed with laughter when he saw Tommy's disfigured face.

"The Beatles came back from Scotland much better musicians," reported Allan Williams. They also came back a band without a dependable drummer. "I'd had a bellyful of Lennon," declared Tommy Moore within a few weeks. "He could be a bloody nasty guy. I think he was sick. He seemed to love watching the fights that broke out in the dance halls between the rival gangs. He'd say, 'Hey, look at that guy putting the boot in there!' He got a sadistic delight out of it all." Whenever Tommy refused to budge from the seat of the forklift he operated in the yard of a bottle works in Garston, the Beatles were in serious trouble because a rock band without a drummer was like a car without an engine. Joey Goldberg, the Beatles' first equipment handler, recalled that every Monday night when the boys would meet at the Jac before going out on the gig, they would ask each other anxiously: "Are we gonna have a drummer?" Three out of four times Moore wouldn't show, and Lennon would have to placate the crowd at the dance hall by shouting: "Does anyone out there fancy himself having a bash at the skins?" One night, at the Grosvenor Ballroom, in a tough industrial district across the Mersey, this dubious ploy nearly led to disaster.

A huge, red-headed gawk named Ronnie, one of the most violent gang leaders in Liverpool, swaggered up on the stage and assumed the drummer's seat. He made an atrocious mess of the Beatles' music and wouldn't get off when the number ended. All night he stayed onstage with the band, showing off for the benefit of his gang, who howled and hooted at the spectacle of their leader knocking the hell out of a fancy drum kit. At intermission John Lennon made a desperate call to Allan Williams, who jumped into his Jaguar and roared through the Mersey Tunnel at over a hundred miles an hour to arrive just as the last set was ending. But by now Ronnie had taken it into his head to become the Beatles' regular skin basher. As little Allan Williams sought to reason with him, saying it would not be right to ace out Tommy Moore—"just a working-class stiff, like yourself, right, skin?"—the Beatles found themselves surrounded by Ronnie's gang, waiting for the signal to go into action. It took a lot of fancy stepping by the nimble manager before the Beatles could make a clean getaway.

Desperate for a dependable drummer, the Beatles tied in now with a very different sort of rocker: Pete Best, an intelligent, well-mannered, but unsmiling and taciturn boy, who looked like a twenty-year-old version of Jeff Chandler. Pete's mother, Mona Best, ran a teen club called the Casbah in the huge, many-roomed basement of her ancient house in Heyman's Green, a very quiet suburb. Pete, who played the club every week with his band, the Blackjacks, had achieved such popularity with the kids that one night in a battle of the bands with Rory Storm and the Hurricanes (whose drummer was Ringo Starr), Pete and his group were awarded the victory by 1,350 cheering fans. (Imagine 1,350 kids assembled in a suburban basement for a rock show!) It was George Harrison, accompanied by his brother Peter, who opened the negotiations with Best. The dickering would have led nowhere but for the fact that at this critical moment the Beatles got their big break: a contract to work for six weeks at Hamburg.

The origin of this history-making engagement lies in the night on which Allan Williams suddenly recognized that his West Indian steel drum band had absconded. When the Jamaicans wrote to say that they were working in the Hamburg's notorious red-light district along the Reeperbahn, Williams was amazed. A calypso band in Hamburg! Why, it was like finding "whales in the Sahara"! So the hard-hustling manager took off for the German port city, arriving with no more German than he had picked up watching war movies. He was lucky because he blundered immediately into the very man he was seeking: Bruno Koshmider, the first importer of rock musicians on the Continent. A former circus clown, with a simian build and a game leg, who embellished his puggish face with an enormous coil of hair that fell over his forehead (what the English called an "elephant's trunk"), Koshmider was highly receptive to Williams's pitch. But when the Liverpool hustler tried to crown his spiel by punching the Play button on his tape recorder, which he had loaded with the Beatles' best numbers, what emerged from the speaker was a jumble of unrecognizable sounds. The golden opportunity was lost—or so it appeared.

A few months later Williams ran into Koshmider again, this time in London. Larry Parnes had canceled without warning a string of desperately needed dates for two bands that Williams was booking. Threatened with a beating if he didn't find work immediately for Derry Wilkie and the Seniors, Williams had dashed down to London and arranged an audition at the Two Is. There he found Herr Koshmider, who had come to England with the express purpose of recruiting fresh talent for his clubs in Hamburg. Williams made a quick deal for Derry and the Seniors, who were soon writing home about their success. A few weeks later Koshmider requested that Williams send him another band to be used for opening his latest club. Allan Williams decided to send the krauts his least marketable group: the Silver Beatles.

RED-LIGHT ROCK

The Club Indra was, until the arrival of the Beatles in August 1960, the best-known strip bar in Hamburg. Advertised by a big elephant suspended across the narrow cobblestoned breadth of the Grosse Freiheit, the room, hung with garish Indian fabric, had featured the highly popular Conchita. Appearing in a red and black flamenco costume, with her hair piled high and crowned with comb and mantilla, she opened her act with a dazzling display of stomps, turns, and arched-back Gypsy attitudes. As the band twanged guitars and clacked castanets, she would fling off first one, then another piece of her clothing, gradually revealing her long, slender legs, high, tight buttocks, and firm, well-shaped breasts. Cheered on wildly by the audience of German johns, she would finally get down to her scanties, which was the cue for the band to strike a stunning chord, as the stage lights went out and a single spotlight focused on the dancer. Reaching up with one hand, Conchita would pull off her hair, and with the other tear off her bra—to reveal that she was a *man!* That was the act the Beatles had to follow.

Hustled out of their van and onto the stage, they found themselves in trouble from their first note. Instead of the natural clang of their electric guitars and the resonant thump of the bass drum, the sounds they produced were puny and muffled. "It was like playing under a load of bedclothes," recalled Pete Best, who quickly identified the source of their trouble in the cocoon-like hangings with which the room was swathed. Even worse was the apathy of the audience, comprised of puzzled-looking men who had come to the club anticipating the usual sex show. The final blow came during the break, when Bruno Koshmider told the boys that the old woman who lived upstairs had complained to the police about the unaccustomed noise. In the red-light district, the last thing anyone wanted was trouble with the *Polizei!*

During the next set the Beatles attempted to rock softly, but no matter how they played, they could not satisfy Koshmider, who kept dashing up to the stage, slapping his hands together like an agitated seal and barking: *"Mach Schau! Mach Schau!"* The show he was demanding was the same uproarious performance he was getting from his other English rockers, the white Tony Sheridan and the black Derry Wilkie, uninhibited young men who used all the tricks they had picked up from the rubber-legged Elvis, the furniture-climbing Little Richard, and the clowning antics of the Bill Haley Combo. The Beatles, by contrast, had always prided themselves on maintaining a cool, laid-back stance. As Lennon explained, "What everybody had done before us was either Elvis and his group or Cliff Richard and the Shadows [who employed choreographed band steps]. Every lead singer had a pink coat and a black shirt and white tie and did ass movements in front of the band. We did the opposite of that. We were cool. We didn't move much. But they didn't want music. They wanted a performance!"

Overnight Lennon had to come up with an act. Nor could he expect much help from his mates. As he complained, "Whenever there was any pressure point, *I* had to get us out of it. They always said, 'Well, OK, John, you're the leader.' When nothing was going on, they'd say: 'Unh-unh! No leader! Fuck it!' So I had to get up and do a show."

The next night Lennon laid aside his guitar and limped onstage like a corkscrew-legged cripple, a Long John Silver, whose virility is enhanced instead of diminished by his affliction. Standing mutely before the audience, he suddenly kicked his lame left leg over the top of the mike, squatting down in a crouch while rotating. Coming up again to face the house, he reached out and collared the mike, throwing it down toward the floor but catching it before it hit by going into a hunched-up Quasimodo posture. Burying his lips in the mike, he intoned in a low, slow, sexually arousing tone, "Be-bop-a-lu-la . . ." From that moment on, John Lennon and the Beatles were on the right path in Hamburg.

But imitating the gimpy Gene Vincent every night didn't solve all of Lennon's problems. Once he had captured the audience's attention, his next challenge was to hold it for hours on end. Downbeat was at seven, save on Saturday, when it was at six; from then until twelve-thirty, the Beatles were expected to perform virtually without a break. Once the boys began drawing crowds, they often played until two in the morning, meaning they were onstage for seven or eight hours straight. Accustomed to working one-hour sets and repeating the same tunes on every show, the Beatles were utterly unprepared for this ordeal. What's more, they discovered that the syrupy stuff that Paul liked to ladle out, like "Red Sails in the Sunset," would not go down with the Germans. So the Beatles were compelled to change their act in two directions, adding a lot of new material and stretching out all their old numbers far beyond the length to which they were accustomed.

If the Beatles had learned their R&B music by playing for years in inner-city clubs in America, they would have known that these songs actually work far better when they are not confined to the three-minute duration of a 45 rpm record. Now for the first time they discovered that when they played a track like Ray Charles's "What'd I Say" for twenty minutes straight, the repetition produced a tremendous change in the emotional atmosphere. For when the group got into the groove—which they tried to make a lot deeper by stomping their feet on the wooden stage—they would gradually build up some of that storefront church atmosphere that is the soul of rhythm and blues, a music that should have been called gospel-blues. Soon the patrons of the Indra were getting off behind this crazy *Negermusik*.

Sensing now what the audience wanted, Lennon urged his boys to indulge in a lot of rough horseplay. He and Paul would stage a mock fight, or one would leap upon the other's back and go charging into George or Stu, toppling him off the stage. Or John might take a great flying leap into the house, a stunt that Rory Storm had developed back home. There were even nights when John and Paul would rouse the drinkers from ringside and, joining hands with them, dance ring-around-the-rosy!

As Lennon got drunk, he would start to send up the krauts. He and the boys had picked up some Afrika Korps caps with swastikas on their peaks. John would goosestep up and down the stage, ending the number with a stiff-arm salute and a ringing cry of *Heil Hitler!* The startling gesture would be followed by a volley of curses and insults that should have provoked a riot but simply made the juiced-up Germans laugh all the harder at the *beknackte Peetles*—the crack-brained Beatles.

After playing the Beatles for seven weeks at the Indra, Bruno Koshmider was forced to close the club because of persistent complaints of noise. Unwilling to lose his new attraction, he offered the boys an extension of their original contract if they would continue working for him down the block at the Kaiserkeller, where they would alternate with Rory Storm and the Hurricanes.

The Kaiserkeller had been a welcome novelty when it opened: a club designed especially for young people. Located in the basement of the Lido Danse Palais, it offered beer, schnapps, and Coke, a place to dance, and a dark, vaguely nautical atmosphere in which the kids could talk and flirt. At nine-forty-five every night, the loudspeaker would blare: "At ten o'clock, everyone under eighteen must leave the club." After that the police might appear to check identity cards.

But within a year of its opening the Kaiserkeller was taken over by the *Schlägers,* or Hitters, a black-leather-jacket motorcycle crowd with their little dolls in crinoline. Soon the club became the arena for nightly punch-ups that took a characteristically brutal turn. At the first sign of trouble a posse of tough waiters with spring-loaded saps would pounce on the offending parties and beat them senseless. Then the bodies were thrown out in the street. So bad was the club's reputation by the time the Beatles arrived that no respectable young man or woman would set foot in the dive.

What ordinary youngsters avoided was absolutely taboo for those refined types called *Exis*—as in "existentialist." The *Exis* were middle-class youths who modeled themselves upon the sophisticated literary-intellectual types of Paris. The uniform of the *Exis* was elegantly casual: a corduroy jacket, a heavy woolen sweater, a scarf, and slipper-like shoes or half boots with rounded toes. Unlike the Hitters or rockers, who wore their hair sweeping up to a tumbling coxcomb, the *Exis* combed their hair down in a slant across their foreheads like school-boys. Just the sight of an *Exi* was enough to enrage a rocker, and the spectacle of a crowd of half-drunk Hitters was enough to make an *Exi* run for his life. Thus it was odd that the Beatles' most appreciative and devoted fans at Hamburg should have been three *Exis*.

Klaus Voorman, Astrid Kircherr, and Jürgen Vollmer were all scions of good middle-class families: Klaus's father was a well-known physician in Berlin; Astrid's father, deceased, had been an executive with the Ford Motor Company in West Germany; and Jürgen's father was a professional army officer, who had died on the Russian front shortly after his son's birth. When they met the Beatles, all three were commercial art students, products of Hamburg's Institute of Fashion. Klaus and Astrid, who were twenty-two, had left the school; Jürgen, only seventeen, was still enrolled. Of the three, Astrid was the most striking in appearance and the dominant personality.

Resembling a snub-nosed St. Joan with her bowl-shaped haircut, black leather clothes, and wide-eyed, impassively staring facial mask, Astrid had been involved for years with Klaus, who had an apartment around the corner from the Kircherr house in affluent Einstudel. But by October 1960, when the *Exis* met the Beatles, the lovers had begun to cool toward each other. In fact, it was a quarrel with Astrid that led to Klaus's discovery of the Beatles.

Wandering alone in the red-light district, where he had gone to forget his troubles, Klaus heard loud music coming from a cellar club. Entering on an impulse, he made his way cautiously through the murk to a table near the stage and seated himself next to a group of rockers, who were costumed in gray-and-white houndstooth jackets, with black shirts and trousers and gray winklepickers. When the band onstage came off, the group at the table arose, mounted the stage, and announced themselves as the Beatles.

These bizarre-looking musicians and their music intrigued Klaus, who like most college students of the day had grown up on jazz. During the Beatles' break he struck up a conversation with them by handing around some record sleeves that he had designed. (Years later he was to design *Revolver*.) John Lennon brusquely directed Klaus across the table to Stu, whom John described as the "artist of the bunch." Then John made funny faces behind Klaus's back, as if to say, "Who's this weird jerry coming the art bit?" But Stu behaved cordially, and Klaus was encouraged to come back to the club, bringing along the skeptical—and frightened!—Jürgen and Astrid.

The Beatles did not carry on at the Kaiserkeller the same way they did at the Indra. Alternating now with Rory Storm, a fair-haired Rod Stewart type, the Beatles had no need to cavort because Rory was an acrobatic performer of the sort who might break a leg leaping from the balcony of a theater onto the stage. So the Beatles felt free to revert to their customary manner and play it cool. Jürgen Vollmer, who was fascinated by John Lennon and never missed a night when the Beatles were in town, recalled distinctly that though Paul showed a certain animation when he sang, John performed with "no gestures while playing the guitar, except for pushing his body slightly forward to the rhythm of the music. *Aggressive restraint*—the Brando type."

It was Lennon's contained but menacing aura that Jürgen sought to capture in the photographs he took the following spring, when the Beatles returned to Hamburg. Unlike Astrid Kircherr's famous shots, which treat the Beatles in the hip fashion style of the day by posing them against primitive-looking carnival machinery, Jürgen's pictures go much deeper. Portraits of the Beatles in their natural milieu, they drew out of the boys, particularly John, not an easy subject, the emanations of their souls. As Lennon observed, "Jürgen Vollmer was the first photographer to capture the beauty and spirit of the Beatles." "Beauty" is not a word that readily associates with John Lennon, but it is the only word for Jürgen's best shot, which was John's favorite picture of himself as a young rocker.

A very romantic picture, the image is that of an idealized street loafer, leaning against a rough brick arch, dressed in black leather jacket and jeans with his hair just beginning to fringe his forehead. What makes the shot remarkable is the dreamy and serene look on John's soft, full, almost feminine face, vaguely reminiscent of the young Bob Dylan's, but offering also that tension between hard and soft, macho and punk, that lent such an ambiguous fascination to Brando's face in pictures like *The Wild One*. Almost as expressive as the face is the quintessentially American body language: one hand in a pocket, the opposite shoulder into the brick, one leg twisted so that the toe of the boot meets the instep of the other boot—like a dancer striking a pose.

The other Beatle who fascinated these visually sophisticated young Germans was Stu Sutcliffe. They saw Stu in terms of another American movie hero: James Dean. "Mystery behind sunglasses" was Jürgen's caption for Stu. Undoubtedly it was infatuation with this mystery coupled with an instinctive awareness of Stu's sensitive and vulnerable soul that inspired Astrid to fall in love with him. The relationship developed rapidly despite the fact that Astrid knew no English and had to rely on Klaus and Jürgen to translate her wooing, for it was she who took the initiative, made the decisive moves, and eventually arranged the pattern of their lives. When the Beatles returned to Hamburg in the spring of 1961 to work at Peter Eckhorn's Top Ten Club, Stu fell completely under Astrid's spell, combing his hair down over his forehead, as she urged, and wearing the effeminate clothes in which she fancied him. One of the pictures she took of them together shows the delicately featured Stu with his shirt tied up in a bare-midriff effect and a big flower thrust down into his cleavage.

Stu's submission to Astrid's domination provoked the derision of the other Beatles, particularly that of Paul, who was always scheming to get rid of Stu because he could never learn to play his instrument. One night Paul said something about Astrid onstage that so infuriated the mild-mannered Stu that he tore off his guitar, dashed across the platform, and belted McCartney in the face, knocking him off the piano stool. As the two boys rolled over and over on the bandstand, fighting desperately, the audience roared with delight.

Stu left the Beatles shortly thereafter, and Paul took over on bass, giving the band for the first time in its history a firm musical foundation. Six months later Stu and Astrid were engaged, and Stu went back to studying art, with Eduardo Paolozzi, a Scottish-born artist, who was greatly impressed by his new pupil's ability

The other Beatles were also occupied with women at Hamburg, but their sex life could be summed up in one word: orgy. Lodged in a couple of unlit cubicles at the back of the Bambi Kino, a cheap movie house near the Indra, the Beatles had fallen into the habit of having a ball every night after work. Pete Best describes how the boys would return to their digs at two or three in the morning to be greeted by the smell of perfume in the dark and the giggling of invisible girls. Often without seeing the girls, the Beatles would begin their nightly romp. "There were usually five or six girls between us," recalled Best. "During the proceedings there would come an echoing cry from John or George along the corridor enquiring of Paul and me, 'How's yours going? I'm just finishing. How about swapping over?' Or: 'How you two doing? I fancy one of yours now!'" On the most memorable night the Beatles had eight girls and contrived to screw them each twice! All this from a band that subsequently got famous singing "I Want to Hold Your Hand"!

Once the game of bedding the Beatles became popular in the red-light district, it assumed a variety of forms. Prostitutes who worked in houses would invite the boys to spend an evening for free. Exuberant hookers would jump to their feet at the Kaiserkeller and hold up their arms in the "fuck you" gesture, shouting, "Gazunka!" Jaded whores would sit coolly at tables near the stage and indicate by wink or nod that they wanted to get it on with the boys. John got the clap, but as he told a friend, "One shot in the butt, and it was gone."

Sex was just one of the recreations offered free to the Beatles. Another was drink, with which the whole district was awash. Cases of beer and Sekt, the sweet German champagne, would be deposited directly before the bandstand, with the implicit demand that the boys guzzle the stuff down before their smiling patrons. John had threatened to become a drunkard at the time of his mother's death. Now he fulfilled the threat. In Hamburg he went for weeks without sobering up. He learned to do everything needful while drunk: eat, screw, change the strings on his guitar. One night, while climbing a flight of stairs, he smashed his leg so badly that he bore the mark for the rest of his life. There was no use of drugs during this first season at Hamburg; according to Best, the Beatles' heavy reliance upon Prellies (Preludin, a kind of speed) dates from their second residence in Hamburg.

As the bitterly cold and dreary winter of North Germany came on, with the icy wind off the North Sea digging its talons into the thinly clad Beatles, the boys began to hurt. They needed cash to buy warm clothes and nourishing food. For a young man like John Lennon, who had always been a hitter and who had long entertained criminal fancies, the solution was obvious. Time and again John had seen waiters taking money out of the pockets of drunken sailors. Why shouldn't the Beatles turn the same trick?

One night a beefy German sailor, who had been plying the Beatles with drink during their show, bought the boys a meal. Riveted by the size of the sailor's wallet, the Beatles decided on the spur of the moment to roll him. When they hit the street, however, George and Paul chickened out. That left John and Pete to make the attempt.

The two toughest Beatles jumped the German in a parking lot. John smashed the sailor in the face, dropping him to his knees. Pete dove for the man's wallet. The sailor was a strong man. Even as Pete fumbled for the wallet, the German regained his feet and knocked Lennon to the ground. Then he thrust his hand into the back of his pants and pulled out a gun. There was no telling from the look of the gun whether it shot bullets or tear gas. Frantically both boys pitched themselves headfirst at the burly German, toppling him while he fired wildly over their heads. John and Pete then beat their man until they were sure they could make their escape, racing up the dark street with their eyes smarting from tear gas.

After running three miles, John and Pete staggered breathless into their quarters at the Bambi Kino. Paul and George were waiting up. "What'd you get?" barked George from his bed.

"Not a bloody penny!" gasped Lennon.

The wallet had been lost in the scuffle. Paul and George burst out in derisive laughter. But the escape from immediate danger didn't relieve the muggers of their fears. All the next day they were on edge, fearful that the sailor would turn up with his mates, seeking revenge. After a week had elapsed, the boys were finally able to relax. They never saw the sailor again, nor were they troubled by the police, until the Beatles were deported from Hamburg after Bruno Koshmider had accused them falsely of setting fire to their quarters. (Koshmider was enraged because the Beatles had gone to work for a rival club owner.) So the matter ended, according to Pete Best. But there was more.

John Lennon disclosed in 1974, in the course of a conversation with his favorite guitarist and hangout buddy, Jesse Ed Davis, that the mugging was not an isolated act but one of a number of adventures in which John had been involved. His victims had not been Germans but English sailors, whom he chose to make it appear had been attacked by nasty Germans. One attack lay heavy on his conscience because he had gone mad and beaten the sailor so badly that John feared he had left the man for dead. Lennon's language was roughly, "God knows if he ever got up again."

Though John could never be sure that his victim had died—and study of the Hamburg press of the time reveals no record of such an event—Lennon lived henceforth with the stain of murder on his soul. By the time he confessed the crime to Jesse Ed Davis, Lennon had brought his guilt under control by balancing it against the certainty of future punishment. He told Jesse he was sure he would die a violent death, because it was his "karmic destiny."

"WHAT BRINGS MR. EPSTEIN HERE?"

Matthew Street is a narrow, curving passage, stuck like a baling hook into the maze of grim old warehouses that converge on the Liverpool docks. Here, every day before noon, in the early Sixties, the kids lined up to enter the Cavern. At the head of the line loomed the massive figure of Paddy DeLaney, a former Welsh Guardsman and steward at the Locarno Ballroom, who worked in the uniform of his trade: tuxedo with cummerbund and diamond studs. When he gave the fans the go-ahead, they scuttled through the narrow entrance and descended crab-wise the eighteen greasy stone steps to the cellar.

The basement of this old produce warehouse looked like a section of subway tunnels. Three parallel barrel vaults, each about a hundred feet long and ten feet wide, ran from front to back, joined by six-foot arch-ways. Illumination was provided by bare red bulbs. Of ventilation there was none, the air reeking of the chlorine used to disinfect the notoriously nasty toilets. The seating consisted of twenty rows of straight-back wooden chairs in the central tunnel. The stage was a low plank platform crowned with a drummer's dais and lit by a couple of white lamps in dish reflectors. The arched wall behind the stage had been daubed amateurishly to simulate the stone wall of a dungeon. Many of the stones bore graffiti, laboriously spelling out the names of the local bands: Rory Storm and the Hurricanes, Ian and the Zodiacs, Gerry and the Pacemakers, and of course, the Beatles.

The presiding presence at the Cavern was Bob Wooler, a cross be-tween a radio announcer and Scoutmaster. Working from a turntable and mike in a corner of the tiny dressing room to the left of the stage, Wooler spun discs while the club filled, interspersing the music with patter, his most famous line being "Remember, all you cave dwellers, the Cavern is the best of cellars." When the Beatles signaled they were ready to take the stage, Wooler announced: "It's time for everybody's favorite rock and *dole* group—the *Beatles!*"

Four figures sheathed in black leather would come charging out of the first arch to the left of the stage and run up the three concrete steps to the platform. Plugging into their amps, they would make a hash of "Johnny B. Goode" in their eagerness to be off. Scrambling the music didn't mean a thing to the fans, whose get-off was the roar of the 30-watt Voxes, which sent the twanging and ratcheting of the electric guitars reverberating off the low brick vaults. With the first notes the girls would start screaming, making so much noise that John Lennon would have to lean into his mike and shout, *"Shurrup!"* That got even more screams. As the boys reached down to turn up their amps to the max, the vibrations in the cellar would become so intense that the peeling whitewash on the ceiling began to fall off, covering the black-clad Beatles with flakes of "Cavern dandruff."

John always stood upon the stage with his legs spread and flexed at the knees, staring the house down with his blind eyes. Once he had put a few tunes under his belt and a big wad of gum in his mouth, he would start to loosen up. "This one's from a musical called *The Muscle Man* [*The Music Man*], and it's sung by Peggy Leg," he would say by way of introduction to Paul's rendition of "Till There Was You." Or Lennon might offer a thumbnail sketch of the Beatles' favorite songwriter: "This is a record by Chuck Berry, a Liverpool-born white singer with bandy legs and no hair." When Paul would go into "Over the Rainbow," batting his brown eyes at Mavis and Edna from the typing pool in the Cunard Building, John would respond by making grotesque faces. Or he might do his Quasimodo, the hunchback, routine, twisting his head over his shoulder and contorting his features into a hideous grimace. Or he might interject into Paulie's sentimental performance a series of queer guitar noises, gazing all the while about the cellar, like a yokel seeing the big city for the first time.

The early Beatles were a human jukebox. They played song after song without rhyme or reason: rock 'n' roll, rhythm and blues, country and western tunes, pop songs, radio themes, music hall novelties, and anything else that struck their fancies. Sometimes they took requests screamed up from the floor. Sometimes they fell to arguing among themselves over what song to play next. Though the boys aimed to entertain, they were just as intent on pleasing themselves. It was precisely their spontaneous humor and free-associative word-and-song play that made their shows so different from what any other rock band had ever done before—or has done since.

The greatest moment would come at the end when the Beatles would embark on a long rave-up based on some funky "rhythm and booze" tune, like "Money," that would give John a chance to holler himself hoarse. For the great secret the boys had brought back from their first trip to Hamburg was simply the old idea of the jam session, whose steadily building excitement sucks the audience out of their seats and compels them to act out the excitement that is boiling up inside the music. As the gospel-blues chant went round and round, gathering fresh intensity every minute, the girls in their black-and-white dresses, billowed out by crinolines, and the boys in their gray crewnecks and dark jackets, would rise in their places and go into the Cavern Stomp. Facing each other but never moving their feet in the dense crowd, they would clasp their right hands and saw back and forth with their elbows. So tight was the crush of writhing bodies and so great the steamy heat they generated—the condensed vapor on the brick arches glittering like ice and trickling down like rain—that often a girl would faint dead away.

As the kids climbed the steep stairs to Matthew Street, the last word they would hear would be Bob Wooler urging them to buy the Beatles' new record. "Remember, folks," he would admonish them: "'My Bonnie' and 'The Saints,' recorded by our very own Liverpool boys with Tony Sheridan!" The record Wooler was pitching had been cut in Hamburg during the Beatles' second engagement in the spring of 1961. Bert Kaempfert, composer of "Stranger in the Night" and artist and repertoire man for Polydor, had taken the Beatles under contract as a backup band for Tony Sheridan, with whom they had been working at the Top Ten Club. A couple of tracks had been released in Germany, but they had not been successful. As John Lennon said of the Beatles' contribution, "It could have been anyone bashin' about back there."

On 28 October 1961, a day that has gone down in rock history, a fan named Raymond Jones took Bob Wooler's advice and walked around the corner to the NEMS shop (Northern England Music and Electric Industries) to order the Beatles' record. The disc proved hard to find because it was cataloged under "Tony Sheridan and the Beat Brothers," but when the manager of the store, Brian Epstein, finally got it in stock, an event he signaled by placing a discreet little sign in his window, he was astonished to find this obscure 45 was outselling the latest releases of Elvis Presley and Cliff Richard. Soon Mr. Epstein was beating a path to the Beatles' cave.

It took an effort of will for Brian to descend the grimy steps to the Cavern. Teenage rock clubs were not his beat. The coddled and pampered oldest son of a prosperous Jewish merchant and the half-finished product of numerous prep schools, Brian was a typical young snob. Though he ran the biggest record shop in the city, he had never taken any real interest in pop music, apart from Broadway musicals.

He must have felt his skin crawl when, clad in his dark custom-tailored suit and accompanied by his personal assistant, Alistair Taylor, he edged into the murky, steamy, noisy, foul-smelling basement, where all the kids were chomping away on "Cavern lunches." Yet despite the prejudices of his class and temperament, Brian Epstein reacted to the Beatles exactly as had the *Exis* at Hamburg. He fell in love with the boys at first sight. Indeed, he was so smitten that when he left the club, he poured into the ears of his assistant a long spiel about taking the Beatles under his personal management and fashioning them into stars!

Peter Brown, Brian's aide-de-camp for many years, insists that Brian's motive was purely erotic: the Beatles were a "personification of his secret sexual desires." Lust most certainly explains the advances Brian made to certain members of the group, starting with the best-looking boy, Pete Best. (Driving toward Blackpool one night, Brian said: "Pete, would you find it embarrassing if I ask you to stay in a hotel overnight? I'd like to spend the night with you." Pete said he'd prefer to go home.) Homosexuality wasn't the only reason why Brian became infatuated with the Beatles, however; there was another motive, just as obvious and urgent as sex. Brian *envied* the Beatles as much as he lusted after them.

A chronically unhappy young man, who had already, at the age of twenty-seven, resigned himself to the thought that no one is really happy, he felt imprisoned by his family and by the petty world of provincial shopkeeping. Time and again he had sought to escape from his ignominious situation behind the counter of a provincial shop. The sight of the Beatles, four young lads without a care in the world, playing their uproarious music, drinking and eating onstage, chivying the girls in the front row, or roughly punching each other's leather-clad shoulders, was enough to set his mind in a whirl. Once he got involved with the band, his identification with them became amusingly obvious. No sooner did he get them into mohair suits than he took to wearing black leather jackets. Up to the day he died, Brian Epstein had no fonder dream than to be taken for the "Fifth Beatle."

Chances, are, though, that Brian had no idea what was impelling him that first afternoon, when he approached the bandstand, to be greeted by George Harrison with a crooked smile and the challenging words "What brings Mr. Epstein here?" What, indeed! Brian was stuck for an answer.

In the weeks that followed, Brian returned to the Cavern time and again to see the Beatles. He also checked out the boys around town. "I wouldn't touch them with a bargepole," growled Allan Williams, whom the Beatles had cold-shouldered after a dispute about money. "If those yobs come around to see Brian," Brian's father told a trusted employee, "tell them he's gone home, and lock the door." Rex Makin, the family lawyer, sneered: "Oh, yes, another Epstein idea. How long before you lose interest in this one?" Brian Epstein had a reputation for being flaky and getting into trouble, but even if he had been firm as a rock and wise beyond his years, he would have had a problem making up his mind about the potential of the Beatles.

The Beatles, for their part, were not all that keen on Brian. Paul's father didn't fancy his son's being managed by him. Aunt Mimi required a special visit from Brian, in which he pledged that he would always treat John with special regard, a promise that he certainly kept. Even though the prospect of benefiting from Brian's position titillated the boys, they couldn't resist the temptation to make fun of their prospective manager. "Antwacky" was their word for Brian—"out of touch." Brian's lack of experience in the pop music business was matched by his total ignorance of rock 'n' roll. But the Beatles were shrewd enough to recognize that at this point in their career the only thing that mattered was getting a recording contract. Pete Best voiced the thinking of the group: "We were nearing the zenith of the Merseyside and faced the prospect of being stuck there, unless somehow we could break through on a national basis. We needed to get aboard a British label if we were ever to escape the Liverpool–Hamburg shuttle." John put the matter more succinctly when he challenged Brian with a blunt question: "Can you buy us onto the charts?" Brian was never sure what he could or couldn't do for the boys, though he talked about the possibilities endlessly. Finally, one day John cut Brian's polished palaver short, declaring brusquely: "Right, then, Brian. Manage us, now. Where's the contract? I'll sign it!"

Brian had no contract in his desk. He was as ignorant of such matters as John Lennon was. Brian was learning the game as he played what proved to be an endless psychodrama with the Beatles. The first sign of his intensely ambivalent attitudes and convoluted emotions appeared during the signing ceremony at the NEMS office on 24 January 1962. After each Beatle had autographed the last page of the management contract by scrawling his signature across the queen's head on a sixpenny postage stamp, Brian surprised everyone by announcing that he was not going to sign. He explained that though he was absolutely determined to do everything in his power to advance the Beatles' career, he did not want to bind them to a relationship that they might someday wish to terminate. So he was committing himself without demanding an answering commitment from them. (The Beatles did not obtain a properly executed agreement until nine months later, when they signed on John's twenty-second birthday, 9 October 1962, for five years, with Brian receiving the customary manager's fee of 25 percent.)

Though Brian claimed that he was leaving the door open to the

Beatles, it's more likely that he was holding it open for himself. Doubtless he believed every word he said, but he was a very conflicted and neurotic young man, who always wanted contradictory things. He loved the grand gesture, the self-dramatizing act of self-sacrifice, but he would usually reimburse himself for whatever he had thrown away by doing something underhanded.

A typical mama's boy of the pet lamb variety, Brian Samuel Epstein had been shaped since birth by the anxious ministrations of his mother, Malka Epstein, known as Queenie (originally because *Malka* is the Hebrew for "queen," but later, because of her manners, mimicked unconsciously by her son). The daughter of a prosperous furniture manufacturer in Sheffield, Malka had been educated in a school dominated by Roman Catholics, an experience that led her to attribute all her subsequent misfortunes in life to anti-Semitism, another trait Brian adopted. Married off at the age of eighteen to Harry Epstein, eleven years her senior, handsome and gentlemanly son of a family of furniture retailers in Liverpool, Queenie went from a school full of anti-Semites to a city full of them. Her social circle was confined to her husband's family, dominated by Isaac Epstein, an emigrant Jew from Eastern Europe, who was accustomed to ruling with unchecked authority. Distanced from her own family in this strange northern city and obliged to accommodate herself to a family that controlled her husband and hence herself, Queenie made her firstborn child, Brian, her intimate companion and her compensation for all the satisfactions she found lacking in her life.

Like John Lennon, Brian Epstein was reared on the women's side of the fence, but instead of having Amazons for his nursery heroes, he had Queenie, a diva-like personality whose big moment every day came in the early evening, when she dressed for dinner. From his earliest years Brian was always present at this ritual, like the eunuch at the harem bath. He was consulted as a matter of course about which gown Queenie should wear, a choice he pondered gravely, as if he were already an authority on such matters.

He was to say later that he could not remember a time when he was sexually normal. He could have added that there was also never a time when he did not feel terribly ashamed of the sexual needs that drove him into profoundly embarrassing and self-destructive forms of behavior. At the age of ten he was expelled from Liverpool College (a boys' school) for drawing obscene pictures. By the time he was sixteen, he had been through no fewer than seven schools. During these endless migrations from one institution to another, he landed once in an academy where some staff member recognized the boy's theatrical flair.

Cast in a school play about Christopher Columbus, Brian invited his parents to witness his moment of glory.

The Epsteins arrived, beautifully turned out and comporting themselves like model parents. They sat through the entire performance, but when afterward they were asked by the headmaster what they thought of their son's acting, both Queenie and Harry confessed that they had not been able to identify Brian among the cast. "Which one was he?" demanded Queenie.

"Why," replied the startled headmaster, "Christopher Columbus!"

This chilling little anecdote goes a long way toward explaining the hapless character of Brian Epstein. The reason his parents couldn't recognize him onstage is that they were seeking him among the minor characters: the courtiers, musket bearers, or Indian slaves. That their son should be the leading man, the hero of the piece, was so alien to their conception of him that they could not accept the evidence of their eyes and ears.

When Brian quit school at the age of sixteen—without taking any of the customary examinations—the only career he could imagine for himself was that of a dress designer. His father rejected this vocation as being unmanly. That left Brian no alternative but to enter the family business as a floor salesman. Even in this lowly capacity, he met with humiliation at the hands of his overbearing grandfather.

Shortly after he turned eighteen, Brian was summoned to military service, becoming the only public school boy who was not recommended for officers' training school. He did obtain, however, one of the most prized postings in Britain—Albany Barracks in Regent's Park. From this billet in the heart of London, he sallied forth every night to enjoy the pleasures of the metropolis. Then disaster struck. Returning one night to the Barracks, he was arrested and charged with impersonating an officer. Later he claimed that the whole incident was the product of an innocent mix-up provoked by the figure he cut stepping from a saloon car dressed in a pinstripe suit and bowler. He said the sentries saluted him by mistake and the military authorities prosecuted him for no real reason.

The truth of the matter was discovered years later in the course of an acrimonious lawsuit between Brian Epstein and a merchandiser named Nicky Byrnes. A veteran of seven years' service in the Horse Guards, Byrnes recognized the absurdity of Brian's account of his arrest, which prompted the ex-guardsman to launch an investigation with the Home Office that immediately elicited the truth. Brian, dismayed by what he called his "hideous uniform," had acquired a smartly tailored officer's outfit into which he would change every night after he went off the post. Transformed from a drab little clerk private into a dashing young "two-pipper," he had taken to frequenting bars where he could pick up young men. If he had behaved discreetly, he could easily have escaped detection, but he started cruising just those bars that were patronized by real officers. Reported as a suspicious character, he was put under surveillance by the military police and arrested one night at the Army and Navy Club in Piccadilly. He would have stood a court-martial but for his family, which by dint of pulling every string it could reach, got his case shunted from a judicial to a psychiatric inquiry, which concluded with the finding that Private Epstein was not fit to stand trial. Discharged from the service on medical grounds, Brian ran for home.

Back in Liverpool, he was given his own furniture shop. He made a good thing of it, much to the family's relief. But he was restless and unfulfilled. Falling in with the actors from the local repertory company, with whom he would drink at night, Brian caught stage fever. Thanks to the good offices of the Liverpool company's director, Brian got a place at RADA, the Royal Academy of Dramatic Arts, England's premier acting school. He lasted three terms at the school and would have gone on but for an unfortunate incident: he was arrested for "importuning" an undercover cop in a public toilet. The Epsteins' next-door neighbor, Rex Makin, happened to be the leading criminal lawyer in the northwest; he got Brian off immediately.

This time, when he came home, Brian was put in charge of the record counter of NEMS's large new store on Great Charlotte Street. He made such a success of it that soon his department occupied most of the building. But he still sought to enliven his life by seeking forbidden pleasures. When he had completed his long day's work, he would sometimes drive out to a public toilet in West Derby. One night a rough-looking character dressed like a longshoreman beat Brian up and stole his valuables. When the attacker discovered his victim's identity from his wallet, he called Brian at home and demanded a large sum of money. Brian ran crying to Queenie, who summoned her next-door neighbor. Rex Makin told Brian that he had no choice but to take the matter to the police, a frightening act because homosexuality at the time was a felony.

The police set a trap for the blackmailer, using Brian as bait. When the trap was sprung, Makin, who was on hand, was startled to discover that the criminal was one of his own clients.

In the trial that ensued, Brian availed himself of a privilege of British law and identified himself before the bar as "Mr. X." Everyone in Liverpool was in on his secret. The trial ended in a conviction. Brian's attacker was sent to prison for three years.

It is often said that the Beatles had no idea that Brian Epstein was gay until years later. The fact is that the boys were wised up immediately by Ian Sharp, who ran into the Beatles at the Kardomah Café on 21 February 1962. When the boys told Sharp the name of their new manager, he snapped, "Which one of you does he fancy?"

John gasped: "He's not like that, is he?"

Sharp joked: "Well, don't bend down to pick up the contract." Within a few days of this conversation, Sharp received a letter from Brian's lawyer demanding an apology and a formal recantation, on pain of a lawsuit.

The last time Sharp saw the Beatles, they were in a cab full of girls coming up Mount Street. "Sharpie!" yelled John, leaning out the window; then, as the cab idled its engine, John and Paul babbled out the news of their impending engagement at a great new club in Hamburg. When they had done, they confessed sheepishly that they had signed an agreement never to speak to Sharp again. As the cab took off up the street, John stuck his head out and shouted: "Sorry about that, mate!"

DEATH IN HAMBURG

As they lifted off from Ringway Airport at Manchester on 11 April 1962, the Beatles were anticipating the greatest moment in their career. They were going back to Hamburg—but not to the old sailor bars. This time they would open what promised to be the world's greatest rock club. The Star-Club was its name, and they were to be its first stars. The Beatles were topping a bill that included Tony Sheridan and Gerry and the Pacemakers and would soon boast such famous names as Little Richard and Gene Vincent. Just as good as the billing was the money—a hundred pounds a week for every man jack! When they weren't rocking, they would be making the good times roll along the Reeperbahn. In fact, the fun would begin that very afternoon, when they were met at the airport by Stu and Astrid.

The Beatles had last seen Stu Sutcliffe in December, when he had brought his fiancée home to meet his mother. The encounter had been disastrous. Both Astrid Kircherr and Millie Sutcliffe were strong personalities accustomed to dominating little Stu. They had collided head-on. Their animosity had grown so extreme, in fact, that Stu and Astrid had to move out of the Sutcliffe house.

Quite apart from this trouble, a lot of concern had been voiced about how ill Stu looked. He said that he had consulted doctors about the terrible headaches from which he was suffering, but no physician had been able to offer a remedy or even a firm diagnosis. John Lennon was not worried about his best friend because Stu's latest letters, running sometimes to twenty pages, offered no cause for concern. They were full of the usual chatter about his work and his pride in the Beatles' success.

When John, Paul, and Pete stepped off the plane, the first person they saw was Astrid. She was dressed, as usual, in black and looked very pale. "Where's Stu?" they shouted.

The words seemed to stick in her throat as she struggled to say: "Stu is dead."

The Fifth Beatle had died in a coma the day before, as he was being rushed to the hospital. "Stuart must have got out of bed during the night," recounted Astrid. "I found him collapsed on the floor and called an ambulance. With the driver I helped to carry him down three flights of stairs. As we raced to the hospital, he became very white and drawn. He was on a stretcher in the hospital lift when a doctor looked down at him and announced that he was dead. They said he had a clot of blood on the brain. I just sat in the hospital for hours, staring at the wall. I felt as though my whole life had been taken away from me."

John became hysterical. "He wept like a child," recalled Pete Best, adding: "I had never seen him break down in public before. . . . He was absolutely shattered. John could be the hard man, violent and abrasive . . . [but] the tragic news that came from Astrid's pale lips utterly floored him."

To the very end, Stu Sutcliffe had lived out the myth of the *poète maudit*. He had suffered head pains so excruciating that he had sought to throw himself out a window, being restrained only by the frantic hands of Astrid and Fran Kircherr. One day he had blacked out without losing consciousness, suffering the horror of being struck blind. More than once he fainted away in his painting class or dropped in the street. Yet despite these overwhelming afflictions, he had stood at his easel night and day, trying to cram into the short time left him the work of a lifetime. For though he claimed to be fit for work, he was convinced that he was dying. Gazing at a white coffin displayed in an undertaker's window, he had cried to Mrs. Kircherr, "Oh, Mum, buy it for me! I'd *love* to be buried in a white coffin!"

The mysterious illness that killed Stu was not diagnosed until after a postmortem had been performed; then the doctors discovered a small tumor on the brain. The lesion lay directly beneath an indentation on the right side of the skull. It had been obviously produced by a traumatic injury. Stu's mother and Allan Williams associated this finding with a beating that Stu had allegedly received at Litherland Town Hall before his second trip to Hamburg, a year before his death. Investigation reveals that the fight was not at Litherland but at nearby Lathom Hall. Stu was trapped in the balcony by a gang of thugs, whom John and Pete drove off, John suffering a broken finger in the punch-up. Pete Best's recollection of the incident is vivid, but he does not recall that Stu was struck in the head.

John Lennon took a very different view of his best friend's death. John believed that he was responsible for Stu's demise. He told Yoko Ono (who repeated the story to Marnie Hair) that he had gotten into a quarrel with Stu at Hamburg. They were standing in the street, and suddenly John was seized by one of his fits of uncontrollable rage. He lashed out with hands and feet. In recounting the incident, he laid especial emphasis on the fact that he was wearing cowboy boots with hard, pointy toes. When he came to his senses, he looked down and saw Stu lying on the pavement. He was groaning, and blood was coming down the side of his face. John could see the wound distinctly on the side of the head between the ear and the cheekbone. Horrified by what he had done, he had taken off running. Paul, who was present with another man, perhaps George, hollered: *"Come back, you bloody bastard! You're a damned fool!"* John never stopped running.

Like the fate of the British sailor whom John feared he had killed earlier in Hamburg, the death of Stu Sutcliffe haunted Lennon for the rest of his life. When he felt his own end was nigh, he told Fred Seaman how completely responsible he felt for Stu's death.

Despite the shock of Stu's death, the Beatles went on to score an important triumph on opening night. The Star-Club proved to be the stepping-stone that carried the band out of the joints and into the big time. Designed for the booming tourist trade that had made the old Tenderloin into the European counterpart of Las Vegas, the Star was located at 39 Grosse Freiheit, across the street from the Kaiserkeller. It took its name from an old cinema out of which it had been carved. The orchestra seats had been floored over to make a polished dance surface, and the ceiling dropped, latticed, and hung with Chinese lanterns, like a beer garden. Rank upon rank of curved Leatherette banquettes provided the seating, and a couple of bars furnished the booze, served by white-jacketed waiters. Operating seven nights a week, from eight in the evening till four in the morning, the club offered continuous entertainment. Every half hour the tabs would part to reveal a fresh act, and if a patron could drink enough beer to hold his table, he could see in a single night as many as ten different rock groups.

During their three engagements at the Star the Beatles got their first and only taste of working for a gangster operator. Manfred Weissleder was a six-foot-seven crop-headed *Starker*, who looked and acted like a sergeant in the SS. He ran his nightclub strictly in accordance with the models provided by old Hollywood movies, even employing a sliding panel in his office (formerly the projection booth) that could be pushed back to survey the action on the dance floor and stage. If Weissleder caught a band goofing off or working with a man missing, he would pick up the phone and bark at his manager, Horst Fascher (a former boxing champ), *"Schmeiss diese englischen Arschlösche 'raus!"* ["Throw these English assholes out!"] The next minute the hapless rockers, crying, "Hey, mate, wot's this all about?," would find themselves being hustled out the back door of the club and told to find their way home—without tickets.

On the other hand, if Weissleder liked an act, as he did the Beatles, he would offer it a chance to work for months at a time in Germany, for once he had made a success of his original club, he established a chain of Star-Clubs clear across the continent that became the greatest rock empire in history. Not only were his musicians provided with living quarters, transportation, and very good salaries, but every man received a gold star-shaped pin that was a powerful protective talisman. Once when Kingsize Taylor was walking along the Reeperbahn, an overeager pitchman seized him by the lapels. Spotting the Star-Club pin, he jumped back a yard and gasped: "I'm sorry—*very* sorry!" No matter what the Beatles did from this time forth, they enjoyed the protection of the Man.

It was a good thing that such a powerful gangster was holding a sheltering hand over the band because John, whose behavior in Hamburg had always been demented, began now, in the wake of Stu's death, to act crazier than ever. Lennon would stroll about the streets in his underwear or appear onstage with a toilet seat about his neck or shove a girl's head into his crotch as he sat on the stage apron playing his guitar. His most outrageous stunt was timed to correspond with the holy season of Easter.

The Beatles were quartered in a flat that faced the Star-Club, which was itself one door from a church and convent. On the morning of Good Friday, when the nuns stepped out of their domicile to enter the neighboring church, they were shocked to behold across the street a grotesque life-size effigy of Jesus on the cross, which John had fashioned and hung from his balcony. As the sisters gazed in astonishment at this sacrilegious display, John started pelting them with Durex condoms filled with water. After he had exhausted his supply of bombs, he pulled out his cock and pissed on the nuns, crying, *"Raindrops from heaven!"*

By this time both John and Paul had steady girls in Hamburg. Paul was involved with a pretty platinum blonde named Erika Huebers, who became pregnant during the Beatles' engagement in the spring of 1962 and came to term during the band's last residence in Hamburg at Christmas. According to Erika, Paul was the father. She gave birth to her daughter in a hostel for unwed mothers on the very day that Paul returned to England. When this impoverished girl, who worked as a waitress, began pleading with Paul to send her some money to support the child, she got no response. She filed a suit in a German court, which dragged on until 1966, when Paul finally gave Erika £2,700. Meantime, his recalcitrance cost the Beatles a bundle because they had to turn down lucrative offers to tour Germany lest the court clamp a claim on their fees. In 1966, after Paul settled the case, the Beatles played Germany for the first time in three years. (Almost twenty years later, the mother instigated a second suit, and Paul had two blood tests, both of which indicated he could not have been the father.)

John treated his girlfriend, who likewise became pregnant, very badly. Named Bettina, she was the fat, jolly barmaid at the Star-Club who figures in all the Beatles' books as the band's most enthusiastic fan. This celebrated Bettina was not always so comically obese. When John met her, she was slim and very pretty, as her photographs prove. It was after she had had the illegal abortion which Lennon demanded that she developed, according to her account, a glandular condition that made her swell up to the size of Mama Cass. But she and John continued to pal around as before, with her paying his bills at the Mambo Shankee Bar, where they hung out with a freaky bunch of whores who gathered about Astrid, including a lesbian called Davy Crockett because she wore a coonskin cap. All the whores were devotees of black magic and disciples of Astrid, whom they regarded as a witch. Astrid was also an admirer of the Marquis de Sade, one of whose books she gave to Lennon.

John's relationship with Bettina was strictly local, a limitation she discovered the hard way when she persuaded Kingsize Taylor to take her back to England with him in the summer of 1963 to see the Beatles in their first flush of success. Arriving at the band's hotel in the Welsh seaside resort of Llandudno, the visitors were informed that the boys were rehearsing at the theater. When the Beatles returned, John took one look at Bettina and cut her dead. Though she had come 1,200 miles to see him, he wouldn't even say hello. He walked straight past her and sat down on the opposite side of the lobby where he switched on his transistor radio. The other Beatles were so embarrassed by John's behavior that they couldn't open their mouths. Only Ringo had the decency to come over to Taylor and Bettina and act normally. Poor Bettina returned to Hamburg, where Taylor last saw her working in the Herbertstrasse, the notorious street where the whores sit in display windows.

Not long after the Beatles opened at the Star-Club, they received a telegram from Brian Epstein. "CONGRATULATIONS BOYS," read George aloud that morning to his badly hung-over mates. "EMI REQUEST RE-CORDING SESSION. PLEASE REHEARSE NEW MATERIAL." Instantly the boys were on their feet, whooping it up. Then one of them shouted: "Where are we going, Johnny? . . ."

Shortly afterward Brian arrived with the story of his coup. The tale began back on New Year's Day, 1962, when the Beatles, tense as four fiddle strings, stepped for the first time in their lives into a professional recording studio. (The Tony Sheridan sides had been taped in an auditorium.) And what a studio! They were suddenly in the big time, reporting to 165 Broadhurst Gardens, West Hampstead, the headquarters of the top British pop label, Decca.

During the next three hours the boys played and sang no fewer than fifteen songs, cutting what was, in effect, their first album, known today as the Decca Audition. Historically it proved to be a most important occasion, for up to this time the Beatles had put nothing down on tape that could give future generations a clear idea of how they sounded before they became famous. Now they were given a free rein in an ideal recording environment and encouraged to go through their whole bag of tricks.

Alas, what emerged was far from being a faithful picture of that legendary band, the early Beatles. A heavily cropped and cockeyed pub shot would be a better description of the famous tape. Far from sounding like a pack of fierce young rockers in full cry, these Beatles come on like a hotel band in the Catskills. They warble sentimental show tunes, like "September in the Rain" and "Till There Was You," or they struggle to rock old chestnuts, like "Besame Mucho" or "The Sheik of Araby." Most startling is the distribution of the vocal honors: Paul sings eight songs (in a voice that cries out for a nasal inhalator), George four, and John—the band's leader and strongest singer—only *two!* All these distorting and dismaying alterations in the Beatles' normal presentation betray the emasculating hand of Brian Epstein, who had already coaxed the boys out of their perfect leathers, putting them into ill-befitting blue mohair suits like junior bank clerks. Now he persuaded the boys to abandon their true character as a rough-'n'-tough R&B band to play at being lollipop entertainers like the Shadows.

Despite its misleading character, the Decca Audition does offer a wealth of information about the early Beatles. The good American accents, the fast, nervous tempos, the eclectic jumble of styles, and the slick, contrived arrangements all found their place in the performance style of the later Beatles. Even at this early date the band can knock off any and every sort of American pop, rock, or R&B record, but their facile mimicry never achieves anything better than a clockwork replica. Their failure to touch the soul of the music they love is most apparent from the fact that they sound so foreign. Listening to a hell-for-leather gallop like "Besame Mucho," you might guess that the Beatles were passionate young men from behind the Iron Curtain, Hungarian freedom fighters, who had learned rock 'n' roll by gluing their ears to the Voice of America.

There is, however, one moment in this fascinating, if wrongheaded, session when you hear a performance of unmistakable originality and authenticity: John Lennon's rendering of "Money." Not just a telling but isolated shot, this track prophesies the whole future course of British hard rock. What it foretells is the end of the attempt to mimic black

America and the rise of a distinctly British style. To appreciate what Lennon does with this disc, you have to flip back to Barrett Strong's original recording: a typical Ray Charles pop-gospel track. Both raunchy and ecstatic ("rock," after all, connotes worshiping as much as fucking), this typical black concoction fuses the erotic and the religious to make an ebullient, life-affirming soul music. In John Lennon's take every feature is reversed, like a photograph going from positive to negative.

John's idea of R&B is to play it tough. He presents himself in song exactly as he did in life: as a hard case with a demand on his lips and a threat in his throat that make it perfectly clear that when he says *"money,"* he means exactly what he says—and will do whatever it takes to get that little girl out there on the hook where she can cop the cash he craves. There's no sexual heat in this guy and no congregational fervor around him. He's a mack man, lean and mean, with a voice like a knife made of cold-rolled steel.

This was the John Lennon who could have led the Beatles forward to become the first great hard rock band of the Sixties. They might have rocked with the tough working-class belligerence of the Who, becoming a group whose musical gestures, seconded by corresponding stage gestures, would have created a rock theater that could have enabled John Lennon to enact the psychodrama seething inside his soul. The machine-wrecking tactics of the Who would have suited Lennon right down to the ground, and eventually he might have written his own *Tommy* (as, in a way, he did with the Primal Scream Album). For what is the famous rock opera about? A boy traumatized by his mother's cheating loses all his senses but the most primitive, the sense of touch. He employs this mute yet passionate faculty to become a pin-ball hero—a symbol of rock 'n' roll. Acclaimed by the world's youth as a pop star, he continues to evolve, becoming first a guru and ultimately a saint. There is the legend of John Lennon, to a T.

But instead of driving forward inspired by the dictates of his true character, Lennon succumbed to the enticements of commercial success. Rather than work to bring the public around to his vision, he adapted himself to the tastes of the mass audience. Granted, when he signed his pact with the devil, he assumed that he could cheat the devil by enjoying the pleasures of success while retaining his soul. Soon he found that he had outsmarted himself. The first and foremost demand of his new career was that he turn himself inside out and impersonate a character that was basically his opposite: a smiling, joshing, immaculately groomed, and buttoned-up pop singer. When he and George bridled at the bit that was soon galling their mouths, they found themselves being taken by Paul on one side and by Brian on the other and led along like tame ponies trotting about the kiddie circuit. Now, for the first time, it became unmistakably clear that the notorious bully and hard case John Lennon—the boy with a tongue that could cut through leather and a temper like a berserker—was behind his bellicose mask an easily manipulated lad, whose strength was no strength because his mind was divided against itself, one half craving his old life in the dives and the other half longing for the big time. So Lennon's protests soon subsided into mere grumblings, and the band's center of gravity began to shift, as Paul and Brian took control of the Beatles, bit by bit, and John, who still retained the title of leader, was jockeyed into a position like that of the lead singer in Paul's group.

Meantime, the Beatles marched off in the footsteps of the ill-fated Elvis. Only instead of having a canny old carny man to coach them and cut their deals, putting half the "now money" he always demanded in his pocket—but at least getting top dollar for his act—they were led down the garden path by that spoiled rich kid Brian Epstein, and straight into the hands of the scheming and scamming old pros of the entertainment industry. Nobody in the history of show business ever took such a screwing.

As for John, he never got over the fact that he sold out. To his dying day he sought to rationalize the betrayal of his gritty muse, arguing one time that going commercial had given him his "freedom"—precisely what it had cost him—and insisting another time that he never really submitted to the commercial yoke because he would always unbutton his collar and pull his tie askew. Such pathetic rationalizations were no substitute for the identity he had lost and would never again regain. For he had been the archetypal rocker, a tough, angry Teddy Boy, punching out drunks and grabbing chicks onstage, while he played or sang any damn thing that came into his pill-popping head. Then, next thing he knew, he was a mop-headed, mod-suited clit-teaser and crowd pleaser, making with the quips at press conferences and doing his twenty-minute clockwork turn on the stage of a vaudeville house. "Stunning" is the word for that turnabout, and "stunting" for its effect. As Lennon lamented in later years, "We sold out, you know. The music was dead before we even went on the theater tour of Britain. . . . That's why we never improved as musicians. We killed ourselves then to make it."

"Selling Out" is the missing chapter in the history of the Beatles. It's the chapter that nobody has ever wanted to write. Yet it's the turning point in the whole story, especially for John Lennon. For it marks the death of Johnny, formerly of the Moon Dogs, and the birth of the famous Beatle John.

THE BIG BREAK

The Decca Audition had been a sop thrown to Brian after he had threatened a boycott of the company by NEMS, the biggest dealership in the north. Dick Rowe, Decca's singles A&R man, had given the job of recording the Beatles to a young assistant, Mike Smith, on a day when nobody wanted to work, 1 January. Smith liked the Beatles, but he preferred the other band he had auditioned that afternoon, Brian Poole and the Tremeloes (once a Liverpool street gang) because they lived only eight miles away at Barking, whereas the Beatles were way up at the Pool. When Brian threw a fit over this stunning rejection—for which he was blamed by Lennon, who charged him with ruining the band's chances by tampering with its music—Dick Rowe decided that he had better give the boys one more chance. Since Brian insisted the Beatles were best heard at the Cavern, Rowe arranged to drop in one night unannounced, so as not to rattle the band.

On the night he chose, the weather was horrible. Finding himself stuck out in Matthew Street with the rain pelting down, the kids jamming the door, and the stink of sweat, piss, and chlorine wafting up the stairs, Rowe succumbed to a natural impulse and said, "Sod it!" Retreating to his hotel, he had a couple of whiskeys and went to bed. Next morning he returned to London without saying a word to anyone, having, in effect, rejected the Beatles twice.

Brian's eventual success in finding another label to paste on his boys was purely a matter of chance. One day, in his bumbling way, he awoke to the fact that it would be better to have a disc than two big reels of tape to demonstrate the band. So he went to EMI's multistory shop on Oxford Street and arranged to have the transfer made. The engineer remarked as he monitored the recording that the material was "not all bad." He offered to play the acetate for Syd Coleman, the managing director of a publishing company controlled by EMI, whose office was in the building. Two of Paul's songs, "Hello Little Girl" and "Love of the Loved" (later a big hit for Cilla Black), impressed Coleman so much that he bought them.

When he learned that the Beatles had no record contract, he dialed an EMI colleague who was looking for new pop singers: George Martin, A&R man for Parlophone. (This little imprint was referred to as EMI's "joke label" because it was known mostly for comedy records and because in comparison with the corporation's internationally famous labels, HMV and Columbia, Parlophone was rather a joke.) It turned out that George Martin was the only producer in the EMI organization who had not yet refused the Beatles.

Next day the baby-faced Brian arrived at the Parlophone office in Manchester Square, sweating out his last chance. If the Beatles didn't make it this time, there would remain only Embassy, the Woolworth label! The man Brian met resembled a British film star, an elegant, cool Prince Philip type, with a studied BBC accent. He reminded the delinquent Brian of a "stern but fair-minded housemaster." Brian made a poor impression on Martin with his preposterous line about a band up in Liverpool that was going to be "bigger than Elvis." The real test, though, was the demo, which impressed Martin as being "either old stuff, like Fats Waller's 'Your Feet's Too Big' or very mediocre songs they had written themselves. But . . . there was an unusual quality of sound, a roughness that I hadn't encountered before. There was also the fact that more than one person was singing."

Chances are that Martin would not have ventured further with the Beatles if he had not been so keen to compete with his opposite number on Columbia, Norrie Paramor, the producer of Cliff Richard. Willing to take a small chance, without even meeting the Beatles, Martin drew up a contract that committed his company to very little. The boys signed as soon as they got back from Hamburg, on 4 June 1962. Two days later they entered the famous studios at Abbey Road to be given a good going-over by Martin, who made them sing standards as well as their own stuff. Again, he was not particularly impressed. "I was going to have to find suitable material for them," he concluded, adding that he was "quite certain that their songwriting ability had no saleable future."

Martin told Brian Epstein that when it came time to record, Pete Best, whom the producer found unsteady, would have to be replaced by a studio drummer. In making this stipulation, the producer had no idea that he was driving the last nail into Pete's coffin. Quite the contrary, Martin assumed that Best was vital to the Beatles because he was the only member of the group who had the looks of a pop star. But it was precisely Pete's brooding beauty that was the cause of his downfall. Back in March, when the Beatles had made their debut on BBC radio, Pete had been mobbed by girls. *Mersey Beat* reported: "John, Paul and

George made their entrance on stage to cheers and applause but when Pete walked out—the fans went wild! The girls screamed. In Manchester his popularity was assured by his looks alone." When the drummer was waylaid by the girls after the broadcast, Paul's father watched the scene with visible displeasure. After Pete had escaped, his hair torn, his new mohair suit ripped, Jim McCartney had said sourly: "Why did you have to attract all that attention? Why didn't you call the other lads back?" He could have been speaking for his son, who fancied himself "Paul Ramone," the Beatles' heartthrob.

That Paul wanted Pete Best out of the band is most likely, particularly in view of the fact that it was Paul who had hounded Stu Sutcliffe out of the band. Ability was not an issue because Pete was regarded by many as the best drummer in Liverpool. By the same token, Ringo Starr's deficiencies became apparent the moment he reported to George Martin, who was astonished to discover that Pete's replacement could not even execute a proper roll. Ringo was promptly replaced by the same studio drummer engaged to sub for Pete. The real difference between Ringo Starr and Pete Best was that Ringo was as homely and uncompetitive as Pete was handsome and self-assured.

For John Lennon had resented Pete's quiet strength nearly as much as Paul McCartney must have been jealous of Pete's good looks. Ultimately the balance of power in the Beatles had to be struck between John and Paul, neither of whom had any use for a third man whose appeal could not be denied or surpassed. Consequently, the odd man out had to get out—and the new man in had to be an odd fellow.

Ringo Starr, whose legal name is Richard Starkey, was an odd duck from childhood. Born 7 July 1940, three months before John Lennon, in the Dingle, which had the reputation for being, after Scotland Road, the poorest and roughest neighborhood in Liverpool, Ringo provided a living demonstration of how temperament is every bit as decisive as experience in the determination of character. In some ways Ringo had an even worse time of it in childhood than had John Lennon, yet he turned out to be the sweetest and most gentle of men. Like John, Ringo was an only child whose father disappeared when he was three. At six he suffered a burst appendix and peritonitis, which kept him in the hospital for an entire year. A poor scholar, he made a bad showing in school and owed what little he learned to the coaching of a neighbor girl, who virtually reared him while his mother worked as a barmaid. At thirteen Ringo got a new dad, a house painter named Harry Greaves, a kindly man who aided his stepson in every way, but Ritchie, as everyone called him, suffered another serious illness, this time of the lungs, that kept him in the hospital for two years. When he got out, he became an apprentice pipe fitter. Then he received his first set of drums from his stepfather.

Working his way up through the local skiffle scene, Ritchie, become Ringo because of his love of finger rings, joined Rory Storm and the Hurricanes, one of Liverpool's most popular groups. It was while they were playing Hamburg in the fall of 1960 that Ringo met the Beatles, hitting it off with them immediately, as he did with everyone, and even participating in a make-your-own record session that produced a cut of "Summertime" sung by Walter Eymond of the Hurricanes.

A little, scrawny fellow, never strong, Ringo was an odd sort to be a drummer because the instrument demands the strength and coordination of an athlete. His face, with its sad beagle eyes and hangdog expression (fringed with a gray-streaked beard), was likewise completely out of character for a pop musician. Actually, Ringo owed his career largely to the fact that drummers were in short supply in Liverpool, the reason being that a drum kit sold for £250, in contrast with the £14 price tag on a guitar. Hence, even the most inept drummer was assured of work.

Before the Beatles took Ringo on, Kingsize Taylor had been about to hire him, simply for lack of someone better. The Beatles were not troubled by Ringo's deficiencies because they were primarily a vocal group that required a drummer who was simply an accompanist. At first Ringo was on probation, working for £25 a week. He also had to take a lot of shit as a new man, particularly from Lennon, who, though he became genuinely fond of his oddly bespoken mate, always treated him with unwitting condescension, calling out: "Hey, Ritchie! Get us a beer! There's a good mate!"

John Lennon could not have been entirely attentive to the final stage in the plot to oust Pete Best because Lennon himself was overwhelmed at this time by a personal crisis. One day, out of the blue, Cynthia informed him that she was pregnant. Lennon reacted like a man who has been informed that he has cancer. "I watched his face drain of all its color, and fear and panic crept into his eyes," reported Cynthia. "He was speechless for what seemed an age. I stared at him, my heart pounding so fast I thought I would pass out.

Finally, John broke the interminable silence. "There's only one thing for it, Cyn. We'll have to get married.'" That snap judgment resolved the crisis, but it opened the floodgates to a sea of future woes.

Cynthia had always wanted to marry John. She had been waging a campaign to make him marry her since the first year. John had escaped from Cyn by running to Mimi. She recalled Cynthia arriving at Mendips one day and the next moment John in tears. "He came down crying his heart out, clinging to me, just as he did as a child. He blurted out, 'Cynthia wants us to get married tomorrow. She's arranged a special license at the registry office. I don't want to get married. *Please!* I don't want to get married!'" Mimi asked Cynthia if what John said was true. She replied that she had come to ask Mimi's permission because John was only nineteen and she was but twenty herself. Mimi took John into the next room and asked him if he loved Cynthia. "He shook his head, saying he wasn't sure. That settled it. I went to Cynthia and, looking her straight in the eyes, said I would not give my consent." Now, three years later, the issue was settled in a manner only too familiar to Mimi, born herself seven months prior to her parents' marriage.

Not till the night before the wedding did John Lennon work up the nerve to confront his aunt. "He came and told me that Cynthia was pregnant. He had two red spots [one] on each cheek. The rest of his face was pallor. My niece [Leila] said under her breath. 'Oh, John!' Two tears came down his face, and he said, 'Mimi, I don't want to be married.' I said, 'John, you won't be told!' He blamed me for being married, after." John asked Mimi if she wanted to attend the wedding. She let out a groan and replied, "I'll say one thing and then I'll hold my peace. You're *too young*! There, now, I've said it. Now I'll hold my peace forever." Neither Mimi nor any other member of the Stanley family was present at the ceremony. Cynthia was so terrified of her mother's reaction that she postponed telling her until the day before Mrs. Powell's departure for Canada.

The wedding day, 23 August 1962, was dark and depressing, threatening rain. Brian Epstein, dressed in a dapper pinstripe suit, picked up Cynthia and brought her to the Mount Pleasant Registry Office. She was dressed in a well-worn purple-and-black-check two-piece suit, a white, frilly, high-necked blouse from Astrid, black shoes, and a handbag. When Cynthia and Brian arrived at the office, they found awaiting them John, Paul, and George, all dressed in identical black suits with white shirts. The boys were giggling nervously. Brian Epstein acted as best man; James Paul McCartney and Marjorie Joyce Powell (Cynthia's sister-in-law) signed the register as witnesses. The moment the ceremony began, a workman in the backyard of an adjoining building started drilling and he did not cease until the ceremony had concluded, quitting as if on cue. "I couldn't hear a word the bloke was saying," complained John as the wedding party ran across the street in the now pouring rain to Reece's Restaurant, where they ate a lunch of roast chicken and soup. Reece's had no liquor license, so the newlyweds were toasted in water. John spent his wedding night with the Beatles, playing the Riverpark Ballroom in Chester.

Marriage was a state that John Lennon had every reason to dread. As an aspiring rock star he believed that having a wife and child would play havoc with his image. "Girl fans really did live in a knicker-wetting sexual fantasy around the stars in those days," confirmed Lee Everet Alkin, secretly married to Billy Fury for eight years. Brian Epstein adopted the same solution for Lennon's marriage as had Larry Parnes for Fury's: Cynthia was to be kept under wraps. But that stratagem didn't relieve John of the burdens he most dreaded: the responsibilities for being a husband and father. Nor should it be overlooked that John was married already—to the Beatles.

By forcing the issue, Cynthia got a husband but lost her man. Henceforth John would elude her for months at a time, and even when he was by her side, he would treat her with either resentment or indifference, acting as if she didn't exist. Meantime, Cynthia was lectured constantly on the importance of keeping the central fact of her life a secret. No home was provided for her because John was intent on minimizing this disaster, not enshrining it in an establishment. After a brief period of concealment at Brian's slip-away pad on Faulkner Street, Cynthia was consigned to Mendips, where she was subject to the tender mercies of Mimi. Until Christmas John's wife shared the ground floor of the house with Mimi's student lodgers, disguising her pregnancy by wearing loose clothing. Though relations between the women were never cordial, Cynthia did win Mimi's sympathy.

The same day Cynthia and John became husband and wife, news of the sacking of Pete Best was splashed across the front page of *Mersey Beat*. Pete's fans were furious. The EMI/Parlophone contract was common news by now in Liverpool; Pete's supporters felt betrayed because their hero had been chucked out at their moment of glory. They picketed NEMS and the Cavern, shouting: *"Pete forever! Ringo never!"* and *"Pete is best!"* Paul and John were attacked by the fans, and George was given a black eye. Brian Epstein could not enter the Cavern without a bodyguard. The brouhaha soon subsided, but the bitterness engendered by the manner of Pete's dismissal—none of the Beatles could look Pete in the eye and say, "You're out!" so the job was dumped in Brian's lap—lingered for years afterward. John Lennon admitted subsequently that they had made a mistake, but it was a characteristic mistake for John, who could never face the music.

Temperamentally Ringo Starr was the opposite of Pete Best. Pete was a jockey drummer, one of those stickmen who are always whipping on the band, making their presence felt at every moment by their tense, urgent pressure on the skins. Ringo was a foundation drummer, a rhythmic bricklayer, who slackened the tension in the Beatles' playing but provided a lot of stolid marching-band sonority, upon which the Beatles began to build layer upon layer of vocal, instrumental, and, later, electronic sound.

The Beatles' first recording session was notable for the fact that it focused upon a song of their own composition, "Love Me Do," an early composition by Paul, which John had prefaced with some bluesy wailing on harmonica suggested by Bruce Channel's recent hit "Hey! Baby." (Pete Best suspected that the melancholy sounds John produced on harp were associated with Stu's recent death.) Considering that George Martin had started off by assuming that he would have to furnish the Beatles with professionally written songs, it is remarkable that they had already persuaded him to allow them to record their own compositions. This was the most important single decision in the Beatles' recording career because it not only got them off on the right foot but soon established an enormously important precedent for other bands to follow, with the result that British rock soon became a music that was wholly created by its performers. In terms of sales, the Beatles' first disc was disappointing. After its release on 4 October, Brian tried to boost the record by placing a huge order for NEMS, but the ten-inch 78 peaked at a disappointing 17. Actually, it was not this first session that counted so much as the band's second visit to the studio a couple of months later, which produced "Please Please Me," the Beatles' first hit.

A John Lennon song, inspired primarily by Roy Orbison but also fed by John's infatuation with the pun in Bing Crosby's famous "Please, lend your little ears to my pleas," the record struck for the first time that note of breezy British pops that became the hallmark of the Beatles. From its opening peal of celebratory bell notes to its tight, bracing harmonies to its echoing vocal entrances, like sailors shouting back and forth as they haul up a sheet of canvas, the song is an irresistible shout of "Bon voyage!" At the end of the session George Martin pressed the intercom button in the control booth and announced: "Gentlemen, you've just made your first number one record!"

TO THE TOPPERMOST OF
THE POPPERMOST

On 2 February 1963 the Beatles stepped into the world they long had scorned. Walking through the stage door of the Gaumont Cinema in the decaying industrial town of Bradford, they were assigned a grimy little dressing room, without heat or hot water. Gazing earnestly into the mirror, the boys applied Max Factor No. 5 until their cheeks were nearly as bright as their pink shirts. Their hair was now in a tight cloche combed down over the forehead (a style that John and Paul had received from Jürgen Vollmer when they visited him in Paris on John's twenty-first birthday). They donned their new stage costumes, bell-bottom trousers with velvet-collared jackets, all in rich burgundy color.

Paul had designed these suits, an act that suggests how completely the Beatles had taken over the job of packaging themselves. Though the press would long insist the Fab Four were puppets in the hands of a "pop Svengali," the reverse was the truth. Every identifiable feature of the Beatles' fabled image, from the famous haircuts to the bum-freezer suits, from the Chelsea boots to the billed caps—to say nothing of such patented mannerisms as the way they shook their hair on a high falsetto note—was the product of the boys' own tastes and invention.

Having given themselves a final once-over, peppered with nervous jests, they picked up their guitars and went out into the wings. They were second on a bill of seven acts, headlined by Helen Shapiro, a "baby girl" singer of seventeen with a voice like Paul Robeson. After all the years of putting down the British pop scene, the Beatles were walking now in the shadow of the Shadows.

The opening act is some poor dolly who is expendable. An offstage voice announces her perfunctorily: "Good evening, ladies and gentlemen. Welcome to the Adelphi Theater, Slough, where Arthur Howes presents this week's show. And here to start the proceedings is

132

Rita Ginch!" The tabs part, and the arc lamp focuses its blue-white blear on the awkwardly poised young woman in front of a two-bit mike, as the pit band, replete with piano and saxophone, sails into some twerpy tune in the style of those hapless days when the pop scene wallowed in the trough between Elvis and the Beatles, a style called in Britain "High School."

The moment the curtains close, the Beatles dash onstage to plug in their guitars and assume their positions. Before the curtains open again, the band strikes up. When the tabs part, the Beatles are in full cry, with John standing alone at a mike on the audience's right, his body rising and falling, like a rider standing in the stirrups, as he shouts the words to "Chains," a month-old hit by the Cookies. Paul and George are cavorting about the other mike, the one craning his neck like a rooster and batting his eyes like Eddie Cantor; the other bending his head bashfully over his guitar when he is not singing into the mike, head to head with Paul. Ringo grins faithfully as he bangs away with his bricklayer's beat atop the unmiked drums.

The young singers on these tours aspired to be all-round entertainers like Tommy Steele, who could not only sing but cut a few steps and do some patter in their act. But the Boys from Liverpool appeared to have no act—to be just a group of engaging lads who sang what they liked and did as they pleased onstage. Actually that was the Beatles' act, and it was every bit as calculated and practiced as the trite routines favored by the other singers.

The Beatles were far too clever to fall into the trap of repeating what other performers had done. They knew they could never move like dancers or look like movie stars or even play their instruments like the American hotshots, so they chose deliberately to present themselves as charming amateurs. "We don't really bother about what we do on the stage," Lennon assured the attractive young Maureen Cleave of the *Evening Standard* just before the tour. "We practice what we call 'grinnings at nothings.' One-two-three! And we all grin at nothing! When we go out with Helen Shapiro, I don't know how we'll manage. I thought I might lie down on the floor like Al Jolson." A fig for professionalism! That was the Beatles' act.

The Beatles' biggest fan on their first tour was Helen Shapiro. Instead of exercising her prerogative as the star and riding in a private car, Helen boarded the bus every morning and sat next to John Lennon, on whom she had a big crush. While Paul and George kept to the rear of the coach, away from the roar of the engine (where they worked on middle eights with their guitars and practiced falsetto "Oohs!"), John sat up front being as ingratiating to Helen Shapiro as he had been to Johnny Gentle. "John spends a lot of time looking after me," confided Helen to the Beatles' new PR man, Tony Barrow, "fathering me a bit, but being very protective in a pleasant way. . . . He's not the brute and the bully that some folk take him to be. . . . Someday he'll make a great dad and a marvelous husband for some woman." Six weeks after Helen Shapiro made this statement, Cynthia gave birth to Julian amid circumstances that fully confirmed John's character as both a brute and a bully.

Life on the road was tedious and uncomfortable. Though the Beatles weren't obliged to sleep in a cold bus in a car park, as did some acts at the bottom of the bill, they spent their nights in grungy bed-and-board establishments that frowned on show-biz guests. Their days were consumed in crawling along bad roads made worse by winter weather. The distances were not great, but an inordinate amount of time was spent traveling. Between two and four in the afternoon the bus would arrive at the venue, and everybody would have a cup of tea and a listen to Radio Luxembourg. Then they would settle themselves in their dressing rooms till show time. Helen Shapiro had a telly in her room, which helped pass the hours. For the Beatles there was always a certain amount of drinking and occasionally a "knee trembler" (stand-up sex) with a "scrubber" (groupie).

The first show was at six-thirty, the next performance commenced at nine; that meant that the day's work did not conclude till about midnight. At that hour the only meal in town was in some steamy little Chinese or Indian restaurant, which pleased Lennon because he had a taste for curry. Then it was back to a cold, damp bed-and-board. Next morning, after breakfast, the bus would honk at the door, and they would be off for Shrewsbury.

In the midst of the tour the Beatles suddenly took off for London. There in a single night they recorded their first album, *Please Please Me.* This tour de force was inspired by George Martin's perception that the band was more effective onstage than in the studio. Hence, he had decided initially to cut their debut album at the Cavern, where the boys would be most confident, profiting from the fanatical support of their fans. But when Martin inspected the notorious dungeon beneath Matthew Street, he recognized that it was a recording engineer's nightmare. Even if the Beatles delivered the greatest performance of their career, the recording would be a sonic botch. Still not willing to abandon his plan, Martin hit on the idea of doing a show in the studio. An audience was out of the question, but the boys could be recorded just as if they were onstage, doing one song hard on the heels of another, without ever once stopping for a ciggy or a cuppa. Martin was confident that if he could once get the Beatles off the ground, they would fly with the same verve they displayed onstage.

The album that emerged from this strenuous experiment was a triumph. From the count-off for "I Saw Her Standing There" to the bawling finale based on the Isley Brothers' "Twist and Shout," the music pours out of the speakers with the immediacy, vivacity, and spontaneity of a live performance. The listener feels himself at ringside, getting sucked up in the effervescent spirit of the young Beatles. Just as enjoyable as the music is the great resourcefulness the band displays in the disposition of its limited resources. Though at this point in their development the Beatles were not yet remarkable as either singers or songwriters, they make up for their deficiencies through their great self-confidence and enthusiasm. They're so delighted by their own cleverness that they become delightful.

The title song, "Please Please Me," jumped on the charts and headed for the top. On the afternoon of 19 February 1963, it rang the bell. Ida "Stevie" Holly, a seventeen-year-old fan, recalls climbing the steps of the Walker Art Gallery that afternoon, late for a date with John Lennon. Suddenly she saw him come whirling through the revolving door crying ecstatically: *"We're Number One! We're Number One! We're Number One!"* Picking Stevie up, he swung her around and then dragged her down the stairs to a battered blue Ford with George at the wheel. In a matter of minutes they were at Brian's office, where all the Beatles were present but Paul. When he arrived, he demanded: "What's all this about?" The moment he heard the news, he sank down on the windowsill and said: "That means we'll have to play the fuckin' Palladium!"

When the boys took off on 9 March for their second tour, starring two American acts, Chris Montez and Tommy Roe, the *Please Please Me* album stood at number three on the charts. Opening night there were screams from the moment the Beatles appeared. Paul turned and smiled happily at the other boys. With each successive tune the audience's excitement mounted, until by the end of the act it looked as though the Beatles might receive an ovation. Then the American hit makers came on, each employing a different style: Chris Montez, a hotshot, shake-'em-up image; Tommy Roe, a straight-on delivery, reminiscent of Buddy Holly. For the first time ever, the American acts could not cut their British competition. Next night the management announced a change of billing: The new headliners were the Beatles. "Hey! We're stars now!" cried Lennon. Then, he added, ironically: "We've got to start behaving ourselves." Actually, the Beatles didn't have to do a thing but keep on pumping out the hits.

Once the hits started coming, Lennon and McCartney joined the ranks of those famous songwriting teams that have always been the backbone of popular music. Their collaboration was unique, however, because instead of dividing the task in the accustomed manner between lyricist and melodist, they took turns writing and revising both words and music. Their special strength lay in the way they complemented each other. If Paul was saccharine, John was acidulous. If John was obsessed with black music, Paul had an ear for lily-white pops. If Paul was verbally constrained, John had a word (or pun) for every occasion. On the other hand, if Lennon was inclined to work to death the same few chords, McCartney could always come up with a fresh change, like the chord that made "I Want to Hold Your Hand." Most important, if John tended to drone away on one or two notes, Paul could loft a phrase into the air that magically assumed the form of an original melody, the pop songwriter's most precious gift.

Though John and Paul were to spend hundreds of hours in hotel rooms, vans, or home studios working hip to haunch, they generally initiated their pieces independently. As Lennon explained, "One of us wrote most of the song, and the other just helped finish it off, adding a bit of tune or a bit of lyric." From the beginning, therefore, Lennon and McCartney songs were divisible into Lennon *or* McCartney songs, the rule of attribution being: If Lennon sings lead, it's a Lennon song. The reason the composers were not distinguishable at first is that they did not approach songwriting as artists intent on expressing themselves but rather as tunesmiths, capable of knocking out any and every sort of record currently in demand. Dedicated followers of fashion, they mimicked each new style or trend as it came buzzing out of that great hive of pop music, the USA.

First, the Beatles copied the male groups, like the Coasters, the Isley Brothers, and the Miracles (with Smokey Robinson); then the girl groups, especially the Cookies, the Shirelles, and Ronnie and the Ronettes. Then came the early Tamla/Motown stars Mary Wells and Marvin Gaye, followed by the rougher sort of southern soul men, James Brown and Wilson Pickett. Most of these performers are still big names, but Lennon and McCartney were affected just as strongly by many now-forgotten groups and singles, such as Rosie and the Originals, the Canastas, the Tams, the Impressions, the Jodimars, along with Derek Martin, Arthur Alexander, Bobby Parker, Major Lance, Chuck Jackson, Tommy Tucker, Lenny Welch, or James Ray—to confine the list to the R&B charts.

The Boys from Liverpool were, like the young Elvis, brilliant students of pop music, who heard everything, understood everything—and filed away anything that might come in handy later. They were motivated by the twin principles of Mersey beat: (1) Anything they can do, *we* can do; (2) if we're doing something the audience doesn't recognize, it's *our* song. In respect to their sources, Lennon and McCartney were no different from the most cynical old hack on Tin Pan Alley. They were quick to nick a lick or make off with anything that they could get away with, which was plenty because they were on the other side of the Atlantic and the material they borrowed appeared typically on obscure R&B sides. Paul confessed jokingly that the Beatles were "criminals," and John, on a radio broadcast in 1974, led the listener straight to the scene of the crime. Spinning an unfamiliar side by an unfamiliar singer, "Watch Your Step" by Bobby Parker, John disclosed that the famous hook used in both "I Feel Fine" and "Day Tripper" was filched from this unsuspected source. On another occasion John convicted himself when he demonstrated a new song titled "Happy Xmas (War Is Over)" for the famous producer Phil Spector. Spector exploded: "That's a direct steal from my 1961 hit with the Paris Sisters, 'I Love How You Love Me'! As John always said, "There's nothing wrong with stealing, providing you steal from the best."

Actually, there *is* something wrong with stealing. You can get caught! Both John Lennon and George Harrison were formally charged in court actions with plagiarism and obliged to make restitution. Lennon spoke the last word on the subject when asked for his opinion of the judgment against Harrison for copying the tune of his most famous song, "My Sweet Lord." "In the early years," John recalled, "I'd often carry around someone else's song in my head, and only when I put it down on tape—because I can't write music—would I consciously change it to my own melody because I knew that otherwise somebody would sue me. George could have changed a few bars in that song, and nobody could have touched him; but he just let it go and paid the price. Maybe he thought God would just let him off." Bright Tunes, the copyright holder of "He's So Fine," a 1963 hit by the Chiffons, sued and compelled Harrison to cough up $587,000. As for the words to "My Sweet Lord," Allen Klein, Harrison's manager at the time, says they were written by George's keyboard player, Billy Preston, who first recorded the song on Apple. (A whole book should be written about plagiarism in pop music, not only to expose the thieves and give belated credit to their victims but to illuminate the fascinating processes by which ideas are spawned and spread in this mental incubator.)

If John Lennon was the music game's slickest pickpocket, he was also a thief with a hole in his own pocket because he always left more at the scene of the crime than he took. While he was concentrating with myopic intensity upon the catchy hook or groovy lick on the latest American release, he instilled unwittingly so much of his northern British soul into the substance of this foreign song that he produced a unique and highly original amalgam. In effect, John's songs are original—save for the part that everybody whistles.

A perfect illustration of the way Lennon anglicized pop music is provided by the Beatles' first great international hit, "I Wanna Hold Your Hand" (thus did John entitle it on the lyric sheet). The freshest coinage of its day, this song was offered in the context of rock 'n' roll, but it is nothing of the kind, nor is it rhythm and blues or country and western. What the song most resembles is a jaunty, snappy British quick march, with its boom-boom-boom-boom oompah echo mounting the scale behind the tune and its rhythm bouncing along like soldiers on parade. Reminiscent of the Scotch-Irish strut of John Philip Sousa, the song's melody, tonality, and rhythm were startlingly original because they came from a wholly different tradition from American pops. Remote from the pseudo-funky atmosphere of the current top forty, the song exuded that keen, clean northern British air that would soon blow up a gale in "A Hard Day's Night."

Yet it won't do to ascribe everything original in the Beatles to their English origins because the most remarkable feature of the band's provenance was its international character. A Mersey beat band that had developed its style in Germany with materials taken from the hillbilly South and the black inner city, the Fab Four embodied the jet age cultural eclecticism of the Sixties long before the new era had found its bearings. To really locate the Beatles, you would have to project a point in space midway between America and India (both formerly parts of the British Empire) and a point in time equidistant between the music hall and the discotheque. You would also have to factor in the tradition of British nonsense, as well as those residues of European avant-gardism that had filtered down to the provincial English art college. A far more heterogeneous mixture than any tapped hitherto in pop culture, the substance from which the Beatles drew their strength was no one tradition nor even a combination of several but virtually everything that was in the air in their day.

While John Lennon was riding to glory on a rapidly cresting wave of fame, his wife was struggling through her lonely and uncomfortable pregnancy. On the afternoon of 6 April 1963, while shopping with her best friend, Phyllis, in Penny Lane, Cynthia began to experience what she took to be labor pains. Rushing back to Mendips, she found the pains subsiding, but she asked Phyllis to remain overnight. After they had gone to bed, Cynthia suddenly let out a great cry! Phyllis leaped up and called an ambulance. The two women, wearing their nightdresses, got into the vehicle and raced off to Sefton General Hospital, where Cyn congratulated herself that she hadn't given birth at home or in the ambulance. All the next day Cynthia lay in pain, her groans growing louder and louder. It was not until 7:45 the following morning, 8 April 1963, that Cynthia finally delivered the baby, who emerged with a big mole on its head and an "awful yellow color" produced by the umbilical cord wrapped around its neck. The infant, named John Charles Julian Lennon, was taken off and kept under intensive care for two days.

A whole week elapsed before John Lennon appeared at the hospital. He rushed into Cynthia's room, babbling excitedly, and picked up the baby. "He's bloody marvelous, Cyn!" John cried. "Who's going to be a famous rocker like his dad?" As this joyful scene was unfolding, a number of women began pressing their faces against the plate-glass window of the room, smiling and pointing at John, a local celebrity. John reacted by getting jumpy and nervous. He longed to make his getaway, but first he had to settle a little matter that was the real cause of his uneasiness.

Turning to Cynthia, he informed her bluntly that he was going off on a short holiday with Brian Epstein. Cynthia was outraged by this astonishing news. How could John go off and leave her with a newborn baby—and with Brian Epstein, of all people? John sneered: "Being selfish again, aren't you?" Then, turning self-pitying, he complained: "I've been working my bloody ass off on one-night stands for months now. . . . Brian wants me to go, and I owe it to the poor guy. Who else does he have to go away with?" With that dubious excuse hanging in the air, John split.

What John didn't dare tell Cyn was how he had been spending his spare time while she was suffering the ordeal of lying in. The Beatles had wound up their last tour at the end of March. Since then they had been hopping about the country, playing dates booked by Brian or recording radio and TV shows. None of these one-nighters was so important that it couldn't have been canceled or rescheduled so that John could have spent some time with his pregnant wife. Actually, John had been in Liverpool just two days after Julian was born, working a gig at Birkenhead, and again, two days later, at the Cavern. Neither time did he go out to the hospital. What was engrossing him during this period was not the little dates he was playing in the provinces but his burgeoning relationship in London with Brian Epstein. Brian was introducing John into the gay world of the West End theater crowd, which took to the young rocker instantly.

Peter Brown, Brian's intimate friend, offers a good account of what John was about while Cynthia was bearing his son: "First, Brian kept John by his side while Brian opened the NEMS office in London, a very busy week, during which Brian probably did a lot of partying. John was later to recall that he enjoyed going to Brian's gay parties because they offered him a glimpse of a world with which John was totally unfamiliar. Feeling very out of place, he would stand in a corner with eyes screwed up and look tough. Naturally, all the men assumed he was rough trade and were all the more attracted to him. Once he had gotten John this far, Brian sought to complete his conquest. He proposed to John that they take a brief trip to Spain, a country with which Brian was always enamored and where he later courted a number of young bullfighters. John agreed to go, but first he made a flying trip home to Liverpool to see the baby." John's flight from the responsibility of parenthood began now to assume the form of a flight from manhood, as he prepared to slip away with a homosexual who he knew was intent on seducing him.

The British press announced on the last weekend in April that the Beatles were leaving for a twelve-day holiday in the Canary Islands. John Lennon went out of his way to make it appear that he would be one of the party, remarking that they would be taking their guitars because, "who knows, we may be able to make those canaries swing!" The other three Beatles did fly to Tenerife on 28 April; a few days later Paul McCartney nearly lost his life, swimming in the sea. Meanwhile, John and Brian went off alone to Barcelona, where night after night, according to Peter Brown, they would sit at sidewalk cafés, playing a peculiar game. "John would point out some passing man to Brian, and Brian would explain to him what it was about the fellow that he found attractive or unattractive. 'I was rather enjoying the experience,' John said, 'thinking like a writer: "I am experiencing this."'"

Soon John was experiencing it not as a writer but as a man. He and Brian had sex. Naturally John was not eager to avow this fact or to explain his motive, but when challenged by Pete Shotton, John came up with an explanation that echoed the line he had taken with Cynthia. "Eppy just kept on and on at me, until one night, I finally just pulled me trousers down and said to him: 'Oh, for Christ's sake, Brian, just stick it up me fucking arse, then.' And he said to me, 'Actually, John, I don't do that kind of thing. That's not what I like to do.' 'Well,' I said, 'what is it you like to do, then?' And he said, 'I'd really just like to touch you, John.' And so I let him toss me off. . . . Yeah, so fucking what! The poor bastard. He's having a fucking hard time anyway. So what harm did it do, then, Pete, for fuck's sake? No harm at all. The poor fucking bastard, he can't help the way he is."

John Lennon the humanitarian, offering his body to the afflicted—a sympathetic picture but one that does not ring true. Far more convincing is the account of the matter that John offered Allen Klein many years later. John told his new manager that he had jerked off Brian because "I had to control the man who had control over our lives and careers." That sounds right, and it conforms with the subsequent history of the relationship, for John and Brian did not confine themselves to a single sexual experiment in Spain. They were sexually involved for the balance of Brian's life, and their relationship was a *controlling* one, with John playing the cruel master and Brian the submissive slave. As for who did what to whom in Spain, Brian told Peter Brown the real story: He had given John a blow job. Lennon couldn't afford to acknowledge that sort of intimacy because it would have stigmatized him as a queer. Indeed, the first time someone got on John about his trip with Brian, John nearly killed the man.

On 18 June Paul threw a big party to celebrate his twenty-first birthday. The event drew every notable musician in Liverpool as well as Paul's "star guests," the Shadows. To get away from the fans, who were besieging the McCartney house on Frothlin Road, the party was held at the home of Paul's Auntie Gin in Huyton. A big tent was erected, and a birthday cake baked, fit for a wedding. With the booze flowing like water, everybody soon drank himself into a state of absolute conviviality. All, that is, save the angry Lennon. He had arrived with Cynthia, whom he introduced to everyone as his "date." No sooner did he begin to drink than he became abusive toward his wife, taunting her before the company and quickly reducing her to the verge of tears.

When Pete Shotton arrived, he found John slumped in a corner, a glass of Coke and scotch in his hand, looking very glum. "Fucking hell, Pete!" cried John, his face lighting up, "Fuck the rest of this party! Let's go get us a drink!"

Shotton had left John to go off to the loo when Bob Wooler came up to Lennon and said, "How was the honeymoon, John?" Taking Wooler's remark as an insulting reference to the recent trip to Spain, John doubled up his fist and smashed the little disc jockey in the nose. Then, seizing a shovel that was lying in the yard, Lennon began to beat Wooler to death. Blow after blow came smashing down on the defenseless man lying on the ground. It would have ended in murder if John had not suddenly realized: "If I hit him one more time, I'll kill him!" Making an enormous effort of will, Lennon restrained himself. At that instant three men seized him and disarmed him. An ambulance was called for Wooler, who had suffered a broken nose, a cracked collarbone, and three broken ribs. Lennon had broken a finger.

John's rampage didn't stop with the fighting. Now it was time for the fucking. Grabbing a girl standing next to him, Lennon began to paw the alarmed young woman. Billy J. Kramer, Brian's new star, barked, "Lay off, John!" Lennon turned on the girl and said something very insulting. Then he sneered, "You're nothing, Kramer. We're the top!"

When Shotton returned, he found John "sitting on the floor with his head cradled in his hands, shielding himself from the daggerlike stares of his fellow partygoers and moaning, 'What have I done?'" He wasn't remorseful, simply fearful that he had fucked up his career. How little shame he felt was manifest when he turned to Pete and suggested that they swap wives for the night.

Next morning Brian Epstein was confronted by the press and the lawyers representing Billy J. Kramer and Bob Wooler. Word of the brawl had reached the news desks of Britain's all-powerful national papers. The Beatles were about to receive their first major publicity—and the news would be bad! Tony Barrow, Epstein's publicist, called Lennon to advise him how to cop out. John was unrepentant. "The bastard was saying I was a bloody queer, so I smacked him one," snarled Lennon. Barrow had had no experience of Lennon at bay. Neither had Brian Epstein, who was dismayed when John refused to go down to London for an appearance on the BBC. "I was afraid of nearly killing Wooler," Lennon explained years later, adding that he assumed he would be slaughtered by the London press.

Actually, the fix was in. The story, which ran on the back page of the *Daily Mirror,* was written by Don Short, who was so simpatico with the Beatles that he soon became one of the key men in their press entourage. He slugged his piece "Beatle in Brawl—Sorry I Socked You" and slanted it along the lines of an apology supposedly offered by Lennon but actually penned by Tony Barrow, who made John say: "Bob is the last person in the world I want to have a fight with. I can only hope he realizes I was too far gone to know what I was doing." Then Epstein disposed of what remained of the crisis by passing the bitter cup to his lawyer, Rex Makin, who had no trouble hushing up the complaints. Bob Wooler was just a little DJ who made his living on the margins of the pop music business; he couldn't afford trouble with the Beatles, who were fast becoming England's hottest pop act. So Wooler settled cheap. For his broken ribs and smashed face, he got two hundred pounds.

The services of Rex Makin were soon required again, when John Lennon committed another and even more ghastly outrage. This incident was witnessed by Alan Davidson, a NEMS clerk, who went to a flat in Leese Street one night to return a tape recorder he had repaired. A party was in progress. "There were lots of girls . . . booze and pills," recalled Davidson. "I got there half eleven or quarter to twelve. I think Brian was there. A row [began] over something. There was an old-fashioned gas fire with fluted porcelain jets. He [John Lennon] grabbed hold of Beryl's hand and shoved it into the fire and tried to hold it there. She screamed. With the amount of booze and the amount of pills that were involved in the party, nobody really took any notice of it. But being cold sober, I took quite a bit of notice. He did hold her hand there. She was badly burned. He let go of her and just pushed her across the room." Commenting on this extraordinary scene, Davidson remarked matter-of-factly: "John Lennon in sober moments was quite a nice person. In drug moments or booze moments he was a thug."

BEATLEMANIA!

Once the Beatles had twanged the nerve of mass hysteria, their lives became a Keystone Kops comedy. The ducking and dodging, the disguises and decoys, the battles between balaclava-helmeted bobbies and short-skirted Beatlemaniacs became one of the most familiar yet absorbing photoplays of the Sixties, the comic counterpart to the war photos that occupied the front pages later in the decade. The first great engagement in the War of the Beatles occurred on 13 October 1963, when the boys topped the bill on Sir Lew Grade's ATV show *Val Parnell's Sunday Night at the London Palladium.*

Reckoning that the fans would gather at the stage door, the police positioned the Beatles' Austin Princess near the theater's entrance. When the boys emerged, they were mobbed by two thousand girls screaming, *"We want the Beatles!"* The police were bowled over, helmets flying and constables reeling. The Beatles hurtled down the front steps and dove into their car, which drove off along Oxford Street with difficulty as first one girl, then another hurled herself in the path of the machine. The boys got their reward next day when it was announced that an estimated fifteen million people had watched the show. All the national papers carried the story on their front pages. One headline read simply: BEATLEMANIA!

From that day on the Beatles were the darlings of the British public and press. Two days after the Palladium show it was announced that they had received an invitation from the impresario Bernard Delfont (Lew Grade's brother) to head the bill at the 1963 Royal Variety Show, performing before Queen Elizabeth, the queen mother, and Princess Margaret. That night the Beatles were playing a typical provincial date at Floral Hall in Southport, a seaside town north of Liverpool. They were besieged backstage by newsmen, who demanded to know if they were "going commercial." The question was highly appropriate because the Royal Variety bill consisted exclusively of the most familiar, family-oriented acts, from Flanders and Swan to Pinky and Perky. John

Lennon knew from that moment he would have to do something outrageous at the show to distinguish the Beatles from the conventional
entertainers he despised.

The story of how John Lennon addressed the audience at the command performance is one of the most familiar of rock legends—and
one of the least understood. The gag was carefully scripted, as were
many of the quips the Beatles uttered "spontaneously." In the original
draft it read: "Will all the people in the cheaper seats clap your hands?
All the rest of you, if you'll just rattle your *fuckin'* jewelry!" This was
John playing the flat-capped prole, the role that earned him the title of
"working-class hero." But no working-class entertainer would have ever
dreamed of saying such a thing before the queen. Only a pampered
middle-class boy who had spent his childhood reading about mad artists who told the "bourgeoisie" to go screw themselves could have summoned the nerve to make such a crack—even with the obscene
expletive deleted. As Aunt Mimi remarked when somebody asked her
what she thought of John's lower-class image, "Working-class hero, my
eye! He was a middle-class snob!"

The Beatles' record sales, which had been strong before these momentous developments, now took off into that hyperspace never before
reached by anyone in Britain. Advance orders for "I Want to Hold
Your Hand" mounted up to a million units. The record jumped on the
chart in the top position and remained number one for six weeks,
straight through the holiday season. Brian Epstein was frantic to cash
in on this great opportunity. The only question was, How? At the last
minute he decided to rent the biggest presentation house in London,
assemble on its stage a pop variety bill and call it *The Beatles' Christmas
Show*. Figuring two shows a night, six nights a week for a fortnight, he
could sell a hundred thousand tickets, grossing fifty thousand pounds.
The beauty of the scheme was that virtually all the money would go
into his pocket because he could buy all the acts from himself for virtually nothing!

For Brian was now what Larry Parnes had been in his day: the master of a whole stable of hot young rock acts, most of them recruited in
Liverpool in the wake of the Beatles' astonishing success and the resultant boom in Mersey beat. Commencing with the Big Three (who soon
defected because they didn't want to go commercial), Brian had signed
to NEMS Enterprises Gerry and the Pacemakers, Billy J. Kramer and
the Dakotas, the Fourmost (the most accomplished of the lot), Cilla
Black, and Tommy Quickly. (Only Kingsize Taylor and the Swinging
Blue Jeans had turned Brian down.) Overnight NEMS had mushroomed into an international management and booking business that
eventually occupied five offices in central London, employed eighty

people, and serviced forty road musicians, all of whom were paid weekly stipends plus allotments for food, clothing, and transportation. Now the trick was to marshal them all behind the banner of the Beatles and score a great show biz coup at Christmas.

Not possessing any real flair for show business, Brian put the whole job of creating the show into the hands of a veteran pantomime producer, Peter Yolland. When he was presented with the idea, Yolland objected immediately: "You cannot call it *The Beatles' Christmas Pantomime* and just put on a string of acts."

"Why not?" bridled Brian.

Yolland explained that the use of the term "pantomime" implied something more than the Beatles' usual turn. "It must have a Christmas theme and be a proper show," he insisted.

"All right," Brian snapped. "I take all those points. What are you going to do?"

Taken aback, Yolland echoed: "What am *I* going to do?"

"Well," Brian retorted, "I booked you as a director. Off you go!"

Six weeks later, on Christmas Eve 1963, three thousand squirming kids, most of them girls, were crammed into the Astoria Cinema, Finsbury Park, the kind of old movie palace that has a proscenium arch boasting a three-dimensional Moorish village with internally illuminated houses. A roll of the drums and a sudden blackout signal the start of the show. As arc spots crisscross the curtains, they part to reveal a movie screen. A Voice booms: "Brian Epstein presents [drum roll] *The Beatles' Christmas Show!*" On the screen flashes a Max Sennett auto race, as the Voice shouts: "By *land!*" A flash of old sailing ships. "By *sea!*" A glimpse of ancient airplanes. "By *air!*" The screen rises to reveal a helicopter pad, as the Voice bellows: "*The fantastic* Beatles' Christmas Show!"

A helicopter descends upon the pad, and out climbs the MC, Ralph Harris, carrying the passenger list on a clipboard. After him emerge about forty people, including Billy J. Kramer, Cilla Black, the Dakotas, each act bowing as it is introduced. "Right!" snaps the MC, after the last act has appeared. "Now you've met everybody in the show," he says conclusively, only to be met by a howl of protest from the house, which suddenly escalates to a scream of horror as the helicopter lifts off! "Oh-oh! Something wrong?" exclaims Harris. "The Beatles? Oh, yes! Helicopter! Back! And now, ladies and gentlemen, introducing the stars of the show . . ." Suddenly the helicopter lifts off again, producing a fresh burst of screams. (This childish teasing was remarkably effective, according to Peter Yolland, who recalled: "By now every seat would be soaking wet. This was a phenomenon unique to the Beatles. Not just this show but on the one-night stands. There would be great big puddles underneath the seats. They would literally lose control.")

The Beatles finally emerge, wearing dark glasses and carrying flight bags (which are blazoned "BEA," as is the helicopter—all part of a deal for free transportation that Brian had cut with the airline). The boys are also part of the tease, for they no sooner appear than they disappear, as they continue to do until the next-to-closing spot. Here the Beatles make their acting debut as pantomime artists by doing a sketch based on the old melodramas about mustachio-twirling villains and maidens in distress. Sir Jasper, top hat on head, bullwhip in hand, is played, naturally, by John Lennon. Irmine Trood, a kerchief about her golden locks, a little bundle in her arms, is impersonated (with profound misgivings) by George, who looks rather like Gracie Fields. Handsome Paul, the signalman (changed to Valiant Paul after McCartney objected: "The fans will think I have a big head!"), is costumed in a railroader's cap, with a red-and-black-check scarf about his neck and his trousers held up by string. Ringo is Snow, appearing in black tights with a newsboy bag over his shoulder, from which he scoops handfuls of confetti, which he sprinkles about the stage and over the principals.

The action is mercifully brief. Irmine presents Sir Jasper with her bundle, crying: "This is yours!"

"Nonsense!" roars the villain. "To the railway lines with you, my girl!"

Tying her to the tracks—while a piano thunders out panic music and the screen shows flickering shots of an archaic locomotive coming head-on—Sir Jasper is confronted suddenly by Valiant Paul, who gives the villain two of the best, dropping him to the ground—where Ringo sprinkles him delicately with snow.

When Paul releases Irmine from her bonds, she cries, "My hero!"— and hands him the bundle, which, when opened, reveals a huge green apple. Blackout!*

The show was an immense success. (It was repeated the following year at the Odeon Hammersmith, where the Beatles did a skit about the Abominable Snowman—who turned out to be Jimmy Saville.) At the end of the performance the boys would run for one of the theater's twenty-seven exits, a different one each night. "If things had gotten too bad," Yolland explains, "we had a plan to take them out of the backyard by helicopter."

All through the year 1963, Cynthia Lennon saw very little of her famous husband. Not only was she kept out of sight at Brian's behest, but

---

*The green apple became in later years the logo of the Beatles' record company, Apple Corps., but the image was actually suggested by the well-known painting of a green apple by Magritte, which hung in Paul's parlor.

she was supplanted by the appearance of a new woman at John's side—the raven-haired, blue-eyed Stevie Holly. Stevie's relationship with Lennon was just the reverse of Cynthia's because she behaved in the opposite manner. When, on her first date with John, he had unzipped her dress "down to the bum," she had spun about and slapped his face. That act won his respect, for, as she soon discerned, he was accustomed to dividing women into two categories: those who offered themselves, whom he called "slags," and those who demanded respect, like his Aunt Mimi, who the perceptive Stevie recognized was "his barrier, his protection, his shield." Stevie's relationship with John did not involve sex, but even so it quickly reached a crisis when she confronted him with the fact that he was secretly married, which she had learned from her irate father, who was threatening to expose Lennon in the press. John's reaction to being found out was loutish defiance. When he heard the word "married," he snarled: "What's that! A fockin' piece of paper!" Then he conceded ruefully, "I had to do it."

1963 was a glorious season for the Beatles and the only time when Lennon experienced the full intoxication of being a star. Songwriter Peter Sarstedt recalled driving around London one night in a Jag with the sunroof open and Lennon standing bolt upright shouting "*I am the King of London!*"

While Lennon was boasting to the press that the Beatles' weekly income was £2,000, Cynthia was living again with her mother at Hoylake, after a spell in a dingy bed-sitting room whose weekly rent was £5.

The principal reason Lennon was so reluctant to have his wife with him in London, where John, George and Ringo shared a luxurious three-bedroom flat on Green Street, Mayfair, was that he was now in the first flush of his affair with Brian Epstein. Peter Yolland recalled that every night after the Christmas show John went off with Brian. As a lifelong member of the British theater world Yolland knew the score. "There was a slightly strange thing going on between Brian and John," he remarked, adding that though they were lovers, "there were others who were being groomed for stardom," an allusion to the other boys in Brian's stable who were paying the customary price for being "brought along." Actually, there was nothing odd about a British rock manager's getting it on with his boys; such affairs were as common in the London pop world as were liaisons between aspiring film stars and studio heads in the old Hollywood of the casting couch. John Lennon was certainly not the only British rock star to exhibit bisexual behavior. Though he was very uptight at first about incurring a reputation for being queer, in time he relaxed and eventually adopted an almost breezy attitude toward homosexuality. When asked in 1972 to contribute something to *The Gay Liberation Book,* he offered a sketch of a voluptuous male nude reclining on a flying carpet, with one hand manipulating an ejaculating penis behind his ass, while the other hand functions as a megaphone through which he chants "Why make it sad to be gay? Doing your thing is O.K. Our bodies [are] our own so leave us alone. Go play with yourself—today."

John Lennon's liaison with Brian Epstein was not confined to sexual dalliance. From the start, Brian took pleasure in showing off his famous rude boy to all his gay friends in the West End theater world. Soon this company included a circle of S/M freaks centered upon a depraved peer who rubbed shoulders with the most dangerous criminals in the kingdom. Brian's guide down the queasy slopes of this hellbent underworld was the glamorous David Jacobs, lawyer for many prominent homosexuals in the capital. As Mario Amaya, art journalist, museum director, lifelong S/M queen, observed: "Jacobs was the lawyer you called if you got into trouble for drugs, sex, etc., the rescue lawyer, gay and show biz, highly popular and successful." Also very kinky.

In the late Sixties, a young man was rescued from crucifixion in Soho. He refused to press charges but years later he took his story to a veteran crime reporter on the *Daily Express*. He named the notorious peer, as well as David Jacobs and Brian Epstein, as the men who ordered his crucifixion, which went well beyond the customary punishment for an informer, which is slashing the snitch's mouth from ear to ear.

There is nothing to suggest that John Lennon was mixed up in this part of Brian's life; but, on the other hand, virtually nothing is known of John's private adventures in this period, the most concealed of his entire life. For the more fame beat down on the Beatles, the more they sought to hide from it and the more Brian, who had suffered grievously from public exposure, worked to shield his boys from scandal. His success owed far less to his own efforts than to the recognition by the British press lords that England's favorite fairy tale was far too valuable to be spoiled by honest reporting. Those journalists assigned to the Beatles soon became members of the touring party, which was the kind of party you wouldn't want to tell your wife about. So the Fab Four were immune to muckraking until they broke their own bubble by declaring in favor of drugs, an impermissible act for a pop group. Thus even though the press was well aware of Brian's passion for John, not a word leaked out. Even years later, when Lennon spoke candidly of his past indiscretions, the most he would say about Brian was: "It will make a nice *Hollywood Babylon* someday about Brian Epstein's sex life."

John and Cyn finally had their honeymoon, thirteen months after their marriage and five months after the birth of their child, in September 1963, when all the Beatles went off on holiday. Brian Epstein sent the not-so-newlyweds out of the country, lodging them in his favorite hotel at Paris, the George V. Soon he joined them there himself. When the brief excursion was over, Patient Griselda was obliged to return to her mother.

Rumors that John Lennon was secretly married to a girl in Liverpool had come to the ears of the press. When John denied the story, the newspapermen staked out the Powell house in Hoylake. When Cynthia was cornered with the baby in a grocery store, she claimed that they had mistaken her for her twin sister. Next day, pictures of Cynthia and the six-month-old Julian, snapped in his carriage with a telephoto lens, were flashed to the fans. Cynthia, who had suffered so long from neglect, began to suffer now from notoriety.

"Of course, we're married—it's no secret!" she bluffed. "I just like to stay out of the limelight, that's all." Just in case anybody got the wrong idea, she volunteered: "John and I were married eighteen months ago. When we were married, there were the usual stories in the papers and show business magazines. All the fans knew where we lived, and I just couldn't stand it, so we moved to live here with Mother."

Despite the need to prevaricate, Cynthia must have felt relieved by this turn of events because it made it impossible for her husband to deny any longer her existence. John, on the other hand, was deeply distressed by the revelation of his true condition. "I did feel embarrassed walkin' about married," he confessed. "It's like walkin' around with your socks on—or your fly open." Brian was likewise dismayed.

Finally, after the first of the year, a dreary little sixth-floor walk-up was found for Cynthia and the baby at 13 Emperor's Gate, close by the Cromwell Road airport terminus. The place was promptly besieged by fans, who mobbed Cynthia and the baby every time they appeared. The flat was also kept under continuous surveillance from the balcony of a youth hostel across the street. One night the terminal caught fire, and the flames flew up dangerously close to Cynthia's windows. Alone and terrified, she called to her aid the Beatles' new photographer, Robert Freeman, who lived in the building. So fared John Lennon's wife at the outset of the Beatles' greatest year, 1964: marooned with her infant son in an immense and intimidating metropolis with no idea of what her famous husband was about.

While John was still struggling to keep the news of his marriage out of the press, Paul was fighting an anxious battle to contain a scandal involving another girl who claimed he was the father of her child. Anita Cochrane, an eighteen-year-old fan, had partied with the Beatles for a year at their slip-away pad at Gambier Terrace. When Anita discovered her pregnancy in June 1963, she tried in vain to get in touch with Paul by registered letters and telegrams. Finally, she recognized that she was not going to get anywhere without the threat of legal action. Only when her lawyer announced he was taking Paul to court did NEMS make an offer equivalent to $7.50 a week as maintenance for the baby. When this figure was rejected, Brian Epstein intervened personally and offered the family $8,400 in exchange for renouncing all claims on Paul. The final settlement was $14,000. The agreement stipulated that Anita Cochrane must never bring Paul to court, never say or imply that he was the father of her child, Philip Paul Cochrane, and never disclose the existence of the contract or its provisions. The problem appeared to have been solved when, a year later, during the great celebration in Liverpool upon the opening of *A Hard Day's Night,* Anita Cochrane's uncle seized on the occasion to distribute among the crowds 30,000 leaflets recounting the story of his niece's affair with Beatle Paul. As Cynthia Lennon quipped, "Paul was the town bull."

In January 1964 the Beatles took off for Paris, where they were booked to play three weeks at the Olympia Theater, France's foremost vaudeville house. Though they were the hottest act in Britain, they were billed third behind Trini Lopez and Sylvie Vartan. A typical Brian Epstein blunder, the booking didn't even pay the Beatles' hotel bill at the posh George V. As for taking Paris by storm, the engagement proved only that the French are a nation that marches to a different drummer.

Opening night was a fiasco. When the Beatles denied the notorious Parisian paparazzi a photo opportunity, the aggressive photographers provoked a backstage brawl that was ended only by the arrival of the police. The Beatles didn't get onstage until after midnight, and then they discovered that their amps were dead. The predominantly male audience enjoyed the *yé-yé* music but was bored by the quieter romantic numbers. Only Ringo went over big, the men shouting his name repeatedly and buying his picture in the lobby at a rate ten to one over the other Beatles. The prospect of spending three whole weeks going through this routine every night would have been unbearable but for the great event that had occurred the preceding night.

Returning from a warm-up show at Versailles, the boys were toasting their opening in champagne and taking eight-millimeter films when the phone rang. A call for Brian from New York. When Brian put down the phone, he gave the Beatles the news that "I Want to Hold Your Hand" had jumped in one week from No. 43 to No. 1! A spate of follow-up calls revealed that in the first three days a quarter million copies had poured over the counters. By 10 January the total sales figure was one million. A few days later ten thousand copies were being sold every *hour* in New York City alone! No foreign record and only two American sides had ever sold at that clip. The Beatles were in a class by themselves. Without any personal appearances or a single live shot on the tube, the Fab Four had conquered the world's greatest record market. The luckiest thing about the news was its timing. In just three weeks the Beatles would be arriving in New York to appear on *The Ed Sullivan Show.* "Where are we going, boys? . . ."

THE BEATLES ARE COMING!

America was ready for the Beatles. By "B-Day," 7 February 1964, over two million copies of "I Want to Hold Your Hand" had been sold. *Introducing the Beatles,* the band's first American LP, was climbing the charts. American stores had begun selling Beatles' wigs, shirts, dolls, rings, lunch boxes, buttons, notebooks, sneakers, and bubble bath. Over a dozen Beatles' novelty records had been released, with titles like "Christmas with the Beatles," "My Boyfriend's Got a Beatles Haircut," and Phil Spector's "I Love Ringo," sung by Bonnie Jo Mason, better known today as Cher. At the last minute Capitol launched a $50,000 publicity blitz. Every disc jockey in the country got a promotion kit that enabled him to interview the Beatles on the air, asking questions from a script and playing the prerecorded answers by John, Paul, George, or Ringo. The climactic gesture was the plastering of America with five million stickers proclaiming: THE BEATLES ARE COMING!

On the morning of their departure for the States the Beatles had to force their way through hundreds of weeping girls at London airport. After a big sendoff at the VIP lounge, where John grudgingly consented to pose with Cynthia, who was making her first public appearance, the party boarded Pan Am Flight 101. Soon afterward, in New York, WMCA, the "Good Guys," announced breathlessly: *It's now 6:30 Beatle time! They left London thirty minutes ago! They're out over the Atlantic Ocean, heading for New York! The temperature is thirty-two Beatles degrees!*

From the moment of takeoff, Pan Am's *Clipper Defiance* was charged with a gay party atmosphere. When a beautiful stewardess with a bust like Jayne Mansfield's sought to demonstrate a life jacket, the first-class cabin was filled with whistles and wolf calls. Paul batted his banjo eyes, and George yelled, *"Will you marry me?"* Instantly the Beatles broke out their cameras—"Swahili Pentax," joked George—and began snapping pictures. Lunch inspired a lot of fresh gags because champagne, caviar, lobster, and smoked salmon were rather a change from the days of beans on toast and jam sandwiches.

Brian got a chuckle out of the discovery that most of the gray-haired businessmen who shared the cabin were actually merchandisers, keen on gaining the Beatles' endorsement for their products. Every half hour a stewardess would deliver to Brian a fresh item for consideration. Taking a sheet of monogrammed notepaper out of his briefcase, he would write a polite note of rejection. Meantime, the plastic guitar or mop-headed doll would be passed about among the Beatles, each boy breaking off a piece until the sample was destroyed.

The only dour note in this silly symphony was struck by the normally upbeat Paul, who asked: "Since America has always had everything, why should we be over there making money? They've got their own groups. What are we going to give them that they don't already have?"

The answer to that question was delivered when the plane touched down at John F. Kennedy Airport at 1:20 P.M. and taxied up to the International Arrivals Building.

As the Beatles emerged from the 707 and descended the air stairs, they were greeted from the building's observation deck by four thousand screaming, placard-waving fans. After the obligatory photographs beside the plane, the Beatles were hustled into the baggage examination area, where they heard an ominous thunder overhead. Gazing up at the glass-enclosed gallery, they saw hundreds of gap-mouthed kids churning about and banging against the transparent walls, like man-eating fish at feeding time.

George was alarmed. "I don't think I have ever been more pleased," he exclaimed, "than when I saw those burly New York Irish policemen." The cops, working in pairs, picked up the Beatles by their elbows and ran with them like display-room dummies. Their destination was the airport's pressroom.

In contrast with the thousands of kids dashing around outside as if on a playground, the pressroom presented an unforgettable picture of irritable and anxious adulthood. Two hundred men and women, bundled in thick coats and fur hats, had been dispatched to the airport that day with orders to get the story of the Beatles' arrival.

The photographers went to work at once, shouting, "Hey, Beatles! Lookie here!" As the flashbulbs popped and the movie cameras whined, the talking press began to bug the Beatles' PR man, Brian Sommerville, for a chance to ask questions. A balding, horn-rimmed, uptight British journalist, later a barrister, Sommerville was no match for the American media. When his repeated requests for silence in court were ignored, he finally blew his stack and started screaming, *"Shut up! Just shut up!"*

Fortunately the Beatles were a lot better at handling the press. Their trick lay in making the reporters play the Beatles' press game. John had invented the game, but all the Beatles had mastered it. Unfolding like a script for the *Goon Show*, it soon had all the veteran reporters chuckling and shaking their heads in amazement:

> Reporter: What do you do when you're cooped up in your rooms?
> George: We ice skate.
> Reporter: What do you think of Beethoven?
> Ringo: I love him, especially his poems.
> Reporter: Was your family in show business?
> John: Well, me dad used to say me mother was a great performer.

The most inquiring reporter in the whole press corps, the only one who scored a scoop that day, was a local disc jockey known as Murray the K—as in Kaufman. Murray had been on vacation in Miami when WINS dragged him back to the wintry North to interview the Beatles. Arriving in his familiar uniform—skintight pants, desert boots, and a straw stingy brim that screamed "tourist!"—the K was thrust into the front rank of reporters, with the other radio men. Hunkering down at the Beatles' feet and thrusting up at them a periscopic mike, Murray started conducting a private on-the-air conversation with the most sincere and naïve member of the group, George. "I love your hat," said George, which was Murray's cue to reply: "Here, you can have it!"

A CBS cameraman infuriated by these underhanded tactics barked, "Tell Murray the K to cut the crap!"

Now it was Ringo's turn to pick up his cue, echoing, "Cut the crap!"

Instantly, John and Paul jumped in, repeating like kids, "Cut the crap! Yeah, Murray!" Thus was born the self-proclaimed "Fifth Beatle."

The Beatles made their getaway from JFK in four black Cadillac gangstermobiles. Tom Wolfe, a reporter then for the *Herald Tribune*, jumped into the car carrying George Harrison and Brian Sommerville. As the convoy raced along the expressway, preceded by two motorcycle troopers and followed by two patrol cars, it was buzzed repeatedly by wildly driving kids. Suddenly a white convertible blazoned "Beetles" rocketed past the Harrison limo. "Did you see that!" cried the horrified Sommerville.

"They misspelled our name," replied the dour George in his glum scouse accent. When they paused for a light at Third Avenue and 63rd Street, George was hailed by a pretty girl, who stuck her head out of a cab that had chased the Beatles from the airport.

"How does one meet a Beatle?" she caroled.

George rolled down his window and replied, "One says hello."

"Hello!" responded the girl, who introduced herself as Caroline Reynolds of New Canaan. When the light changed, she yelled: "Eight more will be down from Wellesley!"

The Beatles' destination was the Plaza Hotel, an absurd accommodation for a rock band but the perfect place for a know-nothing snob like Brian Epstein. As the Beatles approached the old building, they saw that it was besieged by hundreds of kids, who had been herded behind police barricades and were being held there by shock-helmeted cops on steaming stallions. John Lennon's car was escorted to the Fifth Avenue entrance by a mounted detail that put its horses to the gallop. Then, with a short, headlong thrust, Lennon was up the steps and through the revolving door, safe inside the turn-of-the-century marble palace.

Brian boasted that he had obtained the Beatles' reservations through a ruse, by making the requests sound as though they were for British businessmen, like "J. W. Lennon, Esquire." What actually happened was that the manager of the hotel, Alphonse Salamone, after deciding that the Beatles would be more trouble than they were worth, made the mistake of mentioning the matter one night while having supper with his family. The moment his teenage daughter heard the word "Beatles," she screamed aloud and then began sobbing uncontrollably. "It was because of her carrying on," remarked Salamone's son, Greg, "that my father let the whole thing go through." Over and over in youth-indulgent America, the fortunes of the Beatles were determined, for better or for worse, by the demands of teenage girls.

Seeking to contain the damage to his hotel, Salamone assigned the Beatles quarters near the roof, on the twelfth floor, in a wing of ten rooms, which was protected by a police barricade and two men from the Burns Detective Agency. The moment the Beatles got into their suites, they ordered up a supply of their favorite drink, J&B scotch and Coca-Cola. Then, like men set before a lavishly laden table, they proceeded to glut themselves on American TV and radio. Flipping on every television set—but taking care to tune out the sound—the boys stuck into their ears the plugs of their little transistor radios and began to prowl the dial. Naturally they were delighted to find that the news of their arrival was being reported on the air alternately with their records, but what really thrilled the Beatles was the bountifulness of the American media. So many TV channels, so many radio stations, so many voices and accents, so much sound and action twenty-four hours a day! It was the fulfillment of a lifetime of fantasy about America the abundant. When the Beatles got back to England and appeared on *Ready, Steady, Go,* the first question they were asked was what they liked most about the United States. Without hesitation, George replied, "The radio and TV—and drive-in movies."

The first visitors to make it through the security check were the three Ronettes. The girls had met the Beatles recently in London during the course of the Ronettes' tour of Great Britain. One night at a party these sexy little pony girls had tried to teach the tense English boys the latest teen dances, like the pony, the jerk, and the nitty-gritty. Ringo was the only Beatle who gave the steps a try. George was more interested in making out with Mary, and John was hot for Ronnie. By the end of the night the Beatles were talking about taking the Ronettes with them on their next tour. When word of this proposal got back to the Ronettes' record producer, Phil Spector, he went mad with jealousy. Though still married, Spector had determined to make Ronnie Bennett his new wife. Jumping on the first plane to London, he confronted her and warned: "If you go on the Beatles' tour, we don't get married." Then he replaced her with another girl and sent her home to Harlem.

No sooner had Ronnie settled down in her mother's apartment and switched on the TV than she saw the coverage of the Beatles' arrival at the airport. She almost fell out of the chair when she spied the tiny figure of Phil Spector following the Beatles down the steps from the plane. In a flash she realized that Spector had double-crossed her. He had denied her the chance to cop all that great publicity as she walked down those stairs with the Beatles. Meantime, Phil had conned his way aboard the plane so *he* could take the bow. Little creep! Not to be outdone, Ronnie called up the girls, and in a flash they were into their tightest sheaths and heading for the Plaza. Street-smart kids from uptown, they cut through the cops, the house dicks, and the security men to turn up, cute 'n' kissy, right in the Beatles' front parlor.

John Lennon didn't waste any time on idle chatter. As soon as Cynthia's back was turned, he hustled Ronnie into an adjoining bedroom. When he began kissing her passionately, Ronnie was shocked. She had already explained her "scene" to John in London. She was a seventeen-year-old virgin. She was saving "it" for Phil. If she played her cards right, she would be Mrs. Phil Spector! Now, here was John Lennon, the hottest star in the business, coming on to her as if all they had to do was "get down." "John!" she gasped, staring aghast at her steaming lover. "I *can't*!" Lennon, high as a king after that scene at the airport, was in no mood to be rejected. Tearing himself away from Ronnie, he stalked out the room, slamming the door so hard it rattled the windowpanes. Next day he called up and apologized.

George was all set to resume his affair with Mary when suddenly he felt himself coming down with the flu. He complained to his married sister, Louise Caldwell, of St. Louis, that he had a sore throat and felt feverish. Not even "a bit of a throat" could stop him from chatting with his new buddy, Murray the K, who had rushed back to the studio and arranged to do a phone interview over the air. When Brian Epstein learned of this unauthorized broadcast, the first of many by the K, he hit the ceiling of his posh corner suite, facing both Central Park and Grand Army Plaza, far from his madding boys.

Saturday dawned cold and rainy. When the weather cleared, the three healthy Beatles went over to the lake in the park to pose for photographs, accompanied by the press corps and four hundred girls. After eating cheeseburgers at the boathouse, they got into two limos and drove up to Harlem, which they expected would be a colorful place, as befitted the home of rhythm and blues. What they saw was a slum, whose main street was lined with dreary little stores as heavily barred and fenced as those of a frontier town. After this disillusioning vision of black America, the Beatles were carried to the old Maxine Elliott Theater in Times Square, the CBS studio for *The Ed Sullivan Show.*

Sullivan's greatest coup as a TV producer had been presenting Elvis Presley in his first days of fame. So during Christmas 1963 the canny ex-columnist had sat down with Brian Epstein at the Delmonico Hotel and cut a deal for three shows at $4,500 a shot. (Playing with a weaker hand ten years earlier, Colonel Parker had won $50,000 for the same three shots.) Now Sullivan was alarmed by the news that one of the Beatles was laid up with the flu. Assured that George would be well enough to play the show, the lantern-jawed producer growled: "He better be or I'm putting on a wig myself."

Saturday evening the Beatles dined on pork chops at 21. Ringo asked the waiter: "Do you have any vintage Coca-Cola?" Afterward the boys returned to the hotel to feast their eyes on American TV, but Paul deserted the party to pop across the Plaza to the Playboy Club, returning with an off-duty Bunny, with whom he wound up the night at the adjacent Chateau Madrid, North America's foremost Latin American nightclub.

That same night Brian had a little party in his suite with some stud hustlers. A notorious American scandal sheet had prepared for this moment by bribing the hotel staff to tip them off the instant the Beatles got down with their fans or Brian with his rough traders. When the maid made up Brian's bed, she parted the drapes on the window. A daring photographer made his way to the floor above, where he was lowered in a bosun's chair to Brian's window. A couple of days later the prints were in the hands of Nicky Byrnes, the Beatles' merchandiser, who was now dickering with Brian over the provisions of the agreement he had signed some months earlier at London. Byrnes arranged to buy the pictures as well as some shots of little schoolgirls who had secreted themselves in a closet in the hopes of catching the Beatles. He claims credit for having averted a major scandal in America.

At 2:30 Sunday afternoon all the Beatles appeared for the dress rehearsal and the taping of their third Sullivan show, which was to be aired at some future date. 50,000 requests had been received for seats—rather a lot for a theater seating 728. Getting next to the Beatles had now become the greatest challenge to New York's highly resourceful celebrity hunters. Leonard Bernstein had two young daughters who demanded to see the Beatles, and Lenny himself was eager to meet the boys, so when Brian's new assistant, Wendy Hanson, a buxom English girl with a nannylike manner, arrived before the performance, she found the Bernstein girls ensconced in the first row and Lenny showing off upstairs in the Beatles' dressing room. When Bernstein finally left, John turned to Wendy and said: "Look, luv, could you keep Sidney Bernstein's family out of this room?"

Meantime, poor Brian was suffering even worse treatment from the show's gracious host. Walking up to Sullivan, who was scribbling last-minute notes, the Beatles' manager exclaimed: "I would like to know the exact wording of your introduction."

Without bothering to look up, Sullivan rasped, "I would like for you to get lost!"

The historic character of the Beatles' first live performance on American TV (they had been seen on film the night of 3 January on the rival *Jack Paar Show*) was underscored at the start of the program, when Sullivan read a congratulatory telegram from Elvis Presley. (The telegram had been sent by Colonel Tom Parker, eager to cop a little free publicity. Elvis despised the Beatles.) When it was time to bring on the star attraction, Sullivan wound up and made his usual fight announcer's introduction, twirling from the waist and hurling out his hand as if he were hollering, "And in *this* corner . . ." As the Beatles started playing "All My Loving," the camera dollied in slowly from front and center, as did tens of millions of Americans.

What America saw was an image of unaccustomed elegance, standing at the farthest possible remove from the rubber-legged, draped-shape, greaseball vulgarity of Elvis the Pelvis. Accoutered in dark, tubular Edwardian suits that exaggerated the stiff, buttoned-up carriage of these young Englishmen, the Beatles resembled four long-haired classical musicians, like the Pro Musica Antiqua, playing electric lutes and rebecs and taking deep formal bows after each rendition. John Lennon, unsmiling and stiff-backed, looked positively dignified, his aquiline nose and full face giving him the appearance of a Renaissance nobleman. Performing with assurance and betraying no signs of nervousness, the Beatles bore the scrutiny of the cameras and the tension of the occasion easily, even when one of the mikes went dead during "I Want to Hold Your Hand," leaving John suspended in mid-air. The group's strategy was to play it cool, omitting the hard rock and using Paul as lead singer on five out of six numbers, which meant that most of the time the camera was focused on his angelically smiling face.

The rest of the time the screen was filled with astonishing images of Beatlemaniacs, little girls who bounced high in their seats on every beat, screaming, tearing out their hair, and behaving like children during a violent chase cartoon. The fascination of the broadcast lay in the counterpoint between the immaculate British boys, who weren't doing a thing that would provoke such an outburst, and these crazy girls, who were going bananas. Explaining this irrational response was the challenge the program offered its reviewers; none of them accepted it. They ignored Beatlemania like a distracting noise and focused exclusively upon the band, which, they concluded, was nothing very special—in fact, highly disappointing.

The keynote in what became a chorus of dismissive rhetoric was sounded next morning by the *Herald Tribune,* which anatomized the Beatles as "75% publicity, 20% haircut, and 5% lilting lament." *The New York Times* backhanded the group as a "fine mass placebo." The really heavy blows came raining down the following week, when the national weeklies got in their licks. *Newsweek,* which prided itself on its colorful writing, ranted: "Visually they are a nightmare: tight, dandified Edwardian beatnik suits and great pudding-bowls of hair. Musically they are a near disaster, guitars and drums slamming out a merciless beat that does away with secondary rhythms, harmony and melody. Their lyrics (punctuated by nutty shouts of yeah, yeah, yeah!) are a catastrophe, a preposterous farrago of Valentine-card romantic sentiments." But the Beatles could laugh. They were relishing a Trendex rating that estimated they had drawn 73,900,000 viewers—the largest audience in the history of television.

Even after this astounding success the Beatles did not yet regard themselves as all the way home. Their assault on the USA had been planned as a two-pronged attack: First, they were going to hit the *Sullivan Show;* then Carnegie Hall. Oddly the boys worried less about appearing before the entire nation than they did about putting away the 2,780 people who could be seated in the old concert hall. Assuming the Carnegie Hall audience was going to be highly critical, the Beatles demanded an out-of-town date so that they could warm up for the main event. They were booked, accordingly, into an old boxing arena in Washington, D.C., the Coliseum.

On the night of 11 January the Beatles charged toward the fight ring inside a flying wedge of forty red-jacketed ushers. When they appeared beneath the glaring downlights and began adjusting their pitifully inadequate 50-watt amps, they were inundated by a tidal wave of screams, followed by a blizzard of flashbulbs and a hailstorm of jelly beans. "The atmosphere was electric!" babbled Paul after the show. "We came onstage to the most tremendous reception I have ever heard in my life. Our publicist, Brian Sommerville, who is normally a hard-headed businessman, had tears in his eyes as he was rearranging Ringo's drum kit. I told him to go dry up, but the reaction was so overwhelming that even I was on the point of tears!"

Instead of crying, Paul took command of the situation. After being introduced by three local DJs in idiotic-looking Beatles' wigs, Paul MC'd the whole show in a somewhat distraught but charming manner. As the band kicked off with "Roll Over, Beethoven," George singing lead, it was apparent that they were putting everything they had into the performance. Ringo, in particular, played like a madman, revealing a fire that nobody had ever glimpsed before beneath his workmanlike surface. What was especially exciting about the show was its spontaneous character, a product of the chaotic conditions upon the stage. The performing area was an obstacle course, strewn with tripping cables, mikes that went dead, and a rickety revolving drum stand that made Ringo's cymbals totter precariously and his drums slide beyond his reach. As the String Bean Boys went skittering about on their Cuban heels, struggling to find ways to deliver their songs, a crazy *Night at the Opera* choreography emerged that was a lot funnier (and certainly better motivated) than the foolishly admired camera ballet in their first film. Indeed, there were even a few moments when the Beatles regressed to the style they had employed at the Indra or the Cavern, when the order of the night was *"Mach Schau!"*

John instructed the audience to clap and stamp by flapping his hands together like seal's flippers and doing his club-footed spastic stomp. George did his timid little twist routine, as sketchy as a lapdog burying its mess. Ringo shouted the lyrics of "I Want to Be Your Man" while feverishly drumming, like a freshman going through the ordeals of hazing. Paul, radiant with joy, took his left hand off his guitar repeatedly in "I Want to Hold Your Hand" and shook it gleefully, like an ecstatic little puppy dog. By the end of the performance every person in the arena and in the one hundred motion-picture theaters that plugged into the closed-circuit hookup, had imprinted indelibly upon his mind the Platonic idea of the Beatles: four British schoolboys on a lark.

The Coliseum concert established the pattern, though not the standard, for all future Beatles' performances in America. Basically the event was a giant pep rally with salvational overtones. The emphasis was on the vast and frenzied audience rather than on the performers, who were dwarfed by distance, drowned out by noise, and overborne by the aggressiveness of a generation that would soon burst the old boundaries of public decorum and turn rock concerts into festivals of participatory culture. In this mad milieu the Beatles were reduced to marionettes, jouncing about on the distant stage. The Beatles' songs, banged out in the rough-and-ready style of such occasions, revealed their essential appeal as chants and shouts, the sort of thing to sing at a football game, a political convention, or a carnival ball. Ultimately the Beatles became America's foremost cheerleaders.

The moment the Beatles boarded the archaic parlor car that would take them back to New York, they started to party. Ringo, who cut the liveliest figure of any of the group in America, clowned before the cameras of the Maysles brothers. He slithered around and under the seats like an ape. He looped a porter's load of camera gear over his shoulders and staggered down the aisles, shouting, "Excuse me! *Life* magazine! Excuse me!" Next, he appeared strolling through the car in a woman's white fur coat and hat. Later he darted about furtively, puffing on a cigarette, like Pepe Le Moko. Inspired to play the Marx Brothers, the other boys went into action. George lay like a mummy in the overhead baggage rack. Paul shot pictures through the car windows, exclaiming like a fruity fashion plater, "God! How artistic! Railway lines!" John glanced up occasionally from his newspaper to bark, like Groucho, "Funny! Very funny!" The Beatles were now ready for the main event.

On Lincoln's Birthday the Beatles played their first theater concerts in America, a matinee and an evening performance at Carnegie Hall. The promoter, a small-time operator named Sid Bernstein, had sold his 5,700 tickets in two hours. The veteran cashier of the hall estimated that he could have sold enough tickets that day to fill Shea Stadium, precisely what Bernstein began persuading the cautious Brian Epstein to do next. Brian said that he preferred to go slowly and not risk a failure—a very sensible attitude normally but absurd in the face of a Trendex rating of seventy-four million! The promoter tried to milk his sellout by putting 150 seats on the stage. When John Lennon walked out and found people seated virtually within reach, he blew his stack. "It wasn't a rock show," he fumed. "It was a circus, where we were in cages bein' pawed and talked at, touched backstage and onstage. We were just like animals." Lennon was also incensed by the news that New York Governor Nelson Rockefeller's wife, Happy, had turned up at the last minute, escorted by a state trooper, to obtain an unobtainable ticket for her ten-year-old daughter, Wendy. Any assertion of the prerogatives of class enraged the déclassé John Lennon.

Even Murray the K angered John that day, though Murray's Broadway show-biz patter had so charmed the Beatles hitherto that they had taken to greeting everyone by demanding, "What's happening, baby?" But that afternoon their fondness for the K began to curdle around the edges when he insisted upon going onstage before the performance to conduct a popularity poll of the individual Beatles, urging the girls to scream for their favorite after Murray shouted out his name. Ringo beat Paul by several decibels.

It was ironic that the sophisticated New York audience that the Beatles had dreaded should turn out to be a lot of little girls from New Jersey with braces on their teeth. Indeed, nothing in America surprised the Beatles more than how ugly and square were their American fans. Here was this huge and affluent youth population that had absolutely no idea of style or taste. It was very disillusioning.

What explained the Beatles' triumph? The answer goes back to Elvis, who had established the precedent for Beatlemania only eight years earlier. Elvis's phenomonal success in Britain had been based on the fact that he was a working-class hero, and that was equally true of the Beatles, hailed as simple lads from Liverpool who had struck it rich. John was shrewd enough to recognize the value of this delusion; he urged his mates to exploit it by putting on scouse accents and acting as if they had been born to be lorry drivers. Aunt Mimi was horrified the first time she heard her carefully reared ward speaking like a dock worker. When she demanded an explanation, John went into his crookbacked imitation of Fagin, the Jew, rubbing his fingers together greedily and lisping, "Money! Money!"

John was right: by playing up to the image created by the press, the Beatles provided the rising working class of the Sixties with an inspiriting example of British success in the hitherto American field of pop culture.

In the United States the triumph of the Beatles had nothing to do with class but was based rather on the cultural divisions produced by the generation gap. For in every generation since the Thirties, the first decade to be dominated by the mass media—the cradle of youth culture—there has been a distinctive youth consciousness that has both instanced and celebrated itself in a great song and dance cult. At the focal point of these wavelike eruptions has always stood some charismatic hero, like Frank Sinatra or Elvis Presley, but over the years his public has changed. Originally the fads, like swing, began with the young adults and college kids; then they filtered down to the high schools and the junior highs, which got them last and understood them least. By the time of Elvis, this process had reversed itself. College kids took no interest in Elvis Presley; his claque was composed of pubescent or prepubescent girls of eleven, twelve, and thirteen. Colonel Parker spotted this development immediately and insisted that Elvis tone down his act, exchanging his image as the Boy Who Dared to Rock for that of the Boy Who Loved to Play with Dolls, a process that commenced as early as "Teddy Bear." This song, with its combination of

teasing, drollery, and mock passion, was just as crucial to Presley's career as "Heartbreak Hotel" because it provided the ideal formula for
feeding all those thousands of screaming babies who made Elvis the
first King of Kiddie Kulture.

The commercialization of the Beatles in America developed along
precisely the same lines, only more blatantly because by the time the
Fab Four hit the States, they had already been focused into their version of the Teddy Bear image. It was all summed up in that famous
shot, carefully staged by Harry Benson, of the Beatles having a wild
pillow fight in their bedroom, like a gaggle of schoolboys in a dorm.
"Fuckin' imagine four yobbos like us havin' a *pillow fight!*" exclaimed
John Lennon in honest amazement at the way the media had transformed his group of hard-rockers into the very picture of what every
little girl most wanted.

Yet there was a significant difference between the effect produced
by the Beatles in Britain and America, just as there was a difference
between the British and American girls. The latter, being younger on
the average and the products of a more juvenile culture, saw in the
Beatles a subliminal image implanted in infancy by the Saturday-morning cartoons. When the little girls with braces on their teeth were confronted with four identical-looking boys dressed in elf suits with flying
mop tops and making tight-jointed marionette moves, their deepest
and most Disneyized reflexes were excited. Their legendary screams
were simply the cries of a child who reaches out to clutch a new toy and
then, finding it dangling beyond her grasp, explodes in a shrieking,
sobbing, fist-clenched tantrum. Far from panting with lust and dying to
get the Beatles between the sheets, all they really wanted was to prop
these living dolls up on their frilly bolsters because the Fab Four were
as cute as teddy bears!

There is no more revealing clue to the secret of the Beatles' appeal
in America than the astonishing popularity achieved in this country by
Ringo. In Britain Ringo had counted for nothing in the band because
he was just the other boys' stooge. In America Ringo far surpassed the
other Beatles in popularity for the same reason that the most beloved
of the Seven Dwarfs was Dopey. Ringo's fortune was in his face. (His
cute name helped, too.) Looking at him triggered in every kid that
Ugly Duckling complex characteristic of American childhood. Actually,
all the Beatles looked as if they were straight off Disney's drafting
board. That's why they were picked up so quickly by King Features,
which set four teams of animators to work cranking out an endless
series of Beatle flicks for the Saturday-morning cartoons. This same
cartoon character was projected in the Beatles' feature-length films,
whose whole point was to treat the boys like figures in a *Silly Symphony,*
always running running running—and sometimes flying! The transla-

tion into animation reached its apogee in the psychedelic period, when the original fans, now stoned hippies, lay back and let the brilliant German animator Heinz Edelmann pour his Day-Glo fantasies over them, while the Beatles provided a sound track that culminated in "(We All Live in a) Yellow Submarine," a song as cute and catchy as "Whistle While You Work."

So the real Beatles, who saw exactly where their appeal lay, adapted their act to conform with their perceived image. Shaking their hair mops wildly into a force-nine gale of hysterical screaming, they mugged and teased and camped it up like daddy in the nursery. Their music became a junior high rock opera full of jealous tantrums and lonely sighs and breakups and makeups. When they finally felt they were dying amid the steady downpour of jelly beans and baby screams, they changed their tune and image. But children can never have enough.

THE TROUBLE WITH
SUCCESS

A Hard Day's Night, which the Beatles began shooting as soon as they got back to England, was conceived neither as a regular feature film nor even as an exploitation flick. Strange to say, this much admired comedy, often exhibited today in art cinemas, started off as a scam, a ploy designed to enable United Artists to get its hands on a Beatles' album. The unsung heroes of the film were Noel Rodgers (UA's record man in Britain), who cooked up the scheme, and Bud Orenstein (of UA's film division), who cut the deal.

When the idea was spawned in the summer of 1963, Capitol, EMI's subsidiary in the United States, was refusing to release Beatles' records on the grounds that they were unsuitable to the American market. UA's executives in Britain, who enjoyed a much better vantage point, were convinced that the day was fast coming when the Beatles would break big in the States. So they proposed signing the Beatles to a three-picture contract that would automatically entail three sound track albums. Nobody ever dreamed, even in his most golden slumbers, what riches would flow from this simple suggestion, for with *A Hard Day's Night* United Artists got not only the best Beatles' album to date but an enormously popular film, brought in for under a half million dollars.

As UA didn't want to waste money on what was regarded initially as a throwaway item, it engaged Walter Shenson, an independent producer who had demonstrated a knack for making successful little movies on a shoestring, like *The Mouse That Roared.* Shenson was also regarded, as a man familiar with the British and theater worlds, as standing a better chance of putting away Brian Epstein than would have a Hollywood schlockmeister.

The producer recalled that when the time came for him to meet the Beatles, Brian turned up alone, complaining that he couldn't find the "boys." A quick trip to the Beatles' pad in Mayfair discovered them standing in the street, trying to flag a cab. Jumping into Shenson's cab, the boys ordered the driver to take them to Abbey Road, where Gerry and the Pacemakers were recording. No sooner did the cab get under way, however, than the Beatles ordered it to stop at a news kiosk so that one of them could jump out and get the latest press reports on Beatlemania. They made a couple of these jump stops before they reached the studio, tearing the papers out of each other's hands and reading the news as if they, too, were Beatlemaniacs. The quiet, balding, pipe-smoking Shenson was amused at these antics and began to feel as if he were "inside a Marx Brothers comedy." That idea became the keynote of the film.

The most critical problem initially was the choice of scriptwriter. Shenson was apprehensive about tying up his brilliant director, Richard Lester, in the toils of some overrealistic script, but nevertheless he deferred to the Beatles' wishes when they requested Alun Owen, a Liverpool-born writer of "kitchen sink" dramas for television. Owen took his historic mission very lightly, though he did find time to hop over to Dublin for a couple of days in late 1963 to observe the boys at close hand. Then he returned to crank out a script that, whatever its merits as a comic scenario, betrays nothing but ignorance of the Beatles.

A Hard Day's Night looks a lot different today from when it was first released. Then it was primarily a keyhole through which one could ogle the Fab Four. Now you see it for what it was: a travesty of the whole mad phenomenon of Beatlemania. Though the boys are given a few saucy lines in the familiar scene in the railway carriage, the rest of the picture turns on the character of Paul's grandfather, the "clean old man" played with dazzling brilliance by TV star Wilfrid Brambell, whose billy goat face and cut-crystal brogue rivet the viewer and pivot the plot, whose simple farcical point is that this old geezer is a much more outrageous character than any of the boyish pop stars who cause a riot every time they step in the street. Not surprisingly the Beatles were very unhappy about being treated so dismissively. They didn't dare voice their complaints to the American moviemakers, but their beefs did come to the ears of Alun Owen at Swinging London's favorite hangout, the legendary Ad Lib Club.

A Continental-style discotheque located atop the Prince Charles Cinema on Leicester Street, Soho, the Ad Lib was reached by an elevator that broadcast the same music being played on the dance floor. Though the layout was no different from the traditional nightclub, the crowd was always a shock for any experienced club-hopper because it was composed predominantly of startlingly young and strikingly costumed kids, who were wearing the first mod suits and miniskirts that had ever been seen. Instead of the wealthy and famous people who comprised the old café society or the new jet set, these young people had neither means nor position: they were fashion models, fledgling rock stars, hairdressers, commercial photographers, boutique owners or young actors and playwrights. In a word, they were that trendy little group that would soon make a cultural revolution first in Britain and then in America.

They frugged and watusied, hullie-gullied and hitch-hiked on the little dance floor to heavy R&B tracks played on a pair of turntables concealed in a piano case. (Technology was not yet chic.) From time to time, a Jamaican chef named Winston, hired as a tummler, would jump out on the floor with a tambourine in his hand and whip up such a fever of excitement that everybody in the club would spontaneously form a conga line and go shouting and stumbling down five floors to the street, where they all would snake around and go screaming and stumbling back up the steps again to the top floor.

John Lennon wasn't the type for a conga line. He would sit at the Beatles' banquette all night getting drunk and arguing with his mouth against someone's ear. Then he would wind up the evening on the pavement outside the building having a regular Liverpool punch-up. (Fortunately the Beatles' driver, Bill Corbett, was an ex-boxer who would break up the brawls before they produced any serious consequences.)

One night while Lennon was sitting at his table talking to the actress Billie Whitelaw, he got onto the subject of Alun Owen.

"He's full of shit!" stormed John. "He couldn't write his way out of a wet paper bag!" Lennon charged that Owen had missed the Beatles' individual characters completely by confining himself to just one facet of their public image. What galled John especially was having to speak and hear a lot of stupid talk and half-funny humor that would never have come out of the mouths of the real Beatles, who prided themselves on their very special wit, which constantly generated better lines and bits than anything found in the script.

When Owen confronted Lennon with these derogatory remarks, John behaved with characteristic duplicity. "Al, whatever they say, you know I love you, don't you?" blarneyed Lennon.

"Yeah, but what's all this about me not writing my way out of a paper bag?" persisted the offended playwright.

"No, listen, Al," protested Lennon. "She started saying how good you were, so I had to knock you, didn't I? I *had* to knock you. You pay somebody, you got to knock 'em. Nothing personal!" All the same, at the film's premiere, Lennon watched one reel and ran out of the theater, crying, "I can't stand this lot!" Only George remained to the end.

The public's idea of the Beatles as four young lords of pop who delighted in telling the old show-biz types to get stuffed is completely false. They were, in fact, four naïfs from the provinces who knew only one thing with professional assurance, pop music. When it came to anything else, from making movies to making homes, the Beatles felt obliged to put themselves into the hands of the professionals selected by their manager to be their producers, directors, writers, photographers, publicity men, interior decorators, etc. Only when the boys began to realize how inadequate all these people were did they start to take control of their operation, commencing, significantly, by replacing their photographer, Dezo Hoffmann, the guy who took all those corny pictures of the Beatles in highly contrived poses, like a comedy troupe. From control of their photographic image, the Beatles advanced to control of their phonographic image, until, step by step, they reached the most crucial area: the management of their money. But they did not arrive at that vital point until five years after their first film.

The only feature of that movie over which they exercised anything approaching control was the composition of the songs. And here they scored a real film triumph. From the first explosive note of the title song, the listener's head snapped up because he recognized that the band had taken a great leap forward. John Lennon was white-hot by this time, as appears from the story of how he wrote the famous title song.

Late in the production Shenson was still struggling to come up with a catchy title for the film. John told him how Ringo would twist language around to fit his thoughts, citing as a typical example the drummer's phrase for a hard night's work—"a hard day's night." Shenson seized on the expression as a catchy title, adding that the ideal thing would be to embody it in a grabby up-tempo tune that could play through the credits. John asked if the song had to reflect the theme of the picture. The moment Shenson said no, Lennon demanded to be driven home. He arrived at Emperor's Gate well after dark. Early the next morning, Shenson was summoned to the stars' dressing room. He found John and Paul, who must have been up all night working, standing at the ready, guitars in hand. Reading the lyrics off a matchbook cover, they strummed and sang the new title song, thrilling Shenson, who was further impressed the following day, when he received from Lennon a tape of the finished track, cut the night before by George Martin. John Lennon's gale wind of inspiration can still be felt blowing through the song.

The first Beatles' track to win the respect of serious listeners, "A Hard Day's Night" broke through the Mod Moppet image to reveal at last John Lennon's ardent soul. A cowboy gallop spurred by a Wilson Pickett cowbell and underscored by Buddy Holly's tomtoms, then broken in the middle by a deeply twanging speech from the Old Wrangler,

this gallimaufry of borrowed materials sounded completely original because Lennon cast over his pastiche a darkly colored tonal fabric never
heard before in any pop song. The entire composition is written in the
mixolydian mode, an ancient vocal scale abandoned back at the dawn
of modern tonality in the seventeenth century but preserved in British,
Irish, and American folk song. The inspiration for this strange tonality
was simply sincerity. Though cast in the familiar form of the can't-wait-
till-I-get-back-to-you-baby love song, the real theme of the song is
work—the hard, earnest, exhausting labor that men must perform to
survive.

This displacement of the romantic theme was soon to become characteristic of Lennon's compositions even though it went completely
against the grain of the Beatles' success. For once the boys went commercial they adopted the policy of writing nothing but love songs
aimed at the teeny-popper market. The first *one hundred* songs by Lennon and McCartney deal exclusively with the theme of puppy love.
This self-imposed restriction doesn't appear to have caused McCartney
any great discomfort, but it nearly drove John Lennon out of his mind.
His resentment arose not just from the feeling of self-betrayal but from
his sense that he was betraying the music he loved. Think of all the
great heroes of rock: Elvis, Little Richard, Mick Jagger, Jim Morrison,
Jimi Hendrix. What is the thing they have in common, the trait that
constitutes the essence of a rocker? It sure as hell isn't puppy love! It's the
exhibitionistic narcissism of the young macho, preening, boasting, and
flaunting himself with unabashed self-infatuation. That was John Lennon's fancy, too, but he couldn't act on it because he was obliged by his role
as Beatle John to play a high school boy in an endless teenybopper
melodrama. So what did he do? Precisely what any serious-minded artist
does when he finds himself obliged to work in a commercial medium. He
sneaked the real stuff in through the back door.

Lennon's attempt to bootleg the self-intoxicated frenzy of rock 'n'
roll into the sweet and beguiling strains of pop rock is especially clear
in "Any Time at All," the most exciting song in the Beatles' first film
score. Triggered by a pistol-like drum shot, the record fires Lennon's
voice at the listener like a bullet. Every repetition of this bopping figure
crepitates with the same excitement which makes John Lennon sound
like an ecstatic dancing about in the flames, like Little Richard or James
Brown. Lennon's fires are cold flames because he stems from a cooler
culture, but the self-intoxicated thrust of his voice burns with the real
gospel frenzy.

No sooner does John get to the bridge, however, than he suddenly
abandons his macho image and jumps back into his good-guy disguise,
assuring the girl—whom he has obviously forgotten—that he will always be there to take care of her and make her feel loved. His solemn

tone, better suited to a school anthem than a love song, is just a "line" because Lennon often employs this rhetoric when he is being terribly sincere with a girl (as in his first attempt to write a sentimental ballad, "If I Fell," with its portentous block-like tones so full of the earnestness of insincerity). But once John gets past the bridge of "Any Time at All," he snaps back into focus with a voice that cracks like a rawhide whip and whizzes like a lariat. Once again he is experiencing the ecstasy of dancing in the flames.

If the music for *A Hard Day's Night* has nothing to do with the script, that is because most of the songs express the soul of John Lennon—the film score coming as close to a solo album as John ever made with the Beatles—whereas the movie is simply a projection of the Fab Four's public image. Yet there can be no discounting this image because it was immensely important in confirming the Beatles' triumph with the public. In fact, the enormous appeal of the image could be taken as prime testimony to the fantasies of that time, the infatuation with the idea of four cheeky working-class boys, who, beneath their arch and impudent manner, are lovable and innocent children. It is the theme of the Beatles as children that explains their epiphany in the film, which comes not where it might be expected, with the band in full cry on a concert stage or in a recording studio, but out of doors, upon a playing field, where the boys perform the juvenile camerabatics suggested by Dezo Hoffmann's famous shot showing all four Beatles leaping into the air at once.

This notion of the Beatles as sexless and charming children was particularly dear to the hearts of parental America, where nothing was more common in the year 1964 than tributes to the Fab Four from middle-class mamas and papas, who were relieved to discover that for once their children were losing their minds over pop idols who embodied only the most charming and disarming sort of youthful rebelliousness. Many such parents accompanied their children to the first showings of *A Hard Day's Night*, repeating the pattern of Elvis's most successful picture, *Blue Hawaii*, which was also "family." How horrified all those nice mothers and fathers would have been if they could have accompanied the Beatles on their world tour in the summer of 1964 and witnessed the scenes of nightly debauchery. This was the tour that John Lennon summed up with one leering word—"*Satyricon.*"

Down under is where the Beatles perfected those arrangements for procuring and enjoying their fans that would serve the band so well in years to come. Three absolutely trustworthy lifetime employees ran this operation. Big, bespectacled Mal Evans, the Beatles' equipment handler, was the chief procurer. "Mal Evans was very good at picking the right girls," according to Glenn A. Baker's exhaustive and amusing account of the antipodal tour, *The Beatles Down Under*. "After Mal had done his 'You and you and you and, oh, alright [*sic*], you, too' routine," continued Baker, "the sweet young things were corralled in a holding room. It was from this reservoir that Derek [Taylor] and Neil [Aspinall] allocated a continual supply of carnal delight to the tour members who subscribed to the service."

Jim Oram, an Australian journalist who traveled with the tour, observed: "John and Paul, particularly, rooted themselves silly. A seemingly endless and inexhaustible stream of Australian girls passed through their beds: the very young, the very experienced, the beautiful and the plain. In fact, I can vividly remember one spoilt virgin in Adelaide, who proudly took her blood-stained sheet home with her in the morning." Bob Rogers, another reporter who stuck with the Beatles from the moment they landed until they left the country, confirmed Oram: "The boys never, to my knowledge, repeated the dose. They'd rather have a less attractive woman than the same one twice. They had become supremely indifferent to it all, as women and girls continually prostrated themselves. I was convinced that they would all end up homosexuals, out of sheer boredom with conventional sex. There was no pill in 1964 and with the amount of Beatle screwing that went on, I just can't believe that there wasn't an explosion of little Beatles all over Australia in 1965."

The trading of partners that had been typical of the Beatles' days in the back rooms of the Bambi Kino in Hamburg resumed in Australia. Glenn A. Baker recalled that "one young Queensland girl, who married a prominent Woolahra stockbroker and is now a pillar of Sydney society, kept cocktail party guests amused throughout most of the Sixties with her graphic descriptions of being screwed by all four Beatles in one night." Another reporter told the author that he was flagrante delicto when "Derek Taylor sauntered into the room, casually inquiring, 'Would anyone like to meet John Lennon?' The girl slipped out from under me so quickly that I was left doing push-ups on the bed." Baker's investigations revealed that John's crack about *Satyricon* was meant to imply more than mere sexual abundance: "The odd perversion or diversion was certainly not out of the question. Beginning in Melbourne, some mild excremental sports [a euphemism for pissing on girls?] were apparently engaged in and an amusing variety of copulation locations and combinations investigated."

Despite the rule against repeaters, there was a girl who caught John Lennon's fancy. Jennie Kee is today one of Australia's trendiest fashion designers, known internationally for her sophisticated, Pop Art sweaters. In 1964 she was a seventeen-year-old student at Presbyterian Ladies' College. Not a beauty but a girl who knew how to make herself look irresistible, Jennie and a friend stalked the Beatles at the Sheraton Hotel in Sydney. They found a way to jam the elevator and waylaid the boys in the stairwell. They were invited to the nightly party and found it full of airline hostesses. Jennie was dressed in the height of mod fashion. "I wore a tartan suit with leather trim—real Carnaby Street," she recollected with a laugh, "and leather boots with big round [sun] glasses." John couldn't take his eyes off her. When the hour got late, he made his move. "John beckoned to me and said: 'You should stay here,'" she remembered. Stuck for an answer, she exclaimed: "Oh! Big surprise!"

Jennie was relieved to discover that John was not going to treat her in an unpleasant manner. "It wasn't just 'I'm here to lay you,'" she explained, "mainly because I was such a naïve girl. I think he was the second man I'd ever slept with. He was a very, very funny person. We laughed all night. I probably made him sing songs—I would have done all that. I was wearing contacts, and I showed him how to put them in and take them out. He was really sensitive. He knew I was really naïve. That's why I liked him so much. He wasn't macho at all. . . . He *cajoled* me. I kept unbuttoning my dress; then I'd do it up again. Talk about the schoolgirl! I don't think he had been with an Asian girl before. He was very aware of it. He was quite excited by it.

"All night we could hear this *screaming* coming from the next room. . . . I think everybody was whipping everybody. I was a bit shocked. I thought, 'I hope John Lennon doesn't expect me to get whipped because I'm not going to get whipped for anyone!' I was so shy with him. I must say, he must have thought that was terribly attractive. I was not a hardened groupie. This was my first major pull."

The day the Beatles left Australia, thousands of people swarmed over Mascot Airport at Sydney; however, the resourceful Jennie Kee found a way to get out on the tarmac. When the Beatles came rolling up inside a Rolls, John recognized Jennie and shouted, "Get into the reception room!" She dashed inside and was soon discovered by Derek Taylor, who greeted her with the nickname she had received from John, the "Dragon Lady."

Inspired by her encounter with Lennon, whom Jennie still calls humorously the "love of my life," the future fashion innovator went to London in 1967 and got a job at the latest in place, the Speakeasy. One night she bumped into John Lennon, who was accompanied by Cynthia. Recognizing his first Oriental sweetie, John exclaimed: "Ah, I remember! Australia, contact lenses, great night!"

Not long after the Beatles came up from going down under, they returned to the United States for their first American road tour. The second coming of the Beatles was nothing like the first. In February the boys had been handed the country on a vinyl platter. Encouraged to show off and have fun, they had enjoyed a beatboy's holiday. Now, in

August, they were committed to a grueling and dangerous blitzkrieg. Crisscrossing North America at an average rate of six hundred miles per diem, they presented thirty-two shows in twenty-four cities in thirty-three days. Fortunately the arrangements were made not by Brian Epstein—who was much better at arranging supper parties than he was at plotting touring parties—but by a small but efficient New York talent agency, General Artists Corporation (GAC). The paramount consideration was safety. With *A Hard Day's Night* playing simultaneously in five hundred American movie theaters, Beatlemania had now reached its epileptic apogee. To reduce the danger at airports, the party flew by night in a chartered Lockheed Elektra, but even at 2:00 A.M. the terminals would be swarming with kids. The Beatles would emerge from their plane and rush, surrounded by a flying wedge of short-sleeved cops, toward their transport. The hotel that had been foolish enough to book the group (in New York the Beatles were barred from most hotels after the siege of the Plaza) had to be prepared to withstand every sort of attack, from sneaky infiltrations to all-out rushes against the doors and plate-glass windows. In Seattle the Beatles found the ideal accommodation: a concrete tower situated at the end of a pier thrust out into Puget Sound, barricaded by a 350-foot plywood fence and topped with two feet of barbed wire. The famous guests checked in after landing on the roof in a helicopter.

Wherever they stayed, the boys lived under strict house arrest. They would arise in the afternoon and breakfast on cheese sandwiches garnished with bacon strips and washed down with pots of tea. The British papers could always be procured, so as the lads sipped the first of many scotch and Cokes, they would read the news from home or play a hand of cards. When tenderhearted George would suggest they go to the windows and wave at the fans, John would growl: "The best way to see this country is over the blue shoulder of a policeman!" Sometime during the day the visiting celebrities would appear at city hall, where they would receive a vacuous greeting from the mayor and the key to the city, a big chunk of gold-tinted Styrofoam. Then they would meet the press and play the eagerly awaited Beatles word game:

Q: What do you do all day in your hotel room?
A: [John] We play tennis and water polo and we hide from our security.
Q: Ringo, why do you receive more fan mail from Seattle girls than the others do?
A: Because more of them write to me.
Q: Would you like to walk down the street without being recognized?
A: [John] We used to do this with no money in our pockets. There's no point in it.

Getting to the stadium required a Marx Brothers ruse, the Beatles departing from the loading platform in a vile-smelling fish truck or inside a row of laundry hampers. The show was the same every night. Ten to twenty thousand kids, sitting on pins and needles, would suffer through an hour of preliminary events: the hoarse-voiced Dusty Springfield, Bill Black and his Combo (same old doghouse bass player who led Elvis's band) and the mediocre Jackie DeShannon. (The much better Righteous Brothers started the tour but dropped out after a couple of nights because they couldn't tolerate the uproar.) Finally, the Beatles would come jouncing out, four tiny stick figures caught in a jet blast of nonstop screaming.

The Beatles would perform a dozen songs, commencing with John hollering "Twist and Shout" and concluding with Paul hollering "Long Tall Sally." It wouldn't have mattered if they had sung the Lord's Prayer or a string of dirty limericks because nobody could hear them. Ringo declared that there were times when all four stopped playing, and the audience carried right on as if nothing had happened. The fifty-watt Voxes of the first U.S. concerts had now been replaced by hundred-watt models, but what good are hundred-watt amps when you're playing to eighteen thousand banshees in the Hollywood Bowl? If the surging, heaving mob of girls, hyperventilating themselves into chorea, threatened to boil out of the stands and engulf the band, GAC's roadman, the small but aggressive Ed Leffler, would come out onstage and beg for calm.

In New Orleans his appeal came too late.

Over 700 kids stormed the field and fought a pitched battle with 152 cops and 75 Pinkerton men. One girl vaulted the last barrier, like a salmon bucking up a falls, to land sobbing at George Harrison's feet. Finally, a posse of mounted policemen succeeded in lassoing and corralling the maverick fans, but not until the cops had overturned a whole row of crippled girls who were attending the concert in wheelchairs. The band played straight through the riot, with the myopic Lennon peering down between numbers and calling out: "Who's winning now?" By the time the show concluded, the field was littered with casualties, bound prisoners, and badly rumpled police officers, busy now administering spirits of ammonia to the 150 southern belles who had fainted dead away.

The Beatles' escape was always the high point of their day. They would throw down their instruments and dash offstage into a special getaway car. In Toronto some joker let the air out of the tires on the Beatles' armored van. They were transferred quickly to an ambulance full of drunks. As the driver took off with siren screaming, he ran smack into a stanchion. The Beatles were finally rescued by a concerned citizen. At Atlantic City the boys had to clamber down the side of the pier atop which stood the Convention Hall to bound across a raft and up the side of a hospital ship that was their refuge. Never in America, however, did they come as close to serious injury as they did in New Zealand, where the fans came crashing down atop the limousine, nearly crushing the Beatles like sardines in a can.

Getting the Beatles laid without provoking a scandal was a delicate task in the United States, where even a star of the caliber of Chuck Berry had been sent to prison for violating the Mann Act. The customary arrangement was a "party" at which the Beatles would meet either prostitutes, show-biz girls or celebrities, the three types of women adjudged best for the purpose. After a little socializing, each Beatle would pick the two or three girls that struck his fancy and retire to his room. The system worked perfectly during the three years the Beatles toured America, with the sole exception of a night in Minneapolis in 1965. Here the Beatles' procurers packed a motel with female fans, two of whom screwed everybody in sight in order to get to the Fab Four. When the girls awoke the next morning, they ran naked into the lobby, screaming, "Rape!" The police arrived and started flushing all the unregistered girls out of the group's quarters. When they tried to enter Paul McCartney's room, he refused to remove the chain across the door. Threatened with arrest, he backed down and gave up the young blonde with whom he had spent the night. Ed Leffler cooled the beef but not before a police inspector told the press, "Those people are the worst I have ever seen visit the city." The girl who emerged from Paul's room produced an ID that established her age as twenty-one. The inspector told the reporters: "I doubt she is older than sixteen." Some of the girls rounded up for the Beatles' delectation *were* jailbait.

The fourteen-year-old Geraldine Smith, who later became one of Andy Warhol's movie actresses, recalled being picked up on Mac-Dougal Street nine days before the incident at Minneapolis by a spectacular-looking blonde, Francesca Overman, who was Bill Wyman's (of the Rolling Stones) girl in New York. Geraldine, only fourteen, was distrustful when asked, "How would you like to meet the Beatles?" A spunky girl, she decided to brave the challenge. Soon she found herself inside a car with several other girls and a New York *Post* reporter, Al Aronowitz, heading for the Warwick Hotel, where Geraldine found herself next amidst the Beatles. They were tucking into a dinner of steak and baked potatoes, stoned obviously, because John was buttering his spud with his fingers. Afterward they played spin the bottle. When the boys retired to their rooms, somebody asked Geraldine whether she'd prefer to spend the night with Paul or John. She claimed she was a virgin, and the next thing she knew, she was waking up in the dawn's early light covered with Old Glory. If Geraldine had said yes instead of no, John Lennon might have found himself that morning looking at a charge of statutory rape.

Despite the distress of touring, the Beatles did enjoy some unforgettable experiences that first summer in America. The most awesome moment was their arrival at dusk in a helicopter over the Forest Hills Tennis Stadium. As the ship descended, the whole arena began crepitating with thousands of camera flashes, like a giant bowl of lightning bugs. "They're just like the gods!" gushed Brian Epstein to his companion, Geoffrey Ellis. "Tomorrow they could descend in Peru or India!" Brian was getting the picture for once, but he wasn't doing anything about making the picture. The Beatles should have been tracked throughout their legendary first tour by a film crew that would have preserved the flavor of the event, just as *DOA* recorded unforgettably the Sex Pistols' shocking tour of America. One of the best scenes in *Beatles '64* would have occurred that very same night, when, after returning to the Delmonico for supper, the boys responded to a knock at the door and found themselves face-to-face with Bob Dylan.

Already a legend in America, Dylan was just beginning to get through to the Beatles, who had first asked for his records while playing at Paris. Lennon's initial reaction had been violently negative, as the American journalist Pete Hamill had discovered just a couple of months before the American tour, when he was taken to the Ad Lib by Al Aronowitz. Hamill recorded:

> John Lennon came in with Brian Epstein and sat down next to me. Aronowitz was telling them they had to listen to Dylan, and McCartney was nodding, agreeing with Aronowitz, while Mick Jagger got up to dance with a young blonde wearing too much makeup. "To hell with Dylan," Lennon said. "We play rock 'n' roll." "No, John, listen to him," Aronowitz said. "He's rock 'n' roll, too. He's where rock 'n' roll's gonna go. Listen."
> Lennon's mouth became a tight slit. "Dylan. Dylan. Give me Chuck Berry. Give me Little Richard. Don't give me fancy crap. Crap. American folky intellectual crap. It's crap." He was snarling and bitter and hard. He didn't want to talk about music. He didn't want to talk about writing. He looked down the table at Keith Richard. "What the hell are the Yanks here for?" he said. Richard smiled and shrugged. McCartney reached over and touched John's hand. "Ach, come off it, John," he said. Lennon pulled his hand away and turned to me. "Why don't you fuck off?" he said. "Why don't you just get the hell out of here?" "Why don't you make me?" I said. "Hey, come on," Aronowitz said. "Let's just have a good time." "What?" Lennon said to me. "I said you should try to make me get out of here." He stared at

me and I stared back. [Hamill is a stocky ex-boxer.] The Irish of Liverpool challenging the Irish of Brooklyn. Then, as if he had seen something he recognized, he smiled and broke the stare and peered into the bottom of his glass. "Yeah, yeah, yeah," he said quietly, and the moment of confrontation passed. John Lennon left with Brian Epstein.

Now John saw Dylan standing before him, looking just as lorn and waifish as on the cover of his first album. As Lennon sat staring fixedly at the man he recognized instinctively as his greatest rival, Brian inquired graciously what the great singing poet would like to drink. "Cheap wine!" rasped Dylan. When the Beatles offered the yellow Dexies the band took in America instead of their customary white Prellies, Dylan grimaced with disgust and suggested that they smoke some pot. The Beatles confessed that they had never "had" marijuana. (Hashish was easier to get in England than grass.) Dylan was astonished. "What about your song?" he demanded. "The one about getting high?"

Mystified, John asked, "What song?" Dylan started singing "I Want to Hold Your Hand," jumping in just before the famous octave leap, which he rendered: "I get high! I get high! I get *high!*"

"Those aren't the words!" exclaimed John, like Oliver Hardy correcting Stan Laurel. Then he enunciated the correct wording, which was Dylan's cue to be amazed because whoever heard of a guy *hiding* from a girl who turned him on?

Having straightened out the lyrics, the party plugged the cracks under the doors with wet towels, while tootin', tokin' Bob rolled up a bomber. When Dylan handed the fuming joint to Lennon, he passed it directly to Ringo, whom he dubbed "My royal taster." Ringo smoked the joint down to the butt, then went off in a laughing jag. From that night on the Beatles were vipers—the kind who smoke a joint when they roll out of bed at the start of day.

As the tour drove on through the dog days, the Lockheed turbojet, plying back and forth from the Canadian North to the American South, with lots of stops in the Midwest, the atmosphere in the Beatles' detention suites began to turn sour and rancorous. What John Lennon resented most were the pushy, well-connected matrons who would gain admission to the boys' hotel rooms before they could get their heads up, dragging along their metal-mouthed daughters. One day at Las Vegas a girl was admitted to the Beatles' suite and introduced as the daughter of Donald O'Connor. John looked at her intently and said: "Hey, I'm really sorry!"

Half-smiling, the girl replied: "Sorry? What's there to be sorry about?"

Earnestly John answered: "Just heard it on the radio—your dad's dead!" The teenager screamed in horror and then went into hysterics. She had to be sedated and removed from the hotel in an ambulance. Sneered Lennon: "Soft cow!"

That same day John satisfied a deep longing by slipping out of the Sands disguised in a doorman's coat and riding in the back of a caterer's van to the Desert Inn, where he stood beside the highway and stared up at the blacked-out top floor, the residence of Howard Hughes. "That's it!" announced Irving Kandell, the Beatles' program seller, pointing to the heavily curtained penthouse.

As John squinted up the side of the building past all the lighted rooms to the one floor that was dark, he exclaimed: "That would suit me fine! In one place forever instead of this constant traveling. Total privacy. Nobody to bother you."

The tour ended on 20 September with the Beatles making an appearance at the Paramount Theater in New York on behalf of the Cerebral Palsy Fund, an unheard-of act of charity for them since they made it a principle never to give anything away. By this time Lennon's rage against the American public and press had focused to a laserbeam intensity. The Beatles' PR man, Derek Taylor, drew a telling picture of the scene at the Delmonico Hotel after a typically insomniac night, with the sycophants of the press corps sitting around stoned and Murray the K lying half-crocked on a cot—one filmy eye open, the other closed—as John Lennon poured contempt upon the whole retinue and, by extension, on Beatlemania.

FAT ELVIS

By the year 1965 the Beatles had reached an awesome state of grace. In the eyes of the public they could do no wrong. Yet in John Lennon's eyes virtually nothing the band did was right. He was in despair because instead of being able to express himself freely, as he had done in the old days, he was ever more committed to doing whatever the public expected of him. This predicament became acute during the filming of *Help!* The Beatles were manipulated like puppets in this incomprehensible farce and also obliged to concoct a sound track full of corny country and western tunes that Lennon regarded as the nadir of their recording career. "We weren't in control of the movie," he reflected bitterly, "and we weren't in control of the music, either." So John had cried "Help!"—and he wasn't kidding.

What alarmed Lennon most was not the Beatles' loss of control but his panicky sense of having lost control of himself. He had donned the mask of Beatle John in a larky spirit, intent on doing whatever was needed to achieve success. Now he found that he couldn't take the mask off. It dictated how everybody perceived him and consequently how he had to behave. He feared he had lost the capacity to behave in any other way. He had become Beatle John!

All the rest of his life Lennon singled out this time as the worst moment of his career. It was his "fat Elvis" period, the time when he exhibited the full face of a Japanese woodcut and a potbelly that began to protrude through the skimpy cut of his Cardin suits. The actual cause of this unseemly flesh was simply John's diet: toasted cheese and bacon sandwiches at wake-up followed by steak and fries at fallout, washed down by a steady stream of scotch and Cokes. But John regarded the loss of his looks as symbolic of many other losses. "Lost" is the key word in all his descriptions of his plight. He had lost his way, lost his pride, lost his satisfaction, and, above all, lost his soul. Hence, it wasn't just his looks but his whole condition that was reminiscent of the fallen Elvis. Like his old hero, John Lennon was a once-brilliant, rebellious, virile young rocker whom success had puffed up into a fat clown.

The outline of Lennon's spiritual crisis in the year 1965 can be traced in the autobiographical songs he began composing at this time. "I'm a Loser" discloses the crucial fact that Beatle John is not a real person but a jovial mask assumed by a man naturally angry or morose. "Help!" draws the contrast between how easy life was when John was on the make and how bewilderingly difficult it has become now that he is a star. "Nowhere Man," the last and most important of these laments over the failure of success, is one of his most profound and poignant self-images, a song of self-pity.

The whole world listened to these songs, but nobody hearkened to them. The idea of John Lennon—the greatest winner in the pop sweepstakes—as a "loser" was simply unthinkable. Likewise, it was impossible to believe that he was actually calling out for "help" or that he was "nowhere." So the failure of the fans to listen to the Beatles at their concerts was paralleled now by the failure of even the most discerning listeners to grasp the obvious meaning of Lennon's most explicit lyrics. This failure in communication is not surprising because it was part of the whole process by which the public adopted the Beatles as its very special heroes.

Though it is customary to talk about what the Beatles contributed to contemporary consciousness, the truth is that the public imposed its fancies on the Beatles far more successfully than they could ever impart anything to the world. This is the ironic fate of all pop stars. Not so much a communicator or creator as a trigger or target for mass hysteria, a pop star finds his greatest gift is his ability to arouse the collective unconscious, but once he releases this mighty torrent of mental and emotional energy, he is seized and controlled by it so completely that he comes to feel like its slave. The old stars were content to accept their fates, leading lives of mysterious seclusion that left their images spotless, blank screens inviting the projections of the mass mind. The modern star, younger, less disciplined, more self-involved, has often rebelled against the tyranny of his image, behaving in ways that contradict his perceived identity. What the history of the Beatles proved was the futility of such rebellion. No matter what John Lennon did—and he violated every taboo of stardom—he could never shake his image.

John was the first to recognize this distressing fact. He delighted in demonstrating it like a psychologist in a laboratory. If he were out in public with a friend like Pete Shotton and ran into some middle-class, middle-aged matron, who started screaming, "Beatle John!" Lennon would turn to Pete and say: "Watch this!" Then he would gaze scornfully at the woman and sneer: "You stupid old cow! Aren't you ashamed of yourself! At your age! Carrying on in the road in this way! What the *fuck* is the matter with you?" None of those ladies ever heard a word he said.

Another reason John Lennon suffered such a sharp crisis immediately after his great triumph was that he was so ill prepared for success. Unlike the old-time entertainer, who spent half his life climbing laboriously to the top of his profession, getting wiser and tougher at every rung, John Lennon had his most intense experience of fame when he was just beyond college age. What's more, he first experienced success in the classic manner of modern pop stars in a sudden, stunning burst of acclamation, awaking one morning to find himself famous. Like most men who hurl themselves at a goal, sacrificing everything to its attainment, Lennon had never given a thought to what he would do if he reached the "toppermost of the poppermost." Naïvely he had assumed that the payoff would be total fulfillment. Imagine his shock when one day he suddenly found himself standing on the peak, gazing at the promised land. He took one squint and recognized with that quick mind of his that the view wasn't worth the climb. Prone to instant despair, he went straight into a tailspin. At that moment he established the pattern of his entire subsequent life—from infatuation to disillusionment.

Ironically, it was right in the middle of Lennon's "fat Elvis" period that he came face-to-face with Elvis. The Beatles had been looking forward to this encounter since their first arrival in the USA. When the famous telegram was read out to them on the eve of the Sullivan show, they were disappointed that it did not include an invitation to Graceland. "But where's Elvis?" cried John. That line became a running gag among the Beatles during the following year, as they clocked all the times that ol' E eluded their embrace. Colonel Parker, however, was just as intent on having his boy meet Brian Epstein's boys as Elvis was on avoiding this humiliating confrontation. The Colonel hungered for the publicity of a rock summit because he was desperate to hype Elvis's dying career. Without a big hit in years, Elvis was losing now even his B-movie audience. He had just completed his latest "travelogue," *Paradise Hawaiian Style,* when he found himself eyeball to eyeball with the Beatles on the night of 27 August 1965.

As the Fab Four pulled into the parking space in front of Elvis's doughnut-shaped pillbox on Perugia Road, overlooking the fairways of the Bel Air Golf Club, they were surprised to see a crowd of fans being held at bay by the local cops. Who could have leaked the news of this top secret sit-down? Entering the countersunk pad, shaped like a sheikh's tent, they were saluted by the sounds of their latest hits alternating with Elvis's latest misses. The King was holding court, as usual, in his Jukebox Room.

"Oh, there you are!" exclaimed John, with mock casualness, as he approached the Great I-Ham.

Elvis, ensconced on a long sofa amid the chorus line of the Memphis Beef Trust, was wearing his Hollywood regimentals: red shirt, black windbreaker, and skintight gray trousers. Formal introductions were made all around by the beaming triple-chinned Colonel. Then everyone sat down. Instinctively the Beatles assumed the positions of a backup band: John and Paul on E's right, and, on his left, George and Ringo. As the Seabury Salute to the Sons of Memphis and Liverpool continued at high gain, nobody said a word. Elvis, sullen in the presence of those "sons o' bitches" who had toppled him from his throne with their faggy haircuts and Tinkertoy tunes, was not about to make the first move. The Beatles, for their part, felt that youth should defer to age. Finally, the Dream King could take it no more. "If you damn guys are gonna sit here and stare at me all night," he blustered, "I'm gonna go to bed!"

That broke the ice, but now the party sank into the chill waters of disillusionment, for no sooner did John get into conversation with his old hero than he made a terrible gaffe. He said that Elvis should cut some records like his original sides on Sun. To Elvis that suggestion implied that in the Beatles' eyes his career had progressed from its stunning beginning straight downhill! John, from his end, got the impression that Elvis was not just stoned but completely out to lunch.

When the attempt to raise the dead failed, the Beatles bopped back inside their limo. As the car pulled away, John turned to look at the other boys. With a droll expression on his face and his voice gliding up the scale like a water beetle, he demanded: "Where's Elvis?"

John Lennon's escape from Beatlemania was achieved finally through the aid of an unlikely accomplice. The next song John recorded after "Help!" was an obvious knockoff of Bob Dylan titled, "You've Got to Hide Your Love A-way." Embarrassing in its blatant mimicry and lacking all the virtues of its model, this disc provides at least a good clue to what was going on in Lennon's head. Having overcome his initial antagonism toward Dylan, Lennon had swung around onto the opposite tack. Enthralled by the records of his rival, he listened to them night and day. Little Bob now impressed John as a guy who was getting away with murder. Instead of suiting up and serenading the teenyboppers with a pretty vocal style pinked out with "Ooohs!" "Ahs!" and "SSSighs!," this little "Jewboy" wore what he pleased, wrote the most outrageous stuff, and lit into girls in his songs just the way Lennon lashed out at the stupid "cows" in private. Instead of caroling "I Want to Hold Your Hand," Dylan wouldn't have hesitated to rasp "I Wanna Burn Your Hand." Dylan hadn't made it as big as the Beatles, but then, he didn't have to share his fame—or fortune!—with three other guys. So John began thinking that there was a way out of the dilemma of Beatlemania—and little Bobby Zimmerman was the guide.

The first fruits of Lennon's new phase were the songs he wrote for *Rubber Soul,* one of the great growth rings on the trunk of the Beatles. The Boys from Liverpool had always perceived the U.S. pop scene as a board game with brightly colored pieces which they pushed around playfully and confidently the way outsiders—who don't give a fuck because it's all in their heads, not in their guts—can do with another culture's counters. Now the Beatles took the next logical step in their evolution and started writing sustained parodies of this easily mastered, totally predictable music. They kicked off with the currently popular Tamla/Motown sound, which had the double advantage of bringing them back to their starting point in rhythm and blues without putting them up against anything heavier than Berry Gordy's second-generation assembly-line blacks. John Lennon's take on the Dee-troit Sound is found in the two opening tracks, where, like a pop James Joyce, he runs rings around the current American style by inventing a startling new genre—the role-reversed love song.

"(Baby, You Can) Drive My Car" sounds at first like a caricature of Elvis: the priapic hero addressing the groveling groupie. Then you snap to the fact that the speaker is not John Lennon or even a *man* but a hard-boiled, wise-assed American chick, who lays her rap on our hero by talking all on one note (a favorite Lennon stunt), while a hip-shakin', gum-chewin' cowbell (off Marvin Gaye's "Hitch Hike") marks the finger-poppin' time. This broad has an ego as big as Elvis and a line as brassy as the Colonel's. She wants to be in pitchas—natch! A star—no less! When the boy talks about making a living, she blows the idea away but offers him the chance of a lifetime—as her driver. Purely as an afterthought, using the offhand delivery of a girl touching up her hair in the mirror, she throws in the suggestion that *maybe* she'll love him.

With the boy-girl roles totally inverted and the supreme goal of romantic fulfillment reduced to a casual aside, signifying its wholly incidental, utterly insignificant character compared with the narcissistic bliss of being a movie star, the song has reached a level of cynicism that in a Brecht/Weill number would signal the impending downfall of the West. For John Lennon, the prophet of the Sixties, the reversals of convention are as exhilarating and giddy as they would be in a song by Noel Coward. Lennon isn't threatened or appalled by the Modern Woman; he gets off on her brassy self-infatuation with undisguised delight, rounding off each of her raps with a scroll of bluesy melisma that gives her the panache of a soul mama. The kicker comes in the form of a surprise ending.

The girl confesses finally that she really doesn't have a car. Her whole rap has been a *line!* (How typically male.) Now that she has a driver, what difference does a car make? At this moment the Beatles, who have been highlighting the vocal line with harmonies that sound like horns riffing, suddenly transform their vocal instruments into auto horns and drive off like characters in an animated cartoon, going "Beep-beep!"

An even more sophisticated take on the Modern Woman is that embodied in "Norwegian Wood," one of those utterly original songs that only John Lennon could have conceived. For while the would-be sophisticates of British pops, shallow souls like Brian Jones and Mick Jagger, were playing naughty-boy games with the record company censors—the same adolescent game that goes on to this day with wearying predictability—Lennon was employing the new medium of pop song like a serious artist, using it as a lens through which to scrutinize quietly and accurately the character of the strange new life he was experiencing in Swinging London. Always a young man disposed to play hard-to-get with aggressive females, he found during his nights on the town that when he took a girl home, the action was liable to be very different from anything he had known in provincial and old-fashioned Liverpool. Just as "Drive My Car" is his take on the astonishingly brash and self-infatuated women he found in Los Angeles, so "Norwegian Wood" was his rendering of the liberated women he met in the offices and discos of the new London.

"Norwegian Wood" was, as the English knew and the Americans did not, a currently fashionable decorator's phrase, like "Danish Modern," that designated a trendy new style in home furnishing, typified by the use of natural-finished pine. In Lennon's unvarnished tale of Swinging London, girl meets boy and takes him home to her flat, decorated in Norwegian Wood, but so sparsely furnished that she bids him sit on the floor as she plies him with wine and makes all the moves in the mating game traditionally made by males. Finally, when the hour grows late, she announces nonchalantly that it's time for bed. At this point an unfortunate artifice had to be employed to prevent Cynthia from discovering that John was having such an affair and to placate Sir Joseph Lockwood, the stuffy old boss of EMI, who would never have permitted an explicit reference to coitus in a record designed for children. So instead of climbing into the piny bed, the boy spends the night in the bathroom. The climax of the song was not impaired, however: instead of the girl awaking to find her lover gone, it's the boy who awakes to find the girl gone—to work. This leaves him free to build a fire and reflect on how good is Norwegian Wood—which is to say, how much

better it is to be alive in a world where women are free and independent than in that old world, symbolized by the archaic melody, where
women were the responsibility of men.

When John Lennon finished recording "Norwegian Wood," he was
no longer Beatle John, the Man in the Bubble Gum Mask. He was now
the brilliant young innovator who was doing more than anybody in the
music business to transform the rock 'n' roll of the Fifties into the rock
of the Sixties. By adopting the sophisticated technique of song parody,
John broke completely with rock tradition and moved off toward the
urbane and witty style of Noel Coward, eventually one of his heroes.

The split vision of parody, which cherishes and derides its target in
the same breath, had always been characteristic of Lennon's divided
and ambivalent mind. Actually, he had been writing parodies since he
was a schoolboy. His eccentric collections of prose pieces, *In His Own
Write* (1964) and *Spaniard in the Works* (1965), are nothing but sendups
of nursery tales and newspaper stories that John twists into sick jokes
by encoding them in a continuous stream of discombobulating puns.
Spurred on now by the journalist Kenneth Alcott, who asked Lennon
why he didn't employ the same gifts for language in his songs, John
began to bridge the gap between his pop songsmith and his art school
selves. Paradoxically, by viewing his themes on a split screen and writing in double talk, John Lennon really got himself together.

His progress was matched by that of the band—and for many of the
same reasons. For the essence not just of the Beatles but of the Stones
and the Who and most of the great English rock groups was parody.
Excluded by birth from that nearly neurological sense of American
culture that they would have required to make authentic rock 'n' roll or
rhythm and blues, the British capitalized on their imaginative sense of
the music they loved. They selected the salient traits of their models
and discarded everything else, exaggerating and coloring the most
prized features. Ironically, the more a band like the Beatles caricatured
black American music—now entering its soul phase—the more they
captured the authentic traits of this music, which had largely eluded
them back at the beginning of their career, when they were blatant
mimics. Significantly, the only moment in all the Beatles' recordings
when they succeed in conveying the natural warmth and groovy elas-
ticity of genuine black dance music is the A-side of *Rubber Soul*.

Peter Brown claimed that the secret of the Beatles' newly found sen-
suousness was their 'round-the-clock consumption of marijuana, the re-
laxing and euphoric effects of good grass being the perfect antidote for
the kind of high-strung, short-winded jump band jitters that had afflicted the Beatles hitherto. But there were other factors responsible
for the way the boys now got their mojo working, the most important
being the remarkable musical maturation of the twenty-four-year-old

Paul McCartney, who had always exhibited the strongest sense of the parent style and who now offered a take on black bass posturing that is one of the very few occasions in the history of English rock when the boys from Britain showed themselves a match for the boys from black America. In the greatest feat of instrumental playing on any Beatles' track, Paul fused his sense of black machismo with his British sense of courtly pomp and politesse to produce that great basso-bombastico strut on George Harrison's "Think for Yourself."

When *Rubber Soul* was released in December 1965, it won the Beatles a whole new audience. Mature listeners in America, who had hitherto dismissed the group as just another teeny-pop sensation, suddenly pricked up their ears. They recognized the fresh breeze from the Merseyside. For those who had followed the Beatles' career closely, the pleasure afforded by their latest album was heightened greatly by the recognition that the group was boldly progressing, unconstrained by the market forces that oblige most pop stars to go 'round and 'round in the grooves of their first success. Building on the solid foundation provided by their previous achievements—their mastery of American pops, their extensive experience as songwriters, and their growing skill as singers, instrumentalists, and record makers—the Beatles were now beginning to erect that glittering edifice, the Sixties.

THE DOMESTIC BEATLE

The setting of John Lennon's private life during his heyday as a Beatle was Kenwood, a big mock-Tudor house in the Stockbroker Belt, an hour south of London. John's "Hansel and Gretel house" was an odd habitation for a man who despised the pretensions of the upper classes and declared himself a foe of everything "normal." Perched atop a leafy knoll in the posh St. George's Hill Estates—where everybody who counts belongs to the country club and plays a round of golf on Saturday—Kenwood was rife with unpleasant associations with John's youth in Allerton. Just two years after he bought the place for £20,000 and spent another £40,000 renovating it and installing a heated swimming pool, he told the press: "Weybridge [the nearest village] won't do at all. I'm just stopping at it, like a bus stop. . . . I'll get my *real* house when I know what I want." Why, then, had he bought such a place? The answer is that he had followed the advice of his foolish financial advisers, who told him that a big house would gain him a tax advantage and then pointed him in the direction of Sussex.

At the moment of purchase, in July 1964, the Beatles were poised to depart for America on their first tour. It was at the lavish, Belgravia-style blowout Brian gave to celebrate this festive occasion that John took the initial step toward entombing himself in his pyramid. Marveling at the way the roof of Brian's apartment building (Whaddon House, 15 Williams Mews) had been transformed into a beautiful tent house, illuminated with French windows and furnished with tables bedecked with dazzling white linen, silver candelabra, and masses of red carnations, John eased up to Brian's decorator, Ken Partridge, and said in that oddly gliding Boris Karloff voice he employed when being ingratiating: "Did you do all this? Are you Ken Partridge? Could you do a house? Do you do houses?" Before Partridge could reply, John explained: "We've just bought a house. [Turning to Cynthia] Where is it?"

Cynthia replied dimly: "I think it's in Sunbury."

With no more to go on than the knowledge that the house had

twenty-seven little rooms, Partridge went back to his studio in Soho that night and did color renderings of eighteen rooms. Next morning he showed them to John and Cynthia just before they left for the airport. After a quick, appreciative glance at the renderings, John commissioned a total renovation. The upshot was that for the next nine months the family was condemned to live in the dark and dingy attic while their house was torn to pieces and filled with unending noise and dirt and the unwelcome presence of workmen.

Partridge, left entirely to his own devices, designed Kenwood to conform with his notions of how a splendid young pop star should live. Thus, the totally unsociable Lennon was given a lot of reception rooms meant for constant partying, and the man who was lacerating himself for being the "fat Beatle" was provided with a kitchen and dining room fit for a gourmet. Above all, the house was styled according to its decorator's idea of good taste, which meant the taste of a middle-aged bachelor whose most enthusiastic client was Brian Epstein.

John Lennon's only means of assimilating Kenwood was to go through the house like a baffled bird depositing in every room some bit of its nest. In the dark, wood-paneled entrance hall, stacked from floor to ceiling with a job lot of books that John never read, Lennon installed a suit of chased armor crowned with a gorilla's head clenching in its jaws an inverted pipe. (The head was part of a gorilla suit that John said was better than an overcoat because it kept your legs warm.) The lounge was sumptuously appointed with an Oriental rug laid atop the black wall-to-wall carpeting and three lovely sofas disposed so that everyone's eye fell on a costly Oriental screen. John's contribution was a long, crate-shaped credenza housing a powerful sound system (used to play records at inner-city volume) and an early-model color TV that he planted in the fireplace because, he explained, watching the tube (particularly as he did, with the sound off) was the latter-day equivalent of seeing pictures in the hearth flames.

What John couldn't alter, he was glad to give away. The dining room had been papered with mauve felt and hung with illustrations from a rare volume of eighteenth-century French vegetable paintings framed in silver-streaked red lead. When somebody admired these pictures, John snapped: "Take them! They're just a load of shit!" (They were worth thousands of pounds.) The kitchen was Cynthia's province, but it was completely beyond her. Inspired by the Beverly Hills look, it was so modern that it didn't have a stove, that appliance having been supplanted by burners planted flush in a tile counter. When Cynthia confronted the installation, she confessed that she couldn't figure out how to operate the equipment. A man had to be sent out from the city to show her how to press the buttons and twirl the dials. Actually, there was nothing to do with it because the Lennons never entertained and the family ate the simplest foods, John soon becoming a vegetarian.

So swamped by Kenwood were John and Cynthia that they took to living there like the butler and the maid when the family is away: occupying one room at the back of the house and ignoring all the rest. Just a few steps beyond the kitchen was a glassed-in extension that overlooked a steeply terraced garden. John, a sun lover, made this bright, cozy spot his abode, hanging its walls and strewing its cabinets with all his Beatles souvenirs and foreign bric-a-brac. The most important item of furniture, apart from his mother's cottage piano, was a wicker-backed Queen Anne sofa, too small for him to lie upon, where John lay all day, his head propped up on pillows and his feet sticking out the other end. As a comfortable fire glowed in the coal grate and his cat, Mimi, curled up beside him in her plaid kitty lair, John drifted back to childhood. As if to make his condition perfectly clear, he pasted a couple of stickers on the nursery-white cabinets behind his head. They pictured an infant's tender skull over the legend SAFE AS MILK.

By the time the Beatles came in off the road in September 1965, they were in full revolt against touring, which they had come to loathe from the bottom of their stomachs. After one of the hardest-fought campaigns in the history of show business, all the Beatles but John experienced this break as a time of rest and relaxation, a blessed release from their punishing careers. But for Lennon, the end of touring meant total collapse. No sooner did he step off the rock 'n' rollercoaster than he lapsed into a zombie-like state in which he rarely opened his mouth or even remained for long awake.

Not till three in the afternoon would he rise from his eight-foot-square bed. Then he would pad downstairs and go into the kitchen, where the housekeeper would prepare his breakfast, which consisted of those sugar-coated cereals manufactured in America for small children. Grunting and smacking his lips with satisfaction, he behaved with the unselfconsciousness of a hermit in his cell. After breakfast John would take a few mincing steps in his stocking feet into the neighboring sun-room, where he would recline on his sofa, sometimes reading the papers or glancing through the trade mags but more often spending the afternoon gazing like a cat at the telly with the sound turned off, until he nodded out again.

John's craving for somnolence testifies to the terrible depletion of his vital energies wrought by years of rockin' 'round the clock, going for days without sleeping, driven by Prellies and Dexies, travel jitters and stage fright, to say nothing of the long-term effects of chronic rage, paranoia, and nightly hotel-room orgies. Now that he was SAFE AS

MILK, John Lennon became Yawn Lennon. He succumbed to the irresistible longing to soak his poor, parched brain in restorative REM sleep.

John wrote a fascinating song about his slumberous life, "I'm Only Sleeping," a lugubrious strain, reminiscent of the songs of the Great Depression, with a melody that stretches like a cat up and down the aeolian scale in the distant key of E-flat minor. Suggesting a dusky, sensuous, and achingly blissful state of being that owes as much to the effects of inhalation (of potent grass) as it does to exhaustion, the song is as loath to move as was its author, whom it also mimics by breaking off abruptly from time to time, as if the song, like its singer, had suddenly lost consciousness.

As Lennon's Great Lethargy lengthened from weeks into months, inspiring Maureen Cleave to characterize John as the "laziest person in England"—a man so out of it that his first reaction to her call was to ask, like the besotted Falstaff, "What day is it?"—it gradually became clear that his torpor was not simply a case of battle fatigue. John was suffering from boredom and depression. Unlike the other Beatles, who had interests apart from their work, Lennon had none, except for hanging out with Ringo and George, who lived nearby.

When John had moved to the St. George's Hill Estates, Ringo had trailed after him, taking a house at the foot of the hill on which Kenwood stood, where he resided with his wife, Maureen, a Liverpool hairdresser's assistant, and their infant son, Zac. Ringo had delved deep into his backyard to make a sunken garden and added to his mock-Tudor residence a workingman's second home, a snug pub called the Flying Cow, complete to the smallest detail. George resided nearby in Esher, with his girlfriend, Patti Boyd, a young model, in a white bungalow furnished in the clean modern style of Habitat. The oddest living arrangement was the one adopted by Paul, who refused to follow the leader to the Stockbroker Belt. After taking up with a carrot-haired teenage actress, Jane Asher (daughter of a Harley Street psychiatrist and a stage mother who taught woodwind instruments), Paul had moved into a garret room in the Asher home on Wimpole Street. Barry Miles, Paul's best mate, described the star's room as "small and plain with a single window, a large brown wardrobe and a single bed, which occupied most of the floor space. A wall shelf held a couple of Jean Cocteau drawings from the *Opium* series, one in a cracked frame; a volume of Alfred Jarry; and some guitar picks. Under the bed with the chamber pot were a pile of gold records and a presentation MBE [Member of the Order of the British Empire]. An electric bass was propped in the corner, and stenciled on the case in white letters: BEATLES. No room even for records. The few that he had were kept outside on the landing in a rack on top of a chest of drawers next to the amateurly wired bell system that announced whom an incoming call was for. There would [be] three rings for Peter [Jane's brother, a member of the pop duo Peter and Gordon], four for Paul." The influence of the Ashers—a lively middle-class family with a fund of general knowledge and a keen interest in the arts—on Paul and hence on the Beatles was enormously important. It was principally from the Ashers that Paul imbibed that awareness of classic and avant-garde music that led the Beatles to move away from pop rock and launch themselves on the rising tide of art rock.

While Paul was sucking up culture from the London theater and cinema, as well as the art galleries and concert halls, the only things that engaged John, even casually, were expensive toys and the same boys who had shared his childhood at Mendips. In a burst of unparalleled generosity to someone not a member of his family, Lennon bought for Pete Shotton a half interest in a little supermarket on Hayling Island, an hour distant from Weybridge. In return, he demanded that Pete leave his family every weekend and spend a couple of days with John. The drill was: Get stoned in the afternoon in the red and black study (furnished with a world globe that opened up into a full bar), where the boys could shut out Julian and the women. Then, after everyone had gone to bed, they would play all night with John's toys, which included a vast assortment of board games and a lavish layout of electrically powered model cars occupying two rooms in the attic. John sought to heighten the racetrack atmosphere by installing speakers that blared out the roar of accelerating engines, the squealing of tires, and occasionally the explosive sounds of a deadly crash.

After Lennon got his beginner's permit in 1965, the boys would occasionally go out racing real sports cars, like John's mat-black Ferrari, whose plates were blazoned LEARNER. John drove like a kid in a bumpmobile: he trod the gas pedal and turned the wheel; but braking was no fun, and he never learned to shift. This meant that after a good run his cars often needed a new gearbox. What he really craved were the thrills of collision, but he was able to savor this dangerous pleasure only once. When the Beatles were shooting *Help!* in the Bahamas, they took four Cadillacs down into an abandoned quarry, where they roared around sideswiping and ramming each other until the cars were all wrecks—Quarry Men's wrecks.

Usually John left the driving to his huge chauffeur, Les Anthony, a former Welsh Guardsman, chosen as much for his value as a bodyguard as for his driving. Les stayed with John for seven years because Lennon had learned from his first experience with drivers how hard it was to come by a good man. When he and Cynthia had settled at Weybridge, neither of them could drive, so their first concern was getting a car and a chauffeur. John had bought a secondhand maroon and black Rolls-Royce and hired the first man to apply, without asking for references. The driver, seeing that he was dealing with a couple of greenhorns, asked for permission to use the car when off duty. Then he camped out in the machine like a Gypsy in his wagon. If a neighbor hadn't tipped John off, he would have gone on forever complaining about the odor of stale beer and cigarettes that assailed his nostrils every time he got inside his limo, to say nothing of the dubious stains on the upholstery!

The next driver brought along a wife who served as cook. Sizing up how matters stood between the master and his missus, this couple (who soon invited their divorced daughter to move in) would serve John flawlessly, but then, the moment he went off on tour, they would shove TV dinners at Cynthia and Julian, while the servants ate and drank of the best.

Cyn was fortunate in finding at last an ideal housekeeper in Dot Jarlett, a local woman with a need to be needed. Dot started off minding Julian for ten pounds a week and gradually took on the cleaning, the cooking, the fan mail, in fine the whole management of the house and the upbringing of the child—for the same ten pounds!

Cynthia had asked that her mother be allowed to join her in her lonely retreat among the stockbrokers. So from the first Mrs. Powell was a member of the household. "Lowl," as John called her, mimicking the Liverpool working-class pronunciation of Lil (he could never bring himself to call her Mum), was a squat, powerfully built woman of lower-class origin, who exemplified bulldog aggressiveness. Though she served John's turn by relieving him of any responsibility to pay attention to his wife, Mrs. Powell introduced into the domestic drama the unwelcome but inevitable character of the heavy matriarch, the natural enemy of the macho male. She regarded her famous son-in-law as an unregenerate Teddy Boy and wife beater, who lay about the house all day like a besotted lout. John returned the compliment. For years this pair eyed each warily. Nobody wanted to have a scene, so the animosity that John and Lil felt for each other was muted or it discharged itself through their common victim, Cynthia, whom these two would haul back and forth like snarling dogs with a rag in their teeth.

Unable to avow his feelings about his wife and mother-in-law directly, John had recourse to that coded language he first employed when he was a child prisoner at Mendips. "No Flies on Frank" (from *In My Own Write*) appears at first as obscure as "Jabberwocky," but once you have cracked its code, its meaning emerges with precisely the same caveman brutality as John's monstrous cartoons. The hero of the tale awakens one morn to make the dismaying discovery that he is "twelve inches more heavy." His distress is compounded of sexual frustration (the morning hard-on grown twice its normal size) and the dread of obesity (the "fat Beatle"). Descending to the kitchen, Frank confronts his wife, Marion ("the marryin' kind"), who contends it is no fault of hers that he suffers from his "vast burton" (lingua Franka for "bur-then" plus Richard Burton, the sex hero). Frank walks toward his wife, "where he took his head [i.e., skull cum penis] in his hands and with a few swift blows had clubbed her to the ground dead."

Now comes the most interesting part of the story, as Lennon imag-ines the consequences of Frank's attempt to free himself of his wife. After a couple of weeks the body begins to draw flies, which spoils Frank's appetite, even though there are no flies on Frank. So he puts the body in a sack and takes it to his wife's mother, where it belongs. This house-proud lady will have nothing to do with a daughter who draws flies. She slams the door in his face. The story concludes with Frank "lifting the problem back on his boulders," which is to say, his balls.

The other inhabitant of Kenwood, little Julian, was characterized by the women who cared for him as bright, friendly, intelligent, and highly assertive, even bossy. Wendy Hanson was delighted by Julian's Lennonesque way with language. Once when she gave her name on the phone, Julian responded: "Is that like 'windy in the trees'?" And then there was the time he brought home from Heath House Infants' School a watercolor of a blond girl with stars behind her and identified it as "Lucy in the sky." Cynthia never disciplined the boy, so he be-haved like a brat, telling his mother that she was "stupid" or shouting at her, "Shut up!" He was mimicking John, of course. When he was in his father's presence, however, Julian underwent a radical change.

John Lennon had a profound intolerance of children, being too much of a child himself to tolerate any rivals. When Julian would ap-proach his recumbent dad with a request, Lennon would glare at him balefully and growl: "I'm not gonna fix your fuckin' bike, Julian!" Wham! The child would shrink back in terrified silence. That silence, that frozen-faced fear, that shrinking became habitual to Julian when with his father. Ironically, his silent withdrawal was interpreted by John as a sign that there was something "wrong" with the boy. "He's a bit of a dope," John would tell Mimi, adding, "Like mother, like son," while tapping his finger against his forehead.

Cynthia observed John's cruel behavior to their son with her custom-ary resignation because the thing she appeared to fear most was an emotionally charged confrontation. Every day she would go antiques shopping with her mother or to her hairdresser in Bayswater. Often the ladies would have Les drive them up to Hoylake, where Mrs. Powell had kept her old house. Here they would visit with the neigh-bors, and Cyn would go on about her dazzling life in the big city as the wife of a superstar. As Dot Jarlett remarked, "Cynthia was show business, wasn't she?" So she would have liked to have appeared.

Unfortunately she could never gain the attention of her husband, who would go for days without addressing a single word to her. John's emotional withdrawal made him a master of the freeze-out. He wasn't totally out of it, however, because from time to time he would rouse himself and step out into the garden, where he would hail the gardener or the chauffeur or whoever was about, chatting him up and demonstrating how much goodwill he bore to everyone in the world— save his own family.

If John Lennon had not been so childishly dependent on women, he might have ended his marriage at this time. He hadn't wanted to marry Cynthia in the first place. By now he wanted to kill her. He had plenty of money to make provision for her and Julian. He also had the Beatles to fall back upon, as well as the whole world waiting to take him into its arms. So what was he waiting for? John himself couldn't answer that question, but he often asked it. As he told Maureen Cleave in an interview at Kenwood in March 1966, "There's something else I'm going to do, something I *must* do—only I don't know what it is." Trying to discover what that mysterious "it" might be sometimes made John frantic. One night he went into the bathroom and fell down on his knees, as he had been taught to pray as a child. "God, Jesus, or whoever the fuck you are!" he cried. "Will you please, just once, just *tell* me what the hell I'm supposed to be doing?"

FLIGHT TO THE WHITE
LIGHT

One evening in January or February 1966 John Lennon appeared at the Indica Bookshop and asked the manager, Miles, for copies of *The Psychedelic Experience* and *The Psychedelic Reader,* both volumes the work of that troika of renegade American academics: Timothy Leary, Ralph Metzner, and Richard Alpert. *The Psychedelic Experience,* a manual of acid tripping based on the posthumous journeys of the soul described in the *Tibetan Book of the Dead,* was the bible of the LSD cult. As explained in the novel *Groupie,* "the only proper way to trip is to follow Timothy Leary's book . . . and move from phase to phase [until] you reach the point where this White Light hits you with a blinding flash of self-realization." As John reported years later, "I got a message on acid that you should destroy your ego; and I did . . . I destroyed myself."

What Lennon meant by this alarming confession was clarified by another passage in the same interview in which he explained how he recovered his ego—*two years later!* "I started fighting again and being a loudmouth again, and saying, 'Well, I can do this and fuck you!'" In other words, the ego Lennon killed was that rebellious and hostile self that was already crumbling as he lay upon his sofa at Kenwood. What acid did was give that old John Lennon his deathblow, for though he did regain his former aggressiveness when he abandoned the drug, he was never again the same man.

That John Lennon should still have wanted to experiment with LSD in 1966 is remarkable in view of his previous experience with this drug, for if ever a man could say, "Once burnt, twice cautious," it was Lennon talking about acid. Back in 1964, he had tried LSD when the first samples were brought to Britain by Michael Hollingshead, the man who turned on Timothy Leary. Hailed by Leary after his first trip as an "agent for some higher consciousness," Hollingshead had quickly proven himself an irresponsible fool, whose greatest pleasure was to go about at social functions spiking everyone's drink. Appalled by his behavior, Leary decided that the only way to deal with this screwball was to return him to England. Furnishing the Acid Apostle with the two things most needful for his mission—a thousand copies of Leary's writings and a generous supply of Owsley blotter acid—the High Priest saw his quondam mentor off on the *Queen Elizabeth,* reflecting as he left the pier, "That writes off England so far as the psychedelic revolution is concerned for the next forty years!"

No sooner did Hollingshead arrive at London than he established a branch of his Castalia Foundation on Pons Street—and then ran about town, once again spiking everyone's drink. Before he could be locked up in Leyhill Prison (for possession of cannabis because LSD was not yet illegal), Hollingshead furnished Victor Lownes, the manager of the Playboy Club, with a quantity of acid. It was from this stock that the Beatles first partook of the Philosopher's Stone. The go-between was a cosmetic dentist, whose girlfriend was the supervisor of the Playboy Bunnies and hence in a position to ask Lownes for some acid to turn on the Fab Four. Glad to be of service to the kings of pop, Lownes upped with six hits.

A few nights later, after dinner at the dentist's flat, John and Cynthia, along with George and Patti, were served coffee into which the drug had been dissolved. When the dentist explained that he had spiked the coffee, warning that on no condition must his guests leave the apartment, John interpreted the warning as a ploy to inveigle them into a sex orgy. He insisted on leaving immediately, panicking the dentist, horrified at the thought of these famous people driving about London under the influence of a psychotomimetic drug. When George pulled away in his Aston-Martin DB6, the dentist jumped in his car and gave chase. George, a motor racing fan, took up the challenge and hit the accelerator, whipping around corners and plunging down dark side streets, struggling to throw off his pursuer. Finally, Harrison pulled up before the Pickwick Club.

At the club John began to experience bizarre hallucinations. When the table at which he was sitting suddenly elongated, he sought to escape his delusion by heading for the familiar setting of the Ad Lib. But the moment he stepped into the disco's elevator, its red light turned into a fire. The dentist, still dogging his guests, looked like a pig. When someone asked if he could sit next to Lennon, he made the man promise that he wouldn't speak because John couldn't think.

Finally, the party left for George's house, driving at about ten miles an hour, while Patti kept insisting that they get out and smash shopwindows. The moment they got indoors, John fell to drawing, sketching the four Beatles with the caption, "We all agree with you." While Cynthia struggled to throw off the drug, Patti lay down and snuggled with her cat, worried only about how she would explain next day that she was now a different person. Even when everybody had fallen asleep, John continued to hallucinate madly because he had sought to counter the effects of the LSD by taking a lot of speed. His last recollection was of the bungalow turning into a submarine that floated over the nearby eighteen-foot wall with John at the controls.

Lennon was stunned by this experience, but it didn't stop him from dropping acid again in August 1965, when the Beatles spent five days at a house on Mulholland Drive in Los Angeles. This time it was Peter Fonda who pursued the boys with his bad vibes. Having almost died on the operating table some years since, Fonda kept saying: "I know what it's like to be dead." (Lennon used the line in "She Said.") Finally, John told Fonda to shut up. But later, while trying to eat, Lennon found that he could not manage his knife and fork or even keep the food from sliding off his plate. As always when high, John ate with his fingers.

When Lennon returned to acid in January 1966, he was determined to make a controlled flight to the White Light, not to go off on a crazy and dangerous course as in the past. *The Psychedelic Experience* suggests that the novice employ an experienced guide, a sort of ground control who can supervise the trip and straighten out the flight if it veers off in the wrong direction. The basic device for correcting the course is to read aloud to the acid tripper a directional composition written in Wardour Street English. Lennon had no guide available to him, nor was it in his nature to submit himself to the moment-by-moment control of a mentor, so he adopted the other method suggested by Leary, which was to tape-record the instructional screed and play it back the moment trouble develops.

Slipping up to his attic studio, Lennon seated himself before a microphone and opened Leary's large square book to its final chapter: "Instructions for Use During a Psychedelic Session." Punching the red button on the nearest machine, he intoned the following incantation:

> O John Lennon
> The time has come for you to seek new levels of reality.
> Your ego and the rock and roll game are about to cease.
> You are about to set face to face with the Clear Light.
> . . . .
> That which is called ego-death is coming to you.
> This is now the hour of death and rebirth.
> . . . .
> Do not fear it.
> Surrender to it.
> Join it.
> It is part of you.
> You are part of it.

Remember also:
Beyond the restless flowing electricity of life is the ultimate real-
ity—
The Void.

Popping the chemical sacrament into his mouth, John sailed off on his
first controlled flight.

The experience was awesome. "I was suddenly struck by great visions when I first took acid," John recalled, adding, "but you've got to
be looking for it before you can possibly find it." What were those
"great visions"? John never disclosed them. Like most acid voyagers, he
preserved only a vague recollection of the actual experience, but he
never questioned its fundamental value. To the end of his life he maintained that "LSD was the self-knowledge that pointed the way."

Once Lennon's faith in acid had been confirmed, his next move was
inevitable. He set about proclaiming the new gospel in an inspired
composition that would flash like a beacon to the burgeoning counterculture.

Drug songs were nothing new in popular music. As far back as the
Thirties dozens of them were recorded by jazz musicians, including big
stars like Louis Armstrong. These songs, like their counterparts in the
Sixties, were merely descriptive or allusive, often in the snickering style
of an inside joke. What Lennon set out to do in "Tomorrow Never
Knows" (a bad title derived like "A Hard Day's Night" from Ringo's
garbled idiom, where it replaced "You never know what tomorrow will
bring") was not simply to allude to LSD or even evoke its effects but to
proclaim a new revelation, an opportunity for salvation. The earnestness with which he undertook his task is attested by the orthodoxy
of his text.

Virtually every word and idea in this song, originally titled "The
Void" (the term employed by translators of the *Tibetan Book of the Dead*
for the region in which the soul finds itself after death), was derived
directly from Leary's book, starting with the famous first line, taken
verbatim from the instruction for dealing with panic on an acid trip:
"Whenever in doubt, turn off your mind, relax, float downstream." As
for the astonishing musical setting, the origin of acid rock, it is simply
an effort to realize as literally as possible Leary's description of the
sounds heard on acid. Leary wrote that acid produces "swooshing,
crackling and pounding noises." Lennon and Martin followed that description faithfully.

The squiggling, barbed-wire strings *crackle*, the waves of electronic
sound *swoosh*, and a primitive, uppercutting tribal drum *pounds*. John
intended to chant the verses like the Dalai Lama standing before an
assembly of a thousand monks, but this awesome idea had to be aban-

doned for lack of the requisite technology, a failure that Lennon always regretted. Even without the lamasery chorus, the effect was prodigious. By having John sing through a Leslie speaker (a revolving device used customarily to give the acid rock guitar its permanent wave), the ingenious producer made the Prophet Lennon sound like a psychedelic muezzin calling the faithful to prayer.

THE BEATLES BOOMERANG

1966 was the Beatles' pivotal year. At its outset the Fab Four stood supreme upon the summit of success. Objects of hysterical devotion, idealized exemplars of the new youth culture, prophets of where the modern world was heading, the Boys from Liverpool combined within their enthralling image the superstar, the culture hero, and the original concept of the messianic figure.

In ancient times the signs of a messiah were youth, beauty, vitality, and love. His voice was a wondrous voice, and his songs were irresistible. Truly innocent, he was free to trample heedlessly on taboos and violate with impunity even the most sacred law. Just to see him was enough to make you fall under his spell completely and resolve to follow him forever.

To be a messiah, however, is to risk becoming a martyr. This alarming truth was the great lesson the Beatles learned in 1966. Having transcended the level on which even the greatest entertainers had functioned in times past, the Beatles began to suffer now from those deadly threats and lunatic attacks that are the lot of all men who rival the divine. Having harvested a bumper crop of good vibes at their first coming, they discovered as they pressed the vintage that it was tainted with the grapes of wrath. They got their first taste of this sour wine when they arrived on 28 June at Tokyo.

They were met in the VIP lounge by a police official in mufti. He brought them alarming news. Fanatical right-wing students had vowed to assassinate the Beatles in retaliation for their appearance at Nippon Budokan (Martial Arts Hall), the largest indoor arena in the city, which the students claimed was a national shrine to the Japanese war dead. To assure the performers' safety, the Japanese authorities had marshaled the equivalent of two army divisions, thirty thousand uniformed men, to line the route to the city and to serve as guards around the hotel where the musicians were to be immured until it was time for their appearances. Thanks to these extreme measures, the Beatles suf-

200

fered no mishaps in Japan. All the same, the incident—which came as a complete surprise owing to the lack of liaison between Brian Epstein and the Japanese promoter—loomed as a frightening portent. Manila proved to a lot scarier than Tokyo; in fact, it could easily have been the end of the road for the Beatles.

When the band touched down at the Philippine capital on 3 July 1966, they were hailed like the Messiah by the biggest airport crowd ever assembled to greet them—50,000 souls! Expecting to be received with open arms and joyous smiles, the boys calmly awaited the arrival of the welcoming party. Suddenly the hatch swung open, and into the first-class cabin charged a detail of burly military policemen in white helmets. Without a word of explanation, they seized the Beatles and dragged them out of the plane and down the air stairs. "These gorillas, huge guys, no shirts, short sleeves, took us right off the plane," wrote George Harrison, still angry years later. "They confiscated our 'diplomatic bags' [hand luggage containing drugs that by tacit agreement with the authorities was immune to search]. They took all four of us, John, Paul, Ringo and me, without Brian or Neil or Mal. Then they removed us in a boat to Manila Bay surrounded by a ring of cops, guns everywhere . . . straight way we thought we were all busted because we . . . thought they would find all the dope in our bags."

What actually had happened was that the Filipino authorities, after hearing that the Japanese had mobilized thirty thousand men to protect the Beatles in Tokyo, had become highly concerned about the group's safety. Not wanting to appear less careful than the Japanese, the Filipinos had decided to take equally drastic measures. They had scooped up the four Beatles the moment the plane rolled to a stop on the tarmac and surrounded them with two army battalions in full battle gear. Then the party had been rushed to navy headquarters in Manila, where the boys were put aboard a private yacht, on which they were supposed to remain until show time, cruising safely around Manila Bay under escort of a coast guard cutter. The only problem with these measures was that they had not been imparted to the Beatles.

When Brian Epstein saw his boys being hauled off by the soldiers, he went mad. Sorting things out took a lot of time, so it was not until four in the morning that the Beatles were finally liberated from their wealthy host aboard the yacht, Don Manolo Elizalde, who had been showing them off like pet monkeys to a large party of invited guests, a situation that made the Beatles gnash their teeth with fury. When the boys finally got into their suites at the Hotel Manila, they were exhausted.

Next day, the Fourth of July, they slept late. Then they dressed in white suits and drove out to Rizal Football Stadium, where they gave an afternoon and an evening show. The tropical heat was unbearable, and the tumult among the vast audience, many of whom were gate-crashers, was also disturbing. The only thing that consoled the boys during their ordeal was the thought that they could spend the next day lying around in their air-conditioned rooms, before heading home on 6 July. Unbeknownst to the Beatles, however, a crisis was developing that would soon make them fear for their lives. As always, the problem arose from Brian Epstein's incredibly muddled style of management.

While the band was in Tokyo, Brian had received an invitation from Imelda Marcos to bring the Beatles to Malacañang Palace on the morning of the Fourth for a semiofficial reception. The guests were to be three hundred specially selected children, sons and daughters of the country's foremost officials, officers, and businessmen. Imelda, who counted herself a Beatles fan, was especially eager to introduce the Fab Four to her three kids: Ferdinand, Jr. (called Bong Bong), Imee, and Irene, as well as to President Marcos. Obviously this was an honor that nobody could decline. Yet not only had Brian Epstein failed to respond to the invitation, but when the agitated local promoter called on the morning of the Fourth to warn Brian that he was keeping the president's wife waiting, Brian had announced that the Beatles could not be awakened until it was time for them to leave for the stadium. He also instructed the astounded promoter to make clear at the palace that he, Brian, and the Beatles were highly displeased by their reception in the Philippines.

This snub—directed at the dictator of an Oriental state—has to rank among the most audacious feats ever performed upon a high horse. It certainly surpassed by far any impudence toward authority credited to John Lennon. Indeed, it was probably Brian's desperate desire to impress John and the other boys that made him behave so uncharacteristically. For the Beatles had a deep-seated aversion to official functions that dated back to the rough handling they had received at the British embassy when they first played Washington, D.C. Whatever his motive, the effect of Brian's rudeness was catastrophic. On the morning of 5 July the Beatles awoke to find themselves the focus of a national scandal.

IMELDA STOOD UP, FIRST FAMILY WAITS IN VAIN FOR MOPHEADS, blared the headlines of the Manila *Times*. Angry TV commentators denounced the outrageous insult to the Philippine nation. Soon the boys learned that their front man, Vic Lewis, had been dragged from bed the previous night and taken to the palace, where he had been grilled by high-ranking military officers till dawn.

Brian Epstein was horrified when he realized the disaster he had brought down on his beloved boys. He rushed to a local television station, where he went on camera to explain his behavior and make a fulsome apology to Mrs. Marcos. His entire speech was wiped out by mysterious "broadcast interference."

That afternoon a Filipino reporter gained admission to the Beatles' suite and observed their reactions. Paul argued vehemently that the Beatles were not obligated by the first lady's invitation. John was not so confident. He stared out the window at the mob that had gathered below and said thoughtfully: "We got a few things to learn about the Philippines. The first thing is how to get out of here!"

On the morning of 6 July, as the Beatles prepared to leave Manila, they discovered that they were being treated as pariahs. Room service would not respond to their calls. The security guards had been removed from the lobby. The hotel management announced that it would have nothing further to do with its notorious guests. A frantic scramble to make a getaway ensued. Burdened by great amounts of baggage and equipment and without anyone to assist them, the Beatles despaired of reaching their plane on time. Brian put a call through to the cockpit of KLM Flight 862, bound for New Delhi, and extracted a promise from the pilot to idle his engines until they had consumed so much fuel that it was imperative to take off. Then the whole party sweated out a long and unescorted crawl through morning traffic to the airport. When at last they pulled up before the terminal, they recognized that the most dangerous part of the trip still lay ahead.

The police in red sombreros, the military in olive drab, and the raggle-taggle mob had massed before the building, intent on making the Beatles run the gauntlet. "Beatlemania was going on around us," reported George Harrison, "with all the kids screaming and trying to grab hold of us; but with the adults and thugs punching us, throwing bricks, and kicking us as we passed." The airport manager had turned off the escalator, which meant that the Beatles and the NEMS officials had to carry all the amplifiers, suitcases, and instruments up the stairs to the departure lounge. Here the mob overtook their victims. Ringo was floored with an uppercut, and when he sought to crawl into the customs area, he was kicked repeatedly. Brian was also kicked and then thrown down. He hobbled off with a sprained ankle. George and John caught some punches, but Paul broke free and outran his pursuers.

During customs inspection the soldiers took a turn at roughing up the foreigners. When Mal Evans sought to shield the Beatles, he was beaten to the ground. The Beatles' chauffeur, Alf Bicknell, suffered a broken rib and a spinal injury. Every blow struck brought a cheer from the hundreds of Filipinos who witnessed the scuffle through a glass partition.

Finally the Beatles were released. As they dashed toward the Dutch aircraft, they were showered with insults and pelted with missiles from the hundreds of people crowding the observation deck: *"Get out of our country! . . . Nakakahiya kayo!* [Your behavior is shameful!] . . . *Scram! . . . Go fuck yourself!"*

No sooner had the party settled in their seats, thankful to have escaped with their lives, than an ominous call resounded through the first-class cabin: "Would Mr. Epstein and Mr. Evans get off the plane?" Mal and Brian turned pale. Mal, convinced he was about to die, turned to the others and gave them a farewell message to his wife: "Tell Lil I love her."

Outside the plane stood the concert promoter with a Philippine tax official. The tax man required that Brian sign a letter acknowledging that the Beatles owed £5,200 to the Internal Revenue Service. The promoter demanded as the price of the Beatles' release Brian's "brown paper bag money," which was 50 percent of the profits of the two concerts. The terrified Brian handed over the cash, and the plane was cleared for takeoff.

Brian was now at the point of collapse. "How could I let this happen to the boys? How?" he cried to Peter Brown. "I'll never forgive myself. I put the boys in danger."

While Brian was groveling before his conscience, Vic Lewis forced his way up the aisle, brushing past the stewardess, who warned him to sit down and fasten his seat belt. Thrusting his face close to Brian's ear, Lewis barked: "Did you get the money?"

"Don't talk to me about money!" Brian screamed.

"I'll talk to you about money," Vic Lewis snarled. "I'll fuckin' *kill* ya!" Lewis grabbed Brian by the throat, but his hold was broken instantly by Peter Brown, who seized Lewis's hand and forced him back along the aisle as the plane raced down the runway.

No sooner were they aloft than Brian began to vomit. His temperature climbed to fever height. By the time the plane landed at New Delhi, Brian was so ill that he had to be helped down the stairs. The Beatles were furious, but Brian escaped behind an unassailable wall of illness, lying abed for four days, attended by a physician. Meantime, his boys sat in their rooms, smoking, drinking scotch, and rehearsing their grievances.

When they boarded the plane to England, they informed Brian that after this summer they would never tour again. Brian took the announcement as a final and deadly rejection of himself.

By the time the flight landed at Heathrow, Brian's body was covered from head to toe with angry red welts. He was so ill that an ambulance was summoned to meet the plane. "What will I do if they stop touring?" Brian wailed to Peter Brown. "What will be left for me?" Dr. Norman Cowan diagnosed Brian's condition as mononucleosis. He ordered his patient to take a month's vacation. Brian went off to a deluxe hotel at Portmeirion, on the Welsh coast, but just four days after his arrival he was obliged to drag himself back to London. A fresh crisis had erupted in the Beatles' suddenly embattled career.

Back in March, in a profile piece, Maureen Cleave had quoted John Lennon on the subject of religion. "Christianity will go," John had pontificated. "It will vanish and shrink. I needn't argue about that. I'm right and will be proved right. We're more popular than Jesus now. I don't know which will go first—rock 'n' roll or Christianity. Jesus was all right, but his disciples were thick and ordinary."

When these remarks were published in the *Evening Standard*, they didn't stir a ripple because few people in Britain cared what John Lennon thought about Christianity. But when the same words were reprinted in America by *Datebook* in July 1966, they triggered off a holy war fueled not just by the belligerency of true believers in the Bible Belt but by the tendency of many Americans to take the pronouncements of pop stars with the same seriousness they would those of their political leaders, so similar to pop stars. Lennon claimed later that he could have used many other measuring sticks to prove that Christianity was "shrinking," but in actuality he was preoccupied with the idea that he might be the Messiah, if not in this life, then in the next. Comparisons between himself and Jesus always came naturally to his lips.

John's mistake was simply in stating for publication what he truly believed and often discussed in private. By so doing, he violated the taboo that forbids the superstar from calling attention to the fact that he is being treated as if he were the Messiah. The result was an explosion that might well have resulted in Lennon's assassination years before the event and that did contribute to his eventual murder because his killer was a religious crazy from the Bible Belt, who believed that he had been divinely appointed to strike down a false messiah.

What made the "We're more popular than Jesus" brouhaha especially dangerous was its timing. The Beatles were scheduled to do a fourteen-city tour of the States in August, and some of those cities were in the Deep South. Brian Epstein, keen on doing everything in his power to avert another disaster like that at Manila, considered canceling the tour, which would have meant the sacrifice of a million dollars. Nat Weiss, a New York attorney who was Brian's most intimate American friend, as well as a partner in Brian's U.S. management firm, Nemperor, advised the distraught manager not to make a decision until he had assessed the situation at first hand. Nothing Brian saw or said made the prospect of an American tour appear less grave; yet he gave the go-ahead.

John Lennon, who always suffered intensely from anxiety while on tour in the United States, was terrified when he left London—as were all the other Beatles. Prior to the press conference at Chicago that had been planned to clear the air, John broke down and wept. It was an oddly subdued and chastened Lennon who met the press and sought to explain away his remarks, but for once the reporters treated him in an adversarial spirit, bringing the discussion back constantly to the question of whether he would apologize for his blasphemous remarks. John sought by every means to avoid such a humiliating act; finally, he was brought to say that he was sorry.

The tour proved to be a horror. Not only were the Beatles constantly frightened, but they suffered from working in vast ball parks, which they could no longer sell out. Shea Stadium, which had been packed the year before, reported 11,000 unsold tickets. When the Beatles reached Memphis, they received an anonymous phone call warning them that they would be killed during the course of their two shows at the Mid-South Coliseum. During the evening show firecrackers were thrown at the stage. The Beatles reacted instantly, turning to John, half expecting to see him drop dead.

When the tour ended in San Francisco, with a final concert at Candlestick Park on 29 August, it was clear that the Beatles had done their last show. The only person deeply affected by the historic occasion was Brian Epstein, who Nat Weiss recalled appeared "very sad and almost pathetic."

"What do I do now?" demanded Brian despondently. "What happens to my life? That's it! Should I go back to school and learn something else?"

Brian's despair was not just inspired by the fact that his relationship with the Beatles was ending; he was also dismayed by the collapse of NEMS. Until that summer most of his bands had worked regularly, though they were not especially prosperous because they had failed to succeed in the American market. Now the days of the Mersey Sound were past, and the British economy was taking a downturn. Unemployment among the working class was undermining the circuit of workingmen's clubs that was the principal source of income for the lesser British variety acts and rock groups. With NEMS doomed and his usefulness to the Beatles virtually at an end, Brian Epstein felt that his life was over.

Back in England, Dr. Cowan was disturbed by Brian's condition and suggested to Peter Brown that he should move into the house on Chapel Street to keep an eye on his friend. One night Brian retired early; when Brown checked on him, he observed something unnatural in the sleeper's appearance. Shaking Brian, Brown found that he could not wake him. Even a smart slap across his face failed to produce any reaction. Dr. Cowan, reached by phone, said that an ambulance should be called at once. Brown replied that the scandal would be ruinous. The doctor promised to come as quickly as possible.

When he arrived, one look at Brian's purplish face told him that his patient was at the point of death, undoubtedly from a drug overdose. Dr. Cowan, Peter Brown, and Brian's chauffeur, Brian Barret, carried Brian out to his silver Bentley and then raced with him to Richmond Hill Hospital. There his stomach was pumped, and he was revived. When Brian could speak, he claimed that he had just taken one pill too many. After Peter Brown had returned to the house, however, he discovered a note that read: "This is all too much and I can't take it any more." A will accompanied the note, leaving everything to Queenie and Clive Epstein, Brian's brother, with a bequest to Brown. After being discharged from the hospital, Brian was put into a clinic in Putney for detoxification.

The Beatles made their decision to quit the stage despite the enormous and unending pressures brought to bear upon them by both their advisers and their fans. This unaccustomed show of stubbornness was not inspired simply by fear or despair. Quite the contrary, if the Beatles had really wanted to continue touring, they could have found solutions to their problems—the same solutions discovered by other bands facing similar problems. The truth is that the Beatles had no commitment to the stage. The rock hero must be like a lion tamer who every time he enters the cage is prepared to impose his will upon the will of the beast. It was in this will to command that the Beatles were most deficient. They were charmers in an arena where only power is respected. They had never exhibited the theatrical prowess of rock's great showmen, for they lacked alike the riveting intensity of Bob Dylan, the superb poise of the mature Elvis, the flamboyant showmanship of Little Richard, the corybantic ecstasy of James Brown. A mind-mouth-mike act, the Beatles showed to best advantage in an intimate milieu, like the cellar club, where they were free to play instead of being obliged to perform. Listening to a side like "You Know My Name (Look Up the Number)," with its string of nightclub parodies, you recognize how much of what was best in the Beatles, their witty, allusive, spoofy ad-libbing, was lost on the cutting-room floor.

By going commercial, the Beatles had reduced themselves to a formula, like instant rock, that was as utterly unfulfilling as it was ridiculously inappropriate. Far from becoming rock gladiators, they became rock mannequins, immobile, inaudible, almost invisible, standing out in some vast and hysterical arena, no longer the Fab Four but the Four Little Dildos, upon whom their crazy fans brought themselves to climax. No wonder the boys were glad to throw down their guitars for the last time and run off the stage.

Even if the Beatles had continued to tour, they would soon have become a camp act because they had never changed anything but their suits since their days on the British cinema circuit. Yet change, revolutionary change, was the watchword of the rock stage as the Sixties advanced.

Viewed in this perspective, the Beatles' decision to abandon the stage was one of the most sincere and laudable acts of their entire career because it sprang from genuine self-recognition and expressed their true character. Born to play it cool in a cool medium, the Beatles took their stand where they belonged, before a studio mike, where they exercised all the virtuosity and authority that the arena performer exhibits before the mob. Actually, in relinquishing the stage, they made a valuable contribution to rock theater by reviving the idea of radio theater, which is implicit in *Sgt. Pepper*. So it could be said that in the final analysis the Beatles didn't really forsake the stage—they simply put it on the air.

The first practical effect of their decision to stop touring was that, released from the yoke of obligatory performance, they flew off in different directions, intent on their private pleasures or ambitions. In the fall of 1966 George and Patti went for the first time to India, where they met Ravi Shankar and received a mantra from the Maharishi Yogi. Paul and Mal Evans took a sight-seeing trip through East Africa.

John, desperate for something to occupy him, allowed himself to be persuaded to play the part of Private Gripweed in Richard Lester's satiric *How I Won the War,* a dreadful film that proved that Lennon didn't have a scrap of acting ability. The only thing John got out of this bum job was his famous granny glasses. After spending two months out of England, first in Celle in northern Germany, then in Almería in southern Spain, he was glad to get home—where he plunged again into acid. One night, half crazed after a sleepless three-day run on the drug, he stepped out of his black Cooper Mini at the entrance to Mason's Yard and made for the Indica Gallery, where he had been invited to see a show by a screwball Japanese artist named Yoko Ono.

IRON BUTTERFLY

Yoko Ono was born at 8:30 on the evening of a snowy day in Tokyo, 18 February 1933. Her mother was a Yasuda, a name synonymous with the still-powerful zaibatsu, financial, commercial, and industrial conglomerates that have always formed the backbone of Japan's business empire. Yoko's maternal grandfather, Zensaburo Iomi, married the daughter of Zenjiro Yasuda (founder of the Bank of Tokyo) and then was adopted as a son by his father-in-law, a common Japanese practice. Appointed chairman of the family bank and elected to the House of Peers, Zensaburo enjoyed a spectacularly successful career until he incurred his father-in-law's wrath by living like a playboy. Shortly before old Zenjiro was assassinated (by a left-wing fanatic in 1921), he cut his adopted son-in-law out of his will, denying him and his heirs an inheritance of one billion dollars. Thenceforth Yoko's family suffered not only from the loss of great expectations but from the chill that descends upon Japanese who are cut off from the family tree.

Isoko, Yoko's mother, eighth and last of Zensaburo's children, a shy and conventionally pretty girl, received the education of a dilettante, studying painting, for example, with a famous master of the Showa period; unlike her siblings and cousins, who became amateur artists, she elected to exercise her gifts in the social sphere, becoming one of the most successful young society hostesses in prewar Tokyo. Her husband, Eisuke Ono, was a good-looking man of exceptional social accomplishments: a fine dancer and clever go player, a good golfer and drinker, and gifted classical pianist. Of a somewhat lower caste than the Onos, he came from a samurai family, whose lineage reached back to a ninth-century emperor. Educated at Tokyo University, where he earned degrees in mathematics and economics, studying subsequently political science and law, Eisuke was equipped also with the rare ability to speak English and French fluently. In 1927 he joined the Yokohama Specie Bank, thereby commencing the long, slow climb that finally took him to the top of that institution, renamed, after the war, the Bank of Japan.

Yoko's parents met at a mountain retreat of the Japanese upper classes, Karuizawa. Their arranged marriage, celebrated in 1931, was burdened from the start by a lack of affection between the partners and by the demands of Eisuke's career, which obliged him to spend long periods away from his family. No sooner was he married than he was posted to the United States. Yoko, his firstborn, did not see her father until she was three. At the end of each day her mother would point to the framed photograph of Eisuke next to the child's bed and urge her to "Say good-night to Father." Yoko's very name, "Ocean Child," means the child of one who is overseas, far from home.

The Onos were one of the small number of Japanese families that were encouraged to develop a high degree of cultural assimilation with the West both to facilitate business dealings and to qualify them for service in the diplomatic corps. (One of Yoko's uncles, Ambassador Kase, was the first Japanese representative to the United Nations.) In 1936 the three-year-old Yoko arrived in San Francisco with her mother, whose next child, Keisuke, was born in the United States. During the following year, however, Japanese-American relations became so strained over the Japanese attack on the American gunboat *Panay* in China that Isoko returned to the homeland with her children, while her husband was transferred to the bank's New York branch.

Isoko was encharged upon her return with the management of the Yasuda mansion, an imposing establishment that stood on a hill behind the Imperial Palace surrounded by pleasure grounds that boasted a view over one-third of the city. More than thirty servants reported to the mistress of the house, who ruled with a firm hand and a biting tongue.

Little Yoko adored her mother and liked to walk in her steps as she went about the house. In the afternoon, when Mrs. Ono received her lady friends, Yoko would serve the company tea, while her mother extolled her perfect daughter. At the same time Isoko appears to have treated Yoko rather as a plaything, while regarding her almost like an ugly duckling, even going so far as to warn her daughter that she was not pretty enough to succeed in any way save by using her wits. Jealousy may also have contributed to the ill feeling that began to develop between mother and daughter, for Eisuke doted on Yoko and she played up to her father.

In 1940, when Yoko was seven, the family returned to America and established itself on Long Island. Again, the threat of war became so keen that the Onos were compelled to turn about and retreat to Japan. This time Eisuke was sent to conduct the bank's business in Vichy France. His facility in the French language explains likewise his transfer in 1942 to Hanoi, following the Japanese conquest of French Indochina. There, as a respected representative of the Southeast Asia Co-Prosperity Sphere, he functioned throughout the war, while around him millions of Vietnamese starved to death because the Japanese barred the vital shipments of rice from the south. (Isoko told an interviewer in 1982 that her husband was a Class B war criminal, but there is no evidence of this classification in the U.S. National Archives.)

During the years of Japan's triumphs Yoko was given every advantage that could be bestowed on a girl of her generation. She was enrolled at the prestigious Gakushuin School, which accepted only pupils connected with the imperial family or the House of Peers. Subsequently she was transferred to a new academy designed for students who had studied abroad. Founded by Takasumi Mitsui, an Oxford graduate and heir to the Mitsui fortune, this school enlarged and deepened Yoko's growing understanding of Western culture. In addition to the regular curriculum, she received private tutoring in the Christian Bible (her father was Christian), Buddhist scripture, calligraphy, Japanese culture, and Western music and ballet. Eisuke, who had yearned all his life for the career of a concert pianist, measured his daughter's hands when she was only three to see if she was ready for piano lessons. Yoko's German piano teacher told her pupil that she lacked the patience for practice and might do better in the theater.

Yoko resented her elaborate education as much as she did her mother's discipline. "I was like a domesticated animal being fed information," she complained later. "I hated it. And particularly music. I used to faint before my music lessons—literally. I suppose it was my way of escape." But Yoko was not released from school until a big raid by the B-29's struck Tokyo, on 9 March 1944, setting ablaze the city's miles upon miles of wooden shanties.

Isoko took the children, Yoko, Keisuke, and the baby, Setsuko, to a farm house near Karuizawa. There the wealthy city folk fell victim to the starving peasants, who stripped Isoko of her possessions. Yoko claims that she took command of the situation, seizing the produce that the peasants were stealing and doling it out to her family. This story is the first sign of that yearning to be a public benefactor that came to form such a conspicuous feature of Yoko's character.

After the Japanese surrender the family settled in a little house inside the Yasuda compound at Kamakura, a small town on Sagami Bay. After Eisuke was repatriated from Indochina, he worked behind the scenes until he could be installed in 1947 as the general manager and later director of the bank's foreign affairs department. When Yoko was reunited with her father, she was a sensitive adolescent suffering from the problems created by the war. Instead of receiving the love for which she longed and to which she had once been accustomed, she was treated now by her father with an icy reserve. This shocking change of attitude is explained partly by Yoko's conspicuous sexual maturation and partly by the fact that her father was now bestowing his affections on a geisha girl whom he had established as his mistress in a house in another city and by whom he had two children.

Yoko displayed a precociously mature attitude when she returned to school, smoking cigarettes, drinking alcohol, and talking a lot about men. She was also precocious sexually. Her cousin, Hideaki Kase, recalled: "Yoko had an early interest in sex. . . . Before she went to New York, she went from man to man. One of the men was Mr. K., three years older than I. He was going to Tokyo College at the time, and his father held the highest position. Also before going to America, she fell in love with an assistant professor at Gakuishin University." Yoko's most fervent admirer, it is said, was her schoolmate Prince Toshi, younger son of the emperor. In the midst of gossip that the young people might marry, Eisuke was appointed in 1952 general manager of the New York Agency, the name under which the Bank of Japan operated after the war in the United States. The family moved to New York again, settling this time in the attractive upper-middle-class suburb of Scarsdale, where they occupied a conventional ranch house at 74 Charthage Road.

At first Yoko stayed behind in Japan, seizing the opportunity to get free of her parents by insisting that she could not interrupt her studies, which were designed to make her the first female philosophy student in the history of Gakushuin. Yet, late in the summer of the same year, she suddenly threw up her studies and flew to New York. Though she studied writing and singing the next summer at Harvard, it was not until the following academic year, 1953–54, that she enrolled at Sarah Lawrence College, about twenty-five minutes from her home, in the posh suburb of Bronxville. An ideal place for a rich Japanese girl interested in the arts and keen on kicking over the traces of a highly conventional upbringing, Sarah Lawrence was full of arty girls who came from prosperous but eccentric families, who had made their money from show business or had inherited wealth. There were lots of Jewish students, as well as horsy girls from Chevy Chase and WASPy beauties from New England. Hope Cook, who married the king of Sikkim, was a Sarah Lawrence girl, as was Barbara Walters, whose father ran the biggest nightclub in New York.

Very few people who were at Sarah Lawrence in Yoko's day retain any substantial recollection of Yoko Ono. Typical is the response of her "don" or freshman adviser, Katherine Mansell: "I can picture her clearly, but I can't remember anything about her." A former student remarked: "She was small, weird and always wore black." Patricia Bosworth, biographer of Diane Arbus, recalled: "Yoko was the fattest and most sullen girl on campus." Erica Abeel, a novelist who lived with Yoko after they had left the college, found her "kind of sweet, in an Oriental manner. Reminds me now of the people at the Korean fruit stands—a little shy and deferential. She was the campus Jap."

Yoko was not easy to befriend. Richard Rabkin—a Harvard student whose observations have especial value because he was a bit older and progressing toward a career as a psychiatrist—found Yoko "completely opaque. . . . She was scared of other people. . . . If you were a Japanese, that was no good. If you weren't, that was no good. . . . She couldn't be too friendly with men. It required a degree of skill in appearing harmless to make friends with her. You had to be totally safe."

The only person who came close to qualifying as a friend was Yoko's classmate Betty Rollin, subsequently a TV reporter, journalist, and author. Yoko impressed the young Betty as being highly "poetic." Yoko spoke "in haiku," employing a breathy little voice and wobbly English. Everyone knew that she came from a family of high caste, and the connection with the Bank of Japan was bruited about. The girls did not find Yoko pretty because she was big in the bust and the buttocks and bandy-legged, but Betty found her "ethereal" and intelligent. When Yoko's family went off during the Christmas holidays in freshman year, leaving Yoko behind (probably because she refused to accompany them), Betty invited Yoko to stay at the Rollin home in Bronxville. Mrs. Rollin was very sympathetic to this shy little girl who claimed she was being frozen out of her family. In her third year Yoko escaped her family again by moving into a dormitory. She appeared to the other girls to have no social life because she never joined their weekly husband-hunting expeditions to male colleges. In fact, Yoko was consorting with Japanese men sanctioned by her family.

Her original design at college was to become an opera singer and enjoy a career in Europe, a very strange ambition for a young woman who had no voice or musical ability and who usually fainted before her music lessons. Yet it was characteristic of her to think that she could achieve anything she could imagine. Actually, the only evidence of creative ability that she offered at college was a few literary pieces, published in the school paper—fey little fancies spun about fallen stars or grapefruit seeds that glow like stars as the twilight thickens over the picnic table. From these schoolgirl prolusions, it is easy to see why her Harvard writing instructor, an Irish short-story author, concluded that her work was "arty and inauthentic."

At the end of her third year Yoko dropped out of college. Her abrupt departure followed a notorious incident that is still the cause of laughter on campus. Mrs. Ono arrived one day at Yoko's dorm, Gilbert Hall, and began making demands and giving orders that infuriated her daughter. Finally, the mother announced that she was taking Yoko out of college. Yoko tore out of the dayroom, locking the door behind her. When Mrs. Ono discovered that she had been imprisoned, she was compelled to behave in a manner that was highly unbecoming to a highborn Japanese lady, shouting and banging on the door for release. The dean of the college had Yoko on the carpet for this John Lennonish prank. He also demanded to see Mrs. Ono, who refused to return. That was the last of Yoko Ono at Sarah Lawrence.

Yoko met her first husband through Tanaka Kozo, son of the first Christian chief justice of the Supreme Court of Japan. Tanaka was studying at Columbia University when he met one of Yoko's cousins, who took him up to Scarsdale. Perceiving Yoko's enthusiasm for music, Tanaka introduced her to the most outstanding Japanese composition student in the United States, Toshi Ichiyanagi. Toshi was a small, neat man, who walked like a dancer and was very taciturn. He had a girlfriend but broke off with her soon after meeting Yoko. The Onos did not approve of this relationship because Toshi's family was of inferior status, but her parents' disapprobation worked like a spur on Yoko, who persuaded Toshi to allow her to move into his flat in an old brownstone on West 89th Street. The effect of this audacious act on Yoko's family is not hard to imagine. Their efforts to reclaim their daughter were undercut, however, when Eisuke was recalled to Japan in May 1957 to become the general manager of the Bank of Japan.

No sooner was the family out of the country than Yoko and Toshi were married. For a whole year the Onos refused to recognize the marriage; then they changed their tune and returned to New York to celebrate the union publicly with a reception at a small but exclusive hotel on the West Side.

The man Yoko married was her opposite in every respect. The only child of a couple of professional musicians, he was so well trained at home that by the time he reached high school, he was ready to immerse himself in the study of theory with two well-known Japanese composers. Though born only two weeks before Yoko, Toshi had achieved enough by the time of his marriage to satisfy the ambition of a much older man. He had won a whole series of prizes for full-scale compositions and had studied for years in the United States with men of the caliber of Aaron Copland, Boris Blacher, and Goffredo Petrassi. At Juilliard, his principal master was Vincent Persichetti (teacher of Steve Reich and Philip Glass), who always regarded Toshi as one of his finest pupils. After he left Juilliard, where he won the Elizabeth Sprague Coolidge Prize, he took a demanding copying job with Stefan Wolpe, the doyen of "advanced" composers. During the course of an exchange of visits Hilda Morley Wolpe, the composer's wife (and a gifted poet), made some acute observations on the newly married couple.

Yoko and Toshi were terribly poor, she noted. They lived now in a little flat at 426 Amsterdam Avenue, a working-class neighborhood, where their clothes hung out on hooks because there were no closets. Yoko was working for an export-import firm, traveling with Japanese businessmen, acting as their interpreter. She appeared a very conventional young woman, dressed in suits with gloves, wearing high heels and makeup that had been carefully applied. She was supporting Toshi, who had lost his grant from Juilliard. Her manner was "clingy, coy, and flattering." She told Hilda that she was "ageless," and when Wolpe's monumental *Enactments* was performed, Yoko pressed the ailing composer's hands to her breasts as a sign of heartfelt emotion, assuring him that he was the "last of the great composers." Yoko also proved to be a skillful Oriental cook, who took hours to prepare a meal, while her guests waited, but who produced results that were exquisite. When asked about Japanese music, she responded by singing folk songs in a pure little voice, like a child.

Toshi, Hilda recalled, appeared very meek and "squashed down," totally dominated by Yoko. When, during Thanksgiving dinner, Yoko turned on him, berating him in Japanese, he was visibly crushed. Yoko, for her part, complained that talking to him was like "talking to a stone."

Toshi's view of his marriage emerged years later in a Japanese newspaper. He complained that "Yoko was never pleased unless she was treated like a queen. . . . She was selfish and morbid . . . she was indeed an artist, in the sense that she played and spent as she pleased." The reference to playing is most likely an allusion to Yoko's infidelities. She told Marnie Hair that she would get urges to have sexual relations with other men and Toshi would grant her permission, but she recognized that these affairs gave her husband great pain. Yoko's escapades cost her much suffering as well because time and again they resulted in pregnancies that had to be terminated in illegal abortions. "In New York I was always having abortions," she told *Esquire* in 1970, "because I was too neurotic to take precautions. . . . I would go out and have an affair, come back, and 'Oh! I'm in a mess!' My first husband was very kind." Yoko explained the real reason for these repeated abortions to her friend, the former Mrs. Donald Richie (today Mrs. Rutger Smith), stating that love meant to her bearing a man's child. When she fell in love, for the first month she was keen on having a child. "So I go ahead and let it be conceived," she explained. "Then the next month, of course, I don't want it at all, so I have to go ahead and have an abortion." Soon this behavior produced serious medical complications, especially difficulty in carrying the fetus to term.

Many people who knew Yoko in this period believed she had had a child in Japan. Michael Rumaker, a writer who had an affair with

Yoko, observed a "scar on her belly—a tough ridge of purple flesh," which he took for the mark of a caesarian. (Yoko told Marnie Hair: "All my children have been born by caesarian.") Hilda Wolpe recalled that Yoko said she had borne a child. Diane Wakoski, the poet, recollected that the child was in Japan when she knew Yoko in 1961. Yoko's housemate, Erica Abeel, confirmed: "There was a baby. I remember she said to me this curious thing: 'The pain of childbirth is horrendous, and women don't tell each other the truth about it.'"

Yoko's marriage to Toshi established the pattern for her future relations with all her consorts. Her choice has always been determined by the need to have a man rescue her from distressing circumstances. Then the man becomes the instrument of Yoko's baffled ambition to be a world-famous artist. Though Toshi was not famous himself, he had access to the most brilliant and renowned men in contemporary music. Through Stefan Wolpe's principal disciple, David Tudor, Toshi was introduced to John Cage, whose course at the New School he began to attend. Cage introduced Toshi, in turn, to Merce Cunningham, who gave the young composer a job as a rehearsal pianist with his dance company. Next, Toshi encountered La Monte Young, the young genius from the West, who had breezed into New York in 1960 and made a tremendous impact on the avant-garde scene.

As Yoko became acquainted with her husband's new colleagues, she decided to become an avant-gardist herself. Leaving Toshi, she moved into the loft they had rented as a studio at 112 Chambers Street, an industrial area. Here Yoko had an affair with Michael Rumaker that was just as characteristic of her relations with her lovers as was her marriage of her behavior with her spouses.

Rumaker was an accomplished writer who had been institutionalized after suffering a serious emotional breakdown precipitated by intense conflict over homosexuality. He emerged from the mental hospital programmed to find a woman and go straight. When he encountered Yoko at the Land, an artists' colony near Stony Point, he felt that he had discovered a little exquisite who had suffered a fate similar to his own by being "crushed and misunderstood." In *The Butterfly*, his novelistic rendering of the romance, he describes Yoko at first as a girl-woman, shy, mischievous, innocent, twisting an origami butterfly, while reciting a haiku:

> The blossom fallen in the grass
> flies back to the tree—
> No, it is a butterfly.

She metamorphosizes soon into many other shapes, increasingly sinister, until she manifests her innermost self as a Japanese soldier, with

a face of "incredible cunning and stealth, of violence and murder."
Yoko chops off the affair, leaving Rumaker to ruminate over the butterfly that became a bayonet—an "iron butterfly."

Yoko left Michael Rumaker when she fell under the spell of La
Monte Young, who was to exercise over her the most decisive influence
of her entire artistic career. A tiny man, weighing fewer than a hundred pounds, who dressed in cut velvets and elf boots, Young made a
pair with the diminutive Yoko, whose costume was a black sweater and
ski pants with her feet in pointy chukka boots with silver buckles.
Though Young looked like a leprechaun, he fulfilled more than any
musician of modern times, saving Charlie Parker, the American ideal
of the native genius. His compositions, whatever their medium, expressed the ecstatic and unquenchable energy that is the essence of the
American soul. This same energy poured off him in person, inspiring
spontaneous jam sessions, making people collaborate in laborious creative endeavors or in musical jokes. Long before Jimi Hendrix set light
to his guitar, La Monte Young ignited a violin onstage or counted out
beans or engaged in some other prank that made the audience laugh—
or reach for their guns!

Diane Wakoski, the poet who lived with Young, viewed the relationship between Yoko and her lover as one of mutual exploitation:
"He needed an impresario, and she needed a genius." Yoko became an
impresario by offering her loft as the site of a history-making series of
avant-garde performances, organized by Young in the winter of
1960–61. Pronounced "incomparable" and "equal to anything ever
done in Europe" by John Cage, these shows featured a whole congeries
of subsequently famous artists, including La Monte Young, David
Tudor, Robert Morris, Jackson Mac Low, Walter De Maria, Simone
Morris, Christian Wolff, Terry Riley, and Diane Wakoski. Yoko was the
ticket taker, but she found ways to assert herself in performance. Beate
Gordon recalled: "We sat on orange crates. There was a large piece of
paper tacked to the wall. Yoko went to her refrigerator, took a bowl of
Jell-O, and threw it at the paper. Then she took a couple of eggs and
threw them. Then she took some Japanese sumi ink and started finger
painting. Finally, she took out a match and lit the paper. I remember
looking about the rickety loft and thinking, 'I'm going to die!'" Happily
John Cage had advised Yoko to spray the paper with flame retardant.

Basically, however, Yoko identified herself as a poet, a title that
Wakoski found preposterous: "I resented her calling her very bad and
silly writing 'poetry,' and I thought she was hustler, not artist. This,
because she earned her living as a model, seemed to go to bed with all
the men around, and, in fact, never seemed to sacrifice much for her
'art' as all the other avant-garders that I knew did." La Monte Young

took a more tolerant view, allowing that Yoko was "success-oriented" and worked primarily for "recognition" but finding her efforts sincere.

The most important advantage Yoko got from her relationship with Young was the opportunity to get in on the ground floor of what was destined to become one of the most appropriate idioms of modern art, the style that had just been named Concept Art or Directional Art. Directly inspired by the example of Marcel Duchamp, who almost half a century earlier had taken to writing witty surrealist proposals, like "Use a Rembrandt as an ironing board," Directional Art dealt in whimsical conceits. La Monte Young's *Piano Piece for David Tudor #1*, October 1960, reads: "Bring a bale of hay and a bucket of water onto the stage for the piano to eat and drink. The performer may then feed the piano or leave it to eat by itself. If the former, the piece is over after the piano has been fed. If the latter, it is over after the piano eats or decides not to." *Composition 1960 #10* directs: "Draw a straight line and follow it."

The discomforts of the loft on Chambers Street compelled Yoko to seek different living quarters. She took a room in a floor-through at 323 West 80th Street occupied by another former Sarah Lawrence girl, Erica Abeel. Erica was working on a doctorate in French literature at Columbia and teaching in the university's adult education division. Neither young woman was taken with the other's career: Yoko thought Erica was an academic grind; Erica thought Yoko was a phony artist. "I never believed in what she was doing, so I never paid any attention to it," she recalled, adding, "It all seemed like bullshit to me." What gave Yoko and Erica their common ground was the game they both were playing with men.

"It was wall-to-wall fucking," Erica explained with a chuckle. "There was a kind of sexual complicity, talking about men or flirting with men in each other's presence and relating to each other at the same time. It was a big turn-on." Yoko had lovers, Erica observed, "coming out of the woodwork. I always felt she fucked everyone, but I never thought it was something that gave her any pleasure." Yoko often pulled Erica's men because they would call Erica and wind up talking to Yoko. These interceptions didn't trouble Erica because she wasn't serious about any of the men and regarded all the sex play as a joke. Nor was she inspired to retaliate because she viewed Yoko's lovers as "nut cases." Once she came home and caught Yoko in bed with La Monte Young. "I didn't mind," she remarks dryly, "except that it was *my* bed. I thought that Yoko had the hots for me at that time. Just the fact that she wanted my men, who were nothing. . . . What bothered me was how greasy he was—he was very dirty. Greasy ponytail. I changed my pillowcase."

When Diane Wakoski learned about this affair, which had been going on right under her nose, she was shocked. The discovery ended her relationship with La Monte Young.

Yoko left Erica's flat after having run up a phone bill of $700 by talking constantly to Toshi, who had returned to Japan and was active now in the Tokyo avant-garde. When Erica went after Yoko for the money, she was told to meet her former housemate at a sleazy little hotel on the West Side. Erica went up to the room and announced herself, but she was not allowed to enter. Yoko "came out in the hall virtually naked, with just a towel or bathrobe. She gave me a lot of singles and small bills. I was amused. It was a Sarah Lawrence style, like a dorm. She said, 'That's all I can give you now,' clutching her robe. Behind her was this naked Jap, standing there, looking very handsome."

Yoko's last lover during this period was the painter Shusaku Arakawa. He had just arrived from Japan with his few possessions in paper shopping bags and no more English than an infant. Yoko installed the good-looking young man in her loft, where they lived together briefly. While Arakawa stretched canvases for Sam Francis, Yoko sought to enlist the aid of other established artists, including Yayoi Kusama.

Kusama had attracted a lot of attention from the moment she arrived in New York. Her obsessional and psychotic imagery—pieces of furniture studded with penile shapes like bizarrely colored sea urchins—was merely the most tangible element in an oeuvre that also entailed countless examples of performance art and public demonstrations. Though Kusama was perhaps the most important of Yoko's role models, the artist (interviewed for this book in a mental institution in Tokyo) disavowed any association with Yoko, whom she described as a soulless "copycat."

In the spring of 1962 Yoko informed Arakawa that she was returning to Japan. He was very angry at her defection, which made his lot much harder. He recalled her as being very poor and often depressed, intimating that she attempted suicide on more than one occasion. Yoko confirmed that during this period "I thought a lot about suicide—just doing that." At the same time Arakawa observed she was "very hard. She could kill."

GRAPEFRUIT PITS

One morning in March 1962 two dark-suited officials from the Bank of Japan arrived at Yoko's loft to escort her to the airport. After driving to Idlewild, they stood by until they had seen her aboard a flight to Tokyo. Whether Yoko had any inkling of how she was going to be received is not clear; subsequently she claimed that she was virtually kidnapped.

The pretext her family offered for demanding her return was her brother's engagement. Actually the Onos were determined to put Yoko's marriage back together. They had gotten word of her disgraceful behavior in New York and were fearful that the family's name would be smirched. As soon as she arrived, she was installed in a flat owned by the family and occupied by Toshi, who had lent himself to this scheme.

At first the effects of the enforced reconciliation were not bad. Yoko had heard a lot from Toshi about the avant-garde performances at Sogetsu Hall, an elegant little auditorium that was the principal forum in Japan for experimental art. Without wasting a moment, she arranged to present there on 24 May a program titled *Works of Yoko Ono*.

The program was based on *Grapefruit in the World of Park*, a concert collage that Yoko had presented the previous November at the Carnegie Recital Hall. It demanded the participation of a large number of contributing artists, whom Toshi undertook to recruit while Yoko concentrated on hyping the event. She persuaded a local TV station to film all five and a half hours of eccentric performance and nonperformance. The reviews were not favorable, as was to be expected when a piece might consist of the artist coming out and sitting blankly before a piano, which she then pounded for five minutes, winding up her act by smoking a cigarette down to the butt and walking off.

Unfortunately the negative notices caught Yoko at a moment when she was sinking into depression. Already made to feel by her family that she was a bad wife and a bad woman, she was told now that her behavior reflected discredit on the tiny and precariously poised avant-garde establishment. She discovered that she could not attend any sort of social event without being made to feel that she was a pariah. Instinctively she began to withdraw. She went to the theater or the cinema by herself. She walked about the city alone. Eventually she grew so despondent that she was overwhelmed by thoughts of suicide.

"In those days," she explained later, "Mr. I. and I lived on the eleventh floor of an apartment building. At midnight I woke up almost unconsciously and crawled to the window. I tried to jump from the window. Every time Mr. I. quickly pulled me back. It happened almost every night. Mr. I. suggested that it was urgent for me to go to a doctor. I began to think so, too. I am an emotional woman. Although I try to be logical, I can't be satisfied without agreement with my emotions. . . . Part of my mind is very strong, and part is very weak. . . . I pushed myself to the limit. I took drugs. I kept wanting to die. Then I realized I was in a mental hospital." Toshi and the Ono family had institutionalized Yoko to prevent her from killing herself.

She was held for weeks in a padded room under heavy sedation. Toshi visited her constantly and sought by every means to relieve her distress. One day he brought her a visitor from New York, a member of the La Monte Young circle, a young man named Tony Cox. "'There's a guy from New York to see you,'" said Toshi, according to Yoko's account. "'He's a very sensitive man. Maybe you two will get along well. How about meeting him?' I said I didn't want to see anyone. So [Tony] left the flowers [he had brought] for me. But I rejected even that. Eventually the nurse sympathized with the man and said to me, 'Please, just meet him!' I finally decided to meet him because it was a bother to refuse to see him and I was mentally weak. . . . From the doctor Tony learned about the symptoms of my disease and the medication I was taking. He knew about medicine, and he told me, 'The medicine you're taking is very strong, so don't take too much. Also, I can help you get out of here.' He continued to take care of me very much. . . . I was told that he was impressed with my work in New York, and he visited my New York loft while I was in Japan. He wanted to see me in person, so he sold all his possessions and took a boat to Japan to look for me. Now I can say he was my fan."

If Yoko had not been so eager to avail herself of the help offered by Tony Cox, she might have made a few calls to New York and found out who he really was. That discovery might have ended their relationship before it began, thus altering the whole future course of her life.

Tony Cox is the son of two painters who met during the Depression at the Art Students League in New York City. It was ironic that handsome George Cox, who had worked as a Powers model, should have married a Jew because his uncle, Father Ignatius Cox, professor of ethics at Fordham University, was, like the notorious Father Coughlin, a vehememt anti-Semite. There was no irony, however, in Millicent Gootkin, daughter of an English cabinetmaker, marrying a Gentile because she was eager to pass as anything but Jewish—so eager that she had her nose bobbed twice, explaining how dreadful it was to be "Mrs. Cox" and exhibit such a Jewish nose. Tony, born in 1937, grew up during the most anti-Semitic period in modern American history in Bellmore, Long Island, where there were no Jews but lots of German-Americans. In order to pass as just another local boy, he was obliged to conceal the Jewish side of his identity, an experience that may have contributed to his peculiar personality.

As a child Tony was remarkable for two things, according to his aunt, Mrs. Blanche Greenberg: his beauty and his gift for "getting anything out of anybody." His great misfortune lay in being compelled to witness the maiming and crippling effects of a sequence of cancer operations on his mother. When she died, Tony, aged sixteen, took off and vanished. This was the first of a lifelong series of flights and disappearances. It also marked the beginning of Tony's alarming descent into first juvenile delinquency, then criminal behavior.

At seventeen he stole a neighbor's boat, was caught and locked up for several days in the county jail. At roughly the same time he was kicked out of Hoosac, a fancy prep school, the second private school from which he had been expelled. Somehow he contrived to gain admission to art school at the University of Buffalo, but he soon dropped out. When he entered college again, in the fall of 1958, he was, at the age of twenty-one, a second-year student at Cooper Union, an old and unique art institute at Astor Place, gateway to the Lower East Side, which was at that time the most important art community since prewar Paris.

Cutting into the Greenwich Village coteries of John Cage and La Monte Young, Tony found both full of easy marks. The Cage circle included a large number of homosexuals, who were titillated by this handsome, clean-cut young man, who parted his hair in the middle, wore Ivy League tweeds, and gazed at his masters respectfully through horn-rimmed glasses. No sooner did the artists get involved with Tony than they discovered their mistake. On one occasion Tony stole John Cage's car and changed the registration; though the thief was caught, the composer refused to press charges. Meantime, Cox continued his metamorphosis from a nice young painting student to a devious and dangerous underground man. Every step in this process was witnessed by Tony's only close friend, Al Wunderlich, another Cooper Union student, who continued with his studies after Tony, once again, dropped out. In many ways Tony's opposite—naïve, suggestible, totally infatuated by the brave new world of New York—Wunderlich, the good-looking son of a country doctor in Oregon, was destined to become a professor at the Rhode Island School of Design. Between 1959 and 1961, however, he walked on the wild side in the footsteps of his fascinating friend.

The decisive moment in Tony's development came when he got into the drug scene, dealing not only grass and hash but the recently introduced and virtually unknown psychedelics, which were not as yet illegal. Among the people he met in this new circle was Eric Loeb, who had a shop on East 9th Street where he sold mescaline (obtained through a scam run on Hoffman-La Roche in New Jersey), peyote buds from Arizona, and the exotics harmaline and ibogaine, manufactured by Light & Company. Tony also struck up an acquaintance with the Johnny Appleseed of psychoactive drugs, Chuck Bick, descendant of 102 generations of rabbis, whom Tony introduced to another friend, John Beresford, a British pediatrician working in a hospital lab. This meeting had decisive historical importance, for it struck the spark that ignited the great LSD conflagration of the Sixties.

When Beresford was apprised of how easy it was for a medical man to obtain even the most powerful psychedelic, he wrote a letter on hospital stationery to Sandoz in Switzerland and received by mail an entire gram of pure LSD-25—enough acid to stone a city. It was this little vial of white powder, cut with confectioners' sugar by Beresford and his roommate, Michael Hollingshead, that turned on the hip world of New York City and soon led to Timothy Leary's adoption of the drug as the ultimate chemical sacrament. For this decisive act of cross-pollination, Tony Cox deserves a footnote in the history of LSD.

By the summer of 1961 Tony had plunged deep into the criminal underworld. He and an acid-dropping UPI correspondent cut a deal with the Mafia that went wrong. The mob ordered its collector to put the muscle on the boys. Tony and his partner, both new to the game, assumed their lives were at stake. When the hood walked into the apartment on Fourteenth Street they were renting from Al Wunderlich, he got whomped over the head by a lead pipe. Al returned to the pad after his summer vacation to find it spattered with dried blood and gore. Meantime, the mob had put out a contract on Tony, which forced him to go deep underground.

Next time Tony was involved in a violent incident, Wunderlich was present. A friend of Tony's had come to demand repayment of a loan. A hot argument ensued. Tony ran into the kitchen, grabbed a ten-inch cast-iron skillet off the stove, and smashed his creditor over the head. Wunderlich took the victim up to Bellevue, where he got eighteen stitches down the front of his skull. La Monte Young summed up

Tony's reputation at this time: "There were people looking for him. He always carried a knife. . . . Even then he was deeply involved in crime."

In the summer of 1962 Tony fled from New York with the FBI on his tail. He made his getaway by stealing a car from Alan Marlow, husband of the poet, Diane DePrima, boosting a credit card from another victim, and helping himself to all of La Monte Young's publishing fund for *An Anthology,* the basic document of Concept Art. When Tony called Al Wunderlich, who was back home in Portland, from the Montana border, Al warned Tony that the FBI had just left the house. "No problem!" snapped Cox. Then he ordered Al to rendezvous with him on the edge of town. When the two comrades met, the first order of business was putting the white '57 Ford that Tony was driving into an Earl Scheib body shop for a quick change of color. Next day Tony took off to visit his aunt Blanche in Los Angeles. On or about 1 August he sailed for the Orient.

The idea of searching for Yoko Ono in Japan came to Tony, according to his own account in *Radix* magazine, when La Monte Young told him about a young and beautiful Japanese artist who had recently disappeared. The story was that she had returned to Japan. What must have appealed to Tony as much as the glamour of this mysterious Japanese artist was the fact that she was the daughter of a bank president.

On the boat to the Orient, Tony learned from a fellow passenger that a woman artist named Yoko Ono had returned from the U.S. Tony managed to get to see her, but she turned out to be the wrong Yoko Ono—the name Ono is extremely common in Japan. Still, the wrong woman helped him find the right one. His discovery led to dismay, however, when he learned 1) that she was married and 2) that she was in a hospital.

When Tony finally inveigled his way into Yoko's presence, he found her heavily sedated. The drug she was on turned out to be one he knew about. When Toshi asked for Tony's help in getting Yoko out of the hospital, Tony had an inspiration. Buttonholing the hospital's director, Tony explained that he was an art journalist from New York and that it was his intention to write how this famous New York artist was being kept under heavy sedation in this hospital. Did the director want that sort of publicity? The director discharged the patient.

That was the greatest con job in Tony's career. He was so proud of it that he could not resist the temptation to put the whole story into a letter and send it to La Monte Young!

Yoko's release from the hospital did not dispel her depression. "I missed New York so much," she wrote later. "I often met and talked with Tony at a cake shop in Shinjuku [the Times Square of Tokyo]. Tony didn't have any acquaintances either, so he was lonely. Whenever the two of us saw each other we talked about things in New York. We almost cried from loneliness and melancholy."

The cure for Yoko's condition arrived unexpectedly one day in the form of an announcement that Hiroshi Teshigahara (manager of Sogetsu Hall and director of the film *Woman in the Dunes*) had invited John Cage and David Tudor to perform in Tokyo and tour Japan. This meant that Toshi would appear as an assisting artist and Yoko could function as the group's interpreter and guide. Yoko and Toshi told Tony about the tour and invited him to go along. Yoko also made it clear on this occasion that she regarded her marriage with Toshi as finished.

Cage and Tudor performed in October at Sogetsu, employing a number of Japanese musicians and Yoko Ono, who rose above the stage in a chair suspended from the flies and lay on her back atop the piano with her long hair streaming down toward the floor. The balance of the three-week visit was spent touring Japan's cultural monuments with Peggy Guggenheim, who confided in her memoirs: "I allowed Tony to come and sleep in the room I shared with Yoko. The result was a beautiful half-Japanese, half-American baby."

When the tour ended, Yoko moved into a hotel with Tony, who began pressing her to marry him. Yoko's family was alarmed by this development, because it was precisely the sort of scandalous situation they had been seeking to avert. The family promised Yoko that she could have anything she desired if only she would give up this American. "If her parents," remarked Mrs. Rutger Smith, "had not put up such a great objection to Tony—and they were obviously right in their objection to him—Yoko might have left him. She was embarrassed by the situation and didn't wish to further embarrass her family." Doubtless that is what Yoko said, but what she *did* does not suggest embarrassment so much as hostility, for like a bullfighter aiming for the heart of his huge adversary, Yoko delivered a stroke to the family honor that must have made the Onos think they were under a curse. On 28 November 1962 Yoko married Tony Cox at the American embassy in Tokyo—without first divorcing Toshi Ichiyanagi.

A lawyer finally straightened out the legal tangle created by this illegal marriage. The lawyer advised her to divorce Tony, then divorce Toshi, then remarry Tony, if she so desired. The divorce from Tony is dated 1 March 1963, which is only three days from Toshi's second marriage, to Sumiko Watanabe. Yoko married Tony again on 6 June at the American embassy. By this time, the lovers had moved out of the city to a small English-style cottage on a lake, a secluded spot where Yoko could enjoy privacy. Through the influence of her family, Tony obtained a desirable job at a school that taught conversational English. Mrs. Smith recalled that instead of spending the money he earned on food or other necessities, he would use his wages for their art. Once he filled a room with Yoko's poems printed on kites.

Another close friend of Yoko's, Kate Millett, the women's lib writer, then a sculptor married to a Japanese sculptor, recollected afternoons Yoko spent agonizing over whether to abort the child. Mrs. Rutger Smith felt that Yoko's conflict arose from a fundamental fear of commitment: Yoko had an "utter terror of structure; [she was always] hoping something overwhelming would happen to her [but when it did,] she could not tolerate it." Yoko's fear of bearing children was also closely connected to her art, which was all conception and no delivery.

Eventually Yoko was persuaded to have the baby against her will; as she explained: "When I was pregnant with Kyoko, Tony and the doctors frightened me into thinking that I could not safely have another abortion. At the time I decided to have Kyoko, I thought, 'Maybe if I have a child, I'll feel differently,' because society's myth is that all women are supposed to love having children." Actually, an abortion might not have been any more hazardous than the way Yoko decided to bear her child.

Mrs. Smith was told by John Nathan, later of Princeton, who was teaching with Tony at the conversation school, that on the morning of the birth, 3 August 1963, Tony arrived in a frenetic mood and said something like "We've got this baby thing going at our house—wow!" When Nathan asked what he was talking about, Tony declared that he had delivered the baby himself! Alarmed by this news, Nathan jumped into his car and raced to the house. He found Yoko in a heap on the floor, untended. Nathan picked up mother and baby and rushed them to a hospital. According to Mrs. Smith, "Tony had taken it into his mind that it would be fascinating to deliver this child."

The baby emerged unscathed. When Mrs. Smith visited Yoko at the hospital, she showed no resentment over what had happened. The only thing she said was: "I didn't know it would be so difficult."

Yoko's recovery from the delivery was slow. When she was discharged from the hospital, she and Tony moved into a flat consisting of one little room and a kitchen separated by a shoji screen on the thirty-fifth floor of a new building in Shibuya, the Greenwich Village of Tokyo. The apartment and the maid who helped Yoko with the baby were both contributed by Mrs. Ono, who had reconciled herself to the marriage after the birth of the child.

Tanaka Kozo remembered the apartment as "incredibly messy," with dirty dishes piled high in the sink and hermit crabs running loose because Tony was photographing them. Kozo recalled Tony's saying that Yoko reminded him of a girl he had read about who was mentally ill. Yoko summed up her life at this time as the "pits."

The birth of Kyoko had done nothing positive for her parents' marriage. Once Yoko was no longer burdened with her pregnancy, she started attacking Tony. Barbara Ann Copley-Smith, another friend, reported receiving an emergency call from Tony, who said that he was sitting in a bathtub full of blood and glass fragments, unable to find his glasses. Could Barbara Ann come to his aid? When she arrived she discovered that Yoko had trampled on Tony's glasses, in effect, blinding him. Then, he reported, she had held him prisoner in the tub for forty-five minutes by pressing a broken bottle against his jugular vein. This kind of violence was also witnessed by Al Wunderlich when he was reunited with Tony in 1964 in Japan, after having spent a year on a Fulbright grant in India. He found that Tony and Yoko were "trying to kill one another," adding, "I got the feeling that I had walked into the eye of a hurricane."

When Tony and Yoko were not at each other's throats, they were hard at work promoting her art, for their relationship had crystallized into what became henceforth the pattern of Yoko's relations with all men: a starring role for herself and, for the man, the part of producer. What they produced now was *Grapefruit,* Yoko Ono's principal claim to fame, a little collection of word pieces, one to sixteen lines in length, printed in the original edition on five-inch-square pages, sometimes with a Japanese version on the facing page. Though in appearance these compositions resemble poems, they are actually directions in prose that are meant to be acted upon. In the course of the next decade Yoko realized a great many of these scenarios in film, stage performance, or artifacts. Even the simplest of them can be interpreted as a sequence of actions. "Light a match and watch till it goes out" became the script for Yoko's most esteemed film, which examines a match flame at length through the use of an ultra-high-speed camera. The tone of the pieces is likewise consistent, with a sometimes natural, sometimes contrived air of whimsy pervading the collection. Hence, what the pieces attest to in Yoko's character is that side of herself— once so apparent and even now familiar to her intimates—that so entranced Michael Rumaker: the fey little Oriental exquisite, totally out of touch with the world and intent only upon her charming fancies. Yet the turn of a page presents: "Kill all the men you have slept with. Put the bones in a box and send it out into the sea in a box with flowers."

Al Wunderlich participated in a few avant-garde events with Tony and Yoko in Japan; then he found himself in a threatening triangle. Having been assured by both husband and wife that their relationship was at an end, Al had started having an affair with Yoko. The result was that Tony went crazy and began destroying Al's work, while Yoko behaved like a "ball buster." Terrified by these developments, Al took off for home. "I didn't want my life to get ground out at an early age in

Tokyo in a brawl with these two people," he explained. "They were threatening each other with butcher knives."

Yoko was also desperate to get away from Tony and Kyoko and return to New York, for the one thing she had gained through her marriage was the right, as the wife of an American citizen, to reside indefinitely in the United States. After applying for a visa, she busied herself about her final appearance at Sogetsu, *Yoko Ono's Farewell Performance*. Having lost Al Wunderlich, Yoko and Tony pressed into service a young air force medical corpsman, Jeff Perkins. Jeff recalled that he and Tony performed a piece in which they were tied back to back with tin cans and milk bottles attached to them by strings. In total darkness they walked from one side of the stage to the other, seeking to make as little noise as possible. Yoko announced during their progress that she had released two snakes into the house. She added that each member of the audience could light only one match to search for the reptiles.

In the only impressive offering that night, *Cut Piece*, Yoko appeared onstage dressed in formal black, carrying a large pair of shears. Kneeling on a mat and confronting the audience with an impassive face, she invited the spectators to come forward, one by one, and cut whatever they pleased from her costume. The picture of the handsome, aristocratic woman, kneeling before the sharp-edged steel, would suggest inevitably to the Japanese mind the ancient custom of seppuku or harakiri. The duration of the performance, and, consequently, the buildup of tension, were prolonged by the natural reluctance of the spectators to cut more than a bit of cloth from Yoko's costume. How far her shearing went that night is unclear, but on subsequent occasions she was reduced to virtual nudity and sometimes threatened with the loss of her long hair.

Yoko departed from Japan on 23 September 1964 on a Pan Am flight for San Francisco. She gave out the story before her departure that she was going back to New York to complete her studies. Tony remained behind with Kyoko, whom Yoko had proposed to leave with her grandmother, living in a tenement house in a back street.

JULIA: John Lennon's favorite picture of his ~~mot~~her, taken in the summer of 1949, when she ~~was~~ pregnant with his second half-sister, Jacqueline ~~Dyki~~ns. *(Stanley Parkes)*

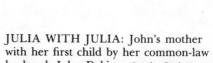

AUNT MIMI, who reared John from the age of five, pictured in their back garden. *(Stanley Parkes)*

~~ME~~NDIPS, the typically middle-class home in ~~whic~~h John was reared in Allerton, a suburb of ~~Live~~rpool. John's room was just above the entry. ~~(Stanl~~ey Parkes)

JULIA WITH JULIA: John's mother with her first child by her common-law husband, John Dykins. *(Stanley Parkes)*

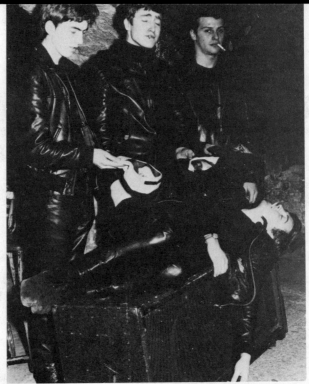

PAUL IS DEAD in 1961, as George, John, and Pete Best
wake him. *(Dick Matthews)*

THE ORIGINAL BEATLES on the bandstand at the
Cavern, its fake dungeon wall imprinted with the names
of the other top Liverpool bands. *(Dick Matthews)*

THE STAR-CLUB, Hamburg, where
the Beatles played with rock greats like
Little Richard and Gene Vincent. *(Ted
"Kingsize" Taylor)*

BEATLE JOHN: The moment he
peeled off his perfect leathers and put
on his first band suit at twenty-one,
John Lennon felt he had sold out.
(Stanley Parkes)

"THE BEAUTY AND SPIRIT OF
THE BEATLES" was John's phrase
for this favorite picture by Jürgen
Vollmer, taken in the spring of 1961
in Hamburg. *(Jürgen Vollmer)*

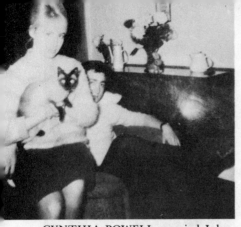

CYNTHIA POWELL married John Lennon in August 1962 but remained concealed at Mendips, where she is pictured with her uneasy-looking husband. *(Stanley Parkes)*

KENWOOD: John's house in the Stockbroker Belt where he said he was just "stopping." *(Ron Ellis)*

FREDDIE LENNON: John's father, forced out of his son's life when John was five, reappeared seventeen years later, at the height of Beatlemania, looking like a long-haired Beatnik. *(Pauline Stone)*

FATHERHOOD: A distressed John Lennon with his first son, Julian, in the garden at Mendips in 1963. *(Stanley Parkes)*

"LIKE MOTHER, LIKE SON" was John's view of Julian, pictured here with a classmate and his mother, after her divorce. *(Stanley Parkes)*

I SAW HER STANDING HERE": Yoko as she appeared when John first saw her at the Indica Gallery in November 1966. *(Iain Macmillan)*

LAST DANCE: After the Beatles' disastrous first date in the London area at Aldershot—eighteen paying customers showed up—John waltzed defiantly with George. *(Dick Matthews)*

RORY STORM, pictured here with John and Paul, was a Rod Stewart–style performer, whose Hurricanes included Ringo Starr on drums. *(Dick Matthews)*

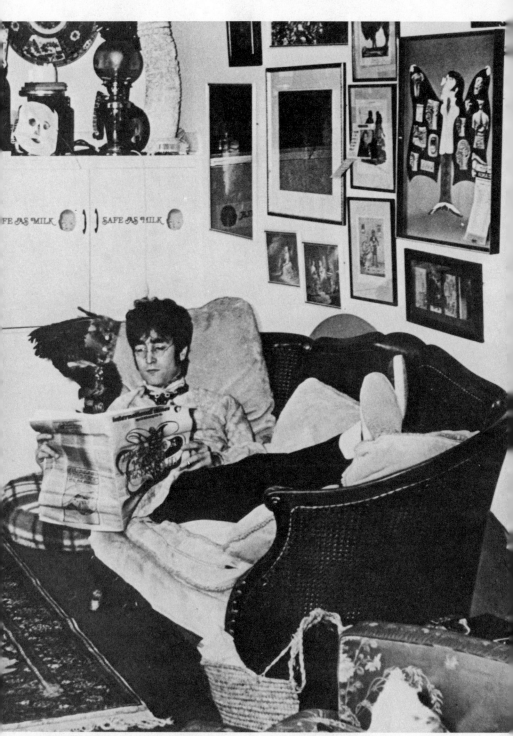

POSITION ONE for John Lennon was lying down with his nose in a newspaper or book, as here in his favorite corner of Kenwood at the end of the Summer of Love in 1967. *(Keystone Press Agency, Inc.)*

INFATUATION with charismatic father figures was typical of Lennon, as his happy expression proclaims in this meeting with the Maharishi Mahesh Yogi, in company with Paul and a skeptical Jane Asher; behind them, an unidentified woman and man; to the right, Ringo and Maureen Starr, and George Harrison. *(Keystone Press Agency, Inc.)*

A TALE OF TWO CITIES

NEW YORK

When Yoko thought of New York in Japan, she wept with the grief of an exile. When she got back to the Apple, she had even more cause for tears. Her return to the avant-garde scene was singularly unsuccessful. She made such a nuisance of herself trying to promote her art that an influential buyer like Ivan Karp of the Castelli Gallery would leave any room where he found her present. Personalities aside, there was an innate difficulty in popularizing Concept Art. By definition, it was intangible. A fashion show of emperor's clothes, it couldn't be treated as a commodity. Yet that was precisely how Yoko sought to push it, offering everyone she met a legal-size sheet of paper headed ONO'S SALES LIST.

The list was simply a catalog of titles arranged in categories and tagged with prices. There were sound tapes of snow falling in India; touch poems priced according to the quality of the material; machines that cried or spoke or kept eternal time; designs for houses through which the wind could blow or into which one could see without being able to see out; paintings to be constructed in the viewer's head; garden sets consisting in holes for clouds and fog; letters and replies; imaginary music; underwear to accentuate special defects; and the unpublished as well as published edition of *Grapefruit*. Ideas, whimsical, amusing, preposterous, but nothing to hang on the wall.

Perhaps the most representative judgment pronounced on Yoko was that of Andy Warhol. One night Andy and his film director, Paul Morrissey, ran into Yoko at a charity benefit. She was standing behind a canvas with a hole in it, shaking hands with people through the hole. When Morrissey asked, "Who is she?" Andy replied, "She's always been around. She's always doing something. She's always copying someone's art."

When all her efforts to promote herself failed, Yoko resumed her relationship with Tony Cox. He arrived early in 1965, bringing with him Kyoko, whom Yoko insisted on boarding out. Tony placed the child with Whitey Caizza, a colleague of his father's, who lived in East Islip, Long Island, with his wife and five children. For nine months the Coxes rarely saw their infant daughter.

Meantime, Tony solved the problem of living rent-free with a typical con man strategy. The Coxes would move into a flat in Greenwich Village and pay the obligatory three months' rent in advance; then, when the next month's rent fell due, they would fail to pay. The landlord would start eviction proceedings, but under New York's housing laws, getting a tenant out of an old apartment is a slow process.

In their eagerness to find some way of gaining attention, Tony and Yoko volunteered to help WBAI, a nonprofit radio station dedicated to cultural programming, which was offering a benefit concert at Town Hall on 14 August 1965. Tony associated himself with Norman Seaman, producer of the event, while Yoko worked as a file clerk. Her job brought her into contact with the station's music director, Ann McMillan, a straightforward and sincere woman, who was dismayed to discover how Yoko and Tony were living in the two flats they occupied in the course of the summer, on Hudson Street and Christopher Street. "I'm not the least bit middle-class-oriented," protested the director, "but boy! it was the *pits*! What a depressing place." Hot as a sauna, dirty as a crash pad, crawling with cockroaches that one visitor described as surrounding Yoko's mute face like exclamation points, these grim little flats were now the home of Kyoko, whom Tony had insisted upon fetching back from Long Island. Since Yoko and Tony were perpetually busy, they often left the child alone, seated on newspapers to absorb her excretions because she was not toilet-trained. Ann McMillan recalled how upset she was when she would enter the flat and find the child in this deplorable condition. "For heaven's sake," she burst out one day. "Why don't you give that child to someone who wants it?" Yoko was actually working hard to achieve that very goal, thus removing once and for all the annoying obstacle in her path.

Tony had a married but childless cousin, Frances Westerman-Collins, who was eager to adopt Kyoko. Only the resistance of her husband—who cautioned that Yoko would change her mind eventually and demand the return of the child—prevented the adoption. Undeterred, Yoko found another couple who were willing to take the risk. This time Tony objected, insisting that Kyoko remain. Because Tony had assumed the whole burden of rearing the child, Yoko was not in a strong position to demand that Kyoko be given up, though everyone agreed that adoption would be more humane than condemning the child to spending her infancy crawling about on urine- and feces-stained newspapers while being overrun by cockroaches.

* * *

Yoko Ono and Tony Cox had come to the end of the road in both their personal and artistic relationships when, in the summer of 1966, a casually offered invitation to an avant-garde congress in London revolutionized their lives. The invitation was tendered by Mario Amaya, a good-looking young man from Brooklyn, who had jumped on the Pop Art bandwagon when it first started rolling and commenced a career that had already made him the lover of an eminent British art historian and eventually raised him to the enviable position of curator of Huntington Hartford's anti-abstract modern art museum in Columbus Circle. (Amaya lost this post by turning the members' lounge into a transvestite cabaret and embezzling the museum's funds.) Amaya was now based in London, where he had founded a new journal, *Art and Artists*, designed to put the phlegmatic British eyeball to eyeball with the bizarre new happenings in the international art world.

The event that Amaya was promoting could have served as the title of his own life: *The Auto-Destructive Art Symposium*. Dashing about New York, handing out invitations, he laid one on Yoko Ono without even knowing her or her work. Though Yoko was hardly in a position to undertake an expensive trip to England just to appear at a symposium, the idea mushroomed into an overmastering obsession. She and Tony were soon battling fiercely over whether or not she should go. Their conflict became so threatening to their relationship that they decided to seek the help of a marriage counselor.

The adviser they chose is known to New Yorkers primarily as the author, producer, and star of numerous Off Broadway musical comedies, but Al Carmines is by profession the assistant minister of the Judson Church, where one of his pastoral duties is counseling troubled couples. When Yoko and Tony first presented themselves, Carmines observed that Yoko "played the Oriental wife—quiet, submissive, catering to the men—but I sensed in her a kind of ambition and drive which she took great pains to hide. . . . The main trouble between them was that she wanted more freedom. She wanted to go to England. Tony was afraid of her having so much independence. He felt that if they loved one another and the child, she wouldn't want to go traipsing off anyplace." Carmines noted that Tony was very possessive. The more he laid claim to Yoko, the more she withdrew.

Carmines was eager to flush Yoko out into the open, so he scheduled a series of private sessions in which he encouraged her to voice her thoughts. When she began to emerge from her shell, she shocked him by appearing a totally different woman. She spoke of her art in a messianic tone, proclaiming it the wave of the future in America and perhaps throughout the world. She was unshakable on the question of going to England. Eventually Carmines concluded: "Yoko Ono has a relentlessness about her own urges that is almost religious , . . . like St. Paul going to Tarsus." As session after session went by and Yoko continued to brush off Carmines's questions, suggestions, arguments—all designed to make her concentrate on the problems of her relationship instead of on the trip to England—he was forced to recognize that Yoko was "a woman of steel . . . one of the strongest-willed individuals I have ever met. . . . I was a little frightened of that, but I was in awe of it."

After two months of counseling sessions, Carmines realized that his work was in vain. "If Yoko wanted the marriage to work, I think they could have done it," he concluded. "Tony, despite his male chauvinism, was willing to do almost anything to keep the marriage together. She was not." At the final session Yoko announced: "I'm going to England next week."

Tony countered: "I'm not sure she's going to England next week."

Yoko retorted: "Yes, I'm going." The Coxes were precisely where they had been on the first day of their counseling. Yoko extended her hand to Carmines and said, "It's been very nice to know you." Next thing he heard about her, she was involved with John Lennon.

LONDON

On a morning in early September 1966 Mario Amaya answered the bell of his flat at 37 Redcliffe Square, Kensington, and discovered on his doorstep Yoko Ono, Tony Cox, and Kyoko. Just arrived after a long journey by freighter from Montreal, the Coxes had no place to stay. About to go out to lunch with art historian Ken Davison, Amaya puzzled on the phone: "What am I to do with these people?"

"Bring them along," drawled the obliging historian.

Soon the party was seated about a restaurant table in Godfrey Street. Davison asked Yoko: "What *is* Concept Art?" Yoko replied with a long rigmarole about going to an ancient bridge in Kyoto, a national treasure, and taking from it a tiny bit. Davison replied: "My dear, wouldn't it be more interesting if you went to the bridge and *didn't* take anything from it?"

"Oh, Tony, Tony!" Yoko exclaimed. "Is brilliant new idea. Mr. Davison says you go to bridge and take nothing from it!" From that time forth, said Amaya, Yoko Ono began producing pieces that did nothing.

One of the Coxes' few London assets was an extensive list of names and telephone numbers of everybody involved in the local art scene. By working these contacts, the impoverished pair obtained invitations night after night to parties that often provided a free meal. One night they met a surrealist artist named Adrian Morris, with whom they achieved instant rapport. The following week Adrian and his wife, Audrey, invited the Coxes to a party at the Morris home, a Georgian house at 52 Tedworth Square in Chelsea. At the end of the night Yoko and Tony gave their hosts a hard-luck story. They said that the flat they had rented was not ready for occupancy and they were loath to lay out the money for a hotel room. Could they stay the night? They stayed not only that night but the entire weekend. When Monday came, they showed no signs of leaving. Morris, who was fond of "Little Yoko," as he called her, allowed the pair to remain in the bedroom they were occupying on the third floor. For the next four months Yoko, Tony and Kyoko lived in a room that Morris described as an "environment." The sheets were never changed. Everything was stained. The floor was littered with photos. Dehydrated condoms hung from a nail. The whole place stank.

In the course of checking out the London art scene, the Coxes soon discovered Mason's Yard, an old coaching yard in St. James that was the sanctum sanctorum of the Underground—the small, loosely knit society of people dedicated to the new counterculture. Entered through alleys that carried the visitor from the busy thoroughfares of central London into a dim and disreputable recess—long the haunt of homosexuals who frequented its notorious public toilet or junkies who would wind up their night's activity with a queasy breakfast at Gus's, the workingman's caf' on the corner (whose mascot was a huge cat covered with grease)—Mason's Yard had suddenly become the in place when the Scotch of St. James opened there, succeeding the Ad Lib as the trendiest disco of Swinging London.

The Scotch was relentless in the pursuit of its decorative theme: bagpipes and claymores, round targes and short pikes covered its wood-paneled walls, the table lamps were brandy balls with plaid shades, the waiters wore tartan waistcoats and trews, and the DJ worked out of an authentic coach that could have carried Waverley to the Highlands. Rock stars regarded the Scotch much as conservative clubmen did their nearby establishments: Brooks, Whites, Boodles, and the Carlton. The disco's management, eager to encourage the custom of the beat elite, would note where each group preferred to sit and attach brass plates to the furniture proclaiming "The Beatles" or "The Rolling Stones." If a rock star arrived while his table was in use, the less desirable guest would be abruptly levitated to another location. Those who wanted to shake a ham had to descend to the cellar, which had a floor so small that if a bottle fell off a waiter's upraised tray, it would bobble about on the shoulders of the dancers until it could be retrieved.

What gave this hot, dark, noisy, and congested basement its cachet was the occasional jam session led by a famous entertainer like Paul McCartney, who once picked up a band consisting of Sammy Davis,

Jr.'s drummer, Dave Clark's organist, and a member of Marmalade, a group whose name was a pun on "jam." Another draw was the surprise appearance of hot new acts breaking into the London entertainment world, like Ike and Tina Turner, or even the debut of some talented unknown destined to fame, like José Feliciano or Joe Cocker.

What brought the Beatles to Mason's Yard was not so much the Scotch as an enterprise that typified more than any other the new underground—the Indica (as in *Cannabis indica*) Gallery and Bookshop. The brain spawn of Paul's housemate Peter Asher (who put up the money) and the two young men who ran the shops, Asher's old school chum John Dunbar, (married to pop star Marianne Faithfull) and Paul McCartney's closest friend, Miles, the Indica was designed to give staid old London a needle-sharp dose of the new wave. Miles was keen on disseminating the beat writers, a mission he had embarked upon back in June 1965 by giving a party for Allen Ginsberg, to which he had invited the Beatles. Before the pop stars' arrival, the notorious American poet had gotten drunk, in which state he was discovered by John and George, who were accompanied by Cynthia and Patti. The fat and hairy author of "Howl" was standing naked in the middle of the room with his underpants on his head and a sign hanging from his penis that read NO WAITING. John Lennon, easily shocked at other men's eccentricities, took one look at the beat bard and murmured imploringly: "Not in front of the birds, man!"

Paul McCartney had demonstrated his support for the Indica by investing five thousand pounds and even lending a hand with the shelf building and wall painting. This was wholly in character for Paul because he was now up to his banjo eyes in the avant-garde, hanging out with Bill Burroughs and lending himself to strange aesthetic experiments. John Lennon, who was still proclaiming himself an "anti-intellectual," regarded the new directions in which Paul was leading the band with profound distrust. As always, however, Lennon proved himself a dedicated follower of fashion, for, as he was to explain many times, the way the Beatles led contemporary taste was not by inventing or introducing anything but simply by picking up the new waves while they were still faint etheric vibrations and then amplifying them powerfully through the medium of the Beatles' popularity. Thus the stage was set for the meeting of John Lennon and Yoko Ono, who were brought together not by chance but by the Coxes' relentless efforts to advance their shared career.

Miles remembered distinctly the day Yoko walked into the gallery and introduced herself: "I recognize now that her distinctiveness came in a typical New York superhustling trait. She really came on very strong and was a pain in the ass." John Dunbar, by contrast, was an easy touch. Today he says that if he had set out to destroy John Lennon, he could not have done better than to introduce him to Yoko Ono. As soon as the Coxes found a patron to underwrite the cost of their show, Dunbar gave them a date. Neither Yoko nor Tony could be bothered with actually making artworks; the pieces they conceived were fabricated by three gifted young students recruited from the Royal College of Art.

One of the first things that Yoko and Tony learned when they started hanging out at the Indica was the connection between the gallery and the Beatles, who always attended the openings and who bought magazines and books from the shop. (John came in the first time asking for something that would describe how to build an orgone accumulator and also for a book by Nietzsche, which he pronounced "Nitchey." George bought illustrated volumes of Tantric art, and Paul, who was decorating a house in St. John's Wood, copies of *Domus*. According to Miles, the Beatles didn't read much, but they got a lot of ideas from looking at pictures.) Naturally this pair of practiced hustlers would not miss out on such a wonderful opportunity to cut into these rich and enormously influential young marks.

Yoko always liked to play her John Cage card, claiming a long and close collaborative relationship with America's foremost avant-garde composer. When she met her first Beatle, Paul, she told him that she was collecting manuscripts for a forthcoming publication by Cage that would reproduce examples of scores by all the great contemporary composers commencing with Stravinsky and concluding, she hoped, with the Beatles. Though her pitch was perfect, Paul McCartney was not about to hand over any of his manuscripts to this pushy little stranger. Instead, he suggested—not without a certain malicious humor—that she would fare much better with his mate John, who was very keen on anything avant-garde.

When the famous night—Monday, 7 November, 1966—rolled around, John Lennon was out of his mind. He'd been without sleep for three days, all that time on acid. Yoko was laying for him. "Yoko took one look at John and attached herself to him like a limpet mine—with much the same destructive effect," recalled Lennon's driver, Les Anthony. "She clung to his arm while we went around the exhibition, talking away to him in her funny little high-pitched voice until he fled."

Lennon rewrote the encounter extensively in later years, as he did every episode in his widely publicized relationship with Yoko. Two moments from the first meeting enlarged themselves to symbolic proportions. One bit entailed climbing a ladder toward a framed canvas attached to the ceiling, from which hung a magnifying glass the viewer could use to read a single word printed on the canvas in small letters. Lennon anticipated that he would read the sort of phrase that he would have put at the end of the climb, something like "Tee-hee!" or

"Fuck you!" He was surprised and pleased to read "Yes." Another celebrated moment occurred when he sought to hammer a nail into a
board provided for this purpose. Yoko wanted to keep her board intact
for opening night. When John Dunbar urged her to relent, she told
Lennon he could drive a nail for five shillings. "Suppose I drive an
imaginary nail for five imaginary shillings," countered Lennon. Yoko
claimed to have been vastly amused at this rejoinder. Actually, she
would have been a lot better pleased if when she ran out of the gallery
to chase John across the yard into Duke Street, he had invited her to
join him. Instead, he excused himself, saying that he had to go to the
studio.

"Take me with you!" begged Yoko.

"No, we're too busy!" snapped the anxious Lennon as he jumped
into his Mini and took off.

When Yoko reported this encounter to Tony, he urged her to press
on and take advantage of this first nibble. Yoko needed no urging. She
set her sights on Lennon and within a couple of days had conned her
way past the guards at Abbey Road and gotten inside Studio 2. Shown
the door, she took to hanging out in front of the building with the
Apple Scruffs, the young girls who spent every night, even in the
coldest weather, camping outside the studio in the hopes of seeing a
Beatle or exchanging a greeting.

One night, when John and Cynthia stepped into the backseat of
their limo, Yoko threw herself between them. Promptly deposited at
her own door, she shifted her beat next to Kenwood, where she hung
about in such dreadful weather that Mrs. Powell took pity on her and
admitted her to the house so that she might call a cab. Yoko took advantage of the opportunity to plant a ring, which she could return later
to reclaim. She also began bombarding John with notes, begging for
money to present her art and threatening, "If you don't support me,
that's it! I'll kill myself!" Cynthia, who had already begun to brood
about this strange little Oriental, was shocked one day when she and
her mother observed John opening a parcel addressed to him by Yoko,
inside which he discovered a Kotex box containing a broken cup
smeared with red paint.

Some men would have been turned off by Yoko's tactics, but John
Lennon was titillated. He was accustomed to being the prey not the
hunter; yet most of the women who had chased him had been types he
scorned: groupies, show girls, whores, and little fans sent up to his
suite like a steak from room service. Never in all the years since his
passionate affair with Cynthia in art school had he been in love or even
seriously involved with a woman. His passion, the strange amalgam of
love and hate that was the essence of his being, had long been focused

on Brian Epstein, whom he confessed years later he had "loved more than a woman."

For a woman to stir John deeply, she clearly had to possess a strong masculine component. Here is where the aggressive Yoko began to tip the beam, which she inclined further by being an Oriental, Lennon's favorite type, and further yet by embodying the New York avant-garde scene, which meant a lot now to John since he had become the leader of the rock avant-garde. In fine, John Lennon was a man upon whom Yoko could work her spell. What's more, he could rationalize that he ran no risk because he held all the cards. He was accustomed to picking up women and boffing them in the back seat of his limo. Why shouldn't he give Yoko a toss?

"John began to weaken," reported Les Anthony. "Came the day when Cynthia went off to the north and Yoko arrived at their house in order to discuss John sponsoring some art show. A business meeting, they said it was. But she didn't go back until the morning, and after that John couldn't leave her alone. . . . In those first days, before John left Cynthia, he and Yoko used to do their courting, to put it politely, in the back of the car while I was driving them around."

How different is this eyewitness report from the Hollywood fantasy that John and Yoko labored for years to impose on the public! According to that account, eighteen months elapsed between the first meeting of these lovers and the consummation of their passion at Kenwood. According to Les Anthony, who was certainly in a position to know, the time between meeting and mating was exactly three weeks.

Once Yoko got involved with John Lennon, her life, already difficult, became even more trying. Tony posed no problem; he encouraged Yoko to go after Lennon. As Adrian Morris observed, "Tony outfoxed himself." Yoko, however, was distressed by John's overbearing macho manner. Accustomed to being treated by Tony as a little princess, Yoko found herself involved now with a very touchy and hostile superstar, who was constantly flying on drugs. "Any woman I could shout down," Lennon remarked years later. "Most of my arguments with anybody used to be a question of who could shout the loudest. Normally I would win the argument, whether I was right or wrong, especially if the argument was with a woman—they'd just give in. And she didn't! She'd go on and on and on, until I understood it. Then I had to treat her with respect." Yoko's greatest strength, however, was not tenacity in argument. Her real attraction for John Lennon arose from the fact that she was ideally suited to play the starring role in his fantasy system.

"I always had this dream of meeting an artist woman that I would fall in love with—even from art school," confessed Lennon. "And when we met and were talking, I just realized that she knew everything I knew, and more probably. And it was coming out of a *woman's* head. It just sort of bowled me over. It was like finding gold. To find something that you could go and get pissed with, and to have exactly the same relationship with any mate in Liverpool you'd ever had, but also you could to to bed with it, and it could stroke your head when you felt tired or sick or depressed. Could also be mother . . . well, it's just like winning the pools." Yoko Ono fulfilled John Lennon's oldest and deepest fantasy: to have again his mother, while at the same time satisfying his yearning for a mistress and a male mate. The switching back and forth across the divisions of gender and the barrier of incest is the key to this relationship, as is likewise suggested by Lennon's odd habit of referring to Yoko by means of the neutral pronoun "it." Yoko Ono existed in John Lennon's imagination as one of those magical creatures in a fairy tale that come to the hero in his moment of need and relieve him of all his problems. The subtext to the Ballad of John and Yoko is "Puss in Boots."

Another fairy tale that is nearly as apt is "Sleeping Beauty" because for years John had been lying about at Kenwood dreaming of the perfect princess, who he imagined would awaken him to passion with the kiss of a Prince Charming. "Since I was extraordinarily shy," he confided, "especially around beautiful women, my daydreams necessitated that she [Yoko] be aggressive enough to 'save me,' i.e., 'take me away from all this.'" Although here he employs the language of the suburban housewife locked up inside an unfulfilling marriage, on other occasions he drew his metaphor from drugs, recalling, "She was coming on, and as she was talking to me, I would get high, and the discussion would get to such a level that I would be going higher and higher. And when she'd leave, I'd go back to this sort of suburbia. Then I'd meet her again and my head would go off like I was on an acid trip. . . . Once I got a sniff of it, I was hooked. I couldn't leave her alone."

By this point Yoko no longer had to be aggressive in her relationship with Lennon. She could revert to a more subdued but no less forceful technique for exploiting the great star's fame and fortune in order to advance her all-important career.

Early in 1967 Adrian Morris finally asked the Coxes to leave. He and Audrey had gone off for a holiday, putting Yoko and Tony in charge of the house. When the Morrises returned, they found their home a mess from top to bottom. Yoko and Tony had been using the place for press conferences and had fouled it so badly that the cleaning woman had given up in disgust and quit the job. Before the Coxes departed, Yoko told Morris that she was in love with a "businessman"—that was her code word for John Lennon—and he was making her life difficult.

Morris observed Yoko on several occasions talking on the phone to her "businessman." At one point she took to her bed and lay there complaining of all the problems this clandestine relationship was causing her. On that note she finally went off with Tony to live in a second-class residential hotel.

Yoko's cousin Hideaki Kase visited her one night early in January 1967, discovering her lying on a big bed supported by several pillows and wearing a white negligee. She had told him over the phone that she didn't want to see any Japanese, but as he was her cousin, he could come around and chat. Tony was sleeping on the sofa, wrapped in blankets. He roused himself when Kase entered the room and then sank back to sleep. Yoko said to her cousin in Japanese: "Don't bother with this man." Then, for the next two hours, they talked. Yoko denounced Japan, remarking, "It's such a worthless country, isn't it?" The Japanese, she complained, were hopelessly unsophisticated and shallow in matters of modern art. Most of the talk consisted of Yoko's boasting of her achievements as an artistic pioneer. She claimed to be the inventor of Flower Power, the founder of the Happening and a lot of other aesthetic innovations then fashionable. Undoubtedly this was the same line that she was feeding John Lennon during those long discussions that got him higher and higher. John had discovered a fellow genius.

Another Japanese who encountered Yoko at this time was Tanaka Kozo, who lived in the same hotel for ten days. Yoko told him that she was sick of the life she was leading and longed to be living in a deluxe hotel. She also spoke disparagingly of Tony, condemning him as a "little man" and admitting that she longed to leave him. But this proud, boastful woman, always contemptuous of men and their pretensions, would not make a move on her own behalf until she had secured a new man who could provide her with everything she coveted: wealth, power, and fame.

PAUL GRINDS PEPPER

The photos of John Lennon taken during the *Sgt. Pepper* sessions are disquieting. Instead of the typical Lennon pub shot—mouth agape, eyes popping, the whole face a clown mask—here is a young man who has suddenly aged about forty years. The eyes behind his granny glasses look like those of dead fish. His dry, droopy mustache belongs on the face of an old geezer. His slumped posture is that of an ancient stage door keeper. Miles, a frequent visitor to the sessions, explained: "John set out to destroy his ego. He made a good job of it."

Ego death, the product of heavy doses of LSD and the *Tibetan Book of the Dead,* could be the reason for John Lennon's sudden metamorphosis into the Superannuated Man. Such drastic changes were to become commonplace in the Sixties as the rock scene degenerated into the drug scene. But two facts make this interpretation untenable. First, John never dropped acid while cutting wax; second, his abject mood blew away as soon as the sessions concluded. So other reasons must be sought, the most likely being either a heavier drug than acid or some intense emotional disturbance. Actually, both factors were at work.

John was choked with resentment because he felt Paul was trying to seize control of the Beatles. This threat had been in John's mind for years, perhaps from the moment he met Paul, because the latter was such an obvious "keenie" and because he was so musically gifted. Only the fact that Paul was younger than John in both age and experience had prevented their naturally conflicting personalities from clashing sooner. Their relationship had also been buffered by the separation of each man's sphere of authority. Paul, a born show-biz hustler, had acted as the band's front man onstage and its de facto manager offstage. John, who fancied himself a proudly aloof artiste, was long content to be the star of the Beatles' records. For years he had gotten all the A-sides on the singles and the lion's share of the album tracks. Singing lead was his symbol of leadership.

Though the public assumed the leading men of the Beatles enjoyed a close personal relationship, this had never been the case. John described them as being like two soldiers in the same foxhole: each man held the other's life in his hands, but when the shooting stopped, they had no desire to remain together. On the road John would bunk with George, while Paul occupied a room with Ringo. There was no more sharing of confidences than there was of living quarters. When asked about Paul's relationship with Linda Eastman, John replied that he and Paul had long since ceased to discuss personal matters. They never socialized together, nor did they move in the same circles. There is only one moment in all the copious literature of the Beatles when you catch a glimpse of how John Lennon really felt about Paul McCartney before their falling out.

They are shooting *Help!* in Switzerland. Having come in from the snow, they're removing their heavy clothing while listening to a tape of their latest songs. After three tracks by Paul, John mumbled: "I probably like your songs better than mine." Doubt, envy, fear concerning who was the better composer—those were John's true feelings about Paul.

When Lennon prostrated himself before the Acid Buddha, he destroyed his carefully maintained balance with his partners. The more passive and withdrawn Lennon became, the more active and engaged grew his rival, who was developing now at an incredible rate and constantly bombarding the other Beatles with his new discoveries and inspirations, from Vivaldi to Stockhausen, from advanced tape-editing techniques to the queer sounds of that protosynthesizer, the Mellotron. Inevitably, Paul became the Beatles' prime mover.

The first product of his ascendancy was the greatest of the Beatles' miscellaneous albums, *Revolver.* This landmark recording completes the transition, already under way in *Rubber Soul,* from rock 'n' roll to *rock,* the term deliberately adopted by the mavens of the music to distinguish the style of the Sixties from that of the Fifties. Rock meant sophisticated and witty lyrics dealing with serious themes. Rock meant a flood of new sounds and musical idioms from every time and place. Above all, rock meant the new psychedelic consciousness and sensibility ushered in by the widespread use of LSD.

The first signal the album gives that we are entering upon a new era comes in its outermost grooves. Instead of hearing a burst of music when the needle starts tracking, we find ourselves listening through an open mike to the Beatles preparing to record, as a Liverpudlian voice counts off (after coughing): "One, two . . ." This cinéma vérité opening—underscoring the fact that *Revolver* is not an impersonally manufactured product but the work of real, live men in a studio—initiated a whole new game in which rock bands began to play around with reality and illusion the way dramatists and moviemakers had long been doing.

The next sign of drastic change was the theme of the initial song— *taxes*. Of all the things that *don't* concern kids, taxation must stand at the top of the list; hence, by firing the first shot of their revolver at the tax man, the Beatles blew a jagged hole in their lifelong identification with the teenyboppers, aligning themselves now with an older, hipper crowd that would appreciate their sour-mouthed complaint as well as their audacity in voicing such grievances through a medium consecrated to love sighs.

As the grooves of *Revolver* unwind, every band offers not just a fresh song but a radically different perspective. The eclecticism of the Beatles, always one of their most striking features, explodes here in a dazzling display of artistic diversity. "Eleanor Rigby" points back to the gaslight era, with its urgently chopping string quartet and Dickensian cast of characters, whereas "Tomorrow Never Knows," with its robot voice chanting over a hubbub of jungle noises, hoedown fiddles, and sore-boil guitar riffs, gesticulates awesomely toward the psychopharmaceutical future. Between these extremes are marshaled a comical street chantey, "Yellow Submarine" (widely regarded as a song about Nembutals, which are yellow and sub-shaped); "For No One," an Edwardian parlor musicale; "Good Day Sunshine," a perky, straw hat, music hall turn; and so on through the greatest variety of musical fare ever heaped up on a pop platter.

Though the Beatles always gave a great deal of thought to how their songs should be sequenced, the effect of tracking through *Revolver* is like seating yourself in one of those metal cars on the Whip, where no sooner do you get rolling in one direction than *wham!* you hit a bumper and go whirling off on a tangent that ends abruptly in another disorienting carom. Obviously you need a little something to cushion your head and loosen up your being so that you can enjoy this trippy inconsequence, but that looseness was now to be presumed in the listener, for the vital link between popular music and drugs forged secretly in the underworld of jazz had now become in the Sixties the universally acknowledged and accepted precondition for getting off to records.

Who was primarily responsible for this hallucinatory album, as full of illusions as the Tunnel of Love? Up until now the answer would have been "John Lennon" because at every point in the Beatles' past history it had been John, with his remarkable sense of where the music and its audience were at, who had boosted the band to their next level of achievement. Now all that had changed. Paul had attained absolute parity with John as a composer by writing "Eleanor Rigby," which, despite its sentimental tone, is just as remarkable as Lennon's best effort, "Tomorrow Never Knows." What's more, as these two songs testify,

John and Paul were not just equals now but opposites, as different in art as they had always been in life.

But it was not simply a case of the Beatles' becoming bivocal. Paul was primarily responsible for the highly innovative use of music and sound, language and verse, production values, and recording techniques throughout the album. *Revolver*, a Columbian journey in search of a brave new world, is inspired, sustained, and infused with Paul's bright-eyed discovery of all the wonders of the London cultural scene, that vast new world that had been opened up to him by his sojourn with the Ashers. The tightly closed and highly defensive Lennon would never have opened himself to all these influences and experiences if Paul had not half seduced, half challenged John to make the effort. Ironically, it was Lennon, once he had been converted, who carried the Beatles' journey of discovery to its farthest reach, but by that time the whole world was tumbling along in the same direction.

By November 1966, when the Beatles began laying down tracks for the album that became *Sgt. Pepper,* Paul McCartney had become the band's de facto artistic director. *Pepper* was from the outset Paul's album. He conceived the idea, wrote at least half the songs, ran the recording sessions, supervised the mixing, and arranged for the precedent-making package. John Lennon was so graveled by this tour de force that he complained bitterly that Paul had gotten the upper hand by employing the tactics of the fait accompli. "When Paul felt like it," grumbled John, "he would come in with about twenty good songs and say, 'We're recording.' And I suddenly had to write a fucking stack of songs. *Pepper* was like that." Even if this account were literally true, as it is not, it would hardly be a crushing indictment of Paul. Indeed, it simply confirms the suspicion that Paul's power was founded primarily in John's growing apathy, which had produced an aversion to work and responsibility. Suppose Paul hadn't come in with his "twenty good songs"? What would have happened to the Beatles? The answer is that they would not have produced the album that brought them their greatest acclaim. Nor would the lethargic Lennon have been inspired to compose some of his most memorable tracks. Clearly Paul was simply stepping into the breach created by John's delinquency in order to hold the band together and keep it moving.

To appreciate how benign was Paul's takeover, judged by the standards of the rock world, all you need do is compare it with how Mick Jagger aced out the founder and leader of the Rolling Stones, Brian Jones. In each case the genius of the band knocked himself out on drugs and became non compos mentis. At that point his highly ambitious lieutenant seized control of the organization and carried it off on a course of which the founder and former leader strongly disapproved. There the resemblance ends, however, for Paul never made the slightest effort to get rid of Lennon. In fact, he kept pursuing John until the last year of John's life, hoping to revive their old partnership.

Though John bitterly resented Paul's takeover, Lennon never confronted this issue squarely. Instead of having it out with Paul, as old partners should do, John sulked and played possum. Lennon wouldn't lead, but neither would he follow; hence, he had no choice but to tune out. This was a fateful act. Not only did it initiate the process that eventually broke up the Beatles, but it also marked the beginning of that long and deadly decline that would eventually destroy John Lennon.

John was not the only Beatle to experience depression during the sessions that produced *Sgt. Pepper.* All the boys but Paul were numbed by this unprecedented ordeal. Seven hundred hours of studio time were logged from November 1966 to March 1967, every minute of it devoted to the Beatles' next annual spring LP. The basic problem was not the direction in which Paul was leading the band but the simple fact that the Beatles had set out to make an album that would extend the frontiers of pop recording without first gaining access to a studio that represented the current state of the art.

Studio 2 at Abbey Road didn't bear the remotest resemblance to a modern recording facility. Constructed in 1931 to make classical records for HMV, it looked like an austere white art cinema whose seats had been removed and whose projection booth had been shoved to one side, where it was reached by climbing a long double flight of stairs. Inconvenient and uncongenial, it was also hopelessly out of date from a technical standpoint. The control board was so crude that just to do a routine playback, the engineers had to repatch the leads, a process that might consume a half hour. The tape recorders were obsolete four-track machines. Nor were there any electronic refinements: for example, when the Beatles wanted that funny speaking-tube effect they exploited on "Yellow Submarine," instead of the engineer throwing a switch to activate a filter, he would give John Lennon a cardboard mailing tube down which he had to holler. At such moments the Beatles were just like radio performers back in the studios of the Thirties, which, in fact, is where they were!

The solution to all these problems was simple; in fact, it had long since been adopted by the Rolling Stones. The Beatles could have boarded a plane for New York, or, better, Los Angeles, and enjoyed the finest recording equipment in the world. How characteristic of them that they did not! Their submission to EMI's parsimonious policy of recording in an obsolete studio is exactly parallel to their submission to United Artists when they were presented with scripts they didn't like or their surrender to the American fans, who drove them off the stage at the height of their career. The Beatles were ambitious, hardworking, highly creative young men, but they were markedly deficient both in practical resourcefulness and in the sort of self-confidence that enables men to make demands and insist upon their fulfillment. Pioneers but never rebels, the Good Guys of Rock made the best of what they were given, even when it made them miserable.

To picture the Beatles during the creation of what is universally regarded as the ultimate masterpiece of the rock age, you must imagine them sitting about in odd corners of a vast and dreary space, like stagehands during a performance of *The Twilight of the Gods.* Most of the time they were idle, whiling away the hours in pastimes like playing chess or cards, drinking tea or eating beans on toast while chatting with their childhood friends or cronies from Liverpool. Paul, meantime, was frantically busy, running up the long staircase to the control booth for a quick conference with George Martin; then dashing down the stairs again to try something out on mike; then summoning the boys to do their parts, until it was time to hear what they had recorded—which meant another long layout. No wonder that on some nights, when the waiting had reached unbearable lengths, John Lennon would suddenly snap out of his trance and thunder up at the control booth: *"What the fuck are ya doin' up there! You're not supposed to be takin' tea breaks! You're supposed to work straight through because we're the fuckin' Beatles!"*

To get themselves through the endless nights, the Beatles had to take something for their heads. It is ironic that the most celebrated work of acid rock should have been created under the influence of a chemical cocktail that dates back to the period when Abbey Road was built. Miles discovered the secret of the Beatles' patience one night when he noticed that all the boys were provided with stoppered test tubes filled with a white powder. When he was offered a hit of this stuff, he inquired cautiously, "What is it?" He was surprised by the answer: "A speedball"—i.e., the classic mixture of cocaine and heroin.

When the Beatles embarked on the long journey that would lead them eventually into Pepperland, they hadn't a clue to where they were heading. Instead of bringing into the studio a sheaf of songs ripened already through performance, they came to work now like jazz musicians, with just the germ of an idea—a title phrase, a hook, a few scrawled stanzas on a piece of paper. Through collective improvisation, they created their songs before the mikes, aided by the steadily increasing contributions of George Martin, who functioned not just as a producer but as a composer, arranger, sound effects man, recording engineer, and instrumentalist. This collaborative process had its good and bad sides. The great advantage was that by composing directly on tape, they cut out the intermediate stage between the concept and the final product. The disadvantage, apart from time-wasting inefficiency, was that the five collaborators were not of one mind. George Martin often had trouble understanding what the Beatles were seeking because they could only describe their ideas in vague, nontechnical language. The four Beatles, for their part, were distinct and unevenly gifted individuals. Given his head, each of them would carry the song off in a different direction.

The solution to this problem was intercommunication, but the Beatles, so glib at press conferences and so chatty among their friends, were not good at imparting to each other their innermost ideas and ideals. Paul came closest to getting what he wanted because he would make the band go through countless takes of his tunes until he achieved perfection. Then he would stand over the engineers, monitoring every moment of the crucial mixing process. John could not tolerate repetition or tedium. He liked to cut records one, two, three! If a thing didn't happen in the first few takes, his impulse was to say, "Fuck it!" He was punished for his lack of persistence by seeing some of his best work mutilated. Here, too, he laid the blame squarely on Paul, asserting, "Paul would subconsciously try and destroy a great song." The song whose destruction John most resisted was "Strawberry Fields Forever."

Lennon composed this famous piece during the six boring weeks he was on location in Spain for *How I Won the War*. (Though John extolled spontaneous composition, adoring those songs like "Across the Universe" that were "given" to him, his best work was usually the product of slow, accretive gestation.) When John got back to London, he demonstrated the new song for George Martin, who found it "gentle" and "lovely." Once the Beatles laid hold of the piece, they began to bang it into the mold of hard rock. You can actually follow this process in the introduction. First, Paul plays groping, otherworldly chords on a Mellotron, while George runs a magical-sounding scale on a silvery Indian table harp—both signals that the song is "out of this world." Then Ringo strikes in with his bricklayer's hands—and the spell is destroyed. Actually, the Beatles can hardly be blamed for missing the point when Lennon himself had no idea what he wanted.

Invariably defined as a song about drugs and/or childhood, "Strawberry Fields" is really about John Lennon's peculiar sense of reality, or, rather, *irreality*, because he insists that you can't tell what is real and you shouldn't bother even trying. This attitude was not simply a product of LSD; it was founded in Lennon's hallucination-haunted childhood, when the most familiar things, like the appearance of his face in the mirror, would change mysteriously. For a lifelong adept at autohypnosis, reality was not something that could be defined in terms of clarity and fixity; it was a visionary flux.

In the depiction of such a shifting and elusive state of consciousness, the first challenge was to find for it a suitable verbal texture. Lennon's solution was simple. He mimicked the stumbling lingo of the hippies, the people of the trance, with their one-step-forward, one-step-back verbal gait. The next problem was how to convey the ambiguity of his meandering mind. Here he had a ready-made instrument in his double-dealing puns. One of the reasons why "Strawberry Fields" was so important for Lennon was because it was the first time that he gave full voice to his puns in song. Thus, in the celebrated bit about his tree, he contrives by playing on words ("up a tree," "out of his tree") to raise the basic questions about his visions: Do they make him higher or lower, wiser or crazier than the normal man? In any event, he concludes, they make him singular.

The central symbol, the Salvation Army orphanage, is really Lennon's hallmark, his chop or griffe. To a traditional pop songwriter, even one of genius, like Paul McCartney, the memory of Strawberry Field would have inspired a song about the joys of childhood, like "Penny Lane," for the environs of the orphanage had provided John with a year-round playground and, in the summer, one of his favorite treats. "There was something about the place that always fascinated John," recollected Aunt Mimi. "He could see it from his window, and he loved going to the garden party they had each year. He used to hear the Salvation Army band, and he would pull me along, saying, 'Hurry up, Mimi—we're going to be late!'" (A charming vignette and especially interesting for its reference to the brass band, which suggests *Sgt. Pepper,* the album for which "Strawberry Fields" was originally destined, on whose cover the Beatles intended originally to pose in the sober uniforms of the Salvation Army.) John's delight in his childhood haunt is suggested by the verbal slip that converted Strawberry Field to Fields, with its strong suggestion of Elysian Fields.

Yet it is highly characteristic of John Lennon that his nostalgic recollection of childhood should turn on a symbol of pain even more than of pleasure. He knew perfectly well that the little girls in blue and white dresses, their straw boaters tied with red ribbons about their chins, were orphans, like himself. Strawberry Field was not simply John Lennon's playground—it was his spiritual home. For the drifting, groping, marginally depressed mood in which he spent so much of his life was the product of his early orphaning, which had cut the ties that bound him to normal life and set him adrift in the existential limbo that was his native element. The weird world that the record evokes does have affinities with drug states, but the drugs had only exaggerated what was always Lennon's natural state of being.

So important was "Strawberry Fields" to John Lennon that for once he rebelled against the way the Beatles had distorted his inspiration. He told George Martin that the track wasn't right: it didn't build, climax, and resolve, as a good record should do, nor did it reflect the hallucinatory vision of the verse. When Martin concurred, John asked the producer to make an arrangement of the sort he had done for Paul's "Eleanor Rigby," which had been one of the first Beatles' records to make use of a classical music texture. Martin complied with a score for beeping trumpets and chortling cellos that became the first and most famous example of a subsequently popular genre that could be called "barock 'n' roll." Lennon was still not satisfied.

Phoning Martin, John said he liked the beginning of the original version and the way the second version continued and concluded. Couldn't they just splice the two bits together? The producer, who could never get over the Beatles' musical illiteracy, replied flatly: "They are in different keys and tempos." Either of those facts would have stopped a trained musician in his tracks. But to John Lennon, Martin's objections were just rubbish.

"You can fix it, George," wheedled John. Then he hung up before Martin could say no.

As it happened, George *could* fix it. He discovered that by speeding up the slower, second version by 5 percent, he could match the pitch and tempo of the first version. The splice is clearly audible just before the entrance of the cellos, but on a track so heavily laden with acoustic impasto, who would notice?

The record that emerged from all these visions and revisions was miles away from John Lennon's original intention, which is why he complained about it till his dying day, vowing that he would record it again and get it right. Instead of being a "gentle" and "lovely" song about drifting back to childhood on a current of wavering visions, the song emerged from a million loudspeakers the world around as a phantasmagoric jumble of incomprehensible images and bizarrely recorded sounds. Like "Heartbreak Hotel" in its day, "Strawberry Fields" communicated far more as an acoustic image than it did as a statement, but what it communicated was a stoned descent into the maelstrom of the unconscious mind.

Ultimately Lennon had to recognize that in seeking to rescue his song from the distorting hands of the Beatles, he had only succeeded in putting it into the even more obfuscating charts and tape decks of George Martin, who was the real author of the record's all-important sound. Hence, Lennon's coldly contemptuous attitude toward Martin in later years may have owed as much to what the producer did as what he didn't do for John's songs. Actually, most of the Beatles were annoyed when journalists began calling Martin the "Fifth Beatle." Giving credit to others was not something that came easy to the Boys from Liverpool, especially when they felt the tension of another mind pulling them into uncharted waters.

After "Strawberry Fields" and "Penny Lane" were issued back-to-back in February 1967, Paul getting the A-side when Brian agreed that "Penny Lane" was the more commercial song, the Beatles had to start almost from scratch again because in economy-minded England it was not considered proper to include singles in albums. After cutting several sides, including what turned out to be the album's concluding track, Paul McCartney had a brainstorm. He proposed that they arrange all the music within the format of an old-fashioned brass band concert, commencing with an overture and concluding with a reprise. Why, he urged, they could even take typical names, like Billy Shears, and present themselves like characters in a play, having a lot of fun with the corny style of such amateurish entertainments. Paul was fresh from a visit to San Francisco, where bands were starting to sport kooky monikers, like Big Brother and the Holding Company or Country Joe and the Fish. Getting into the same spirit, he came up with a marvelous camp title: *Sgt. Pepper and His Lonely Hearts Club Band.*

Nothing could have been more characteristic of Paul McCartney than the idea of *Sgt. Pepper* because even though he was the Beatles' avant-gardist, at heart Paul was an old-fashioned entertainer. A nostalgist who delighted in recalling the world of his boyhood—his most perfect and profound song being his exquisitely bright and shining vision of Penny Lane—he was at his best composing musical genre paintings that captured some treasured feature of common English life. In particular, he doted on that old-fashioned show biz typified by cheery morning radio shows, breezy, wisecracking film romances, and spivy-looking singing stars, Paul Ramone types, crooning and mooning in front of lines of hard-hoofing pony girls. Though he had come to fame as one of the leaders of a band that signaled the shape of things to come, Paul McCartney was at heart, like Al Jolson or Maurice Chevalier, a singer of sunshine songs.

Hence, the paradox of *Sgt. Pepper,* which was offered and received as the voice of the brave new world of the Sixties but which, when examined twenty years later, appears to lie squarely in the mainstream of popular music, reaching back at least as far as Gilbert and Sullivan. The theme of the album is pure pop: the celebration of the ordinary life of ordinary people, the keynote being struck by Ringo, the modern Everyman, with his "With a Little Help from My Friends." This song was Paul's final contribution (with a little help from John) and his most significant statement. It conveys perfectly that self-dismissive, muddling-through attitude that has always been the rhetoric of the common man in Britain and that also epitomizes Paul's public persona—"Little me, the multimillionaire." Likewise, when you strip off *Pepper's* Day-Glo cellophane wrappings—its bright metallic clangors, palimpsested sound textures, and slick segues—what you discover underneath are a style and an attitude that are more old-fashioned than newfangled. A song like "She's Leaving Home" is positively Victorian, a gaslit episode from an old melodrama, with the girl slipping out the door of the paternal home to run off with a highbinder in the motor trade, while her poor old mother and father are left keening in high, cloying falsettos. There are, to be sure, a few exotic diversions as John steps through the looking glass of "Lucy" and George unfolds his Indian prayer mat, but these are merely the odd spices thrown into the homely pepper pot. The whole album is Paul—until the End.

Then, out of nowhere, comes sailing in, like a ghost ship with an ice-encrusted bowsprit, the bleak, despairing, yet resigned voice of John Lennon, sounding the eternal note of sadness and offering a view of ordinary life, culled from that day's *Morning Mail,* that totally annihilates and eventually blows up Paul's jolly Toby Mug vision. As Lennon unfolds the surrealistic jumble of the newspaper page, death stares from one column and from the next the kooky image of 4,000 holes in Blackburn. The death is described in terms of drugs that blow the mind and of a world-weariness that makes death seem a welcome release. The holes inspire a dirty pun. The song's bridge, a fragment fished out of Paul's song bag, offers a hectic glimpse of another ordinary citizen of Pepperland rushing to catch the morning bus to work. This breathless bit of footage, resembling a TV commercial, crosses John's tragic strain with as little logic as the succession of items on the newspaper page. The next time Lennon's sweeping theme returns, it leads on to the insinuating phrase about turning on, which then whirls away like a wheel spinning off its axle. Transformed into the ominous sound of a dynamo being brought up to speed, the infernal machine reaches through its vertiginous rotation a terrifying climax when, finally, it explodes. The last chord, struck by many hands on a piano, is allowed to resound, decay, and float away, like a puff of smoke. It resolves into an E major chord employed traditionally in Western music to symbolize heaven.

Sgt. Pepper was released into a cultural climate hot and fecund with fantastical ideas and beliefs. The hippies, inspired by their yearning to recover the imaginative core of life, sat pondering the album's mystifying cover through the smoke of joss sticks and Thai sticks, like monks poring over an allegorical illumination. What they read into the illustration was precisely what lay uppermost in their minds: the currently fashionable doctrine of death and rebirth. Interpreting the two sets of Beatles depicted, every analysis in the rock journals or the underground press laid great emphasis on the contrast between the drab black-and-white waxworks Beatles standing beside what appeared to be a grave and the gloriously psychedelic Beatles in their dazzling satins, like wet-winged butterflies sprung from withered chrysalises. Triumphantly the pop pundits proclaimed the old Beatles dead and buried, the new Beatles reborn and risen. *Pepper* was sacred music, a hippie *resurrectus*. What a pity that the release date was not Easter!

All these farfetched interpretations fall to the ground at the touch of history. The album's cover designer, British Pop Artist Peter Blake, recalled that when John and Paul approached him (on the recommendation of Robert Fraser, a gallery owner who coveted the custom of the new rock stars) they had only the idea of a band concert in a park. "You could have a bandstand and a crowd," remarked Blake, inspired immediately with the vision of the "magic crowd" (to which Paul also lays claim): a mass of faces, familiar and unknown, in photomontage. Blake suggested that the Beatles make up a list of the faces they would like to see in the crowd, while Blake and Fraser made up their own lists.

Ironically, it was Blake, the painter, who chose the only pop singer: Dion, of Dion and the Belmonts, along with Leo Gorcey and Huntz Hall of the Dead End Kids, a couple of British comedians, and his friend, the American Pop Artist Richard Merkin. Robert Fraser, who had introduced Pop Art to England, chose the painters he admired, led by the proto-Pop iconographer Richard Lindner. George Harrison put into the crowd a whole tribe of unknown Indian gurus, including the Maharishi Mahesh Yogi. Some faces, like Lenny Bruce and Terry Southern, were favorites of all the Beatles; others were stock icons displayed in every poster shop. The most eccentric list was composed by Lennon, who relished this game. John chose Jesus and Hitler; Aleister Crowley, England's foremost occultist; Stephen Crane, a writer to whom he never again alluded; and Albert Stebbins, an old Liverpool football player, who was a favorite of Freddie Lennon's. Ringo was the only member of the group who made no contribution. He declined the invitation, remarking, "Whatever the other guys want is fine by me."

The process of composition was casual. There were a few rough sketches, but most of the work consisted in collecting and processing the images, which was done by Blake's wife, Jann Howarth, also a Pop Artist. After the photos were assembled, they were blown up to life size, then mounted on hardboard and cut out as silhouettes. Hand-colored and propped up like a piece of stage scenery, the final product was a freestanding mural on a scale far greater than the photo conveyed. The nearest object to the camera actually lay twenty feet distant.

Once the artists had erected the mural, they started arranging three-dimensional objects in the foreground. Each Beatle brought in his toys. Paul contributed a collection of musical instruments. Blake owned a waxworks effigy of Sonny Liston, which made him think it might be fun to have Madame Tussaud's Beatles looking at Sergeant Pepper's Band, whose drum had been embellished by a fairground painter. The emblematic flower bed (which Americans mistook for a grave) was a stock feature of a British pub. Blake ordered the blooms for the night scheduled for the shooting, planning to arrange them in a symbolic design, as is customary. When the Beatles canceled the session, the flowers did not survive in sufficient quantity to realize the original design, so a fifteen-year-old florist's helper offered to arrange the remaining blossoms in the shape of a guitar. Thus, the famous design was realized through improvisation coupled with happenstance.

While all this work was in progress, Brian Epstein was having fits. He feared that outsiders were getting into the act and that he was losing control over the project. On the other hand, when it came time to clear the budget for the fancy package, Brian couldn't face the music. He stepped aside in favor of Robert Fraser, whose merchant banker family was on good terms with Sir Joseph Lockwood, the head of EMI, whose business background lay in flour milling. Fraser confronted Sir Joe in EMI's impressive boardroom. "You're Lionel Fraser's boy, aren't you?" rumbled the director. "What are you mixed up in this rubbish for?" Fraser mumbled and stammered like a schoolboy. "How much is this gonna cost?" thundered Sir Joe.

"Fifteen hundred pounds, sir," mumbled Fraser.

"*Fifteen hundred pounds!*" exploded the irate director. "I can hire the London Symphony Orchestra for that!" (Indeed, he would be asked to do that very thing next.)

Lockwood had every reason to be angry: An EMI album cover was usually a publicity shot dummied up by the art department at a cost of about twenty-five pounds. Only when the Beatles agreed to reimburse the company for the full fifteen hundred pounds if the album failed to sell 100,000 copies did he give his consent to this outrageous demand. He didn't spare Fraser, either, inquiring shrewdly: "Who is this photographer, Michael Cooper? Is that you, too?" Cooper was, in fact, Fraser's partner.

At 8:00 P.M. on 30 March 1967 the Beatles arrived at Michael Cooper's studio at 1 Flood Street in Chelsea, where they changed into their dazzling nineteenth-century bandsman's uniforms, especially tailored by Burman's Theatrical Agency from the brightest comic opera satins and adorned with the most elaborate braid and frogs, hats, and custom-cobbled orange-and-yellow patent leather boots.

The shooting occupied three hours, during which the Beatles posed in a variety of attitudes, while Robert Fraser's companions filled the air with the enticing aroma of Moroccan hashish. The Beatles were delighted by the whole adventure, so delighted that they wanted to go on adding new elements to the package. Now, instead of a single LP, they decided to offer the public a double album, packed like a Christmas stocking with hippie toys: uniform badges, a T-shirt, and cutouts. At that point the alarm bell sounded at EMI.

Lord Shawcross, one of the company's directors, learned what the new package was to contain and instantly began to raise objections. A double album was out of the question. Packing into the sleeve all sorts of oddments would make it impossible to stack the merchandise. Worst of all, in his eyes, was the notion of covering the album with pictures of famous and obscure entertainers. Every one of these people would have a right to sue. The company stood to lose a fortune in litigation. The whole project was in jeopardy. These arguments made such an impression on Brian (who had been resistant to the idea from the start) that he sought to persuade the Beatles to abandon their cherished design. When they flatly refused, Brian panicked. He called up Wendy Hanson and told her that she must come back immediately to sort out the problem of the photo releases.

For the next month Wendy did nothing but contact agents and managers, seeking the necessary signatures. Some of the stars, like Shirley Temple Black, a big shot at the United Nations, asked a lot of sticky questions. Others were unavailable, like Karlheinz Stockhausen, who was on a boat in the Pacific. Leo Gorcey behaved like a Dead End Kid, demanding money. He was airbrushed out, as was Gandhi, whose face was considered too sacred for such company. Hitler was in, but Jesus was out because of John's notorious remark. Mae West answered the form letter with a challenging inquiry: "What would I be doing in a lonely hearts club?"

The final battle was waged over the credits. First Paul said, "No credits!" Then Robert Fraser persuaded Paul to acknowledge the work of Peter Blake and Michael Cooper. But no one else save George Martin was mentioned, though scores of musicians, technicians, and other ancillaries had made contributions to the project. "Paul is very stingy about credits," Fraser explained, "because he wants to give the impression that he's done it all himself." The day was not far distant when that would be the correct impression.

Sgt. Pepper was the shout heard 'round the world. Overnight it recharged the Beatles' aura with the electricity of Beatlemania: only now the glow around the band was a psychedelic glory. A monument to the Sixties, the album glows with the excitement of an age that felt it had the whole world at the tip of its knob-turning, pill-popping fingers.

Though the hippie pundits labored to load the album with a great freight of portentous meanings, the record owed its success to the same inexplicable enchantment that makes any tune go 'round and 'round in your brain. 'Round and 'round went *Pepper* that summer both at home and on the air, where the DJs took to flipping it over as if it were a double-headed hit single, a tribute to Paul's skill in making this clutch of ill-matched tunes a seamless whole.

Paul's triumph was, however, a Pyrrhic victory, for *Pepper* marks the beginning of that deadly quarrel between the Beatles' leaders that would ultimately deprive the public of the greatest songwriting and record-making team of modern times. The wrath of Lennon had now been ignited. It would smolder for another year; then it would suddenly flame up, wiping out everything that had been achieved through a decade of grueling work, stern self-discipline, close cooperation, unflagging inspiration, and, above all, total dedication to the ideal of reaching the "toppermost of the poppermost." *Pepper* is what goes on the top.

THE SUMMER OF LOVE

The in place during the summer of 1967 was the Speakeasy, a basement club at 30 Margaret Street, just behind Oxford Circus. Decorated originally in the style of *Bonnie and Clyde,* with a wreath-crowned coffin for a reception desk and black walls adorned with Al Capone murals, the club had celebrated its opening with a St. Valentine's Day Massacre party. But once hippies started traipsing about the city, strewing blossoms, tootling flutes, and babbling nursery songs like crackbrained Ophelias, the hustlers who ran the joint decided to make a quick change. With a single wave of the whim wand, they transformed their ominous dive into an Indian pavilion, swathed in paisley-patterned cotton and glaring with Day-Glo pinks, oranges, and greens. Instantly the club caught on.

Every night, 'round about midnight, it received down its coal shute stairs the beat elite. All of London's leading groupies, admitted without charge to bait the suckers with their beautiful faces and bodies, paraded through the bar-restaurant to reach the small back lounge. Here, enthroned on comfortable sofas and easy chairs, were the princes of the rock world: John and Paul, Mick and Keith, Pete and Moonie—all stoned and gazing with mixed emotions at a tiny stage, upon which appeared each night some new rock prodigy.

One night it would be Jimi Hendrix playing Superspade. Wearing a dazzling regimental purchased from I Was Lord Kitchener's Valet and with an electric Afro crowning his acid zombie face, Jimi would execute all those coiling, menacing cobra moves that made Elvis Presley look like your uncle's mustache. His favorite stunt was to thrust his Stratocruiser between his thighs, while extorting from it an undreamt-of range of excruciating Iron Age sounds, as he mowed down all these hip white English kids with his huge, swiveling, screaming electric cock.

Another night the new star might be Arthur Brown, king of the English hippies, attired in flowing tribal robes, his face covered by a silver mask and his head crowned with a pair of flaming horns that made him appear like a cruel Mayan chieftain arriving for the sacrifice or a great Teutonic devil about to celebrate Walpurgisnacht. (Brown didn't confine his performing to the stage. One night he entered the back room wearing a Chinese warlord's costume and carrying an African spear. Spotting Kit Lambert, co-manager of the Who, Brown hurled his weapon. When the assegai sank quivering into the tabletop, Lambert reeled back in horror. While fighting the Mau-Maus in East Africa, he had seen a fellow officer impaled by just such a spear.)

Sarah Kernochan, later winner of an Academy Award for codirecting *Marjoe*, recalled that on her second night as a waitress at the club, the Beatles appeared. "They were dressed uniformly in either Indian gear or velvets. That was the way Swinging London togged out at the time. Within three weeks after I started, everyone wore bells around their necks. John was completely engulfed with girls. He was just cramming them in his face, just trying to cover as much of himself as possible with girls."

Her recollection of Lennon during the Summer of Love bespeaks a vastly different public image from any he had displayed in the past. Just a couple of years before, when he frequented the Ad Lib, he had always sat in a corner, "keeping himself to himself." If anything happened to excite his ire, he would erupt in physical violence. Now he seemed a different man.

Indeed, everybody commented on how much John had changed. Ivan Vaughan, a childhood friend who had spent a lot of time with Lennon during the *Pepper* sessions, observed: "Even a couple years ago the old animosities were still there: refusing to talk to anybody, being rude, slamming the door. Now he's just as likely to say to people, 'Come in. Sit down.'"

Pete Shotton rejoiced at the change in John, which confirmed Pete's contention that his friend was at heart a lovable man. "Today John is not trying to prove anything," opined Pete. "He doesn't have to be number one—that's why he's so happy." Even John celebrated his change of heart by writing the theme song of the Summer of Love, "All You Need Is Love."

John himself ascribed his revolutionary change of character to acid, claiming the drug had given him a new breadth of vision and the philosophic mind. John Dunbar seconded this idea, maintaining that Lennon had been liberated from the clogs of the past and translated onto a higher spiritual plane. Actually, it was not so much acid as it was the enormous quantity of the drug that Lennon consumed that wrought this remarkable change. At the peak of his acid addiction John was consuming LSD at a rate that blows a man clear off the charts of the known drug world. "I must have taken a thousand trips," he confessed. "I just ate it all the time like candy." When you take that much acid, you stop tripping because the brain is denied the four or five days it requires to recharge after each dose. Diurnal acid dropping produces an effect rather like XTC, the "love drug." Hence, instead of mental pinwheels, the tripper feels himself bound in affectionate communion with everything he sees, like Titania embracing an ass.

Without his love drug, John would never have been able to participate in the merry masquerade of the Summer of Love. For though he was one of the Sixties' greatest heroes, he was no Love Child. His temperamental affinities were rather with the Angry Young Men of the Fifties, with whom he often compared himself, or with the Me Generation, whose narcissistic pursuits he embodied and defended to the end. None of the values championed by the hippies—hanging loose and loving everyone, grooving on simple pleasures and performing manual tasks, or losing your identity by merging with mankind at some great festival—was congenial to John Lennon. Yet Lennon, who often called himself a journalist, was highly conscious of the mood of the moment. So it must have been with a great sense of relief that he discovered that so long as he ate his candy, he could go along for once with the crowd.

Cynthia was astonished by this sudden change in her husband's character. The John she knew had always been extremely antisocial and particularly detested entertaining at home. Now, she reported, "he would return home following a recording session and nightclubbing with a flotsam and jetsam he had picked up on the way. They would all be as high as kites. John didn't know them, and neither did I. They would spend the night raving and drinking and listening to loud music, ransacking the larder and dossing down all over the house." Cynthia recognized that if she didn't go with the flow, she would soon be left behind, so after being endlessly exhorted by Lennon to turn on, she tried acid again. The experience was another nightmare, its worst feature being the images she formed of John as "a slimy snake or a giant mule with razor-sharp teeth, leering and laughing at me."

John's unappeasable appetite for LSD inspired next one of the most concealed enterprises of the Beatles' organization: the Great Acid Smuggling Expedition. The goal of this caper was to procure a lifetime supply of the finest LSD available, the product of the renowned Augustus Stanley Owsley III's secret laboratory. The cover for the move was provided by the Monterey Pop Festival, to which the Beatles sent a camera crew even though they knew the film rights had been purchased by an American company. The idea was to use the crew's abundant baggage to conceal the contraband. When the filmmakers returned to London, after their apparently futile journey, they were carrying in their airtight lens cases a large quantity of a clear fluid of unimaginable potency. By late June John Lennon had standing on the shelves of his sun-room two pint-size bottles of nearly pure lysergic acid.

Eventually, that summer, John got rid of his family by packing them off for a holiday at Pesaro, on the Adriatic coast of Italy. Free to live like a bachelor, he spent most of his time with John Dunbar, whose marriage to Marianne Faithfull had ended when she went off with the Stones. Every afternoon the Lennon limousine would come rolling down Bentinck Street, where Dunbar lived with his parents, creating a sensation by its appearance. The once-black Rolls-Royce had been scratched by sand and road grit when John was filming in Spain; when Lennon announced that he was going to have the car sprayed, Ringo suggested that it be done in the style of a fairground carousel. A BBC scene designer working with a paintbrush transformed the Rolls into the most famous icon of Flower Power: a pumpkin yellow coach, its roof emblazoned with the signs of the zodiac, its sides embellished with bunches of red flowers of the sort you see on an old tea caddy.

If the car looked bizarre from the outside, the view from inside was even more outlandish. Lennon made it a practice to pour everyone who joined him in the back seat a cup of tea from a thermos that had been spiked with LSD. Then, as the travelers journeyed out of the city and through the suburbs, everything would turn weird outside the tinted windowpanes. Not just the sense of sight but that of time was radically altered, existence being slowed to the trancelike largo of the haunting record forever blasting from the stereo speakers: "Whiter Shade of Pale."

If, on the other hand, John was in his mischievous Magic Christian mood, he would throw a switch and activate the powerful speakers concealed inside the front wheel wells. Out of these instruments would blare the sounds of barnyard animals, planes landing, or Peter Sellers doing a mock election broadcast. Lennon would double up on the back seat, convulsed with laughter at the effects of highly realistic train recordings, which sent pedestrians hurling themselves into shop doorways.

During that zany summer art began dictating to life. Every day brought some startling novelty. One night Lennon and Dunbar were ensconced in the lounge at Kenwood, staring at the color TV mounted in the fireplace, when the flames revealed a riot of body-painted, joss stick–brandishing freaks, holding wassail in a vast Victorian pleasure palace. Focusing their flaccid minds on the screen, Lennon and Dunbar identified the locale as the Alexander Palace, the occasion as the *Fourteen-Hour Technicolor Dream.* Instantly Lennon summoned his pumpkin coach. When the adventurers, enveloped in dark, concealing cloaks, arrived at the immense old building atop a hill to the north of

the city, they were astounded to find themselves in an indoor fairground so large that a rock band could play at one end without inter-
fering with the sound of another rock band at the opposite end. In the
middle stood a towering helter-skelter or spiral slide, about sixty feet
high, down which the freaks came shooting like children in a playground. On the walls were the amoeba shapes and exploding fly eyes
of a fabulous light show. On the floor was an igloo, from whose side
hippies were dispensing banana skins, the makings of a mellow yellow
high. After forty-two bands had played in the course of this one night,
the dawn was saluted by Pink Floyd, poised on a scaffold before a rose
window, shrieking out the strains of "The Piper at the Gates of Dawn."

That a man as paranoid as John Lennon was able to endure such a
promiscuous crush of people was another of the miracles wrought by
acid. But soon Lennon began to suffer from a new fear: that people
would suspect him of being a stoned freak. To conceal his mental de-
rangement, he adopted a simple but effective disguise. When addressed by a stranger, John would *smile*. "If you look happy, nobody
ever questions," Lennon instructed Dunbar, demonstrating his always
impressive grasp of human psychology. Actually, as Dunbar observed,
Lennon's smile was a lot closer to a grimace. When he came bearing
down on a stranger, enveloped in his long black cloak, his lips drawn
back exposing his teeth, the effect was rather like that of Nosferatu
welcoming a guest to his castle in the Carpathians.

The black cloaks that English rock stars began to sport at this time
were just one of the many items of flamboyant apparel that appealed to
their imaginations. With the lids flying off the clothes chests of the
past, the wardrobe of a London rock star soon became as extravagant
as that of an old-time opera star. The goal of hippie fashion was to take
the most farfetched things and assemble them ingeniously so as to
achieve a novel but convincing "look." Nobody exhibited a greater flair
for this combinative style than John Lennon. He never appeared to be
flaunting himself in his glad rags. In fact, the only times John appeared
to be overdressed or ill-costumed were when he was obliged to wear an
outfit that had been designed by someone else. At the press party for
Sgt. Pepper, John was the most eccentrically but tastefully dressed man
in the room. He wore a green, frilly, flower-patterned shirt with maroon cord trousers, yellow socks, and cord shoes, rounding off the en-
semble with a sporran. When a reporter asked John, "Why the
sporran?" Lennon offered one of those utterly reasonable replies that
left the questioner speechless: "As there are no pockets in these trousers, it comes in handy for holding my cigarettes or front door keys."

The merry masquerade of the Summer of Love lasted no longer
than the unnaturally warm weather. Eventually, having taken scores of
trips, Lennon and Dunbar began to burn out. First, the vivid colors

and startling hallucinations that had fascinated them originally faded into the light of common day. Then they discovered that they had lost their sex drive. (Dunbar characterizes Lennon on acid as "monastic".) Finally, they found they were having trouble maintaining their upright posture. Every time they got high, they were forced to bend over at the waist and go about on all fours, like the higher apes. Even worse were the persistent patches of angst. Dunbar's warmest memory of Lennon relates to one such occasion. Dunbar was starting to panic when John leaned over and said: "It's the same for us all."

While John Lennon was freaking out behind acid, Yoko Ono and Tony Cox were driving their joint career like alternating pistons. In January 1967 they had moved into 25 Hanover Gate Mansion, a stately Edwardian apartment house, with wrought-iron balconies and gilded bird-cage elevator. The building was going co-op, and while it was being emptied, some temporary rentals had become available. For the equivalent of $200 a month, Yoko and Tony had six rooms with lofty ceilings, ornate moldings, and French windows that opened on Regent's Park. An identical flat across the hall was taken by the Coxes' friend from Japan, Dan Richter, who was working on Stanley Kubrick's *2001*, choreographing the first scene with the apes and playing the principal ape.

Yoko had the whole flat painted white and carpeted the salon in the same color. No furniture was installed lest it break up the space. Day and night an endless stream of visitors, most of them avant-garde artists, talked, ate, drank tea, or conducted business while seated on the floor. "Yoko would hold court," recollected Richter, "while Tony scurried around. He always gave the impression that he was doing everything; she always gave the impression that she was doing nothing. But Yoko was probably doing more than Tony because she has a mind like a steel trap and never stops. . . . Tony was self-effacing. His name was not on the poster. He would do the physical labor, organizing, selling. There was nothing of the artist in his role. He was her promoter . . . She was like an absolute princess all the time. No problem about being served—she's samurai! . . . Tony liked to create secretly and be the power behind the throne. Yet they thought of themselves as equal. . . . They always needed a fog machine or three hundred pairs of scissors. . . . Tony was always asking me if I could bring home a camera from the studio, or if I had one, if I could get two. . . . There might be a bang at the door and the people downstairs saying that their ceiling had just fallen in. We'd climb through the window and find that there was nobody in the apartment and there's a bathtub that's been running for two days."

Tony's greatest talent was for hustling money. "Tony would go into a bank," recalled Richter, who was invited once to watch the game, "and tell the official that he was an officer of a foreign film company. A letter of credit was arriving in two days from such and such a bank. Now he wanted to open an account. As he was leaving, he might mention casually that he would like a book of checks to prepare his work. The English weren't ready for this sort of thing. . . . Tony has always looked innocent and honest. . . . He can look you straight in the eye and lie. . . . His secret is religious fervor—ardent, direct, undeniable. . . . Tony is a bank manager's bad dream."

Tony soon persuaded some mark to put up the money for a film. The project was to be produced jointly by Tony and Victor Musgrave, a man of many gifts: journalist, critic, and poet; gallery director and filmmaker; psychosomatic therapist and chess master. His principal contribution to the picture was the use of his house in Mayfair as the studio for the bizarre production. The film, titled originally *Film No. 4* but known to the public as *Bottoms,* was supposed to show in full-screen close-up 365 naked asses in action. To obtain this many volunteers in a short time and organize the work of filming them all, the Coxes had to have help. In February 1967 they ivited a young California couple they had met recently, Tim and Robin Rudnick, to move into the flat at Hanover Gate and live there free in exchange for their help in making the movie.

Their first theater of operations was UFO (Unlimited Freak Out), which advertised itself as "London's first psychedelic ballroom." Located originally in a black cellar at Covent Garden, the club's house band was the unknown Pink Floyd. Yoko performed there on one of the four small scaffold stages. She would pick a man and woman out of the crowd and put them into a bag, back to back, asking them to describe their sensations with the aid of a mike. Or she would cut a paper dress off a girl, using a scissors fitted with a contact mike, every snip making a loud, metallic sound that delighted the audience, as Yoko sheared the girl down to her panties. One night the crowd was astonished to see John Lennon appear with Yoko to make a public appeal for volunteers to appear in *Film No. 4.*

If it seems surprising that so many people should volunteer to have their asses filmed, the reasons may be sought in the story about the Frenchman who sent a photograph of his ass to all his friends as a Christmas card—a stunt that John and Yoko copied in 1972. When asked why he would do such a shocking thing, the Frenchman replied reasonably that first, your ass is generally in better shape than your face; second, your ass offers the great advantage of novelty; and third, your ass is a more intimate offering than your face because everybody sees our faces whereas only those we love see our asses. In any event, a great number of artists, writers, models, and other such folk offered their buttocks to Yoko's camera.

It was characteristic of Tony's operations that the whole business was efficiently conducted. A late-night van service shuttled the volunteers from UFO to the house in Mayfair and back to the club. When a subject arrived, he was ushered into a little dressing room, where he was asked to remove everything from the waist down. Then he was brought into the studio, a small sitting room with a cozy fireplace illuminated by silk-shaded sconces. In the middle of the floor stood a six-foot turntable, on one side of which stood the subject, supported and guided by an L-shaped armature that extended like the tines of a carving fork before and behind the waist. Before the subject hung a white backcloth; behind him were a shuttered floodlamp and a little sixteen millimeter camera on a tripod. A few minutes were spent teaching the person how to walk on the turntable; then, once he was stepping smoothly, Tony would shoot about twenty seconds of film.

Bottoms turned out to be one of those works whose original intention—Yoko said it was "an aimless petition signed by people with their anuses"—was the least important factor in its public reception. What it "meant" was entirely what the public, press, and film censor made it mean. The Board of Film Censors launched the little film on the path of notoriety by denying it a license. Tony went mad with what he regarded as a snub by the establishment. Yoko's answer was to picket the film censor's office. She issued a call for supporters but found none. When she arrived with an armload of daffodils, which she planned to hand out, she found, to her delight, that a swarm of reporters and TV cameramen were awaiting her under the eyes of seventeen policemen. That night Yoko appeared on the tube, and the London bureau of *Time* filed a story.

On 8 August *Film No. 4*, granted a special license by the Greater London Council, had its premiere at the Jacey Tatler in Charing Cross Road. The performance commenced at 11:30 P.M. as a benefit for the Institute for Contemporary Arts. Lots of VIPs attended. *Bottoms* was a picture after an Englishman's heart, for no country is so addicted to anal humor. The first glimpse of all those asses—big and little, flat or protuberant, pear- or heart-shaped, bland or brown, bare or hairy, immaculate or spotty—was enough to bring down the house. Despite a heavy canning by the critics, *Film No. 4* played for a whole season, first at the Jacey Tatler and then at the Time Cinema near Baker Street. For John Lennon, *Bottoms*—which he called *Many Happy Endings*—was a hilarious confirmation of his view of Yoko as an unrecognized genius.

BRIAN BREATHES HIS LAST

Brian Epstein was never more unhappy than during the Summer of Love. He had begun the year by announcing that he no longer wanted to manage NEMS because his only satisfaction came from working with Cilla Black and the Beatles. His once-booming business had fallen off so badly that after having been offered $20 million for the firm in his heyday, Brian was now constrained to sell 51 percent to Robert Stigwood, manager of the Bee Gees, for a mere half-million pounds. At that point, Brian put himself into the hands of Dr. John Flood, a psychiatrist, who committed him to the Priory, a sanatorium near Roehamptom.

Chronically afflicted with depression and insomnia, Brian had experimented with many drugs, including heroin, going so far as to have his conservative business suits fitted with an inner pocket divided into a series of dips, each of which could hold a different pill: the first a Prelly, the second a Seconal, the third a Carbrital, the fourth a "black beauty" Biphetamine, the fifth a tab of acid, etc. No matter how dark the room or how dim Brian's wits, he could reach into his pocket and select by touch the drug he required for the next tug on his chemical yo-yo.

Reluctant to endure the discomfort of kicking, he underwent a sleep cure. Knocked out for an entire week, he was fed intravenously while his body adjusted itself to its new chemical balance. When he awoke, he didn't feel much better than when he went to sleep. As the great Charlie Parker remarked about a similar cure, "They can take it out of your body, but they can't take it out of your mind." Brian's mind was especially troubled by the thought that his contract with the Beatles was due to expire this very year, on 8 October 1967.

Financially he had nothing to worry about because he had swindled the Beatles the previous November, when he renegotiated their contract with EMI. The new contract was designed to run for nine years, and though Brian knew that he might not be managing the group longer than the current year, he had cut himself in for 25 percent of the Beatles' earnings forever. None of the Beatles had troubled to read the agreement. After all, they had always trusted Brian completely. Wasn't he a perfect gentlemen? Didn't he love his boys more than life? What had they to fear? When the Beatles learned later what Brian had done, they were deeply shocked. They hadn't realized that he was running scared.

Whether the Beatles would have given Brian the sack is a question that cannot be answered with certainty, even at this late date. Allen Klein, the group's next manager, insisted that Brian was doomed, but Klein's information came from John Lennon, who was adroit at tailoring his statements to suit his listeners. Since Lennon was responsible for hiring Klein, he might have wanted to make it appear that Klein would have gotten the job no matter what happened to Brian. Paul, on the other hand, had involved himself ever more closely with Brian in the management of the Beatles because he recognized the danger to his interests posed by Brian's relationship with John. Miles witnessed what may have been the last business meeting between Paul and Brian, late in the Summer of Love. Brian had come over to Paul's newly furnished house in St. John's Wood to discuss the plan for the Beatles' projected TV show, *Magical Mystery Tour*. What was uppermost in the manager's mind was assuring that all the Beatles got their fair share of the honors: "We must find more for Ringo to do. . . . We must arrange to involve John here. . . . George could do this bit nicely." Clearly, by the end of his tenure, Brian's primary function was keeping all the Beatles happy by soothing their easily injured egos. This was a role whose importance Paul, the diplomat, would especially appreciate because he was keen on preserving at least the semblance of unity as a means of avoiding a final showdown with John, who was becoming more difficult to deal with every day. With the very existence of the Beatles at stake, Paul would not have been eager to dismiss the only man who represented their solidarity.

In July Brian's father died suddenly while on holiday at Bournemouth. Brian went into a decline immediately, developing one symptom after another. When his mother complained that she didn't know what to do with herself, Brian urged Queenie to visit him in London, staying at his elegant white four-story Georgian house at 24 Chapel Street in Belgravia, near the Irish embassy. Brian, aided by the ubiquitous Ken Partridge, had lavished great pains on this dwelling. The drawing room was light and airy, hung with Venetian paintings and canvases by Malcolm Lowry, who was enjoying a vogue at the time. The dining room was draped in green silk, and around the table were set six superb fanback chairs inlaid with tourmaline, coral, jade, and turquoise.

Partridge had also found Brian a rare Carver chair, in which Ringo had sprawled one night at supper, his leg over the arm and his fingers busy picking the stones out of the nearest fanback. When Brian exclaimed, "Oh, don't do that!" John Lennon barked: "He fuckin' *paid* for them! He can do what he likes!"

The challenge to Brian's customary life-style posed by the presence of his mother was enormous. But he rose to it. Instead of crawling home from the gambling clubs at three in the morning and drugging himself to sleep at dawn, he reverted to the regimen of his childhood. He awoke when his mother entered his room in the morning and drew the drapes. Mother and son breakfasted in the bedroom, with Brian propped up in bed and Queenie sitting at a side table. Brian would bathe, shave, dress himself smartly, and set off for the office like any successful executive. In the evening, instead of a seduction supper with a lot of wine or a night of cruising Piccadilly Circus for rough trade, the Nemperor would come home to dine. He and his mother would watch TV until ten. Then they would take a cup of cocoa and retire to bed.

When Queenie left on Thursday, 24 August, Brian breathed a sigh of relief. Now it was time to play. That very night he went to supper with Simon Napier-Bell, the young, good-looking manager of the Yardbirds, an unabashed hustler who was keen on getting out of Brian everything that could be learned about the Beatles.

When they came back to Chapel Street, Brian tried repeatedly to seduce Napier-Bell, who was not physically attracted but was eager to continue the relationship because it offered such obvious advantage for a man in his line. Declining an invitation to spend that weekend with Brian in Sussex, Napier-Bell offered to come down the following weekend. When he joked, "You would have to promise not to molest me," Brian exclaimed, staring meaningfully into his guest's sultry green eyes: "Good gracious, I couldn't promise that! Besides, think of the fun you'd have trying to stop me."

While Brian was trying to get laid, the Beatles were heading for nirvana. That same night they attended a lecture by the Maharishi Mahesh Yogi, familiar to Londoners from posters in the underground advertising his book *The Science of Being and the Art of Living.* The holy man had announced that the solemn moment had come when he must bid farewell to the vanity of the material world and retire into the immaculate silence in which alone is to be heard the primal om. Patti and George Harrison, who had already met the guru in India and later at meetings of his Spiritual Regeneration movement, alerted the other Beatles that this was their last opportunity to sit at the feet of the master.

Arriving at the Park Lane Hilton, where the maharishi was residing, the Beatles found an overflow crowd in the ballroom. Indians in garish Terylene suits and nylon saris rubbed shoulders with drably attired British folk. The Beatles were ushered to the front of the assembly, where a flock of earnest devotees sat in lotus position, holding their hands cupped upward with their eyes cast down. The holy one came onto the stage dressed in Indian robes that contrasted sharply with the dark business suits of his British disciples. Seating himself on a deer-skin in the center of a semicircle of straight-backed chairs, the ma-harishi called for five minutes of silent meditation. As the Beatles looked on self-consciously, embarrassed by the sotto voce gossiping of the old ladies about them, the suspense built, until, at last, the guru spoke.

Talking in a high-pitched voice, interspersed with odd little giggles, he launched into an endorsement of transcendental meditation. "This practice," he warbled in a high, reedy voice, "will alone bring one to the complete fulfillment of one's life." Demanding but "one half hour a day," transcendental meditation's effect could be detected immediately. "Rejuvenation is there!" enthused the monk. "Within two or three days, the face of a man changes." The maharishi's claim must have made every Beatle zoom in on the old man's face. God knows, he wasn't any beauty. His complexion was dusky, his nose broad, his hair long, greasy, and unkempt, his beard a cotton boll stuck on his chin. Yet the man was right! He *had* a glow in his face.

Such was the faith he inspired that immediately upon the conclusion of his talk, the Beatles mounted the platform, and while the business-suited entourage kept the faithful at bay, the eager young pop stars offered themselves to the yogi as his latest converts. Not one to drop a cue, the maharishi invited his world-famous novices to join him next day aboard his private railroad coach, which was to take him to Bangor, Wales, where he was giving a five-day course. Delighted, the Beatles accepted the invitation and left their first private darshan bab-bling with excitement.

The following afternoon the Beatles, accompanied by Mick Jagger and Marianne Faithfull, turned up on the platform at Paddington Sta-tion. Waylaid by press and TV, the stars had to fight their way to the guru's coach. Breathing a sigh of relief, they were suddenly alarmed by desperate cries of *"John! John!"* Cynthia had been held back by a po-liceman, who assumed she was a fan. Now she was running down the platform, shouting. Just at that moment the train began to move.

John thrust his head out the window and yelled: "Run, Cynthia, run!" Cynthia ran her heart out, but she could not catch John.

On Saturday the maharishi addressed his following in the au-ditorium of a teacher's college. Seated on a sofa, he was flanked by

England's most famous young men. When the question period was reached, the Beatles witnessed for the first time the suspicion and hostility with which the holy man was regarded by the British press. Being masters of the press conference, the boys began to ward off the mocking queries of the reporters, answering with such spirit that the maharishi's followers were moved to spontaneous applause. Then came the bombshell that rewarded the press for their daylong vigil. The Beatles, represented by Paul McCartney, announced that they were renouncing drugs. "It was an experience we went through," said Paul. "Now it's over. We don't need it anymore. We think we're finding new ways of getting there." Paul's goal in making this widely publicized renunciation was to offset the wave of bad publicity that had broken over the Beatles earlier in the summer when Paul told *Life* that he had experimented with LSD. Now the Beatles' diplomat redeemed himself and the band.

Sunday felt, for once, like a holy day. The Beatles promenaded across the campus with their ladies, including the tardy Cynthia, discussing the great new spiritual adventure upon which they were embarking. Soon they would be leaving for India and the maharishi's ashram at the foot of the Himalayas. There, in that intensely spiritual atmosphere, they would be initiated into the final mysteries of the cult. After that . . .

The persistent ringing of a telephone inside a nearby dormitory was violating the peace of the Sabbath. "Someone had better answer that," admonished George.

Jane Asher took the call in a public phone booth. It was Peter Brown. "Call Paul to the phone," he ordered.

When Paul answered, Brown said somberly: "I've got bad news."

On the same Friday afternoon that saw the Beatles leave London with the maharishi, Brian Epstein had driven off in his silver Bentley, with the top down, bound for his country house, Kingsley Hill, at Rushlake Green, Sussex. He was planning to spend the weekend with Peter Brown and Geoffrey Ellis, another old friend and colleague. That very night, according to Wendy Hanson, Brian was going to have an orgy with some boys brought down from the city. Sad to say, the boys failed to appear. When Peter Brown arrived for supper, he found Brian in a dark mood, which was not lightened by all the claret he drank. At the conclusion of the meal he made a number of calls to London, trying to pull more boys. When none of these efforts proved successful, he got into his car about ten and headed back to town. Peter Brown, anxious about Brian's driving while drunk, called Chapel Street around midnight. Antonio Garcia, the butler, informed Brown that Brian had come home safely and gone straight out again.

On Saturday Brian did not awake until five in the afternoon. He called Peter Brown in the country and said that he was going to have breakfast, read the mail, watch *Juke Box Jury*, and then drive down to Sussex. Brown, troubled by the groggy tone of Brian's voice, urged him to take the train instead of driving. Brian agreed, but he did not appear that night.

It was not until noon on Sunday that anybody made an effort to find out what had happened to Brian, which is very odd in view of the fact that he was due at Kingsley Hill on Saturday evening. It is especially hard to believe that Peter Brown, who had evidenced such concern about Brian the previous night, did not pick up the phone and find out what had befallen his friend.

What finally happened, according to Brown, was that Antonio called first Brown and then Joanna Newfield, Brian's secretary, and reported that Brian had not emerged from his room since the previous evening and was now locked in his bedroom with the intercom off. Joanna recognized the potentially sinister implications of his report. She tried to get in touch with Brian's personal physician, Norman Cowan, but the doctor, she discovered, was on holiday in Spain. Next, she called Alistair Taylor, Brian's oldest employee, who agreed to meet Joanna at Chapel Street.

By the time Joanna arrived, Peter Brown—who had been out to lunch with Geoffrey Ellis at a pub near Kingsley Hill—had called back and spoken with Antonio. Brown's attitude was that the servants were panicking foolishly—an odd line for a man to take who had found Brian near death in similar circumstances. Yet Brown told Antonio that there was nothing to fear and ordered him to call Alistair Taylor and warn him that he was coming on a fool's errand. When Antonio relayed this conversation to Joanna, she was not satisfied. She called Brown herself. Now he changed his tune. He advised Joanna *not* to call Norman Cowan—whom Brown assumed was in town—but to ring up instead Brown's own doctor, John Gallway, who lived "two blocks away in Belgravia." In fact, Dr. Gallway lived a couple of miles away at 23 Ovington Garden, Knightbridge.

By the time Dr. Gallway arrived, a considerable number of people had assembled at the house on Chapel Street: Antonio and his wife, Maria, Brian Barrett, the chauffeur, Alistair Taylor, and Joanna. The question was: What should they do? Brian had locked the double oak doors to his bedroom. No matter how much noise they made, they could not rouse him. When Joanna called Brown again, he told Gallway to break down the door. As Antonio and Barrett laid their weight against the oak leaves, Brown stayed on the phone, listening to the grunts of the servants and the cracking and splitting of the wood.

As soon as the doors were forced, Joanna and Dr. Gallway entered the dark bedroom. Joanna saw Brian, dressed in pajamas, lying on his right side, curled up in the fetal position. Before she could look more closely, the doctor seized her and forcibly evicted her from the room. Undismayed, Joanna announced to the staff: "It's all right. He's just asleep. It's fine."

But what Dr. Gallway saw was not so fine. Blood was oozing from Brian's nose and the sheet beneath him was soaked with bodily excretions. His heart had stopped. The cause of his death appeared obvious: Everywhere the doctor looked, he saw pills, pills, pills, in vials and boxes, on shelves or in cabinets next to the bed. The whole scene proclaimed suicide.

When Dr. Gallway emerged from the bedroom, he looked, according to Joanna, "all white and shaken." He announced that Brian was dead. Then he picked up the telephone receiver. "He couldn't get any words out," wrote Peter Brown. At that moment Brown heard Maria scream, *"Why? Why?"*

Everybody was quick to assume that Brian Epstein had killed himself, because he had made attempts on his life before. This interpretation was flatly contradicted, however, by the pathologist's testimony at the inquest. He attributed the death to drug poisoning but not to the massive dose that a suicide would take. Analysis of the contents of Brian's stomach indicated that he had taken six Carbritals to alleviate his insomnia. This was probably his normal dose because he had built up a tolerance that had brought him close to the lethal level. The pathologist concluded, therefore, that Brian had died of an accidental overdose, and the coroner endorsed this finding. Scotland Yard, however, was uneasy about Brian Epstein's death—with reason.

The true circumstances surrounding Brian Epstein's death were deliberately concealed. The key was supplied by Brian Sommerville, the lawyer who had served as the Beatles' PR man in 1964. He disclosed in a tape-recorded interview for this book that Brian Epstein was not alone on the last night of his life, but had with him in his bedroom a Coldstream Guardsman, to whom he had been introduced by Sommerville. It was this man who discovered that Brian was dead. When pressed to provide more details, Sommerville balked, insisting only that Brian's death was not a suicide and warning that even if the guardsman were discovered, he would never talk.

David Jacobs, Brian's lawyer, told Wendy Hanson that he was the first man to enter Brian's bedroom after his death, though no one else reported his presence at the scene. He even boasted of having removed from Brian's bed a tattletale article by Paul's ex-housekeeper that had appeared in the Italian press. It's not likely that Jacobs stopped with such a trivial precaution. Jacobs would have known how to prejudice the coroner's judgment by removing and planting evidence that would point to a finding of misadventure. The enormous number of pills found on the premises and the brandy bottle near the bed figured prominently in the inquest; yet according to the pathologist's report absolutely no alcohol was found in the body and no significant amounts of any other drug.

As the amount of bromide found in Brian's body was not so great as to make death inevitable, the question arises whether there were any other circumstances that might have led to his death, which was ultimately caused by anoxia, or the diminution of oxygen to the brain.

According to the buzz of the London gay world, Brian Epstein died of asphyxiation produced by a mask over his face. Such a death would have entailed no violence and left no telltale marks. If the S/M paraphernalia or women's clothing or other evidence was removed, it would be virtually impossible for the coroner to reconstruct the manner of death.

Ironically, the man who may have suppressed the evidence of Brian's suffocation died himself of asphyxiation just sixteen months later, found by his servant strung up in the garage of his weekend home at Hove. The parallel went even further, for like Brian Epstein, David Jacobs had suffered a breakdown from drug abuse and been confined to the Priory. When discharged, he displayed symptoms of extreme paranoia, insisting in the days before his death that six prominent show-biz people were out to get him. Wendy Hanson learned from her gay friends that Jacobs actually died in the course of an S/M ritual when, having submitted to the noose to produce a hanged man's erection, he fell victim to an evil prank. One of Jacob's torturers kicked the stool out from under his feet. Immediately thereafter, the lawyer's lover, according to Mario Amaya, went into hiding.

The last word on the subject of Brian Epstein's death must be spoken by Simon Napier-Bell. This shrewd fellow was in Ireland when the news broke of Brian's death. Instantly he rushed back to London, inspired by a hunch that Brian had left a message on his new flame's answering machine. Napier-Bell's instinct was sound: Brian had left not just one but a whole series of messages. The first one was recorded the Friday morning before his departure for the country, and the next one that same night when he returned to London, with further messages extending the series, until the calls ended late Saturday night, presumably not long before Brian met his death. What was most striking about these communications was the way they transformed themselves (owing doubtless to the effect of drugs) from messages directed to Brian's newest love to messages that could only have been meant for Brian's greatest love. As Napier-Bell wrote, "Brian was finding life vacuous and unchallenging. And in North Wales, the giggling guru was stealing the last vestiges of his influence over the person who'd meant the most in his life. I wasn't the only one who'd gone away that weekend." As the recipient of these important messages decided not to impart them but simply to use them to tease his readers, the closest we can come to Brian's last recorded words is to quote their recipient's impression of the whole sequence:

> After dinner on the Friday he'd driven back from the country and phoned me. "I had a premonition you'd come back to see me. If you have, call me back at once. Please."
>
> Later he called again. "You shouldn't have gone away." His voice was slurred. "I asked you not to. I thought I might have changed your mind. I want to talk to you again like before."
>
> After that there was a succession of messages which must have been left on the Saturday. Some of them didn't seem to be for me, in fact, I'd prefer to think that they weren't. The last one was particularly muddled and seemed to touch on things that had no connection with our brief relationship.
>
> Perhaps it was just that I had an answer phone and Maharishi's holiday camp didn't.

Perhaps.

MÉNAGE À TROIS

The love affair Simon Napier-Bell alludes to so coyly was, of course, that between Brian Epstein and John Lennon. Being privy to the gossip of the gay world, Napier-Bell probably knew about this relationship before he met Brian. Even if he did not, Brian's conversation during supper would have told the tale. At one point he confessed that he "feared he had lost John forever." He did not disclose, however, what had inspired this despairing and lovelorn mood.

Yoko Ono told Marnie Hair that just before Brian's death John had come around to Chapel Street. Something had aroused his passion, and he had behaved in his accustomed manner, seizing Brian's arm and twisting it up behind his back as he bent him forward. John was preparing to bugger Brian—or was actually flagrante delicto—when Queenie, hearing the sound of a tussle, walked into the room. Horrified to behold her son being sexually molested, she rushed out and called the police. When John heard the call going out, he panicked. Dashing out of the house, he jumped into his car and ordered Les Anthony to drive around to Peter Brown's place in Mayfair. Bursting in upon the Beatles' man of affairs, John demanded that arrangements be made immediately to get him out of the country.

Meantime, the police arrived at 12 Chapel Street—as they had done on many past occasions for similar reasons—where they were met by Brian. Speaking with his best West End accent, he assured the officers that the call had been a false alarm. His mother, in delicate health owing to the recent demise of his father, had discovered her son in a playful tussle with an old friend and had misconstrued the situation entirely. Brian offered the officers his apologies and showed them to the door.

When he was confronted by the press after Brian's death, John parroted for public consumption the maharishi's line: that death was the gateway to a better life. In his heart Lennon felt fear. For Brian had functioned like a mother to John, coddling him, shielding him and getting him out of trouble. Now John's surrogate mother was dead. "I was scared!" Lennon confessed later, adding, "I thought, 'We've fuckin' had it!'" More likely what he felt was: "*I've* fuckin' had it!" For the pattern was all too familiar. Once again, as in childhood and youth, John had been abandoned and left to fend for himself by the person to whom he had looked for love and protection. A clear sign of how closely Brian was identified with Julia in John's mind is the fact that Lennon did precisely the same thing after his manager's death as he had done after his mother died: He held a séance conducted by a medium that was attended by all the Beatles, who, as was their wont, never disclosed what transpired.

At such a critical moment it was natural that John should turn to Yoko because he had already developed a grand illusion about her wisdom and powers, regarding her as an almost magical being who could fulfill his every need and solve all his problems. Now his need of her became so great that he could no longer allow their relationship to exist in limbo; instead, Lennon demanded that Yoko make a commitment to him.

Ironically, at this very moment Yoko was experiencing a crisis no less serious than John's, in fact, one that threatened her very life. Insight into her predicament is provided by Tony Cox's younger cousin Jodie Fridiani, who was a guest of Tony and Yoko's at the time. Jodie, a nineteen-year-old college student on holiday in Europe, had decided on the spur of the moment to pop over to London to visit Tony, whom she hadn't seen since she was eleven. No sooner did she arrive at the flat near Hanover Gate than she was led into the kitchen by Yoko, who began to pour out all her woes. She confessed that she was living in fear of her life and that of her daughter. Tony was becoming violent. Yoko longed to leave him, but she was afraid that if she told him she was going, he might kill her. Having blown Jodie's mind with this appalling revelation, Yoko set the girl a task. She told her to get on the phone and start calling around to all the hardware stores in the city to find a small, elegant hammer—what the English call a toffee hammer—so that Yoko could copy it in glass. No sooner had Jodie settled down to this odd job than Tony appeared and took his cousin aside to ventilate all his troubles.

After a week of listening to these alarming confessions, Jodie decided to leave the Cox household and travel north to Edinburgh, where the famous festival was in progress. When she came back to London early in September to board a flight for the States, she decided to say good-bye to Tony and Kyoko. She found Tony alone in the flat. "Where's Yoko?" Jodie asked.

Tony replied bitterly: "She's with John Lennon."

Yoko wasn't just spending the afternoon or evening with John; she had been gone so long that Tony had changed all the locks on the doors.

Up to this time John and Yoko had been simply having an affair, taking their pleasures covertly in the back seat of a limousine or wherever opportunity offered and enjoying long heart-to-heart talks. After their abrupt elopement their relationship was established formally as a kind of ménage à trois in which John was recognized by Tony as Yoko's lover and John, in exchange, provided the money to support Tony and Yoko.

The obvious question is why Yoko and John didn't plight their troth and have done with their hopelessly unsatisfactory—in Yoko's case, dangerous—marriages. The answer is that none of the principals was ready as yet to upset the status quo. Though John was eager to enjoy a new life, he wasn't ready to accept the serious consequences of divorcing Cynthia and provoking a public scandal. Though Yoko would have given a lot to be released from her harrowing relationship with Tony, she had to be cautious about pressing John lest she alarm him and lose him. Though Tony resented Lennon's becoming Yoko's acknowledged lover, he had no other means of bailing himself out of the flood of legal complaints that could send him soon to prison. Now, for the first time ever, he and Yoko were free to address their next project with the confidence born of knowing that they had an angel.

Half-a-Wind, which ran from 11 October to 14 November, was Tony's and Yoko's most ambitious effort. When the visitor entered the Lisson Gallery at 68 Bell Street, he beheld a number of objects mounted on white stands. An ordinary bottle, titled "Flute Song for John," was priced at £200. Yoko explained: "I just fixed that price because I don't want to sell it." On another white stand were four stainless steel spoons, titled "Three Spoons." The catalog listed a piece, "Hammer a Nail Painting," that proved nonexistent. Queried about the omission, Yoko laughed and replied: "I think it would be very good for someone's mental health to buy something that didn't exist!" The most interesting work was not these exhibits but three detached "environments," a concept totally unfamiliar to London gallery visitors.

The first of these environments was the "Half-a-Spring-Room," above the gallery. It contained a great variety of objects, all of which had been halved and whited. Not only was there half-a-bed, covered with half-a-sheet and half-a-pillow and flanked by half-a-chair, but nearby there was also half-a-washbasin with half-a-toothbrush and half-a-mug. The half-witted decorator had furnished the room with half-a-radio and half-an-ironing board. Half-a-bookcase contained half-pots, half-pans, and a half-kettle. All that was lacking was half-a-loaf, which is better than none.

Down in the basement was "The Stone," an environment originally exhibited in New York. Its most significant feature proved to be its use of a black bag, into which the visitor was urged to crawl and then disrobe. That idea had come to Yoko one night in Japan, when she tuned out of a social gathering by putting a piece of fabric over her head through which she could see without being seen. But the image of the stone came to Tony when he saw a figure crouching inside the bag: The shape reminded him of those black rocks found in Zen gardens.

"Backyard," the third environment, was like a Happening. To reach it, the visitor followed a white line that led out of the gallery and down the street to a drinking club. After taking some refreshment, he was supposed to pick up the trail again and follow it back to the gallery to a room where Yoko sat cross-legged in the corner. Before her was a tray of labeled keys, reading "Half-a-footfall," "Half-a-year," "Half-a-word." Yoko would announce to each arrival: "Choose a key, and I will whisper a message in your ear." The message was always a single word in Japanese.

This same space was called "The Blue Room" because, as the program explained, if the viewer stared at it long enough, the room would turn blue. The only objects in the room were large, empty chemical jars, standing on a shelf. John Lennon had suggested, according to the catalog, that Yoko sell the missing half of all her objects in bottles. The jars on the shelves were labeled, accordingly, "Half-a-Chair," "Half-a-Room," "Half-a-Life," etc. This was the wittiest idea in the show.

After the Lisson show, John Lennon began to turn up more frequently at Hanover Gate. Dan Richter recalled seeing the chauffeur-driven car standing outside the building on numerous occasions. It was at this time that Dan and his wife, Jill (who held a degree in medieval literature from the Sorbonne), were introduced to Lennon by Yoko. "John was on his best behavior," Dan observed, "trying hard not to appear rich." This meeting marked the beginning of a relationship that eventually ripened into the closest friendship that John and Yoko enjoyed in England. The more Lennon appeared at the apartment, however, the more agitated became Tony Cox. As Richter explained, "Tony had originally encouraged Yoko to go after John, but when he saw the two of them getting involved with each other, he didn't like it."

Shortly before Christmas 1967 Yoko and Tony rounded out their year's activity by attending the International Film Festival at Knokke-le Zoute in Belgium, where they intended to exhibit *Bottoms* in the short film division. They found the normally staid competition beset by a radical spirit. A militant Happening artist, Jean-Jacques Lebel, dedicated to the goal of sabotaging "all that is 'cultural,'" had decided to disrupt the proceedings by staging a spontaneous nude beauty contest. Arriving in the judge's chambers bare-assed naked and carrying squares of paper inscribed with their competition numbers, Lebel's merry crew, including Yoko Ono and Tony Cox, sought to drive the bearded, scholarly-looking judges to some discrediting excess. But the judges maintained their dignity while the photographers had a field day snapping pictures of naked filmmakers. Not content with appearing in the nude in publications sure to be seen by her family, Yoko seized on the occasion to send home a special greeting. Running into a Japanese film critic, Shigeomi Sato, she gave him a phial containing an amber fluid, with orders to take it back to Japan. "What is it?" asked the unsuspecting critic.

Tartly Yoko replied: "My piss!"

During that fateful fall and early winter the Beatles were busy digging the pit into which they would topple with *Magical Mystery Tour*. The idea for the show had burst full-blown in Paul's brain while he was flying across the United States in April. Turning to Mal Evans, Paul had dictated the outline. When he presented the plan to the other Beatles, they were not enthusiastic; in fact, John was enraged: "I was choked that he'd arranged it all with Mal Evans and had all this idea going. And he comes in and says, 'We're going to do this. Would you write that bit?'" So far as John was concerned, *Magical Mystery Tour* was *Sgt. Pepper* all over again. Only there was the great difference that this time the Beatles were going far beyond the art they had mastered to experiment with one of which they knew next to nothing.

What was driving Paul, of course, was the need to find some way to satisfy the public's demand that the Beatles make themselves visible again. The obvious solution was to make Beatles III, the last film called for in their UA contract. Bombarded with proposals, the boys had been best disposed toward making a picture in which they would represent four aspects of the same man, Paul having gone so far as to engage the notorious Joe Orton to rewrite the script. The result was predictable. Cautioned by Walter Shenson that the "boys shouldn't be made to do anything . . . that would reflect badly," Orton reflected: "I hadn't the heart to tell him that the boys, in my script, have been caught *in flagrante*, become involved in dubious political activity, dressed as women, committed murder, been put in prison, and committed adultery." Not far off the truth of John Lennon's life but hardly the thing for the Beatles.

After a meeting at Paul's house on 1 September to discuss the future of the group, John plunged into the *Mystery Tour* and worked hard for months as writer, performer, director, and editor. His principal contribution was his masterpiece, "I Am the Walrus." He wrote this famous lyric by putting a sheet of paper into his typewriter and adding a line whenever the spirit moved him. How different is this patient, passive way of working from the Tin Pan Alley approach of earlier years, when he would eagerly snitch something from the latest American releases and then piece and patch like a typical tunesmith hammering away at his tinker's anvil. Now he had learned to lie back comfortably on the nourishing breast of the media, making his mind a sticking paper for bits of radio chatter, TV commercials, newspaper headlines, the siren of an ambulance, the babbling of a child—any and all the impressions that constitute the ordinary day of an ordinary person. When it came time to compose, he had learned that he could drop a hook down into this mass of material and draw up into consciousness just those few precious images that he required.

Though this method of composition courted the accidental and the ephemeral, the song brought to burning focus every resource of Lennon's mature art, commencing with Lewis Carroll nonsense and including childhood recollections (the image of pus dripping from the eye of a dead dog is actually a line from a schoolboy chant), ambient noise (the rising/falling ostinato of the introduction was suggested by a European police siren), acoustic collage, and the inevitable Mersey beat. The brooding opening, worthy of a pop Beethoven, is reminiscent of the sound track of a grimly realistic black-and-white film of the late Forties, one of those *On the Waterfront* toughies whose credits roll up supered over shots of grimy old warehouses, decayed docks and rusty freighters, all underscored with a deep, foreboding sound—harshly distorted by the lousy movie theater sound system. Then the Lennon voice strikes in with hammerlike force, that cold, flinty, quarry man's voice that was John's most compelling vocal tone, chanting rather than singing because he didn't give a damn about the tune when he had words that were this strong.

Lennon's delivery is imbued with his master passion, rage, which he inflects across the entire infrared range from mocking and cursing to jeering and sneering. In no other recording does he strike such a perfect balance between language as speech and language as action. You can practically see him grimacing and gesticulating as he spits out the words against the concussive backbeat. The double edge on Lennon's mind is also clearly revealed, as one moment he taunts the medical experts who condemn dope smoking while the weedheads laugh up their sleeves, and the next he gibes at these same stoned jokers, whose oh-so-hip snicker is choked with strangling smoke. This same trick of mind impels him to telescope the crabby-looking fishwife and the Brigitte Bardot sex goddess, who melt and meld in the flames of his Juvenalian wrath, as do the very sexes in the act of undressing—"knickers" being not just an article of feminine apparel but one of the British gay world's favorite taunting words. In fine, for the first time ever, John Lennon unlocks in the "Walrus" that crazy attic in his mind where he had always stored the grotesque imagery that first emerged in his teen-age monster cartoons.

Such an unremittingly angry song cried aloud for relief, which Lennon provided with a soothing lyric theme, reminiscent of Ralph Vaughan Williams, that is one of his most haunting and felicitous phrases, appearing like an island of pastoral calm in a raging brainstorm. The domestic garden imagery it projects not only provides an escape from the teeth-bared ravings that precede it but also serves as a transition to the blubbering, gurgling noises of the Walrus himself.

After he had recorded the song, Lennon discovered by rereading the ballad of "The Walrus and the Carpenter" in *Through the Looking Glass* that he had misremembered Lewis Carroll's poem: "It was only later that I realized the Walrus was a big, fat capitalist eating up all the oysters." Unconsciously, John may have been thinking of another big, fat, black, seafood-gobbling creature with great white tusks—Lennon's lifelong favorite Fats Waller (i.e., "Walrus"), author of that cunnilinguistic classic, "I Want Some Seafood, Mama!" (The other moniker that John adopts, the "Eggman," turns out likewise to entail an identification of food with sex because it was Lennon's nickname for Eric Burdon of the Animals, notorious for cracking eggs on the naked bodies of girls to whom he was making love.)

The lengthy fadeout of the "Walrus" displays the most imaginative and sophisticated use of sound montage in all of Lennon's work. What makes it so effective is not the lavish resources he employs—the symphony orchestra, the twenty-voice choir, or even that "Shakespeherian Rag" from the BBC. The art lies in the composition, which suggests a long aural tracking shot, up close at the start, following the inconsequent sequence of programs across the dial, until the focus enlarges finally to the sublime perspective of a great dish antenna reaching out across the universe.

In "I Am the Walrus," John Lennon finally found an artistic formula and a creative mystique that suited him perfectly, along with the means to reconcile his habitual lethargy with his need to be productive. Yet in the process of releasing himself from the toil of his old Tin Pan Alley routine, he actually imposed upon himself a discipline more drastic than any he had practiced in the past. For now, like a religious devotee or monk, he was obliged to submit, day in, day out, to that most exacting Zen: a self-annihilating immersion in the mundane.

"DEAR ALF, FRED, DAD, PATER, FATHER, WHATEVER"

Shortly after his twenty-seventh birthday, 9 October 1967, John Lennon made one of those impulsive, self-reversing moves that sprang from his deeply conflicted nature. After a lifetime of regarding his father as little better than a Bowery bum, John invited "the ignoble Alf" to reside at Kenwood. What made the decision even more startling was Lennon's recent history with his father.

Freddie had popped up three years before, in April 1964, after an absence of seventeen years. He had been urged to declare himself publicly by his brother, Charles, and by his fellow workers, who exhorted him not to tolerate the defamatory lies about him that were being disseminated by the press. Two reporters from the *Daily Sketch* had arranged the initial meeting with John. The poor old kitchen porter strode into the dressing room of his world-famous son at the Scala Theater, where the Beatles were shooting *A Hard Day's Night*—and both men did a double take!

John experienced the weird sensation of staring at a man whose face foretells exactly how you will look thirty years hence—particularly if you are down on your luck. For though Freddie had retained his jaunty air, he had lost his teeth and acquired the manner of a raffish hobo. Otherwise, he was astonishingly like John, save for his height, being a half-head shorter owing to childhood rickets that had stunted his legs. The facial resemblance was remarkably close: the same long, narrow nose, terminating in flared nostrils; the same small, almond-shaped eyes under heavy brows; the same narrow, finely carved lips; and the same elongated facial mask, framed by a firm, square chin. And when Freddie opened his mouth to speak, he projected the very sound of John's voice in the same lilting Liverpudlian intonation, but with a rather more cosmopolitan accent because the former merchant mariner had spent so much of his life in foreign travel.

If John was amazed by the resemblance between himself and his dad, Freddie was no less impressed by the likeness he perceived between John and Julia. "He was so much like his mother, I was quite astounded," he reported; "He even wore the kind of scowl that his mother might have done in a situation like that, where she felt she had reason to resent. . . . I stuck out my hand to shake his, but John just growled at me and said suspiciously, 'What do you want?' I told him I didn't want anything, seeing how hostile he was. John retorted, 'You never bothered about me before, why now?' I suspected John thought I was jumping on the bandwagon, that I'd only come out of the woodwork because he was a star and could help me.

"But I asked him, 'Isn't being your father enough?'"

Evidently it was. Father and son were soon chatting amiably. Freddie displayed his customary joie de vivre, recounting his life in an amusing style that sometimes sparkled with puns. (He was given to saying things like "My son is an idol, but he thinks I'm simply idle.") After just twenty minutes, however, Lennon was summoned to do an interview with the BBC. Next day he was enthusiastic about Freddie when he described him to Pete Shotton. "He's good news!" declared John. "A real funny guy—a loony, just like me!"

Like father, like son. That idea became the positive pole of John's highly ambivalent attitude toward his rediscovered parent. The negative was John's ineradicable resentment at having been abandoned as a child. This was the stronger force, and its power explains why after this promising first meeting, John did not invite Freddie to a return engagement. On the other hand, John, who was very stingy, fell into the habit of sending his old man from time to time a few pounds. One of these remittances betrays John's confusion about how he should regard his father. The salutation reads: "Dear Alf, Fred, Dad, Pater, Father, Whatever."

A year later Freddie, working now at a hotel near Esher, told a reporter, "It's not a bad life, really [he was paid £10 a week plus room and board], but what I'd like is a bit of recognition. . . . I would like to meet my daughter-in-law and the kiddie. I would like to see John again and explain things to him my way." This plea for attention had the opposite of its intended effect. John complained bitterly that his father was "blackmailing" him through the press.

It was not the papers that brought Freddie to John's door next, but the Gordon Mills Organization (managers of Tom Jones, Engelbert Humperdinck, et al.), one of whose hard-hustling agents, Tony Cartwright, had persuaded Freddie to sign a contract and become a recording artist. When Freddie Lennon fulfilled the ambition of a lifetime by recording a blarney-tongued recitation of his life and hard times for Pye, entitled, "That's My Life," John reacted with characteristic ambivalence, playing the record constantly at Kenwood because he got a kick out of the idea that his father was the block off which John had been chipped, while at the same time plotting with Brian Epstein to have this "embarrassing" exploitation of the Lennon name suppressed in both Britain and America, where it actually made the charts.

This treacherous act outraged Freddie Lennon, who had a temper and a tongue to match his son's. One day in February 1966 John opened the door at Kenwood and found himself again face-to-face with his father. What freaked John wasn't so much Freddie as the man who was with him, Tony Cartwright, whom John considered the root of the evil and treated accordingly, slamming the door in his face. A few weeks later John used the occasion of a newspaper interview to continue his attack on Freddie, announcing publicly that when his father had turned up, John had "shown him the door." Now Freddie's younger and very devoted brother, Charles, took a hand in the game, writing John a scathing letter in which he told him to stop listening to Mimi's lies and learn the truth about his childhood, which Charles proceeded to disclose: the facts of Julia's infidelity, her illegitimate child, the double play at Blackpool—Freddie to Julia to Mimi—in fine, the whole ugly story. John did not respond, but the truth sank in.

In October 1967, when Freddie returned to Kenwood, after being fetched to the house by Les Anthony, the old man was received effusively by John, who displayed nothing but affection and pride in the father he had so long detested. Staggered though Freddie was by this startling change of face, he contrived to make the most of the opportunity. He said they should invite Uncle Charlie because his birthday was nigh. In no time this long-forgotten relative was ushered into John's presence, and was hailed with "Happy birthday, Uncle Charlie!" Before the astonished Charles could utter a word, John gushed: "Isn't me dad grrreat!" Struck dumb by this amazing display of filial piety, Uncle Charlie failed to reply. "Did you hear what I said?" John demanded.

Finding his tongue at last, Charlie answered: "John, I've been waiting for that many a long year!"

As the men drained their lagers, the women bustled about, tending to them in the grand old subservient manner. One of these women was Freddie Lennon's latest love, Pauline Jones, a nineteen-year-old university student who had taken a holiday job at the Toby Jug and met there a middle-aged kitchen porter—who instantly captured her heart! Undoubtedly Pauline was looking for a father, hers having died not long since, but what really made her fall for Freddie was simply the fact that he was the merriest, most charming and entertaining human being she had ever met. So Pauline, an attractive as well as a highly intelligent girl, had assumed the role in Freddie's life once played by Julia. Imagine the effect of that discovery on John Lennon! It must have taken a supreme act of will for him not to bolt out the door and run down the hill to Ringo's house, crying, "My old man's fucking a Beatles' fan!" Cynthia had an entirely different take on Pauline. She saw this young woman as the solution to a pressing problem.

In the wake of John's recent commitment to Yoko Ono, he and Cynthia appear to have arrived at a tacit agreement that each would go his own way. Cynthia had taken to spending her evenings in London, where her mother was now living at Ringo's flat on Montagu Square, after having given up the house that John had bought her at Weybridge. As Cynthia was so often out late at nights, she required a resident baby watcher. So she invited Pauline to move into Kenwood, where she would care for Julian and perform some secretarial duties.

What Cynthia was really about at this time is hard to make out, but what must be understood in the first place is that she had long been in the habit of going out at night with escorts like Brian's friend Terry Doran, who were regarded as friends of the family. In this manner Cynthia was enabled to enjoy certain social pleasures without John being obliged to do anything that was not to his taste. Now, according to Vivian Moynihan, the press officer of NEMS, reports were received that Cynthia had been seen about with her hairdresser, whose shop, Curl Up and Dye, was in the vicinity of the flat on Montagu Square. Miles confirms that there was a flutter among the Beatles' women, who all rushed to Cynthia's defense. John hit the ceiling when he heard the gossip and threatened a divorce. Brian Epstein went into action immediately, and succeeded in calming John and smoothing matters over.

The ill humor produced by this disturbance may have accounted for the spooky and tomblike atmosphere at Kenwood, which impressed itself on Pauline Jones the moment she moved in, late in October 1967. Freddie had moved out already, having spent three uncomfortable weeks in the house, during which time he hardly ever saw John, who was busy working on *Magical Mystery Tour* as well as on Yoko's show at the Lisson Gallery. Now Freddie was living in a little apartment in Kew, which John had provided, along with a place on the Beatles' payroll that paid twelve pounds a week, a sum calculated to match Freddie's income as a kitchen porter. Pauline, who had thought she was moving into a family home, discovered now that she was condemned to spending virtually all her time alone because John and Cynthia were either absent or else behaved like ghosts. Pauline recalled:

> My impression of John was that he was totally withdrawn into himself when he was at home—unsmiling, cold and unapproachable. He seemed high-strung and tense, yet expressed nothing of himself to the household. His thoughts and feelings

appeared tightly guarded. He would rise about 10 A.M. and take a breakfast of mushrooms on toast, the only meal of the day he ate at home, prepared for him by Dot, which he would consume in total silence save for a good deal of lip-smacking and grunting. He would then leave for London in the Rolls, chauffeured by Anthony, usually not returning until late at night. Cynthia was clearly hurt and insecure as a result of his behavior but had begun to establish a social life of her own.

Pauline observed that Cynthia "would frequently return home even later than John and so as not to disturb him would sleep in one of the spare bedrooms. On the occasions when she went to bed early, it was John who would come home late and sleep in the spare room, so the nights they shared the marital bed were few or none."

After Christmas Pauline left Kenwood because she found it difficult to manage the badly spoiled Julian. Also, she was so disturbed by the weird vibes in the house that for the first and only time in her life she began to fear, as she lay abed of nights, ghosts and intruders. Meantime, Pauline's mother was making her daughter's life miserable, even going so far as to have her declared a ward of the court, which meant that Pauline could not marry without judicial permission until she attained her majority. Pauline, suffering now from stomach cramps and even blackouts, decided to move in with Freddie at Kew. Then, one night in January 1968, an incident occurred that put the whole notion of like father, like son into startling perspective.

That evening Freddie went with Pauline to a club in London that all the rock stars patronized and got a "skinful of drink," which fired up his temperament and loosened his tongue. Then who should walk in but Cynthia with a strange escort! Freddie, who had always assumed that his daughter-in-law was a sweet Lancashire lass completely dedicated to John, was shocked to behold her in the company of another man. Instantly his painful memories of Julia's infidelities assailed him. Confronting Cynthia, the old boy gave her a piece of his mind. At the climax of his tongue-lashing, he told her that if she were so free with her favors, she ought to give him a little piece! Cynthia was horrified and humiliated. Never again would she speak to Freddie Lennon.

Next morning John, who had gotten an earful of the incident, stopped on his way to work to give his father a good going-over. Freddie, anticipating the worst, refused to open the door. For five minutes Lennon stood out in the hall, ranting and raving about the damage such indiscretions could cause his reputation. Finally, seeing he was getting nowhere, be bellowed: *"Keep your fucking mouth shut or the bloody feud will start again!"*

John calmed down soon and even provided the money to fight Pauline's court action against her mother; he also paid for the three weeks that Freddie and Pauline were obliged to spend in Edinburgh, establishing residence in Scotland so they could marry despite the ban imposed by the English court. When the happy pair had a baby, David Henry Lennon, born 26 February 1969, John bought them a little house in Brighton for £6500. But for the next three years he saw nothing further of his father.

DOES GOD LIVE IN OLD MEN?

Jet age pilgrims, the Beatles flew from England to India in February 1968 to join the maharishi at his ashram. After landing in New Delhi, they journeyed by jeep 140 miles to Rishikesh. The holy city on the Ganges, lying at the foot of the snow-covered Himalayas, was "thronged with saffron-robed sadus [*sic*] and disciples in white dhotis; naked, mud-bedaubed hermits holding begging bowls; Hindu women with mascara-encircled eyes and henna-palmed hands," reported Evelyn Ross of the *Guardian;* but the Beatles saw virtually nothing of the real India. Mounted now on donkeys, they pushed straight through the pungent city, until they reached the steep gorge of the river, where they crossed on foot a modern suspension bridge that brought them to the wooden gates of the Meditation Academy. Here they found not the primitive shelter of twigs and leaves prescribed by Hindu tradition or the free tuition that it is the duty of the holy man to provide but instead a $350-a-day Western-style resort hotel, where each Beatle was assigned a chalet with hot and cold running water, four-poster bed, and electric heaters. As Ringo observed, "It was a bit like a Butlins Holiday camp."

Those pilgrims serious about the spiritual life were awakened rudely at three in the morning by a loud banging at their doors. After splashing the cold water of the sacred river on their heads and eyes, they gathered in a dimly lit, incense-scented hall, where they meditated for two or three hours before dawn, concluding their exercises with chanting and body yoga. After a sparse vegetarian breakfast, they repaired to a network of tiny caves hollowed out under the temple to continue their meditations in private until the midday meal. A dose of hard labor in a hot, steamy laundry or a clammy public toilet was prescribed for the afternoon as a counterpoise to the morning's spirituality.

But just as the physical rigors of the ashram had been replaced by the comforts suitable to rich foreigners, so the traditional regimen was softened to cosset the golden geese. "It wasn't a hard life," Ringo told

Melody Maker when he returned to England after just ten days. (Ringo disliked the food, and Maureen was maddened by the mosquitoes.) "We used to get up in the morning—not particularly early—and go down to the canteen for breakfast. Then, perhaps, walk about a bit and meditate or bathe. There were lectures and things all the time, but it was very much like a holiday. Really, his meditation center is all very luxurious." As for cleaning toilets, John Lennon shocked the more pious sojourners by covering the lavatory walls with dirty drawings.

Whom did the Beatles find at the ashram? The clientele of such establishments is primarily prosperous widows or divorcées. At the academy there were seventy Westerners, most of them rich old ladies from Sweden because the maharishi had a center at Malmö, as well as some pretty girls from California and several pop stars: Donovan, Mike Love of the Beach Boys (who subsequently toured with the maharishi), and Mia Farrow, who was recovering from her brief marriage to Frank Sinatra. Everyone wore Indian attire: saris and pajamas, kurta tunics and sandals, with so many beads and bells that they jingled as they walked. In the group photograph printed in the Beatles' fan mag, the celebrities and their women are lined up in the bright sunlight, with the dark little guru and the blond movie star in the middle. Cynthia stands at one end, looking, with her tinted glasses and garishly patterned pants, like a schoolteacher on a holiday. John Lennon poses at the opposite end, dressed in loosely hanging garments, bearded, bespectacled, and smiling more contentedly than anyone else.

John loved the Meditation Academy because it offered him all the things he craved: privacy, protection, an absence of demands, and an atmosphere highly conducive to mental tripping. He insisted upon living apart from Cynthia, occupying a one-room stone bungalow carpeted with an old rug, upon which he sat for hours every day, supposedly meditating but actually composing songs. "I was going humity-humity in my head," he recalled, "and these songs were coming out. For creating it was great! It was just pouring out!" Ironically, the songs created in this serene and spiritual climate were for the most part reflections of the neurotic and decadent life John had been leading before he came to India. "I'm So Tired" reflects the insomniac exhaustion produced by night after night of acid tripping. "Yer Blues" describes a mood of suicidal depression. "Happiness Is a Warm Gun" contains a repeated line about craving a fix. John had brought his London head to Rishikesh.

Throughout the Beatles' visit to the Meditation Academy the British press was observing the ashram and filing reports that appeared in the trade mags and national newspapers. The music reporters, whose jobs depended on promoting the Beatles, were properly respectful, but the general press ridiculed the goings-on at the camp as hokum and struggled to expose the maharishi as a crook. The Beatles defended their saint, John remarking, "They had to kill Christ before they proved He was Jesus Christ."

Actually, the Beatles had gotten a taste already of the exploitative tactics of the "giggling guru." They had discovered before they left for India that the maharishi was negotiating with ABC-TV to star in a show on which he had promised to deliver the Fab Four. When a warning from Peter Brown had made no impression on the old man, Paul and George flew to Malmö to make clear that they would not participate in such a program. The maharishi, an old hand at evasive tactics, smiled and double-talked his way through the encounter, behaving like a tolerant father hearing out his cranky children. "They are wonderful lads." The old man beamed, "They make me so happy." What he really hoped was that they would make him immensely rich. He demanded, for example, that all his disciples pay him a yearly tithe equal to one week's wage. The money went into a Swiss bank account under the maharishi's own name. Once he had hooked the Beatles, the guru began to speak of a worldwide network of meditation centers that could accommodate millions of people. When pressed about his business ambitions, the wily guru would explain that he had to be active now because soon he would "retire into silence."

The Indian idyll unraveled rapidly at the end. First, Paul and Jane left, evincing their less than total commitment to the maharishi. Then John sent for his great friend Alex Mardas, a young Greek who had enthralled the gullible Lennon by posing as an electronics genius who required only a bit of financing to produce a series of inventions that would revolutionize the Beatles' lives and career. Among the amazing devices he offered John was a car paint that would change color at the flick of a switch, an invisible curtain of ultrasonic vibrations that would shield the Beatles from the screams of their fans, an electrostatic wallpaper that would make any room into a total sound chamber, and an artificial sun that would illuminate the night sky by means of laser beams. Magic Alex was the right man to expose the maharishi. He knew a lot about police work because his father was a major in the Greek secret police. When he took a gander at the maharishi, he became suspicious. Soon Alex discovered that the old boy was busy seducing one of the pretty girls from California. When John and George refused to credit this scandalous accusation, Alex set a trap for his man.

Next time the monk was alone with his adoring disciple, Alex made a noise outside the bungalow. He observed the maharishi give a guilty start and rearrange his clothing, then send the girl to her quarters. That night Alex and the young woman sat up late with John and George, going over her experiences with their spiritual leader. George waxed indignant and refused to believe that his master was caught with his dhoti up. But John Lennon was quick to see that he had been duped. (Subsequently one of the maharishi's foremost disciples, Linda Pearce, revealed that she had been seduced by the guru when she first went to India as a twenty-two-year-old virgin. "When I asked him about his celibacy," Mrs. Pearce recalled, "he said: 'There are exceptions to every rule.' We made love regularly, and I don't think I was the only girl.")

By the end of the nocturnal powwow, it was decided that the Beatles should pull out the following morning. Alex was detailed to line up the transportation; the women were told to take only what was necessary. Anticipating serious trouble with their saint, the Beatles were planning to cut and run.

Next morning, John recalled, "The whole gang charged down to the hut. I was the spokesman, as usual, and said: 'We're leaving.' He asked why, and I said: 'Well, if you're so cosmic, you'll know why.' The maharishi gave me a look that said: 'I'll kill you, you bastard!'"

Meantime, Magic Alex was having a lot of trouble with the local drivers, who complained that if they took the job, the maharishi would put a curse on them and ruin their lives. Finally, two men volunteered themselves and their vehicles.

The cars were so decrepit that every few miles they broke down. When one car developed a flat that could not be fixed—because the driver didn't have a spare—the other car went ahead to get help. John and Cynthia sat for three hours in the baking heat, waiting for George and Patti, meanwhile fearing that they were suffering under the maharishi's curse. Eventually they were rescued by a couple of Western-educated Indians, who recognized the famous Lennon face. John was in a rage by the time he reached New Delhi, but such was his fear of the maharishi that he curbed his usually uncontrollable tongue. He left India without uttering a single angry word in public.

When John Lennon got back to England, he announced: "We made a mistake. What could be more simple?" That was how John often excused his errors, but his words belied his heart. John was like the little boy who wakes up on Christmas Eve and walks into the living room to discover that Santa Claus is really his father. Actually it was good for John to realize that the maharishi was a man with fleshly desires; Lennon was far too prone to belief in miracle men. The bad thing was his reaction to this revelation: Instead of seeking the real reasons for his happiness under TM, John turned his back on the whole experience, which was a shame because the maharishi had worked wonders with John Lennon. For the first and only time in his adult life John had gotten off booze and drugs. He had enjoyed the rare experience of sustained exaltation. In just two months he and the other Beatles had written *thirty songs,* virtually the whole substance of the White Album.

Imagine the market value of thirty songs by the Beatles in their prime! The maharishi could have told his famous disciples the same thing New York analysts tell their patients when they want to raise their rates: "I have increased your earning capacity." The ultimate joke was that though Lennon had insisted that every little gofer at Apple contribute a tithe of his meager wages to the guru, John had conveniently forgotten to pay his tithe!

GROUNDS FOR DIVORCE

Aboard the plane, flying home from India, John began drinking hard liquor for the first time in months. As the booze melted his inhibitions, the rage that lay at the bottom of his soul, like sulfuric acid under a wax stopper, began to fume up. For no apparent reason, he started telling Cynthia about all the women he had fucked during the eight years of their marriage. The hundreds of girls John had screwed on the road, as many as seven in a single night, counted for little in his confessions. What he concentrated upon, according to Peter Brown, were the women whom Cynthia would recognize. Then he got down to women whom Cynthia knew personally, explaining that the reason this one turned up unexpectedly that night at Kenwood or that one behaved so oddly in the restaurant was that John was carrying on with her behind Cynthia's back. Whether his motive in making this confession was to goad Cynthia into suing for a divorce or to punish her for some real or imagined indiscretion makes little difference; the fact is that he hurt her horribly without helping himself one bit.

Baffled in his desire to break free, John took off on a tremendous drug binge as soon as he got home. He dropped acid and smoked tea. He popped pills and drank whiskey. He tooted cocaine and horned heroin. Having discovered that the faith that obviates the need for drugs was itself just another deceiving opiate, he felt justified in kicking out the jams. Within a month he was so fucked up, he could have been declared non compos mentis.

As always at a moment of crisis, John longed to retire into seclusion. So just two weeks after her return from India, Cynthia found herself leaving the country again, this time in the company of Magic Alex and Jenny Boyd (Patti's younger sister), bound for Greece. John engaged Pete Shotton as full-time companion, obliging him to leave his wife and family and move into Kenwood. Having effected this comforting exchange, John resumed the acid-inspired games he had played the previous summer with John Dunbar.

It was ironic that just at the moment when Lennon was declaring himself a philanderer and an adulterer, he should be spending all his time in the company of his childhood playmate. Actually John had little use for women save as whores or mothers. A born fantasist, he was more lustful in his mind than he was in reality, a fact that explains his farcical encounter at this time with Brigitte Bardot.

John had been infatuated with the famous sex goddess since adolescence, having made love to her countless times with a practiced hand while lying on his bed, gazing up at the ceiling, where he had assembled a life-size picture of the bikini-clad actress by pasting together pages torn, one at a time, from a weekly newspaper. Even as late as 1964, when the Beatles arrived at Paris, John stated publicly that the only person he was intent upon meeting in the great city was the French sex queen. So imagine how John Lennon felt when Apple's PR man, Derek Taylor, announced that Bardot was in London and dying to meet the Beatles! (The previous year she had sought to hype her fading career by offering to play in a Beatles' remake of *The Three Musketeers*.)

"Grrreat!" exclaimed John, but in the next breath he asked: "Where are the others?" When he learned that none of the Beatles was in town, he panicked. He couldn't possibly handle a meeting with Bardot alone. Even when Derek Taylor offered to accompany John, he was still groping for support. He proposed they do a little acid first: "Not so much to get out of our heads but just a sparkle!" That was a fatal decision because by the time Lennon and Taylor reached the Mayfair Hotel, they were bonkers.

Taylor, betimes, had sought to pave the way for his friend and employer by ringing up Bardot's personal assistant and explaining that John Lennon had just returned from a long pilgrimage to India, where he had sat at the feet of the Maharishi Mahesh Yogi. Taylor suggested that the most suitable way to receive the great rock star would be in a room furnished with cushions, filled with flowers, and resounding to the music of Ravi Shankar. Nothing impresses the great more than great demands. When Lennon walked into Bardot's sitting room, he found that it had been rearranged to make it resemble an Indian pavilion.

No change in decor could relieve John Lennon's anxiety or enable him to regain control of his addled pate. Without saying a word, he sank down upon the cushions in the lotus position and shut his eyes, as if to meditate. For the next half hour he remained in that position without uttering a word. Brigitte Bardot was not enchanted by this bizarre behavior. Having anticipated the arrival of all the Beatles, she had invited several pretty girls, designing to take the whole party to a chic restaurant for supper. Now she was stuck with just one Beatle, who was in another world, and a flunky who resembled Ronald Colman. When she tried to make conversation with "Ronald Colman," it turned out he could not speak a word of French. In fact, he was having trouble saying anything in English! Finally, Bardot could no longer tolerate this impossible situation. Raising her voice, she addressed the strange figure squatting on her floor: "India appears to have made quite an impression on you."

"Don't ask questions," John snapped. "Feel the vibes!"

Throwing up her hands, Bardot went back to talking in French to her female friends, who were now joined by a couple of hastily summoned men.

Two hours later Bardot made a second attempt to arouse Lennon from his trance. She proposed that they all go to Parkes, a very chichi restaurant on Beauchamp Place. Lennon and Taylor were both horrified by this suggestion because Parkes was a tiny place owned by some Liverpudlians. If they turned up there in the company of Brigitte Bardot and a lot of flashy-looking young women, word of the evening would fly all over town and get into the papers, which would mean bad press for Lennon and a nasty scene at home for Taylor. John replied that he could not upset his delicate state of mind, which portended an important spiritual experience, perhaps a revelation. He suggested that Bardot go to supper with her friends. "When you get back," promised John, "I shall have written a song for you." There was nothing for it. Brigitte Bardot had to go to supper with an escort composed principally of women.

When Bardot got back late that night, she could hear the Indian music blaring down the hall long before she reached her door. Walking into the sitting room, she stopped short. There, sprawled across the cushions like a bum on the sidewalk, lay the great John Lennon, surrounded by a litter of empty beer bottles. When Bardot went into her bedroom, she was startled again—this time by the spectacle of "Ronald Colman" laid out cold across her counterpane. Having reentered the sitting room, Bardot started shaking Lennon roughly. He struggled valiantly into the upright position and tried to sing something. After a few bars he toppled over and went back to sleep.

Early next morning John was delivered to Kenwood by Les Anthony. Pete Shotton was dancing with impatience to hear the night's adventures. "What happened? What happened?" he demanded.

John glared at his old friend and finally barked: "Fucking *nothing* happened! It was a fucking terrible evening," moaned John, "even worse than meeting Elvis."

John Lennon's crazy encounter with Brigitte Bardot was of a piece with everything he did during this period of drug madness. A couple of nights later John and Pete were tripping on acid and struggling to make tapes of ambient noise on the Brunell machines in John's attic. When John got tired of assembling what was later released as "Revolution 9," he sat down cross-legged on the floor to have a heart-to-heart with Pete. John spoke for a while of his disillusionment with the maharishi; then he lapsed into his characteristic silence. As Pete eyed a large photograph of Brigitte Bardot, imagining all the things *he* would have done to her if he could have enjoyed John's recent opportunity, he noticed that his friend was making slow, whirling movements with his arms and hands, as if he had wings.

"Pete!" John breathed, in an awed whisper. *"I think I'm Jesus Christ!"* Pete had not been John Lennon's comrade all his life for nothing.

Almost matter-of-factly he replied: "What are you gonna do about it?"

Without a moment's hesitation, John declared: "I've got to tell everyone! I've got to let the world know who I am!"

Pete protested: "They'll fucking kill you; they won't accept that, John!"

John was not to be dissuaded. "That can't be helped," he retorted. Then, pausing to take thought, he asked: "How old was Jesus when they killed him?"

Pete was stuck for an answer. Finally, he estimated (just one year short): "I reckon he was thirty-two."

John started counting laboriously on his fingers. Then he exclaimed: "Hell! That gives me about *four years!*"

As dawn broke in the quiet Sussex suburb, Lennon declared: "First thing tomorrow, we'll go into Apple and tell the others." Then he and Pete fell exhausted in a heap atop each other. When they awoke, they found Dot Jarlett standing over them. Startled to be discovered in this embarrassing situation, John jumped to his feet. "Oh, Christ!" he swore. "She'll think that we're fucking each other."

Woozy Pete, the perfect straight man, replied: "Why on earth would she think that?" Then, seeing the chance for a gag, he added: "We've got our clothes on, for a start."

Lennon didn't laugh. Instead, he started making preparations for a board meeting.

That afternoon the inner circle of the Beatles' organization—Paul, George, Ringo, Neil, and Derek—met with John and Pete in Lennon's office. All arrived in a mood of keen expectation, wondering what could have inspired the normally passive Lennon to ring the alarm. John rose from behind his desk and addressed his colleagues. "I've got something very important to tell you all," he began. "I am Jesus Christ come back again. This is my thing." He demanded that Apple prepare a press release immediately announcing His return. It is a sign of the awe in which John was held by his closest associates that nobody ventured to challenge him. They sat there stunned for a moment; then they all agreed that this was a most important announcement. But they cautioned that they would need time to reflect on its meaning and decide what steps should be taken by Apple. On this note the meeting was swiftly adjourned.

John was still in the grip of his delusion when he and Pete went into a restaurant for supper. They were addressed by a genial middle-aged man, delighted to find himself standing next to the famous pop star. "Really nice to meet you," said the man. "How are you?"

John replied without dropping a beat: "Actually, I'm Jesus Christ."

The man didn't turn a hair. "Oh, really?" he replied. "Well, I loved your last record. Thought it was great!"

When John and Pete got back to Kenwood that night, the first thing they did was smoke some dope, adding another dimension to their drug dementia. At that point Lennon became restless, a sure sign that he would stay up yet another night. He said: "I fancy having a woman around, Pete. Do you mind if I get one in?"

Shotton welcomed the suggestion because it would allow him to get some sleep.

"I think I'll give Yoko a ring then," said John, who, despite his condition, was wily enough to disguise the fact that he was deeply involved with the little Japanese artist whom Pete had met at Apple.

Shotton wasn't so wiped out that he didn't react. "So you fancy her then?" he challenged.

"I dunno, actually," said John, playing it dumb. "But there's something about her—I'd just like to get to know her better." Then, with a suggestive leer, he added, "And now's a good time to do it." Put that way, the idea lost its oddity and became just another horny little romp.

When John ushered Yoko into the house, he gave no sign that he had more than a casual acquaintance with this woman whom he had summoned forth in the middle of the night, like a groupie. Everybody went into the lounge and sat about uncomfortably, with Yoko appearing very ill at ease and incommunicative. Pete remained just long enough to keep up appearances and lend John emotional support; then he departed.

John and Yoko went up to his attic studio and began making the tape that was issued later as *Two Virgins*. While John threaded the reels and manipulated the controls, Yoko sat before a microphone and made her usual assortment of noises. At some point during the night John suggested that they drop acid. Stoned, beguiled, delighted to have found such a marvelous game, the pair played till dawn, when they climbed into bed and made love. The only remarkable thing about this celebrated night is what happened the following morning.

Pete arose early and went down to eat breakfast. He discovered John
in the sun-room, wearing a brown kimono and eating a boiled egg and
tea. When Pete remarked on John's early rising, John replied that he
had not yet slept—and then asked Pete if he could go out that day and
find him a new house. When Pete asked why, John put his cup down
emphatically and replied: "I want to go live in it with Yoko."

The startling declaration struck Shotton as just another symptom of
the drug-induced craziness that had inspired Lennon to assert twenty-
four hours earlier that he was Jesus Christ. Yet John, sitting there in his
kimono, with the remains of breakfast before him, did not appear like
a man whose thoughts were flying away with him. "I want to go live in
it with Yoko," he repeated, as if to confirm what he had just said.

"Just like that, John!" whispered the awestruck Shotton.

As if a button had been pressed on his brain, John shot back: "Yeah,
just like that! *Just like that!* This is *it*, Pete. This is what I've been waiting
for all me life. Fuck everything else! Fuck the Beatles, fuck me money,
fuck all the rest of it! I'll go and live with her in a fucking *tent* if I have
to!"

With that Lennon jumped to his feet—and so did Shotton, crying,
"This is incredible, John!"

"It *is* incredible," echoed Lennon, who was feeling now the rapture
of a man facing the supreme moment of his life with all his doubts
resolved. "It's just like how we used to fall in love when we were kids,"
he went on. "Remember when you'd meet a girl and you'd think about
her and want to be with her all the time, how your mind was just filled
with her? Well, Yoko's upstairs now, and I can't wait to get back to her.
I felt so hungry that I had to run down here and get meself an egg—
but I can hardly bear to be away from her a single moment!"

That very evening Yoko moved her things into Kenwood, surprising
Dot Jarlett by the inadequacy of her wardrobe. Next morning John set
out to repair this defect, thrusting a heavy wad of money into Shotton's
hand and ordering him to take Yoko shopping. Pete's next assignment
was to confer with a real estate agent and find a country estate within
fifty miles of the city that had a lot of land. Price was not a consideration.

By the time Cynthia got back to Kenwood, that inveterate fantasist
John Lennon had already divorced her, married Yoko Ono, and settled
down with her on a magnificent country estate. The only thing John
had omitted to do was inform his wife of her changed status. The upshot of this failure was that when Cynthia got home, she had an experience straight out of a horror movie.

"It was eerily silent," she recalled, as she approached the house with
Alex and Jenny. Nobody was about: not Julian or Dot or the gardener.

The first thought that went through her head was that there had been an all-night party and everybody was dead asleep. Seizing the knocker in the shape of a woman's derriere, she knocked loudly on the front door. There was no response. Finally, she opened her purse and took out the magnetically coded card that activated the special lock. At that moment Cynthia discovered that the door was unlocked. Entering hesitantly, followed by her friends, she stood in the dark, wood-paneled foyer and shouted up the stairs: *"John! Julian! Dot! Anybody home!"* There was only silence and the weird light that came through the closed drapes on the windows in the lounge. Turning to the right and making her way through the dining room and kitchen, Cynthia stepped into the sun-room—and froze!

Sitting on the little Queen Anne sofa in a green and white terry-cloth robe, his hair disheveled, a cup of tea in his hand, was John Lennon. Facing him, with her back to Cynthia, was a tiny woman with a great bush of black hair, her body shrouded in a black silk kimono. "It was like walking into a brick wall," Cynthia said, adding: "It was as if I didn't belong anymore." The truth was that she *didn't* belong anymore. Without her knowledge she had been eliminated.

After a silence that seemed to last forever, John said, "Oh, hi!" coolly taking a puff on his cigarette.

Cynthia was now so freaked out that she opened her mouth like an automaton and began to recite a little speech that she had prepared on the plane. "I had this great idea!" she gushed. "We had breakfast in Greece, lunch in Rome, and Jenny and Alex and I thought it would be great if we all went to dinner in London to carry on the whole holiday."

Impassively John Lennon replied: "No, thanks." At this moment, Yoko turned around and gave Cynthia "a positive, confident look."

"It took my breath away," said Cynthia. "I wasn't angry. I was just absolutely shattered. . . . So instead of starting a battle and asking questions about what was going on, I felt I had to get out of there immediately."

Rushing upstairs, Cynthia started packing as if for a trip, even though her luggage was still in the car. Passing the guest bedroom, she spotted a pair of Japanese slippers on the carpet.

Fifteen minutes after arriving home, she was going out the door. "I took John's silence," she observed, "as saying: 'Don't interrupt this fantastic situation. Get lost! You're spoiling things.'" Having received John's tacit command, Cynthia thought only of obeying. Without a murmur of protest, she abandoned home and husband to another woman and left in the company of two people whom she knew only socially.

Alex and Jenny offered to put up Cynthia in the little mews house they shared as friends in central London. After her first day as guest, according to Peter Brown, "Cynthia sat up with Magic Alex most of the night, drinking wine and talking at a candlelit table in his apartment. She had never trusted Magic Alex before, but she needed someone to talk to desperately that night and she poured her heart out to him. Many bottles of wine were finished by dawn, when she crawled into bed with Alex and made love to John's best friend."

Three days later Cynthia phoned Dot and announced her intention of returning to Kenwood. When she arrived, she found John awaiting her. Yoko had vanished. "I can't understand why you went off," protested Lennon, who acted very "warm and welcoming." "What have you been up to?" he demanded, as if Cynthia's abrupt disappearance had been some utterly inexplicable event. Cynthia challenged John immediately to explain what *he* had been up to with Yoko.

John was well prepared for the question. He explained with a show of complete unconcern that his relationship with Yoko was purely intellectual. When Cynthia sought to probe a little deeper into the liaison, John clammed up and refused to say anything more about the matter, save for assuring Cynthia that she had nothing to worry about.

Cynthia was not satisfied by his assurances. "I see a great similarity between you and Yoko," Cynthia insisted, and noticed John blanch. "John, there's something about her that's just like you. Look, you may say these things about Yoko, that she's crazy, just a weird artist, but there's an aura about her that's going to click with you."

No matter how much Lennon protested his lack of love for Yoko, Cynthia remained unconvinced. As she said, "I knew I had lost him."

This conviction explains what happened next. When Cynthia asked John if she should cancel the family holiday, which was to be spent with Mrs. Powell and Julian at Pesaro, John replied: "No, no, you go ahead and have a lovely time." Somehow Cynthia persuaded herself that her absence would not have a decisive effect on her marriage. She rationalized that it would be a terrible thing to disappoint Julian.

Yoko had meanwhile gone back to Tony to work out the final arrangements for their separation. "She owed Tony a lot," observed Dan Richter, who was present at this moment. "He got her out of the mental hospital. He kept her going, raised money for her shows, promoted the tickets to London, went after all the publicity, found backers for her films, borrowed money from the banks." The payoff Tony demanded was a flat 50 percent of everything she got out of Lennon. A contract embodying this demand was drawn up by Tony and signed by Yoko. "She felt she owed him," explained Richter, who served as a witness: "I think she also felt she could break the agreement later if she wanted to."

*   *   *

Once Tony had been placated and Cynthia had left for Italy, Yoko was free to return to Kenwood. Lennon considered his marriage at an end, save for the legal formalities. Without troubling to warn his wife, he started stepping out with his new woman. On 15 June, John and Yoko offered their "Acorn Event" at the National Sculpture Exhibition at Coventry Cathedral. The concept was the planting of two acorns to symbolize the "uniting and growth of our two cultures," a trivial little act yet prophetic of future events, for though devoid of substance, it proved rich in consequences, all of them negative, starting with a sharp quarrel with the cathedral authorities that climaxed in an astonishing burst of rage from Yoko when the canon dared to challenge her notions of art and concluding with the absurdity of posting guards over a second pair of acorns when the first were exhumed by the fans. The press did not get wind of this event until too late, but three days later, when John and Yoko arrived at the National Theater to attend the opening of Victor Spinetti's adaptation of Lennon's books, the reporters were set to pounce.

John Lennon emerged from Pete Shotton's white Jaguar togged out in a white silk jacket and flowered shirt with black trousers, Giving his hand to little Yoko, who was dressed in white, save for a black vest, Lennon was suddenly stopped in his tracks by the cries of the reporters, who came surging in from all sides accompanied by flash-popping photographers. *"Where's your wife? Where's Cynthia? What happened to your wife, John?"* shouted the newsmen, snapping like dogs at their cornered prey.

"I don't know!" exploded Lennon as he marched Yoko into the theater. Soon he was engrossed in the play, which was highly successful. Next day, however, when he saw the picture in all the papers of him holding Yoko by the hand and read the copy which implied that he was either estranged from his wife or cheating, he was troubled. What John felt was as nothing, however, compared with the shock and shame that Cynthia experienced when she read the English papers.

Another woman would have rushed home to confront her husband and save her marriage. Cynthia, who dreaded emotional confrontations, took to her bed, where she remained for days. Finally, one night she went out with the owner's twenty-eight-year-old son, Roberto Bassanini, a big, hearty, handsome man of whom she had become fond during a previous visit. Next morning, when they returned to the hotel, they found Magic Alex awaiting them.

When Alex had Cynthia alone, he told her that John would be very interested to learn that she was not moping about like a rejected wife but carousing with a handsome young bachelor. Having thrown her on the defensive, he announced next that John wanted a divorce in order to marry Yoko Ono. If Cynthia made a fuss or didn't cooperate, John had vowed to "take Julian away from you and send you back to Hoylake."

Even Cynthia could not tolerate such threats. "Suing me for divorce!" she burst out. "On what grounds is he suing me for divorce?"

"John is claiming adultery," Alex replied coolly. "I have agreed to be corespondent and testify on John's behalf." Then he reminded Cynthia of that night when she had crawled into his bed, drunk at dawn. Having dropped that bombshell, he left at once for London.

No sooner was he out the door than Cynthia was closeted with her mother. Mrs. Powell must have come close to apoplexy when she heard of her detested son-in-law's evil designs. When Cynthia announced that she was going home the next day, the redoubtable Lil said that she couldn't wait that long. That afternoon she was on a plane bound for England.

When Mrs. Powell arrived at 34 Montagu Square, she was surprised to discover a bouquet standing by the door. Opening the envelope, she read: "Beat you to it, Lil." John was enjoying his long-yearned-for revenge.

The same detective who had kept an eye on Mrs. Powell must have also tipped off John's solicitor because when Cynthia returned the next day, within five minutes of her arrival she was served with a divorce petition. Calling Apple, she asked to speak with John. She was told it would take two weeks to arrange a meeting with her husband. Impulsively she grabbed her mother and son and drove down to Kenwood. She was met at the door by John and Yoko, dressed identically in black. John, who had been delighted to play the spymaster from the security of his home, was totally unprepared for a face-to-face encounter with his wife. When Mrs. Powell told Yoko, "I think you should go in the other room and leave these two together," John cried out like a frightened child: "No, Yoko! You stay here!"

Cynthia broke down immediately and began to weep. What was distressing her was the prospect of being publicly branded as an adulteress. She insisted that she had never liked Magic Alex, and that far from wanting him to make love to her, she had been bewitched by candles and black magic. John kept explaining that he had no choice but to sue on grounds of adultery if he were to avoid the sort of publicity that would damage his career. After arguing for fifteen minutes over who had committed adultery with whom, Cynthia finally made the point with which she should have started. "You're totally unjust in putting me on the spot when *you're* the one breaking up the marriage," she cried.

Lennon, desperate to end the scene, answered only: "We better put it in the hands of the solicitors and get it all sorted out." John suggested also that Cynthia move back into Kenwood with her mother and

Julian, leaving the Montagu Square flat for his use. When Lillian Powell insisted that her daughter should not be left entirely on her own, Lennon shouted, "This is *my* house! You get out!"

At the next meeting between John and Cynthia, which concerned the vital matter of the property settlement, both parties were accompanied by their lawyers. After the session Pete Shotton, who was living still at Kenwood, asked John how the meeting had gone.

"It was just fucking nonsense!" Lennon cried in exasperation. "Every time I tried to say something to Cyn, her lawyer would interrupt and say I wasn't allowed to speak to her. I could only talk to my lawyer, who'd speak to her lawyer, and he'd speak to Cyn! Finally, I just said: 'Look, Cyn, just take whatever you fucking want. Sort it out among yourselves, let me know, and I'll fucking give it to you!'"

Cynthia knuckled under and allowed John to sue her for adultery. Having made this painful concession, she was entitled to demand a generous settlement. Instead, she conspired against her own interests by calling John up on the sly and telling him they should reach a private agreement because her attorneys planned to "screw him out of hundreds of thousands of pounds."

Once John recognized what this divorce could cost him, he disavowed his earlier offer and started beating Cynthia down, shouting, "My last offer to you is £75,000. What have you done to deserve it? Christ, it's like winning the fucking pools!"

Still, the divorce would have proceeded smoothly if Yoko had not become pregnant in September. This event made a mockery of Lennon's charge of adultery. So the parties were obliged to exchange roles, and Cynthia wound up suing John, which gave her the whip hand. Needless to say, she never put the leather to John's tender hide. He got off lightly with a settlement of £100,000 plus £2,400 annually for Julian's maintenance. The trust fund established for Julian was just as ungenerous. It provided for the payment of £100,000 when his son reached the age of twenty-five—provided John Lennon begot no more children. In the event John had another child, Julian's provision was to be halved. John did surrender all his custody rights to Cynthia, but that was a welcome sacrifice.

On 8 November 1968, just two weeks after John Lennon announced publicly that Yoko Ono was pregnant with his child, Cynthia Lennon was granted a divorce. "Cynthia was amputated from the Beatles with ruthless speed and precision," wrote Peter Brown, who added: "Few Beatles' employees or friends dared to show her support or speak out against Yoko, lest the wrath of Lennon fall on them."

The only old friend in the Beatles' circle who offered Cynthia any support or sympathy was Paul. "I was truly surprised when one sunny afternoon Paul arrived on his own," recalled Cynthia, adding: "I was touched by his obvious concern for our welfare and even more moved when he presented me with a single red rose accompanied by a jokey remark about our future: 'How about it, Cyn? How about you and me getting married?'"

Julian Lennon and Kyoko Cox were victims of the divorce. Henceforth John saw his son only rarely and Yoko made absolutely no effort to see Kyoko. At first, the child spent a lot of time in the home of a sympathetic friend, Maggie Postlewaite, who was provided by John with a telephone number to call in the event of an emergency. But the one time Maggie dialed the number, it proved useless: a telephone answering service took the message but refused to call the Lennons. Neither John nor Yoko called back. Kyoko was terribly hurt when she discovered that she could not talk to her mother, even on the telephone. Maggie had to call Tony, who came around the next day to collect his daughter.

Yoko's divorce from Tony cost John Lennon more money than his divorce from his wife. John agreed to pay all the joint debts of Yoko and Tony, which came to a whopping £100,000. The extent of Tony Cox's individual payment is unclear, but Tony's brother, Larry, recalled that Tony had a "lot of money" when he left England. For tax reasons, the payoff was arranged to appear as an assignment from Apple Films to purchase cameras and hire a boat for filming in the Virgin Islands, where residence for the purpose of divorce can be established in six weeks. The divorce decree, dated 30 January 1969, tied up the last loose ends in the complicated tangle of affairs. All the loose ends but one: the custody of Kyoko. "The questions of the care, custody and control of the minor child, Kyoko, shall be left open for the future determination of a court of competent jurisdiction," stated the decree. Why was so vital a matter left up in the air? According to Allen Klein, who came on the scene at this time, John Lennon, having relinquished custody of his child, demanded that Yoko follow suit. Yoko, however, wanted a loophole left open through which at some later date she could reach out and make a claim on Kyoko.

HEROIN HONEYMOON

Long before John and Yoko had obtained their freedom, they were enslaved by heroin. Yoko told Marnie Hair that John had been on the drug for a long time before he hooked her, adding that he could withdraw from anything, but she could not. To the press, she offered another story, explaining years later: "John . . . asked if I ever tried it [heroin]. I told him that while he was in India with the maharishi, I had a sniff of it in a party situation. I didn't know what it was. They just gave me something and I said, 'What was that?' It was a beautiful feeling. John was talking about heroin one day and he said, 'Did you ever take it?' and I told him about Paris. I said it wasn't bad. I think because the amount was small I didn't get sick [i.e., nauseated]. It was just a nice feeling. So I told him that when you take it—'properly' isn't the right word—but when you do a little more, you get sick right away if you're not used to it. So I think maybe because I said it wasn't a bad experience, that had something to do with John taking it." More important than who turned on whom was what happened next.

"Spanish Tony" Sanchez, a hustler intimate of the art dealer to the rock stars Robert Fraser (imprisoned for heroin after he was busted with the Rolling Stones in May 1967), spent a lot of time that summer with John Lennon, watching him get high with Brian Jones and Keith Richard, both notorious addicts. "John, I feared," wrote Sanchez, "seemed to be following Brian into a world where drugs dominated everything. [Lennon was using heroin, cocaine, and hashish, as well as LSD, marijuana, and Biphetamine pills.] He called almost daily to see if I could help him get hold of dope. . . . Once he aggressively insisted I supply him with heroin. He sent his chauffeur to my apartment to get it. I was so annoyed at the way he was pressuring me that I accepted the $200 proffered by the driver and gave him a stash containing two crushed aspirin. That, I thought, should stop him pestering me once and for all. Next day John was back on the phone asking for more.

'What about the last lot?' I said. 'Oh, I didn't think very much of that,' he said. 'It hardly gave me a buzz.'"

Ringo's flat in Montagu Square had witnessed plenty of drug craziness even before John and Yoko moved in. Decorated by Ken Partridge as a honeymoon nest, it had been trashed by Jimi Hendrix, who went out of his mind one night and threw cans of paint all over its watered blue silk hangings. Ringo had scrapped the original decor and painted the place stark white. Now it got another dose of junkie squalor. "They lay in the basement of Montagu Square almost all July that simmering summer, submerged in self-inflicted stupor," recalled Peter Brown. Soon the apartment appeared a "pigsty, a junkie's haven of rumpled sheets, dirty clothes, newspapers and magazines heaped all over the floor." The most striking object was a collage by Richard Chamberlain composed of newspaper clippings of the Rolling Stones' bust. As John and Yoko lay stoned, gazing at this minatory montage through the smoke of joss sticks, they were contemplating unwittingly their own doom.

Yoko recalled that she and John lived on a diet of champagne, caviar, and heroin. John said that they lived in "a strange cocktail of love, sex, and forgetfulness." It's unlikely they were ever closer or happier together, for though they appeared to be wallowing in stupor and squalor, they were actually experiencing a bliss that is unimaginable save to those who have tasted of their love potion. As they lay peering at the world through their TV window or making love or stumbling about stoned, they melted and merged into one another. Symbiosis was the miracle heroin wrought upon these narcissistic lovers, who celebrated their love by acting as if they were one person in two bodies.

Heroin's other effect on Lennon was to trip him back to infancy: "I felt," he declared. "like a baby wrapped in cotton wool and floating in warm water." (In his caricatures of this time he depicts himself naked and floating on clouds.) As a swaddled infant, his whole world had been his mother. Now it was natural that his earliest feelings about his mum should revive and mingle with his love for Yoko. That is the burden of the remarkable "Julia," which John recorded that summer, testifying better in song than he ever could in mere words to the precise nature of his infatuation with Yoko.

The first thing that strikes the listener is the uniquely warm, relaxed, almost cooing tone of John's voice as he calls out his mother's name in an access of love and joy, like a baby holding its arms up to be kissed in the bath. In this song John is again the sweet child who flourished before he was traumatized by Julia's adultery and subsequent abandonment of him. Just as remarkable as the emotional tone is the musical idiom, so reminiscent of the ease and sensuousity of the oceanside, which is the hallmark of the Beatles' most talented contemporary, Antonio Carlos Jobim. John Lennon never had a good word for the Brazilian composer, but with John's genius for associating words and music, concepts and images, it was natural that he should slip instinctively into Jobim's style the moment he started invoking his mother, whose name he joins directly with that of Yoko, the "Ocean Child."

With this resurrection of the tender infant buried for so many years under the disguising layers of the school bully, the adolescent Teddy Boy, the Merseyside rocker, and, finally, the triumphant but bitterly unhappy international pop star, John Lennon reversed the whole course of his spiritual development. Hitherto his view of women had been utterly contemptuous, his favorite line being "Women should be obscene, not heard." Now he suddenly abandoned his masculine swagger and swung around to the opposite tack, either adopting the baby role or making a passionate identification with the female, particularly the man-hating Yoko.

This startling revolution was signaled first by an art exhibition offered by Lennon at the Robert Fraser Gallery on 1 July 1968. The theme of the show was John's notorious obsession with cripples and the deformed. Far more significant than the theme was the treatment, slavishly copied from the style of Yoko Ono's exhibitions.

On opening night the critics, reporters, and VIPs arrived at the gallery on Duke Street to find the exhibition room entirely empty. At the far end of the gallery a large white canvas disk had been affixed to the wall. It was inscribed in a tiny hand: "you are here." This was the title of the show, which was dedicated "to Yoko, from John, with love." The phrase and the white dot were taken from the maps in the subway, the same conceit explaining the location of the show, down a flight of stairs in the basement.

Here the spectator found an eerie gathering of life-sized effigies of crippled or spastic children, standing with braces on their legs or sitting in wheelchairs, holding donation boxes and accompanied by various animal figures appealing on behalf of homeless dogs or the mentally retarded. The theme was a familiar one for Lennon, but what was notable was the complete absence of that hysterical humor of horror and rage that would froth out of John's mouth when he would reflect upon the way the Beatles had been presented with blind and lame children and entreated by frantic mothers, crying, "Go on, kiss him! Maybe you'll bring back his sight!" By mimicking the deadpan tone of Yoko's art, John Lennon had actually throttled himself.

Lennon's next public appearance was on 26 July at Mick Jagger's twenty-fifth birthday party. The celebration was coordinated with the opening of Vesuvio, a club owned by Tony Sanchez in conjunction with Jagger and Keith Richard. "Mick flew in dramatically at the last minute, with the first advance pressing of *Beggars' Banquet*," reported Sanchez. This was "the album the whole world was waiting to hear, for this was a record on which the band's entire future hung—'If they can't make a good record by now,' the music business was saying, 'they never will.' Everything was perfect for the party. The club looked beautiful with huge silver bowls of Methedrine-spiked punch plus plates full of hash cakes, which had become a craze, and little dishes with hash for people to smoke beside every hubble-bubble pipe." Sanchez was worried, however, because Tottenham Court Road police station was only three hundred yards away. If the police appeared at the party, they could bust every pop star in Britain. As the celebration took off, he quickly forgot his anxieties in the mounting hubbub.

"As Paul McCartney walked in," Spanish Tony recollected, "everyone was leaping around to *Beggars' Banquet,* which—with tracks like 'Sympathy for the Devil' and 'Street Fighting Man'—was far and away the best album of the Stones' career. Paul discreetly handed me a record and told me, 'See what you think of it, Tony. It's our new one.' I stuck the record on the sound system, and the slow, thundering buildup of 'Hey Jude' shook the club. I turned the record over, and we all heard John Lennon's nasal voice pump out 'Revolution.' When it was over, I noticed that Mick looked peeved. The Beatles had upstaged him."

The birthday party turned quickly into a drug bacchanal as everyone, including the staff, became deranged on the potent hash cakes and brain-searing punch. Late in the evening Lennon, "looking as though his eyes were going to pop out of his head," staggered over to Tony Sanchez and asked him to call a cab. Sanchez promptly dispatched a doorman on the errand, but when he didn't come back, it became necessary to send out another man. Meantime, Lennon got angry and started shouting, "What kind of doorman takes half an hour to find a taxi on Tottenham Court Road?" Frantically Sanchez sent off his third and last man. When he, too, failed to return, Spanish Tony's mind suddenly flashed a picture of the police standing outside the club, picking off his men as they emerged, one by one. Actually, the doormen were so stoned that when they got out in the street, they forgot what they had been sent to do and wandered off. One of them woke up twelve hours later in a rose bed in St. James's Park.

Lennon was bellowing like a mad bull when Mick Jagger asked him what was the matter and instantly produced the keys to his midnight blue black-windowed Aston-Martin DB6. Sanchez told his cousin to drive John and Yoko home. The lad, an ardent Beatles' fan, ran to accomplish his mission. Once behind the wheel of the highly sophisticated automobile, the poor boy discovered that he couldn't even find the ignition keyhole. While he sweated over the dashboard, Lennon fumed in the lavishly upholstered back seat. Suddenly he was startled by the sound of a knocking on the window next to his head. Squinting through the tinted glass, he beheld a huge policeman standing at the curb. John was carrying in his pocket a vial of cocaine. Terrified of being busted, he eased the bottle out of his pocket and dropped it on the floor of the car. As it turned out, the bobby was simply trying to be of service. He showed the driver how to switch on the ignition, and the party sped off into the night.

John started scrabbling around on the floor, trying to find his coke. "This is Mick Jagger's car," he muttered. "I can't just leave my coke rolling around on the floor of his car. It isn't fair!" Just at that moment a sudden acceleration sent Lennon sprawling off the seat. Flashing with fresh rage, John yelled: "Stop the car! We're getting out! I'll walk home, if I have to. You find the coke and keep it."

"Revolution" marked another departure for John Lennon: his first attempt at a political song. The original track, which John called "Revolution 1," had been inspired by a demonstration that summer in front of the American embassy in London that Lennon had witnessed on TV. His initial musical response to the revolutionaries was to send them up by adopting the tone of the cynical uncle who says, "So, sonny boy, you want to be a man?" and then, after leading the kid on for a while, suddenly turns on him and crushes him with a devastating refusal to have anything further to do with him or his ideals. Yet, only a second after Lennon warns the revolutionaries that their demonstrations will lead to violence and that therefore, they must count him out, he cancels the key word by crying "In!" Which way it was to be John simply couldn't say, because he was radically ambivalent about radicalism, as the further history of "Revolution" reveals.

For now, having taken a shy at politics, Lennon rebounded from this experiment by proceeding directly to the opposite extreme and producing his most purely avant-garde musical composition, "Revolution 9." Commencing with the long fade-out to "Revolution 1," he superimposed on the basic track a whole series of tape loops and cassette sounds culled from EMI's tape library, interspersing them with a weird-sounding voice that repeatedly intones, like an engineer testing a mike: "Number nine!" The resultant montage was strongly reminiscent of John Cage's work in the early Fifties.

Next, Lennon combined these two very interesting but totally disjunct experiments on one disc and offered it to the judgment of the other Beatles. Led by Paul, they rejected the record, saying that it wasn't good enough to be a Beatles' single. This sentence both hurt and enraged John, who felt that some of Paul's recent sides, like "Lady Madonna," were simply trash. But instead of sticking to his guns, Lennon caved in completely. Not only did he surrender the A-side to McCartney, but he went back into the studio, where he turned "Revolution 1" into "Revolution 2," by speeding up the tempo and injecting some hot piano playing by session-man Nicky Hopkins. The effect was to transform his slowly uncoiling, deeply sarcastic political put-on into a trivial up-tempo pop tune, just good enough to be the flip side of "Hey Jude."

"Revolution 1" found a home eventually on the White Album, the extraordinary compilation of avant-rock compositions by all four Beatles that John Lennon regarded as the band's single greatest achievement. Measured song by song, the White Album is vastly superior to *Sgt. Pepper,* but it would be an odd fan who cited this huge two-LP collection as his favorite because the anthology fails through its very success. Though it displays at exhausting length the Beatles' now-astonishing virtuosity in every genre of late-Sixties pop song art—rock parody ("Back in the U.S.S.R.," "Why Don't We Do It in the Road"); childlike pastoral ("Dear Prudence," "Blackbird"); Pop Art phantasmagoria ("Helter Skelter," "Bungalow Bill"); pop surrealism ("Glass Onion," "Happiness Is a Warm Gun")—the kaleidoscopic bedazzlement of all these competing pieces is too much for anybody's head. In contrast with *Pepper,* where Paul had artfully arranged a clutch of heterogeneous and often mediocre songs into a seamless and eloquent whole, the Beatles' richest songbag tumbles forth its contents without rhyme or reason, becoming a textbook demonstration of how the parts can be greater than the whole and more can be less.

At the same time the Beatles were packing the stark white, serially numbered albums of their latest release with mental pinwheels, John and Yoko were fighting to release their first LP, *Two Virgins.* As devoid of art and substance as the Beatles' album was overflowing with both, this soiled air filter would hardly have been noticed but for its astounding cover.

John claimed that it was his idea that he and Yoko should pose on the front and back of the album in the buff, but he was simply repeating the nude photos of Tony and Yoko at Knokke-le-Zout that had appeared in magazines like the *Tulane Drama Review.* Oddly, the uncropped photos show a third virgin—a short bearded young man. When the pictures and the tape arrived at the Apple office for submission to EMI, Peter Brown thought they were a joke and locked them away in his desk. Weeks later, when John called to check on the progress of the album, Brown sought to dissuade Lennon from going through with the project. John brushed aside the warnings, because, as he later declared: "I wanted people to be shocked."

"Paul hated the cover beyond words," reported Brown, "and took it as a personal affront, probably just as John had planned it." When Sir Joseph Lockwood got an eyeful of the photos, he, too, refused to believe that John was in earnest.

At a meeting with John, Paul, and Yoko, Sir Joseph was asked by John: "Well, aren't you shocked?"

The EMI chief replied: "No, I've seen worse than this."

John weighed in quickly: "So it's all right then, is it?"

"No, it's *not* all right," snapped Sir Joe. "I'm not worried about the rich people, the duchesses, and those people who follow you. But your mums and dads and girl fans will object strongly. You will be damaged, and what will you gain? What's the purpose of it?"

Yoko replied: "It's art."

Sir Joe retorted sharply: "Well, I should find some better bodies to put on the cover than your two. They're not very attractive. Paul McCartney would look better than you."

A compromise was finally effected whereby EMI would press the album and the Beatles' company, Apple, would undertake its distribution.

When the first shipment of records reached the States (released by an obscure label with the curious name Tetragrammaton, i.e, the four letters that signify the name of the divinity in Hebrew), the merchandise was seized by customs in New Jersey and impounded. At the trial for obscenity that followed in Newark, a number of expert witnesses endeavored to make a case for the album. Professor Albert Goldman of Columbia University testified that the cover photos were "in the tradition of Christian iconography depicting Adam and Eve before the fall." The old judge was not impressed, and the record company lost its case. Only a few thousand copies were sold, discreetly wrapped in brown paper bags.

Far more serious than the seizure of the records in the United States was the impact on public opinion in Great Britain, where the Beatles had always been adored as four charming innocents. Now the fans were invited to examine in the raw the simian-looking Yoko and the beat-looking Lennon (whose large uncircumsised penis was conspicuous). The effect was one of shock and revulsion, followed by a universal "Yuck!" After this damning verdict had been delivered, Lennon remarked ruefully: "I guess the world thinks we're an ugly couple."

John and Yoko outraged the British again in October, when Lennon announced that Yoko was pregnant with his child. Now people everywhere were beginning to think he had run off the rails, for first he had ditched his sweet English wife to take up with this dubious Oriental, and now he had gotten his woman pregnant before either of them had obtained a divorce. What would he do next? The answer was not long in coming. Within a fortnight John and Yoko were busted for drugs.

* * *

Unlike everyone else in Swinging London, the Beatles had always been above the law. One night at the Speakeasy, the narcs who constantly snooped about the club wearing hippie clothes and long-haired wigs busted a whole party of people in the company of John Lennon. *"I'm with them! Why don't you arrest me?"* screamed Lennon as the cops hauled his friends away. Now all that changed. There appeared a nemesis from whom even the most privileged pop star was not safe: Detective Sergeant Norman Pilcher, an antidrug zealot (later sentenced to two years in prison for planting evidence), targeted John Lennon as his next big case. Fortunately for John, there was a man on the drug squad who played the game both ways. He tipped off Lennon early on the morning of the raid, 18 October 1968.

When Pete Shotton arrived at Montagu Square that morning, he was astonished to find John vacuuming the carpet. Lennon told Pete in a resigned tone that he was expecting the police momentarily and that there was a good chance that they would find something because Jimi Hendrix had lived in the flat. Then John went into the bedroom. Shotton, an ex-cop, rummaged expertly through pockets, drawers, and medicine cabinets. As he worked, he heard an argument brewing up between John and Yoko. She was demanding that Pete leave immediately. Shotton departed, taking with him the bag from the vacuum cleaner.

At eleven fifty-five the bell rang. Yoko went down the hall and opened the door into the vestibule. A woman standing outside the house announced that she had a registered letter for Yoko Ono. Opening the house door a crack, Yoko saw instantly that the woman was no postal employee. Slamming the door, she ran back into the bedroom to warn John, who quickly flushed his heroin down the toilet while shouting to Yoko: "Call the solicitor!"

Another officer, who identified himself as Nigel, hollered through the window of the basement floor of the two-story flat: "Let me in!"

Lennon answered: "What do you want?"

"It's the police!" cried the cop.

"But you're not allowed in that way," answered Lennon, stalling for time.

"Let me in or I have to break in!" cried the officer.

"That won't be very good publicity," quipped Lennon.

"We have got a warrant!" insisted Officer Nigel.

"I want to read it," demanded John, who had learned a thing or two by listening to his junkie friends.

The female officer obligingly unfolded the warrant and held it against John's bedroom window. He went through a pantomime of reading.

Yoko, meantime, had gotten through to their lawyer, who promised to come over immediately. John was now asking for time to get dressed because he and Yoko were clad in nothing but T-shirts. By this point three cops had started breaking down the front door, and Officer Nigel had contrived to open and climb through the bedroom window. Sergeant Pilcher came charging into the room, crying, "Right! I've got you for obstruction of justice!"

Immediately the police began searching the flat, soon aided by two dope-sniffing dogs, led in by their handlers. When the Lennons' lawyer, Nicholas Cowan, got to Montagu Square, he found the flat swarming with police. The search yielded the following evidence:

1. Exactly 27.3 grains of hashish in an unsealed brown envelope in a blue trunk in the bedroom
2. A cigarette case with traces of hashish on the floor of the bedroom near the window
3. A cigarette-rolling machine with traces of cannabis on top of a mirror in the bedroom
4. Exactly 191.8 grains of hashish in a binocular case in the living room
5. Two bottles of pills containing amphetamines
6. A half gram of morphine

When Peter Brown arrived at the flat, alerted by a call to Apple, he found John "ashen-faced and frightened, chain-smoking cigarettes." Brown witnessed John and Yoko being marched out through the waiting mob of photographers and put inside a police car. Just as John and Yoko were being taken off to be booked, Paul McCartney got through to Sir Joseph Lockwood, who agreed to call Paddington Green police station and advise John how to comport himself. By the time Sir Joe got through, John had regained his nerve. "Hello!" he answered. "This is Sergeant Lennon. Can I help you?" John and Yoko were soon bailed out and escorted through the mob outside the court to their waiting car.

The following morning the Lennons appeared at Marylebone Magistrate's Court for a hearing of the charges against them. News of the bust had carried the time and location of the hearing, which was on a Saturday, when everyone was free to attend. When the Lennons arrived at the small court in a bronze-colored sedan, they were mobbed by hippies and housewives, who engaged each other in a shouting match. As a hippie roared, *"Good luck—God bless you both!"* a working-class woman screeched, *"Get your 'air cut!"*

Standing in the dock, John and Yoko made a striking appearance. He wore a military-style uniform, with narrow black trousers and a black tunic buttoned up to his neck. His long brown hair swung at his shoulders. Yoko was dressed in dark trousers, fur coat, and tennis shoes. The hearing, scrutinized by the press from the visitors' gallery, lasted only five minutes. Sergeant Pilcher read the charges; John and Yoko were remanded on bail till 28 November. When they left the court, their car was not at the curb. The mob closed in, as the bobbies fought to drive it back. Yoko huddled at John's side and claimed later to have been struck in the head with a rock. Finally, they were bundled into their car and sped off to Paul's house.

Yoko was rushed to Queen Charlotte Hospital on 7 November, when it began to appear that she might lose her baby. John moved into her room, sleeping upon an air mattress laid on the floor and hardly leaving the building for two weeks. When it became apparent that the fetus would die, John obtained a stethoscopic microphone and recorded the final heartbeats of the unborn child, whom he named John Ono Lennon II. (The recording was included in *Life with the Lions*.) John's extreme concern about Yoko and his distress at the loss of the child were deepened by guilt. As Yoko told her assistant, Arlene Reckson, years later, the miscarriage had been triggered by a beating she received from John. On 23 November the dead fetus was removed. Five days later Yoko appeared again with John at Marylebone Magistrate's Court.

John had decided to plead guilty to possession of hashish because he feared that if he and Yoko fought the charges against them and lost, she would be deported. This was a highly imprudent decision because with his immense resources and unique social position, Lennon might well have beaten the rap and thus averted the endless battles he fought later with the American immigration authorities. Once Yoko was released, the only question before the court was what punishment to mete out to John Lennon. Precedents in such cases ranged from relatively small fines to the nine months in prison that had been given John Hopkins, the Cambridge-educated scientist who was a founder of the *International Times,* the underground newspaper, and Pink Floyd. As John Lennon stood before the bar on the morning of 28 November he had every reason to be fearful.

Solicitor Martin Polden offered a plea for clemency, declaring that Lennon had renounced drugs completely when he became a devotee of transcendental meditation the previous year but had overlooked some cannabis secreted in certain items, like the binocular case, that had been delivered recently to Montagu Square from his previous residence in Sussex. Having laid that story on the court, he rounded off his address by making the customary statement about his client's having "given pleasure to millions." The magistrate quashed the obstruction of justice charge and fined the defendant £150 plus £21 in court costs. Then he warned Lennon that next time he was found guilty of such an offense he could be sentenced to a year in prison.

No sooner had John and Yoko resolved their legal problems than they were evicted by Ringo's landlord, who had obtained an injunction forbidding his tenant to permit the flat to be used by "One John Lennon and/or one Yoko Ono Cox." John and Yoko decided to return to Kenwood, which was standing empty. Cynthia had left the house, complaining that it was too painful to continue living in a place so charged with memories of her marriage. She did not depart, however, until she and her mother had stripped the place of everything of value. Not content merely to haul off the silver, china, and furniture, they ripped up the black wall-to-wall carpeting—heavily stained by John's numerous cats—exposing yards and yards of forbidding-looking nails. It was to this procrustean bed that John and Yoko returned, carrying all her art pieces, which they dumped in one room.

When the house was put on the market, the property correspondent of the *Evening News* gained access to the premises under pretext of being a prospective buyer. Next day the paper's readers were regaled with an exhaustive account of the "mad, mad, mad, mad world of John and Yoko."

"The first hint of what lay within," wrote the reporter, "was the front door knocker. It was shaped like a naked woman. Freudian? Just you wait!" Then he cataloged all the half-assed objects from *Half-a-Wind,* as well as the inventory of *you are here.* The account made great copy and confirmed everybody's worst suspicions about the mental condition of John Lennon.

Actually, John and Yoko were not occupying the whole house. "The two of them lived in the bedroom," reported Les Anthony. "They'd even built a small kitchen upstairs. Not that Yoko ever cooked. She'd never wash a cup, even if there wasn't any staff downstairs. In the early days they used to eat a lot of rice, but even cooking a bit of that, she'd burn it. When I went to pick them up, they'd say: 'Do us a favor and wash up.' And what a job it was with everything burnt."

Like most junkies, John and Yoko preferred to spend their lives in bed. They camped on John's eight-square-foot pad. Around them was a Sargasso Sea of books, magazines, and newspapers, tapes and records, dirty underwear, and discarded clothing. With a color TV and a film projector, they had plenty of images on which to batten. For decor they stuck up their nude photos framed in a couple of condoms filled with stale piss. In this condition they hibernated until Christmas.

The day before Christmas the Apple offices were the scene of an elaborate party for the Beatles, their staff, and children. Because no one had seen John and Yoko for two months, their unexpected appearance caused a sensation, particularly because they came dressed up as Father and Mother Christmas. Though he appeared wan and gaunt, he presided calmly over the distribution of gifts to the kids, muttering through his fake beard, "Ho, ho, ho!"

On New Year's Eve the Beatles always held a party at Cilla Black's flat on Portland Place. This year the party was a bummer. Brian Epstein, Cynthia Lennon, and Jane Asher all were missing, Jane having broken off her engagement to Paul when she came home unexpectedly from a tour and found him with an American girl, Francie Schwartz. John and Yoko were also missing, having gone to a party given by Michael Boyer, a young promoter associated with an experimental community center, the Arts Lab. After starting off at the Lab, the party had wound up at Boyer's home in Islington, where Lennon turned to the promoter, whom he barely knew, and told him with tears in his eyes that he was the only person he had met in years who wanted nothing from his friendship.

Lennon had many reasons to weep on New Year's Eve. He was strung out on heroin. His image was besmirched. His son was traumatized. His relations with the other Beatles and with EMI were in jeopardy. After years and years of adulation, he had become a target for public indignation. What's more, there was a devastating irony in his fate.

All through his years of fame John Lennon had been longing to fall in love and actually experience the bliss about which he was always singing. Then he had developed his great passion for Yoko and sacrificed everything to possess her. "I really believed," he confessed later, "that all you need is love." Yet from the moment he started acting on that cherished conviction, he had suffered one disaster after another.

GET BACK!

Around noon on 2 January 1969 the Beatles began arriving, one by one, at the cold and cavernous Stage One of Twickenham Studios outside London, the site of many happy scenes from *A Hard Day's Night* and *Help!* The four young men who appeared that day, however, were hardly recognizable. The relentlessly turning kaleidoscope of pop fashion had now brought them into focus as hirsute hippies with rough hair down to their shoulders, a big fruit vendor's mustache on Ringo and on Paul the massive black beard of a mountain man. The strangeness of their appearance as they gathered about the breakfast table on the sound stage, set by Mal with toast, cornflakes, and tea, was as nothing compared with the changes that had occurred in their minds. John, who appeared with Yoko clinging to his arm as if she had him under arrest, was stoned blind and proclaiming through every pore of his body: "I don't give a shit!" George was tense and angry because he felt the band was about to take a giant step backward. Ringo was depressed because Paul had given him such a hard time during their studio sessions the previous year that he had come home one day and told Maureen tearfully that he was out of the band. The only man who hadn't changed essentially was Paul, who arrived a half hour late because he had tried to reach the studio by public transportation, both to save money and to prove that he was still one of the people.

The reason they all were gathered in this unlikely place at this unaccustomed hour was that Paul had decided to make a last-ditch effort to pull the Beatles together again after each had gone his own way on the White Album. Reasoning that the band that tours together stays together, he had sought first to persuade the boys to go back on the road—even if they just played a string of dance halls up north! Since nobody could face another tour, Paul came up next with with the idea of a single remarkable event that could become a TV show. No such event offered itself, however, so finally Paul and his director, Michael Lindsay-Hogg, proposed a series of exotic locales, like an oasis in the sub-Sahara or a Roman amphitheater at Tripoli. "I'm warming to the idea of asylum," quipped John, but it looked that first day as though the pale Beatles would soon be getting some sun in Africa.

Meantime, they had agreed to start laying down the tracks for their spring album, taking as their theme the latest trend: rock 'n' roll revival. The idea was for the Beatles to go back to their roots in Hamburg and Liverpool, playing again all their old favorites plus some of the early songs they had never recorded. Paul had persuaded the boys to begin their labors at Twickenham so that footage of them at work could be used as cutaways in a concert film or as material for a documentary.

But no rock band, least of all the Beatles, can afford to allow the public to see how it works. The habitual obscenities, the use of drugs, the malicious comments about all sorts of people, and the backbiting among the members of the group could destroy the band's cherished image in one reel. What's more, the intrusion of the cameras into such an intimate activity was bound to make everyone close up like a clam. Working at a film studio also meant that the Beatles had to reverse their normal hours: Instead of getting to the studio between 7:00 and 10:00 at night and knocking off before dawn, they now received their wake-up calls from Mal at 8:30 A.M. in order to get through the morning traffic and arrive by noon. Then, surrounded by a strange crew, they were obliged to make music in a frigid airplane hangar while being filmed before a white cyclorama on which played washes of colored light. After a couple of days in this depressing milieu, everybody was pissed off, and the future of the project was shrouded in gloom.

These problems were nothing, however, compared with what happened when Yoko got into action. She made it clear from the start that she was not going to join the other members of the entourage in sitting quietly outside the range of the cameras. If there was to be a TV show, she was going to be in it, as close to center stage as possible. Not only did she arrive on John's arm, but she never relinquished it. Even when John lowered his butt onto the narrow perch of a piano stool, Yoko butted in on the same unaccommodating roost. Not content merely to sit with the boys, she was eager to sit in with them, jamming and acting as one of them, especially when it came to bossing around Mal, whom she sent constantly to the canteen with orders for fish or steak, salad or coffee. At one point she had an easel set up next to the music stands, at which she made a great show of painting while the Beatles played. She even had the nerve to offer the band suggestions on their music.

In later years John and Yoko filled the media with outraged complaints about how the "others" had treated poor little Yoko during these sessions. The gist of their charges was that the Beatles were macho pigs who could not tolerate the idea of a woman's asserting herself as their equal. The fact of the matter was rather different. The Beatles actually let Yoko get away with murder because they were afraid of provoking John. They fluttered about like helpless little birds trying to protect their nest from a predatory cat. John complained: "Paul was always going up to Yoko and saying, 'Why don't you keep in the background a bit more?'" Clearly that was not an unreasonable request.

"Yoko sees men as assistants," remarked John Lennon wryly in one of his last interviews, speaking from years of experience. Specifically he could have added that she saw them as supporting artists, fund-raisers, and press agents. It followed that this was to be John Lennon's fate if he sought to fulfill Yoko's ambitions, but there was one great obstacle to the achievement of Yoko's program: the Beatles—especially Paul. For years Paul had jockeyed John through project after project precisely the way Yoko would do when she had supplanted him. Ousting Paul would have been an impossible task but for the long history of barely suppressed conflict between the leading Beatles. Their rivalry was the band's weak point; by now it threatened to become their breaking point. Yoko was shrewd enough to see the weakness, and so was Paul. What the film shows is a Paul McCartney who is walking on eggs. But Paul, like Yoko, was born to dominate. Behind his Robin Goodfellow mask of charm and insouciance beat the iron heart of the power tripper. What's more, unlike Yoko, Paul had the talent and experience that gave him every right to command. Always the most commercially attuned of the Beatles, Paul's famous songs, like "Michelle," "Yesterday," and "Eleanor Rigby," got the most airplay and earned the most money in publishing royalties. Now while John was succumbing to drugs, Paul was hitting his commercial peak, constantly coming up with "monsters," the sorts of hits that are no sooner off the mastering lathe than they are blaring out of every loudspeaker in the world. "Hey Jude," "Get Back," "Let It Be," "The Long and Winding Road"—every track was enough to make a lesser man's reputation.

Paul had the tunes, and he had everything else he needed to make them into finished products, in contrast with John, who once confessed that every time he went back to recording he had to learn the board all over again, like a forgotten lesson. So is it any wonder that Paul got a little bossy, betraying his impatience with Ringo (who had gotten worse over the years) or with an uptight, crib-book guitarist like George, or a sullen, apathetic drug addict like John? Paul, after all, was the guy who had been running this band for years, and now he was watching it run right off the road. Naturally there were moments when he took a deep breath and said to Yoko with the utmost politeness but not without a shade of menace in his voice—"Get back!"

Unfortunately Paul went a bit too far with George. Again, Paul's behavior was understandable. In that great age of the guitar star George Harrison had not kept up. In fact, he had come to resemble the Beatles' filling station attendant. In would drive John or Paul with their latest song, and all George would do was check their breaks and run a couple of squeegee notes across their windshield, sending them out again without any of that high octane that other bands got from their electric pumpers. On this day George bridled under Paul's spurring and declared: "I'll play whatever you want me to play—or I won't play at all! Whatever it is that'll please you, I'll do it!" The words were obliging, but the tone was threatening. Next moment George split for lunch, driving back to Esher. As he walked through the door, he announced: "I've quit the group. The Beatles are over!" He didn't stay away long, but his walkout was the signal for John and Ringo to veto Paul's plan for a TV show. When George returned, bringing Billy Preston, a young black keyboard player from Little Richard's band, the group decided to confine its efforts to the album and the documentary.

At this point John Lennon launched an ill-considered counterattack. He proposed that Paul take charge of the film and leave the album to him. Then he sought to retaliate against Paul for "overproduced" albums like *Pepper* by decreeing that this album must not be canned but candid music, rock *au naturel*. "[John] said there was to be no echoes, no overdubs, and none of my jiggery-pokery," reported George Martin. "It was to be an 'honest album' in that if they didn't get the song right the first time, they'd record it again and again until they did. It was awful. We did take after take after take. And John would be asking if Take Sixty-seven was better than Take Thirty-nine." It was a preposterous approach for a band that had long since abandoned spontaneous music making in favor of the wiles and guiles of the studio, also a band whose playing and vocalizing had deteriorated so badly of late that it sounded like a campfire sing. So the man who really led the Beatles to disaster, doing endless takes of "One After 9:09" (a song Lennon wrote when he was seventeen), was not the much blamed Paul but John.

After ten miserable days at Twickenham the Beatles left the bleak, midwinter sound stage for what they fancied would be the finest studio in the world: the magnificent seventy-eight-track facility that Magic Alex had been building for months in the basement of their headquarters at 3 Savile Row. But when they arrived, they discovered that work on the studio had only begun! The costly German tape recorders were still in their shipping crates, and there wasn't even a hole to run the wires from the control console to the studio mikes. The shock of outrage should have blown Magic Alex out of the Beatles' lives forever, but the gullible Lennon continued to have faith in his magic man, insisting still that he was a genius.

The Beatles' Bataan ended after what John called "six weeks of misery," on 30 January 1969. At noon the band climbed onto the roof at Savile Row for what proved to be their final performance. Paul had insisted that the film contain at least a token concert. So the Beatles had measured the shortest distance between public and private and had hit the roof. Clothed in furs and macs, surrounded by their crew and entourage, they took their stand amid the chimney pots and counted off "Get Back." The moment the sound of their amps began ricocheting among the world's most renowned collection of custom-tailoring establishments, all hell broke loose.

Clerks and miniskirted office girls rushed out into the chill street or climbed onto neighboring rooftops. Traffic stopped as the lunchtime crowds gathered below No. 3, craning their necks as they searched for the invisible musicians. Master tailors with half-glasses sliding down their noses and limp tape measures around their necks phoned the local constabulary. In a last, impudent, nose-thumbing act of self-assertion, the Beatles disturbed the peace.

They also caught fire, John hurling himself into the performance like a rock Paganini, his long hair blowing back in the breeze, his noodly body, hugged by a brown fur jacket, bending at knees, waist and neck like a serpent, as he wrestled with his guitar and shouted the words of the songs into the mike. Jouncing on his sneaker-clad feet and smiling happily, Lennon got off on the kookiness of the occasion, trying even harder than Paul to end the film with a burst of the old raving.

Finally, when the rooftop show was over and everybody was retreating from the mikes, John turned around and addressed those present: "I'd like to say thanks on behalf of the group and ourselves—and I hope we passed the audition!" Not bad. Not great. A stock bit of irony—but a sad little epitaph for what had been the most triumphant career in the history of show business.

THE BEATLES GO BROKE

"We haven't half the money people think we have. . . . We're losing money. If it carries on like this, we'll be broke in six months." So declared John Lennon on 18 January 1969, putting his business in Fleet Street. Like his musical cry for "Help!" three years before, Lennon's financial SOS was not taken seriously. Nor is it any wonder. For years the press had been detailing the financial triumphs of the Beatles, with the result that the Fab Four were presumed to be the wealthiest young men in the world. In terms of gross income this estimate was accurate. As of December 1968, the Beatles had earned (according to an Arthur Young audit) $154 million. Yet John Lennon had not exaggerated: the Beatles were virtually broke.

The only man who read Lennon's distress signal correctly was Allen Klein, manager of the Rolling Stones, the Kinks, and Donovan. Klein, a professional accountant, knew from long experience that even the most successful entertainers often wind up in grave financial trouble because of extravagance, mismanagement, or cheating. Time and again he had opened the books of some famous act and discovered that the star, living in luxury and acting as if he hadn't a care in the world, was actually teetering on the edge of bankruptcy. This had been the case with Elvis, who, if he had lived just one more year, would have gone bust.

Klein was also alert to Lennon's signal because the manager of the Stones aspired to manage the Beatles. "I got 'em!" he had shouted when he heard the news of Brian Epstein's death, but he was dead wrong. Eighteen months elapsed without his getting his foot inside the door. Meantime, Paul McCartney had started living with Linda Eastman, whose father, Lee Eastman (no connection to Eastman Kodak), was a New York attorney, deeply involved in music publishing and the art world. At Paul's urging, the Beatles had engaged Eastman's son and partner, John, to represent them in their business dealings. But when it started to look as though Paul might marry Linda, John Lennon set about looking for a manager who would not be his partner's brother-in-law. That search led quickly to Klein, who remembered the astonishment he experienced when he first dialed Lennon's private number and heard the famous voice singing to the tune of "Three Blind Mice": *"We're not home! We're not home! Leave your name! We'll call you back—maybe!"* Klein left his name, and on the night of 27 January he opened the door of his lavish suite at the Hotel Dorchester to welcome John Lennon and Yoko Ono.

Allen Klein was a man whom many feared, as is clear from John Belushi's parody in Monty Python's *The Ruttles.* Puffed up like an adder and so muscle-bound that he can barely walk, Belushi's Klein enters his office like a German tank plowing through a Russian barn; as his employees shrink in horror before his basilisk stare and golem stride, he disappears inside his lair with a couple of huge bodyguards—whom he throws out the door!

It was this Killer Klein image coupled with rumors of stock rigging, double-dealing with the Rolling Stones, and some IRS violations that haunted Klein from the first day he got involved with the Beatles. Actually, the accusations constantly aired in the British press came to very little: The run-up in the stock of Cameo-Parkway was due more to ineptitude than sharp practice and the Stones' principal complaint was simply that they rarely saw their manager. As for the IRS convictions, they were for failing to file small sums in payroll deductions, a case of negligence rather than of fraud. But in England, Klein was not in a good position to defend himself because he was perceived as a cunning and ruthless New York Jew—THE TOUGHEST WHEELER-DEALER IN THE POP JUNGLE, as one newspaper headline blared—out to rip off a national treasure.

John Lennon must have been startled the night he finally met the man who had generated this ominous aura; in fact, people with far less perceptiveness than Lennon are surprised when they first encounter Allen Klein because instead of a saber-toothed tiger with a phone in either paw and murder in his heart, they discover a stocky little guy with a distant resemblance to Buddy Hackett dressed in slovenly clothes and sneaks, who looks as if there's nothing he'd rather do than run out in the alley and play a fast game of one-on-one. His image as the sloppy little whiz kid from New Jersey galled the well-groomed British business establishment, but it immediately enthralled John Lennon. Compared with the gleaming Jack Kennedy style of John Eastman, Allen Klein came across as a fuckin' working-class hero!

Presenting himself much as he actually was was one part of Klein shtick—the most obvious part. Less conspicuous was the enormous care with which he studied his prospects. "I'm not that smart," he modestly averred, denying his most undeniable virtue: "I just prepare well." And how had he prepared for this historic occasion? When the Lennons came in, all tense and nervous, Allen had it fixed that they could sit right down and have a little nosh, which would immediately put everybody in a nice cozy relationship around the table. And the meal turned out to be a vegetarian's plain boiled dream, flawlessly catered to Lennon's queasy tastes.

Even better than the veggies was Klein's choice of table talk. John Lennon recalled: "The early thing that impressed me about Allen—and obviously it was a kind of flattery as well—was that he went through all the old songs we'd written, and he really knew which was *my* song and which Paul's. He'd say, 'Well, McCartney didn't write *that* line, did he?' And I'd say, 'Right!' You know? That's what really got me interested—because he knew what our contributions were to the group. Most people thought it was all Paul or George Martin [how about that assumption!]. And he knew all my lyrics, and he understood them—not that there's much to understand—but he was into it and he dug lyrics. So I thought, 'Well, anybody who knows me this well—just by listening to records—is pretty perceptive.'" So Klein's preparation paid off. Not only did he demonstrate his appreciation of Lennon's talent, but in doing so, he buffed up Lennon's easily tarnished ego by reminding him of all the great things he had done in the past. That reminder was worth a lot to a man given to self-doubt.

The skill that Klein exhibited in dealing with the prickly and unpredictable Lennon was just as apparent in the way he handled Yoko Ono. Never once did he exhibit a trace of that male condescension that drove Yoko crazy when she had to deal with the Beatles or their entourage. Klein spoke to her with precisely the same respect that he evinced toward John, implying that he saw them as equals. Lennon was as gratified by the way Klein made no difference between him and Yoko as by the way Klein constantly distinguished between a Lennon line and a McCartney line. So Klein didn't have to wait long for his reward.

After a couple of hours John said: "Listen, Allen, would you manage Yoko and me?" The words echoed that meeting seven years earlier, when Lennon had cut short the discussion by exclaiming: "Right, then, Brian—manage us!" Only now vastly more was involved than the fate of four unknown boys eager to land a recording contract. Nor could Lennon speak any longer for the others. He had to warn Klein: "You cannot manage the Beatles because they're already signed with Eastman."

Klein was not dismayed by this revelation. As he said, "You can always fire your lawyer." But he didn't offer his immediate assent, even though his financial situation was only somewhat less pressing than Lennon's. For though Allen Klein gave the impression of enormous

wealth with his £500-a-day hotel suite and his £100-a-day limo perpetually parked before the Dorchester, the truth was that he had only a
few hundred thousand dollars in his corporate account, and only that
week his right-hand man had told him: "You had better sign the Beatles or
you'll find yourself going out of business." No matter. Allen Klein was a
born crapshooter—and a born optimist. He knew when he was hot, and
he knew when to pass. Now he played it cool, replying that he would be
happy to manage the Lennons—but going no farther.

"Well, what do we have to do?" challenged the impetuous Lennon.

"I think we should sleep on it tonight," answered Klein.

"What's the matter?" snapped Lennon. "Don't you want it now?"

"Sure, of course." Klein smiled.

"Well, what do I have to do?" John demanded.

"I think that what we really should do," Klein answered, finally persuaded to pass, "is write and inform those individuals that you have
direct contractual relationships with—tell them that you have asked me
to look after your things and send them notes. But before you do that,
call them so that it won't appear as if it is a cold and impersonal
change."

Klein had his assistant, Iris Keitel, standing by in an adjacent room
with her typewriter, but he decided to adopt a less business-like approach. Having gone into the room, he came out carrying the machine,
which he set upon the floor with some paper. At three in the morning
Yoko typed out the notes to Sir Joseph Lockwood at EMI, Dick James
at Northern Songs, Clive Epstein at NEMS Enterprises, and Harry
Pinsker at Bryce, Hanmer. The message ran: "I've asked Allen Klein to
look after my things. Please give him any information he wants and full
cooperation. Love, John Lennon."

By pushing Allen Klein into the ring to confront John Eastman, John
Lennon was really preparing to square off against Paul McCartney.
What would happen when they came to blows was prefigured in
the initial encounters between the rival managers. On 3 February the
Beatles held a meeting at which they voted three to one to engage
Klein to look into their affairs, overriding Paul's opposition. The boys
met next with Klein and Eastman. There was no contest. When Eastman said that he would like to accompany Klein to his meeting with Sir
Joe, Klein turned him down flat, insisting that he must have a free
hand to manage the Beatles' business, just as Eastman should enjoy the
same freedom as their lawyer. Eastman summoned his father to the
next meeting with Klein. As usual, Allen Klein was well prepared.

When Lee Eastman appeared in the conference room, he exuded
that hale-and-hearty self-confidence typical of the old business ace who
lunches regularly at the WASPy Grill Room of the New York Harvard

Club. But no sooner had he seated himself with his son and future son-in-law than he had the carpet jerked from under him. Allen Klein commenced the meeting by announcing with a teasing little smile on his lips that he had recently done a bit of detective work. He had been rewarded with an interesting discovery: Lee Eastman had started out in life with a different name. Until he was graduated from Harvard, his name had been *Leopold Epstein!* John Lennon exploded in a Goon-hyena laugh. Then, quick as always to find the soft spot and needle it till the victim screamed, Lennon set about his work. For the balance of the meeting both he and Klein insisted on addressing Eastman as "Epstein." "Well, Mr. Epstein," or, "No, Mr. Epstein," or "If I had a name like Epstein," they went on, until finally the normally affable lawyer freaked out.

Leaping to his feet and staring down at his adversary, Eastman poured out his rage, denouncing Klein as a crook, a boor, a con man. "He called me everything he could think of," recalled Klein. "I just sat there and let him come out of the woodwork. He showed everybody what he was: emotional, pedantic, patronizing." Eastman, having vented his spleen, stormed out of the room, followed by his son and prospective son-in-law.

Violent as was Eastman's anger, it could not hold a candle to John Lennon's fury. "He was an animal! A fuckin' stupid middle-class pig!" ranted Lennon. "He thought he could con me with fuckin' talking about Kafka and shit, and Picasso and de Kooning, for chrissake! I shit on them!" So began the long war that would destroy the Beatles.

Although Paul disliked Allen Klein every bit as much as John hated the Eastmans, Paul finally agreed to empower Klein to make a thorough investigation of the Beatles' business. Nobody could have faulted that decision. Klein owed his original success in the music business to his unfailing ability to ferret out missing money.

For two months Klein sat at Apple, surrounded by a mountain of papers. When he finished his accounting, a giant neon sign flashed on in his mind. It read: SCHMUCK!

Brian Epstein, that little Lord Fauntleroy in long pants, had really done it! He had taken the greatest property in the history of show business and pissed it away in one bad deal after another. The whole thing was a nightmare. Every arrangement was wrong; every percentage inadequate. The worst thing was that the Beatles *were* broke, and most of what they had lost was gone *forever*.

To understand how badly Brian had fucked up, you had to take in turn each source of income and follow the money.

EMI RECORD DEAL

The Beatles' primary source of income was the royalties they earned from the sale of their records. These earnings were governed for the first five years of the group's recording career by the provisions of the contract that Brian had obtained from EMI when the Beatles were still four unknown beginners. Naturally the terms weren't very good; in fact, they were appalling. The royalty on a single, for example, was exactly one British *penny*, which rose by a farthing (one-quarter of a penny) each year after the first, to reach the grand summit of two pence per record. Translated into the terms of the Beatles' principal market, North America, the contract authorized EMI's U.S. subsidiary, Capitol, to pay the Beatles on an album that retailed for four to five dollars exactly *six cents*. The normal rate would have been from twenty-five to fifty cents.

There was an obvious remedy, however. In the music business it's common to renegotiate beginners' contracts once the artists start earning the company big money. But here is where Brian was most delinquent. He would not consider going back to EMI to get a fair deal even when the Beatles took off like a rocket and pushed up the company's earnings in 1964 an incredible *80 percent*! Why not? Because, Brian insisted, he was a "gentleman," and a gentleman does not go back on his word—even if his clients are taking a screwing! So for three miraculous years, while the Beatles were the most profitable act in the history of the record business, they continued to be paid as if they were unknown beginners.

Finally, when the contract expired in June 1965, Gentleman Brian got his chance. What did he do with it? Absolutely nothing. So overwhelmed was he by all the different proposals made by his financial advisers that he stalled the negotiations for *a year and a half*. Meantime, the Beatles turned out *Help!*, "Yesterday," *Rubber Soul,* and *Revolver*— all without a contract! At last, on 26 January 1967, they signed the agreement that had taken so long to frame. It provided a sizable increase in royalties, from six to forty cents on a Capitol album, as well as a bonus of one million pounds; but the royalty was still inadequate, and the bonus was merely the money the Beatles had earned during the period when they were working without a contract. Even worse were the provisions governing production quotas and exclusivity. The Beatles bound themselves to turn out two albums and three singles a year for the next five years, but they remained under exclusive contract to EMI for the next *ten years*. In other words, Brian had bartered the band's entire foreseeable future for an increase that left them still far short of where they should have been years before.

PUBLISHING

The Beatles' music publishing business was embodied primarily in Northern Songs Ltd., established on 26 February 1963 by Dick James (born Richard Leon Vapnick), a washed-up pop singer turned hole-in-the-wall song publisher, who became the luckiest man in the history of the industry. Getting in on the ground floor on the recommendation of George Martin (who was too ethical to take a proffered percentage of the publisher's share and consequently sacrificed a fortune), James set up a typical artist's company, reserving 50 percent for himself and his accountant and financial backer, Charles Silver, and offering 50 percent to Lennon, McCartney, and Epstein, who divided their share 40–40–20. (In 1966 the Beatles' portion was increased to 55 percent in exchange for extending their contract to 1973.) To avoid taxes, John and Paul assigned the writer's share of their songs to Lenmac Ltd., owned by them and Brian 40–40–20. For the record, John and Paul were signed to Lenmac as contract writers.

In February 1965 Dick James took Northern Songs into the market, where it did quite well. In the consequent reshuffling of the old arrangements, Lenmac sold out to Northern, providing it with all rights in the first fifty-six Lennon-McCartney songs. In return, John and Paul received £140,000 each (actually unpaid royalties already in the pipeline) plus 15 percent of Northern's shares, with a further 7 percent to NEMS and 1.6 percent to George and Ringo collectively. This was a tax-free capital gain, but it didn't represent what it should have because Lenmac had been underevaluated owing to the fact that its all-important American affiliate had never been audited. Now John and Paul set up a new company, Maclen Music Ltd., to house their future compositions, signing a seven-year agreement with Northern to handle the publishing of these songs.

SUBPUBLISHING

The international renown of the Beatles enabled Dick James to get into subpublishing in a big way, by either establishing companies abroad or entering into agreements with foreign publishers. The typical Beatles split with a foreign publisher was 85–15 (15 percent to the foreign house), but when Dick James controlled the foreign company, the split was 50–50—a revealing difference. The money that came back to Britain from foreign earnings was divided equally between the publisher and the writers. Since the United States was the Beatles' biggest market, the band's American company, Maclen Inc., became the key element in Dick James's operation. By retaining 50 percent of what this company earned in America and adding this sum to his half of the 50 percent returned to Britain, James succeeded in holding on to 75 percent of the Beatles' income from their largest source of publishing revenue.

Somebody must have blown the whistle on this practice because just before Brian Epstein's death, when the publishing contract came up for renewal, James wrote a highly ambiguous letter to Maclen Ltd.—

which is like your right hand corresponding with your left—in which he said that henceforth 85 percent of the American revenues would be transmitted to England, with only 15 percent remaining in the States. In this same letter, however, he inserted a sentence which ran roughly: "You will receive your money as before." Dick James induced John and Paul to sign this letter, which had the effect of making them confirm the old arrangement under color of changing it in their favor.

In 1986 an English court handed down a landmark decision on such subpublishing practices. After reviewing the relationship of Dick James and Elton John, the court ruled that the publisher's way of doing business was improper and illegal. (Shortly thereafter Dick James bent over at a card game to retrieve a card he had dropped and was smitten by a fatal heart attack.)

TOURING

Brian Epstein was so overcome by gratitude when Arthur Howes booked the Beatles on their first little package tour that he gave the promoter an option on all future tours of England by the Beatles. Enjoying a monopoly, Howes was in a strong position to hold down the band's price. The Beatles never received more than 50 percent of the take, even though Howes could sell out his houses by merely announcing the main attraction.

Brian's only recourse was to book shows that he produced himself, like the Christmas pantomimes. But these entailed a clear conflict of interest, because Brian was both buyer and seller, virtually all the talent coming from the NEMS stable. What's more, when the Beatles worked for their manager, they worked for peanuts. In America, where the tours were run by GAC, the deal was a 60–40 split against a guarantee of $25,000 per show. This was a standard break, but clearly, after their first, incredibly successful, tour, the Beatles could have gotten a bigger piece of the pie.

Brian's ultimate solution to the problem of increasing the Beatles' earnings makes a mockery of all those glowing accounts of how "honorable" and "upright" he was. A close friend, Peter Brown, has revealed that Brian always left every date with his "brown paper bag money," the big chunk of cash that the promoter skimmed off the top without reporting it to the tax collector. Exactly how Brian divied up this unaccountable money will never be known.

MOVIE DEALS

When Walter Shenson and Bud Orenstein met Brian Epstein for the first time, they planned to offer him 25 percent of the net profits on their picture, but being seasoned businessmen, they first asked Brian what he wanted. Puffing himself up in what he took to be the manner of a City magnate, Brian replied: "I wouldn't consider anything under 7.5 percent." Fortunately for the Beatles, the deal was reviewed by Brian's lawyer, David Jacobs, who demanded 25 percent.

Actually, any percentage of net as opposed to gross profits is fool's gold in Hollywood because of the movie companies' notorious book-keeping, which results in even successful pictures showing only small net yields. Because none of Elvis Presley's films ever earned him any-thing in profits, Colonel Parker insisted on getting his money up front, in a big guarantee, commencing with $250,000 on the first picture and rising swiftly to $500,000 against 50 percent of net. The Beatles were paid only $15,000 a man to make their first film. They were lucky, however, because the combination of a low budget, modest marketing costs, enormous box-office receipts, and, above all, an honest producer earned them eventually a lot of money: $7 to $8 million on their first two films in the years between 1964 and 1980.

MERCHANDISING

A phenomenal act like the Beatles could anticipate making a pile of money by licensing its name and image for exploitation by manufac-turers of paraphernalia. A man named Nicky Byrnes, with no previous experience in this business, copped the Beatles' merchandising rights in 1963 in exchange for 10 percent of the take. When Brian saw what a bonanza Byrnes was mining in the States, he insisted upon renegotiat-ing the deal. The ensuing scuffle alarmed the manufacturers, who can-celed their orders en masse, causing the Beatles to lose millions in potential earnings. Meantime, both Byrnes and Epstein went on issuing conflicting merchandising licenses that triggered a spate of costly re-turns.

Epstein tried to throw all the blame on Byrnes, suing him and being sued in turn. Brian had no case, but he could not afford to lose. So he engaged Louis Nizer, allegedly for $1 million, and told him to push the action to the limits. In the next three years the Nizer organization filed 39 motions, every one of which was rejected by the court but each of which cost Byrnes a bundle. Byrnes retaliated by denouncing Epstein to the IRS, claiming that Brian was slipping the profits of the American tours out of the country without paying the requisite taxes. The IRS responded by attaching $1 million of the Beatles' 1966 concert earn-ings, holding the money until 1976.

The punch line of the merchandising story is that the contracts were negotiated not with the band's company, The Beatles, Ltd., which held the rights, but with NEMS, which did not possess any proprietorial rights whatsoever, being simply a management organization. This basic confusion about mine and thine in the relations between Brian Epstein and the Beatles can be discerned in other dealings. Allen Klein discovered that Brian's American company, Beatles U.S.A., Ltd., wound up holding *Magical Mystery Tour*, to which it had no title. It was revelations of this nature that finally persuaded John Lennon that Brian Epstein was crooked.

TAX SHELTER

No matter how much the Beatles earned, their net income was bound to be but a tiny percentage of their gross so long as they were subject to Britain's incredible 94 percent income tax. The primary challenge to Epstein, therefore, was not making money but holding on to what the Beatles earned. The obvious answer was a tax shelter. Dr. Walter Strach, of the entertainment accounting firm of Bryce, Hanmer, established in the Bahamas a company named Cavalcade Productions that was owned 50–50 by the Beatles and Walter Shenson. The idea was to capitalize the company with £100,000 and then post the completion guarantees for *Help!*, which would enable the company to sequester the profits of the film beyond the reach of the American or British revenue services. Brian sought the advice of Lord Goodman, a wealthy real-estate developer, who was Harold Wilson's lawyer. When Goodman learned that the Beatles were involved in a tax shelter, he warned Brian that when it came out, it would make the boys look bad. The insecure and shamefast Brian, horrified at the thought of appearing a moneygrubber, took Goodman's advice and dismantled the Beatles' shelter. Harold Wilson rewarded the boys for their unwitting sacrifice by making them all members of the Most Honorable Order of the British Empire. Brian told the Beatles that they received the award for "increasing trade."

INCORPORATION AS APPLE

When the tax shelter was dismantled, an alternative method had to be found to reduce the burden of taxation. The Rolling Stones had adopted the practice of residing abroad for a year whenever the law permitted them to spend their foreign earnings outside England without paying British taxes on the money. Brian rejected this device in favor of another, far more questionable alternative: incorporation with an eye to going public. By a deed of partnership dated 19 April 1967, the Beatles sold 80 percent of themselves (exclusive of their films and music publishing) to Apple Corps, Ltd., which became the majority partner in a newly created partnership, The Beatles & Co., which replaced The Beatles, Ltd. as the group's basic business entity. As payment, the group received a tax-free capital gain of £800,000 plus salaries and the opportunity to charge off many of their personal expenses to the company, which would now be the official owner of their homes, cars, etc. But £800,000 was an absurdly low estimate of the

Beatles' total worth, which should have been measured in millions. Actually the figure had been suggested by the immediate availability of the $1 million in cash that EMI was about to give the Beatles as a bonus for signing their new recording contract. A much better arrangement would have been to evaluate the Beatles at a more appropriate figure, like £4 million, which would have given each Beatle £800,000. Apple could have paid the money as it became available. As it turned out, once the boys had discharged all their debts, they were left pretty much where they started. Only now, all their future earnings were tied up in a corporation, which would make it much harder to recoup their money in the event the band broke up.

When Allen Klein gazed down at the bottom line of the auditor's report, he saw two figures that loomed up like tombstones. One was the Beatles' net income for 1968—a pitiful £78,000. The other was the Beatles' indebtedness to Apple, from which they had been obliged to take advances just to pay their bills. John was in the hole for £64,000, Paul for £66,000, and George and Ringo for £35,000 each. Clearly something had to be done quickly or the Beatles would come under pressure to start selling their remaining assets.

Klein's first target was NEMS, owned now by Queenie and administered by Brian's brother, Clive. NEMS continued to receive 25 percent of the Beatles' income, but it no longer performed any significant service. The obvious remedy was a buy-out, a procedure that John Eastman had already initiated by going with the Beatles to Sir Joseph Lockwood and asking for a loan of £1.25 million, the stipulated price. Allen Klein advised the Beatles against taking this road, warning them that they would have to earn £2 million to repay the loan. He told them there was a good chance that he could get NEMS for free because Clive Epstein might not want to go through the litigation that the Beatles could launch on the basis of Klein's audit. The grounds would be fraud, mismanagement, self-serving, overreaching, and conflict of interest.

John Eastman agreed that delay was advisable. On Valentine's Day he sent a note designed to stall Clive Epstein: "As you know, Mr. Allen Klein is doing an audit of the Beatles' affairs vis-à-vis NEMS and Nemperor Holdings, Ltd. [successor to NEMS]. When this has been completed, I suggest we meet to discuss the results of Mr. Klein's audit as well as the propriety of the negotiations surrounding the nine-year agreement between EMI and the Beatles and NEMS."

Clive read the writing on the wall. There was no time to be lost. He must immediately get out of this nasty business. Getting in touch with Leonard Richenberg of Triumph Trust, Clive sold NEMS for about £750,000.

Allen Klein reacted to this unforeseen development with characteristic swiftness and boldness. Walking into Richenberg's office, Klein congratulated his opponent on being a smart man. Then he told him that he wasn't as smart as he believed because the audit had disclosed the existence of enormous debts that Epstein had incurred back in the days of touring. What's more, there were so many lawsuits pending that defending against them all might bankrupt Triumph. Richenberg replied by showing Klein the door. Undismayed, Klein wrote a letter to the firm that collected the Beatles' royalties, Henry Ansbacher and Company, instructing it to remit the moneys henceforth to Apple Corps.

Triumph Trust responded by taking EMI to court. Meantime, more than £1 million in sorely needed royalties were deposited in a Lloyd's bank awaiting the outcome of the dispute. Richenberg sought next to strengthen his case by commissioning a Bishop's Report, which produced a lot of information that made Allen Klein look bad. All this stuff was leaked to the *Sunday Times,* which published it in a blistering article. At this point, with his bluff called and his nose bloodied, Allen Klein recognized that he would have to change his tactics and enter into serious and prolonged negotiations with Leonard Richenberg. Just at that moment a sudden crisis blew the whole Beatles' organization sideways.

John Lennon was lying abed one morning in March, reading the papers, when his eye fell on an item that jolted him bolt upright. Dick James and Charles Silver, the men who ran Northern Songs, had just sold their 32 percent of the company to Sir Lew Grade of the Associated Television Corporation (ATV), which already owned 3 percent. So Sir Lew's share of the Beatles' song bag now amounted to more than the Beatles' 30 percent. John went wild with rage and summoned Paul from East Hampton and Klein from Puerto Rico in a desperate effort to seize control of the company before it could be taken over by the detested Grade, the fat-cat, cigar-sucking boss of the British entertainment industry. What had inspired James to his treacherous act was fear that the Beatles would break up (he had no faith in them as individual writers), coupled with dread of Allen Klein. Actually, John and Paul had invited this disaster by resigning from the board of Northern Songs and relying on as their representatives lawyers and accountants who worked for Dick James.

The five-month battle that commenced now between the Beatles and Lew Grade was greatly complicated by the intervention of a third party, the so-called Consortium, consisting for the most part of financial institutions that owned or bought up shares in Northern Songs and then combined to play the middle between the contending giants. Sometimes the Consortium inclined toward ATV's stock offer, sometimes toward the Beatles' offer, which was strengthened at one point when Allen Klein, reacting to Paul's refusal to pledge his shares as collateral, threw into the scales 45,000 shares of MGM, worth about £650,000. Every time a deal was set, some fresh development would knock down the house of cards. Meantime, Klein was busy working out the purchase of NEMS, which also held 5.4 percent of Northern Songs.

In July 1969, Klein came close to fulfilling his boast that he would get NEMS for nothing. For the 90 percent of the company they did not own, the Beatles paid £750,000 in cash and £300,000 in frozen royalties plus $50,000 for NEMS's share of the Beatles' film company, Subafilms Ltd. (first two films plus *Yellow Submarine*), as well as 5 percent of the Beatles' gross record royalty from 1972 to 1976. Triumph bought in turn the 10 percent of NEMS owned by the Beatles for stock convertible for £420,000. Though it would appear that the Beatles wound up paying more than they got, the Triumph shares were worth $400,000 *tax-free*—the equivalent of £4 million before taxes!

Klein was destined to go down in defeat in the contention over Northern Songs. On 9 September ATV finally succeeded in buying out the Consortium, thereby obtaining 54 percent of the Beatles' music publishing. Undaunted, Klein fought on, struggling to save something from the debacle. He negotiated stubbornly with Lew Grade, using as his leverage the threat that the Beatles would pull out and leave ATV with a wasting asset. What Klein was after was the American publishing, which he claims was right in his hand when once again Paul McCartney balked (on the advice of the Eastmans) and the Beatles were obliged to sell out, losing the marketing rights (but not the royalties) in 160 of their songs, while remaining obliged to write 6 songs a year till 1973. For their 35.5 percent of Northern Songs, they received equivalent value in 10½ percent ATV Loan Stock. John exchanged his 644,000 shares for stock in the face amount of $1,288,000, redeeming the stock for cash on 31 October 1974. Paul, who had started buying up shares on the sly before things got tough, received proportionately more.

The emotional shock of loss of control to John and Paul is incalculable. The financial value was established pretty clearly in 1986, when Michael Jackson bought ATV's publishing catalog, whose principal item was two hundred Beatles songs, for $47.5 million.

In May Allen Klein had signed a three-year management contract with the Beatles after Paul was outvoted three to one. Klein asked for 20 percent of any gross income earned beyond that mandated by the contracts in force before he took control. Subsequently, he enjoyed the full support of all the Beatles in his most important task: the renegotiation of the EMI contract, which still had eight years to run. His bargaining power was generated by a provision of the contract that stipulated that the Beatles would cut ninety sides. Owing to the intense activity during the period of the White Album, the band was close now to fulfilling its quota. If EMI wanted the boys to continue producing, it would have to provide a fresh incentive. Allen Klein is regarded by even his worst enemies as one of the best negotiators in the music business. When he finished dealing with Sir Joseph Lockwood, the Beatles had a contract that elicited praise from even the grudging mouths of the Eastmans.

Under the agreement, dated 1 September 1969, the Beatles' American royalty would rise for the next three years from 40 to 57 cents not just on new releases but on "all existing product." (This paved the way for the lucrative reissues that Capitol produced in the Seventies.) After three years the royalty would jump up to *72 cents* an album—nearly double what the Beatles were currently receiving. The only proviso was that the band's two previous releases had to have sold not less than a half million units each. The most important change the new deal entailed, however, was not the royalty increase but a radical change in the way the Beatles did business.

Henceforth Apple would become the proprietor of the Beatles' records in the United States, licensing Capitol to manufacture and distribute the product. This was the kind of deal that Klein had negotiated for the Rolling Stones, and it was to become the ideal of every major band. Its primary advantage was the absolute control it conferred on the Beatles, who now became in effect their own record company, with all that entailed in terms of policing the sale of their product. The tax advantages were also great because by keeping the American earnings in the United States, the Beatles would avoid paying the British taxes, which, heightened by surtaxes, could go as high as 110 percent.

With this total recasting of their all-important record contract, Allen Klein succeeded finally in putting the Beatles in the driver's seat. If they fulfilled their commitment to two albums and three singles a year plus one repackaged album—and if they maintained their customary sales level—they would have the kind of money with which they had always been credited.

TALKING HEADS IN BEDS

On 14 March 1969, as John and Yoko were being driven out of London in their white Rolls-Royce, they decided to get married. "Intellectually, of course, we did not believe in getting married," explained John, "but one does not love someone just intellectually." So, impulsively, impatiently, as he always behaved when he had to make a major decision, John Lennon took the most decisive step of his entire life. Shouting through the plate-glass window to Les Anthony, John demanded to know if it was possible to marry on a Channel ferry, for the car was headed in the direction of Southampton. When Les replied that he had no idea, John ordered him to drive back to Southampton to make inquiries, first dropping them at their original destination, the waterfront bungalow at Poole that John had purchased in 1965 to get Mimi away from the fans at Mendips.

It was richly ironic that John's impulse to marry should have mastered him on the road to Mimi, for no one could have been more averse to the idea than his aunt. When John had first brought his Oriental princess to visit his aunt, she had seethed with rage at the sight of this little Japanese, with her great mop of unkempt hair. No sooner had Yoko stepped out on the patio to enjoy the view of the harbor than Mimi turned to John and snapped: "Who's the poison dwarf, John?"

Normally such an insult would have brought John Lennon to a boil, but with Mimi, he was wont to play a pacifying game. Laughing mirthlessly, he replied, "Oh, Mimi!"—as if to say, "How can you say such a terrible thing?"

Only Mimi wasn't just saying it. She was as serious as a heart attack. She told John that he was a fool to get involved with this "Yo-Yo." What could he possibly see in her? Didn't he realize what sort were the Japanese? Mimi, who had felt contempt for Cynthia, felt a much stronger emotion toward Yoko—loathing.

For this reason John did not reveal his momentous decision. Mimi would learn of John's marriage just she had learned of Julia's marriage—when it was too late to prevent. Meantime, John danced with impatience, awaiting a ring from Les. When the call came, it made John even more irritable. The only boat on which you could marry, reported Les, was an oceangoing steamship. As it happened, a liner was scheduled to depart in just two hours. *"Why didn't you book when you were there?"* barked Lennon at the hapless chauffeur. When Les called back again, he was obliged to report that it was too late to make reservations.

John ordered Les to return immediately. His new orders were to drive straight through to Paris, the ideal place for a honeymoon. The faithful but grumbling chauffeur got his master as far as the gate at Southampton ferry—but there they were stopped for lack of passports. Wild with frustration, John grabbed the nearest phone and called his office. He told Peter Brown that he wanted to marry within the next half hour! Brown wrestled with the problem, but the only place he could find that offered instant matrimony was Gibraltar. John didn't want Gibraltar. He wanted Paris. So he hired an executive jet and flew to Le Bourget. There he enjoyed his second honeymoon before his wedding, a nice variation on his first Paris honeymoon, which had followed the birth of his son.

John Lennon's sudden rage for matrimony was not an inexplicable impulse. Quite the contrary, it was a clear case of not wanting to be outdone. Only two days before, the papers had announced the surprising news of Paul McCartney's marriage to Linda Eastman. Not even Paul's closest friends had anticipated the event, but its cause was readily understood: Linda was four months pregnant. So Paul became the third Beatle to "do the right thing." The ceremony was performed at the Marylebone Registry Office, with no other Beatle present. Normally such an event would have made the front pages, but it was bumped off by the even more startling news that George and Patti Harrison had been busted that same day for possession of 120 joints.

John promptly described Paul's marriage as the "dry run" for his own. As had happened so often in the past, both partners did the same thing at the same time because they were in the same boat. (When Paul played "Hey, Jude," John cried: "Grrreat! It's me!" Opening his eyes wide in astonishment, Paul protested: "No! It's me!") What a pity Paul and John could not have enjoyed a double ceremony! The symmetries were perfect.

Linda Eastman was, like Yoko Ono, a product of the haute bourgeoisie. Like Yoko she had lived in Scarsdale and attended Sarah Lawrence. Now she was, like Yoko, divorced and the mother of a six-year-old daughter. Like Yoko, she had been involved with a lot of famous young men, both as a rock photographer and a groupie. She had also had to work just as hard as Yoko to get her Beatle, encountering sometimes violent resistance. (When she had moved into Paul's house in St. John's Wood in the fall of 1968, he confided to Miles: "I hope it doesn't become a problem because the last time she was here, I had to throw her suitcase over the wall.") Perhaps the greatest irony lay in the fact that Linda had been attracted originally to John, just as Yoko later boasted that she could have had Paul.

John and Yoko spent four days at Paris secretly. Then they called Alistair Taylor at Apple and told him they needed transportation to Gibraltar and cash. He met them at Le Bourget with a chartered jet and then had to flag the departing plane down on the runway when he realized he still had the money in his pocket. When the witnesses to the marriage, Peter Brown and a friend, David Nutter, met John and Yoko at the registry office, they found the couple clothed in virginal white. John wore a white sweater, trousers, a long corduroy jacket, and tennis shoes; Yoko was costumed charmingly in a white knitted minidress, sneakers, and a big, floppy-brimmed hat.

During the three-minute ceremony, John stood with his hand in his pocket, smoking a cigarette, while Yoko fidgeted uncomfortably and Nutter kept clicking his camera. Within seventy-five minutes of their arrival on the Rock, Mr. and Mrs. John Lennon were flying back to Paris. John was in high spirits, entertaining Peter Brown and David Nutter with a continuous stream of dirty jokes. Yoko remained silent and pensive throughout the flight.

The French press had been tipped off to the Lennons' marriage. When John and Yoko stepped into the arrival lounge at Le Bourget, they were surrounded by hundreds of people, all eager to hear the famous couples' first statement. "We are both tremendous romantics," proclaimed John, when they got back to their luxurious suite at the Plaza Athénée. "We should have liked to have been married by the Archbishop of Canterbury, but it was impossible because they don't marry divorced people."

Yoko chimed in: "This man rabbiting on about 'Do you take this woman to be your wife'—it was a tremendous experience. Marriage is so old-fashioned. It's like dressing up in old clothes."

Shortly thereafter, returning from lunch with Salvador Dali, the Lennons were set upon by a pack of screaming girls, who started hugging and kissing John. Horrified, Yoko leaped out of the car and screamed at the girls to stop. She told them that they could not behave in this manner any longer. John Lennon belonged now to Yoko Ono.

A few days later the Lennons popped up in Amsterdam, where they held the first of the famous bed-ins at the Hilton Hotel. The idea of harnessing the publicity generated by their marriage for the promotion of peace made perfect sense—after John had explained it a few times.

The concept was a witty example of the Lennons' evolving philosophy
of life as art and art as life. Treating their honeymoon as a public event
was itself a topsy-turvy joke. At the same time, they were exploiting
(and confirming) their reputation as a couple of notorious screwballs.
As John recalled the first bed-in, "These guys were sweating to get in
first because they thought we were going to be making love in bed—
naked, bed, John and Yoko *sex*!" Yet when the reporters were gathered
about the bed, they found a couple of white-clad figures who looked
like patients in a hospital delivering a message that could have been
issued by the pope at Easter. "What we're really doing," said John, "is
sending out a message to the world, mainly to the youth, to anybody
who is interested in protesting for peace or protesting any form of
violence." John summed up the message in one colloquial phrase:
"Give peace a chance."

As the phrasing of John's famous chant suggests, the model for all
the Lennons' peace propaganda was Madison Avenue advertising. John
believed deeply in the power of images and slogans to affect the mass
mind. He was sure that during his years as a Beatle he had mastered
the techniques of manipulating the media, and of course, he had a very
able partner in this work in Yoko Ono, who had devoted her life to
self-promotion. So once the Lennons embarked on their peace mission,
they organized their efforts exactly the way a radio or TV station does
its daily broadcast schedule. After a breakfast of tea and toast, the Lennons would go on the air from 10:00 A.M. to 10:00 P.M., presenting ten
one-hour programs a day. The only significant interruption in the daily
broadcast schedule occurred in midmorning, when the Portuguese
chambermaid would roust her famous guests so that she could change
the sheets, an operation that was duly photographed and often telecast.
Otherwise, no interruptions were permitted in the rigidly maintained
schedule of operations.

Every hour a fresh crowd of reporters and photographers was admitted to Studio Bed Peace, where they sat on the floor or stood with
their cameras and notepads, recording the performance. John and
Yoko would take turns speaking, exactly like those teams of male and
female hosts on breakfast television in the States. The resemblance was
not perfect, of course; not only were John and Yoko a pretty weird-
looking pair of co-hosts, but they were also strangely impassive because
they were strung out on junk. In fact, even at close quarters they appeared more like images on a black-and-white screen than they did
flesh-and-blood people.

Neither John nor Yoko had anything interesting to say about peace,
though they spent hundreds of hours discoursing on the topic. Yoko
Ono filled the media with great dollops of cotton-candy double-talk.
Her principal philosophic influence appears to have been the notion of

the "guilt we all share." Here, in Amsterdam, the first city in Western Europe to feel the destructive fury of the Luftwaffe, she was speaking to a population that for four horrible years had been subject to the exactions, the penal discipline, and the slave labor levies of the Nazis— and what did she say? "When Nazism persecuted the Jewish people, that wasn't only Hitler who did it, or Germany who did it, but just a symbol of everybody in the world who had the feeling of persecution of Jews—you see? . . . If there's war suddenly, that's our fault, you know." What a lesson for the Dutch!

Actually, it would have been unreasonable to expect that either John or Yoko would have had anything to contribute to the discussion of peace. John had no understanding of or faith in the political process. When warned that if the Beatles bought a Greek island as a retreat, they would be playing into the hands of the fascist regime of the colonels, John had replied, "I don't care if the government is all Fascist or Communist. . . . They're all the same." Never once in his entire lifetime did John Lennon cast a ballot or regret that he hadn't done so. Yoko was even less political than John, if that be possible, having never before uttered a word about such issues. Yet she was clearly the instigator of the bed-ins, her model being, most likely, Yayoi Kusama, the artist Yoko credited with teaching her the importance of nudity. Kusama's demonstrations against the Vietnam war had taken the spectacular form of her appearing naked in the citadels of American capitalism, such as the New York Stock Exchange or the Federal Treasury. If Yoko had not been married to a man as basically reserved as John Lennon, the bed-ins might have taken a much more drastic form. Also, they would not have been confined to bed.

However the bed-ins are judged as a contribution to world peace, they were highly effective in overcoming all the bad publicity the Lennons had received. No better device could have been found for exorcising the nasty image of John and Yoko as drug-crazed adulterers than the image of saintly white-clad peace gurus, exhibiting themselves without a trace of prurience in their marital bed.

The media, which had tuned out John and Yoko a year before, went gaga over the bed-ins. Overnight the new image caught on, and cartoonists everywhere had a great time putting ill-sorted people 'twixt the sheets. Yet at the same moment that the public and the press were amusing themselves at the Lennons' expense, John and Yoko were becoming the heroes of a new constituency—the worldwide antiwar movement. Like all political activists, the war protesters took their allies and icons where they could find them. If John and Yoko were willing to spend their honeymoon sitting in bed twelve hours a day pleading for peace, they were ipso facto peacenik heroes, which further encouraged the Lennons.

Even if the inspiration for the bed-ins originated in John and Yoko's desire to refurbish their badly tarnished image, their continued dedication to the cause, which soon assumed the form of an obsession, implies some deeper motivation. In John Lennon's case, this ulterior motive is not hard to figure out. For from his very first interviews in Amsterdam, Lennon made it clear that for him demonstrating for peace was the same thing as demonstrating against violence. To the Dutch press John asserted: "I'm as violent as the next man, and I'm sure Yoko is just as violent. We're violent people, you know. I prefer myself when I'm nonviolent." This was a remarkably candid statement, but it revealed only half the truth. John Lennon was *more* violent than the next man, and he knew it. That John was, in fact, seeking to purge himself of blood guilt by proclaiming a crusade against violence, was brought out clearly in one of his last interviews, when he remarked: "It is the most violent people who go in for love and peace . . . I am a violent man who has learned not to be violent and regrets his violence."

After a week in bed John and Yoko went to Vienna, where they had been invited to witness the TV premiere of their film *Rape,* the theme of which was the relentless pursuit of an attractive woman by a film crew. Checking into the Sacher, the elegant old hotel behind the Opera, the Lennons prepared their next publicity stunt. First they plastered a handsome crimson-walled public salon with placards proclaiming BAGISM, BED, PEACE, TOTAL COMMUNICATION, STAY IN BED, GROW YOUR HAIR, IT'S SPRING, I LOVE JOHN, I LOVE YOKO. Then, while the representatives of the media gathered in the hotel lobby, John and Yoko returned to their room and fashioned the white bedcover into a sack. "We came down the elevator in the bag," John recalled, "and we went in and we got comfortable, and they were all ushered in."

The Viennese journalists were puzzled to find a huge white sack lying upon a low table. When they realized that this bag contained the world-renowned John Lennon and Yoko Ono, they were nonplussed. "It was a very strange scene," continued John, "because they'd never seen us before or heard—Vienna is a pretty square place. A few people were saying, 'C'mon, get out of the bag.' And we wouldn't let 'em see us. They all stood back, saying, 'Is it really John and Yoko?' and 'What are you wearing and why are you doing this?' We said, 'This is total communication without prejudice.' It was just great! They asked us to sing, and we sang a few numbers. Yoko was singing a Japanese folk song, very nicely, just very straight we did it. And they never did see us."

With the bed-ins, John and Yoko established a wholly new identity. Henceforth they would not be merely stars or celebrities; they would join that new class of pop eminences represented best by the "Pope," Andy Warhol, and the "Rabbi," Allen Ginsberg, popular and controversial artists who had evolved into commanding public figures because their greatest talent was for self-promotion. John and Yoko were even better endowed for this role, being such stuff as myths are made upon. Their myth received its title now from a hastily scribbled song about their honeymoon—"The Ballad of John and Yoko." An undistinguished example of Lennon's diary style, this composition tells how the perfect lovers have been pilloried in the press, busted by the cops, persecuted by the other Beatles and, finally, forced to hide away. John was so paranoid by now that even such a slight and predictable impediment as the refusal of the immigration officers to allow the couple to board the Channel ferry without passports inspired him to raise the cry of crucifixion.

This complaint would be amplified and broadcast in every direction in the years to come, until it became the most basic feature of Lennon's life. It evinced itself most clearly in the way he dealt with criticism. Every day he would subject to minute scrutiny everything said in the media about himself and his wife. After identifying the critical voices, he would take appropriate countermeasures. These would range from chewing out a writer or commentator on the phone to sending a vicious letter to an editor to making a cutting and embarrassing remark (like an allusion to a woman writer's thick legs) on radio or TV. John was absolutely convinced that people were out to get him—and he was just as determined to get them in turn.

After their honeymoon, John and Yoko decided to reverse their field: instead of hiding out at home, they would go public full-time as leaders of a world peace crusade. To achieve this ambitious goal, they needed a large, well-equipped office and a staff at their command. They found exactly what they required as a base of operations in the handsome and lavishly appointed Georgian house at 3 Savile Row that was the headquarters of Apple Corps.

Apple was inspired originally by the accountants' demand that the Beatles found their newly established business entity on real commerce, like a string of apparel shops. The first embodiment of the concept was Apple Clothing, a chic fashion boutique designed and stocked with delightful clothes by the premier artificers of hippie fashion, the Fool. The second manifestation was radical: in May 1968 Apple issued a call to young artists to submit their work for possible funding and development. Hundreds of demos, manuscripts, treatments, and designs came pouring in upon the Beatles. Paul and George signed up and produced such gifted newcomers as James Taylor, Mary Hopkin, and Badfinger; John spent a couple of weeks auditioning people whom he viewed with

undisguised contempt and then washed his hands of the whole business. Meantime, the boutique, which had lost a lot of money in its first
eight months of operation, was being led back toward profitability by
John Lyndon, when one day—after the appearance of an article in the
press that mocked the Beatles for turning into rag merchants—Yoko
Ono made an impassioned appeal to the group to close down the shop.
"John," Yoko demanded, "we must get rid of this ridiculous shop.
John, it is good to give it all away, *all away*!" As Lyndon looked on,
astounded: "Yoko drove right over the Beatles and persuaded them in
twenty minutes to shut down the store."

The decision was disastrous, for in addition to costing the Beatles
£112,000 in stock, plus the expense of renovating the building, etc., the
company forfeited the price of the fall merchandise, which had already
been ordered. When the shop was thrown open to plunder on 31 July,
the foremost looters were John and Yoko (John loved Apple and had
been its principal advocate). Toting great hobo packs of clothing, they
loaded up their white Roller. John had a marvelous time, exulting: "It
was just like robbing!"

Now, having made no further contributions to the business since
that happy day, John Lennon suddenly reappeared at Apple in the
spring of 1969, like a king returning from exile with his queen, and
took command of the entire establishment. One day the staff of thirty
would be dispatched to find acorns, which the Lennons were intent on
sending to world leaders as peace symbols. Another day everyone
would have to answer all the mail that came pouring in as a response to
John and Yoko's latest appeal. "Media saturation" was the Lennons'
goal, according to the "house hippie," Richard DeLello: "Cajole, convert, argue, bully, but keep saying it over and over again. Peace! Peace!
Peace!"

Barraging Europe with peace appeals was not the best way to
achieve peace because it was the Americans, not the Dutch, French, or
Viennese, who were at war with the Vietnamese. So one day late in
May John and Yoko arrived at the dock from which the *Queen Elizabeth
2* was about to sail, accompanied by Kyoko Cox, Derek Taylor, Tony
Fawcett (their new assistant), a two-man film crew, and twenty-six
pieces of luggage. When they presented their passports to the emigration officials, they were shocked to learn that their application for a visa
to the United States had been rejected automatically because of John
Lennon's conviction for possession of hashish. Undismayed, the Lennons drove out to Heathrow and boarded a BOAC flight to the
Bahamas. No sooner did they arrive at the hotel at Kingston than they
recognized that they had chosen the wrong place from which to conduct a media blitz. Again, they changed course, flying north to
Toronto, where, after being detained for two hours at the airport, they

were admitted. On 26 May they stretched out in bed on the nineteenth floor of the Queen Elizabeth Hotel in Montreal, prepared to saturate the media.

Derek Taylor estimated that during the one week the Lennons held forth from their bed in Montreal, they spoke with an average of 150 press people daily and called more than 350 U.S. radio stations to talk peace. During one remarkable conversation, an announcer at KPFA at Berkeley was seeking the peace guru's advice in the midst of a tremendous student battle with the police over the so-called People's Park. When he was told the students demanded that John say what to do, he grew alarmed and exhorted them to use their heads to avoid a fight. As is clear from the original version of "Revolution," John was highly ambivalent about whether he wanted to be counted in or out of the explosive radicalism of the day.

The most important Happening at Montreal was the composition and recording of "Give Peace a Chance." Lennon wrote this song during the bed-in and then decided impulsively to record it on the spot. A portable four-track recorder was rushed to his bedside, and a chorus of fifty fans recruited from outside the hotel. When word of the session went out, John was joined by a group of celebrities: Timothy and Rosemary Leary, Tommy Smothers, Petula Clark, Murray the K, Dick Gregory, as well as an ecumenical trio comprising a priest, a rabbi, and the Canadian chapter of the Radha Krishna Temple. Pasting the words on the wall, John led the singing vigorously from his bed, the room blazing with the hot white lights of a film crew.

Lennon envisioned himself at this moment as standing squarely in the tradition of the American civil rights movement. "In me secret heart," he confessed, "I wanted to write something that would take over 'We Shall Overcome.'" "Give Peace a Chance" took wings immediately because it voiced what was uppermost in millions of peoples' minds.

CRACK UP!

KENWOOD, JUNE 1969

"You're going to drive!" snapped Yoko. John bowed to his wife's command as if he were Uncle George submitting to Aunt Mimi. Then he sat contemplating the unwelcome task that lay ahead of him. He had to drive virtually the entire length of Great Britain, from Sussex to Sangobeg, at the northernmost tip of Scotland. For a man accustomed to lolling about on the back seat of a limousine, listening to rock, gazing at the telly, and feeling the euphoria of his acid thermos, it was a big order. Why was it necessary? Because Yoko had decided to make John *"act like a man."*

That phrase was constantly on her lips now that they were married. The words embodied precisely the same complaint that Yoko had made to Al Carmines years before about Tony Cox. John simply wasn't a man! What makes a man? Well, the most obvious thing, as Yoko saw it, was that a man should be able to do all the things she was afraid to do—like driving a car.

John must have felt rumblings of foreboding the moment he acceded to his wife's demand. Though he rarely drove, he had managed to have quite a few accidents, all of which had been hushed up by the police. What was his problem? It wasn't just his bad vision or his short attention span or his drug addiction. The real trouble was that anything requiring the slightest degree of motor coordination imposed a heavy burden upon Lennon. If he had been examined by a neurologist, the doctor would have been obliged to put a tick next to virtually every symptom on the list of "multiple developmental defects": poor coordination; jerky, spastic movements; reversing letters in reading and writing; inability to perform simple acts like driving or operating domestic appliances. (But what about his guitar playing? Wasn't he one of rock's greatest rhythm guitarists? That claim would be hard to judge from the Beatles' records because John is always hidden inside

350

the mix. You hear Paul on bass, George on lead, Ringo on drums—but where is John? It is not until later years, when he struck out on his own, and later still, when his demos came floating to the surface, that you could finally judge Lennon as a guitarist. And then two things are unmistakable: he plays with an iron-fingered rigidity that summons up visions of Parkinson's disease, and when he departs from rudimentary strumming to essay melodic figures he betrays a clumsy ineptitude.)

John would never have undertaken to drive any distance but for Yoko's insistence. In fact, the whole excursion was totally out of character. It arose from a rare paternal impulse triggered by the announcement that Tony was sending Kyoko to Britain for a visit. Instantly, John conceived the idea of a sentimental journey to the scenes of his childhood with his son and Yoko's daughter. It's easy to imagine the relish with which he anticipated showing them the Cavern or Woolton or his old haunts in Liverpool 8. When they had done the sights of Liddypool, they could drive up to Edinburgh, where Aunt Mater was still going strong with Uncle Bert. Then would come the best part of the trip: the journey to the Highlands, the region where John had experienced his happiest moments as a child and the first strong stirrings of his vocation as an artist. At the Sutherlands' sheep croft near Durness, Julian and Kyoko could enjoy all the things that had delighted John as a child: the primitive, earth-hugging house, the northern sea, and the windblown heath with its wild beauty.

Sad to say, what should have been a relaxed and trippy experience, a deliberate courting of all those spontaneous reminiscences that going home can evoke in the mind of an artist, became now an act of torture on the wheel. The folly of Yoko's insistence that John play the chauffeur was obvious by the time they got to Liverpool. John was having trouble with the shift on his green-and-yellow Mini (chosen to avoid recognition). Pulling into a service station, he asked the mechanic to have a look. The man reported that John had destroyed everything in the gearbox.

Les Anthony drove up immediately with John's other everyday car, a white Maxi, which Les offered to pilot for the balance of the trip. Yoko would not hear of Les driving. Poor John had to resume his masculine duties and haul the family up the road to Edinburgh. What's more, instead of staying in first-class hotels, Yoko decreed they stop in dreary bed-and-board establishments, where, she insisted, they would not be recognized.

Somehow John—tense, jerky, fighting to keep his mind on the road—got the family up to Bert and Mater's sheep croft near the village of Sangobeg. Here John found his old playmate Cousin Stanley Parkes, with his attractive wife, Janet. John could relax at last. Only he couldn't! Yoko would not condescend to the level of these common folk, John's family. She withdrew behind her mask of inscrutability. "Yoko would sit in the corner and hardly say a peep," complained Stanley. "I could never get anything out of her—just stupid little sentences. Nobody in the family liked her. When John took her down to the pub, where he met people he had known in childhood, the locals said she was an 'apparition.' Her daughter was a precocious little brat— a horror! She absolutely browbeat Julian. My mother got on Yoko and said, 'You shouldn't let that little terror overpower Julian.'"

The contrast between John's and Yoko's children *was* startling. Kyoko talked like a stoned adult and behaved as imperiously as her mother. Julian was as silent and hapless as a blob. A newspaper photographer in Edinburgh snapped a remarkable picture of the Lennons with their plaid-clad kids. Before the heavily bearded John sits Julian, without a ripple of expression on his face, his eyes averted from the camera, an impassive baby of six. In front of Yoko hunches six-year-old Kyoko, her two bold black eyes confronting the camera like gun barrels.

On the first day of July, Mater urged John to show Yoko the most impressive scenic feature of the district, the Kyle of Tongue, a deep glacial bay of spectacular beauty. Stanley explained to John that the road was only one lane with a lay-by every sixty yards. If a car appeared from the opposite direction, John should make for the nearest lay-by or allow the oncoming driver to pull off first. John took off with Julian riding beside him in the front seat and Yoko sitting with Kyoko in the back seat. Driving around Loch Eriboll, a deepwater port ringed with bare hills, John reached the Kyle and began cruising along its shores.

Looking up the road, he saw a car approaching. Neither vehicle was moving rapidly. Visibility was perfect. Suddenly John panicked. He flung up his hands as if he had been galvanized. The white Maxi hurtled off the road and slammed into a ditch. They all were thrown forward violently, striking their heads against the dashboard, the windshield, or the side walls of the car.

What happened next enraged Yoko every time she thought about it, for years to come. John forced his way out of the front door and, dragging Julian after him, got free of the car. When he realized that he wasn't badly hurt, he seized the boy and began dancing about like a mad troll. *"We're alive! We're alive!"* he caroled gleefully. Yoko, stunned, bleeding from facial wounds, suffering pain and hearing the howls of her child next to her, was furious that John had no thought for her. What she failed to realize was how relieved John must have felt at this moment. He had to know he need never drive again.

The other motorist picked up the Lennons and carried them twenty-five miles down the road to Lawson General Hospital at Golspie. Here a surgeon set to work, X-raying them all for concussions and fractures as well as sewing up their wounds. Yoko was the worst hurt. She required fourteen stitches in her face. As she was again pregnant, an X ray was taken to determine the condition of the fetus, which proved secure. Kyoko got four stitches in her lip, and John received seventeen stitches in his head. Julian suffered only from shock and was released soon in the custody of Mater. The Lennons were kept under observation for five days because the serious consequences of collisions, like subdural bleeding, are sometimes slow to declare themselves.

The moment the news of the crash went out on the wire, Cynthia headed north, escorted by Peter Brown. Ten minutes after their Viscount took off from Glasgow Airport, en route to Aberdeen, a full-scale emergency developed aboard the plane. Vibrations of unknown origin rattled the pressurized cabin. Glasgow Airport prepared for a crash landing, but the pilot contrived to get the ship back on the ground without mishap. Shaken but determined, Cynthia retrieved her son from Mater without saying a word to John or Yoko.

When the Lennons were discharged from the hospital, they were flown home in a helicopter. Yoko staggered out of the plane and took to her bed. A few days later the wrecked Maxi was hauled onto the property. When John looked inside, he was fascinated by the blood all over the seats, particularly in the back seat. "Oh, grrreat!" he enthused. "Don't touch it!" he commanded the astonished Les Anthony. "Leave it just as it is!" Eventually Yoko got the idea of putting the car atop a concrete pedestal in front of the living-room windows so that when the family looked out on the lawn, they would feel grateful for their survival.

John and Yoko weren't allowed much time to recuperate because John's presence was urgently needed at the studio, where the Beatles were at work on *Abbey Road.* John groaned at the prospect of cutting again with Paul, but with the new royalty rate about to take effect a lot of money was at stake. Yoko insisted on being present at the sessions despite doctor's orders that she remain in bed until she recovered from the back injury she had suffered in the crash. So on the appointed day a huge bed from Harrod's was delivered to Abbey Road. For the next couple of weeks Yoko lay within its comfortable folds, knitting, reading, or sleeping but always keeping a Mimi-like eye on John. Meantime, the Beatles, once again under the supervision of George Martin, labored as late as four in the morning. The result of their highly professional efforts was a highly professional album.

Abbey Road marks a deliberate reversion to the Beatles' middle-of-the-road manner, Paul's aim being, as John saw it, to produce "something slick to preserve the myth." The B-side of the album is an extended medley of the sort Paul is so clever at producing, which gathered up all the scraps of unfinished songs that had accumulated over the years on the Beatles' workbenches. John took a very dim view of this contrivance, complaining that "none of the songs had anything to do with each other, no thread at all, only the fact that we stuck them together." Actually, the medley tracked very smoothly and soared off like a kite sustained by a powerful updraft of show-biz nostalgia. But it was nostalgia for the movie musicals of the forties, when the Beatles were babies. What gives here in the year 1969? The answer lies partly in the culture, saturated with Pop Art nostalgia, partly in Paul McCartney's soul, wedded to a show-biz imagery he had glimpsed in early childhood. The final product was prophetic of Glam Rock, the next big trend in pop music.

Abbey Road succeeded perfectly in giving the impression Paul wished to convey that all was well with the Beatles. But the long-impending crisis was fast coming to a head. One night Paul chose to stay home and enjoy a candlelit supper with Linda rather than go to the studio. When Lennon realized that he had turned out for a session that was not going to happen, he grew so enraged that he had himself driven to Paul's house, where he climbed over the front wall, barged into the living room, and tore off the wall a painting he had done at art school and given to his partner years before. As Paul and Linda gaped in astonishment, John put his foot through the center of the canvas.

A VOTE FOR PEACE IS A
VOTE FOR LENNON

One Friday afternoon in September 1969 John Lennon picked up the phone on his desk and found himself listening to a young Canadian promoter who was pitching a stadium concert starring Chuck Berry, Fats Domino, Gene Vincent, Bo Diddley, and Little Richard. As those famous names reverberated in Lennon's mind, he suddenly remarked: "The only way we would come is if we could play." *Play!* The promoter had only been hoping that John would attend. Would the Beatles, who hadn't performed publicly in three years, turn out now on the spur of the moment to play in the *Toronto Rock and Revival Show* at Varsity Stadium? The idea was too good to be true. Next thing the promoter heard was Lennon barking to his staff: "Get me George on the phone. . . . Get me Clapton!" Then John explained that he would come with Yoko and an all-star band, but since they had less than thirty-six hours to get themselves together and across the Atlantic, he was going to ring off right now!

The long-haired hippie at the other end of the line was stunned. He rallied quickly, however, because he was a born hustler. John Brower, twenty-three-year-old scion of a distinguished family that had long stood at the forefront of Canadian politics, had gone to school with the sons of all the best families, but then he had taken off for California, where he had tried to make it as a rock musician. Coming home dead broke, and with a wife and kid to support, he had borrowed some money from his rich friends and promoted this concert—which was turning out to be a terrible bomb. Only 800 tickets had been sold to a stadium that holds 20,000. The lawyers were urging the backers to declare bankruptcy when somebody suggested that Brower call John Lennon, known to be crazy about old rock 'n' roll acts.

Lennon's promise to appear should have guaranteed an instant sellout; instead, it was like the big check that nobody will cash. When Brower called the radio stations to give them the thrilling news, they didn't believe him. "Don't bullshit us," they sneered. "We know the tickets are soft!" So the kid called Apple again, and this time he taped Tony Fawcett reading a list of the people who were coming: John Lennon, Yoko Ono, Eric Clapton, Klaus Voorman. Jesus! What more could you want? Now the stations said: "You guys are really desperate. You've got somebody with an English accent faking a phone call."

Allen Klein didn't help much either. "It's bullshit!" he told the press. "They're not going on."

By this time, with the hour hand on the clock slowly lowering the show into its grave, Brower was frantic. He called Lennon again and taped *his* voice. Still, no dice! Finally, some DJ in Detroit played the tape over the air—and the show was saved. Ten thousand tickets were sold on the day of the concert. Meantime, John Lennon had decided *not to go!*

After spending all night searching for Eric Clapton, on whose support Lennon had counted, John had crashed at 5:30 Saturday morning. When Clapton was finally roused from a narcotized sleep, he rushed to the airport but arrived too late for the morning flight. He and the other musicians, bassist Klaus Voorman and drummer Alan White, called John's home for instructions. Lennon was so kacked out he couldn't get out of bed. "Send them roses, love from John and Yoko, but we can't make it," he mumbled, and hung up.

Clapton was furious. Grabbing the phone, he called again and barked: "Listen, motherfucker—I'm not at the fuckin' airport for a joke! You guys get your asses out here—or don't ask me for any more favors, ever!" The Lennons and the Richters arrived in time for the 3:15 flight.

The long haul over the ocean witnessed a comical effort to rehearse with unamplified electric guitars, which only produced the annoying discovery that Lennon could not recollect the lyrics to any songs save those he had sung at the Cavern. Then John and Eric began to sicken. Junkies, they needed a dose of their medicine, but they feared if they got high, they might not be able to play. They decided to tough it out. Soon John was down on his knees in the toilet, puking up his skinny guts. To soothe his ragged nerves, after each bout of vomiting, he would smoke a joint with his no-trace technique: After each toke he would put his face in the sink and press the drain release, which would suck the smoke down the pipe. Finally, at 4:00 P.M., the plane landed. After a hassle with the emigration officers because Yoko had not been vaccinated, the strung-out British rock stars stepped out of the terminal and straight into a horde of black-leather-clad bikers—the Vagabonds, Canada's counterparts of the Hell's Angels.

The pixie-faced Brower had planned Lennon's reception like a rock Ziegfeld. No sooner did the heavily bearded white-suited apostle of peace appear with his Oriental missus, clad in a long orange gown with a red silk jacket, than the bikers went into a replay of reel one of *The Wild One.* They roared down the highway to the stadium, where they drove straight onto the oval, raising their leather-gauntleted fists in acknowledgment of the hysterical cheers of the fans. With forty bikers before and forty behind the royal coach, Lennon arrived like a king. The royal treatment ended abruptly when he was hustled into a cold, raw concrete locker room beneath the stands. At that moment he felt his Jones comin' down.

Always terrified before a public appearance, John had done some crazy things at times like this. Once, in the heyday of the Beatles, he had declared that he was not going onstage until he had gotten his nuts off. His aides had to run around to the house and grab the first girl they saw. Hustling her backstage, they handed her over to John, who ripped off her panties, threw her up against a wall, and raped her. That was the old John Lennon, a smoldering young hitter who sometimes erupted into a terrifying werewolf. Now he was just a poor sick cat, desperate for something to get his head up.

"Can you get us some coke, man?" John asked Brower in a confidential tone.

"No problem!" snapped the young impresario, beside himself with excitement. "Dennis, six Cokes over here, right now!" he yelled. Then, turning with the grin of a man of power on his face, Brower saw John and Yoko give each other a look that wailed: "What have we got ourselves into this time?"

"No, no!" Yoko piped. "Coke for the nose!" making as if to snort something off the back of her hand.

Suddenly Brower snapped to the fact that he was being asked to supply *hard drugs!* He didn't know what to do—but he couldn't afford to fail! So he ran out on stage and grabbed the mike.

Speaking in a deep announcer's voice, he intoned: *"Attention! Dr. Sneiderman! Dr. Sneiderman! Please go to the backstage area."* Then he ducked around to meet a swarthy little guy named David Sneiderman, who arrived scared out of his wits.

"What is it, man!" he gasped. "Is it a bust?" When he heard what was wanted, he cried: "Oh, my God! I thought you were trying to *warn* me! I had coke! I had hash! I threw them on the ground when I heard." Dashing back to his discarded stash, he returned soon with the desperately needed medicine. Brower laid the stuff on John and Yoko; then he watched them scuttle into the bathroom. When they emerged, they didn't look so green.

Now Lennon had to go through a big hassle with Little Richard, who demanded the coveted next-to-closing spot. It's one thing to worship old rock stars from a distance; it's quite another to let them upstage you. John turned Richard down flat; then he had to deal with Jim Morrison, who was making the same demand. The prospect of going on *after* Morrison scared the hell out of Lennon. So Brower read the riot act to Jungle Jim. Finally, John and the hastily named Plastic Ono Band walked out onto the stage "terrified and shaking," according to Clapton, who had just been resuscitated after throwing up and passing out.

The MC ordered the tower lights doused and yelled at the fans to light matches. As everyone held his breath, the emaciated and hirsute hero explained that his band had never played together before; then he kicked off with "Blue Suede Shoes," following it up with his old Mackie Messer number, "Money." In this piece and "Dizzy Miss Lizzy," John showed that he still knew how to phrase those golden oldies—but he simply hadn't the vocal power to put them across. After slogging through "Yer Blues" and the not-yet-released "Cold Turkey," which he had to read off a paper held by Yoko, Lennon was glad to sing "Give Peace a Chance" and hang it up.

Now Yoko got her chance. She had ducked into a white bag at the start of the set, holding a mike through which she had joined the band by producing sounds like tape chatter. Now with her face glowing with joy—in contrast with John's expression of apathetic melancholia—she proceeded to take over the whole show. Hurling herself into a wordless rave-up titled "Don't Worry, Kyoko (Mummy's Only Looking for a Hand in the Snow)," she yodeled for twenty minutes straight against a vigorous riff and then a ululating drone of feedback produced by the band laying their guitars against the amps. Soon the hard-core fans in the front rows were shouting obscene insults at the stage and walking out in protest. Yoko was very upset. As John helped her off, he sought to comfort her. "Don't worry, baby," he pleaded. "I'll make it up to you!"

This embarrassing fiasco would have brought another man to his senses, but Lennon was so thrilled by the mere fact that he had braved the stage without the Beatles that he told Allen Klein on the return flight that as soon as they landed, he was going to announce his departure from the group and the establishment of a new band with Eric Clapton and Klaus Voorman. Klein, who had just spent the toughest nine months of his life trying to save the Beatles, must have felt like opening the emergency hatch and stepping out. Instead, he kept his cool and persuaded John at least to wait until they collected their big advance from Capitol. What Allen couldn't do was curb John's impulse to kick Paul's teeth down his throat.

At the Beatles' next meeting Paul renewed his pleas for unity. To everything he suggested, John turned a deaf ear, until finally Paul was reduced to asking, "When all is said and done, we're still Beatles, aren't we?"

"Ah, fuck!" sneered John. "I ain't no Beatle!"

"Of course, you are!" scolded Paul, like a hurt and angry parent.

"I'm not!" cried John, the eternal child. "Don't you understand?" he insisted. "It's over. *Over!* I want a divorce, just like the divorce I had from Cynthia! Can't you get it through your bloody head?" Then, pausing, he confided: "I wasn't gonna tell you this until after our new record deal, but I'm leaving the group." Paul and the other Beatles stared at John in amazement. "It feels great," John went on, gaining conviction from the sound of his own voice. "It feels like a divorce. It's a great relief now that I've got that off my chest. I'm glad I told you!" Then, without allowing another moment for discussion, John turned on his heel and rushed out of the office and down the stairs, followed by Yoko as he shouted: *"It's over! Finished!"*

On 9 October, the date of John's twenty-ninth birthday, Yoko was rushed to King's College Hospital for an emergency blood transfusion. Four days later the papers carried the news that she had miscarried again. To recover from the ordeal, John and Yoko flew to Athens and boarded a yacht that Magic Alex had rented for them. The last time the Beatles had gone sailing on the Aegean, during the Summer of Love, John and George had sat out on deck every night chanting the Hare Krishna mantra under the stars while accompanying themselves on banjo-ukuleles. Now John and Yoko, having sworn to purge themselves of every form of filth, from drugs to dung, sought to combine kicking with fasting by subsisting on a diet of pure water. The result was one explosion of violence after another, with John wrecking the master cabin and knocking the hell out of Yoko.

When the unhappy couple got back to London, they issued the *Wedding Album,* an elaborate celebration of their happy marriage. The lavish package contained a copy of the wedding license, a plastic wedding cake slice, a portfolio of John's sketches of the wedding ceremony and honeymoon, a postcard from the Amsterdam Hilton, a strip of photo machine snapshots, and a huge two-sided poster composed of David Nutter's photos of the wedding and the flight to Paris. Part fan mag and part souvenir program, part concept art and part avant-garde "box," the album lacked only one thing—music. On the A-side, John and Yoko took turns screaming each other's name; the flip side reproduced a typically tedious press interview.

* * *

John Lennon's next stunt made headlines in Britain. On 25 November he returned his MBE medal, with a note to the queen, reading: "Your Majesty, I am returning your MBE in protest against Britain's involvement in the Nigeria-Biafra thing, against our support of the American troops in Vietnam and against 'Cold Turkey' slipping down the charts. With love, John Lennon." This impudent gesture outraged public opinion anew and inspired many people to denounce Lennon, beginning with his Aunt Mimi, atop whose TV set the cherished medal had long reposed.

By this point, however, Lennon didn't give a damn what his countrymen thought of him because he no longer saw himself as a citizen of backward little Britain. John Lennon was now a world figure and even though the days of rock heroes on the front pages were over, Lennon could qualify in the new arena of high visibility—the politics of peace. Politics, religion, and show business were all coming together now and thereby creating the ideal conditions for John Lennon's metamorphosis from pop hero to peace leader. Thus it was with a genuine sense of rededication that Lennon appeared at Toronto on 16 December 1969 to announce the *Music and Peace Conference of the World*.

The goals of the festival appear fantastic today, but in that time, when the counterculture was at its peak and the worldwide youth movement had been roused to a messianic sense of its mission through Woodstock, such grandiose schemes seemed perfectly feasible. "Bigger than Woodstock" was, in fact, the phrase by which the festival was habitually described, because John and Yoko wanted to revenge themselves upon Woodstock, which had refused to present the famous couple in place of the Beatles. Originally scaled at a half-million people, later upped to two million, the festival would be a vast be-in, encamped upon a well-wooded and watered site called Mosport ("motor sport"), a car-racing track forty miles from Toronto. To entertain this immense horde, John Lennon intended to assemble the greatest bill in rock 'n' roll history, which he would top by appearing side by side with Elvis Presley, while the global village eyeballed the action via satellite TV.

Though the festival would be a mind blower, it would not be an end in itself; quite the contrary, it would simply be the climax of Year One AP ("After Peace"). During the first months of the year millions of ballots would be distributed in every country on earth. The ballots would offer people the basic choice between war and peace. Every vote for peace would be a vote for Lennon. When the election was over, the international Peace Party would set up headquarters in each country, and John Lennon would fly from one center to another as the world peace leader. In fact, even as he proclaimed the festival, giant billboards were being unveiled in a score of major cities around the globe announcing in bold black letters: "WAR IS OVER! If you want it. Happy Christmas from John and Yoko." If everything worked out, John Lennon would bring peace on earth, goodwill to men, single-handed.

The organizer of the festival, John Brower, had been busy for months stage-managing John Lennon's apotheosis. As soon as John had made his announcement to the media, Brower carried off his star to the ten-acre estate of Ronnie Hawkins, near the Toronto Airport. An old-time rock 'n' roller (whose band, the Hawks, had once contained all the members of the Band), Hawkins was trying to make a big comeback on the strength of rock 'n' roll revival. His publicist, Ritchie Yorke, a Canadian journalist, was John Brower's partner in producing the peace festival.

No sooner did the Lennons head off for Hawkins's house than they found they were being chased by a reporter and a photographer who were so desperate to score a beat that they drove straight through the gates of the estate in pursuit of their prey. That was too much for the hot-tempered Brower, determined to protect his stars. Jumping out of the limo, the promoter confronted the journalists in an angry face-down that swiftly escalated into a fight. Brower smashed the picture snapper so hard that he knocked five teeth out of his mouth and broke his jaw. Next morning, the local press blared: PEACE FESTIVAL STARTS WITH BRAWL AT RONNIE HAWKINS' FARM. With one blow, Brower had revealed Lennon's hideout and beckoned the world to his doorstep.

From the moment John and Yoko stepped through the door, they turned Hawkins's mock-Tudor mansion upside down. Three extra phone lines were run in for the duration, the direct line to Apple being kept open twenty-four hours a day to avoid hassling with the overseas operators. Two macrobiotic cooks stood by in the kitchen to prepare at any time the Lennons' food, which consisted primarily of brown rice and bean shoots. Reporters and broadcasters entered and left the house in shifts because John and Yoko stopped working only once— when John mounted a snowmobile for a gag and the damn thing ran away with him. During the visit, Ronnie Hawkins suffered every sort of insult, from seeing his children poring over the muff-diving imagery of Lennon's erotic lithographs to discovering one night that his famous guests had gone to sleep with the water running in their tub, an oversight that brought down the ceiling over the kitchen.

John Lennon, for his part, was furious at Elvis for his repeated refusals to take Lennon's calls.

The Canadian visitation came to its climax a few days before Christmas. First, John met, at the University of Toronto, Pop's greatest pundit, Marshall McLuhan. The dialogue of star and seer testified to Lennon's ability to hold his own with even the fastest, subtlest, and most off-the-wall intellectual. "Language is a form of organized stutter," proclaimed the philosopher of media, getting the game off to a typically stunning start. "Literally, you chop your sounds up into bits in order to talk. Now, when you sing, you don't stutter, so singing is a way of stretching language into long, harmonious patterns and cycles. How do you think about language in songs?" Most men, after a service like that, would have been speechless. Not John Lennon.

Stone cool, he replied: "Language and song to me, apart from being pure vibrations, is just like trying to describe a dream. And because we don't have telepathy, we try and describe the dream to each other, to verify to each other what we know, what we believe to be inside each other. And the stuttering is right—because we *can't* say it. No matter how you say it, it's never how you want to say it."

Bravo! A perfectly played set. As the Lennons got into their white Rolls, McLuhan waved good-bye, calling out, "These portals have been honored by your presence."

The next summit conference was with Pierre Trudeau in Ottawa. A week of intense behind-the-scenes negotiations had gone into this encounter. Brower was keen on having the meeting because he recognized how much cooperation he was going to require from the government of Ontario in mounting his immense festival. It would strengthen his hand enormously if the project had the blessing of the prime minister. Trudeau, for his part, had been persuaded that it would look good for him to receive the Lennons as representatives of the youth constituency—precisely the same reasoning that had made Nixon so well disposed toward Elvis.

Handling the media exploitation of the event required a deft hand because the government would not tolerate any unseemly hoopla. So it was agreed that there would be no preliminary announcement. On the appointed day the press would be alerted at the last minute and given its shot before the public was aware of the event. The night before the meeting the Lennons left Toronto quietly by train, traveling in state aboard a glass-domed observation car fitted with sleeping and dining accommodations and rigged with international communications gear. Again, young John Brower showed that he knew how to showcase his act.

At 10:30 A.M. on 22 December, the media were informed that Pierre Trudeau was about to receive John Lennon and Yoko Ono in the office of the prime minister. Over fifty photographers rushed to the Parliament Buildings. John had costumed himself in a black Cardin suit, wide black silk tie, and swirling black cape, copping the sartorial glamour of the great FDR at Yalta. Government aides ushered the Lennons into Trudeau's oak-paneled office. The prime minister suggested that they commence by inviting in the photographers. Trudeau was pictured shaking hands with John and giving Yoko a hug. Then the PM signed for the press to retire, and the doors of the office closed on the three principals.

If Marshall McLuhan, with his profound absorption in media and his Joycean turn of mind and tongue, was the ideal interlocutor for John Lennon, Pierre Trudeau was the most ill-suited person imaginable. A cloistral figure, who never watched TV or went to movies, the austere Trudeau was notorious for holding himself apart from life as it is really lived. He was visibly nervous when he began his conversation with the Lennons, which took the form of quizzing John about his poetry, his life as a Beatle, the generation gap (an issue in Trudeau's family that became an open wound when Margaret Trudeau got involved with the Rolling Stones), and the Lennons' efforts on behalf of peace. "We talked about everything, just anything you can think of," reported John. "We spent about forty minutes—it was five minutes longer than he'd spent with heads of state!" At the conclusion of the conversation Trudeau said that John and Yoko had given him a positive feeling about the future of youth and its ability to bring peace to the world. Lennon felt just as positive. "If there were more leaders like Mr. Trudeau," he told the press, "the world would have peace."

The encounter with Trudeau confirmed Lennon in his grandiose view of his new mission. "The meeting was a confirmation to John," explained Brower, "that he was acceptable on an international political level. He believed this was the cornerstone on which he could begin to create plans for happenings in every country around the world. . . . John was a very political animal. The thing that politics did and that fame as an entertainer *didn't* do was provide you with an engine for propagating your theories and beliefs. The one thing John would have liked more than anything else was his own political machine. Even though he would profess that politics is bullshit, he just wouldn't call it 'politics.' He'd call it 'peace.'"

COSMIC ROCK

When Ronnie Hawkins got the $5,000 phone bill for the week that John and Yoko had been his guests, he noticed among the many unfamiliar places on the chits the name of Ålborg, a little town in Jutland, on the bleak northern tip of Denmark. This is where Tony Cox was living with his new wife, Melinde Kendall, the blond, bespectacled daughter of a prosperous family in Houston. Tony had met Melinde after returning to London from his postmarital cruise in the spring of 1969. They had been married the following summer at Bellport, Long Island, in a formal church ceremony, in the presence of both the bride's and groom's families, with Kyoko serving as flower girl. That fall the Coxes had left for Denmark, at the invitation of an old friend of Tony and Yoko's, Aage Rosendal Nielsen, who got the newlyweds a teaching job at a little experimental school, Norden Fjord World University.

There had been bad blood between Cox and the Lennons ever since the auto crash in Scotland because John and Yoko had refused to send Tony the medical reports and X rays of Kyoko. Now the Lennons offered to smooth things over by coming to Denmark to pay Kyoko a visit and to discuss her custody. It was two days after Christmas when John and Yoko stepped off the little plane from Copenhagen—and found themselves in a setting for a horror movie.

Tony and Melinde were living in a remote farmhouse surrounded by miles of empty fields buried under deep snowdrifts and raked by Arctic winds off the North Sea. The Lennons, fresh from the comforts of England, suddenly found themselves completely cut off from the outer world, without so much as a telephone. Nor did they find Kyoko running out to greet them. Tony had sequestered the child until he could hammer out the terms of the visitation.

The moment John and Yoko stepped through the door, Cox must have gone to work on them. Indeed, in the light of his subsequent statements and those made by John Lennon, it's easy to imagine his rap. He would have explained that since he had last seen the Lennons, he had gotten into some very heavy stuff that could make an enormous difference in their lives. Melinde had been a member of a psychic cult located at Harbinger Springs near San Francisco, whose leader, Dr. Don Hamrick, was a brilliant man who had written some amazing books. He was a key figure in the effort to promote contact between humankind and extraterrestrials. Hamrick had already made contact with space people in Norway. He could put John and Yoko in touch with the ETs, too. (What Tony wouldn't have said, at least at first, was that Hamrick believed the best way to promote communication between spacemen and earthmen was through the Beatles. He reasoned, sensibly, that nobody on the planet had the hold on people's minds possessed by the Fab Four, who had functioned time and again to introduce new modes of consciousness, like LSD and TM. Hamrick had ordered Melinde, who claimed to be a witch, to do everything in her supernatural power to promote this linkup.)

As Cox warmed to his theme, he must have finally proposed that instead of merely paying a visit, the Lennons consider going into a retreat. They could spend a couple of weeks cleaning out their bodies and minds through fasting and meditating; then they could go on to some heavier stuff, like energy exchange and mental telepathy. They could fly in Dr. Hamrick, who would cure them of their tobacco addiction. And they could fit right into the work that Tony was doing now. As they could see, he had rigged the whole house with video cameras and monitors, the idea being to make a total tape record of their daily life, including even the most intimate activities performed in the bathroom and bedroom. As for drugs, they didn't have to be uptight. Tony had some acid, and Melinde had made a Moroccan concoction called *majoun,* a black, sticky paste that was the same thing as hash oil. Tony liked to put it on his toast in the morning.

For three weeks the Coxes and the Lennons were isolated in their remote farmhouse. When the first visitors arrived, they reported that Tony and John had bonded tightly, and the women were playing demure supportive roles. The talk was that henceforth both couples would live and work together. John was even saying that it might be a good idea to get rid of Allen Klein, who was causing so much dissension, and make Tony their manager.

The first indication John Brower received that Lennon was on a new kick came in a phone call from Denmark. Lennon ordered Brower to arrange transportation to Ålborg for Dr. Don Hamrick, living in the vicinity of Toronto. Brower discovered that Hamrick was living at Peterborough, Ontario, under the alias Z. Charneau.

Around this time Brower received another order from Lennon:

"Get me the dirt on Allen." Worried what these strange requests might portend, Brower and his partner, Ritchie Yorke, decided to visit Denmark. Just before they set out, they were warned by Ronnie Hawkins that Allen Klein was out to "bury" them. The boys didn't take that expression metaphorically. When they arrived at the White House Hotel in Ålborg, the snow-covered little town at the end of the world, they were alarmed to discover under their door a note that read: "Blue peace to you and love, Z." Immediately they began to hear weird horror-movie music playing inside their heads. Ringing up Tony Fawcett, quartered in the town but barred from the Lennon-Cox farmhouse, they demanded to know what was happening. Soon John was on the wire, chuckling and assuring the boys that "Dr. Z. just wants to be friendly." Then they got another call, from Z. Charneau, who invited them to his room.

"I'll never forget," declared Brower, "when Z. opened the door to the room. Both Ritchie and me started to squirm and scratch. We felt like spider webs came out of the room and went onto us. We weren't drunk or stoned. Yet we both had this same, incredible feeling. Hamrick was more than an eyeful. He was about six-foot-three with hair like Baby Huey, long, stringy gray hair. He was wearing shorts but no shirt. He said hello, and then he turned. He had a hole in his back as big as my hand. His spine was showing, and you could see one of his lungs pumping. There were white strings going up and down. The flesh was laced with stitches. Ritchie and I just gasped. He said he had had major surgery in London a month ago. They had wanted him to stay for a couple months and recuperate, but after a week he left. He said he was taking care of himself. His face was very white. He spoke very slowly with a sort of German accent. This guy was obviously dealing from a different deck.

"He immediately begins to tell us that we're part of a very important time in the evolution of man. He goes into a heavy rap about how space people are watching everything that is going on. They are very pleased with the opportunities being made now to contact human beings, and they regard John Lennon as an important person. John had been taken already to northern Norway and been taken up in a spaceship. The next thing Hamrick does is take us over to this table, and here's this scale model of a little Buck Rogers city. It's floating mysteriously about a foot above the table. He runs his hand under it and says, 'I have been given by the space people the antigravity secret. We're building a city above Brazil in the clouds. This is the model and it illustrates the power.'"

That night, while having supper in a restaurant atop the White House hotel, Brower and Yorke got their next surprise. The maître d' came over and handed Brower a bill from a hairdresser, explaining that John Lennon had said Brower would accept the charge. In a few minutes Brower was face-to-face with the hairdresser herself, a young Danish girl who told him a crazy story. She had been summoned that day to the farmhouse where the Lennons were living. "When I got there," she repeated, "Mr. Cox asked me to cut off Kyoko's long hair. Then John Lennon gave me his passport and asked me to cut his hair just like it was in the picture [the photo had been taken in the summer of 1967 before John went to Greece]. So I began, and Yoko started to cry. Next John asked Yoko if she would have her hair cut. She looked horrified and said, 'No!' . . . When John asked a second time, she said, 'Yes.' . . . Then it was Kyoko's turn to cry."

Four hours had been spent cutting everyone's shoulder-length hair to a length of two inches. John was still not satisfied and demanded that he be trimmed to the length of Mia Farrow's hair, four-fifths of an inch.

As John Brower listened to this latest report on Lennon's behavior, he was seized by an overpowering conviction that everything that had happened to him since he stepped off the plane in Ålborg had been carefully arranged by Lennon to blow Brower's mind. Determined now to beat Lennon at his own game, Brower ordered the astonished hairdresser to cut off his shoulder-length locks immediately.

The next morning Brower and Yorke drove out to Tony's isolated farmhouse—with no idea of what they would discover. When they walked in the door, they found John and Yoko, Tony and Melinde sitting around a table looking as if they had been carved from stone. They were all saucer-eyed and crop-headed. The only thing that moved was the fuzzy-headed Kyoko, who stared up at the two strangers and said: "I'm really a girl!" Then the young men noticed that whole house was pervaded by a strange odor that reminded them of flowers and incense. It had apparently been created during the preparation of the black sticky stuff that Melinde was now passing about in a saucer. When Brower tried some of this preparation, he found himself getting so high that he was virtually out of his body. Taking a turn about the house, Brower checked out the bedrooms. The moment he spied the TV gear, he thought: "Closed-circuit wife swapping!" Then he went back and sat down next to Lennon, who was so stoned that when he delivered his opening lecture—on the importance of destroying empty symbols, like long hair—he failed to notice that his promoter's hair had been sheared off already.

Since Brower had last seen his star, a tremendous change had come over John Lennon. Whereas before everything had been world peace, now everything was space and cosmic consciousness. The galactic perspective on the festival proved to be a lot different from the purblind view of a mere earthling. Now John was insisting that the festival be *free,* even though he had stated in writing as recently as 9 December that only a portion of the profit was to be set aside for a peace fund. When Brower asked how they were to find the money to entertain gratis half a million people for three days, Lennon spoke airily of getting donations from private corporations or a subsidy from the Canadian government to promote the image of "Young Canada." Brower felt that he was walking on thin ice when it came to disagreeing with Lennon because he had witnessed so many appalling demonstrations of John's terrible temper. "John was filled with rage that was with him every moment that he lived," observed Brower. "When he really let it out, he was mercilessly scathing. I tell you, you did not want to be at the other end of that barrage. I never saw anybody stand up to him. *Never!*"

Now as Brower and Yorke sat gloomily in the kitchen, contemplating the vast new problems that would be created by this startling demand for a free festival, who should walk into this weird farmhouse at the end of the world but the very man they had been warned was out to "bury" them—Allen Klein!

Brower and Yorke had faithfully executed Lennon's order to "get the dirt on Allen." As Brower explained: "Being the naïve idiots that we were, we went out and canvassed everybody in the industry. People opened up to us because they thought: 'Here's my chance to communicate with John Lennon.' Basically everybody's comments on Klein were the same. 'A very brilliant numbers man, he's never going to come out of anything a loser. Though he may profess artistic sympathies, his game is to get in there and get the cash—and anybody who thinks anything else is crazy!' Of course, we assumed that this was something that was going to be treated with the utmost confidence—top secret! [But] Klein wasn't in the house three minutes, when Lennon reaches over and takes the dossier we had prepared on Klein and says: 'Well, here, Allen, this is what everybody thinks of you. Take a look at this!' Ritchie and I thought, 'That's it! We're going to be buried within fifty yards of this farmhouse.' Klein was very cool. He flips through the thing and smirks and says, 'Oh, yeah, he *would* say that!' Then he looks over at us and says: 'Did you enjoy putting all this information together, boys? I wouldn't have thought you would have had time enough. Surely you're too busy with your little festival.'"

The Danish summit didn't accomplish much. Lennon told Brower and Yorke to prepare a plan for producing a free festival or at most a "free-for-a-dollar" event. They were instructed to have their proposals ready for submission on 1 March. They were also given to understand that Tony Cox would be playing a part in the festival management, along with the people from Harbinger. The more Lennon talked, the more dictatorial he sounded. Finally, the young hippies were astonished to see their hero lean across the table to Allen Klein and, bringing his fist down on the board, announce: "Hitler was *right*, Allen. Hitler was *right*! You've got to *control* the people." On that note the boys from Toronto went out into the cold world on an impossible mission.

When they got back to their poster-plastered office in Canada, they received a call from Tony Cox, who informed them that Lennon had decided to add to the planning staff a couple of people who would assure that the festival had the proper cosmic orientation. He mentioned Don Hamrick and his chief disciple, Leonard Hollahan. Then he dropped a name that went off in Brower's mind like a bomb: David Sneiderman. Brower felt that if Sneiderman were associated with the festival, it would never get the approval of the attorney general of Ontario.

The whole peace bubble burst finally at a tumultuous meeting late in January 1970 at the Jefferson Airplane's house in Haight-Ashbury, where Brower had gone to cool out the West Coast band members, who were pissed off because Lennon had not invited them to perform at the festival. Brower made the mistake of allowing Sneiderman and Hollahan to attend the meeting as Lennon's space senators. It was Hollahan, a gung ho freak with long red curls, who dressed like Oscar Wilde in purple velvet, who really broke up the meeting. After going through a long rap about the imminence of a hookup with ETs, he produced plans for a "kosmic kraft" that looked like a bubble-bodied helicopter with a huge inverted dish instead of a rotor. Explaining that the vehicle operated entirely on psychic energy, he announced that John and Yoko were going to arrive at the festival riding in this engineless wonder. *"This is bullshit!"* shouted Paul Kantner of the Airplane. "Space people and air cars! If that's what John and Yoko want— *fuck them!"*

Jann Wenner also freaked out. He had been ballyhooing the festival on the front page of *Rolling Stone* and offering his unlimited support. Now he suddenly saw himself sitting way out on the end of a twisted limb. "How could you do this to me!" he kept gasping in Brower's face. The promoter didn't know which way to turn.

Two days later, on the afternoon of 26 January, John Lennon awoke in England with the words of a cryptic little song running around inside his head. Its key phrase was an expression of Melinde's, "instant karma." A hippie expression, meaning "immediate retaliation," it struck a chord in Lennon's mind because it voiced his conviction that we must pay for the wrongs we do in *this* world. After jotting down the verses on the paper he kept by the bed for this purpose, Lennon padded downstairs and seated himself at the piano in the sunroom. Paul would have come in handy, but there was no Paulie, now, so

John's cue was: "Go for what you know!" Instinctively he began pounding out his favorite chord sequence, the steplike motif of "Three Blind Mice"—ironically, the very same phrase he had used for the totally different concept of "All You Need Is Love." Magically the words fell into place. Fearful that he would forget what he had done, John sang the strain over and over again, until he had fixed it firmly in his mind. Then he picked up the phone and called Apple, thus setting in motion one of the fastest and most brilliant productions of his entire career.

Lennon summoned to the studio George Harrison, Klaus Voorman, and the drummer Alan White, but he wanted all the help he could muster, so he took advantage of the presence in London of Phil Spector, requesting that he, too, come by. John himself set off for the studio late in the afternoon, stopping along the way at a piano store, where, without getting out of the car, he ordered that one of the instruments in the window be trucked out to Abbey Road, pronto. By seven that night the band was laying down the rhythm track, but when they got to the next stage—overdubbing the vocal and instrumental solos—they stuck fast. Lennon was crying, "Help!" when in walked Phil Spector.

Though John had never worked with Spector before, he installed the producer immediately behind the console and went back to singing with the band. When Spector called the musicians into the booth for the first playback, Lennon recalled: "It was fantastic! It sounded like there were fifty people playing." By beefing up the sound, Spector had not only made the band sound bigger but had made Lennon's voice sound more powerful, which is what John had always clamored for from George Martin. Every time John heard a straight recording of himself, he cried out in anguish: "*Do* something with my voice! Smother it with tomato ketchup!" Smothering music with extraneous sounds was Phil Spector's specialty; hence, from the moment of that first playback, Lennon must have felt that he had finally found the right producer.

Meantime, Spector, recognizing doubtless the importance of this opportunity to cut deep into the Beatles—the very band that had put him out of business—started coming up with all his favorite tricks. At one point he had Lennon playing one piano while White and Harrison hammered at either end of another piano and Voorman comped on an electric keyboard. At another point in the session, Spector ordered White to lay a bath towel over his tomtom. Finally, Phil decided to heighten the contrast between the chorus and the refrain by employing a vocal chorus in the latter. A couple of gofers rushed out of the studio, making for the Speakeasy, where they quickly rounded up a chorus of revelers, who came back to the studio and sang their hearts out for the fun of it. By dawn the track was finished.

When the tape came blasting out of the studio monitors, everybody stood about in awe. The steady tramp of the massed keyboards, underscored by the rolling thunder of the drums, produced a doomsday atmosphere into which the ominous-sounding Lennon intoned his warnings like Jehovah.

Despite everything he had done, Spector still wasn't satisfied. "Can I take it back to the States and overdub violins on it, John?" he demanded. Lennon refused, point-blank—but that didn't stop Spector. Though he had to surrender the original tape to EMI, the copy he sent to Capitol was surreptitiously remixed, and into the runoff groove was scratched PHIL & RONNIE. "It's the only time anyone's done *that!*" joked John, who was so infatuated with his new producer that though he could read the names in the groove, he could not read the writing on the wall.

Before Lennon left the studio that morning, he ordered Tony Fawcett to call John Brower and play him the tape. Brower received the call around midnight in a bungalow at the Beverly Hills Hotel, where he was closeted with some reporters from the underground press. Thrilled by the title (Brower's company was Karma Productions), the young promoter assumed that Lennon had written a song to plug the festival. Shouting to the writers to pick up on the extension phones, Brower pressed the receiver against his ear. He was dismayed by what he heard, for the record's message was embarrassingly clear. Lennon was saying that we are not put here on earth to build ourselves up to be superstars (or, by implication, superpromoters!); the goal of life is symbolized by the real stars, the heavenly bodies that shine serenely down upon our crazy little planet. Far from giving the festival a boost, Lennon was dismissing it as a colossal ego trip.

Shortly thereafter Brower called Lennon and told him that it was utterly impossible to produce such an immense event without charging at least twenty dollars a head. Lennon went through the ceiling. He chewed Brower out on the phone and then dismissed him with a curt telex: "We want nothing to do with you or your festival." A couple of months later *Rolling Stone,* which had turned on Brower overnight and was now intent upon discrediting him, printed a piece by John Lennon in which he sought to explain his role in the ill-fated festival, which had received an immense amount of publicity all over the Western world and was a major source of embarrassment to Lennon. He heaped all the blame for the festival's demise on Brower and got righteously indignant over the way everyone had violated the faith that only *he* had kept, crying: "Have we forgotten what vibes are?"

By the time the article ran he had not only blotted out of his mind his true role in the festival but had turned his back on both his peace crusade and his faith in the cosmos. For Lennon was now embarking on a new cycle that would reveal once and for all that he was a man with peace on his lips but war in his heart.

NERVOUS PROSTRATION

In February 1970 John Lennon suffered a quiet nervous breakdown. He didn't crack up: he simply took to his bed and refused to see anyone but Yoko. When he lapsed into a similar state years later, he provided a striking description of his condition: "I'd lie in bed all day, not talk, not eat, just withdraw. And a funny thing happened. I began to see all these different parts of me. I felt like a hollow temple filled with many spirits, each one passing through me, each inhabiting me for a little time and then leaving to be replaced by another." Nobody could have explained better what it means to go to pieces.

The fragments into which Lennon broke were his subpersonalities, the submerged selves that manifested themselves vividly in his music. Think of any famous Lennon record and instantly there will echo in your mind the distinctive persona that John employed for that particular song: the plaintive, spaced-out voice of "Nowhere Man"; the urgent, breathless voice of "Help!"; the drowsy, languorous voice of "I'm Only Sleeping"; the angry, mocking voice of "I Am the Walrus"; the sly, put-on voice of "Bungalow Bill"; or the childishly innocent voice of "Dear Prudence." These vocal masks are not just moods or attitudes: they possess the depth and solidity of character. What's more, they associate with the incessant alterations in Lennon's visual image that often inspired picture editors to lay out strips of head shots, in each of which John Lennon appeared a different man. For just as every Lennon song demanded a new voice, almost a new singer, so every Lennon pub shot demanded a new look: mop top/bright smile/Cardin suit or granny glasses/stern mustachio/psychedelic satins or shaggy face/cropped head/bib overalls. Viewed from one aspect, these changes suggest the cultural chameleon, the dedicated follower of fashion; viewed from another, they imply the now-familiar but inadequately understood phenomenon of multiple personality.

According to the psychiatric textbooks, multiple personality develops in response to childhood trauma, the mind acting like a sponge that once saturated with suffering must be set aside and replaced with a fresh sponge. Dissociation was written all over John Lennon, whose portrait could be laced with cracks or comprised like those computer-generated pictures out of countless little frames or facets. Normally, John held himself together through the force of his manias, his obsessions, which by focusing his whole being on a single, passionately desired goal, reduced his incoherence to a minimum.

But when he went off into his dream-like states of self-hypnosis, he would start to come apart. As he told the Beatles' official biographer, Hunter Davies: "If I am on my own for three days, doing nothing, I almost leave myself completely . . . I'm up there watching myself . . . I can see my hands and realize they're moving, but it's a robot that's doing it. . . . It's frightening, really."

It was at such times that Lennon's submerged selves would appear, each one clamoring to be "I." Not the multiple personality's usual collection of incomprehensibly various beings, Lennon's personae were manifestations of his conflicts and consequently appeared in antithetical pairs, like the "monk" and the "performing flea." Though John never described these ghostly selves explicitly, it is clear that they clustered around the two poles of his being: his obsessive-compulsive hunger for action and his lethargic and spaced-out enjoyment of reverie. The imaginary Lennon would be in turn a pirate captain or a slumbering babe.

When Lennon's anxiety about having lost contact with reality became alarming, he would bring himself back to earth by a simple expedient: "When it gets too bad," he told his biographer, "I have to see the others." The value of the Beatles to him at such moments was that they were "someone else like me." In other words, the Beatles embodied the identity that John Lennon was always losing.

But their own identity was by no means simple. Consider how various were the ways in which the public perceived the Beatles. Initially everyone saw the Fab Four as one man repeated four times. Soon, however, this perception was superseded by the vision of the Beatles as four different men wearing the same costume, which is how they were seen by the typical fan, who then identified with his favorite Beatle. The more sophisticated Beatle watchers, however, had yet another take on the group: they saw the Beatles as *one man with four different faces*. This was an idea that appealed to the Beatles themselves, but it raises a basic question: who was that man?

The best clue is provided by the finest description ever written of the Beatles as a collective identity. According to British Pop critic Nik Cohn, the most remarkable thing about them was their self-sufficiency, which was the product of their perfect complementation, each Beatle interlocking with and counterbalancing the others like the works in a

Swiss watch. "Lennon was the brutal one," Cohn observed, "McCartney was the pretty one, Ringo Starr was the lovable one, Harrison was the balancer. And if Lennon was tactless, McCartney was a natural diplomat. And if Harrison seemed dim, Lennon was very clever. And if Starr was clownish, Harrison was almost sombre. And if McCartney was arty, Starr was basic. Round and round in circles . . . and it all made for a comforting sense of completeness." Exactly. But what was the source of this dialectical completeness?

The answer is that the Beatles were created by John Lennon, who fashioned them in his own image. Virtually every one of the epithets that Cohn employs to characterize the various members of the group could be applied to Lennon alone. John was *arty* as well as brutal; after all, it was he not Paul who spent three years at art college. On the other hand, John sought to be *basic*, playing the lucky layabout, a role that brought him close to Ringo, as did the fact that John was also *clownish*. But behind his clown's mask, he confessed, he wore a frown, which made him resemble the *somber balancer*, George. Yet John was also *lovable*, for who else in the history of show biz has ever done so many outrageous things and still retained the affection of the public? *Pretty* he wasn't—but beauty is not a character trait. As for the two terms that seem least applicable—*diplomat* and *dim*—they are not so alien as might appear because Lennon often displayed a distinct flair for diplomacy, for example, when apologizing for himself or the group, and in any matter that he couldn't grasp intuitively, such as business affairs, he proved himself deplorably dim. Hence, if the Beatles were one man with four different faces, that man was John Lennon.

The Beatles not only incorporated all the elements of John Lennon's fragmented personality but they harmonized these elements perfectly, which enabled them to achieve total self-sufficiency. Theirs was the very same quality that the Stanley sisters had exhibited during John's childhood; it was, therefore, his ultimate ideal. Yet, by the same token, it was precisely the quality in which he was most deficient, for his basic failure was his inability to function as a mature and independent human being. Thus by losing himself in the Beatles, Lennon found himself; contrariwise, by divorcing himself from the Beatles, Lennon lost himself forever.

Lennon's rupture with the Beatles was ultimately a case of psychic suicide. With one blow he cut away his creative partner and his band, which is to say his art and his family. At the same time, he lost his hold on reality and found himself back where he started—an orphan, living alone in a big house with an overbearing matron. No wonder he broke down. As Dan Richter reported, "John was asking himself—'Who's going to take care of me now?'"

The answer, presumably, was Yoko. But she was also beginning to have second thoughts about this marriage. She had married a man who she could presume would become her rocket to fame. But now, instead of helping her attain stardom, he was behaving like a sick child and casting her in the role of his mother. For a woman who had spent her whole life fleeing the responsibilities of motherhood, this was an intolerable situation.

John Lennon's breakdown was exacerbated by his drug addiction, for now that his honeymoon on heroin was over, John was seeking a divorce; but he found it hard to obtain and impossible to finalize. Mistakenly assuming that getting off drugs entailed nothing more than abstinence, he had made an heroic effort to kick heroin back in August when he first moved into his new home, Tittenhurst Park. He had had himself roped to a chair, leaving only one arm free to hold a cigarette. Pinioned in that position, he had sat for three whole days, alternately burning and freezing, crying out in agony or begging for release. He recorded the whole ordeal with clinical accuracy in "Cold Turkey," a giant step along the path to total candor that was always the high road of John Lennon's career.

A chant not a melody, sustained over a bass that booms like an amplified heartbeat and sung in a "white-nigger" voice that bends its vowels blue, the song is sliced into staves by the frailing of Eric Clapton's acid guitar, each stanza offering a lurid flash of Lennon's desperate plight. At the end, he goes off into half-terrified, half-nauseated screams, anticipating the Primal Scream Album by a year, although another six months were to elapse before he ever read about this novel therapy.

Soon John was back again on junk, a relapse that inspired him and Yoko to put themselves into the hands of Dr. Michael Loxton, from nearby Virginia Water, who came highly recommended by Dan Richter. Today, a man who won't take a drink, far less an addictive drug, Richter suffered terribly in the old days from his habit. Then he discovered methadone, recently introduced into England as the answer to the increasing population of registered drug addicts. A synthetic opiate invented by the Germans during World War II and named Dolophine in honor of Adolf Hitler, methadone was the latest in the long line of chemicals that have been hailed as cures for the heroin plague. Like all the others, commencing with cocaine, the new drug proved to be almost as bad as its antagonist. Experience soon demonstrated that though Dollies will sate the junkie's craving for horse, smoothing out his day and transforming the way-out street criminal into the docile outpatient, the legally condoned drug produces many of most alarming effects of its deadly rival, including the fatal dangers of an overdose or a prenatally addicted newborn baby, destined to go into convulsions six hours after delivery. In time to come, John and Yoko would complain bitterly about their enslavement to the drug that was supposed to set them free.

On 5 March the Lennons checked into the London Clinic, 20 Devonshire Place, an expensive private hospital where wealthy addicts could safely change their drug habits. Their cover story was that Yoko had to undergo an operation following complications produced by her latest miscarriage. The steady stream of visitors to the sick room included Magic Alex, reporter Ray Connolly, and Michael X, a Trinidadian agitator whose Black House had recently benefited from a public auction at which John Lennon had offered two hanks of his and Yoko's hair.* Not a single picture of this event appeared in the press, a sure sign that the English public was now fed up with the Ballad of John and Yoko. Michael X demonstrated his appreciation for the Lennons' support by bringing to the hospital a suitcase full of marijuana. John was glad to have the weed, but when he saw the doctors preparing to give Yoko an injection, he shouted, according to Ray Connolly, "Don't give her that! She's a junkie!" After the famous couple returned to Tittenhurst, on 29 March, the press announced that Yoko was two months pregnant and expecting a baby in October.

The final blow to the already prostrate Lennon was delivered by Paul. After being completely out of touch for months while living on his farm in Scotland, McCartney rang up one day to announce that he was leaving the band and bringing out an album on his own. John was stunned by the news. First, it enraged him because when he had wanted to announce his break from the Beatles, he had been prevailed upon to keep his mouth shut in the interests of the group. Just as disturbing was the recognition that Paul's defection meant the band was gone for good. After all, it was one thing for the ambivalent Lennon to announce he was quitting—John might have had second thoughts and probably was having them now that he recognized how desperately dependent he was on the Beatles—but if Paul, the one who had fought the hardest to keep the group together, was quitting, then there was obviously no hope of a reconciliation. As if all this were not

---

*The Lennons' relationship with Michael X marks the beginning of their fateful infatuation with the criminally inclined demagogues who sprang up in the radical climate of the late sixties. Michael Abdul Malik was a onetime pimp and slumlord muscleman whom the British government deported to his native Trinidad. There he was tried and convicted of a double murder. Though the Lennons were hardly in a position to investigate the charges against him, they insisted that he had been framed. Having visited him in Port of Spain in April 1971 and arranged for a thirty-thousand-dollar advance from Apple for a book he never wrote, they paid for his three appeals and addressed statements on his behalf to the English public and to people with influence in government. He was executed on 16 May 1975.

bad enough, the timing of Paul's album, scheduled for release on 17 April, could not have been worse. On 20 April United Artists was launching the Beatles' film *Let It Be,* accompanied by a sound track album that had been produced by Phil Spector out of the tapes the Beatles had abandoned. Ringo also had an album, *Sentimental Journey,* scheduled for release. If all these products hit the market at once, the Beatles would be involved in ruinous self-competition.

John and George sent Ringo, as the most nearly neutral party, on an embassy to Paul. When Ringo rang the bell, Paul insisted his old mate stand out on the stoop and state the nature of his business. After Ringo was admitted to the house and began his rap, Paul exploded. "He went completely out of control," testified Ringo. "He shouted at me, prodding his fingers towards my face, and said: 'I'll finish you now!' and 'You'll pay!' He told me to put on my coat and get out."

What really got John's goat was the press release for Paul's album, titled, significantly, *McCartney,* and featuring Paul on all the instruments normally played by the other Beatles. Leaked to the media on 10 April, this handout created a worldwide sensation. Couched in the form of an interview, it answered all the questions on everybody's mind with curt, cold negatives:

Q. Will Paul and Linda become a John and Yoko?
A. No, they will become a Paul and Linda.
Q. Do you miss the other Beatles and George Martin? Was there a moment, e.g., when you thought "Wish Ringo was here for this break"?
A. No.
Q. Do you foresee a time when Lennon-McCartney becomes an active songwriting partnership again?
A. No.
Q. What do you feel about John's peace effort? The Plastic Ono Band? Yoko?
A. I love John and respect what he does, but it doesn't give me any pleasure.

PAUL BREAKS UP BEATLES . . . NO BEATLES WITHOUT PAUL. The shouting headlines echoed and reechoed the world around as the public, totally unprepared for such a startling announcement, went into shock.

Nothing could have demonstrated more dramatically and conclusively that the golden era of the Sixties was over. Now there was nothing to do but struggle to understand how such a disaster had befallen the world's most beloved entertainers. The consensus was that the Beatles had broken up because they had finally grown up. Although this naïve analysis was flatly contradicted by the facts—all the boys had long since married, three of them were fathers, and one had gotten a divorce to remarry—the thoughtless press reduced the Beatles crack-up to a chorus of "That Old Gang of Mine." Invariably these simpleminded obsequies concluded by quoting the last line of the Beatles' last recording, the familiar phrase about the equivalence of the love you give and take. Though the line had the right cadence for a kiss-off, it was hardly the last word on the subject.

The real reasons for the Beatles' breakup were clearly apparent in their latest film, *Let It Be*. Even though Paul had edited the footage carefully to put the best face on things, the picture was a muddle of boredom, lassitude, and incomunicativeness. There wasn't a scrap of real dialogue—save for under-the-breath asides—and the group's playing and singing were deplorable, save for Paul's perfectly framed solos. Nor was the album any better, despite the work lavished on it by Phil Spector. Even the greatest mixologist can't make mediocre tapes into knockouts, particularly when he is constrained to play it close to the vest. On only one track, "The Long and Winding Road," did Spector succumb to his itch to inflate and orchestrate. Paul complained bitterly that his work had been ruined, though the arrangement caught perfectly the note of Academy Award ceremonialism in the song. When the album won the Beatles their only Academy Award, for best film score, Paul flew to Los Angeles to collect the Oscar.

While John and Yoko were suffering through this time of emotional distress, their house was being pulled down about their ears. Tittenhurst Park (bought for the Lennons by Maclen for £145,000 in May 1969) was a Georgian manor house set amid seventy-two acres of rolling woodland. Like many old mansions, its interior was a warren of little rooms, which didn't suit its new owners, who aimed to convert the place to the country equivalent of Andy Warhol's Factory. Ordering the internal walls ripped out, the Lennons set about installing all the equipment required to make professional-quality films and records. A sixteen-track studio was built, complete with echo chambers and temperature- and humidity-controlled storage vaults. Projection rooms were provided for sixteen- and thirty-five-millimeter film. Editing suites, darkrooms, and even a billiards room for idling musicians rounded out the specs for what John called Ascot Studios.

Yoko yearned for the spaciousness of a New York loft, so the entire ground-floor front was consolidated into a single space carpeted with a quarter million dollars' worth of white rug from China. John craved proximity to water, which meant digging a pond, lining it with rubber matting, and stocking it with fish—which were killed by the matting. Upstairs the Lennons demanded a huge revolving bed (which never worked), whose coverlet was a replica of a phonograph record. The round bed was echoed by a circular bath big enough for two, ogled by an overhead TV camera.

The labor for all this demolition and construction was provided, at George's suggestion, by a score of saffron-saried Hare Krishnas, bossed by Dan Richter, who had moved onto the estate with Jill and their children, Sasla and Misha, to become its manager. The founder of the Hare Krishnas, A. C. Bhaktivedanta Snila Prabhupad (a retired pharmaceuticals executive), was installed in a Victorian assembly hall near the house, which he transformed into a Hindu temple. John grew to hate the Hare Krishnas because they were quarrelsome and inept. As they washed the windows, bobbing their shaved pates and smiling, John would bob and smile back, muttering in response to their repeated "Hare Krishna, Hare Krishna!" the Lennonesque antiphon: "Fuck you, fuck you!" When the swami demanded the deed to the temple, Lennon threw the whole lot off his property. Then he settled down to brood in the glass-enclosed extension of the kitchen, where he puffed on his cigarettes and drank his tea as he gazed out at the barren trees dripping with cold rain.

HOLLYWOOD HEALER

John Lennon was sinking toward his nadir when one day he found his salvation in the morning mail. Opening a hefty padded envelope bearing an American postmark, he extracted a book with a startling title, *The Primal Scream.* "Just the title made my heart flutter," he declared. "Then I read the testimonials—you know: 'I am Charlie so-and-so. I went in, and this is what happened to me.' I thought, 'That's me! That's me! It's something better than a tab of acid and feeling better.' I thought, 'Let's try it!' But I'd been so wrong in the past, with the drugs and the maharishi, that I gave it to Yoko. She agreed with me. So we got on the phone." The ultimate impulse buyer, John Lennon made even the most important in a snap. What decided him this time was the word *"Scream."*

That highly charged word acted like a trigger, releasing Lennon's extraordinary powers of association. The first thing it made him think of was Yoko, whose trademark was screaming. Then John thought of all the screaming he had done from the days when he shouted himself hoarse hollering "Twist and Shout" down to his recent record, "Cold Turkey." Screaming was likewise the sound on which the Beatles had risen to fame. So what the hell! John didn't need to read this book to know it was offering him the right answer; he just had to read the title. "I never would have gone into psychotherapy," he explained, "if there had not been this promise of this scream, this liberating scream."

Arthur Janov, into whose hands John Lennon was about to commit himself, was not a psychiatrist. He was an aggressive forty-six-year-old psychologist from Los Angeles, who had spent twenty years in private and institutional practice, until one day he had a eureka experience. He witnessed a young male patient regress violently to infancy, thrashing about on the floor of the office, crying and slobbering like a baby, as he cried out: "Mommy! Daddy!" What impressed Janov most about the incident was the unearthly scream that came out of the man at the beginning of the seizure and the born-again attitude he displayed at the end of this startling episode, when he proclaimed: "I can *feel!*"

Janov built up from this experience a theory and practice that he was convinced would revolutionize the whole profession of mental health. He believed that if he could trip a patient back to his early childhood and make him scream forth the pain he had experienced when his wants were not fulfilled, all the distorting and deadening defenses that the patient had subsequently built up to avoid feeling this original pain would be blown away and a new man would start forth, free again to feel the bliss and grief of life.

Primal therapy was strikingly similar in concept (though not in technique) to the cathartic therapy with which Sigmund Freud had began his career as a healer back before the turn of the century. Freud had soon abandoned the idea, and it was the consensus of analysts since that this method was unavailing because the spectacular "breakthroughs" it produced were really products of the analyst's suggestions and the patient's desire to please. Also, experience teaches that while catharsis does produce a momentary sense of relief or cleansing, the emotional abscess that has been lanced soon fills up again.

Questions of medical theory were not really Janov's forte. He was primarily a healer, who saw himself like Wilhelm Reich, as an inspired maverick who had discovered a panacea. Janov claimed to cure not just neurosis but "homosexuality, drug addiction, alcoholism, psychosis, as well as endocrine disorders, headaches, stomach ulcers, and asthma." It must have been a good day for Janov when he heard the distinctive voice of John Lennon on the wire from London asking for help because Janov himself needed all the support he could muster to overcome the skepticism that had been voiced by the medical profession concerning his method. Already he had begun to appeal to the general public, which often takes its cues from pop stars, by sending prepublication copies of *The Primal Scream* to celebrities like John Lennon and Mick Jagger. It wasn't long until Janov, accompanied by his attractive wife and assistant, Vivian, was on his way to England.

When Janov arrived at Tittenhurst, he created a sensation. The staff was expecting some bespectacled old coot, like doctors on Harley Street. Instead, they beheld a man in his forties who had the looks, clothes, and charisma of a movie star. His stress-lined face, handsomely hawkish in profile (in full face, querulous and sad), was framed by a mass of curly pepper-and-salt hair styled in an expensive French poodle version of the black man's natural. His clothes were Benedict Canyon casuals: a baby blue V-necked cashmere sweater over heather gray slim-line slacks. Most remarkable was his manner, which proclaimed, "I, Sigmund Wilhelm Janov, have come six thousand miles to cure the world's greatest pop star. Lafayette, we are here!"

John and Yoko had been living for the past twenty-four hours in bated-breath anticipation of what the doctor would do when he arrived. They had followed his instructions as closely as their self-indulgent temperaments would permit. They had separated for twenty-four hours, a feat, almost as drastic as parting Siamese twins. They had not watched TV (an act of wrenching self-discipline for John) or talked on the phone (that must have made Yoko frantic) or smoked cigarettes (no more than a pack for Lennon) or taken any drugs (save for their maintenance doses of methadone). Now they were ready to meet their savior. The whole future course of the therapy was probably affected by its first minute, when instead of ministering first to Yoko, Janov blundered by going straight to the star.

After the two-hour session Janov offered his diagnosis: "John was simply not functioning. He needed help." Ditto Yoko. "Help" didn't mean soft words and hand-holding. Far from it! "I believe the only way to eliminate neurosis is with overthrow by force and violence," declared the radical doctor. As the Rommel of the couch, Janov was accustomed to doing battle from his first encounter with the enemy and routing him in the same amount of time it takes the conventional shrink to work up his full diagnosis. Whereas other therapists measured time in terms of years, Janov talked of a three-week intensive course and a six-month long-term cure, with a year being the outermost limit to which his treatment extended.

To get results in this brief time, the doctor had to act boldly. The patient had to be yanked out of his natural milieu and subjected to sensory, emotional, and cognitive deprivation. Janov insisted that John and Yoko separate. They put up at adjacent hotels, the Inn on the Park and the Londonderry. Encouraged to surrender to the promptings of their bodies, they developed an overwhelming craving for ice cream. Dan Richter remembers calling the deli in Ascot and ordering crates of ice cream in every flavor, particularly chocolate for John and hazelnut vanilla for Yoko. At night, when the famous patients would sit down with their staff at the long refectory table in the kitchen, there were cartons of ice cream everywhere.

Janov acted next as family counselor. When John disclosed his extreme ambivalence toward Julian, whom he hadn't seen since the previous July, Janov urged the delinquent father to pay a visit to his son. If the therapist had known more about the family situation, he would have recognized that this was a suggestion fraught with danger. Yoko objected vehemently to John's visiting the boy, saying, "It isn't fair for you to be able to see Julian when I can't see Kyoko." She may also have feared that with the marriage running on the rocks, John might take it into his head to go back to Cynthia. After all, nobody knew better than Yoko Ono how suggestible was John Lennon. Actually, there was nothing to fear. John had no eyes for his former wife; in fact, now that he had finally gotten away from her, he could hardly believe that he had lived with her for so many years. What's more, Cynthia was about to marry Roberto Bassanini, who would shortly open a restaurant in London.

Julian must have been terrified that day when his father came climbing up the stairs in Cyn's new house in Kensington. When John came downstairs again, it was tea time. He was sitting with cup in hand, describing primal therapy, when the phone rang. It was Val Wilde, the housekeeper at Tittenhurst. Highly alarmed, she reported that Yoko was threatening to take a fatal drug dose because John was spending so much time with Cynthia. John slammed down the phone and dashed out into the street, where he shouted to Les Anthony, "Quick, let's go! The silly bugger's threatening to commit suicide!"

When John and Les reached the house, they dashed upstairs to the bedroom. "She was lying in bed, looking as if she were at death's door," recalled Anthony, adding, "Personally I thought she was putting it on—but it wasn't a bad performance, and it stopped John from going to see Cynthia again."

What Dr. Janov made of this incident is unknown. It certainly demonstrated the potential for conflict between John Lennon's psychotherapist and John Lennon's wife. Undeterred, Janov plunged on with his daily marathon sessions, breaking them off in mid-April only after having persuaded John and Yoko to put their lives on hold and follow him out to Los Angeles, where they arrived on 27 April.

Perhaps the oddest thing about primal therapy was the fact that its founder, the man who believed the cure for countless illnesses lay in screaming, could not scream himself. In fact, he could barely talk. Arthur Janov had suffered for years from a throat condition that had been surgically treated but never cured. The result was that he spoke very softly and tended to be taciturn. His wife, Vivian, did the talking at the press conferences where Janov showed films of his work. First, you would see a woman primaling in a session; then, four months later, she would appear standing happily in her kitchen, slicing a salad and buttering bread, smiling out of a deep inner peace.

After screaming, crying was the most important note of primal therapy. Art and Vivian Janov were always crying. Right in the middle of an important interview with a major news magazine, Vivian might touch on some theme close to her heart, and suddenly break down and start weeping. Her tears symbolized Janov's basic message: "You're really at bottom just a sad little baby. So why don't you cut the shit and come out with it?"

Crying was every bit as appropriate to John Lennon as was screaming. In fact, if Lennon had searched the world for a psychotherapist, he could not have found a man to whom he could have related more naturally than he did to Art Janov. For the doctor was a musician as well as a healer, a jazz trumpet player whose hero was Miles Davis— another guy who can barely talk. And Janov was also a political man, who had run for office in Palm Springs. He urged the Lennons to go further into political activism, and they heeded his advice.

The course of primal therapy was clear and direct. First, the patient was prepared through a series of private sessions, in which Janov employed the traditional Freudian "blank screen" posture but instead of encouraging an aimless pouring forth of thoughts and feelings, he directed the patient to act out those scenes from his past that appeared especially significant. It was at these moments that Janov would urge the patient to primal.

The subdued tone of the private sessions offered no clue to the extraordinary atmosphere of the group sessions, which were the essence of the cure. Three times a week, on Tuesday, Thursday, and Saturday, as many as thirty patients would gather inside one of the two five-hundred-foot offices at 900 Sunset Drive. The Saturday morning session, run by Janov himself, was the high point of the week.

The patients—predominantly youthful middle-class men and women—came dressed for physical freedom, like a Beverly Hills exercise class. They assumed various positions about the room, standing, sitting, or lying on the carpeted floor. Janov, dressed in shirt and slacks, would say: "Who's got a feeling?" Somebody would speak up, recounting a disturbing scene from his childhood. As if on cue, the other patients would swing into their primaling rituals. Where, a moment before, an exercise class had been about to begin, now there was *Marat/Sade*!

On one side of the room a couple of husky guys, raging and crying, would start punching holes in the Sheetrock wall with their bare fists. Over there, in the corner, a mature woman in leotard and tights would curl up in the fetal position and start sucking her thumb. A paunchy middle-aged man would scream out his pain so violently that he made all the fat on his body vibrate. As the uproar mounted, with cries of "Daddy! Mommy!" rending the air and tears streaming down faces contorted by sobbing and gasping, Janov would move about the room, working quietly and efficiently, like a doctor in an emergency clinic.

He might make one patient go further into her fit. To another he would flash a sign that meant: "Hit the deck!" His assistants went about wiping tears and offering cues to generate fresh outbursts. The screaming, the crying, the violent physical behavior would continue without letup for two hours, until the room resembled a nursery or day-care center filled with oversize infants throwing tantrums—an illusion heightened by the introduction of a man-size crib and huge teddy bears and baby dolls.

Bobby Durst, son of a Times Square real estate magnate, was in therapy at the Primal Institute all through the summer of 1970. He recalled his astonishment when he walked into the "snake pit" for the first time and saw in the midst of all these distraught patients the familiar shapes of John Lennon and Yoko Ono. John primaled by getting down on the floor and rocking back and forth violently as he screamed and moaned, calling aloud for his mother and father. Yoko lay still in one spot and shivered.

The Saturday session concluded with a period of conventional group therapy, which gave patients like Durst an opportunity to question John and Yoko directly about their emotional problems. Durst remembered that John seemed preoccupied by two themes: mother and religion. He was convinced that his mother had truly loved him, but he had been separated from her by his father. John dwelt on one scene in particular, an occasion when he and his mother were about to go off to church and were forbidden to leave the house by his father. (Freddie Lennon did, in fact, view religion as the "opiate of the masses" and was quite vehement on this theme.) After rehearsing all his grievances against his father, John would wind up his complaint by asking rhetorically, "So what do I do about it today? I give him *money*!"

When the session concluded, around noon, all the patients would troop out of the building and walk up the Strip to Bob's Big Boy, where they would eat hamburgers, John Lennon's favorite American food. John impressed everyone as being remarkably modest and ordinary. After lunch the Lennons would get in their limousine and retire to their rented house at 841 Nimes Road in the hills of Bel Air. "We'd go down to the session, have a good cry, and come back and swim in the pool," John recalled, summing up the routine maintained for four months. "You'd always feel like after acid or a good joint, sort of in the pool tingling, and everything was fine. But then your defenses would all come up again—like the acid would wear off, the joint would wear off—and you'd go back for another fix."

In India it had been the cynical Magic Alex who had disillusioned Lennon and inspired him to flee from the place where he had been so happy and productive. In Los Angeles it was Yoko Ono. "Janov was a daddy for John," she said years later. "I had a daddy . . . but I saw his hypocrisy. So when I see something that is *supposed* to be so big and wonderful—a guru or a primal scream—I'm very cynical." Yoko claimed that she had saved John from the dreadful fate of being exploited by Janov, who brought video cameras into the room when they were primaling. Actually, there was a video camera in Janov's group sessions from the day John and Yoko arrived. It was understood by every patient that if he did not wish to be filmed, all he had to do was step aside. John and Yoko were always among those who moved out of the camera's range. So the cameras were not the real reason for the Lennons' abrupt and angry rejection of Janov. The truth was far more drastic. "I can tell you," Allen Klein confided, "Janov wanted John to leave Yoko."

"Janov was tough," reported Lennon, "but he was no match for Yoko. She watched everything he did. She figured it all out, and she learned to do it better." Or, as Yoko put it: "I did primal therapy with him. I watched him go back to his childhood. I know his deepest fears." Yoko was also lucky. At the height of her struggle to discredit Janov, she found an unexpected ally in the Immigration and Naturalization Service, which refused to extend the Lennons' visa. In September John and Yoko flew back to England, arriving there just a month before Lennon's thirtieth birthday.

Though John Lennon had spent only four months in therapy, a very short time as such treatments are usually measured, he had profited enormously from the experience. He recovered from a serious nervous breakdown, learned lessons about himself that he never forgot, and found the material for his most important album, for, as was his wont, John had been steadily transmuting the insights he obtained through therapy into a new collection of songs. Even months after he had abandoned Janov, he continued to primal every day and to say: "It [primal therapy] was the most important thing that happened to me besides meeting Yoko and being born." Breaking off therapy was, therefore, a terrible mistake because it meant throwing away what proved to be his last chance to come to terms with the deadly mental and emotional problems that soon laid waste his life.

It was also highly dangerous to abort the therapy without first finding some way of putting the lid back on the Pandora's Box that the treatment had ripped open. Janov warned Lennon that he was heading for trouble. The nature of that trouble became apparent the moment John had his first face-to-face encounter with his father.

THE WRATH OF LENNON

"*To be opened only in the event I disappear or die an unnatural death.*" So ran the inscription on the envelope that Freddie Lennon deposited with his solicitor after his terrifying encounter with his son on his thirtieth birthday. For months after that traumatic event, Freddie and Pauline went about in fear of their lives because John had threatened to have Freddie shot and his body dumped at sea. "His countenance was frightful to behold," reported Freddie in the letter, "as he explained in detail how I would be carried out to sea and dumped 'twenty, fifty, or perhaps you prefer a *hundred fathoms deep*?' The whole loathsome tirade was muttered with glee, as though he were actually participating in the terrible deed." Helpless in the face of such insane rage, Freddie had done the only thing in his power. He had written out a complete account of the incident and put it into the hands of his lawyer. If worse came to worst, at least there would be this mute witness to John Lennon's patricidal designs.

"Malignant" was the right word for John's behavior. For first, he had called his father, to whom he had not spoken in more than a year, and sweet-talked the old man into coming up to Tittenhurst for a family birthday celebration. Once Freddie had agreed, John set about preparing for him a nice Tony Perkins motel reception. Freddie was met by Diana Robertson, the Lennons' attractive secretary, when he and his wife and eighteen-month-old baby pulled up before Tittenhurst's imposing porter's lodge. Diana escorted the little family up the long, curving driveway to the house; then she told them to wait in the porte cochere, while she went inside, presumably to get further instructions. As Freddie cast his eye over the property, which he had never seen before, he got an eerie feeling. Perhaps it was the sight of the smashed-in white Maxi perched on its concrete pedestal, or perhaps it was simply the ghostly appearance of the whitewashed manse. However it was, he formed an impression of the place not as a home but as a lavish mausoleum.

When the secretary returned, she led the family into the big country kitchen and bade them wait again. Freddie and Pauline sat down at the long dining table, putting the baby on the floor so that it could crawl. Again, Freddie got that weird feeling—actually going so far as to say to Pauline: "This place positively reeks of evil!" At that moment John and Yoko made a startling entrance, circling down from the ceiling like a pair of bats, as they descended a spiral staircase.

John looked grim, and the pupils of his reddened eyes were dilated. The moment he sat down, he fixed his father with an angry look and growled: "Start worryin'! Go on! Start worryin'! Get your fuckin' cards! [National Insurance cards, the British equivalent of "Get your walking papers!"] Keep your fuckin' self and—*get out of my life!*" The last words were torn out of John's throat like a convulsive scream. They so drained him that he fell back in his chair, shaking from his exertion.

As Freddie stared at his son, shocked as much by his appearance as by his tone—John was wearing a fiery red beard and appeared to be completely demented—Pauline broke down and started crying. Between sobs she sought to explain to John that his rage against his father was unjust. Her efforts to defend her husband only succeeded in further infuriating Lennon, who sneered between clenched teeth, "Mind your own business, you stupid cow!" Then he brought his fist down on the table with shattering force. Yoko sat through this violent scene stone-faced, saying nothing.

Finally, Freddie found his tongue and sought to placate his son, conceding that he was partly to blame for what had happened when John was a child. Far from pacifying John this concession only fanned his flames afresh. Now he embarked on an incoherent account of his recent treatment in America, where, he explained, he had spent a vast amount of money to be taken back again to his childhood so that he could experience all over again the horrors of his earliest years. As he recounted this ordeal, his voice rose time and again to the same horrible scream, his face going to pieces from the force of the emotions he was pumping up. Soon it became clear that he was not only enraged but possessed by a terrible *fear*. He compared himself to Jimi Hendrix, Jim Morrison, and Janis Joplin, all of whom had recently died unnatural deaths. John insisted that he, too, was destined to an early grave. Finally, at the peak of one outburst, he roared: *"I'm bloody mad! Insane!"*

Now that John's rage had been ignited, it ran like a powder train from one target to another. He denounced his mother as a "whore," shocking Freddie deeply. He ranted against Mimi. Finally, he lit into Paul McCartney. Little David Henry, alarmed by the uproar, was clinging anxiously to his mother's legs. Suddenly John pointed at the child and screamed: *"See what will happen to him if you lock him away from his parents and shut him up with a fuckin' mad woman! He'll end up a raving lunatic, like me!"*

"I sat through all this completely stunned," wrote Freddie, "hardly believing that this was the kind, considerate, happy Beatle John, talking to his father with such evil intensity—but much worse was to follow. It was when I alluded to the fact that I had never asked him for financial help and was quite prepared to manage without it that he flew into another abominable outburst, accusing me of using the press to force him to help me. He threatened that if I were to speak to them again, particularly about our present discussion, he would have me 'shot.' There was no doubt whatsoever in my mind that he meant every word he spoke."

Terrified, Freddie and Pauline fled from Tittenhurst. The week following they were informed by Apple that they would have to vacate their little house at Brighton, which had been put in their name for tax purposes but which John now wanted to repossess. Freddie was only too happy to comply because by so doing, he would sever the last tie to his mad son. Not till he was lying on his deathbed did Freddie Lennon hear again from John.

John Lennon's *Psycho* attack on his father was the climax of all the primaling he had done in Los Angeles. Through therapy he had dug down to the deeply impacted rage that had been smoldering inside him since childhood. Now his wrath came spewing out on precisely those people who had the greatest claim on his love and compassion. No one was immune to his mad-dog attacks, nor were any of his assaults provoked by their victims.

If releasing Lennon's anger meant that a lot of people caught hell, it also meant that the lifelong shackles on John's imagination were struck off. Lennon's muse had always been a muse of fire, a howling devil that dwelt in a pit of molten lava at the bottom of his soul. Its liberation was marked by an eruption of sound and fury, of primitive images and ideas, that corresponded closely with what psychiatrists call "primary process" material—the stuff of nightmares, psychotic episodes, and bad acid trips. This perilous stuff had churned about inside John for years, giving off pungent vapors and occasionally producing a burst of irrational violence. It had imbued Lennon's personality with a dark, saturnine hue and given even his most commercial work an acidulous tone. For the most part, however, it had been sternly repressed, its only licensed expressions being in the coded language of Lennon's private writings or the grotesque contours of his cartoons. Even so disguised, behind the masks of verbal nonsense or sick humor, it had been disquieting, particularly when he started recording tracks like "Cold Turkey," on which his voice rang with the cold fires and burning ice of hell.

When, at long last, his demonic spirit found release through the screams of primal therapy, out came roaring the voice of inspiration. The Primal Scream Album (*John Lennon/Plastic Ono Band*) is the greatest work of Lennon's entire career because it represents the only time when he reached down to the bottom of his soul and yanked to the surface his hidden self. A startling album, as shocking in its self-pitying infantilism as it is in its savage brutality, the whole composition can be seen as a series of vortically whirling or despondently blue self-portraits dedicated to Vincent van Gogh's severed ear.

Lennon believed that the basic cause of his sufferings was childhood trauma, a recognition he symbolized in the album's frame, which consists of two songs about his mother: the first track a reenactment of the horror of being abandoned by her and the last track his numbed acknowledgment that she is dead, the ultimate abandonment. These archaic-sounding pieces suggest the symmetry of this carefully contrived album, which mirrors the themes of its A-side on its B-side: "Mother" (A1) is answered by "Remember" (B1) and "Hold On John" (A2) echoed by "Love" (B2) and so on. The design is not, as in *Sgt. Pepper,* a brilliant feat of sequencing. Quite the contrary, the form of the Primal Scream Album is generated organically by the emotional polarities that pattern and power the LP. The primary oscillation is between fear and rage, Lennon's master passions, which are fused in the primal scream, triggered by terror but choked by infantile fury.

The other balance struck in this artful, if brutal, album is that between past and present. Therapy didn't inspire Lennon to focus exclusively on his painful childhood; it also drew forth his thoughts and feelings about his unhappy current life and the deplorable condition of his world, the now decadent culture of the Sixties. Hence, John's vicious attacks on his parents and family are echoed by no less savage attacks on the fans and freaks who he felt were persecuting him and Yoko in the name of brotherhood, to say nothing of British society, which had only recently pilloried and ostracized the Lennons.

Almost as remarkable as the materials out of which the album is composed are the artistic resources that Lennon employed to render his themes. Governed by a determination to spit out his perceptions and passions without any of the softening or seduction typical of popular music, Lennon pared his poetry down to the barest, starkest language, while restricting the music to the fewest possible instruments (his own piano and guitar plus Voorman's bass and Ringo's drums) and the most rudimentary musical building blocks: the drone, the riff, the shout. Basically the album is written in two contrasting idioms. The songs of fear or despair are rendered in the style of black gospel, with Lennon using his voice like a soul singer to make the church-like atmosphere *ring* with bluesy cries that end in swirling worry notes or *split* with desperate screams. The songs of rage and resentment are set to a primitive kind of rock, all backbeat and fuzz-buzz guitar, with the voice hurling itself against the cannibal beat with the fury of a berserker.

Though most of the songs sound like those of a man talking to himself, sometimes with teeth-bared rage, sometimes with lisping baby prattle, and sometimes in hysterical agony, there is one moment on each side, in the next-to-closing band, when Lennon pulls himself together and addresses his audience like an actor playing a scene. The backdrop for "Working Class Hero" could be a shebeen in Liverpool 8, late at night, with the speaker deep in his cups, leaning over the bar and spilling out his words in a tone that threatens at any moment to explode. The music is a low-pitched guitar thrum, reminiscent of those old Scottish ballads, like "The Foggy Dew," whose ominously swaying rhythms mimic the movements of the kilted "Ladies from Hell" marching forth grimly to do battle against their British foemen. The performance is one of Lennon's greatest because instead of surrendering to the temptation to rant and scream, he restrains himself, making his points by lowering rather than raising his voice, his anger flashing forth for only a moment at the end of each stanza, like a spark struck from a spur.

As Britain's most famous working-class hero, John Lennon speaks with the enormous authority of his perceived identity. He sees the worker as being just as enslaved today precisely as he was in his forefathers' time. Only now he is drugged not just by religion, the "opiate of the masses," but by those modern narcotics free sex and television. (How's that for a whiff of Welsh Chapel!) As for what it feels like to be a working-class hero, Lennon sneers when he reflects on what the brave and brainy—including himself!—have had to do to get that bit of ribbon on their chests or those initials after their names. What makes this song radical is not its politics but rather the singer's determination to smash through politics in order to come to grips with the unchanging human condition.

If "Working Class Hero" is a barroom ballad for Saturday night, "God" is a sermon for Sunday morning. What Pastor Lennon has to say is even more startling than the message of Liverpool Johnny. Instead of urging his followers to keep the faith by which he and they have lived through their great days together, he convenes them now to witness an elaborate and ritualistic recantation of their entire creed. In one awesome act of apostasy, John Lennon renounces, rejects, and consigns to oblivion all the hippie shibboleths that were the credo of the Sixties: Jesus and Buddha, Elvis and Dylan (now called "Zimmerman"), the Bible and I Ching, magic and mantra, Kennedy and Gita (The "Man of Miracles," whom John and Yoko visited in India in late 1969). All these revered figures are treated like altar steps leading to the shrine of the generation's greatest idols—the Beatles. Needless to say, Lennon doesn't believe in the Beatles any more than he does in all the other saints of the hippie calendar. After completing his breathtaking renunciation, he pauses dramatically; then, altering his voice, to that of a small, hurt child, he confides that the only thing in which he now believes is himself, adding, as an afterthought, the name of his wife.

The song's farewell begins movingly with the announcement that the Sixties were a dream now dead. But no sooner is the thought of loss, decay, or death set going than it is met by its counterpoint: the concept of rebirth. But what John Lennon presents as his reborn self is merely his primaled-out self, that sad little boy destined not many years hence to retire to his bedroom, where, with the aid of his drugs and toys, he will dream away the rest of his life. Having reduced his world and himself through the irresistible power of his negativity to his solipsistic essence, John Lennon is obliged to lay down his Magical Minstrel's wand and confess that he can no longer lead his people because he no longer knows where he or they are going.

The angry, nihilistic, and despairing mood projected so uncompromisingly in the Primal Scream Album asserted itself next in the famous *Rolling Stone* interview (reprinted as *Lennon Remembers*), unquestionably the most provocative, passionate, and profound statement ever given the press by an entertainer. Printed in two successive issues of the magazine (21 January and 4 February 1971), while John and Yoko were in New York on a three-week visa, this extraordinary outburst rocked the public and dismayed the Beatles' fans. For suddenly, out of the mouth of their former leader, the Beatles—those innocent and cherished singers of a generation's cradle songs—were revealed as the *Beastles,* the "biggest bastards on earth."

Determined to smash the myth once and for all, John set to work with a vengeance. He exposed the legendary tours as drug-debauched orgies organized by the Beatles' poncy staff and protected by the police. The charming Brian Epstein was characterized as a tantrum-throwing "fag." The Beatles' authorized biography by Hunter Davies, published in September 1968, was dismissed as "bullshit," all its home truths deleted at Aunt Mimi's insistence. Paul was the villain of the piece. He is portrayed as a scheming, self-aggrandizing show-biz hustler, who timed his announcement of the Beatles' breakup to "sell an album." As for the Beatles' fans, John depicted them as "an ugly race" and their successors, the hippies, as "uptight maniacs going around wearing fucking peace symbols." His final judgment of his days as a Beatle was summed up in one phrase: "I resent performing for fucking idiots."

The most shocking feature of this great confession was not Lennon's savaging of the Beatles but his scornful dismissal of the Sixties. Lennon recognized that though the era had been a great adventure of the imagination, one of those rare moments that make a crack in the mundane shell, its effect on reality had been ultimately nil. Despite the immense claims made on behalf of this time—that it marked the return to Edenic innocence, redeeming the world after five thousand years of "irrelevant" civilization—the truth was, according to Lennon, that "Nothing happened except we all dressed up. The same bastards are in control. . . . They're doing exactly the same things, selling arms to South Africa, killing blacks on the street, people are living in fucking poverty with rats crawling all over them . . . it's just the same only I'm thirty and a lot of people have got long hair."

Pelting Paul McCartney with mere words could never satisfy John Lennon. It was inevitable that eventually he would go for the muscle. John got his cue early in 1971, when the High Court ruled upon a writ that Paul had issued against the other Beatles. The motive for this action was Paul's conviction that Allen Klein was stealing the Beatles blind: this despite the fact that (1) Paul signed all the contracts that Klein negotiated, save for the management contract; (2) Paul profited directly from the increases in earnings that were the fruits of Klein's labors; (3) this additional wealth was so enormous that *in one year Allen Klein got the Beatles more money than they had earned in their entire career.* Nevertheless, Paul was determined to oust Klein and replace him with the Eastmans, so he adopted the only device available to him, which was to tie up the Beatles' income through a lawsuit, thus assuring that no more money would flow through Klein's hands, at least in England. Paul based his case against the other Beatles on four grounds: (1) that the Beatles had long since ceased to work together as a group; (2) that his own artistic freedom was jeopardized by their partnership; (3) that no accounts of the partnership had been prepared since the Beatles had formed Apple; (4) that the other Beatles had sought to impose on him a manager whom he found unacceptable. McCartney's lawyer also cast a lot of aspersions on Klein, asserting that he had paid himself out of funds to which he had no title and that his reputation was so bad that he should not be entrusted with the stewardship of the partnership's assets. The court ruled on 12 March 1971 that until the dispute could be resolved, all monies paid to Apple in Britain should go into the hands of a court-appointed receiver, with each Beatle receiving a living allowance. Eventually this account swelled to more than £5 million. The Beatles, meantime, were each receiving £5,000 a month.

When John, George, and Ringo left court that morning, they were sullen and depressed. They saw no way out of their predicament. Klein had sought to buy out Paul by offering him 25 percent of Apple in cash, but the deal foundered on the question of who should pay the enormous capital gains tax. As John and his mates got into Lennon's new white Mercedes Pullman, John had a sudden inspiration. Turning to Les Anthony, he demanded: "Do we still have those bricks in the boot—the ones for the garden?" When Les confirmed the bricks were still in the trunk, John gave the direction for Paul's home at 7 Cavendish Avenue in St. John's Wood.

Arriving at the house, staked out as usual by a gaggle of Apple Scruffs, John scaled the garden wall and opened the gate from the inside. Then he returned to the car and seized a brick in either hand. As George and Ringo got out of the limo to watch the action, John marched back into the front yard and hurled one brick after the other into Paul's bay windows, shattering them completely. Then all three Beatles hopped back in the white Mercedes and made their getaway, laughing uproariously.

John's next caper was no laughing matter. In fact, it could have put him behind bars. What made it so appalling was not the risk to which it exposed him but the cruelty it betrayed. Of all people, John Lennon should have been the last to involve himself in a plot to steal a child from the parent who had reared it, because he had suffered this trauma himself and never gotten over it. Yet when Yoko decided upon kidnapping Kyoko as the surest means of getting the child back into her possession, John not only endorsed the scheme but participated in it wholeheartedly. Yoko claimed later that she had been advised by a lawyer that if she could once get her hands on Kyoko, she would have an easy time persuading the courts that the child belonged with her mother. Unfortunately for Yoko, the court in which the case was first heard was in a Latin country, where, in contrast with Anglo-Saxon sentiment, it is the father, not the mother, who is regarded as a child's natural guardian.

Whether Yoko was desperate for Kyoko or whether she simply wanted revenge against Tony is an open question. As Allen Klein observed, as long as Tony had Kyoko, "Yoko felt that Tony had power over her."

It was not till March 1971 that the Lennons were able to locate Tony, thanks to information supplied by Don Hamrick, who was living quietly in the Dordogne. Hamrick revealed that Tony had been traveling through Spain and was currently residing with the Maharishi Mahesh Yogi in Majorca.

Armed with this information, the Lennons and Richter chartered a Briton Norman Islander and flew to Palma, where they checked into the Melia-Majorca Hotel. After reporting to the British consul and consulting with a local lawyer, who did not appear to understand the case, the would-be child stealers discovered Tony's whereabouts. He was living in a half-finished resort hotel on the other side of the island at Manacor, where the maharishi had gotten bargain rates for his ashram. When Yoko called Tony, he consented to a visit—but only if she came alone.

Next morning John and Dan deposited Yoko at the maharishi's quarters and drove off—only to double back and approach the building stealthily. Slipping into the hotel unobserved, they made their way up to Yoko's room. There they spent the day lying low, going into a closet when they wanted to converse. When Yoko returned, she reported that Kyoko was being cared for at a nearby children's camp. Now the Lennons were ready to make their move.

On Friday, 23 April, at three in the afternoon, Richter drove John and Yoko to the children's camp. They found Kyoko at play, watched over by a local woman. According to Richter, Yoko approached the little girl, who ran at once to her mother's outstretched arms. But according to Allen Klein, who arrived at Majorca a few days later, it was Richter who actually took the child, acting on Yoko's orders. Whoever made the snatch, the moment the infant minder saw what was happening, she started screaming for help. Richter recalled: "I knew we'd get busted."

There was nothing for it now but to get back to Palma as quickly as possible and then get out of the country. John and Yoko were so fearful of being spotted that they lay on the floor of the car, holding Kyoko. Once the child realized that she was being taken away from her father, she began to panic. Richter, racking his brains for some way to avoid arrest, pulled off the road long enough to call the English vice-consul, who agreed to meet the Lennons at their hotel.

Eager to establish an alibi, John and Yoko sent for a doctor, claiming that Kyoko had a sore throat. Meantime, Dan went out to buy the barefoot child a pair of sneakers. When he returned, he found the lobby full of cops in cocked hats. Tony had told the Guardia Civile that the Mafia had kidnapped his daughter. John and Yoko were taken by the Criminal Brigade to their headquarters for questioning. As Dan Richter sat outside the police chief's office, he was confronted suddenly by Tony. "I've got John by the balls this time!" exulted Cox. "This will cost him millions!"

By eight that night news of the bust had reached the world press. In London a desperate scramble ensued to get reporters to Majorca. At the same time frantic efforts were being made to rescue John and Yoko. Les Perrin, the Apple press representative, called Allen Klein in New York and told him the Lennons were in jail. Klein phoned Peter Howard, an Apple lawyer who spoke Spanish, in London. Howard chartered a Learjet and took off for Palma, accompanied by a staff drawn from Apple and EMI.

At eleven that night, after being held for four hours at the police station, the Lennons were brought before a magistrate and interrogated in a formal hearing. In a reckless mood John Lennon confessed to kidnapping Kyoko. This potentially devastating testimony was taken down by a stenographer to be submitted later in court. Having confessed to the crime, John and Yoko were now arrested and deprived of their passports.

The next problem the magistrate faced was the disposition of the child, who by now had become highly agitated. Taking Kyoko into a private chamber, the judge asked the seven-year-old what she wanted. "I want to see my daddy," Kyoko replied without hesitation. At three in the morning the judge declared the hearing at an end.

The case was remanded to the court at Manacor. The accused were ordered to report to the jurisdiction on the first and fifteenth day of every month until the case was called. As people filed out of the courtroom, they were greeted by the press, which had been waiting outside for hours.

Tony and Melinde emerged first, with Kyoko riding atop her father's shoulders. As the Coxes stepped into the street, all smiles, they were applauded by a group of friends. Afterward John and Yoko appeared, visibly gloomy, to return by car to the hotel.

Allen Klein arrived the following Monday or Tuesday to take control of the situation. He recalled that by this time Dan Richter had left the country because he was being threatened by the Spanish police, who wanted to take him into custody for his part in the crime. For the next twelve days Klein wheeled and dealed. He negotiated with Tony, while having him watched by private detectives. When the discussions broke down, Tony and Melinde slipped out of Majorca with Kyoko, suffering a minor accident on the way to the airport. Once the Coxes had left, there was no point in John and Yoko's remaining, but because they had no passports, they could not leave. What's more, their case was now about to be heard at Manacor. Here Klein was more successful. He found a local lawyer, a swarthy man named Señor Pinha. The lawyer had a relative who worked for the court and who, in a clear act of corruption, was bribed to alter the written record of John Lennon's testimony so as to make it less incriminating. Thanks to Klein, the Lennons did not suffer punishment for their crime.

When John and Yoko got back to Tittenhurst, they immersed themselves in the utopian realm of *Imagine*. This album was the most commercially successful and critically acclaimed of all John Lennon's post-Beatles efforts—which doesn't speak well for the tastes of either the public or the reviewers. Lennon himself remarked that the album had "chocolate on it for public consumption." The famous title song is a hippie wishing well full of pennyweight dreams for a better world—a far cry from the searing vision of the Primal Scream Album. The only track that qualifies as full-potency Lennon is "How Do You Sleep?" which surpasses the title song in every way save for mere tunefulness.

"Imagine" suffers from a piano accompaniment as monotonous as a student in a practice room and a vocal delivery with a hook-shoulder turn as feeble as a hymn sung in a Quaker parlor. The put-down of Paul (actually an answer to McCartney's mild criticism of Lennon in "Too Many People") is powered by an ominous riff (reminiscent of *Tommy*) which generates a steadily mounting tension that reaches its peak when it is answered by the Shanghai gestures of the Spector Philharmonic. Sustained by this steady, measured tramping out of the gripes of wrath, John Lennon comes on in his most laid-back, drink-in-hand, back-against-the-bar, size-'em-up and put-'em-down tone of voice. Sad to say, after this tremendous buildup, the sensational climax of the composition was aborted.

What happened was typical of Lennon, who was always being persuaded by somebody that he shouldn't put out his records as he imagined them. In this case John had planned to set Paul up through a series of mocking verses and then knock him out of the ring with a savage blow aimed straight at the Beatle's most sensitive spot. The first line of the capper couplet said that Paul's only important achievement was writing "Yesterday"; then, for the second line, John planned to scream: *"You probably pinched that bitch anyway!"* Allen Klein, who was standing in the booth next to Phil Spector, was so horrified by the likely consequences of that libel that he demanded that John pull his punch and use an alternate rhyme—which Klein improvised on the spot—that reduced the great moment to a hapless anticlimax.

Lennon never got "Yesterday" out of his system. It always remained a source of annoyance because it was the Beatles' biggest hit, and Lennon despaired of ever writing anything so popular. What deepened his chagrin was the universal belief that he *had* written the song. Didn't it say: "By John Lennon and Paul McCartney"?

Imagine, the album, begot *Imagine,* the film, the first full-length rock video. As most of the songs were directly inspired by the circumstances of Lennon's life, it made sense to illustrate them from his life: so John and Yoko took over a TV profile of them that had been started by a British network and transformed it along the lines suggested by the moody and surrealistic videos for "Penny Lane" and "Strawberry Fields," as well as by the zany humor of *Magical Mystery Tour.* Their basic difficulty soon declared itself, however, in the incongruity of each successive sequence. Assuming their art was their life, what was its style? The footage runs the gamut from newsreel documentary to glamorous-phony perfume ad, leaving the viewer in a quandary. Are they—you ask, watching them march through the streets on behalf of the magazine *Oz* (busted for obscenity) or against the war in Vietnam—dedicated do-gooders? Or are they mysterious Pop decadents, as they appear in those strange scenes in which they engage in enigmatic rituals, riding in a black hearse or eating white chess pieces while dressed up like characters in *El Topo*?

Basically what they come across as is rich kids at play. For now that they had evened out their lives on methadone and learned to primal, the emotional steam that had once driven them was beginning to turn back into water. Without a cause or a crisis to stir them to passion, they appear condemned to wander aimlessly in limbo, Tittenhurst Manor manifesting itself as another Strawberry Field. And just as John had played about the girls' orphanage as a boy, so he and Yoko appear like children amusing themselves at home with expensive toys and costumes, pretending to be glamorous grown-up lovers, Hollywood Pop stars, yet constantly betraying through the awkwardness and silliness of their flirtations and embraces their inability to imagine real love and passion.

The only successful sequence in the hour-long picture is that designed to accompany the title song. John and Yoko, dressed in black capes, walk slowly down a tree-lined road through thick fog. They enter Tittenhurst with the song's opening notes. Cut to John, clean-shaven with a short haircut and wearing a white tennis sweater, sitting at a white baby grand, singing the song, while Yoko, dressed like Cleopatra in a long white gown with gold rope belt and headband, opens the shutters one by one in the huge white-carpeted drawing room. There is a momentary gaffe when John, seated in his lavish mansion, sings of the joy of owning nothing, but as the room grows brighter and brighter, the effect of emergence from the gloom of the present into the light of a utopian future is gracefully conveyed. This clip became the Lennons' most familiar promotion piece. It projects their most appealing stance—as idealists who sought to dispel the depressing atmosphere of the Seventies with faith in a better world.

APPLE KNOCKERS

Nothing that happened to John Lennon after his marriage to Yoko Ono made so great a difference in his life as his removal to New York. "I love New York. I should have been born in Greenwich Village." So spoke John after he had settled in the city, but that was a far cry from how he felt during his first visits. Though he paid the Big Apple the dubious compliment of calling it the "modern Rome," he found it highly intimidating. Even in the tight little world of Swinging London, the Beatles had felt themselves naïve provincials—imagine how they felt in New York! No man could ever conquer the capital of the modern world the way the rock stars bestrode London. What's more, there were so many stars in New York that even a man more confident than the self-doubting Lennon might have been daunted. Hence, there can be no question that, if left to his own devices, John Lennon would never have settled in Big Town but would have remained content to ogle the city from time to time through the tinted back window of a stretch limo. It was Yoko who conned John into becoming a Manhattanite.

Yoko had many reasons for wanting to return to the city she regarded as her home. Unlike John, who hated the English but loved England, Yoko had no use for the country where she had been derided in the press and maligned by public opinion. Nor could she have ever been content living in another small island nation like Japan. Yoko has always craved to be at the center of things; she was born to be a "Roman." Likewise, she is one of those people who feel that life stops when you step off the island of Manhattan.

Quite apart from these personal preferences, Yoko may have had another, more compelling motive for removing Lennon from his native country. So long as John lived in England, surrounded by all the people with whom he had spent his life, Yoko could never be sure that someone might not pop up to jostle her hold on John. Once she got him to New York, that danger would be drastically reduced.

*   *   *

Yoko started easing John into the Big Town as early as December 1970, when the Lennons were staying at Ronnie Hawkins's estate. Her basic strategy was to find John a congenial and knowledgeable guide, somebody who could polish the Apple and make it appear bright and tempting. The man she selected was an ideal choice: Howard Smith, writer of the "Scenes" column for the *Village Voice.*

Smith was surprised by Yoko's first call because though he hardly knew her, she came on as if they were old comrades, exclaiming, "Oh, Howard, we have been through so much together!" What lay behind this odd chumminess was simply the fact that Smith had once published a few good words about Yoko's art. As he observed, "To Yoko's way of thinking, the only reason for anyone to praise your work is because they like you personally." What surprised Howard even more was the picture Yoko painted of John Lennon and his attitude toward the city. "She was trying to convince John to come down to New York, if they could get a visa. She wanted to make sure everything went terrifically for John so he would love New York and be convinced that he should move here for good. John was afraid that he would be a small fish in a big pond. Yoko wanted to live in the U.S. and be in the swing of things. She kept calling back and saying: 'I've told John so much about you,' or, 'John is fascinated with you.' Finally she suggested I come to Ronnie Hawkins's farm. I agreed on condition that I could do an interview for my radio show on WPLJ.

"We arrived in a blizzard," Smith continued. "I got two and a half hours with John on tape. He said that people shouldn't smoke dope, but he had a joint in his hand. Afterwards he admitted that he lied because otherwise, he wouldn't be able to get a visa. I was quite surprised at his candor, but I learned this was a basic element of Lennon. John opens up very fast. Yoko never opens up. The longer you know her, the more suspicious she is of you. With him, he wants to tell you every thought on his mind every second." The next time Howard heard from Yoko was in November 1970, when she called to announce the Lennons' imminent arrival.

From the moment John and Yoko checked into the Regency Hotel on Park Avenue, Howard Smith became their cicerone, showing them where to shop, where to eat, where to hang out. At that time the in place was Max's Kansas City, a storefront bar with booths, leading into a backroom steak-and-chick-pea parlor, where everybody sat around in the weird glow of neon sculptures, dimly seeing and being dimly seen. Howard called up Mickey Ruskin, the owner, and got him to reserve the best booth, where the Lennons would enjoy privacy but could ogle the crowd. "John loved it," recalled Howard. "Despite his insecurity, he dug the action. Yoko put up a wall and decided there was something wrong, to protect herself and her sense of art."

One of the fixtures at Max's was Andy Warhol, then at the peak of his fame, thanks especially to the sensational publicity he had received when Valerie Solanas nearly assassinated him and Mario Amaya at the Factory in June 1968. As a rock star Lennon belonged in Andy's pantheon because rock was the heartbeat of "Pop," the spirit that Warhol worshiped like the life-force. Yoko, on the other hand, he scorned as a virtual caricature of that dreary, overserious, Europeanized avant-garde that had either been co-opted or simply blown away by the tumultuous energies of the Sixties. So contemptuous of Yoko was Andy that he applied to her his most damning epithet: "corny!" No matter what Andy thought of Yoko, however, he couldn't throw away a chance to earn $25,000 doing one of his "portraits" (a reworked photograph run through a commercial silkscreen process), so he promoted a party for these rich apple knockers at the absent Ken Nolan's loft, with the hostess Baby Jane Holzer, Tom Wolfe's "Girl of the Year" in 1965. (Baby Jane puts down the "fat" Beatles all through Wolfe's powder-puffy piece, comparing them unfavorably with the "skinny" Stones; hence, she is the most likely source for Lennon's bête noire, the image of himself as the "fat Beatle.")

When Andy and Yoko finally started haggling over the portrait (as well as a real estate deal in SoHo), neither could prevail over the other. "Talk about exploitative artists!" exclaimed a Warhol intimate. "Andy from day one was trying to sell John and Yoko a portrait. They felt they were so famous that he should do a portrait of them for free. Or they would give him permission to do their portrait and he could make multiples and make lots of money. So they engaged in this mano-a-mano struggle to see who was going to exploit whom the most. Andy was annoyed and began to say bad things about Yoko. Yoko said bad things about Andy in print—part of her homosexual Mafia bit. Andy was more interested in Mick Jagger anyway because he wanted to run around with Bianca. She was the kind of international jet set type that Andy really loves."

So the man who had carried pop music into the world of the avant-garde and the man who had brought the avant-garde to Pop were kept apart by Yoko's hostility. But John was intrigued by Warhol for the same reason that he had been fascinated by Dylan: both Yanks knew how to get away with murder. Warhol was the most famous artist in the world, yet all he had done to earn his fame in Lennon's view was color photos and point a movie camera at somebody sleeping. "Andy's way is rather nice," remarked John appreciatively: "He doesn't do anything—just signs it." Lennon wanted to turn that same trick.

*   *   *

It took John Lennon three visits to the Apple before he summoned up the courage to step out of his protective bubble and take his first uncertain steps along the sidewalks of New York. This historic event occurred on 3 June 1971, while the limousine was stopped for a light at the corner of Sixth Avenue and Eighth Street, the crossroads of Greenwich Village. Looking at John Lennon gazing like Little Boy Blue at the passing scene, Howard Smith exploded with exasperation. "This is crazy! Let's get out and walk!" Yoko objected instantly to leaving the security of the car. Howard drove over her, shouting to the chauffeur: "Tom, meet us in an hour by the arch!"

"OK," rasped the man, in a Rodney Dangerfield voice, "but are you *sure?*"

"If worse comes to worst," snapped Smith, like an impatient mother replying to a nagging infant, "we can duck into a shop and tell them to lock the door." With that he unlocked the door of the limo and released John Lennon, who was soon strolling through Greenwich Village, feeling, probably, like he was walking naked through Piccadilly Circus.

The first thing that caught John's eye on the Village's principal shopping concourse was a shoe store displaying sneakers embossed with the Stars and Stripes as well as matching socks. "My God!" he exclaimed. "We've got to buy these for friends in England. They'll love them!" So they trooped into the shop, finding it crowded with weekend customers. The moment the first salesman looked up at the new arrivals, his mouth fell open, and he hollered, "It's John Lennon!" Instantly every clerk dropped his shoeboxes and walked like a sommambulist toward the famous star.

The customers did not object because everyone was fascinated by the spectacle of a Beatle shopping. John and Yoko, accustomed to such reactions, sat down nonchalantly and began ordering breathtaking quantities of merchandise. They urged Howard and his girlfriend, Sarah Kernochan, to follow suit, offering to pick up the bill. When the party left the store, they were toting a couple of huge shopping bags and were very pleased with themselves.

No sooner did they step onto the pavement than Yoko turned automatically and handed her big bag to Howard, while John turned at the same time and gave his bag to Sarah. Howard flushed with rage at the thought of being treated like a servant. "What the fuck are you doing!" he snapped at Yoko.

The little woman whined, "We can't carry this!"

"And *I* can!" ejaculated the six-foot-two Smith, apoplexy in his voice. Then, suddenly reasonable, like the good mother, he suggested, "If you want, we'll *spread* the load." I'll carry something, and so will Sarah, *but*," he added firmly, "we're not gonna carry *all* your things!"

Yoko retorted: "That's why I wanted to keep the limousine! You see! You see how hard it is without having that limo *right there!*"

Howard gave her a good maternal comeback. "Look at the street, Yoko," he lectured. "Look at all the people carrying packages. Now, how come *they* can carry them and *you* can't?" Yoko went right on complaining until they met the car at Washington Square.

A couple of days after the shopping expedition, Smith arranged for John Lennon to "discover" David Peel, a well-known street singer whose stand was at Washington Square Park. Raucous-voiced, punk tough, always togged out in patched jeans and a T-shirt embellished with some cheery little emblem, like a skull and crossbones, Peel liked to come on with black lenses and bared fangs like those angry blind men you bump into in the subway. But instead of chanting to a funky street beat, his band, the Lower East Side, scraped fiddles and twanged banjos as if they were working a hootenanny back in the folksy Fifties, when Peel, a Puerto Rican kid from Brooklyn whose real name is David Rosario, first came up out of the subway and discovered Greenwich Village.

Far from being an unknown genius of the gutter, as Lennon was to ballyhoo him, the hard-hustling bard of the bikers, winos, and freaks had already enjoyed his fifteen minutes of fame. Recorded by Elektra in the Sixties (when he changed his name to Peel under the inspiration of the mellow yellow craze), his first album, *Have a Marijuana*, had sold a tidy 75,000 copies. All the same, Howard Smith wasn't taking any chances with this curbside audition: he coached Peel on how to act when Lennon discovered him.

The moment the silver Lincoln Continental bearing the stars hove into sight, Peel went into his most outrageous number: "The Pope Smokes Dope." John Lennon broke up. He sang the song for the rest of the day, and before it was over, he was telling Smith how he was going to produce his new find on Apple.

John was thrilled by this fresh contact with the street. When he and Peel were told to move along by a cop outside the Fillmore, John practically creamed. They'd been *rousted*! Ah, he could see it all now! He was about to get back to his roots in the tough underground world of a great port city: Liverpool, Hamburg, and now New York! What a line he could run out for the press! And what a line the PR people back at Apple could run for him: "John Lennon is back on the street!" Ha! That would show Paulie a thing or two!

That same day Howard Smith announced that he was going to interview Frank Zappa. "Wow!" exclaimed Lennon, with that boyish enthusiasm that was one of his most engaging traits. "I've always wanted to meet him. I really, really admire him."

Puzzled, Smith snapped: "In what way?"

"He's at least *trying* to do something different with the form," explained Lennon. "It's incredible how he has his band as tight as a real orchestra. I'm very impressed by the kind of discipline he can bring to rock that nobody else can seem to bring to it."

Recognizing that Lennon could not reach out to Zappa, Smith asked: "Do you want to meet him?"

"I'd *love* to meet him!" echoed Lennon.

Smith then proceeded to give the Lennons a quick briefing on the notorious Zappa personality. "He's passive-aggressive," explained Smith. "He wants you always to feel ill at ease in his presence."

Armed with this useful knowledge, John and Yoko drove down with Howard and his engineer to 1 Fifth Avenue, half hotel, half NYU dorm, a favorite roost for touring bands, where they prepared to beard the man Smith called the "Bartok of Rock."

When Zappa, tall and saturnine, wearing a Zapata mustache, opened the door, Howard greeted him by casually announcing: "I brought somebody along."

Zappa glanced at John and Yoko with a practiced deadpan and said as casually as if he were acknowledging the engineer: "Oh, hi, glad to meet you."

But Zappa's band reacted very differently. They leaped out of their chairs and rushed to meet the great star.

"Lennon was very deferential to Frank," observed Smith. "John acted like 'I may be popular, but *this* is the real thing.' Yoko acted like Frank Zappa had stolen everything he had ever done or even thought from her. 'Yes, yes, yes,' she would say, 'I did that in 1962.' Zappa just ignored her. He didn't care what she said." What was really on Zappa's mind was that night's show, which was to mark the closing of the greatest rock theater in the world, the Fillmore East. Bill Graham was shutting down the old house because it was impossible to operate it profitably in that period of skyrocketing fees for rock stars. When the subject of the show came up, Howard remarked casually to John and Yoko, "Why don't you join Frank tonight onstage?" Zappa's band howled with delight. "Frank looked deadly at me," reported Smith, adding, "He couldn't decide whether it was a good or a bad idea."

John's response was characteristic. "I haven't played in a long time," he pleaded. "I wouldn't know where to begin! We'd have to rehearse!"

"Not with Frank's band!" interjected Howard sharply. "You wouldn't have to rehearse at all!"

Now Howard could see that Zappa was accommodating himself to this abrupt suggestion. "It finally got through to Frank that this could be big. So he said to Lennon: 'I think we know your stuff.' The guys in the band were saying: 'Are you kidding! We know every chord!' Frank said, 'Yeah, I don't think that would be any problem. Do you know any of our stuff?' Then John and Frank discussed technical matters. Finally, they all agreed."

Howard sensed that John and Yoko would never show up unless he kept a grip on them till show time. Zappa had suggested that they appear at the end of the second show, about two in the morning. Howard's idea was to deliver them to the theater at the last minute, lest they get too nervous sitting around backstage. Even with this precaution, he saw them go to pieces the moment they left the studio after their interview with him that night. "John and Yoko were nervous wrecks. It was like young kids going on with the big boys for the first time. He was a wreck! A wreck! And she wasn't much better. She was very nervous about getting up with a band as artistic as that. After all, they screamed, too! In the limo going downtown all you heard was: 'What shall we wear? Are you sure we have the right thing on?'"

Howard's response was: "What's the difference? Zappa's guys wear anything."

Arriving at the stage entrance, the stars were rushed inside and stashed in the right stage box, which housed the theater's sound board. "John and Yoko started changing clothes the minute I got them into the box," recalled Howard. "She was putting on his shirt; he's sayin', 'Gimme your belt!' It was high school! Finally, one of them said, 'We can't go on unless we get cocaine!' So I went out and wandered around until I found a dealer. With the money they gave me, I bought some coke. They did up about a gram. That did the trick. Now they could function. Without that they might not have made it."

It so happened that the Fillmore East house photographer, Amalie Rothschild, an earnest, ambitious young filmmaker, had rented for the weekend a sixteen-millimeter camera to shoot a film on legalized abortion. When she discovered that John and Yoko were going to perform, she decided to make an unauthorized record of the show. Standing in the sound booth and using a zoom lens, she captured with her two eleven-minute magazines most of the event.

Zappa had completed his third encore before a screaming, standing audience at 2:00 A.M., when the stage lights blacked out. People were slowly getting out of their seat when suddenly the lights went back on. For a moment nobody believed what he was seeing. There before them, plain as day, were John and Yoko! John was wearing a fawn-colored chamois suit and the red, white, and blue sneakers he had bought the day before on Eighth Street. Yoko was wearing a black blouse open to the cleavage and jeans slung 'round with a cartridge belt. The moment the kids recognized the Lennons, they went mad.

They climbed atop their seats, stood on the armrests, and screamed out their lungs. Zappa stood scowling at the house, obviously thinking: "These scumbags! What the hell do they know about music?"

John, holding a red guitar and chewing a wad of gum, kicked off the impromptu set by announcing that he was going to sing a song that he used to do at the Cavern. Though he appeared withdrawn and uncomfortable, talking into the mike as if it were a speaking tube, no sooner did he get into the Olympics' "Well (Baby Please Don't Go)," with the drums beating an ominous dirge and John giving his voice a crying, pleading tone, than he had the audience firmly in his grip. Then a strange and distracting noise was heard that became increasingly loud and intrusive. Sounding like a malfunctioning electric guitar, this annoying noise echoed and travestied every one of Lennon's perfect phrases. It was Yoko, horning in on John's act. Paradoxically, while she was projecting herself vocally as such an intrusive presence, she was presenting herself visually in perhaps the most attractive manner she ever achieved on the stage, appearing youthful, pretty, sexy, and expressive, as she moved her body in a sensuous manner and opened her arms wide. Lennon, by contrast, looked as if he would have given a lot to be somewhere else.

The next number, which consisted in shouting repeatedly the word "Scumbag!" to an acid rock rave-up, ended in a long runoff, during which John was supposed to make his guitar drone with feedback. Trying to turn this simple trick cost him such an effort that he came off looking like a Boy Scout building his first fire. When he finally got the guitar humming, Yoko was shrieking from inside a bag that the band had dropped over her head. John, signaling "You don't need me any more—take it away!" slipped into the wings. Yoko complained for years afterward that once she was helpless inside the bag, John had abandoned her.

When the Lennons discovered a few days later that their New York stage debut had been filmed, they were frantic to get their hands on the footage. Amalie Rothschild was summoned to the Plaza, where she got an eyeful of superstardom. "My immediate impression was of ostentatious wealth with no care for what it really represented," she recalled. "There were lots of costly clothes thrown around with no regard for their value, and on top of the TV was a stack of hundred dollar bills a couple inches high under a paperweight." When the Lennons asked her how much she wanted for the film, emboldened by their obvious unconcern about money, she asked for a Stienbeck editing console, worth about $12,500. John and Yoko agreed immediately, asking only that she throw in some stills because they "showed a lot of warmth." Amalie Rothschild's other impression was of John's extraordinary lack of manual dexterity. She spent twenty minutes trying to show him how to operate the very simple Bolex camera that he had just been given by Jonas Mekas, but Lennon could not master either the camera or a light meter. It was clear to Rothschild that being so inept made John reluctant even to try. He was resigned to being helpless.

John and Yoko made their headquarters in New York at Allen Klein's ABKCO office, on the top floor of a forty-one-story bronze-glass megalith at 1700 Broadway, a couple of blocks north of the Brill Building, along the modern Tin Pan Alley. The Lennons were totally infatuated with Klein at this time, vying with each other in interviews to pay him the highest tribute. "I love him," John would say, "he really has made me secure. . . . I have money for the first time ever."

Then Yoko would talk about how Klein was "creative," a "genius," yet behind his image as the brash street-smart hustler, he was "shy and quiet."

"And so insecure," John would echo. "He was an orphan. How insecure can you get with nothing to hang on to?"

Klein, for his part, was thrilled by his success with the Beatles, whom he regarded as a class act in comparison with the crude Stones, and he still clung to the idea of getting the Beatles back together, at least in the recording studio. Meantime, Allen, John, and Yoko were the happiest talent-manager combination in show business.

One day Klein suggested that the Lennons join him in auditioning a young singer named Bette Midler, who had been working to a gay crowd at the Continental Baths but who was now about to appear in an Off Broadway play. Saul Swimmer, ABKCO's film producer, recalled: "Bette was going to play Rachel Lily Rosenbloom, a girl who lived across the street from Barbra Streisand in Brooklyn. There's a song in the play called 'Dear Miss Streisand,' where she writes a letter to Barbra, like Judy Garland with 'Dear Mr. Gable.' I brought Bette into Klein's office, and John and Yoko were there eating breakfast. Bette sang her heart out, and right in the middle of the performance, John said: 'Any more toast?' It didn't mean a thing to John, who ate through the whole audition. Yoko gave Bette the evil eye. When Bette left, John said, 'Look at that face!' Yoko said, 'Look at that body! Are you kidding?' Within two days Yoko went and recorded a song titled 'Mrs. Lennon.'"

Around the same time George Harrison turned up at Klein's office. George had a lot of new songs that he wanted to demonstrate for John. They both got guitars and went into an empty room to play and sing. Al Steckler, who was running Apple at the time, was enjoying the session when the door opened. "Yoko barged in," recalled Steckler, "and saw what was going on and started doing her screeching. John said, 'Get the fuck out of here!' He picked her right up and took her, stumbling over a chair, and tossed her out of the door and slammed it. Then they went back to playing on their guitars."

In July, after the Lennons had returned to England, a series of events occurred that blew John in and out of New York so violently that it wouldn't have been surprising if he had reverted to his old dread of the city. The drama began when John discovered that he could not get a visa to St. Thomas, where Yoko's custody case had come up in the court at Charlotte Amalie. For any other couple, the solution would have been simple: Yoko would have attended the court proceedings, which required only her presence, and John would have awaited the outcome at home. But John could not tolerate a moment's separation from Yoko, so Dan Richter improvised a clever scheme to get around the immigration ban. First the Lennons flew to Antigua, which is in the British Commonwealth. There they engaged a small plane to take them to St. Thomas. Before they took off, Richter called a couple of radio stations in the Virgin Islands and told them that John Lennon would be arriving at such and such an hour but was facing a showdown with immigration. He would appreciate all the support he could get from his fans. When the little plane put down at St. Thomas, it was mobbed by Beatlemaniacs. The authorities judged it best to admit Lennon.

On 26 July Tony Cox's lawyer appeared in place of his client to challenge the jurisdiction of the court and demand that the proceedings be transferred to Houston, where Tony was currently residing. This was a blunder. If Tony had testified, citing all the reasons why John and Yoko were not fit parents for Kyoto—their drug addiction, Lennon's drug conviction, and their attempt to kidnap the child—he might have won. By declining to appear, he cut the ground out from under his own feet, making it inevitable that the court would rule, as it did, that Yoko was entitled to custody of the child.

John, Yoko, and Dan Richter left the courtroom in a jubilant mood, and even enjoyed a couple of days' vacation. Now that they were inside the territorial limits of the United States, there was no reason why they shouldn't proceed to New York. When changing planes in San Juan, however, they ran into trouble. Customs insisted upon going through the mountain of luggage with which the Lennons traveled, and immigration, noting the narcotics conviction on John's visa papers, insisted on searching him. When they turned up a bottle of methadone tablets, they demanded a strip search. By the time John had persuaded the customs men that he was legally entitled to carry the methadone, somebody had made off with most of the Lennons' luggage. Wealthy people can bear such losses better than most, but what shocked John and Yoko was the theft of a case that contained all the Ono family jewelry, which

Yoko had obtained from her mother. On that sour note, the Lennons arrived in New York City.

When John Lennon got back to the Apple, he was primed to spend every minute hyping *Imagine*, an album that could boost him to the top of the charts for the first time since he had left the Beatles. But instead of being able to concentrate on his own career, he found himself being swamped by the emotional turmoil that had been generated by *The Concert for Bangla Desh*, the huge benefit performance at Madison Square Garden that had been arranged by George Harrison to relieve the flood- and famine-ravaged countrymen of George's musical guru, Ravi Shankar. Right up to curtain time the fate of this eagerly anticipated event hung by a thread because George was terrified by the responsibility of headlining a show of this size, and the surprise guest star, Bob Dylan, kept blowing hot and cold. The final crisis came when Eric Clapton—upon whom George was relying to get him through the ordeal—shot up some junk that had been cut with talc and collapsed. Lord Harlech, father of Clapton's girlfriend, Alice Ormsby Gore, appealed to Allen Klein for help. Klein called Dr. William Zahm, the neighborhood physician who prescribed for everybody at ABKCO. The doctor drove down from his suburban home that weekend and straightened out the famous guitar star with methadone. At that moment the Lennons discovered their connection in New York.

By now Lennon was being pressured from all sides to appear at the concert. Klein wanted John to join George and Ringo because that would put pressure on Paul to appear, in which case Klein stood a good chance of realizing his ultimate ambition—to make Beatles III. Footage of the afternoon and evening shows could be intercut with flashbacks to the days of Beatlemania to produce a picture sentimentally entitled *The Long and Winding Road*. George wanted John to show up because he needed Lennon's support badly and felt entitled to demand it after all the help he had given John over the years. The heaviest pressure of all came from Yoko, frantic to get out on the huge stage and bask in the publicity this great event would receive. This great concert, with its combination of pop glamour and humanitarian benevolence, was a dream come true for a woman who had always yearned to be perceived as a public benefactor.

John Lennon took a totally negative view of Bangla Desh, characterizing it as "caca." He had always detested benefits of any sort, which helps explain why the Beatles in the course of over 1,400 public performances played for free only once or twice. In John's eyes, benefits were like blow-out patches on old tires: If you do one today, you'll have to do another one tomorrow. Meantime, everybody associated with the event was making money, save for its star. What was really galling Lennon at this moment, however, was not the demand that he play for free but the spectacle of Allen Klein working around the clock on behalf of George Harrison.

John had been consumed with jealousy ever since the astonishing success of "My Sweet Lord" and George's four-record album, *All Things Must Pass,* released in November 1970, just a month before the Primal Scream Album, which collected a lot of respectful notices but did poorly in the stores. For months John couldn't turn around without hearing George's goony hymn coming out of the nearest loudspeaker. Now here was little George, whom neither John nor Paul had ever regarded as a peer, stealing the limelight again—just at the moment when John was about to release his own chart topper! What's more, even if John were to be big about it and get out there on the stage with George and Ringo, what would happen if Paul showed up? Everything John had said against the Beatles for the past two years would be wiped out in a single afternoon. The myth would be reborn! So the answer had to be no.

But could Lennon resist Yoko? Only two or three times in all his years with her was John able to prevail over his wife on a major issue. In fact, the only way he could say no and make her swallow it was by working himself up into a violent fit—precisely what he did around dawn on 31 July 1971, the day before the concert. That morning Dan Richter was jarred awake by the ringing of the phone at his bedside. It was John announcing that he was leaving for the airport immediately. Richter threw on his clothes and rushed next door to the Lennons' suite. The moment he entered the sitting room, he saw what had happened.

John had wrecked the place. He had thrown everything that was loose against the walls and overturned all the furniture. He had also attacked Yoko, who had evidently fought back savagely, just as she used to do with Tony. John bore a deep gash over one eye that had probably been made when his glasses were torn off and thrown on the floor, where they were discovered later twisted up like a pretzel. After Dan assured himself that Yoko had not been hurt, he left the Park Lane with Lennon. Stepping out onto Central Park South, they found the city being lashed by a violent rainstorm, whipped up by an offshore hurricane. It was hard to get a cab, but finally Dan flagged down a beat-looking hack that carried them out to JFK. Lennon was so intent on making his getaway that he jumped on the first plane leaving for Europe, a flight to Paris.

When Richter got back to the hotel, Yoko informed him that she was going onstage the next day *without* John. Dan tried his best to talk her out of this unseemly act, but finding that he could not bend her will, he gave up and called Allen Klein, who soon had his hands full making

Yoko see how bad it would look if she were to make a solo appearance. For one thing, it would drive George crazy; for another, it would enrage the fans, who would see it as a confirmation of their worst fears. Klein finally got Yoko to agree not to go onstage, but then he had to start all over again to persuade her to return to her husband in England. "What for?" she demanded. "I love it here!" At that moment, for the first time in his entire relationship with John and Yoko, Allen Klein got the basic message of their marriage: *"He needed her a lot more than she needed him."* Eventually Yoko allowed herself to be convinced that it would be in her own best interests to fly home that night. After all, she didn't have to stay there any longer than it took to cool out John and turn him around again.

When John arrived in Paris, he got a suite at the George V and then considered going out and picking up a whore. He was inspired by anger, of course, but there was more to the thought than just the desire for revenge. John was frustrated sexually. Just a few months before, when he was in Majorca, he had told Allen Klein how disappointed he was in Yoko as a woman. "I don't want to fuck her!" he grumbled. "When I married her, I thought she was a real wild broad. Yoko is a *prude!*" So John opined. All the same, he did not feel free to go out and get laid. He knew that he could not cheat on Mother without being assailed by terrible guilt. So he gave up the idea and next day flew back to London. When Yoko arrived later that same day at Tittenhurst, she found the house filled with roses, John's peace offering.

Thus the wrath of Lennon rose up and smote him just when he should have been thinking not of his petty private war with Paul or his jealousy of George but of his duty and destiny as one of the great heroes of his generation. Ironically, just at the moment when Lennon was knocked out by his rage, his mighty opposite, Bob Dylan, revived after a long layout and stepped forward to take the place abandoned by John. The effect of Dylan's surprise appearance was awesome. A small, wry figure in a Levi's jacket and baggy brown pants, carrying a D-size Martin guitar and wearing around his neck his orthodontic-looking harmonica holder, he stepped out on the broad stage of the Garden and angled himself awkwardly yet confidently into the cheering circle of twenty thousand souls.

Gazing earnestly up at those Ice Follies arc lamps as if they were the flyspecked Mazdas of some country juke joint, raising and lowering his hard-edged nasal voice with the weary sincerity of another Woody Guthrie, Dylan suffused the hall with white soul. The irony, the anger, the strep-throat abrasiveness of the old Dylan were magically transmuted into a keening melancholy, an Okie Dust Bowl antiphony to the unthinkable agonies of Bangladesh.

Dylan went from song to song, from truth to truth, that afternoon, with the steady eye-on-the-star assurance of a great spiritual captain. When he finished, he stepped back into the shadows without saying a word. Behind him he left thousands of exalted young people determined afresh to follow that small, shy figure, so durable, so wise, so determined to survive. As for John Lennon, nobody gave him a thought.

THE CONNING TOWER

The St. Regis Hotel, home to John and Yoko after their return to New York on 13 August 1971, was an incongruous setting for a man who espoused radical causes, identified with the underprivileged, and sang about the joys of having nothing. John Jacob Astor's marble, bronze, and crystal palace on Fifth Avenue is a monument to the grand old American dream of living like a king. When you step into the glittering lobby, you are instantly transported to the palatial splendor of Europe in former centuries. The gleam of old money comes off the marble floor and runs up the burnished brass screens of the ornate reception desk until it is lost in the dazzle of the crystal chandelier suspended from the trompe l'oeil ceiling. The same sheen of old gold reflects from the little Elsie de Wolfe boutiques that surround the lobby, and it lies heavy on the walnut-paneled library. Even the wine cellars, down among the foundations, are redolent of class and cash. Replicas of the vaults in a famous French abbey, these well-stocked *caves*, true even to their gilded gothic lettering, have provided the setting for many a café society cocktail party served by waiters dressed in hooded monk's robes.

Mr. and Mrs. John Lennon occupied as a matter of course the best rooms in the house. Their spacious sitting room on the top floor boasted a mottled brown marble fireplace ripped out of an Italian palazzo, and their elaborately swagged and festooned French windows framed a prized view of Central Park. Even the marble-lined bathroom contained a collector's item: a 1904 French marble washstand of austere beauty. But John and Yoko quickly reduced their costly accommodation to their accustomed state of junkie squalor.

The Lennons had returned to New York this time charged with a sense of a special purpose. No longer content to shop or hang out with celebs or show up as surprise guests at 2:00 A.M., they had set their sights on becoming the new leaders of the New York avant-garde. This bold ambition had been spawned by Yoko's fairy tales about her early years on the downtown scene. She had painted fascinating pictures of a brilliant society of underground artists who lived in barren industrial lofts, where they created out of sheer genius the seminal ideas that subsequently became trends, then schools, and finally fortunes realized in the New York art market. Yoko's role in this world, according to her own account, had been that of brilliant but unacknowledged innovator. Single-handed, she had invented Concept Art, the Happening, Minimalist film, Flower Power, and, as a cofounder, Fluxus, the most wayout art movement since Dada. Sad to say, she had been denied the credit she deserved by a cabal of homosexual artists and gallery owners, who resented the fact that the greatest mind among them belonged to an Oriental woman. Now, with John Lennon's help, she would attain at last her rightful position.

Immediately the Lennons unleashed from their command post high atop the St. Regis an astonishing blitzkrieg. By dint of working around the clock, hiring highly motivated people, and employing every artifice of media manipulation, John and Yoko established themselves overnight as the hardest-charging, hardest-selling of avant-gardists.

Basic to their high-pressure operation was the limitless service provided by their newly indentured bondswoman, May Pang, a young Chinese-American girl, who was a gung-ho rock fan. So that she could be at her masters' beck and call twenty-four hours a day, May had moved into the room adjacent to the Lennons' suite after her predecessor, Lindsay Maricotta, a pretty girl fresh out of Smith, was fired by Yoko for daring to sit next to John at the Grotta Azura.

May's day would begin at ten, when she would knock on the Lennons' door and then call room service for their breakfast of cinnamon toast, coffee, and tea. John and Yoko could not get out of bed until they had received their methadone, illegally prescribed by Dr. Zahm, who would add their doses to the prescription of another patient, an ABKCO employee. (The good doctor also provided his famous clients with "B-12" shots—vitamins laced with speed—which he likewise dispensed liberally to the Lennons' staff to keep them working around the clock.) Once John and Yoko were "up," they would inspect their production line.

Extending down the marble-lined corridor from the master suite were a whole series of bed-sitting rooms that had been converted into ad hoc offices, labs, and shops. Here labored unstintingly all the technicians who were charged with the great task of realizing John's and Yoko's concepts. Joko Productions, the Lennons' film company, occupied one room. It's director, big Steve Gebhardt, an architect turned filmmaker, spent his life bent over a Stienbeck editing console, along with his sound-technician partner, Bob Friess, and Steve's editor and wife, Laura Lesser. Their goal was to turn out a film a week, this breathless pace having been set for Gebhardt from the moment he was hired during the Lennons' first visit to New York. At that time they had knocked out in just two weeks *Up Your Legs Forever* (same anatomy lesson as *Bottoms* but a different part of the body) and *Fly*, which recorded the perambulations of a winged insect in the crotch of a naked and supine woman.

Earlier, in England, Lennon had made a string of Andy Warhol-style films, starting with *Smile:* fifty-two minutes of Lennon sticking out his tongue, raising his eyebrows, and smiling in a garden, with bird cries for a sound track. Then came *Two Virgins,* celebrating the Lennons' consubstantiality by slowing transforming John's face into Yoko's. *Erection* followed: eighteen months of shooting stills of a building under construction, so that all the images could be run together finally to show the structure rapidly rising. Getting it up was Lennon's basic theme. *Self-portrait* he described as: "My prick, that's all you saw . . . but it dribbled at the end. That was accidental. The idea was for it to slowly rise and fall—but it didn't." *Apotheosis* was a gaseous variation: A camera attached to a helium balloon rose straight up into a cloud—producing five long minutes of white-out.

The Lennons had flown to Cannes in May 1971 to exhibit their work before an audience of cineasts. These sophisticated viewers raised such a ruckus during the eighteen silent minutes of *Apotheosis* that Lennon ran out of the theater in despair. *Fly* met with a somewhat better response because, as one reviewer observed, "the fly exhibited a degree of hammy exuberance, rubbing his forelegs and strutting about, that was astonishing in one so small." Asked what were his favorite motion pictures, Lennon replied with characteristic candor: "I really prefer watching TV to movies." Yoko had first tasted fame, however, with *Bottoms,* so she was dead set on making a great name for herself in pictures. Indeed, now that Andy Warhol had retired from the screen, the Lennons were confident they could swiftly become the world's leading underground moviemakers, an accomplishment which would justify them in buying a Hollywood studio.

Another room on the seventeenth floor of the St. Regis served as the photo studio of Iain Macmillan, a pale, puffy-eyed young man, who had shot (from Paul's specifications) the famous cover for *Abbey Road*. Iain had been flown in from England to realize Yoko's inchoate scheme for a one-woman show at the Museum of Modern Art. Not an actual exhibition, this was to be a Concept Art show—but Yoko could never come up with the concept. Then, one day, sitting up in bed with John, holding court, she got into her obsession with flies and suddenly plucked the idea out of the air. She ordered that a bottle full of flies, equal in volume to her body, be released in the sculpture garden of the MOMA. As the flies escaped, Macmillan was to follow them and photograph them all over the city. When he asked how he would know which were Yoko's flies, she replied that they would be scented with her favorite perfume, Ma Griffe.

After the original plan proved unfeasible, poor Iain was confronted by an even worse task. He recalls being stuck for hours inside a polyethylene tent into which a thousand flies had been released. After taking countless close-ups of these insects, he was able to superimpose their images on shots of familiar New York scenes and landmarks so as to make up a 116-page catalog for the imaginary exhibition. The real fun began when Yoko announced the show in the *Village Voice* and sent her gofer, Peter Bendry, a bearded little English hippie, to walk back and forth before MOMA inside a sandwich board advertising the nonexistent show. When people began entering the museum, holding in their hands the catalog they had received from the man in the sandwich board, the staff was not amused.

Fly became the title of Yoko's next album, which was a tit-for-tat complement to John's *Imagine*. Most of the same musicians were employed, but Yoko injected the novelty of a band of crude mechanical instruments—self-beating drums and violins that hung from music stands—designed by Fluxus artist Joe Jones. When the album was released, John and Yoko went on the Howard Smith show to hype it. John outdid himself in the extravagance of his praise for Yoko's music, comparing her with Little Richard. As Lennon was one of the most discriminating listeners in the whole history of rock music, the question is whether he was sincere in his praise or was conning the public.

The answer lies partly in the fact that John Lennon believed that anybody could be famous—and not just for fifteen minutes. Though in one humor he might describe himself as a genius, when he got on the opposite tack, he would treat his gifts dismissively, for John knew that in many ways he was mediocre. He couldn't compare for looks, voice, or stage presence with an Elvis, nor did he have a great songwriter's gift for a tune. He certainly wasn't much as a guitarist, and even his verses were pretty slight as poetry. So Lennon lived, as do so many pop idols, with the perpetual awareness of the enormous incongruity between what he was and the impact he had made. Hence, he could say sincerely that Yoko should be famous because fame was a wholly irrational condition. What's more, John was a great believer in the power of publicity. He was confident that if he really put enough effort into the job, he could shove Yoko down the public's throat. The alternative to this attitude—acknowledging that Yoko was in no wise his peer as an artist—was simply intolerable because their relationship was founded on the idea that they were the same soul in two persons. Parity was an indispensable condition for their symbiosis. So ultimately it didn't matter what Yoko was by objective standards. She *had* to be what John imagined her to be: his fellow genius.

The Lennons' campaign to take over the New York avant-garde was, therefore, in large measure, a publicity campaign designed to persuade the public that, as John told May Pang, "artists like Yoko, not the Beatles, were the true visionaries." To make sure that message was transmitted faithfully by the press, John and Yoko developed a system for putting away reporters and interviewers. First, the journalist would be felt out by May Pang, who would report his predelictions to Yoko. Then he would be given the privilege of spending some time alone with Lennon, who would bleat about the dreadful way that his wife had been abused by the English press, thus arousing the reporter's sense of justice and his protective impulses. Finally, Yoko would meet a man who was nicely set up for her pitch, which she would tune to fit his prejudices.

When the Lennons really wanted to ingratiate themselves with a journalist, they could do even better. Jill Johnston of the *Village Voice* recalled that John and Yoko sent her a dozen roses, invited her to their room at midnight, and took her shopping one afternoon on Eighth Street, where they insisted on buying her a pair of shoes. The proffered intimacy boomeranged, however, because the more Johnston saw of the Lennons, the less she liked them. "Yoko played the greedy *grande dame,* going from store to store, demanding, 'Gimme this, gimme that!'" Johnston reported, while John "appeared to be courting attention, as if he needed a shot of it between limo rides."

What Yoko really wanted was not an article here or a review there but a whole issue of a magazine devoted primarily to her, as *Rolling Stone* had devoted itself to John the previous year. *Crawdaddy,* a rock publication fallen on hard times, had just changed hands. Just as desperate as Yoko, it capitulated to her demands that she choose her own interviewer and that she have final approval of the copy. Yoko selected Henry Edwards (ironically, the same man who later wrote May Pang's memoirs). Why? Because Yoko had turned up a statement by Edwards that the three outstanding Minimalist artists were Tony Smith, Robert Morris—and Yoko Ono. What the humorless Yoko failed to perceive was that Edwards's use of her name was not intended as a compliment but as a joke.

Edwards's first appointment with Yoko was scheduled for the supper hour. When he arrived at the Lennons' suite, he found her lying abed with the sheet up to her chin and her long black hair down the bedclothes. She was in shock after having just learned that Simon and Schuster was not going to give her a four-color jacket for its edition of *Grapefruit.* Lennon was sitting atop the bed cross-legged, watching an oldie-goldie rock 'n' roll show on TV. Totally oblivious of Yoko's suffering, every once in a while he would exclaim with juvenile fervor: "That's a song I used to play, Yoko!"

She would reply in the tone of a depressed but indulgent mother: "It's a very nice song, John."

After forty-five minutes of absorption in the TV screen, Lennon picked up the phone and ordered supper from room service. He asked for three steaks, without troubling to ask Edwards if he wanted to eat steak. When the waiter rolled the meal into the room and lifted off the silver covers, instead of serving the steaks on plates he began to slice them, acting obviously on orders from the kitchen. John stopped the man and instructed him to cut the meat up into little squares. When the steaks had been piled up in bowls, like Alpo, the Lennons fell to eating them with their hands.

No sooner had the meal ended than there was a knock at the door and a gruff voice growling: "It's me!" John and Yoko brightened up instantly, like kids about to receive their Christmas gifts. In walked their chauffeur, Tom Basalari, swarthy and unshaven, looking decidedly beat. "How many did you get?" crowed Yoko.

"I got three—but what a job!" moaned the ex-narc. (Basalari had been indicted and suspended from duty for an alleged drug offense committed while serving on the Harlem detail. At this time he was awaiting trial. He was later convicted.) Putting down the big sack he was carrying over his shoulder, he extracted three battered old wooden medicine chests. It turned out that he had been riding up and down the subway system, looking for toilets that still had their original chests. When he found one, he would rip it out of the wall and put it in his bag. The idea was that John and Yoko would make out of these cabinets art pieces that would symbolize New York City. The transformation from urban detritus to avant-garde art would be achieved by affixing to each chest a plastic tag. They had a little machine of a sort found in kindergartens that made the tags, which read "John and Yoko."

Edwards spent a month conducting his interviews. During that time he got a pretty clear idea of how things stood between John and Yoko. When Yoko desired to converse with him, she would say: "Let me give John something to do, and then we can talk." Often this distraction was not necessary because John would nod off and sleep through the evening. Edwards concluded: "There is a public out there and that public has substituted the myth of John and Yoko for the vacuum in their own lives. The Lennons are a mythic couple and they love it. They love having their pictures taken; they love publicity; they love success." He also recognized, as he wrote later in the May Pang book, that "for the press and for anyone who would listen, John and Yoko spoke with total conviction about how much they loved each other, how much support they gave each other, and how wondrous was their devotion to each other. They said it; they meant it; they believed it—they were *on!*"

But when the camera was switched off or the tape recorder stopped rolling, the stars sank back into their normal selves and exhibited a marked indifference to each other. As May Pang observed, "They spent enormous amounts of time in bed together, but they rarely kissed or touched. As far as I could see, there was nothing sensual about their relationship." Basically Edwards found Yoko sympathetic. He saw her as this "nice, sensitive, artistic lady married to a rather boorish rock star." This is precisely the image that Yoko projected in the three-hour made-for-TV program she authorized in 1985. There can be no question that it was exactly how she saw her relationship with John, for whom her favorite word was "clod."

The interview that emerged from Edwards's lengthy commerce with Yoko was just what she ordered. It was *Ono Remembers*. Though she was on her best behavior, this lengthy screed is full of her undisguisable self. At one point she discusses Janov's views on physical defects, which had inspired John to say that his myopia was a product of his childhood sufferings. Yoko's version of this same delusion is even more bizarre. Speaking of her diminutive stature, she fumed: "I am a small woman because people repressed me when I was young. My bones stopped growing because of the repression that surrounded me. Did you ever realize that the great aggressors in the world, Napoleon, Hitler, are all physically small people who have been repressed." Think about it!

WATER ON THE BRAIN

The climax of the Lennons' campaign to become the leaders of the New York avant-garde was reached at Syracuse, where in October 1971 Yoko Ono had a hung one-woman show at the Everson Museum of Fine Arts. Housed in a fortresslike cast-concrete structure by I. M. Pei, the Everson's collection consisted for the most part of American ceramics and those contemporary American painters that had received the stamp of approval of the art establishment. Attendance was poor, and the attitude of the community one of indifference. To remedy these conditions, the trustees had hired recently a dynamic young director, whose mission it was to stir things up.

Jim Haristhis was ideally suited for the role of gallery guerrilla. A tall, twangy-voiced Texan, he showed his stuff the moment he was introduced to the famous John and Yoko. Between bites on a cheeseburger in a Madison Avenue coffeeshop, he offered the Lennons one-sixth of his annual budget plus the full resources of the museum—seven galleries and a sculpture court plus an auditorium, three equipment rooms, a studio, souvenir shop, and parking lot—for a solo show by Yoko Ono, with John Lennon as guest curator. It was an offer the Lennons couldn't refuse. It was also a hard order to fill.

Normally only a major artist who had been productive for thirty or forty years could have undertaken an exhibition conceived on such a colossal scale. Even a prolific master would have had to reach out in every direction to bring together all the requisite components, borrowing work from other museums and private collectors, to be supplemented by unsold pieces, things recently completed, models, sketches, photographs, etc. Yoko Ono was in a totally different position. Her most distinctive work consisted of concepts or scenarios sketched out in terse instructions. She had also done a fair number of performance pieces and some films. But the only physical objects she could present would be little oddities, like her smile boxes—which smiled back at you—or the bifurcated furniture from *Half-a-Wind*. All this stuff had been kept in a single room at Tittenhurst. The history of Yoko's show at the Everson, therefore, is actually the story of how fifty thousand square feet of gallery space was filled by an artist who didn't have enough work to occupy more than a single bedroom. No wonder the show was titled *This Is Not Here.*

Yoko's only recourse was to convert all her concepts into solid three-dimensional objects, an enormous task, made especially difficult by the vagueness of her directions. What's more, she had but six weeks in which to fabricate all these pieces and perfect their installation. Such overwhelming demands would have defeated most people. Not our Yoko! She was confident that she could summon up a whole museum full of as yet unmade art simply by conning one man, the late George Macuinas.

A legend in the avant-garde, Macuinas was the founder of Fluxus, an art movement named for a bowel movement and defined by him as the "fusion of Spike Jones, vaudeville, gag, children's games and Duchamp." What this meant in practice was filling boxes with oddments from the odd-lot shops on Canal Street or designing kooky graphics with lots of camp copperplate or contriving bizarre rituals, like Fluxus weddings, divorces, and funerals, while meantime recording every little Flux fart as if it were an act of Congress.

A classic underground man, Macuinas lived in a basement at 80 Wooster Street that was half wood shop, half junk shop. Piled helter-skelter all about the premises were boxes of glass eyes, WWII gas masks, cartons of processed food, and even rabbit droppings. A man of terrifying mood swings, Macuinas shot himself full of cortisone every day to control his chronic asthma. To soothe his flayed nerves, he played Gregorian chants. When you flushed his toilet, you got another sound—a hysterical laugh.

The oddest feature of Macuinas's pad was its primitive security system. The door to the basement bristled with razor-sharp paper-cutter blades thrust out like samurai swords. The back wall of the bedroom was fitted with a submarine's escape hatch. The eccentric artist often ducked out of this hole in disguise, for he delighted in getting himself up as a woman or even a bride, a role he played at his own topsy-turvy Flux wedding. What obliged him to resort to these tricks was his work as the pioneer developer of SoHo, where at this time he was busy converting factory lofts into artists' studios for next to nothing. Trained originally as an architect, he created through his enterprise millions of dollars in real estate values while being relentlessly persecuted by state and local building authorities. He was also destined to receive a horrible beating from an irate contractor that cost the visionary builder an eye.

Macuinas was perfect for Yoko's purposes because first, he was a former admirer, who had told his mother when Yoko exhibited some burnt-holed canvases at his short-lived Almus Gallery in 1961 that he wanted to marry the Japanese artist. Second, Macuinas had at his command a whole network of carpenters, mechanics, and building supply houses and possessed the knack of making these people work fast, well, and cheaply. Not only could he turn Yoko's fancies into slick, stylish, carefully crafted objects, but as a graphics designer he could also create all the print pieces for the show, designing the poster, the catalog, etc. As it turned out, the single most impressive artifact inspired by the exhibition was a typographic composition, about the size of a newspaper, that reproduced chockablock every notice and review ever received by Yoko Ono in America or in England. Displaying a welter of typefaces and print sizes, old photographs and illustrations, funny headlines (often punch lines), this fascinating coagulation epitomized better than anything else the show's spirit of avant-garde homage.

Yoko's strength as a con artist—a title in which she gloried—was not exhausted by persuading George Macuinas to drop everything in order to make things that weren't supposed to be there. She had many other tricks up her sleeve. In late September one thousand artists received in the mail a printed sheet of paper enclosed in a plastic envelope. When removed, it proved wet. It read: "Yoko Ono wishes to invite you to participate in a water event by requesting you to produce with her a water sculpture, by submitting a water container or idea of one which form [*sic*] half of the sculpture. She will supply the other half—water. The sculpture will be credited as water sculpture by Yoko Ono and yourself." The response to this solicitation was about 10 percent, which, judged by the standards of the direct-mail business, was extremely good. Soon the Everson was receiving a steady stream of odd-looking objects designed to hold Yoko's water.

By adding the enormous demands of the Everson show to all the other work in progress on the seventeenth floor of the St. Regis, Yoko produced a Marx Brothers effect. Night and day the incommodious bed-sitting rooms of the turn-of-the-century hotel were jammed with people who worked with the determination of fanatics—or speed freaks. Steve Gebhardt, still busy reducing the hundred thousand feet of *Imagine* to fifty-eight minutes, was ordered to prepare a whole new series of film loops and programs for the gallery show. Iain Macmillan was now doing photographic sleight of hand to make John's face merge with Yoko's face on a rotating record label. And there was even a room in which a seamstress bent over a sewing machine all day fashioning the Lennons' chamois clothes.

Yoko was not content simply to exhibit her art at the Everson; she was also keen on peddling souvenirs in the gift shop. So, in addition to her countless calls to artists and journalists, she had to haggle with garment district types, who were printing up vast quantities of black T-shirts and bath towels blazoned in white lettering: YOKO, JOHN, MRS. LENNON, THIS IS NOT HERE, YOU ARE HERE, FLY, UP YOUR LEGS FOREVER. Another of Yoko's conceptions was an E-shaped box, which, when unfolded, offered from its many compartments such goodies as a copy of *Grapefruit,* glass keys, Monopoly money, newspaper clippings, etc. The price of this Fluxus-inspired object was $100.

So busy were John and Yoko, as they sought to supplant Andy Warhol as leader of the New York avant-garde, that they missed an ideal opportunity to commune with their prototype Salvador Dali. The clown prince of modern art, with his antennalike mustachios and gold-capped cane, had been popping up recently in a stage box at the Fillmore East, where he always got a circus intro from Bill Graham and a good hand from the rock fans. For the fall season he had taken up residence, as he had done for decades, at the St. Regis, where he could be found having a late breakfast every morning at the King Cole Bar and Grill while his manager's pet ocelots stood guard at the entrance. What would have been most valuable to John Lennon would have been the recognition not of how similar were the ambitions of old and new avant-gardists but of how astonishingly alike were he and Dali in personality, for the Spanish surrealist was the English pop star's alter ego: childish, timorous, given to wild enthusiasms and current fads, totally self-absorbed and utterly dependent, like a little boy, on his aggressive, domineering, and proprietorial wife, Gala. And what could Yoko have been thinking when she lost this chance to solicit an "astounding" water piece from the world's greatest master of such wacky shtick?

While John and Yoko lay abed conceiving ideas, George Macuinas labored to such good effect that he fabricated all the pieces and got them installed at the Everson right on schedule. Three days before the opening, John and Yoko appeared at the museum to lay claim to the work. Even for a man as devoid of ego as Macuinas, this was certain to be a tense moment, for as his friend and fellow Lithuanian Jonas Mekas explained, "He would give everything he had to others. Yet he was extremely stubborn, and she was just as stubborn. So their disagreements were absolute." They were also explosive.

The day before the opening, Yoko and Macuinas had a violent fight. Every witness to this battle offers a different explanation of its origin: Kevin Harrison—the hippie plumber who was installing a maze of twenty-foot-tall Lucite panels in the basement—insists that the quarrel broke out over his job; Jonas Mekas says the battle was joined over some natural-finished wooden boxes that Yoko demanded be painted white; Almus Salcius, Macuinas's principal confidant, offered the most likely explanation. Macuinas was on retainer, but his costs for materials, workmen, transportation, etc., had gone way over budget. Hence, he was facing a wipeout. When he recognized that Yoko was not going compensate him for his cost overrun, he not only blew his stack but threatened to fill the Everson with illuminating gas and blow them all sky high!

Next moment he dashed out of the building and down the main drag, where he found a barbershop. Leaping into the chair, he ordered the barber to shave his head. Then he returned to the museum and demanded transportation to the airport. En route the car crossed a major southbound highway. Macuinas threw open the door while the car was in motion and hurled himself outside. Miraculously he landed on his feet. Sticking out his thumb, he bummed a ride home. He and Yoko exchanged acrimonious letters, but they did not speak to each other again for years.

The opening date for *This Is Not Here* had been calculated to coincide with John's birthday, Saturday, 9 October 1971. The day before, a mass press conference was staged in the museum's auditorium. When John and Yoko walked onstage, they were greeted with a barrage of flashbulbs and a spontaneous rush of people to the stage apron, as mikes and cameras were thrust at the stars from every direction. Yoko was wearing the same costume in which she had been photographed for the past three days: black turtleneck and hot pants with black boots, beret, and a brown plaid jacket whose lapels parted to reveal a long gold chain sustaining a gold medallion. Her speech went straight to the point. "In this show," she declaimed as John pushed her hand-held microphone closer to her mouth, "I'd like to prove you don't need talent to be an artist. Artist is just a frame of mind. Anybody can be an artist. Anybody can communicate if they're desperate enough. There's no such thing as imagination of the artist. Imagination, if you're desperate enough, can come out of necessity. . . . This show is the work of a very untalented artist who is desperate for communication."

On that cue hundreds of guests and journalists were turned loose to examine the show. What they found was one of the most elaborate and costly installations ever seen outside the major art centers of America. The $100,000 allocated by the Everson had been supplemented with $70,000 of John Lennon's money. What his wealth bought was a show that didn't miss a bet.

As the visitor entered the lofty glass-ceilinged sculpture court, he encountered first a dialogue between Yoko and John conducted through side-by-side pieces. This colloquy took the form of you-say, I-say contradictions. Thus, Yoko's "This window is 2,000ft wide" was answered by John with "This window is 5ft wide," and Yoko's "Stay until the room is blue" was countered by John's "Get out when the room turns blue." The badinage continued to the point at which Yoko announced the title of the show, *This Is Not Here,* only to be contradicted by John with the title of his last show, *You Are Here.*

As the visitor followed the large route map, he wandered from one whimsical notion to another, like the booths of a fun fair. "Portrait of John Lennon as a Young Cloud" turned out to be a bed on which the spectator lay and stared up through the skylight—on a day of pelting rain. "Lennon Tour Tickets" was a volley of inside jokes for Lennon fans; for example, "ticket to visit John and Lee Eastman to give your copyrights away." In the adjoining space was a "Vending Arcade" of spoofy machines supposed to dispense acorns, air, tears, and metal slugs. A whole gallery was filled with small "Part Paintings" of "cloud, glacier, moon, Ku Klux Klan, smog, albino, smoke, diamond from the Affair of the Diamond Necklace, harvest moon, star, snow, white corpuscle, White House, soda, sodium, rhodium, Battle of the Bulge, Mona Lisa's mole, Man with the Iron Mask, jig-saw puzzles."

Ascending the monumental spiral staircase to the second level, the visitor found a gallery dedicated to all Yoko's past pieces, including the "Eternal Clock" (which has no bands), the all-white chess set, the apple on a pedestal (which someone ate and then replaced with the core), blank canvases for the spectator to paint upon, and some novelties like the "Danger Box (put your hand in at your own risk)," which proved to be a box filled with rubber prickles. The adjacent gallery, "6th Dimension," contained a Happening. Every visitor was obliged to don a gas mask with blacked-out goggles. Then, after being asked if he preferred mineral, vegetable, or animal food, he was given something to eat and encouraged to crawl through an obstacle course.

By far the most interesting exhibit was the "Water Event." This extraordinary collection was worthy of P. T. Barnum's famous museum. Though the general level of wit was not much higher than the water level of the pieces, the sheer miscellany of this hydrocephalic aggregation was delightful. John Lennon's water piece was one of the best. Labeled "Napoleon's Bladder," it consisted of a strange pink mass inside a clear plastic bag. Other Beatle offerings included a milk bottle from George and from Ringo a green plastic garbage bag full of water, bearing the legend: "This sponge was caught off the Lybian coast, taken to the Kalymos Island and prepared. It is filled with British water. When it dries it will be a sponge caught off the Lybian coast, taken to Kalymos Island and prepared and filled with water from another land." Not a bad parody of Concept Art.

Dylan sent a copy of *Nashville Skyline* in a fish tank, a hillbilly Atlantis. Tim Leary sent a capsule. Isamu Noguchi made an elaborate pun by offering a rock—the title of Yoko's first environment, John's music, and Noguchi's favorite sculptural material. The same punning spirit informed the most admired contribution: a VW Beetle convertible, which the artist Bob Watts filled with water to produce a "Water Beetle." At the other end of the scale of substantiality, though not of wit, was the novelist John Barth's contribution: a slip of paper reading "The water you make is equal to the water you take."

The Maginot construction of the Everson made it one of the few museums that could have withstood the onslaught of Lennon's fans. On opening day eight thousand kids lined up in the rain outside this gallery that normally didn't see eight thousand visitors in a year. These kids were not the peace-loving hippies of the Sixties but the Brat Pack of the Seventies. They didn't give a flying fuck about Concept Art or Yoko Ono. They had come to see John Lennon. Once the Levi's-clad horde began pouring into the Everson, the museum's officials suddenly recognized that they were confronting a potential disaster. Giving Yoko's lib-lab philosophy of Everyman as artist a radical twist, the kids smashed and trashed, defaced and looted the exhibition.

"Water was the theme of the show and water was soon everywhere, from leaking objects, faucets, overflowing toilets," reported Henry Edwards. As the watery chaos spread, May Pang sat with a grim John and Yoko in the museum library. "They had been up for days," she recalled, "and were both very cranky. The staff would appear with reports of the latest damage. 'They just broke the glass hammers,' someone reported. 'Do you know how much those fuckin' hammers cost?' John scowled. 'Thousands apiece.' 'If they were broken, that was the way it was meant to be,' Yoko replied sullenly but with a kind of Zen calm. 'I told you to put 'em under glass,' retorted John. 'I told you to put the whole fuckin' show under glass. I told you not to let 'em touch everything. I told you they'd break whatever they get their fuckin' hands on!' he shouted. Yoko was impervious. 'What was meant to be was meant to be,' she said again. A museum aide suddenly appeared. 'Another toilet is overflowing.' 'I suppose that was fuckin' meant to be, too,' said John. 'Yes,' said Yoko. 'Yes.'"

To hype the show, Yoko had set afloat rumors of a Beatles' reunion. By the end of the day the word was out that the Fab Four were going to jam inside the museum at midnight. Long before that hour another mob of kids had massed outside the building and was clamoring for admission. The show's creator, David Ross, rushed over and was appalled by what he saw. The situation struck him as "one of the great potential disasters, like the Warhol opening in Philly"—the famous occasion when Andy Warhol and Edie Sedgwick were nearly crushed to death by a crowd. As Ross ran around, trying to head off the stampede, the kids decided to take matters into their own hands. They broke down the steel doors and rampaged through the building. After marauding for hours, they were quieted finally when Allen Ginsberg, who had been attending Lennon's birthday party across the street at the Hotel Syracuse, got the kids chanting. After the riot subsided, the museum was a mess. Yoko was obliged to consolidate what remained of her show in a much smaller—and better guarded—space.

When John got the final damage report, he quipped: "I guess it's *not* there!"

Yoko was thrilled by all the publicity that her show had generated, but she was infuriated by the many artists who were angry with her because their pieces had not been installed correctly or had been destroyed. Another source of resentment was the exclusionary lines that Yoko had drawn all about the show, marking out zones where only this or that class of people could enter. This sort of arrangement is characteristic of Japanese social functions, where an elaborate pecking order is maintained, but to a group of New York artists and journalists no greater provocation could be offered. So fierce was the resentment against Yoko that John finally advised her to call up some honest and well-disposed person, like Howard Smith, and ask him for his frank opinion of her problem.

Howard remembered distinctly the night he got this surprising call. "John says you're the only one who's honest with me," Yoko began. "I know I haven't been good to you lately. [When Howard left his hotel room the night of John's birthday party, he had been steered by a group of policemen past the door of the Lennons' suite and ushered into the elevator. This made him so angry that he left the hotel immediately and went to a friend's farm nearby.] What I want to know is, What is it that people don't like about me?" To John, in another part of the room, she called out, "John, is that right? Did I ask the question right?" Then, turning back to Howard but shifting to the third person, she repeated: "Why don't people like Yoko? John and I have been arguing about this. He said you would tell me truth. You knew me before I was John's Yoko."

Hardly believing his ears, Howard replied: "You really wanna hear, Yoko?"

Breathlessly she answered, "Yes, yes, yes!" adding: "Especially the museum! Why everybody hate me when I was so nice that I let everybody come to my wonderful event?" Howard took a deep breath and plunged.

"Yoko," he said, "nobody likes to be strangled by the person they're talking to. When people talk to you about art, music, whatever it is, you feel you know more about it than any human being on the face of the earth—which you *may*! Let's assume you *do*! Let's assume you're as good an artist as Michelangelo. Nobody wants to have Michelangelo's hands around their neck, squeezing their windpipe until they admit you're Michelangelo! And that's what it feels like, talking to you about art. Even me, who's a fairly strong-willed person, feels like I have to flee from your presence. You're choking me! You have me in a hammerlock! You're gonna gouge my eyes out unless I admit that you're the greatest artist. . . ."

Yoko cut him off at this point, screeching, *"I am a fantastic artist! You mean I'm not a good artist!"*

Suddenly Howard recognized that he had stepped into the steel-jawed trap that he had just been analyzing. As his lips tightened with exasperation, he could hear Yoko yelling at Lennon: *"John! John! Howard says I'm nothing but a lousy shwew* [shrew]. *I am not! John, am I loud shwew that chokes people?"*

John hadn't the faintest idea of what had inspired this outburst, but he yelled back: "No, you listen to Howard. He's telling you the truth!"

Yoko screamed. *"Ahhhh, John! You ganging up on me!"*

ROCK 'N' REVOLUTION

Several weeks after the opening of the Everson show, John and Yoko had supper with Jerry Rubin at Serendipity. Sitting in a room that looks like a cross between an old-time ice cream parlor and a rummage sale, the famous couple laid a proposition on the bearded little coxswain of the New Left that blew his mind. "Yoko says that they want to live in New York and do things," reported Rubin, who habitually recounts the past in the historic present, like one of Damon Runyon's "guys." "John says he wants to put together a new band. He wants to play, and he wants to give all the money back to the people. I was so ecstatic that I embraced them."

Rubin's glee was not inspired simply by his delight in welcoming a new convert to the fold. By late 1971 the top banana of "Guerrilla Theater" was registering an ominous drop in his Nielsen ratings. Not only had the mass media grown tired of his frenzied antics, but within the ranks of his own party, the Yippies, a revolt was being fomented by a formidable adversary, Thomas King Forcade, a brilliant but unstable young man with a distinct relish for violence. Rubin, condemned by his own rule—"Never trust anyone over thirty!"—was witnessing the formation of a splinter group called the Zippies, whose motto was: "Put the Zip back into Yip." The Zippies would soon celebrate Rubin's thirty-fourth birthday by presenting him with a big white cake—smashed in his face!

Just as John and Yoko had sought to lead the avant-garde after it had been co-opted by the art establishment, so now the naïve and ill-informed Lennons were jumping on the radical merry-go-round just as everyone else was about to jump off. Actually, it had taken only one phone call to pull the Lennons. Back in June when Jerry saw their picture in the New York *Daily News*, he had called up ABKCO. Within two hours Yoko had called him back. The following Saturday afternoon—on the same weekend John and Yoko performed with Zappa—Rubin was standing under the arch in Washington Square with Abbie and Anita Hoffman, awaiting the stars. When their limo rolled up, the radicals piled in and rolled down to St. Mark's Place, headed for Hoffman's pad—whose every room had been bugged by the feds. "John was very playful," recollected Rubin. "As we passed the cops, he would lie down on the floor of his limo, wave his red, white, and blue sneakers out the window, and shout, 'Look! I'm a patriot!'"

The first meeting, which lasted five hours, was devoted to everyone's convincing everyone that all were on the same wavelength. Rubin talked about "how the Yippies had been applying Beatles' tactics to politics, trying to merge music and life. We talked about their bed-in as a Yippie action. All five of us were amazed at how we had been into the same kinds of things all these years." Rubin discovered John's political attitudes could be packaged as two slogans: "It's us against them" and "We can do anything."

During the months that followed, John and Yoko had been too busy with all their other projects and problems to make a major contribution to American politics. But once the tumult of the Everson show had subsided, the restless pair decided on a complete change of front. Instead of blitzing the New York art world, they would concentrate their energies on radicalism. Symbolic of their shift in priorities was their change of address. On 1 November they moved from the top floor of New York's most aristocratic hotel to the basement of a shabby apartment conversion in the West Village.

The Lennons' new pad at 155½ Bank Street, a decrepit old house with a blank gray facade, was a sunken loft. After passing through a dark, narrow service section and pulling aside an American flag, you entered a two-story backyard extension that resembled a bohemian painter's studio. The serrated skylight was connected to the floor by a spiral iron staircase painted muddy green. A huge crib bed, with a headboard made of a dark church pew, jutted from the white brick wall like a platform stage whose prompter's box was a big color TV set.

No sooner was John Lennon installed in this minimal habitation than he began dreaming of no possessions. When the New Yorker Talk of the Town came around to check out the new arrivals, John recited his vows of poverty. "I don't want that big house we built for ourselves in England," he protested. "I don't want the bother of owning all these big houses and big cars, even though our company, Apple, pays for it all. All structures and buildings and everything I own will be dissolved and got rid of. I'll cash in my chips, and anything that's left I'll make the best use of. Yoko is a three-tatami woman, and she's been working on me to get rid of the possessions complex, which is something that happens to people who were poor, like myself." Yoko chimed in to say that since she had been reared in great wealth, it was natural for her to yearn for the simple life of the poor artist in Greenwich Village, which she had enjoyed so much in earlier years. Possessed now by this altruistic spirit, the Lennons turned to the task of liberating the workers and arousing youth from its capitalist-induced apathy.

Just as John was vowing to give away all but the most essential possessions to "libraries and prisons," he was relieved suddenly of the necessity of giving away even what he most prized. One night the bell rang, and Lennon, violating the first rule of survival in New York, opened the door without first identifying the caller. In slouched two wasted-looking junkies, mumbling something about "collecting." As John froze with fear, these two cats started ripping off the pad. They boosted the color TV, which Lennon begged them to leave, and they took a Dali lithograph off the wall. They also snatched up a small antique table, just for good measure. No sooner were they out the door than John realized with horror that in the drawer of the table was his address book, which contained the locations and phone numbers of all those radicals who were in hiding, including Tim Leary, who was living in Switzerland after his California prison break, and Dana Beal, the inventor of the smoke-in, who was wanted by the FBI. Calling Tom Basalari, John poured out his woes. The veteran narc put the word on the vine, and in six hours Lennon had his book back, as well as an explanation of the heist. It turned out that the previous tenant of the pad, Joe Butler of the Lovin' Spoonful, had welshed on a gambling debt. The outraged bookie had sent a couple of needy boys down to take up a collection.

That winter John and Yoko held court lying naked in their bed of state, while their honored guests perched on its sides. The king and queen of the counterculture showed no sense of shame, even when they had to exhibit their nudity. (Joe Butler was astonished by Lennon's body: "John was amazingly flabby. Even though he wasn't heavy, he didn't have any muscle tissue.") Jerry Rubin, acting as the royal couple's majordomo, began introducing his radical comrades into the presence. These heavily bearded and roughly clad worthies arrived at the bohemian throne room like a reprise of the Chicago conspiracy trial: Dave Dellinger, who would soon defect to the boy guru Mahari Ji; Huey Newton, who would trade threats of murder via radio with Eldridge Cleaver in Algeria; Bobby Seale, who had been bound and gagged in the Chicago courtroom; and Rennie Davis, the movement's greatest organizer, whose tip had been infiltrated recently by an FBI snitch, "Crazy Annie" Collegio. Soon John Lennon could say that he had been to bed with the entire leadership of the New Left.

The political jam sessions at Bank Street, which sometimes raved on for ten hours at a stretch, concluded finally on an audacious note: the decision to star John and Yoko in a "revolutionary road show" that would meld rock music, avant-garde happenings, radical rhetoric and protest demonstrations in a hippie jamboree. The tour would kick off on the East Coast early in the summer and rock across the country, until it wound up in August at San Diego, where the Republican party would be holding its presidential nominating convention. There the revolutionaries, charged up with the excitement of their triumphal progress and acting as the spearhead of a great youth crusade, would have their final showdown with the Nixon administration. When some-one inside the Lennons' circle tipped off the government to this plan, the administration saw it as the work of the Chicago Seven, who were using John Lennon as sucker bait.

The officials in Washington couldn't have been more wrong. Those present at the sessions testify that the leading architect of the plan was none other than John Winston Ono Lennon, who was the only man among them accustomed to projecting actions on such a grandiose scale.

Actually, Lennon had conceived the idea of the revolutionary road show in the wake of *The Concert for Bangla Desh*, whose success had impressed him deeply. In September 1971 he had proposed in a letter to Eric Clapton to put to sea aboard a big ship (financed by EMI) with a gang of rock musicians, recording engineers, film technicians, and—most important!—a ship's doctor. The plan was to sail from Los Angeles to Tahiti, rehearsing, recording, and filming all the while. Each man would be encouraged to bring along his woman and children so that the whole company would resemble a Swiss Family Lennon. After they had enjoyed a couple of weeks of fun under the palms and hibiscus blossoms, they would resume their cruise tour, with the aim of playing all the countries behind the Iron Curtain. John and Yoko would assert themselves politically, but nobody else was expected to share in these activities. Now, after the spark sessions at Bank Street, the priorities were reversed, and politics took precedence over music. The first test of the revolutionary road show came much sooner than anybody had anticipated.

On 10 December 1971 a rally was scheduled at Ann Arbor on behalf of John Sinclair, the leader of the local hippie community and head of the White Panther party, whose program was "rock 'n' roll, dope, and fucking in the streets." Sinclair had been locked up in prison on a bum rap—ten years for selling two joints to an undercover narc. (It was, however, his third conviction.) Hence, the title of the rally: *Ten for Two*. When Jerry Rubin persuaded John Lennon to appear at this event, John decided to use the occasion as a trial run of the film and record-ing units that would be tracking him across the country that summer. He ordered Joko Productions to truck its cameras and sixteen-track tape gear to Crysler Stadium in Ann Arbor to film the whole rally.

John and Yoko also taped a radio pitch that guaranteed a sold-out house—15,000 freaks.

Topping the bill at a radical rally on behalf of Ann Arbor's most notorious extremist was a much more provocative act than John Lennon recognized. Sinclair's community of "freeks" was by this time the last great stronghold of radicalism in "Amerika." What's more, unlike the highly publicized hippie squatting grounds in Haight-Ashbury or the Lower East Side, Ann Arbor was not a congeries of street people clinging to the underside of a great metropolis. Quite the contrary, these freaks were the lawfully constituted government of the city. In a remarkable election the hippies had won control of the City Council and, as their first and most symbolic act, reduced the penalty for possession of marijuana to a five-dollar fine. At Ann Arbor both sides of the counterculture had found fulfillment: on the one hand, the forklift drug dealers and the dynamiters of CIA facilities and, on the other, the founders of food co-ops, medical clinics, and crisis centers for drug victims and runaway kids. By the same token, no town in America was under more intense surveillance from the forces of law and order. To appear as the champion of revolution in Ann Arbor was to say as emphatically as possible: "Count me in!"

Ten for Two turned out to be the last blast of the counterculture. For seven hours straight Crysler Stadium rocked alternately to explosions of light and sound or buzzed with the boredom and frustration of long lulls, during which technicians struggled to wire up the next act. Meantime, the arena's aisles were patrolled by drug dealers, hawking every high and low in the hippie medicine chest, particularly grass broken off kilo-size bricks.

John Sinclair had honed as the cutting edge of his White Panther party a frenzied band, the MC5 (= Motor City), whose drummer used to play so violently that a man had to be posted next to him to set upright the drums and cymbals knocked down during the course of each rave-up. Now the MC5's successors, a covey of half-naked, superbly hirsute boys called Up, were the principal purveyors of the Methedrine Beat. The joyous fervor of their music was betrayed, however, every time one of the movement's preposterous, ego-tripping leaders stepped onstage and started ranting.

These soon-to-be-forgotten demagogues lent the rally an unforgettable air of self-parody. The most ridiculous of the lot was Bobby Seale, chairman of the Black Panthers, who made his entrance heralded by a phalanx of bad-assed bodyguards, like a ghetto gangster arriving at a big sit-down. After huffing and puffing in the manner of an old-fashioned black preacher, Chairman Bobby delivered himself of this capper line: "The only *so*-lution to *po*-lution is a people's humane re-*vo*-lution!" Got that, bro?

The one deeply affecting moment in the entire night was a phone call from John Sinclair in prison. As Sinclair spoke to his wife, Leni, and his four-year-old son, his voice carrying plaintively through the stadium's huge speakers, he broke down and sobbed uncontrollably. For a few stunning moments all those high and happy freaks experienced the pain of a caged man.

Not till three in the morning did John and Yoko come on, having been preceded by Phil Ochs, Bob Seger, Archie Shepp, Commander Cody, Stevie Wonder, and David Peel and the Lower East Side, who insisted on doing a full set of his street hollers despite the angry protests of the crowd. When John and Yoko joined Peel and Jerry Rubin, they didn't comport themselves like the king and queen of the counterculture. They looked embarrassed and out of place, like the couple from downstairs who have come up to ask: "Could you hold it down a little, please?" John's tone was totally at odds with the bombast that had filled the air all night. "We came here tonight," he said quietly, "to say that apathy isn't it. And that we can all do something. So Flower Power didn't work. So what! We start again."

Then, employing an acoustic guitar, Lennon sang the jinglelike "Attica State," followed by "Luck of the Irish," its harsh words counterpointed against a melancholy music hall melody, and Yoko performed her feminist pep song, "Sisters, O Sisters."

The only interesting piece in this clutch of agitprop pieces was Lennon's plea for John Sinclair's release. An archaic, rural strain, twanged out on a National Steel guitar and intoned with folkie sincerity, this bit of hip primitivism came to climax on the plea phrase, repeated no less than fifteen times.

The crowd, though radical in politics, was primed for entertainment. It had waited seven hours to see and hear the legendary John Lennon. Now when he walked off after performing four unfamiliar tunes, the whole audience rose up in protest. It felt cheated. But to the Lennons, the great thing was that they had testified to their commitment. Pleasing an audience was something that entertainers worried about—not the king and queen of the counterculture.

On the Monday following the rally, John Sinclair was released while he appealed his conviction. The Michigan Supreme Court had based its decision on a vote in the state legislature three days earlier to reduce the maximum sentence for possession of marijuana to one year.

The Lennons were delighted by what they took to be their first political success. They stepped up the pace of their activities, appearing in rapid succession at a benefit for the victims of Attica at the Apollo Theater, at the trial of the Harlem Six, and at a street demonstration on behalf of the IRA. (John had taken to identifying himself as Irish, whereas in fact, he had been reared by the Stanleys, who were Welsh in

origin.) The drift of Lennon's political development was toward ever
more drastic causes and actions. Even Jerry Rubin had to concede that
"John was more radical than I was in this period. He would joke about
their earlier projects, saying, 'She's the one who's into peace and love.'
He was angry, really angry. He ranted and raved about the police."

Lennon's growing infatuation with revolutionary violence was most
clearly revealed in his friendship with A. J. Webberman, the
"Dylanologist" and leading member of the Rock Liberation Front, dedicated to saving rock from commercialization. John had started off by
attacking Webberman in the *Village Voice* for his persecution of Bob
Dylan, whose house on MacDougal Street Webberman had picketed
with signs reading SLUM LORD and whose garbage he had ransacked
looking for evidence of Dylan's enigmatic character. But when Webberman turned up with his gang at Allen Klein's office to demonstrate
over the distribution of funds from the Bangladesh concert, Lennon
abruptly reversed himself. He invited the feisty street scholar to a sit-
down at Bank Street, where he quickly became infatuated with this
hammerheaded personality who exhibited in every word he spoke the
enormous strength that comes from having nothing to lose.

Like David Peel, whose album *The Pope Smokes Dope* Lennon was producing at the time, Webberman insisted on treating the great star as if
he were just another cat on the corner, not only lecturing Lennon
about his political duties but even offering suggestions for improving
his lyrics, which Lennon occasionally adopted. John, in turn, got off on
using his outrageous new friends as hit men. When Peel announced
that he was going to cut a song that expressed his disillusionment with
"Bobby Zimmerman," as Peel insisted on calling Dylan, Dylan turned
up at the studio to lodge a protest. Everybody snickered knowingly at
Dylan's appearance and the company that was keeping him: He was
wearing on a warm spring day a coat, hat, and scarf, and for protection
he had brought along two bodyguards from the violent Jewish Defense
League. "We can't do anything about David's music, and in any case, he
loves your music," Lennon assured Dylan; meantime, on a sheet of
paper, John caricatured his rival in an image from Peel's song "super
Zimmerman" as a squat, big-bellied figure with a Z on his jersey and a
pair of outsize balls.

The relationship between Lennon and Webberman blossomed
swiftly into that between a social subversive and a wealthy sympathizer.
Though Lennon preached publicly against violence, he had no scruples
about supporting it privately. When an IRA man, smuggling hashish
into the United States to pay for terrorist guns and bombs, contacted
Lennon, looking for someone to take his weight, Lennon introduced
the smuggler to Webberman, who reciprocated by turning Lennon on
to Northern Irish Aid, a front for the IRA in New York. This outfit

told Webberman: "You did the greatest thing in the world for us. You got us thousands of dollars in contributions." (Among other things, John assigned NIA the royalties of "Luck of the Irish.") When the political conventions commenced in the summer of 1972 in Miami, Webberman arranged to take two busloads of Zippies across state lines to disrupt the proceedings—precisely the same act for which the Chicago Eight had been indicted. Lennon paid for the expedition, giving A.J. $2,000 in cash and buying a full-page ad in the *Yippie Times* for *The Pope Smokes Dope*.

"Lennon believed in violence," attested Webberman. "Otherwise, he wouldn't have introduced me to people like the IRA guy. He knew something was gonna happen in Miami—that it wasn't going to be altogether peaceful. He gave us the money nonetheless. They *did* finance the riots in Miami—that happens to be the truth."

Lennon would doubtless have gone much farther in this same direction if he had not been braked to a halt by the Immigration and Naturalization Service, which demanded his deportation in March 1972. Overnight John found himself in a highly precarious situation. His status in the United States was that of a guest for whom an exception had been made. Though legally ineligible for a visa owing to his drug conviction in England, he had been given a special waiver after Allen Klein had prevailed upon his congressman in Riverdale, Jonathan Bingham, to pull some strings at the State Department. With no firmer toehold than that provided by a sixty-day visa, John Lennon had set out to make a revolution in America. That the government should seek to get rid of him—not as a dangerous political foe but as a powerful lure in the hands of the same people who had incited the riots at the Chicago convention—was such a natural and inevitable development that one wonders why all the politically hip people around Lennon didn't anticipate the problem before it arose. Once Lennon felt the heat coming down, he and Yoko began to audition immigration lawyers. They soon found a winner in Leon Wildes.

A conservative, scholarly Orthodox Jew, Wildes had no idea who John Lennon was when they first met. The lawyer regarded the star just as he would any other client, observing shrewdly that "he was one of those guys who close in for a second on a decision and, if everything seems OK, say yes, and run away from it, as though he really didn't want to get involved. *She* was the one who dug deeper and deeper."

John and Yoko never leveled with their attorney. They told him only those things that would "motivate" him. They never said that they wanted to settle permanently in the United States; their line was that they just wanted enough time to settle the child custody issue. They denied that they were drug-addicted or had agreed to participate in the revolutionary road show. Naturally they said nothing about slipping money to the IRA or the Miami convention wreckers. Perhaps their most prejudicial act of concealment lay in failing to identify the hairy young men who sat around their bed like disciples when Wildes conferred with his clients. One of those men was a Judas.

The Lennons' decision to tell their lawyer nothing that would reflect adversely on themselves blinded Wildes to the real issues in the case. It also caused him to say things before third parties that normally he would not have disclosed. Asked whether he pressed the Lennons for the truth about all these sensitive issues, he conceded: "I never discussed those things with John at all, maybe because I didn't want to get the answer or I didn't think he would tell me the truth or I would feel the same motivation. I had a real motivation to help these people. I would have had very serious problems if I had felt that he was doing something to overthrow the government. It's not like representing someone in a criminal case, where you have a duty to do whatever you can for them. I could just withdraw from the case." Yoko's gift for manipulating people to her advantage did not fail her with Leon Wildes. He believed that the Lennons were innocent victims of the anti-drug zealots in the government, who were exercised over the appearance of an alien with a drug conviction at a rally on behalf of a drug felon.

Wildes's strategy was simple: He said that he would apply for permanent residence, stressing the fact that this was a case of the reunion of a family, one of the basic concerns of immigration law. Yoko was eligible for permanent resident status as the mother of an American child. If she got this status and the government denied it to John, the government would appear guilty of breaking up a family. Wildes instructed Yoko to say when interviewed by the press: "I am being forced to choose between my child and my husband." Both John and Yoko qualified for residence under a provision called "third preference," based on a statute that reads: "presence in the U.S. is potentially beneficial to the American economy or general welfare." As for the drug charge, though Wildes didn't know what "hash" was, he knew that it was not explicitly mentioned in the drug statute. What was not forbidden could not be the cause of exclusion.

Wildes soon discovered that the customary procedures and arguments would not meet with a sympathetic reception in this case. When he approached his old friend Sol Marks, local director of immigration, the lawyer got a chilly reception. Years later Wildes discovered that Marks was taking his orders directly from Washington. What had prompted the government to go after John Lennon was a now-notorious memo from the Judiciary Subcommittee of the Senate Internal Security Committee prepared by Senator Strom Thurmond's staff and sent to Attorney General John N. Mitchell. The memo, dated 4 February 1972, noted the Lennons' appearance at the John Sinclair rally, but its primary emphasis lay upon the plan to conduct a national tour starring Lennon that "will pour tremendous amounts of money into the coffers of the New Left and can only inevitably lead to a clash between a controlled mob organized by this group and law enforcement officials in San Diego." Clearly the attorney general had gotten in touch with Immigration and Naturalization, which had issued an order to get John Lennon out of the United States as quickly as possible.

All the information in the memo is attributed to an anonymous "source," who was obviously well informed about the deliberations at Bank Street. Though Lennon knew nothing of this memo until it surfaced years later in the course of litigation, he was not unwary at this time; in fact, he told everyone that his house was being watched and his phones were being tapped. Tom Basalari scoffed at these allegations and insisted that during the time he worked for the Lennons, there was absolutely no evidence of surveillance, a point that is qualified by that portion of the FBI file on the Lennons that has become public through Freedom of Information Act inquiries. The agents were instructed to keep an eye on Lennon, but their reports betray such ignorance of him even in simple matters like his address that it was obviously a blurry eye. Actually, the only area in which John and Yoko were vulnerable was their drug addiction. Lennon was back on heroin, but that summer he would try a new cure. Once the legal machinery for deporting them was set in motion, however, it ground on for years, creating one crisis after another and imposing on the Lennons a siege mentality.

Whatever the truth of the matter, it is apparent that John Lennon's sudden disillusionment with his political guru followed the pattern established by his sudden disillusionment with his religious guru, his psychiatric guru, and all the other saviors in whom he had placed his faith. A man perpetually in search of help, John focused his quest instinctively on charismatic father figures—precisely what the fans did to him, investing him with the wisdom and spirituality that they were seeking. Needless to say, Lennon's saints were not all they claimed to be, but the greater truth is that they *did* fulfill Lennon's expectations so long as he kept the faith. What most disillusioned him was not the discovery of some deceit they had practiced on him but rather his recognition that they were men, not demigods, and that they were making demands on him.

It was also typical of Lennon that once he had enjoyed the thrill of baiting the squares by playing the radical, he should not only abjure his political commitments but pour scorn over the whole idea of himself as a political man. In 1980 he summed up his radical phase in devastating terms: "I dabbled in so-called politics in the late Sixties and Seventies more out of guilt than anything else. Guilt for being rich and guilt for thinking that peace and love isn't enough, and you have to go and get shot or get punched in the face to prove I'm one of the people. I was doing it against my instincts." He stopped doing it, however, the moment it went against his interests. In the spring of 1972 John Lennon turned his back on politics to focus on the two most distressing features of his private life: the loss of Kyoko and the burden of drug addiction.

PUBLIC BENEFACTORS,
PRIVATE PERSECUTORS

Around 1 June 1972, when they should have been plugging *Some Time in New York City,* a weak new album that needed all the hype they could give it, John and Yoko disappeared. For an entire week they maintained a communications blackout. When they broke surface, they were on the opposite side of the country, calling from a borrowed house at Ojai, California, the Shangri-La of the original *Lost Horizons* and for many years the retreat of Krishnamurti. The Lennons had not returned to spiritual pursuits. Their cover story was that they had driven across the country with Peter Bendry behind the wheel of their green Chrysler station wagon to see America. The truth was that John and Yoko were again playing Bonnie and Clyde.

To understand this latest caper, you have to flash back to the previous summer, when Yoko was granted custody of Kyoko by a court in the Virgin Islands. At approximately the same time Tony was also granted custody of the child, on a temporary basis, by a court at Houston. Both courts stipulated that the other parent should enjoy the customary rights of visitation. When Yoko had sought to visit Kyoko in December 1971, a conflict ensued that brought the whole custody issue to a sad and destructive conclusion.

The Houston court had ruled that Yoko could have access to her daughter only on condition that she post a $20,000 bond as a guarantee that she would not remove the child from Harris County without authorization. Yoko was also instructed to renew her acquaintance with Kyoko gradually, by spending a weekend with her during which the child was restored each night to her customary home. Once these preliminary conditions were met, Yoko was free to take her daughter out of the county every other weekend and for ten days at Christmas.

When the Lennons arrived on 19 December for the preliminary visitation, they discovered that Tony Cox was not going to give them a second chance to abduct his daughter. Tony knew that a $20,000 bond would not deter John and Yoko, so he sought to delay the execution of the court's order by demanding that the Lennons meet with him first in the presence of his fundamentalist minister, Austin Wilkerson. At the meeting John and Yoko behaved in their most charming manner, Yoko going so far as to say that she would be content to see Kyoko in the presence of other people. Mr. and Mrs. Wilkerson, for their part, revealed that they had been harboring the little girl at their home on Woodbrook Street in Timbergrove. They invited John and Yoko to visit them the next day, but instead, the Lennons flew back to New York, where they denounced Tony to the press and announced that they were suing for damages.

The following week the Wilkersons noticed that their house was being watched by strange men stationed at either end of the block. One afternoon two big black limousines pulled into their driveway. Out stepped a posse of New York attorneys clad in dark suits. They demanded admission to the house. The minister and his wife stood in their door and refused to admit the strangers. After a sharp altercation the lawyers gave up and drove away.

Locate, survey, and enter: that was the strategy John and Yoko had been employing against Tony ever since the failure of their kidnapping attempt. When they had learned that he had returned to the States and was living somewhere near his father at Bellmore, they dragged old George Cox into court in a vain endeavor to make the father disclose the whereabouts of his son and granddaughter. When that move failed, they went to work on Tony's brother, Larry, who was living with his wife in Brooklyn Heights.

Larry received an urgent call one day from Allen Klein, who insisted that he drop everything and rush over to the ABKCO office on Broadway. No sooner was he out of the house than a private eye rang the bell. When Larry's wife opened, she found herself face-to-face with a burly stranger who had his foot in the door. "*I know you know where they are!*" shouted the detective as he shouldered his way into the house and started searching the premises. To avert possible prosecution for this flagrant violation of law, Yoko apologized, insisting, as she was to do more than once, that she had no idea how her detectives operated.

When Tony Cox had moved to Houston in July, the Lennons' spies quickly located his apartment in the Memorial district, about ten miles out of town. Immediately the apartment was staked out. Paul Mozian, ABKCO's director of artist relations, recalled going down to Houston on three separate occasions with private eyes. Tom Basalari recollected: "We sat on the place a couple of days lookin' for the kid. No way we could get near the place." What they would have done if they could have gotten near, Basalari wouldn't say.

Once Yoko had brought suit against Tony, the court at Houston ordered Cox to produce Kyoko. When he equivocated, the judge sentenced him to five days in jail at Christmas. Tony went to the lockup carrying a Bible and a prayer book. Next morning he woke up screaming for his child. Meantime, Tony's lawyer and Yoko's lawyer rushed to the appellate court to obtain writs of habeas corpus—one to free Tony and the other to produce Kyoko. Tony's lawyer won the race. The day after he entered jail, Tony walked out. The judge renewed his demand that Cox produce his daughter. At the same time he told Yoko that if she wanted to see her child, she would have to come to Houston.

John and Yoko arrived the day before Christmas, carrying a copy of their latest release: "Happy Xmas (War Is Over)." Anticipating a joyous meeting with the child, the Lennons had put into the mix a whispered "Merry Christmas, Kyoko!" They failed to reckon with Tony Cox's determination. When the court convened on 27 December, neither Tony nor his lawyer was present. Next day the judge ordered the sheriff to arrest Cox. The order came too late. On Christmas Eve the great escape artist had slipped out of town with his wife and child.

Immediately John and Yoko set up a tremendous hue and cry, and Tony became the target of a national manhunt. Defying the Lennons was not something to be done lightly. John and Yoko were armed not just with the power of the law or the weapons of wealth but with the immeasurable resources afforded them by John's immense popularity in the United States. With unlimited access to the media, they were in a position to revive the search by presenting Yoko as the grieving mother bereft of her only child and John as the distraught husband, deeply concerned for his ailing wife. The ordinary American was eager to help John and Yoko. Many people reported Tony's movements to the sheriff at Houston.

Tony Cox recognized that the only way to maintain himself underground was to go to ground in a community committed to saving him. Through his Christian affiliations he had discovered a powerful cult called the Church of the Living Word or the Walk. One of those charismatic churches whose members surrender their individual autonomy to the authority of a masterful leader, this cult was the earthly kingdom of a onetime pastor and "doctor of theology" named Robert Stevens. The headquarters of the Walk was at Granada Hills in the San Fernando Valley. This was Tony's first hiding place, and this is where the Lennons sought to trap him, their house at Ojai being just a half hour's drive from the Walk.

Like most amateur adventurers, the Lennons were very clumsy with their cloaks and daggers. After a month of vain endeavors to snatch their elusive prey, during which time they trashed the beautiful house in which they were staying and were expelled by its irate owner, John and Yoko got word that Tony was in Sausalito. Immediately they rented a house in Mill Valley from the proprietor of the No Name bar in Sausalito and summoned to their side Steve Gebhardt, who arrived with his wife on the Fourth of July, carrying $10,000 in cash and two of John's guitars. The Lennons were planning on a long stay.

It was not with Gebhardt, however, but with Craig Pyes that the search flared for a moment into an exciting chase. Pyes and his partner, Ken Kelley, were hippie journalists who had just established a monthly magazine, *SunDance*, designed to compete against *Rolling Stone*. Jann Wenner aroused Lennon's ire by publishing an unauthorized book, titled *Lennon Remembers*, comprising John's primal scream interviews. Wenner even had the gall to send Lennon a copy inscribed "Without you, this book could never have been done." When John learned about *SunDance*, he offered to contribute a monthly column in the hope the new magazine would drive *Rolling Stone* out of business. On the strength of Lennon's name, Pyes and Kelley had rounded up enough support to go into business in San Francisco. Pyes assumed when Yoko called that the Lennons wanted to check out his operation. Instead, they asked him to spend the next week driving them around the Bay Area in his ancient VW, the classic coffee can on wheels. One day Pyes discovered what they were all really doing.

"There's Tony!" gasped Yoko as John nearly snapped his head off trying to confirm the sighting. Nobody else saw Cox, but they all tumbled out of the car and dashed into the lobby of the apartment house at which Yoko was pointing. Finding the lobby empty, Yoko ordered Pyes to knock on the apartment doors.

"Excuse me!" he said to the first startled housewife. "This is John and Yoko—you may know them! They would like to look out your windows because there is someone in the street they're looking for, but they don't want to stand in the street and cause a riot." Flabbergasted, the woman mutely signed her acquiescence as John and Yoko charged into her home and peered about suspiciously. Then they dashed to the windows and craned their necks outside, searching for Tony. Seeing nothing of him, they finally retreated to their coffee can, ordering Pyes to drive to a neighboring playground.

One day Yoko asked Pyes if he knew of an acupuncturist in the area. (Acupuncture was illegal in California but practiced by the local Chinese.) Pyes introduced Yoko to a Dr. Hong, who lived in San Mateo County, south of the San Francisco airport. The doctor was built like a fireplug, talked like a boastful old soldier, and kept a bottle of whiskey on his desk to steady his hand while he inserted his unsterile needles. The Lennons told Dr. Hong that they were desperate to get off methadone, which they had learned to their dismay was more addictive than heroin. ("We got off heroin cold turkey in three days," John informed Pyes, "but we've been trying to shake methadone for five months!") The other ailment for which they were seeking a remedy was the drying up of their sex life. Hong, who had never heard of the Beatles, assured his new clients that he could cure their illnesses quickly. But it was necessary that they move into his house and put themselves completely in his hands.

For a week the Lennons lived in Dr. Hong's little pink stucco house, John sleeping on the sofa in the living room, which reminded him of the way he had spent his last years at Mendips. Hong took his patients off methadone abruptly, countering their sufferings with his needles and dosing them heavily with those old-fashioned vitamin pills that look—and taste—like little asphalt footballs. To strengthen their sexual energies, he fed them herbal teas and two-hundred-year-old ginseng root in little cubes that tasted like licorice. When no treatment was in progress, the doctor encouraged Lennon to play his guitar, or Hong would perform himself, showing off his prowess with the Chinese pike. (A kung fu master, the doctor taught self-defense at the local police academy.) When John begged Hong to show him the best way to protect himself in the street, the 65-year-old Chinese gave the 31-year-old Lennon some lessons in the martial arts.

Three days after their immurement commenced, the Lennons received a visit from the SunDance Kids. Ken Kelley was astonished by the difference six months had made in John's and Yoko's appearances. "John had shrunk, and Yoko had grown," recalled Kelley. "Lennon looked a foot shorter and very tiny. Yoko's hair had been short when I had last seen her; now it hung to her tits." Kelley observed that: "John was grateful to be released from drugs. He was anxious to go back in the world and do things." The next time Pyes and Kelley came visiting, they were told that the cure was complete.

From the little tract house in San Mateo County, John and Yoko moved to the elegant Stanford Court on Nob Hill, where they received Geraldo Rivera, a New York TV reporter who had just done an exposé on conditions at Willowbrook Hospital on Staten Island, in New York City, a facility for mentally handicapped children. To aid the hospital, Rivera had conceived of a red-letter day that would focus on a visit by the children to Central Park, each child to be accompanied by a guardian who would establish with his charge a one-to-one relationship. The day would be crowned with a pair of pop concerts at Madison Square Garden headlined by John and Yoko and filmed for transmission later on the ABC network, which would pay $300,000 for the Lennons' services, which they would donate to the hospital. According to Steve Gebhardt, John and Yoko felt they were being exploited by Rivera, but in view of their immigration problems, they decided they had better cooperate.

BURNOUT

The John Lennon who appeared at the Garden on 30 August 1972 was gaunt, tight-lipped, and wired on coke as tight as an E string. He wore blue-lensed blind man's glasses, an old army shirt with its tail out, and a sweat rag dangling down his ass. Though he looked like a man who had steeled himself for a trying task, he was for once completely in command of the stage. Yoko was relegated to a sideshow, pounding away on an electric keyboard and singing a couple of solos. All the rest of the show turned on John Lennon, superstar.

One to One would demonstrate that John Lennon had finally found his natural stage style in raw and violent psychodrama. His enactments of "Mother" and "Cold Turkey" were the high points of both afternoon and evening performances, the drug withdrawal song triggering off a burst of primaling as John threw up his hands like a desperate suppliant while flashing from his face the unmistakable look of a hysterical child. "*Hysterica passio!* down, thou climbing sorrow!" had always been the epigraph for Lennon's life, but it had taken a lifetime for his frantic soul to worry its way through the mask of Beatle John and burst forth onto the public stage.

Now Lennon stood once again at a point in his career where, if he had simply driven straightforward along the natural track of his development, he could have become the leader in the next phase of pop music: the Age of Decadence, which would soon spawn punk, new wave, rap—all those brutal, almost psychotic styles that mirrored Lennon's fractured soul. No other star of that day was so capable of bringing the decade's Theater of Cruelty to its savage apogee. Yet once again John Lennon failed to heed the summons of his genius. Instead, Lennon abandoned the stage, save for a few inconsequential guest shots. It was as if by primaling at the Garden, he had blown out his flame forever.*

---

* The video of *One to One*, issued in 1985 as *John Lennon—Live in New York City*, is an important document not only because it records Lennon's last major stage performance but because it shows clearly how Yoko Ono has functioned as the custodian of the Lennon archive. Although the concert was edited originally under Lennon's supervision by Steve Gebhardt

The atmosphere at the after-the-show party at Tavern on the Green was depressing. Allen Klein, who had been obliged to paper the house with 5,000 free tickets to give the appearance of a sellout, was at daggers' points with Yoko because the show had confirmed him in his long-held opinion that the public did not want to see John Lennon performing with Yoko Ono. Yoko was enraged by Klein's attitude. From that moment on, relations between the stars and their once-idealized manager rapidly deteriorated. When his latest contract extension expired in March, Klein was dropped. For this self-destructive decision the Lennons marshaled a host of rationalizations alleging that Klein was intent on becoming a bigger star than his clients, that he wasn't producing for them anymore, and that he threatened to remain forever at loggerheads with Paul and the Eastmans. But the Lennons could not have picked a worse time to discharge their manager, for they now had urgent need of his skills.

That spring the long-awaited jump-up in the Beatles' royalties was supposed to go into effect, but the increase was in jeopardy because of the Beatles' failure to meet their sales quota: a half-million copies of each of the last two albums released before the target date, 31 August 1972. The next-to-last album, *Wild Life* (Paul's first with his new band, Wings) almost fulfilled its quota, but the Lennons' *Some Time in New York* (which John had insisted upon rushing out before the deadline) had bombed, selling only 272,041 copies. Klein had stepped into the breach immediately by negotiating a two-month extension of the original schedule, but before the amendment could be signed, he was ousted. Instead of replacing him with a new manager, John, George, and Ringo decided to engage individual representatives—or, as Lennon put it, "the Apples became Pairs." At this point Capitol's president, Baskar Mehon, finding himself confronting three little Kleins who were demanding that his company give the Beatles their increase without any concessions on the band's part, declared the Beatles in default and refused to authorize the increase.*

---

and broadcast on 15 December 1972, Yoko discarded the authorized version and reedited the tapes to cut Lennon down to size while building herself up proportionately. First, she replaced the powerful evening performance with the inferior matinee, which John had derided as the "rehearsal," thus substituting a bad Lennon performance for a good one. Then she stole the show from Lennon at every turn by constantly cutting away from him, even at his greatest moments, to show herself banging away at an electric keyboard. After the tape was released by Sony, Adam Ippolito, the keyboardist of Elephant's Memory, brought suit against Yoko, alleging that she had not played one note of the music that she appeared to be making because her electric piano had not been plugged in.

*Amazing to say, this is where the matter has remained to this day. For fifteen years the Beatles' big royalty increase has not been paid, with the result that the account has swollen to more than $10 million. After the introduction of Beatles' CDs in 1987, the amount was destined to grow much larger, perhaps as great as $20 million. At this writing, all the Beatles but Paul have combined to sue Capitol, but the issue is in doubt because the court must decide whether having rejected the deal they were offered in 1973, the Beatles can reverse themselves after all these years and demand with justice the terms they once spurned.

The royalty jump-up was just one of the serious problems that John and Yoko faced after they dismissed Klein. In fact, they now found themselves completely at sea because for years they had been totally dependent on their manager not only in business matters but in every sort of personal problem that demanded resourcefulness or practical judgment. Klein had babied his famous clients. Now the babies were suddenly without their daddy. Nor was it easy to replace a man like Klein. The next best thing, the Lennons decided, was Klein's former right-hand man, Harold Seider, who they engaged on April Fools' Day 1973. A small, brisk, bright lawyer with a straight-to-the-point way of thinking and talking, Seider was temperamentally the opposite of Klein, which is basically why he had resigned from his post as chief corporate counsel of ABKCO back in 1971. Unlike Klein, Seider had no desire to play Santa Claus. In fact, he turned down the job of manager, remarking dryly, "I didn't want to take out their cleaning." Seider defined his role as that of adviser or counselor in matters of business. He hired the Lennons the best accountants and lawyers he knew; then he settled down to wean them from their financially irresponsible lifestyle.

Seider saw Lennon as a "moocher." So long as John didn't have to reach in his own pocket, he didn't care how much he spent. That was how in recent years he had squandered millions of dollars. John simply sent the bills to Klein and let him worry about paying them. Now Seider demanded that his client assume full financial responsibility for every expenditure he made, even insisting that John sign all the checks every month—a sobering experience that soon changed Lennon's profligate ways. Lennon became so anxious about money that he began to behave like a skinflint, challenging even the most necessary expenditures. Seider explained to John that their goal had to be, on the one hand, establishing "income streams" that would enable him to live comfortably without the need to grind out "product," while, on the other hand, cutting his yearly expenses down to a reasonable figure, like $300,000. To achieve this goal, everything that was financially unproductive had to go, commencing with Joko Productions. As for the long-term goals, everybody in the Beatles' camp had now decided that it no longer made sense to maintain Apple. Therefore, it was high time to set the lawyers to work on the dissolution of the company and the distribution of its assets among the four partners. That would be a big job, and Seider's role would be purely advisory. He would provide information, advice, and expertise, but the responsibility for making all the final decisions would rest squarely on John Lennon's shoulders.

Seider also had to be careful of his own reputation. As Klein's former counselor the lawyer had a potential conflict of interest; likewise, as a vice-president of United Artists Record Management (which gave him permission to work part-time for John Lennon) he had another potential conflict. Though Seider walked the straight-and-narrow line of moral and professional rectitude, there can be no question that in John's and Yoko's eyes Seider's chief value lay in the fact that he knew Allen Klein and his business inside out. The Lennons were preparing to go to war with Klein. Seider was their secret weapon. When they unveiled it, they blew their former manager's mind.

At this point in their career the Lennons could have taken off their peace symbols and sewn on the double cross, for their dealings became double-dealings. Two film deals illustrate their business morality. In 1971 A. D. Pennebaker wanted to put into distribution his documentary record of the Varsity Stadium show, *Sweet Toronto*. The Lennons had cut a quid pro quo deal with Pennebaker, authorizing him to make use of the footage he had shot of them in exchange for the right to release his sound track recording as a John and Yoko album titled *Live at Toronto*. The album made a lot of money, selling an amazing 750,000 copies, but when it came time for Pennebaker to profit from his end of the deal by releasing *Sweet Toronto*, the Lennons went back on their word, demanding a sizable sum to release the footage. Too poor either to pay or to sue, Pennebaker had no choice but to withdraw his film. It was finally released two years later, without the Lennons, as *Keep On Rockin'*.

An even worse instance of double-dealing was *Ten for Two*, the film of the John Sinclair rally. When Steve Gebhardt had finished editing the picture, Leon Wildes reviewed it. He told John and Yoko that as far as Immigration and Naturalization was concerned, it was poison. Instead of explaining this verdict to John Sinclair, who would have sympathized with the Lennons' plight as a fellow victim, Yoko contrived a phony scheme to take her and John off the hook. Having summoned the impoverished Sinclair and his wife to New York, Yoko kept postponing the meeting until two hours before the couple were scheduled to fly back to Detroit. Then they were summoned to the bedside. When they arrived, Yoko greeted them with a long harangue about the oppression of women. "We couldn't figure out where she was coming from," recalled Sinclair. "John Lennon hardly said a word during the whole meeting. Then she announced that we had to accept that all the money was going to female causes. We were dumbfounded. Yoko insisted that she would distribute the money herself and didn't have to account for it to anyone."

This was an outrageous ultimatum because scores of people, including all the other entertainers at the rally, had donated their services on the assumption that the proceeds of the film were to be divided equitably among the various charitable organizations that had organized the event. Sinclair was infuriated not only by this unilateral decision but even more by the Lennons' obvious condescension. "You'd have to see them in their fucking bed," he recalled. "It was just like *you* were the peasant and *they* were royalty. It was humiliating. I've been beaten and probed in my orifices—but this was *really* humiliating!" What Sinclair didn't recognize was that John and Yoko were in panic flight from their political commitments. They didn't care whom they trampled upon just so long as John saved himself from the unbearable fate of being deported from the United States.

On election night, 7 November 1972, Jerry Rubin assembled his friends at his pad to watch the returns. John and Yoko had promised they would come after they finished work at the Record Plant, where Yoko was cutting a two-record solo album, *Approximately Infinite Universe*. An enormous and costly undertaking, this recording had consumed almost every night for two months, including some marathon sessions that ran up to eighteen hours. As news of Nixon's victory came pouring into the booth, John got loaded on tequila. He was enraged at the prospect of Nixon's reelection because Lennon assumed it meant he would be kicked out of the country. His fury was also fueled by his growing antagonism toward Yoko, whose singing had inspired John to dub her the "Japanese Mrs. Miller." By election night, relations between the pair had become so bad that all the musicians were convinced that John and Yoko were heading for a breakup.

When the session wound up at four in the morning, John was dangerously drunk. He was "cursing with a vocabulary that would have been the envy of a Liverpool sailor," reported Bob Gruen, the Lennons' house photographer and gofer, adding, "It's the only time I ever heard so many cursewords in such a torrential flow." As the group headed down to Rubin's apartment on Prince Street, Gruen observed that Lennon "was outrageously angry at everything."

The party at Rubin's pad had started on a high note early in the evening, as Judith Malina of the Living Theater recorded next day in her diary, but after McGovern's concession, the mood had grown glum. Those guests who remained at 4:00 A.M. were gathered about the TV, watching the Nixon totals pile up, when suddenly they were horrified by a terrible scream, obviously the sound of a man in agony. At that moment John Lennon burst into the flat, wild-eyed and unshaven, alternately crying out in pain and hollering like a Beatle, *"Yeah, yeah, yeah!"*

As an actress Malina was impressed by the depth of Lennon's passion and his remarkable ability to utter cries that came from the core of his being. As a woman she observed that Yoko was wearing a floppy hat and a brown leather coat with a gold sheriff's badge on the breast over a loose linen jumpsuit of the latest design. Though Lennon never stopped cursing in his raspy voice and leveling accusations at these people, whom he now regarded as false prophets who had misled him, even going so far as to denounce them all as middle-class Jews, Yoko never lost her cool. She unwrapped a package of cocaine, from which those partook who were not swigging down vodka and tequila from the bottle.

One after another the guests sought to calm Lennon, Rubin trying to steer him into a room with a water bed, but John reacted violently to being treated as a nut case. Instead of cooling out, he kept spitting out his pain and disillusionment over the failure of the revolution, over the very idea that there could *be* such a thing as a revolution. When Julian Beck sought to reason with John, he could not be made to listen, denouncing everything Julian said as bullshit.

Finally, Lennon found himself sitting face-to-face with Judith Malina, a tiny woman. Gazing into her eyes like a lunatic, he snarled: "I want to cut you with a knife!" When she didn't flinch, he repeated the threat even more menacingly, declaring that he wanted to see blood flow. When he still got no satisfaction from his victim, he rose unsteadily to his feet and lurched toward the door, where he bellowed: *"I'm going to join the Weathermen! I'm going to shoot a policeman!"*

After that night, according to Steve Gebhardt, "John Lennon went into his room and didn't come out for six months."

OUT OF THE DRAGON'S
LAIR, INTO THE LION'S DEN

"Hi! I [beat] wish [beat] to [beat] book [beat] you. My name is Yoko. Y [beat] O [beat] K [beat] O." That's how David Spinozza, the hottest guitar slinger in the New York studio system, recalled the beginning of the relationship that finally drove him crazy. David thought that somebody was putting him on that July afternoon in 1973 when he walked into his pad on East 70th Street and flipped on his answering machine. Punching out the phone number, he cocked his ear for the answer. Imagine his surprise when the wee-voiced woman on the other end of the line turned out to be the wife of John Lennon.

Even more amazing was the reason for her call. She was going to cut a whole album of her own stuff. She wanted Spinozza to contract and lead the band. She'd even got a little list of studio men. They were the best and busiest players in town. David loved the sound of all those aces going down. What made him grimace and squirm, as he scribbled the names, with the phone stuck under his chin like a fiddle, was the recollection of the last time he got involved with a Beatle. That was back in the spring of 1971, when he got a call from the woman he calls the "Queen of the Groupies," Linda McCartney.

The queen was so confident that any musician would snap to attention at the mere sound of her name that she barely troubled to identify herself. "What's this for?" Spinozza had demanded, not having caught the name.

"My husband heard of you," drawled Linda in her carefully cultivated British accent. "He wants to get together with you and play with you and check you out because we're going to make an album."

David still didn't click. "I'm a studio musician," he snapped. "You can check me out on hundreds of dates. There's no need to get together. You can book me through my service. Just call Radio Registry,

452

and say you want David Spinozza, two to five, seven to ten, which guitars—and I'll *be* there!"

"No! You don't understand!" cried Linda. "My husband . . ."

Before she could say another word, Spinozza exploded with exasperation. "What's this with your *'husband'?*" he shouted. Finally, Linda got across the fact that she was the mouthpiece of Paul McCartney. That revelation only made matters worse because now Spinozza recognized the true purport of the call. "What's this," he barked, barely able to utter the hateful word, "an *audition?*"

That's where Paul had made his first mistake, calling up Capitol and saying, as if he were in London, "Get me five top men on each rhythm instrument—piano, bass, guitar, drums." New York studio men don't play auditions. They regard themselves, justifiably, as the most accomplished all-'round musicians in the world. They boast that they can cut the first-desk men in the symphony, the improvising soloists in most jazz bands, any instrumentalist on the pop scene, and certainly any rock 'n' roll player ever born. As one of the young lions of the studio, Spinozza had displayed the attitude of his pride. But he had been curious about the famous Beatle, so he had gone over to a dirty loft on Tenth Avenue, where he found Paul with a three-day growth of beard, Linda, and the kids. Billy Lavoina, a veteran drummer, had just been asked to play. "You know, Paul," Lavoina replied in a sarcastic tone, "I hear *you* sometimes play drums, so why don't you play for *me?*"

The whole scene had disgusted David. "Here I am meeting Paul McCartney," he recalled, "and he played these basic rock 'n' roll things—ching, ching, ching. It was embarrassing! He had to sing every note or hit it on his guitar, like the three notes of the major seventh. He didn't even know what the chord was called. He called it the 'pretty chord'!" Spinozza did work for weeks on *Ram,* but when the gig was over, he gave a sneering account of the experience to *Melody Maker,* objecting particularly to Paul's keeping his children in the studio till four in the morning.

So it was with mixed feelings that David Spinozza went to meet Yoko Ono on that day in July 1973.

First thing Spinozza did was ask to see the music. Yoko handed him a sheaf of neatly typed pages. Each song was written in verses with a chorus—but there wasn't a note of music! Above the words might be written "G minor, D, G," but it was impossible to imagine what she had in mind. Yoko was mimicking the way John wrote, but John would always bring his guitar and demonstrate the song. When Spinozza asked Yoko to sing her songs, what came out was something that sounded like a Japanese version of "Jingle Bells." Spinozza's instinctive reaction was to snap: "Are you kidding?"

But for a studio man, a gig is a gig. The pay is high, and the chal-

THE LIVES OF JOHN LENNON

lenge is often to make something of nothing. Day after day Spinozza took his tape recorder and music paper to his meeting with Yoko. Notating her stuff was a nightmare. She could not sing in meter. "Yoko!" he would burst out. "Will you count it off and sing in time so I can hear where you're hearing the beats?" Soon he realized that there was no point in writing down the melody because she might not stick with it at the session. So he would score bar lines and insert chord symbols. The idea was to keep the score wide open and fill it in as the date unfolded.

The fun really began when they got into the studio. The band was a dream. Rick Marotta was the favorite drummer of every act on the road. Andrew Smith and Bob Babbit had been until recently the boss rhythm section at Motown. Michael Brecker would soon be the hottest tenor man in the USA. Arthur Jenkins, the mallet man, was an elegant cat with a very hip take on soul. The pianist, Kenny Ascher, was also a songwriter (which would come in handy), and the bassist, Gordon Edwards, was admired for his work on a fusion band called Stuff. With David Spinozza on lead guitar and other fine people coming in to do special jobs, Yoko Ono would be surrounded by a million dollars' worth of talent. But no music!

The solution was to pass out lead sheets and encourage the musicians to make up the score as they went along. Yoko sat in a chair chain-smoking Kools. The moment she started singing, they would be off the chart. "Make it a 6/4 measure instead of 4/4," Spinozza would order, and everybody would scratch away at his sheet. Or Yoko would say: "I want more drive here." David would translate, telling the drummer to do a fill or the bass player to let his last note ring. The biggest problem was where to put the downbeat. Yoko had no sense of time. The musicians were obliged to shift their attack constantly to fall in with her first note. Despite all these obstacles, the musicians turned out track after track of highly listenable instrumental music, the best of it in a sophisticated soul style, like pastel funk.*

The more Yoko worked with David Spinozza, the more she came to dig him. Swarthy, straight-backed, sternly mustachioed, Spinozza looked like a young Turk, though he was actually from a working-class Italian family in Brooklyn. Already he enjoyed a great reputation not only for his playing but for being a "player." He would startle the other musicians with his tales of racing dirt bikes, an absolute no-no for guys who can't afford the slightest injury to their hands. He also boasted

---

* Yoko's previous two-record album, *Approximately Infinite Universe,* was created in much the same manner, with Adam Ippolito of Elephant's Memory performing the same tasks as David Spinozza. "She'd come in with lyrics typed out," he recalled, "and she'd get me in one studio while the band was gettin' a sound, and I'd put the chords in the right places where the words fell. . . . [We] did all the horns, the arrangements, and she would take credit for the arrangements on the record cover."

that he had scored three ballerinas in the Balanchine company. While the boys had to strain to imagine what those dancers, with their rock-hard asses, could do in the sack, they didn't have to do anything but glance across to the next music stand to see what Spinozza brought to these encounters. He was notorious at the studio for whipping out his king-size shlong. (When I told a studio man that I was going to interview Spinozza, he exclaimed: "That guy! Christ, I've seen his cock more times this year than I have my own!") So famous is Spinozza for his spontaneous cockouts that when he stepped onstage to receive the award for best studio guitarist, all the cats in the audience were anticipating the Spinozza Salute. At the conclusion of his brief, modest acceptance speech, he paused dramatically; then he snapped: "And . . . no! I'm *not* gonna whip it out!"

Yoko has always admired ballsy little guys. In fact, the way her close friends recognize that she's attracted to a man is by catching her putting him down for being short. So as the weeks wore on at the studio, she must have started musing on what she could do with this little stud. That was the theme of the last and best song on the new album, *Feeling the Space*. "Men, Men, Men" is a put-on of macho males, the kind of guys who yearn for women who are "animals." Sung in a breathy Jackie O style, the song turns the tables on these guys by treating *them* as sex objects, complaining about the fact that their jeans are too loose, their boots too short, and their faces too aged. The track winds up with a little gag that is a classic of kidding on the square. Yoko calls out to her pet male, telling him that it's time for him to come out of his cage. When he answers, like Caspar Milquetoast, you recognize the voice of John Lennon.

Though John was willing to lend himself to a gag, he wasn't up to working any longer as one-half of the duo of John and Yoko. He had spent most of the last six months laid out in his bed at Bank Street, stoned on heroin and drunk from drinking crate after crate of Colt 45. When Harold Seider had gone to the flat to talk business with Lennon, the lawyer found his client sunken-eyed, emaciated, unshaven, looking as if he had just gotten out of a "concentration camp." Seider had interpreted Lennon's condition as a burnout produced by Yoko's relentless blitzing of first the art world and then the radical scene. He recognized that John had a need to "hibernate." Lennon had used this long layoff to review his position both as an entertainer and as a husband. His conclusion, as regards the first issue, was, as he confided to May Pang: "I've tried to push Yoko for the past few years, and it doesn't seem to work. I'm a little tired now. The best person for Yoko now is Tony." Those words signaled the end, at least for the next seven years, of the team of John and Yoko. They also signaled the revival of John Lennon. In July John gave another signal by shaving his head.

Once Yoko recognized that John had withdrawn his support, she had to cast about for another male helper because Yoko needed a man the way a ballerina needs a partner: to lift her, spin her, and show her off to best advantage while she camps it up before the public. Now that her old partner was off sulking in the wings, she had to find some strong new hands to go around her waist.

When she discovered that David Spinozza was breaking up with his wife, she began to write David some helpful letters, offering good advice. Then, toward the end of the session each day, there would be a few minutes when Yoko and David could chat and flirt without attracting notice. May Pang detected this dalliance immediately, but she could be relied upon to keep her mouth shut. Nobody else was allowed inside the studio.

Yoko's problem was what to do about John. Recently John had humiliated Yoko at Jerry Rubin's flat by taking Jerry's girl into an adjacent room and fucking her. It was probably this outrage that inspired Yoko to adopt a drastic but characteristic solution to her problem. She had grown up watching her father nipping off to enjoy his geisha. So what could be more natural than getting a geisha for her husband, some nice young Oriental woman whom Yoko could totally control? As she reflected on the matter, she recognized that she had the ideal woman already in her employ—little May!

During the three years that May Pang had slaved for the Lennons, she had been put through every conceivable test for obedience and loyalty. May was so eager to please that she could be manipulated without even the prospect of reward. She had sacrificed her whole life to her employers, working recently, for example, all day for Yoko at the studio and then returning to work all night on John's new solo album, *Mind Games*. She ate on the wing, slept an hour at a time, went home only to change clothes, and assumed so much responsibility that after she was dismissed, her duties were divided among no fewer than four employees. Reared in a Catholic parochial school, May was a goody-goody who regarded Yoko as a mother and had never exhibited the slightest romantic interest in John. Short of some woman fresh off the Yasuda estates in Japan, May Pang was the perfect choice for concubine.

May recalls that she was sitting one August morning at her desk in Apartment 72 of the Dakota,* humming "Mind Games," when she

*The Lennons had moved into the Dakota in June 1973, renting Apartment 72 from the actor Robert Ryan. Since the death of his wife the year before, he had been uncomfortable in the flat. The Lennons agreed to pay $300 over the monthly maintenance charge of $1,500, with an option to buy in three years. A year later Ryan died, and his estate asked the Lennons if they wanted to exercise their option. Seider agreed on condition that the asking price of $125,000 be reduced. When Lennon was offered the nine-room apartment (worth $2.5 million today) for $105,000, he asked Seider, "Can we afford it?" The lawyer replied: "You gotta afford it."

looked up and beheld Yoko standing before her in a long, blue-checked flannel nightgown, with her feet bare, her hair down and a Kool in her hand.

"Listen, May," she said, "John and I are not getting along. We've been arguing. We're growing apart." May was surprised by Yoko's bluntness but not by what she said. It had been obvious for weeks that the Lennons were going through a bad patch. They never seemed to be together, and if their paths did cross, they would not acknowledge each other. There had even been talk of their attending the Masters and Johnson sex clinic. Still May was totally unprepared to hear what Yoko said next: "John will probably start going out with other people." As May's mouth opened in surprise, Yoko said, with a significant lilt in her voice and look in her eye: "May, I know he likes you."

May sputtered a protest, but Yoko continued, unperturbed. "May," she said reassuringly, "it's *OK*. I know he likes you. If he should ask you to go out with him, you should go." May was aghast. She was a naïve little girl whose sexual experience had been confined to one affair—with the drummer of Badfinger. The thought of Yoko Ono, whom she regarded virtually as a mother, handing over her husband—who was the greatest man in the world, *John Lennon!*—was enough to make May's granny glasses frost over. Speaking in that hard, resonant tongue used in the streets of Spanish Harlem, where May had grown up, she started reciting all the reasons why fucking around with John Lennon was definitely *not* "OK." John was married to Yoko—right? John was her boss—right? John was . . . Forget it! No matter how many objections May threw up to this insane idea, Yoko went right on laying out her cards.

Only now Yoko shifted her ground slightly and started coming on like May's aunt, an older, wiser woman concerned about May's personal happiness. "Life isn't all work," explained the workaholic Yoko. "You're entitled to some fun. You should have a boyfriend. Wouldn't you rather see him with someone like you than someone who would treat him rotten?" That was a shrewd hit, and it compelled May to agree for the first time with some of Yoko's pitch. Basically, however, there was nothing that Yoko could say that would turn May Pang around. The thing was wrong, as May saw it, so she wasn't going to do it. Period!

When Yoko saw that May would not listen to reason, she decided to act as if her suggestion had met with complete agreement and now the only remaining issue was how to implement the agreed-upon course of action. "I think tonight when you go to the studio would be a good time for you to begin," remarked Yoko calmly. "Don't worry about a thing," she added. "I'll take care of everything." With that mysterious admonition hanging in the air, Yoko turned on her heel and vanished from the room.

At noon Yoko was back, punctual as a cuckoo clock, to announce again that May should begin her new assignment as John's mistress that very night. To May's relief, John treated her at the studio just as he had for years, paying her no heed. The following night, however, he acted like another man. No sooner did the pair step into the elevator at the Dakota than John seized May and kissed her passionately. "I've been wantin' to do this all fuckin' day," panted Lennon as May shrank back in shock. Yoko had released her pet male from his cage and pointed him at his prey.

For three nights running, John insisted on taking May home. Two nights she warded him off, but on the third he dismissed the limo and took May uptown to her flat in a cab, which left them alone on the curb. After pleading to be admitted to her apartment, he pressed home his advantage once he was inside the door. After a bout of tears and the usual expressions of anxiety—which John countered by telling this powerless girl how anxious the encounter was making *him* feel—May allowed John to climb with her into the sack, where he exhibited a wonderful tenderness.

Once her initial resistance had been overcome, May Pang recognized that there was nothing she wanted more than John Lennon. She decided that she would take what was offered so freely. After a couple of weeks of making love every night with mounting pleasure and passion, May was obliged to concede that she owed this undreamed-of happiness entirely to her lover's wife.

John was sexually famished. Both he and Yoko were burnt out from years of hard drugs, overwork, emotional breakdowns, quack cures, and bizarre diets, to say nothing of the effects of living constantly in the glare of the mass media. It was no coincidence that he turned at this moment to a twenty-three-year-old, high-energy, working-class lover. May Pang was ideal. John could recapture his youth through his new love without jeopardizing his marriage.

Early in September Yoko went off to a feminist congress at Chicago. John seized the occasion to fly the coop. Attaching himself to Harold Seider, Lennon insisted upon accompanying his adviser home to Los Angeles, taking along May Pang.

But John was not so rebellious as to leave home without first notifying Mother. Anticipating a very violent reaction, he was astonished to get a very low-keyed response, which he took as his go-ahead.

Why didn't Yoko nip this startling defection in the bud? Many answers suggest themselves: She knew John couldn't survive long without her and would soon be back; she didn't dare say no at the last minute because he might not obey; she experienced a pang of delight on hearing his announcement and thought: "Good! Let the bastard go!" This last hypothesis is the best supported by what happened subsequently, for once John stepped out the door, Yoko barred it behind him. "She felt with John out of the picture her career would take off," explained Harold Seider. She must also have thought that with her husband out of the city, she could enjoy herself much more freely.

When John and May arrived in L.A., they ran into a serious obstacle. Seider explained to Lennon that he was broke. He had been living on money borrowed from Allen Klein plus his £5,000 a month from the Apple receiver. There was also some income from other sources, but it was barely enough for Yoko, who now demanded that $300,000 be made available to her for the duration of the separation as "security." The upshot was that John Lennon was finally free—but obliged to live on nothing!

Seider got Capitol to advance Lennon $10,000 in walk-around money, making him promise to spend it very slowly. John got the message and gave a brilliant demonstration of the art of freeloading. He lived in fine houses, did costly drugs, and ate in the best restaurants whenever he pleased without ever once putting his hand in his pocket. In contrast with Yoko, who could never bear to appear concerned about the price of anything, John Lennon was delighted to see other people pick up the check.

Starting all over was always one of the great themes of the life of Lennon. Every time he got on a new kick, whether it was LSD, transcendental meditation, or primal therapy, he confidently expected a rebirth. Now he got another shot at going back to the starting post. He imagined himself living in L.A. like a penniless young musician with nothing but his guitar and his rock 'n' roll sweetie. It was an enchanting prospect. John had spent his whole life a married man. From his early twenties he had been burdened with all the trappings of fame, which have the paradoxical effect of diminishing rather than increasing a man's sense of freedom and self-satisfaction. Now he wanted to get back to basics. Forget about being a culture hero and concentrate on himself. It might be a simple life—but it would be fun!

Symbolic of Lennon's change of life was the name he adopted. Dropping "Ono," which he had substituted for "Winston" at the height of his infatuation with Yoko, he reverted now to his once-detested English name, but he redeemed it by adding a ribald epithet, "boogie," an expression, like "jazz" or "rock 'n' roll," that equates hot music with screwing. Thus was born that rockin' rake and king of the street cats, Dr. Winston O'Boogie.

John might have had a wonderful time in L.A., but he could not go a day without running his head into a noose. The first thought that entered his mind was to cut a new album with Phil Spector, a collection of Fifties rock classics, the songs that John had loved when he was a kid. It seemed like a perfect idea for a rock star who was starting over, and now was the ideal moment, when he was between major projects and set to ball. Within forty-eight hours of his arrival John was laying out the plan to Phil.

Spector's first reaction was to snap: "Who is in control of this album?" Replied John: "You are."

Unsatisfied, Spector insisted: "Do I have *total* control?"

John answered: "Yes. Yes, you do. I only want to be the singer in the band. I want you to treat me just as you did Ronnie in the old days."

With those fateful words John Lennon summoned up the first of the three Evil Fairies who determined the course of his Lost Weekend.

The situation into which the hapless Lennon had blundered could not have been more wickedly ironic. Here was one of rock's greatest stars begging to be treated the way Spector had handled little Ronnie Bennett when she was first breaking onto the charts. What Lennon had in mind, of course, were the records Ronnie had made *before* she became Spector's wife. Once Spector had "total control" over Ronnie, he had not cherished her talent or fought to advance her career. Far from it! With Ronnie at the peak of her fame, hits all over the lot, Spector had retired her, dropping her into obscurity the way a chess player removes a piece from the board. It was precisely Phil's mania for *total control* that turned Ronnie's life into a gothic horror story.

The story began the day Miss Veronica Bennett of Harlem became Mrs. Phil Spector of Beverly Hills. Ronnie thought she had made the biggest score ever racked up by a girl in her position. "I was the only girl who ever married the boss in the music business," she boasted, adding: "Not even Diana Ross married Berry Gordy." But instead of being allowed to pursue her career or bear children, as she wanted to do, Ronnie suddenly found herself in prison. As a lover madly jealous, as a husband Phil Spector became an ogre. He turned his gloomy old Spanish colonial mansion into a Bastille, with brick walls and barbed wire, prison yard floodlights, burglar alarms, and attack dogs, to say nothing of karate-killer bodyguards and Phil's sinister trademark—the heavy piece carried in a shoulder holster.

No sooner did Spector get his hands on Ronnie than he put her in purdah. She was never allowed to see another man. If she had a little chat with the cook, she would find Phil lurking on the service staircase, eavesdropping. If the masseur came to work on Ronnie, he was obliged to rub her in a blacked-out room and she was ordered to wear a one-piece bathing suit. Any sort of trip outside the walls was frowned upon, save for a week with her family every other month. Normally Ronnie was permitted to leave the house for only twenty minutes a day, and then only on condition that she prop up in the front seat of the car a life-size replica of Phil Spector smoking a cigarette! When Spector proved sterile, the couple adopted a male baby of mixed blood. Phil insisted that Ronnie tell everyone, including her family, that the child was theirs. Ronnie endured it all—until her mother made an alarming discovery.

One day Phil took Mrs. Bennett down to the basement and showed her a glass coffin. He said that if Ronnie ever left him, he would kill her and put her on display, like Snow White. At that point Mrs. Bennett told Ronnie: "You're gonna have to get out. But you're gonna have to sneak it. You can't jerk your hand out of the lion's mouth. You've got to *sliiiiide* it!" And out she had gotten.

Now, here was John Lennon, fresh from his captivity at the Dakota, free at last from his masterful missus, sticking his head straight into the lion's mouth!

Once Phil had obtained full control of the album, he put John and May on hold. An entire month elapsed before they were summoned to the studio. During that time they put together their new life on the Coast. Lou Adler, the famous record producer, offered Lennon the use of a house in Bel Air. The young lovers got wheels when John bought May on her twenty-third birthday an $800 1968 Plymouth Barracuda. They even obtained an assistant when May's friend Arlene Reckson, a New York designer, offered to come out and help in exchange for room and board. A lot of local people, including many celebrities, sought to meet Lennon, but he remained aloof, associating exclusively with Spector, who would come over at night with this guitar and his amyl nitrate to run through old rock tunes.

The illusion of freedom which John and May enjoyed when they arrived in L.A. was soon dispelled by Yoko's insistent presence on the telephone. She called day and night. She also sent her informers, like Elliot Mintz, a local DJ and celebrity interviewer, to find out what was happening. Above all, she gave John and May endless orders concerning how they were to comport themselves in public.

Basically what Yoko was seeking was protection for her cherished image. John was instructed to tell the press that Yoko had kicked him out for misbehaving. He was likewise forbidden to do anything that might suggest that he and May were having an affair. Yoko suggested that John and May travel in separate cars, and she insisted that May keep up the pretense that she was merely John's secretary, even in front of their closest friends. What astounded May was the way John submitted to these demands. The only way he could imagine defying Yoko was to do things behind her back. He told May that their best bet was to make it appear that they were obeying Mother because that would enable them to do as they pleased—in secret.

The next major concession Lennon made was to public opinion. He asked Tony King, a charming but lightweight British PR man, for his ideas on promoting *Mind Games*, set for release on 16 November. Like a typical flack, King told Lennon that he must persuade the public that he was *not* the angry man he had appeared to be in the famous interview in *Rolling Stone* or in *Some Time in New York*, which contained songs like "Woman Is the Nigger of the World" that had dismayed the publicists at Capitol. King's advice reflected the prejudices of the day. In the Fifties Lennon's anger would have been applauded as a sign of how much he *cared*, but since the advent of the Love Generation, anger had become to Americans what sex was to the Victorians—the most dreaded and shameful of human emotions. What King didn't reckon with was the fact that John Lennon *was* an angry man who had spent years discovering how to channel his anger into his work, where it had inspired his masterpieces. To advise him now to shut himself back up inside the box that had contained the Beatles was to miss completely the basic thrust of John's personal and professional development. But Lennon, troubled by weak sales (caused by weak songs), complied with King's suggestion and told the press he was merely an entertainer. Then he witnessed his new album rise to No. 9, with the single peaking at a disappointing 18. Though he had failed again, John professed to be pleased, telling May, "Now they know I don't automatically make number ones all the time. . . . The pressure's off me to keep producing."

Meantime, John and May were hearing through the grapevine that Phil Spector had hired this or that player for the upcoming sessions. Lennon's requests were confined to his favorite engineer, Roy Cicala (who brought his assistant, Jimmy Iovine) and the drummer, Jim Keltner, plus another local player with whom John had been longing to work for years, Jesse Ed Davis.

Lennon had met the exotic-looking Davis (a full-blooded Kiowa Indian with a B.A. in English literature from the University of Oklahoma) back in December 1968, during the filming of the *Rock 'n' Roll Circus*, a disappointing TV show that Allen Klein had refused to release when he recognized that all the guest stars—the Who, Jethro Tull, Taj Mahal, Plastic Ono Band—came over better than the program's headliners and hosts, the Rolling Stones. One evening, while the musicians were killing time in the dressing room, John had started singing some of Elvis's early sides; every time he hit the guitar break, Jesse Ed (Taj Mahal's guitarist) would chime in with a perfect rendition of Scotty Moore's original solo. When John shifted from Elvis to Carl Perkins, he found Jesse still tracking him flawlessly, with every lick at his fingertips. That sort of knowledge was enough to set any man up forever with John Lennon, who saw rock 'n' roll as a vast reservoir of licks out of which a smart songwriter could scoop an endless series of hits. Even if Jesse had not been a brilliant player—fast but smooth, with a beautiful singing tone that he could sharpen to ringing steel when he got into bottleneck blues—he would have been a valuable resource man for the rock 'n' roll album.

The real problem with the new project lay not in its personnel but with Lennon's failure to define his purpose in artistic as opposed to personal terms. It was all very well to go back to his roots in the Fifties—but then what? A successful reinterpretation is basically no different from an original recording because it projects such a fresh view of its source that it produces the effect of a new song. But John Lennon had rarely cast such a transforming spell on an old side. His approach, which shows to best effect on the Larry Williams covers he cut in the mid-Sixties, was to steep the hot original in his own dry-ice temperament, quietly putting his stamp on the tune, like a good editor working on a manuscript with which he deeply empathizes. Now John was in a totally different mood. He wanted to rock out and shout, to rip it up as he had done in the good old days at the Cavern. That meant that instead of subtly one-upping his originals, he was going to compete with them on their own terms, an approach that wasn't likely to get him very far with either the music or the critics, who by now were pretty hip to the oldie goldie classics.

Ultimately what lay behind the rock 'n' roll album was not simply John Lennon's current mood but that of the rock world in general. Actually, there has never been a rocker who wasn't haunted by the thought that nothing has ever surpassed the original rock 'n' roll. The basic reason for this perpetual hankering after the past is simply that rock has not developed organically like jazz, by generating layer after layer of more sophisticated music out of its original core. Rock has advanced by fitting on the sturdy little chassis of the basic beat an endless series of trendy new bodies, like the sporty shell of the Karmann Ghia on the undercarriage of the Volkswagen. This was precisely the way Lennon viewed rock: as a kind of conveyor belt upon which you can shovel anything. But now it was time to go back to the beginning to revitalize and confirm the fundamental commitment—if he could just figure out how.

During the tense hours before the first recording session, early in November, John found himself being distracted by endless calls from Yoko. First she announced her intention of cutting another two-record album. Then she informed John that she had booked a week at Kenny's Castaways, a club on the Upper East Side, where she would work with a studio band fronted by David Spinozza. At the same time that she was proposing these costly projects—a double album could set Lennon back $150,000—she kept deriding the rock 'n' roll album and attacking Phil Spector. By the end of the day Yoko had shaken John so badly that he asked May Pang: "Do you think I'm doing the right thing?"

When John and May got to the A&M Studio, located on the old Charlie Chaplin/United Artists lot, they hadn't a clue to what they would discover. Spector had cloaked all his activities in paranoid secrecy. John was sure that Phil would have mustered no more than eight musicians. Imagine his astonishment when he saw twenty-seven men file into the huge Studio A! Every man was an outstanding soloist and some were big names: Jose Feliciano, Leon Russell, or Steve Cropper, the guitar star of the Memphis Sound. Massing men of this caliber in a giant rock band was a bizarre and unheard-of act, a consummate example of Phil Spector's lifelong love of overkill.

The session began with Spector making a characteristically dramatic entrance, arriving late and wobbling into the studio atop his lifts, a pistol showing prominently in a shoulder holster. He was followed by a big middle-aged man with a beard, his minder, George, the only bodyguard in the world whose basic job was to protect other people *against* his employer. The musicians, who were being paid triple scale, gave Phil a cheer. After greeting each man personally, Phil snapped: "Let's set up!"

Although Spector had spent more than a month putting this session together, not even the simplest preparations had been made at the studio. As the clock ticked on, orders had to be issued to provide the players with chairs, music stands, and lead sheets. Finally, Phil took guitar in hand and ran down the first tune, "Bony Moronie." Though the song is little more than a walking bass, Phil insisted that the band rehearse this elementary exercise. When he had satisfied himself that the best players on the West Coast could recite their ABC's, he went into the booth and commenced the mind-numbing ritual that occupied the next six hours. First he had the rhythm section play its part for three hours straight. Then it was the turn of the horns and finally the guitars. Not till three in the morning did Spector announce that he was ready to record the vocal track.

John Lennon had endured this ordeal because he wanted to discover how Spector built his legendary Wall of Sound. Now Lennon demonstrated how he worked. Stepping behind the singer's baffle, he announced: "I'm singin' this for May!" Then he insisted that she sit beside him. Knowing exactly what he wanted, John completed his takes within half an hour.

"Playback!" announced Phil through the intercom. For the first time that night the mob of musicians heard the results of their labors.

Out of the studio speakers came a plodding, leaden, joyless track, full of calculated fuzz and buzz, with mewling little licks from a pedal guitar that sounded like a hungry cat. Lennon's voice had a fierce rasp and bite, exciting at first but impossible to sustain. The song, meant to rock like a walking beam, shlepped along like the Volga boatmen until it reached its welcome fade. The great Phil Spector had laid an egg.

Spector's entrance on the second night was even more dramatic than his debut. This time he appeared before the astonished musicians costumed as a clinician, with a long white lab coat and a stethoscope hanging about his neck. Brandishing his pistol in one hand and a bottle of Mogen David in the other, he wobbled around the studio, talking manically to the players. The excitement produced by his appearance did not continue once he had stepped inside the booth. As the relentless grind resumed, all the men who were not working left the studio and began to hang around in the halls. A&M Studios is next door to a Safeway Market. The juicers ducked over to the store and came back with bottles of wine. The heads lit up joints and passed them around. Soon the whole session, apart from the few musicians who were working, became a party whose tone grew increasingly drunken and ribald.

Lennon had done very little drinking during the first session, though he had armed himself with a flask of vodka. Now he started passing a gallon of Smirnoff back and forth with Jesse Ed Davis, thus giving the signal for all the players to pull out their jugs and drink openly. As May Pang and Arlene Reckson looked on in dismay, the musicians got loaded and John began to get rowdy. He swaggered over to May and kissed her macho style, running his hand up inside her blouse. Then he went into the booth and yelled at Spector, who was driving everybody crazy with his time-consuming procedures. When Spector ignored John's complaint, John picked up a headset and smashed it on the console. Soon a fight broke out between the producer and a musician who was shouting: "I've been here five hours, and I've only done twenty minutes' work!"

Once again it was not until two or three in the morning that John went behind the baffle with May and laid down the vocal track of "Angel Baby" in a half dozen quick takes.

The violence that had been building inside John Lennon all night came bursting out the moment he left the studio. It struck so fast and unexpectedly that it stunned May Pang. She recalled that John was walking unsteadily toward the parking lot when suddenly he cast a drunken look over his shoulder at Jesse Ed Davis. Running over to him, Lennon gave Jesse Ed a passionate kiss on the mouth. Not to be outdone, Jesse Ed grabbed John and kissed him back. Lennon screamed, *"Faggot!"*—and knocked Jesse flat on his ass.

At that moment Phil Spector roared up in his old Rolls-Royce with George at the wheel. Roy Cicala was following in his car. Phil leaped out and threw May Pang into the Rolls. Then he pushed John into the back seat of Cicala's car, ordering Keltner and Davis to sit next to John and Arlene Reckson to get into the front seat beside Cicala's assistant, Jimmy Iovine. Both cars took off at once for Lou Adler's house. As they sped along the hushed streets of Bel Air, May could hear John screaming in the car behind her: *"May! Yoko! May! Yoko!"*

The moment John had realized that he had been separated from May, he had gone berserk. He had yanked Arlene's hair like a child. He had tried to kick out the windows of the car. Davis and Keltner sought to restrain him, but he had displayed extraordinary strength, pulling out Keltner's hair by the handful. When the cars screeched to a stop before the house, Arlene jumped out and ran toward May, shouting, "John's gone mad!"

May wanted to put John to bed at once. Spector ordered her to sober him up first with coffee. He warned that John was still highly dangerous. No sooner were the words out of Phil's mouth than John lunged for the little producer's throat. Instantly Spector was on his feet issuing orders. Big George seized Lennon from behind and frog-marched him upstairs to the bedroom. Bang! went the door. May heard John screaming, *"Gimme back my glasses, you Jew bastard!"* Inside the bedroom George was tying Lennon's hands to the bedposts with neckties from the closet. The bodyguard showed his professional skill by tying Lennon facedown. If he had been left lying on his back and the booze had made him nauseated, John Lennon might have suffered the fate of all those other famous drunkards—Malcolm Lowry, Tommy Dorsey, Jimi Hendrix—who choked to death on their vomit.

When Lennon found himself being tied down, with his ass up in the air, he flashed back on his sex scenes with Brian Epstein. "I thought, Phil is gonna fuck me up the ass!" he told Jesse Ed the next day. Instead of fighting and screaming, John suddenly changed his tune. Now he whined: "Please let me go, Phil. Be my baby! I'll sing your song great, Phil!" Then John started singing "Be My Baby."

The implacable Spector was not satisfied until Lennon had been firmly secured. Then Phil gave the signal for a fast pullout. As he went through the house door, he turned his little shaded face up at the terrified girls and said: "Wasn't it a terrific session?"

No sooner was Spector out the door than John began screaming, *"Untie me, May! You had better untie me or else!"* May and Arlene were panic-stricken. They didn't know what to do. May was afraid to release John because he might turn on her. Suddenly they heard sounds of rending and tearing upstairs. Then there was the crash of broken glass. John had gotten loose and hurled something through the window. The next moment he appeared at the top of the staircase. Without his glasses, he looked blind and weird. The neckties that had bound him were trailing from his wrists. Squinting down the stairs, he screamed: *"Yoko, you slant-eyed bitch! You wanted to get rid of me! All this happened because you wanted to get rid of me! Yoko, I'm gonna get you!"* With that he came stumbling down the stairs and lunged for May.

Screaming with terror, she ran out the door barefoot and took off down Stone Canyon Road toward the Bel Air Hotel. Arlene was running after May, when suddenly, a jeep driven by two boys came roaring around a curve and nearly struck May. Screeching to a halt, the boys shouted at Arlene: "What's going on?"

Arlene replied: "She took some acid!"

Meantime, May had reached the hotel, where she ducked into a phone booth. Even at this desperate moment she did not violate the code of her service to the Lennons by calling the cops. Instead, she rang the engineers for help. Then she went out front in the parking lot, where she and Arlene could hear John howling and moaning in the darkness. *"Why doesn't anyone love me?"* he cried out in anguish. *"Why doesn't anyone love me?"*

Finally, help appeared in the form of Tony King, whom May had called while Spector was having John pinioned. Pointed in the right direction, he approached Lennon, calling out, "What's the matter, John?" The sound of a sympathetic English voice must have relieved John's fears because he broke down immediately and started sobbing. Tony took John into his arms, as one would a frightened child. Rocking and soothing him, he quieted John's spastic motions.

Finally John's fit ended in a flood of tears. *"Nobody loves me,"* he sobbed. *"Nobody loves me!"*

PING PONG PANG

Kenny's Castaways was one of those maritime mock-ups in the East Eighties that catered to the Swinging Singles. Contrived to resemble a raunchy dockside bar in Key West, strung with dusty nets and dry corks, this saloon had been given a queer twist by the installation of row upon row of stiff old church pews facing a tiny corner bandstand. On the opening night of Yoko Ono and the Plastic Super Ono Band, a capacity crowd of a couple of hundred sat crammed together in those pews buzzing so loudly that they could barely hear David Spinozza's musicians playing a quiet but swinging version of "Killing Me Softly." The buzzing got much louder and crested in a wave of applause when the star of the evening made her eye-opening entrance.

Starting at the rear of the room and brushing past every table and pew in the house, Yoko Ono strutted up to the stage, wearing a costume that made a loud and provocative statement. The white-clad apostle of peace had tricked herself out like a Seventh Avenue hooker. She wore black leather hot pants with knee-high black leather boots, jacked up on spike heels. Her black satin blouse was boldly unbuttoned, revealing a Grand Canyon of cleavage. Chains glinted around her waist, and stones flashed in her ears. Her hair was teased as high as a guardsman's beaver, and her face painted as flamboyantly as a cigar store Indian. Grabbing the mike off the stand and catching the beat of the band, now grinding out straight black funk, she reared back and let rip with a bloodcurdling scream that sounded like Bruce Lee in *Enter the Dragon*. Then she bent double, as if seized by an abdominal cramp, and started gasping out the words to "What'd I Do?," a song that creates a great sense of urgency without any sense of purpose.

Having seized the audience's attention, Yoko settled down to the theme of her show, which was her new image as the heroine of the man-hating wing of women's liberation. As she launched into songs like "Angry Young Woman" and "Men, Men, Men," her dominatrix costume began to make sense. To drive the point home, she employed props and even did a bit with her bandleader. After waving over her head a pair of panties, which she invited the men in the audience to try on, she thrust the mike at Spinozza, demanding, "Do you have anything to say?"

Mumbling with embarrassment, the stern-looking guitarist delivered his stooge line: "I love women."

"Ohhh!" exclaimed Yoko sarcastically, turning back toward the audience. "Men don't have much to say anymore—but we give them the chance anyway." Then she went into the strangely prophetic "Coffin Car," inspired by Jackie Kennedy, which describes a widow riding in a funeral cortege and being hailed by the public, which recognizes her for the first time as a wonderful person. Hatred for men and fantasies of noble widowhood—those were the themes of Yoko Ono's bizarre nightclub act.

After the show Judith Malina and Julian Beck went back to Yoko's dressing room—banked with costly flowers and littered with costumes, props, cases of royal jelly and filled with cigarette smoke—to offer their congratulations. The sentimental Judith, whose knowledge of the Lennons' relationship was gleaned almost entirely from the media, was prepared to find Yoko dying of a broken heart. Naturally she found what she was seeking. Her diary records Yoko's explaining that at first she had sought to picture every hour what John was doing but that now she was struggling to stand on her own feet and lead her life alone.

The fact was that Yoko had spent the entire day on the phone with John.

Yoko was convinced that her little offbeat appearance at an East Side singles bar was going to grab the attention of the media. What she feared was that at this moment of glory John might spoil her triumph by letting the cat out of the bag about their separation. Again and again that day she had rehearsed him in the party line. He was to tell the press that Yoko had kicked him out of the house because he had been a bad boy. That line would save her face. It was typical of John that he raised no objection to this humiliating confession. All the same, the strain of dealing all day with Yoko's importunate demands had told on him and may help explain his bizarre behavior in the afternoon.

Elliot Mintz, who made his living by interviewing celebrities, had persuaded Lennon to do something utterly out of character by lunching with David Cassidy, then at the peak of his fame as star of *The Partridge Family*. Afterward the party had driven up to Mintz's place in Laurel Canyon, one of those houses that stand on stilts and are reached by riding up on a little funicular. May and David were standing at the window, chatting and admiring the impressive view, when John, who had been reclining on the sofa, suddenly stood up and stalked out of the house. In a flash May was at his side, demanding, "Are you all right?"

It was obvious that something was troubling John, but all he would say was: "I want to go home."

When John and May got back to Harold Seider's house (to which they had returned after wrecking Lou Adler's place), John gave his mistress the freeze until it was time to leave for the studio; then he left without her. When he got back that night, he was half drunk. May implored him to tell her what was wrong, impulsively throwing her arms about him. Angrily he broke out of her embrace. When she persisted, he grabbed her long hair and snapped back her head like a rag doll. "Do you know what you did?" he demanded.

"I don't! I don't!" she wailed.

Gulping down a big slug of vodka, John coughed up the choke pear that had been gagging him since lunch. "You flirted with David Cassidy."

As May denied this ridiculous accusation, John started circling her like a menacing animal. While he paced, he rapped out the carefully compiled evidence of her betrayal: (1) She had met Cassidy outside the house when he arrived; (2) she had ordered the same dish as Cassidy at the restaurant; (3) she had stood at the window with Cassidy, talking to him intimately. "I always knew you would cheat on me, and now I have the proof!" screamed John as he worked himself up for the kill. "Don't you know who I *am*?" he demanded. *"I'm John Lennon!"*

Seizing May's eyeglasses, John tore them off her face and stomped them on the floor. Then he grabbed a camera he had bought her and smashed it. Finally, he started running around the house, destroying everything that lay in his path. As he hurled vases into walls and toppled pieces of furniture, there could be heard above the sounds of smashing crockery and cracking wood the persistent ringing of the doorbell. *"Are you all right?"* shouted Arlene from outside.

Distracted by this unexpected interruption, Lennon ordered that Arlene be sent away. When May replied that Arlene was living in the house, Lennon seized May's handbag and dumped its contents on the floor. Snatching up the keys to the car, he said, "Tell Arlene to drive the car away or I'll smash it!" Arlene drove off.

"I'm callin' Yoko!" John yelled when May returned. "I'm gonna tell her everything," he warned, like an outraged child. When his call came through, Yoko was in her dressing room at Kenny's. She was just about to go on. "You were right!" John shouted the moment she answered. Then, signaling May to pick up the extension phone, John started telling Mother everything that naughty May had done that day.

Mother was too busy to listen. "I have to give my show," she snapped. "I'll call you later." Lennon heard the receiver clatter in its cradle.

Blocked by Yoko, John swung his guns around on May. For the next half hour he denounced her as a fortune hunter and a gold digger. While he was abusing her for exploiting him, he revealed inadvertently how much he and Yoko were exploiting May. She learned now that her salary had been stopped the day they left for Los Angeles. What's more, Yoko had told John to spend no more than a thousand dollars on May. May saw at once that Yoko had been poisoning John's mind against his mistress. Her insight was soon confirmed when Yoko called back and May, ordered again to pick up the phone and listen, heard John say, "You were right, Yoko. She doesn't treat me like a star. Tell her that you told me she was a fortune hunter."

Yoko was caught in a trap. She giggled nervously. "May," she said in a tone that meant "Aren't we being silly?" "You know how people say things when they're drunk!"

When John realized that Yoko was not going to help him, he suddenly turned against her, too, denouncing her bitterly. Then he slammed down the phone. When Yoko called back, he refused to answer. After kicking the instrument across the floor, he collapsed across the bed.

May sat up all night, crying.

Next morning, when Lennon got up, he was still angry. "We're goin' back to New York. Make the arrangements!" he barked. A couple of hours later they were on their way to the airport with Arlene and Jimmy Iovine. Jimmy sought to relieve the tension by making jokes. Lennon never cracked a smile. All he would do was repeat endlessly, "That's it! It's over! That's it! It's over!"

Only it wasn't over. It was just beginning. Twenty-four hours after John and May had arrived in New York, they were on the plane flying back to Los Angeles. What had happened? Nothing, really. John went back to the Dakota, poured out his woes to Yoko, and fell asleep. At eleven that night Yoko called May from Kenny's and assured her that everything was fine. "Are you sure?" asked the bewildered May.

"You don't have a thing to worry about," replied Yoko. "I'm not gonna fuck him."

Sure enough, May got a call from John the following morning. He was contrite and apologetic. He said that he didn't know what had come over him. All he wanted to do was go back to California with May. Having learned a few things from her recent experience, May asked Lennon whether it was *he* who wanted to go back or whether Yoko was sending him back. John insisted that he was making his own decision. That was good enough for May. When she got back to L.A., however, she discovered only one difference. Spector couldn't stand the effects of the nightly debauch, so he had reduced the frequency of the sessions from every night to every other night and then to once a week. This stretch-out had the effect of giving Lennon even more time to get loaded and make trouble. Jesse Ed Davis has many recollections of this period.

One day Jesse, John, and May went to Westwood, where they spent the afternoon eating, drinking, and going to the movies. At this time there was a commercial on TV that amused John. Three swishy boys would appear and introduce themselves: "Hi, I'm Charlie . . . I'm Scott . . . I'm Dennis—we're the Wilson Brothers from the House of Suede!" As luck would have it, on this day Dennis Wilson of the Beach Boys spotted Lennon sitting in a beanery. Coming up to John, who was drunk and not wearing his glasses, Wilson said, "Hi, John! I'm Dennis Wilson."

John looked up and drawled, "Yeah, from the House of Suede—right?"

Dennis just hung his head and shook it. Then he walked away, crushed.

Another night John grabbed Jesse and his woman, Patti, demanding, "Have you ever seen *Enter the Dragon* with Bruce Lee?" When it turned out they hadn't, John carried them down to the Los Angeles Theater on Main Street, in the heart of Los Angeles's skid row. A heavy rain had driven all the winos inside the movie house, where they were sitting around, swigging out of their bottles. John upped with his jug of vodka and a carton of orange juice. But just as they were getting into the good part of the picture, with Bruce Lee knocking men over like tenpins, the roof caved in! A torrent of water came cascading into the theater. Jesse Ed had stood up to leave when suddenly the manager appeared. He gazed up at the ceiling, shook his head, and went out again. Meantime, the picture never stopped. Jesse sat down with his friends, and they watched the last three reels through a waterfall.

After a session on yet another night John, Phil, and Jesse went to eat at the Brasserie in Sunset Plaza. John and Phil were trying to outdo each other in their drinking. They were into vodka and champagne, drinking under the table, shooting jets from the bottles into each other's mouth. When the food came, they were so blasted that all they could do was play with the stuff, throwing it at each other or sticking it in their ears. As Jesse Ed looked about the restaurant, he could see that the people witnessing this incredible scene were struggling to persuade themselves that the man making such a fool of himself was *not* John Lennon.

Finally, John and Phil got really nuts. They mounted the table and rolled around on the food. Then they started a game of "I bet you can't do this!" One flipped a fork in the air and caught it. The other raised the ante by making the fork turn twice or three times before catching it. At last Phil screamed, "I bet you can't do this!" With that he flipped over backward in his chair and struck his head violently on the floor.

John said: "You win."

In November the Spector sessions ended when neither John nor Phil could decide what to do next. May Pang breathed a sigh of relief, but then she noticed that John was acting oddly. One day, as they were preparing to visit San Francisco, she pressed him to say what was wrong. "It's over!" he announced firmly. Aghast, May demanded an explanation. John could not offer a reason. Instead, he told Arlene that he would pay to send her and May to Europe. The young women declined the offer and went to San Francisco, as planned. Then they trailed back to New York, broke and at loose ends; in May's case, despondent. Lennon, with the last restraints upon him removed, went berserk.

Jack Douglas, an engineer who had developed a good relationship with Yoko, recalled that she offered him money at this time to spy on John in L.A. Jack declined, but when John invited him, Douglas flew out to the Coast with his wife. He soon witnessed a scene that reminded him of the terrifying conclusion of *The Day of the Locust*.

Lennon was drinking one night at the new "in" place, On the Rox, a club atop the Rainbow disco. A crowd of fans was shouting up at the club from the parking lot, demanding that Lennon appear. Incensed by their demands, John got so hot that he kicked out the window overlooking the lot. Then he started screaming at the fans, *"You want me, ya fucks! You want me!"* Just about to hurl himself down upon the crowd, he was seized from behind by Jack Douglas and Jim Keltner. Breaking free, Lennon dashed downstairs and burst out into the lot, where he started throwing punches right and left. The fans hit back. By the time Jack and Jim came running out of the building, Lennon had been swallowed up by the mob. Plunging into the melee, they grabbed John, still hitting and cursing, and dragged him into the back seat of a big black Caddy. As Jack floored the car, Lennon went for the door. Checked in his attempt to escape, he suddenly jackknifed and kicked out the back window with his boots, sending shards of glass showering down over everybody.

The appalling exploitativeness and violence with which John Lennon treated May Pang raise the question: why did May tolerate such abuse? The explanation lies in her family history. May's father, a laundry worker, was often seized by fits of uncontrollable rage. Big, strong, he intimidated everyone about him. Born in China, he had married there but came to this country without his wife and their baby daughter, the sister May was never to know. When he finally sent for his wife, he ordered her to leave their daughter behind and purchase instead a male child to be reared as their son. Obediently she carried out his orders. When May was born in the United States, the father was disgusted. He belted her around just as freely as he did his wife, and the adopted son, imitating his father, attacked May when she was an infant with a hot iron. By the time May was nine, she was suffering from stomach ulcers.

Eventually her mother, recognizing that women were not treated the same way in America as in China, began to fight back against her husband's oppression. Sometimes when May came home from school, she would find the floors glittering with shards of broken glass. Caught in the middle and batted back and forth like a Ping-Pong ball, May became the family mediator. Her mother and father were finally reconciled but May was destined to repeat the whole experience and play the same part in the Lennon family.

And May was still part of the family because after a couple of weeks in New York, she recounts in her book that she was persuaded by Yoko to go back to L.A. once again, this time to see John through an emotionally disturbing reunion with his former wife and son. Cynthia had called John recently and said: "Do you know you have a son?" It was a good question because John hadn't seen the boy since the Lennons left England. Smitten with a rare pang of paternal guilt, Lennon had acceded to the visit on condition that Julian come to him. Because Julian was only twelve, Cynthia was obliged to accompany him, and for a week she would be in the same city as John.

John Lennon was totally mute the day his family arrived. After he and May picked them up at the airport and delivered them to the Beverly Wilshire, he fled. Next day he managed a visit of two hours. Meantime, Yoko grew so alarmed by Cynthia's proximity to John that she clocked a record number of phone calls—twenty-three in a single day!

The third day was the real test: John was scheduled to take Julian to Disneyland. Informed that he was to go off alone with his dad, the boy panicked and hid behind the sofa. Finally, he was persuaded to come out but only on condition that he be accompanied by his mother. The tension eased once the party reached the amusement park. Julian rushed from one attraction to another, dutifully followed by John and Jesse Ed, who were doing a little toot. May and Cynthia chatted amiably, each recognizing that the other posed no problem. Though Cynthia was no longer living with Roberto Bassanini, whom she would divorce by year's end, she made it clear that she had no designs on

John. She was extremely concerned, however, about Julian, who was now showing plainly the effects of prolonged neglect by his father.

The whole group gathered for supper a couple of days later at the home of Mal Evans's girlfriend, Frances Hughes. John and Cynthia were enjoying reminiscing together when she remarked that she had always wanted another child by John. Instantly John got defensive, volunteering some surprising news: "I can't have another child. . . . I have a low sperm count because of the drugs I've taken." The party broke up shortly afterward, but all the way home John brooded on Cynthia's remark, which he interpreted as a confirmation of Yoko's warnings. Yoko, for her part, was greatly relieved by word of this contretemps. She told Arlene Reckson, who was now in Yoko's employ, that she lived with the fear that John would divorce her and treat her just as shabbily as he had Cynthia. "Imagine!" exclaimed Yoko. "She was the mother of his child!"

The day after the dinner party John ran amok. Jesse Ed Davis preserved a vivid recollection of what happened. "I lived over on the beach at Venice with Patti and her little boy, Billy. He and Julian are the same age," he recalled. "John and May were going to pick up Julian from Cynthia and come down to our house so the kid could play in the ocean. John and May showed up two hours late without Julian. They had had a hassle with Cynthia, who wouldn't let them have the kid. So John was in a bad mood. He just wanted to take *anything*! I had some little miniwhites, like Bennies. He swallowed a bunch of those and got all wired up. Then he went down to the liquor store and bought a big bottle of vodka. We got back to our house and just got shit-faced.

"Jim Keltner called up and said, 'Why don't you come join me and Bobby Keyes [a horn player on the Spector sessions] for dinner at this restaurant, Lost on Larrabee?' So we drove over in May's car. By the time we got there, we were so blasted! Everybody else was straight, and they ordered dinner. John and I just looked at the food. There was a friend of mine, Jim Cataldo, who came along to dinner. He was an artist and a racquetball player kind of athlete. He stayed straight because he knew we were all fucked up. Meanwhile, we kept gettin' more and more drunk, orderin' drinks. Then we went down in the basement, which had a coed bathroom.

"There was a sanitary napkin machine on the wall. John pulled one out. It had a little tape on the end. So he stuck it on his forehead. When we got back upstairs, everybody said, 'God, John! Take that shit off your head!'

"John said, 'Naw, it's mine. I want it!'

"Annie Peebles was closing at the Troubadour that night. She had a hit record, 'I Can't Stand the Rain,' that John really liked. So we drove over there, and John walks in with this Kotex still stickin' on his head. When the waitress came over to take our order in the big round booth by the door, she saw we were drunk. She refused to serve us. 'Whaddya mean, you won't serve us?' says John. 'Do you know who I am?' The waitress gives him a disgusted look and says, 'You're some asshole with a Kotex on your head.' Well, we had to order our drinks through the other people. We got more drunk. We would have been in the prone position if it hadn't been for this little bit of toot I brought along. That was the only thing that was keepin' us alive.

"When Annie Peebles came out on the stage, John was sittin' up on top of the back of the booth. Annie was sort of foxy-lookin', so John starts hollerin', *'Annie! Annie!'* He figured she'd recognize him, but with the stage lights in her eyes, he must have sounded like any drunk. So when she doesn't answer him, he starts hollerin', *'Annie! I wanna suck your pussy!'* Next thing I remember is these two big arms grabbed me around the shoulders from behind. Picked me up and carried me out. I ended up on the curb, and there was John! Some other big guy had carried him out. They left May and Patti in there to pay the bill. They came out pissed and said that when we got thrown out, the audience stood up and cheered. So John says: 'Let's go to the house and have a nightcap.'

"On the way there May said, 'I think we should take Patti and Jesse back to their car.'

"'No!' John growled. 'I wan' 'em to come over for a drink!' She got pretty insistent about it. He went for her. He grabbed her around the throat and started choking her. Then he stopped choking her, and he tried to get out of the car. Jim Cataldo, who was driving, grabbed John and pulled him back in. Then John went for May again! Jim pulled John's hand off her neck and saved the day.

"When we got back to Harold Seider's apartment, we came up from the street into the kitchen. There's a light hanging from the ceiling. John said, 'I don't want this light on!' He picks up a skillet and smashed the globe. Glass flew everywhere.

"May started screaming, 'Oh, no! Oh, no! Don't do that!' We *laughed*. We thought it was funny. So we decided to play Keith Moon on Harold Seider's apartment. [Moon was the greatest housewrecker in the history of show business.] We demolished the whole place. Just turned it into smoking rubble.

"We even went upstairs to the bedroom. John thought the mattress was Roman Polanksi. He ripped the mattress up and pulled all the stuffing out. Just demolished the place. Finally, we came back downstairs, and there was nothing left to break but this big marble ashtray. We threw it and couldn't break it. All this time we continued to drink and snort a little coke. When we realized there was nothing left to break, we said, 'Let's wrestle!'

"We started rolling around on the floor. When you're that drunk, things turn serious quickly. It turned into a full-on fight. John was incredibly strong! He got me in some kind of a hold behind my back that I could not get out of, like a full nelson. And he started to kiss me on the mouth! He was laughin' and kissin' me on the mouth. I was strugglin' to git away and I couldn't git away. Then he stuck his *tongue* in my mouth. God! So I *bit* him. Bit him on the tongue. That pissed him off. So he grabbed the marble ashtray that we couldn't break and banged me on the head. Knocked me cold.

"Patti was screaming—I've been told—'You killed him! Oh, my God! He's dead!' That's about all the neighbors needed to hear in that apartment building because they had heard all the smashing and crashing. Now to hear some chick scream, 'He's dead!' They called the cops.

"John said, 'He's not dead! We'll just throw water in his face.'

"So he went in the kitchen to find something to put water in, but we'd smashed everything.

"In the refrigerator there was a big carton of orange juice. He comes back in and throws that in my face. That woke me right up. Orange juice in the eyes and nose and mouth. I came up coughing and spluttering. 'We need to bandage his head,' says John. He goes over to May's purse and pulls out this Nikon camera that she kept and pulls out the film. He wraps my head with the big long roll of film, with the little yellow plastic film can hangin' off one ear. And the damn cops come in!

"They've got shotguns out. They're lookin' for Charles Manson. We sobered up real quick. I'm laying there with orange juice dripping off my head. Film around my damned head. One of the cops is an Indian guy. He comes over to me and says, 'Aren't you Jesse Ed Davis?' Never mind that I look ridiculous sitting there. He's proud to see another Indian in such distinguished company. He's givin' me the fan treatment!"

May Pang recalled that when the sheriff's men announced themselves, John fled upstairs to hide in the bedroom. When a cop asked, "What about upstairs?" May darted up the steps and confronted John.

"You've got to come down," she insisted. "If they come up and get you, it will be worse."

May had been followed by a cop with his gun drawn. When he saw John Lennon, he froze. When John appeared downstairs, the whole posse turned their flashlights and guns upon him. Then they, too, turned to stone. Finally, the youngest and most naïve cop spoke. He said humbly, "Do you think the Beatles will ever get together again?"

"You never know," John answered nervously. "You never know."

Finding nobody dead, the cops left, followed by Jesse Ed and his people. May was seeing them off from the driveway when she heard John shouting up in the bedroom, *"It's Roman Polanski's fault!"* Dashing back into the house, she arrived in time to see John prize one of the legs off the four-poster bed. Then he seized the television and threw it against the wall. Grabbing a lamp, he used it to smash a mirror. Yanking out a dresser drawer, he dumped its contents on the floor. Then he fell to ripping and rending the clothes, like an enraged animal. When May sought to calm him, he seized a jade necklace that he knew she wore at her mother's behest and tore it off her neck, trampling it underfoot.

May began to panic. She called Yoko for help. While she sketched in the situation, Yoko could plainly hear the sounds of demolition. "Call Elliot Mintz," she snapped and hung up.

When May echoed, "Elliot?" the name clicked like a trigger in John's sodden brain.

"I don't want that Jew bastard in my house!" shouted Lennon. "I'll kill him if he comes through the door!"

Next morning, when John awoke amid the rubble of Harold Seider's apartment, he claimed to remember nothing. Nor was he contrite about the havoc he had wrought. The only thing that affected him was the sight of his Martin guitar, which had been broken. "This is the first time in all these years," he exclaimed, "I ever destroyed anything that belonged to me."

By December 1974 the John Lennon/Phil Spector rock 'n' roll sessions had become the talk of Hollywood. The drinking and drugging, the violence and injuries had become so scandalous that A&M finally booted out the famous recording star and his producer. They moved their nightly party, like a floating crap game, to the Record Plant West, but no move could alter the character of the sessions, which were bound to end in a fateful explosion. One of the best witnesses to the final phase of this ill-starred collaboration was Mac Rebennack, better known as Dr. John, the only white man ever to totally master the black R&B style of New Orleans. A little rowdiness wouldn't have troubled this great hero of the street one bit, but what did bug him was the sycophancy displayed by his fellow musicians, who lent themselves without protest to Lennon's self-destructive antics.

"Instead of sayin', 'Hey man, you're fuckin' up your own date,'" rasped Dr. John, "they let it happen! It was the first time in my life that I ever felt sorry for a producer. There was nuthin' that Spector could do. He would try to dole out the lush to John—and the cat would have it smuggled in. Next night Phil would get somebody to make sure that

John didn't drink more than a certain amount. Then the cat wouldn't cut till he had his taste. But when he had his taste, he *couldn't* cut! He'd sit on the floor and act shitty. His attitude was: 'Look at me, Mom, and watch me fuck up the shit!' He broke a man's horn. You don't fuck with nobody's ax. It's like fuckin' with somebody's woman! He bit Danny Korchmer on the nose. He knocked a tooth outta Jesse Ed Davis's mouth. He was nice to my face. But when I had to take a leak, he said I was goin' to shoot up. Now, I'd be *damn* sure I was clean when I went to the studio because I was on parole and I didn't want to be violated. John was the one who dirtied up the scene. One night he had some hustling chicks from Hollywood come over to deliver drugs. There could have been a bust from cops following those girls because they were always on the edge of trouble. John was the kind of cat who would invite trouble to the session. He wanted to be part of the street, but he didn't see that there was elements in the street that could destroy him."

The sessions ended on a spectacular high note. One night Phil Spector, John Lennon, and Mal Evans were standing in the studio hall talking, when Mal said something about having injured his nose. Instantly little Phil up and punched the gentle giant square on the schnozz. "Watch that!" cried Mal as he put his hand to his nose.

"Watch what?" screamed Phil. "*You* watch it!" With that, Spector whipped out his pistol and fired a round into the ceiling. The noise was deafening. Suddenly, after months of making excuses for Spector's crazy behavior, Lennon recognized that he was dealing with a dangerous man. Unfortunately it was too late to save the album.

When the Christmas holiday ended and John was ready to go back to work, he got a call one night from Spector. "The studio has been burnt down!" announced Phil. Lennon was startled, but he believed Spector until he called the studio and learned that it had *not* been burned down. The following Sunday Spector called again. "Hey, Johnny," he began, but before he could get any further, Lennon cut in.

"Oh, there you are, Phil! What happened? We're supposed to be doing a session."

Spector lowered his voice to a conspiratorial whisper and confided: "I got the John Dean tapes!"

Startled, Lennon gasped: "What are you talking about?"

Suddenly Phil cried: "The house is surrounded by helicopters. They're trying to get them!"

Deciding to go with the bit, Lennon asked: "What are *you* doing with them?"

Phil knew the answer to that one: "I'm the only one that knows how to tell whether they've been doctored or not!"

Now John got the message. "What he was telling me, in his own sweet way, was he had my tapes . . . locked in the cellar behind the barbed wire and the Afghan dogs and the machine guns. So there was no way you could get them." Yet John did try every way to get them. He sounded a red alert at Capitol, but nobody could dig Spector out of his burrow.

Eventually it became clear that Spector had used John Lennon's commitment to cut the rock 'n' roll album as bait to inveigle Warner Brothers into signing a major deal with him. Now, with all sorts of people demanding an explanation, Phil put out the story that he had been severely injured in a motorbike accident and was lying up in a sanatorium. This was a ruse that Phil had often employed, sometimes going so far as to have himself swathed by a Hollywood makeup artist in heavy casts and bandages.

Phil Spector's cop-out left John Lennon all revved up with nowhere to blow. John had run away from New York intent on returning to his past as the hard-living lead singer of a hot new band. But instead of recapturing the thrill of bygone days, Lennon had landed in a mess even worse than the one he had fled. Floundering about at the start of the new year, without a compass or rudder, he was totally at sea until he fell under the spell of another, slicker hustler—the second evil fairy.

DARING YOUNG GIRL on the flying trapeze is Yoko
Ono at Sogetsu Hall in 1962, appearing as an ancillary
performer in an avant-garde concert given by John Cage
and David Tudor. *(David Tudor)*

YOKO on 88s with John Cage at the keyboard.
(David Tudor)

FLOWER POWER'S MOST FAMOUS ICON: Lennon's tea-caddy Rolls with his driver, Les Anthony. *(Les Anthony)*

HONEYMOON BREAKFAST 1969 in Amsterdam, site of the first bed-ins. *(Les Anthony)*

KICKING meant cropping his hair for John Lennon. He collapsed from the combined stress of the Beatles' breakup and the changeover from heroin to methadone early in 1970, but he rallied for this one appearance on *Top of the Pops*. (© 1984, Chris Walter, Retna Ltd.)

TITTENHURST MANOR, the Georgian mansion surrounded by seventy-five acres of ornamental trees, was Lennon's last and grandest residence in England. (*Tom Hanley*)

THE IMAGE: John and Yoko planned to announce their arrival in New York in 1971 by plastering this picture over the biggest billboard on Times Square. *(Iain Macmillan)*

COUNTERIMAGE: When the Lennons arrived in New York for the first time, they were greeted by this caricature by David Levine, which illustrated an *Esquire* article, "John Rennon's Excrusive Gloupie." *(David Levine)*

GOOD INJUN, BAD INJUN: John and his favorite guitarist, Jesse Ed Davis, a full-blooded Kiowa Indian, give a red brother a little coke at Disneyland. *(Jesse Ed Davis)*

THE LOST WEEKEND: John broke the news that he had left Yoko and was living with May Pang by striking this pose for the photographers at the Troubadour in L.A. on the night of the Smothers Brothers' comeback in 1974. Harry Nilsson sips a "Milk Shake," a.k.a. brandy Alexander. *(Camera 5 inc.)*

THE FOUND WEEKEND: After nine months of madness in L.A., Lennon returned to normal in New York with May Pang for the next nine months, celebrating Christmas with Julian in West Palm Beach. *(Michael Brennan, copyright Scope Features)*

NODDING OUT AT THE INAUGURAL: Lennon couldn't keep his eyes open during the big show for President-elect Carter at the Kennedy Center for the Performing Arts, but Yoko and Sam Green, who arranged the expedition, were not suffering from John's problem, which he explained as "20 or 30 cups of espresso a day." *(Ken Regan, Camera 5 inc.)*

AS JOHN LENNON autographs a copy of *Double Fantasy* for Mark David Chapman, Chapman watches, smiling. Six hours later, Chapman shot Lennon to death. *(Paul Goresh)*

"SHE LOOKED MARVELOUS!" said Yoko's closest friend, Marnie Hair, when she joined Yoko and Sam Havadtoy for an intimate New Year's Eve supper a year after John Lennon's death. Havadtoy had moved into Yoko's apartment six months earlier and has lived with her ever since. They are pictured here at Sardi's in April 1987. *(© 1987 Ron Galella)*

HARRY THE HUSTLER

If you're sitting in Harry Nilsson's ultramodern multimillion-dollar aerie atop Bel Air, you don't have to be persuaded that he's well off. His high-shouldered, sharply angled residence, poised across the road from Elvis Presley's old mock-Tudor barn at Rocca Place, is one of those go-with-the-flow designs that don't have rooms but offer "spaces" that flow up and down, in and out, like a Happening or an environment. The living-room space extends beyond a plate-glass wall onto a launching platform that makes you dream of taking off and hang-gliding down over those dry hills to the ocean. The den space satisfies the opposite craving, to burrow down into the ground, until you wind up in a snug little cockpit lined with all the gear you would need to cut your own demo records. Considering that Harry not only built this elaborately designed house but owns much of the adjacent land, you're bound to ask yourself: "How did this cat get all this bread?"

The answer is by no means obvious. Unlike most famous singers, Harry Nilsson has never been a public performer. His whole career has been confined to the recording studio. Nor has he had a lot of hits. His sophisticated early albums, like the one on which he paid graceful tribute to the Beatles, were not commercially successful. His last albums were bombs. Actually there was only one album, *Nilsson Schmilsson*, that rode high on the charts. Sure, Harry wrote some songs that other people made hits. Yeah, he's done some work behind the scenes for the movies. But when you put it all together, it doesn't add up to wealth. Not till you learn that Harry has done all his business dealing by himself do you get a clue to his financial success. Harry has always been a helluva hustler—and his greatest hustle was John Lennon.

The books about the Beatles give the impression that Nilsson got tight with Lennon as soon as Harry's first album, *Pandemonium Shadow Box*, was released in 1967. But the fact is that the only Beatle with whom Harry was friendly in the old days was Ringo. He and Harry and Keith Moon used to go partying in London. They recognized each other as men who loved above everything else that good old Rip 'n' Roar! That wasn't John Lennon's scene. Harry was never close to John or even on good terms with him until Lennon came out to the Coast. Then things changed.

And even then it was not until Ringo appeared in February 1974, moving into the lower half of the duplex suite that John and May were occupying at the Beverly Wilshire, that Harry got his big chance. Those were the days of the great brandy Alexander cult. Ringo had discovered this drink and was laying it on all his friends like a hot tip on the market. "Have you ever tried a brandy Alexander?" he would inquire earnestly, giving you those sad beagle eyes. "It's really good," he would insist. "But one thing about it," he warned, "when you have it, ask for *double brandy*. You've got to say, 'Give me a brandy on the side,' because they never put enough in. Then you give it a sip to get it down, and then you pour it in. Then you've got yourself a proper drink."

Soon it become the custom for Ringo, Harry, and John—and whoever else was in town, like Terry Southern, Keith Moon, Roger Daltrey, or Mick Jagger—to assemble around a table in the middle of the El Padrino, a taproom decorated as a tack room, at the back of the hotel. Their arrival would signal the bartender to start shaking up triple brandy Alexanders, one trayful of drinks following hard on the heels of the next because this tipple went down like a milk shake.

John Lennon was always enthralled by strong personalities, and Harry Nilsson was one of the strongest. Though Harry shied away from the public stage, in private he was rarely off the stage. Particularly when he sat behind a table in a bar, he became one of the most relentless performers in Hollywood, a compulsive mimic and chatterbox, broadcasting night and day like a radio whose dial is being twisted by a restless hand unable to find the right station. Harry quickly cast his net over the impressionable Lennon, drawing him into Harry's own self-destructive life-style, which consisted primarily in heavy drinking and 'round-the-clock partying. Though he was at the peak of his career, Harry lived like a man who is desperate to chase his blues away. In fact, all the stars of the bar at the Beverly Wilshire were in the same boat. They were youth stars beginning to feel their age, married men in trouble with their wives, or single men with hectic love lives.

John Lennon was constantly assailed by guilt. With the rock 'n' roll album locked up in Phil Spector's basement, John had to find himself a new project—but what? He was so exhausted creatively that he was down to playing over and over some song he admired, letting the chords seep into his mind until he could stretch a new line across these borrowed changes. His last original album, *Mind Games*, had been a bust; in fact, John regarded everything he had cut since *Imagine* as "dog shit."

Faced with the choice between squeezing out more dog shit or simply getting drunk and playing trivia every night with Harry, John finally came up with a make-work project. He suggested to Nilsson that they collaborate on a new album: Harry would be the star, and John would be the producer.

Instantly, the two drinking buddies became business partners, and all the other boys began clamoring to climb aboard the bandwagon. Ringo had to play drums. Keith Moon had to play drums. With Jim Keltner, that made three drummers for openers. Obviously the album was going to be a tub-thumper, a drunken, off-the-wall, old-gang-of-mine party record. Still, it was better than nothing—and they could charge their bar bills to the production budget!

It was while John and Harry were in the first flush of their new enterprise that they made that famous stink at the opening of the Smothers Brothers. About three weeks before the show Yoko had called and told John that on her birthday she had been royally laid by David Spinozza.

John appeared to be unaffected by the news, telling May Pang, "I was beginning to worry that she would never get it." But Yoko's words set a time bomb ticking in John's madly jealous mind.

When he arrived at the Troubadour with May and Harry 'round about midnight on 13 March, well before the second show, he was already half loaded and seething with anger. When somebody yelled, "Where's Ono?" John shot back: "Suckin' Ringo's cock!" Ushered into the VIP section, where they found a celebrity claque, including Peter Lawford, Pam Grier, Jack Haley, Jr., and Alan Sacks, producer of *Welcome Back, Kotter,* the threesome booked their orders for triple Milk Shakes. When the drinks arrived, John downed his in a single gulp. "Let's have another round," he proposed expansively. Then he began to hum "I Can't Stand the Rain," an ominous sign. Harry joined his voice with John's and soon both singers were performing happily, while accompanying themselves by banging spoons and knives against the glasses and salt cellars.

"That's really wonderful," gibed Peter Lawford. "You'd be a great opening act for the Smothers Brothers." John responded to this crack by seizing Peter Lawford's Milk Shake and downing it.

Having stolen the spotlight with their exhibitionistic behavior, Lennon and Nilsson were surrounded instantly by photographers. John Lennon had an instinctive talent for camera miming. When the spirit was upon him, he could shoot a look, a pose, a gesture into the lens that said it all. Now he decided to send Yoko a little message, acknowledging the news of her birthday present. Grabbing May Pang by the throat, he pulled her toward him and planted an Apache dancer's brutal kiss on her lips. As the flash cubes exploded, the photographers shouted, "Who is she?"

John smiled at May and crowed, "The secret is out!" Then he ordered two more Milk Shakes.

The Smothers Brothers were an object of liberal sympathy in Hollywood because of the way they had been booted off TV. This night was supposed to mark the beginning of their great comeback. The moment they stepped onstage, they received an ovation. But when the cheering and applause subsided, John and Harry could still be heard singing— louder than ever and without any sign of stopping. Harry was egging John on, shouting at him, "They love you!"

Lennon was determined to have his fun. A lifelong heckler, he shouted: *"Hey! Smothers Brothers! Fuck a cow!"*

Soon Lennon was alternating between loud singing and shouted obscenities. Occasionally he'd vaunt: *"I'm John Lennon!"* Peter Lawford told John to shut up. Alan Sacks told John to shut up. No matter what anybody told John, his answer was: "Fuck you!"

Now people all over the packed club were shouting back at John, "They were fucked over, and now *you're* fucking them over! . . . How will *you* sleep at night?"

Finally, Ken Fritz, a mild little guy who managed the Smothers Brothers, came over to the table. He was hopping mad. "Look," he shouted, "we've worked hard for this, and I'm not going to let you fuck it up!" With that, he grabbed John's shoulder.

John reared up instantly, overturning the table with a crash of shattering glass. Spinning around, he caught Fritz with a hook to the chin. Fritz swung at Lennon, as the crowd roared. Before either could throw another punch, Peter Lawford came charging in with a group of bartenders and waiters. Forming a flying wedge, they gave John and Harry the bum's rush. The hecklers were hustled through a furious crowd, whose members threw punch after punch at John Lennon.

When John and Harry came flying out of the club, they ran head-on into a knot of people in the parking lot. There was a lot of pushing and shoving. John wrestled a parking attendant to the ground and fell atop him. A woman photographer began screaming, "He hit me! He hit me!" (She claimed later in a lawsuit that Lennon had belted her in the right eye.)

When John, Harry, and May, who had slipped out unnoticed, finally got inside their car, Harry demanded that they drive to the house of a friend who was having a party. "I don't want to go!" growled John, who had lost his glasses in the melee. "Then I'll go with May!" shouted Harry, making a drunken lunge for her.

"Get your fuckin' hands off me!" she shrieked.

Stunned, Harry fell back. Then they drove to the party, where John and Harry finished off the evening by serenading the astonished guests. When the night ended, May Pang was so disgusted with the team of Lennon and Nilsson that she took them back to Harry's apartment and dumped them.

Next morning Yoko started burning up the phone lines. Calls detailing John's misadventure had poured into the Dakota the preceding night. Yoko heaped all the blame for the incident on May, who was too exhausted to defend herself. When May went down to the hotel lobby, she saw the morning paper had headlined the story and printed the picture of John kissing her. Next day the Los Angeles bureau of *Time* filed a story that made its way into the magazine. The copy began "John Lennon has separated from his wife Yoko Ono, and is living it up in L.A.," but what counted was the picture: John is kissing May with such force that he appears to be sucking out her soul, while his sinewy hand holds her neck as if she were a rag doll. With this one shot Lennon summed up his whole relationship with May Pang and reduced Yoko Ono to his "ex."

That day John watched apathetically while Harry Nilsson—who had not slept a wink the night before—repaired Lennon's damaged image. Harry sent the Smothers Brothers a load of beautiful flowers with a note of apology, signed "From John, with Love and Tears." Nilsson also insisted that they go to the Troubadour and offer their apologies directly to the owner, Doug Weston. When gossip columnist Joyce Haber implied that Lennon might have been out of his mind on drugs—a charge that could have had an adverse effect on John's immigration case—Nilsson arranged for Haber to receive a call from a "friend," who placed the blame for the incident squarely on Demon Rum.

The night after the fracas, Lil, one of Harry's two steady girlfriends, broomed into town and joined the Roaring Boys. A sophisticated, good-looking, highly ambitious writer and filmmaker, Lil had gotten involved with Harry in the course of cutting a record album that she hoped would lead on to a career as a pop star. The first thing she observed now was that Harry was so busy scamming that even while he slept, his "coke foot" never stopped tapping. Next, she sized up the relationship between John and May, pinning it as a pimp turning out a new whore. John encouraged May to dress like a tart, with her blouse unbuttoned to the midriff and gold chains hanging all over her breasts. "He was very titillated by her," Lil recalled. "He had his fingers in her, hand on the ass, hand in the blouse. She was a fox. He liked having that squirmy, puppyish, sexy little koochie dancer. I could tell that this was not how she usually dressed or behaved, but he was turning her into a sex kitten."

How the two famous singing stars rallied after the Troubadour scandal is best heard directly from Lil's lips because she was both an observer and a participant in what became the wildest—and most dangerous—moment of the Lost Weekend. "John and Harry had corralled all these people to play on Harry's album," she recalled. "It was all on John's head, but he didn't want to take the responsibility. John wanted to feel that he was just along for the ride. He kept wanting Harry to take the responsibility. Harry was too busy destroying his voice. [Nilsson had developed laryngitis, but instead of guarding his voice, he insisted on drinking more than ever and shouting at the top of his lungs.] Finally they had a sudden realization that they were fucking up. So they decided to go to Palm Springs to clean up. I thought they meant they weren't going to take anything, and they were going to play tennis. We went to this square hotel, a real athletic club. Horrible! Mal Evans drove us down, with his lady friend and her kid—the first night they had a helluva fight.

"John and Harry tried not to take anything for about two hours. They hadn't brought any coke or acid or anything. So they didn't have any way of getting into trouble, save for liquor. Two hours into the trip, they were looking for trouble. I don't remember what we did the first night. I suppose we all got very drunk and went to bed. I do remember that they never saw daylight. It hurt their eyes. May did some sunbathing. The boys slept till three or four and then put on sunglasses. So we were looking for something to do when somebody recommended that we take the tram up the side of the mountain.

"We had a few beers and went on the tram. We were just going to ride up and come down, but I had a severe attack of acrophobia on the way up. I thought I was going to throw up. My knees were trembling. So we couldn't go right back down. We stayed up there in the bar, from seven in the evening until it closed. The people in the bar weren't just a bunch of tourists and their kids. They were singles or up there for illicit rendezvous. There were a lot of high jinks in the air.

"John and Harry were wearing matching slouchy patchwork denim porkpie hats and dark glasses. John was always afraid of being recognized, but he and Harry would be unhappy if they *weren't* recognized. So John went over to the jukebox and found some Beatles' records, which he played over and over again. Sure enough, we were recognized and people started coming over to us. Finally, we had to leave the bar, but the tram was not ready to go down. May and I were wearing short shorts that are cut to show your cheeks in the back. John and Harry were playing games with us, passing us back and forth. The other people saw that, which explains what happened when we got on the tram.

"Everyone from the bar crowded into the last tram. We were surrounded and couldn't move. Harry and John were still playing their little games with our buttocks. Except that after a while, it became obvious that there were many more than four hands on us. At that point we realized things were getting out of hand. I remember some fifty-year-old grandmother shouting at Harry, 'Bite my tit! Bite my tit!' The whole tram was going wild. Everyone was getting very aggressive about touching us. But nobody could get any closer. They were just pressing their bodies against us as hard as they could.

"When we got to the bottom, Mal had the limousine waiting there with the door open, as if he knew this was going to happen. So the moment the tram door opened, we were off and running at full speed—with the entire tram after us! It was exactly like *Hard Day's Night*. We screeched off in the limousine. Instead of going back to the hotel, we went to a boutique, where May charged up about a thousand dollars' worth of clothes. The boutique had free wine. So the boys got even more drunk. They bought themselves some more patchwork denim things. We got back to the hotel too late for room service, which closed down about eight. So Harry and May went off for groceries.

"John and I got into the little Jacuzzi on the front lawn of the hotel. I don't know what happened then because I blacked out. Harry was very upset with me when he came back. Harry and May were both very angry, but they got in the Jacuzzi with us. I don't know what May said to John, but she was being whiny and spoiling his fun. Suddenly he had both his hands around her throat. He was squeezing as hard as he could. I couldn't believe it! We didn't do anything for a few crucial seconds. Then Harry decided that May had had enough and dragged John off. The guard came out at that point and made us get out of the Jacuzzi.

"We had gotten into some other trouble that day. Harry had to go to a clinic to get a shot for his throat. He was constantly taking antibiotics and swilling them down with cognac. So they didn't do him any good. His vocal chords were starting to hemorrhage. He was spitting blood. We came back to the hotel and started getting into crazy *Kama Sutra* poses on the front lawn. I remember I was sitting down for a photograph when a jet of water came shooting up between my legs, like a bidet. They had turned the sprinklers on us! It was just like they do when they're trying to stop dogs from fucking. The hotel was going to throw us out. They didn't care who the hell John was.

"Up in the room John picked up May and threw her across the room into a wall! It wasn't May he was angry about. It was something about women. He used to turn on women like that. I don't doubt he pulled some of it on Yoko in the early days. Cynthia and May *are* infuriating in a way because they don't have any character.

"The next thing I remember is that John, Harry, and I were in bed together. May had run off crying because she had been beaten to a bloody pulp. I don't remember any of that, until the next morning. Then I remember something John said: 'I don't want to be in love. It hurts too much.'"

The weekend concluded with Mal's driving everyone back to L.A., where Harry took Lil to the airport and then hung around to welcome his other love, Una, who was coming to visit him on her Easter holiday from college. John no sooner got back than he was presented by the hotel with the bill for March: a whopping ten thousand dollars! The money could be charged off to the album budget, but John was very unhappy about incurring all the expense of entertaining his friends. So a couple of days later he came up with a fresh idea. "There should be an asylum somewhere for aged rock 'n' rollers," he suggested. "Then we can all be put in padded cells where we belong. We should all rent a house and live together. Then we can watch Harry, save money, and make sure all the musicians get to the studio on time when we begin to work on Harry's album."

Harry picked up on the idea in a flash and arranged for the rental of the now-notorious house where Marilyn Monroe had her assignations with Jack and Bobby Kennedy. No. 625 Pacific Coast Highway is a big old house built by Louis B. Mayer and planted on the beach just north of the Santa Monica ramp. Here on April Fools' Day gathered the inmates of Dr. Winston O'Boogie's rock 'n' roll asylum. In addition to John and May, the patients included Harry and Una (a pink-faced Irish college student, who is now Mrs. Nilsson); Klaus Voorman with his hefty black girlfriend, Cynthia Webb; Keith Moon; and Ringo Starr and his business manager, Hillary Gerard (who looked like a California biker—one of those tattoo and gold tooth types, with a bald pate and long, lank hair framing his satanic visage).

The moment John started functioning as Harry's producer, the rhythm of the Lost Weekend altered because John straightened up and refused to go out on nights with the boys. When the recording sessions at the Burbank Studios (which still involved plenty of juicing) concluded around midnight, Harry and Keith, Ringo and Hillary would go off to the Rainbow or On the Rox, while May would drive John and Klaus back to the house. In the morning the straight people would get up at a normal hour and be served breakfast by the Mexican couple who kept the house; then, as the afternoon commenced, the victims of the previous night's action would slowly begin to appear, like the walking wounded. The most amusing appearance was always made by Keith

Moon, who would come downstairs dressed like a German general in a long brown leather coat, a long white aviator's scarf with a pair of field glasses slung about his neck. When he turned around, you could see his bare ass.

As the recording proceeded, Harry Nilsson's once beautiful and inexhaustible voice began to break. Conventional medicine having been defeated by Harry's life-style, John suggested that his star try the services of Dr. Hong. To make sure that Nilsson got back in time for the session, Keith Moon was detailed to take the patient to San Francisco. Keith was hardly the man to play medical orderly. When the two rockers showed up at Burbank that night, late for the session, they were both dead drunk. John shouted to Keith: "Is he any better?"

Moonie answered: "No, but he's full of holes!"

Once the tracks had been cut, John and Harry set to work to mix the album. Every time they would finish a track, Harry would say he wasn't satisfied and insist upon mixing it again. You can hardly blame him. His voice sounded horrible, the music was mostly self-pitying mush, and the playing was nothing special. Basically, *Pussy Cats*, as the album was titled, was an embarrassing mess. John was not the type to spend months in the studio. Once he saw that Harry would never make an end, John grabbed the tapes and took off for New York, where he figured he could wind up the project in a hurry and get Harry out of his life.

The moment Harry saw the bird had flown, he sobered up fast. He jumped on a plane and chased after John. The moment he arrived at the Apple, he grabbed Lennon and, after a few rounds of get-together drinks, talked him into playing shill to Harry's hustler.

Harry's triumph on the morning of his arrival is recalled by Lil, who got the story straight from Harry's mouth the moment after he staged this brilliant scene:

"I saw Harry and John about eleven o'clock in the morning, right after their meeting with Ken Glancy, the president of RCA. They had arrived around nine o'clock, which is when Harry called me and told me to meet him at the Pierre. Harry marched John, whom he had gotten drunk, straight into the RCA offices that morning. To understand what happened, you have to know that Rocco Laginestra [a former president of RCA] was like an uncle to Harry. He loved him to death. Before Rocco was deposed, he had negotiated a contract for *five million dollars* for Harry. Five albums. And after Harry delivered each album, RCA had to give him in cash something like $800,000! Really lush. Then there was some shuffling around at the top. Gil Beltron, then Ken Glancy came in. Harry's contract was sitting in a drawer, unsigned by RCA. So that morning Harry marched in with John and came into Ken Glancy's office, unannounced. Ken had never met

Harry and was only recently installed as president. I daresay he was shaking in his boots when those two walked in.

"Harry said: 'We've flown in with these basic tracks. This is going to be the album of the century.' Then he puts the tape on and turns up the volume as far as the dial would go. They had three drummers—a wall of noise. Ken's mouth fell open. Then Harry said: 'This is gonna be a big album for you guys, but I'm gonna leave the company! You know why? Because you had a contract sitting here for nearly a year! And you guys have never signed it! So I'm mad! I'm *mad*! If I were gonna stay with this company, I would bring John with me. His contract is gonna be up soon at Capitol." John, being drunk, nodded mechanically when Harry looked over at him. Harry said: 'I'm gonna bring Ringo, too! I could. But I'm not gonna because you still haven't signed the contract.'" With that, Harry turned on his heel and walked out of the office, taking with him the legendary John Lennon.

"So when they came over to the Pierre," Lil continued, "John hurled himself across the lobby and sank his head into my crotch. Kneeling down in the fucking reception area! Just glad to see a friend because Harry had been putting him through all this nightmare, politicking. When we got upstairs, John threw himself across a bed. Harry got straight on the horn to his lawyer, Bruce Grakal, in L.A. Harry, drunk as he is, is always completely lucid when it comes to his deals. So he was on the phone to his lawyer, who aids and abets him in everything, telling Grakal the incredible tap dance that he had just done. 'Now you get on top of this,' he said, 'because I know they're gonna be reading that contract right now as we speak.' And sure enough! It was signed two days later."

Harry the Hustler had made his big score.

FREE FALL

When John Lennon returned to New York, he didn't bring along May Pang because he didn't want anything to interfere with the reconciliation he was now desperate to achieve with Yoko. What was making John run home to Mother wasn't love; it was fear. John was in a panic because he recognized that if he continued to rock around the clock with Harry Nilsson, Ringo Starr, Jesse Ed Davis, and Keith Moon, he would fly out of control again—and this time he might do something terrible. "I don't wanna be fucked up!" he cried out in anguish to May Pang before abandoning her in L.A. "It scares the hell out of me!"

No sooner was John back in the Apple, however, than he discovered that Yoko would not allow him the sanctuary of the Dakota. In fact, she refused even to see him unless it was in the company of other people. So John grabbed Harry and Lil and told them that they were going to be his chaperons during a meeting with his wife, but that as soon as he gave the signal, they were to excuse themselves and leave him alone with her.

The meeting commenced in a very chilly atmosphere. Yoko retreated behind her mask of impassivity. Harry was drunk, as usual. When he recognized that Yoko was giving him the freeze, he cast an imploring look at her and croaked: "Whaddya wan' me to do, Yoko? Suck yer cock?" That was such a direct hit that even the Great Stone Face turned up the corners of her mouth. John and Lil virtually killed themselves laughing, as much from a sense of relief as from appreciation of Harry's kamikaze wit.

Once their laughter had subsided, however, the mood went right back to the Ice Age. John sat on pins and needles until he could give the high sign. Finally, the moment came. Harry and Lil excused themselves and left. But before the elevator could lumber up the shaft, John's voice rang out from behind the glass-paned door of the flat: "Hold on! I'm comin'!" When he got out in the hall, he grimaced despairingly and confessed that Yoko had asked him to leave.

By refusing to take John in out of the cold, Yoko gave Harry a perfect chance to draw Lennon back into the dissipated life-style he was trying to escape. The only difference between New York and Los Angeles was that with May Pang off the set there was no limit now to the lengths that Lennon could go once he got back to rockin' 'n' reelin'. For the whole month of May 1974 the Lost Weekend became a free fall.

John and Harry holed up in Rooms 1604-5-6 of the Hotel Pierre on Fifth Avenue, across Grand Army Plaza from the Plaza Hotel, where the Beatles had made their first landfall in America. About one every afternoon the two rounders would start to get their heads up as Harry rolled over in bed and called room service for their breakfast: two triple brandy Alexanders and a tray of hors d'oeuvres. Until the cocktail hour the boys would nosh on Vienna sausages impaled on plastic toothpicks and batter-fried shrimp dipped in cream sauce, washing these tasty tidbits down with an ever-renewed supply of Milk Shakes. Anybody who knocked at the door of their suite was admitted. Once the word got out, all sorts of people showed up.

Some of these uninvited guests were celebrities in search of celebrities.

In the evenings John and Harry would go over to the Record Plant East at 321 West 44th Street and continue work on Nilsson's album. One night Paul Simon and Art Garfunkel arrived to harmonize behind Harry. They hadn't sung together in four years. What brought them to the studio was simply the chance to work with John Lennon. When the session got under way, the famous duo had a lot of trouble coming in on cue. They spoiled take after take. Lennon was very polite and forbearing. Harry Nilsson was infuriated. "You're fucking it up! What's the matter with you?" he snarled. Garfunkel turned on Simon and accused him of coming in wrong. Simon retorted that it was Garfunkel's fault. Everybody had been drinking, so the argument soon escalated into a tremendous cuss fight. Finally, the job got done, but so badly that the track could not be used.

When the hour grew late, Harry would always want to go out on the town. His addiction to Milk Shakes had given him a red nose and a fat Shmoo body. Because he never shaved and was dressed slovenly, he looked like an alley wino. Still he possessed the capacity to go for days without sleeping, a faculty that Lennon was losing with age.

One night the Rover Boys turned up at the Algonquin Hotel, where Derek Taylor was staying with the British jazz singer and pop writer George Melly, who was flogging his latest book. John came into the suite "baying for broken glass," as he sought to smash the chandeliers. Then he and Melly, a Liverpool Jew, like Brian Epstein, nearly came to blows. The intruders were persuaded to go away, but at two in the morning the phone rang in the room of Melly's female flack. It was Lennon. "He demanded sex with her," recalled Melly. "She replied: 'I'm asleep. Go away!'"

One morning John and Harry found themselves around breakfast time in Greenwich Village. They headed for Jimmy Day's, on the corner of West 4th Street and Barrow, an old-timey saloon that serves food. Lennon was recognized on the street by a kid from Brooklyn named Tony Monero, who came on so strong that John invited him to have a drink. Tony was beside himself with joy. He described John as looking like a "stallion," but his photos of John with the gang at the bar show Lennon looking scuzzy: unshaven, slovenly, with shades over his eyes and a big flat cap pancaked on his head. In his hand he's holding the street king's scepter: a bottle in a paper bag. Tony recalled that John went up to each girl and said: "I'm John Lennon. Suck my cock!" Finally, he turned to Tony and said, "Hey, Tony, suck my cock!" It was all the same to John—and it was all nothing! That's exactly how Lil read Lennon after making it with him in Palm Beach and now again in New York.

One night she went up to the suite only to discover that the rooms were empty. "I waited and waited," she recalled, "until John came in alone. He said, 'Harry took me around to some whorehouse, and it's just not what I feel like. I just don't want to do that.' Then he begged me to go to bed with him. So I did. He didn't seem to be that interested in the fucking part, although we did that. He wanted to be held basically. He was definitely a wimp. He seemed a little frantic and desperate. He really wanted the closeness more than he wanted to do the act. I don't even recall that he came. He wanted to go through the motions [he went down on her] and be enveloped. He wanted to be taken care of." When Harry got back, Lil left John's bed and said nothing about what had occurred. She didn't feel she owed Harry a thing because he had spent the evening with a bunch of whores. Next morning she left for the country.

That evening Harry called Lil and announced, "We've got the crabs!" John had told Harry about sleeping with Lil and had upset Harry terribly. He had concluded that Lil was responsible for giving them both the itch.

John got on the phone and said: "What are we gonna use? KY jelly?"

Lil was amused by the situation. She suggested that they adopt the classic cure. "Douse your bush with gasoline," she advised them. "Then light it with a match. When they come running out, you stab them with a knife!"

*   *   *

John Lennon's behavior during his last month with Harry Nilsson marks the low point of the Lost Weekend. Anybody whose knowledge of John was confined to that time would have had to judge him in the terms that Lil employs, dismissing him as a "wimp," or else see him, as did Harry Nilsson and Jesse Ed Davis, as a real "player." The one image degrades Lennon, the other is meant to exalt him; but neither is accurate because these people could see in Lennon only the image they projected on to him and he reflected back to them.

When John was with the street people, he was the epitome of the street, just as when he was with Marshall McLuhan he was the epitome of the pop pundit, or with Pierre Trudeau, the epitome of the peace politician. Interview a score of people who interacted strongly with Lennon and you will get a score of Lennons, each one a man highly congenial to your source. Clearly, John took his identity from the company he kept. Thus the real John Lennon was only as real as his latest infatuation and always a man who was up for grabs.

In later years, when John and Yoko rewrote the Lost Weekend to make it conform with the other stanzas of the Ballad of John and Yoko, they represented Yoko saying to John every time he wanted to come home, "You're not ready yet." The truth was just the opposite: It was Yoko who was not ready to take John back. While he was shivering with the fear that he would go crazy again and kill somebody or himself, she appears to have been calculating how she could prosper without him. For after all this time and despite the enormous advantages she enjoyed, she had still not consolidated her relationship with David Spinozza.

She had tried everything to make herself attractive to him. She had started wearing cosmetics again and fancy underwear. She had put herself out to flatter David and soften his resistance with costly gifts. One day he would receive a new dirt-racing bike. The next, he would be presented with an original work of art. Once Yoko and Arlene tramped all over the city photographing anything that contained the magic word "David"—like a sign for Mogen David wine. When David complained that Yoko got her lipstick all over everything, she countered by smearing a white cup with the same lipstick, embedding it in Lucite, and presenting it to him, lavishly wrapped, as "Lipstick Piece."

At the same time that she was feeding David sugar, she was quick to give him a dose of gall. She treated him as an animal trainer does his beast: with a constant alternation of the carrot and the stick. Yoko had unerring aim for David's soft spots. He enjoyed, for example, quite a rep as a young stud. Imagine how he felt when Yoko would look at him with the deep-etched contempt of six generations of Japanese aristocrats and sneer: "You're an uptight asshole!" Or even deadlier, she would take careful aim at that highly sensitive spot where studio musicians harbor the thought that they've sold out their talent for a lousy paycheck and an old man's pension. Then she'd give him a good Bruce Lee chop with: "You never wrote one song from the heart in your entire life!" Suddenly the hotshot of the studio would see himself as a drone in a jingle factory.

Yoko's kiss-'em-'n'-kill-'em tactics had worked wonders on the desperately insecure John Lennon. The Boy from Brooklyn, however, was made of tougher stuff than the Boy from Liddypool. Even when Spinozza did heel over from the impact of Yoko's bombs or torpedoes, he would quickly right himself. Then he would experience a burning sense of resentment. As he said, "No woman ever made me so angry." Next, he would start looking for Yoko's soft spots, which weren't hard to find if you weren't intimidated by her Wizard of Ono bluff.

Spinozza observed, for example, that Yoko was a split personality. One moment she would be the wistful little Japanese princess talking airy-fairy stuff about love and peace and clouds on the ceiling. Then the phone would ring, and "*Hi!*"—the spacy little Flower Child would suddenly become the hard-bitten Dragon Lady. "He's just trying to fuck me!" she'd spit into the receiver, sounding exactly like some mean little hooker standing out on Columbus Avenue in a phone booth.

Spinozza also noticed that Yoko had a very peculiar attitude toward people in general. She was always seeking the love and tribute of the world, working day and night to become a famous person; yet her basic attitude toward society was summed up in the phrase "They're just a bunch of assholes!" She talked about John Lennon as if he were a mere newcomer to the world of art, where she had long since made a great reputation. Eventually Spinozza would say: "Why do you keep putting his name on everything you do and dragging his name into everything you say? Why don't you go out on your own if you're so sure you don't need him?"

All these points of contention might not have counted for much if Spinozza had found Yoko physically appealing. Unfortunately she was not his type. He even denied having slept with her, contradicting what Yoko told John at the time and, later, her intimate friend Sam Green. Yoko maintained she had slept with Spinozza three times, the scene of their lovemaking being the mattress on the floor of the White Room.

The surest sign of her failure to attract David as a woman was his growing involvement with Barbara, a pretty young girl who aspired to be an actress. Yoko was not dismayed by this development. She made friends with Barbara and sought to work out an accommodation. This tactic scored no more points than her other mind games.

By May, when John came back to New York seeking a reconciliation,

Yoko was singing the blues. Harold Seider remembered going over to the Dakota to talk with her and sitting in the bedroom, where she lay upon the bed contemplating her image in a mirrored wall. "I can't even get laid," she complained. "I'm Yoko Ono—I can't go out and out and pick somebody up and fuck them. I can't even fuck a truck driver without somebody claiming that they fucked Yoko Ono." Harold wondered if she was enticing him. Feeling powerless to control her life, she simply cast about for a new source of power. What she found was the occult.

MOTHER'S LITTLE HELPERS

Japanese ladies are notoriously susceptible to the lure of soothsayers. Yet, it wasn't an Oriental who introduced Yoko to New York's leading clairvoyant—it was Harry Nilsson's woman, the intelligent and sophisticated Lil. When she told Yoko how this man could look into the future, she jumped up from the restaurant table and darted into a phone booth. Next afternoon, huddled into the corner of a stretch limo, she was on her way down to Little Italy.

Frank Andrews lives in a modest house on Mulberry Street facing the churchyard over whose wall Robert De Niro vaulted in *Mean Streets*. Small, plump, dark-haired, dressed in jeans and T-shirt, with a soft face masked by shades, Andrews looks like a boy-man. As he greets a visitor, a pack of silky little brown dogs yap and skitter about his legs, like familiars. Obligingly he explains that his pets are papillons, the sail-eared lapdogs of Louis XIV, and illustrates his point by opening a book and displaying a picture of *Le Roi Soleil* surrounded by prancing little dogs. As he ushers his guest to a comfortable seat, his discourse flows smoothly from the bookplate to the golden-glowing Biedermeier furniture standing about in the otherwise bare rooms of his dollhouse. Then, having settled himself, he recounts matter-of-factly his recollections of Yoko Ono's first consultation.

She comported herself like an attentive little schoolgirl, copying everything Andrews said into a mottled black-and-white notebook. Just as she was rising to leave, he checked her. Murmuring in a semi-trance, he said: "Your husband sleeps in blood."

"What do you mean?" she gasped.

"I don't feel he has a happy ending," explained the visionary lamely. Then, struggling to sharpen his psychic gaze, he added: "I see him covered in blood."

After that warning Yoko insisted that John consult with Andrews. He was opposed to the idea but relented, on condition the psychic come to him. Andrews held a two-hour session with Lennon in the kitchen at the Dakota. It was an unpleasant experience. Every time Andrews spoke the truth, Lennon would sneer: "You read that somewhere!" Despite his hostility and distrustfulness, Lennon plied Andrews with difficult questions. "Will the Beatles get together again?" he demanded.

"No, but I see them on Broadway," Andrews replied. John snorted derisively, but Andrews points to *Beatlemania* as the fulfillment of his prophecy.

"Will I receive my green card?" asked John. When Andrews assured him that he would, Lennon retorted, "Of course, I will—after all the money I have paid to lawyers!"

Next John asked, "Will I make it to forty?"

Andrews smiled and replied: "You've got at least till forty-four."

When they got onto the theme of love, Andrews suggested that Lennon was troubled by his homosexuality. "Why do you dress Yoko up as a boy?" he challenged. John was enraged at the suggestion, rejecting it violently. "I see a baby being born," observed Andrews. John conceded that it was possible that May Pang might bear him a child.

The session ended with a palm reading. Andrews found Lennon's palm lined with signs of conflict and madness. He concluded that Lennon was a "Saturnian" type, with a pronounced tendency to sadomasochism. Not till the men were ready to part did John get up his nerve to ask the question that lay nearest his heart: "Will Yoko and I get together again?"

Andrews cautioned: "It might not be a good idea."

John snapped, "Don't tell her that!"

Once Yoko was launched on the sea of the occult, her yearning for fresh revelations became insatiable. Anyone who claimed to discern the future in a glass of water or a pile of colored stones had a claim on her attention. Eventually these auditions turned up a man who, whatever his powers as a psychic, was undeniably a very astute reader of character. Oddly, he owed his introduction to Yoko not to his real ability but to his reputation as an exorcist.

Yoko had concluded that her apartment was haunted after she had experienced a number of severe anxiety attacks during her first winter alone. Arlene Reckson recalls being awakened repeatedly in the middle of the night by calls from her employer. "I'm on the windowsill!" Yoko would gasp. "Can you come right away?" Arlene would throw on her clothes and dash down to the limousine sent to fetch her. When she came charging into the flat, she would find her boss looking and acting no different from usual. After a cup of tea the two women would go to sleep: Arlene on the mattress in the middle of the White Room; Yoko in the bedroom.

By May Yoko had decided that her problem was the ghost of the previous owner's wife, Mrs. Robert Ryan, who had died in the apartment. One of Yoko's hippie assistants gave her the name of an exorcist. When the tiny Yoko met John Green, on 14 May 1974, she was instantly impressed. A virtual giant, Green stood six feet seven and weighed 290 pounds. Though he looked as if he could handle anything, he was, in fact, an exceedingly cautious man.

Venus is the rising sign of John Raymond Green (born 11 December 1947) and the symbol of his function, the female task of protection. Green discovered his psychic powers while studying art education at the State University at New Paltz. Broke one day, he offered to read a girl's palm in exchange for a cup of coffee. The moment he gazed into her hand, he started flashing pictures. The girl confirmed that his reading was amazingly accurate.

After marrying a classmate and teaching school for a year, Green came to New York and got a job at *Financial World*, a Dell magazine. In 1971, by reading another Dell publication, a little book by Susan Roberts titled *Witches, U.S.A.,* Green discovered the man destined to become his master, Joseph Lukach. "Joey" is described in Roberts's book as an effeminate and childish creature: a 250-pound ball of tallow, draped in garish tunics, garlanded with strings of bright beads and beringed with green scarabs and golden pentangles. Yet, as the book explains, Joey was recognized at the age of six months by the high priestess of a Dominican voodoo cult as one of those rare beings who have the "power," a view that has been echoed by countless people who have known Lukach over the past twenty years.

Wendy Wolosoff, the woman with whom John Green began living in July 1974, after the breakup of his marriage, recalls meeting Lukach at a *balata,* or Santería festival, on All Souls' Day (1 November), the day sacred to Babalú Ayé, the chief priest of the Afro-American cults. The gathering, curiously reminiscent of *Rosemary's Baby,* was held at the posh apartment of a wealthy client on East 73rd Street. An altar had been erected and draped in yellow and black. Huge bowls of peanuts were set out, and vases filled with chrysanthemums. Cigars and rum were much in evidence. The guests feasted on chicken and yucca, black beans and rice. At midnight Joey moved to the altar. His dark, luminous eyes glowed forth from his ivory skin. Standing before the painted statue of St. Lazarus, the Catholic icon for this African spirit, Joey went into a trance. He stumbled suddenly, a sign that he had been "mounted" by Babalú Ayé, who is a cripple. Joey blessed the jugs of water that had been set upon the altar by people seeking psychic healing. Then he gave way to Josephina, a creature even more obese, clad in a white satin pants suit. She started wrestling with a devil that had crept into the womb of a pregnant woman, possessing the fetus. There was a violent tussle. The woman shrieked. Josephina was flung across the room. The call went up for a crucifix. Joey was wearing a cross of black wood on a chain of plastic silver beads. As he removed the cross and handed it to Josephina, she murmured: "It's a good thing he was loaded!"

This was the milieu in which John Green served his apprenticeship in sorcery.

Green was a very different sort from his master. A Roman Catholic by birth and a Jesuit by natural affinity, he was reluctant to learn too much or venture too far. He said that in magic it was vital to know who you were and what you were seeking, for a man who becomes too deeply involved with the power can be destroyed by the power, especially if he abuses the power. Green's attitude toward serving the powers provoked a *babaluae* with whom he was studying umbanda to remark, "I'll bet we take you in here, teach you everything, and then you leave!" Green agreed—and left. Because of his refusal to submit to the discipline of a cult, his education was confined to white magic: reading the tarot deck, preparing charms, weaving spells, doing psychic healing, and performing *despojos,* or spiritual cleansings. Subsequently, he went further.

On the day he first set his huge foot inside the Dakota, Green was clad from head to toe in immaculate white. As bustling and proficient as a party caterer, he converted a table in the White Room into an altar, with three burning tapers at its center. At the cardinal points of the compass he set the symbols of the four elements: fire to the east, represented by a bowl of Florida Water, a cheap cologne; air to the west, symbolized by vials of volatile essences; a bowl of holy water to the south; and at the north, a jar of consecrated salt, symbolic of earth.

The ritual commenced with Green igniting fire. Raising the flaming bowl aloft with both hands, he invoked Babalú, the gatekeeper. "I ask the archangel Raphael for protection from all evil that approaches from the east," he intoned. As the light blue flames danced eerily, he turned to Yoko and requested that she lead him to the entrance of her dwelling. Arriving at the quaint half-glassed door of the apartment, he censed it up and down, back and forth, with the bowl, sealing it against the intrusion of evil spirits. Then he made the circuit of the entire apartment, taking care to enter every room and corridor, to open every closet and drawer, exposing all these spaces to the influence of fire.

He repeated the same ritual with each of the other elements. With air it was his practice to uncork in a westerly direction vials containing oils with magical properties. Upon an appropriately colored silk scarf, he would pour tuberose, which affords protection against the dead; heliotrope, which lets in light; and gardenia, guardian of human relationships. Then he would go about the apartment, flicking his bright cloths into one dark corner, then another, until the whole dwelling was suffused with exotic fragrances.

But no sooner had John Green assured Yoko that she was no longer afflicted by a curse than she began to insist that she could still feel the evil spell. Now she demanded to meet with John Green's master, the man about whom he had spoken with such respect. So the 250-pound Lukach came to bat for the 290-pound Green.

Another sorcerer might have seized on this opportunity to take the famous Yoko Ono away from his apprentice. Joey behaved honorably. He verified Green's findings and assured Yoko that her apartment was "clean." It was Green's impression that Yoko was still not persuaded and was actually quite annoyed with both magicians because they had failed to detect the ghost of Mrs. Robert Ryan. In fact, Yoko did find means to address the ghost. She met with Mrs. Ryan's daughter, Anita, and told her, "I spoke with your mother's spirit. She's fine."

Despite the unsatisfactory outcome of the *despojo,* Yoko came now to rely increasingly on John Green as a tarot reader. Though he was considered an outstanding reader, the reason he became indispensable to Yoko lay less in his skill in interpreting arcane symbols than in his capacity for solving pressing problems. Gifted with the kind of mind found ideally in business advisers, attorneys, and psychotherapists, Green could cut through the emotional static produced by a crisis to focus sharply and shrewdly on the essential issue and its possible solutions. Though he employed adroitly the complex symbolism of the tarot deck, what the cards offered Green was a lens through which he could scrutinize his clients. His greatest strength was simply the fact that he knew how to deal with his new client.

Green found Yoko a tense, frightened, masked, and duplicitous personality. He observed how she chewed her nails down to the quick, how she threw herself into the corner of a sofa or chair (crossing her arms and legs as if to make herself even smaller), how she spoke in whispers and always wore sunglasses. She would invent codes for everything, which would confuse Green so badly that often he didn't know what she was talking about. Even when she spoke directly, she would generally say the opposite of what she thought. Green's way of dealing with this difficult client was to adopt the impassive, impartial, impersonal mask of the Park Avenue psychoanalyst. He affected a calm, reasonable, sympathetic tone that was often far from how he felt. He was unflappable by design. Because Yoko saw that she could never shake Green, in time she came to rely upon him completely. The tarot man was a massive symbol of stability.

Green's enormous bulk and passive disposition led him to spend most of his time lying down. Propping himself up on pillows so that his feet would not hang out beyond the end of Wendy's sofa bed, he would consult with Yoko by means of a phone with a long cord that he could keep next to him at all times. When the phone would ring, no matter what the hour or the condition of Green's mind—sodden with a half gallon of Gallo wine or flying on LSD—he would roll over onto his elbow and lay out his deck of Waite-Rider tarot cards. To accommodate Yoko's barrage of anxious questions, Green adopted the simplest spread, the seven-card Solomon's seal: six cards at the points of a Star of David with a seventh in the center. He also delivered his responses with the brevity of a telegram. After each reply he would announce like a robot: "Question?" After hearing every answer, she would say: The other thing is . . ." This stock phrase became in John Green's mind the symbol of Yoko Ono. It represented her relentless compulsion to discover new perils in her path.

At the same time that John Green was insinuating himself into the pilot's chair next to the captain of spaceship *Lennon,* another curious figure was sliding into the navigator's seat on the other side of the highly insecure Yoko. This was Takashi Yoshikawa, owner of Taste of Tokyo, in those days a dim little restaurant on West 13th Street whose only distinction was a slide show of the Japanese capital. Yoko had known Yoshikawa for years because he was the leading practitioner in America of the ancient Japanese science of *katu-tugai,* or directional taboos. As every reader of the Japanese classics knows, Orientals have always believed that certain directions are propitious for siting buildings or taking journeys, whereas other directions are considered highly dangerous. Yoshikawa is the author of a system that combines geomancy with astrology and numerology. Working with maps and compasses, he asks for dates and addresses, which he translates into their Japanese equivalents, writing them down like chicken scratchings. After interpreting them according to his system, he pronounces on whether a given movement will bring good luck or bad, suggesting alternate directions for movements that are taboo. Yoshikawa boasts that he was responsible for John and Yoko's reconciliation. Certainly it was during their separation that Yoko became so dependent upon him that she could never again make a move without consulting her "directional man."

Once Yoko had established her network of psychic consultants, she began running by them every idea that came into her head. They received hundreds of calls at all hours of the day and night. Since they never consulted together and they all were flying on different beams, their counsels were hopelessly contradictory. Soon it became as difficult for Yoko Ono to make a move as it was for the Dalai Lama to leave his palace at Lhasa. Then she began to recognize that she was not making the most opportune use of her oracles.

If she could persuade everyone with whom she had to deal, starting with her husband, that the occult was real and that magic *worked,* she could control these people by manipulating the prophecies of her psychics. Instead of appearing to impose her will on someone she wanted to obey her, she could say that the behavior she was demanding was the will of the stars, the cards, the numbers, or whatever occult authority she chose to invoke. Once she achieved that illumination, Yoko was relieved of the burden imposed by all her mismatched auguries. Henceforth her clairvoyants and card readers and geomancers stopped being a hindrance to her operations and started acting as Mother's little helpers.

LIKE NORMAL

In June 1974, after John and Harry had finished their whiskey-voiced album *Pussy Cats*, May Pang returned to Lennon's side and Harry Nilsson left it, forever. This was the signal for one of those sudden reversals in behavior that constitute the basic pattern of John Lennon's life. Overnight, Lennon the alley cat transformed himself into Lennon the domestic cat.

Rejecting an offer by Yoko to rent them a flat at the Dakota, John and May found the apartment of which every New Yorker dreams, a charming little penthouse on Sutton Place at 434 East 52nd Street. John's building was the last before the street comes to a dead end overlooking the East River at River House, the poshest address on the East Side. Lennon's most famous neighbor on the block was a woman who had always fascinated him, Greta Garbo.

In furnishing this $750-a-month pad, John and May looked first to their comfort. On one side of the living room, which boasted a working fireplace and a door that let upon a terrace with a river view, they installed a king-size platform bed, with a nineteen-inch Sony Trinitron at their feet and a remote-control channel selector for John's restless hand. The spare room they prepared for Julian's visits, May having persuaded John that he should pay more attention to his son. The rest of the flat was sparsely furnished but luxuriously carpeted with the white rug from Tittenhurst, across which bounded two vivacious kittens, Major (white) and Minor (black).

May Pang encouraged John to eat, reviving his long-repressed appetite with spicy dishes from the Jade Tang Restaurant or with special treats delivered to the apartment by May's mother—whom John refused to meet, pleading a "mother problem." Soon Lennon was restored to his normal weight and recharged with the energy he had lost through years of malnutrition. Every morning he would be up by ten and enjoying a breakfast of bacon and eggs. On Sundays May would prepare him a special English breakfast, with beans on toast and blood pudding, a dish the quondam vegetarian relished. John would have all the British papers delivered and would go through them avidly, smoking his Gaulois and drinking cup after cup of coffee, as he ogled the "Screws of the World."

After breakfast Lennon would take his stand before the massive Altec speakers in the living room, intent on reviewing the previous night's work. Listening with his head bowed in deep concentration, he would whoop with delight when he heard something particularly good. Anything that didn't come off would make him turn and say: "Call the studio and see if we can straighten out this track tonight."

Perhaps the most surprising feature of John's behavior was the way he began to pick up all the threads of his past, which had been severed when he married Yoko. Not only did he resume relations with Julian, but he started corresponding for the first time in years with Mimi, even entertaining the thought of having his aunt come over and stay with him as a houseguest. Mimi besought John's help with his youngest sister, who now styled herself "Jacqui" and was living like a hippie with a man to whom she wasn't married but by whom she had had a son named John. "I was looking for a family," John told his sister Julia, a schoolteacher, one day on the phone, "and it turned out I had one all along."

John's real family was the Beatles. Hence, it is not surprising that one day he should clap his hand across the receiver and say to May: "Can you stand having Paul over tonight?" May wanted nothing more than to see John reunited with Paul, even though the McCartneys had treated her in California with unconcealed condescension. What was worse, the moment May's back was turned, Paul told John that he had spoken recently with Yoko and was sure that John's marriage could be saved—if John would humble himself before Yoko, get down before her on bended knee. John gave Paul a withering glance and told him that he didn't know what he was talking about. So shaken was Paul by this rebuke that he spilled a glass of blood-red wine on the pure white rug. "It's good for the carpet," drawled John coolly, laying a firm, restraining hand on May's shoulder as she rose instinctively to protect her home.

John also got tight again with Mick Jagger. Mick had proven himself the unrivaled winner in the rock 'n' roll survival stakes by demonstrating his remarkable ability to ride simultaneously the runaway horses of relentless work and relentless play. Though he ground out as much "product" as a Paul McCartney, Mick was always flying somewhere to party it up with the liveliest members of the jet set. Married to Bianca Pérez Morena de Macias, a former fashion model, Mick had a daughter, Jade, on whom he doted, but he never allowed his marital status to interfere with his bachelor fun. He always showed up with a pretty bird and a bottle of Beaujolais. His talk would be gossip, gossip, gossip, including the latest dirt on George Harrison, whom Ringo had caught in bed with Maureen, while Patti was living with George's best friend, Eric Clapton. *"Where have I been!"* John would cry out at each fresh—and delicious—dish.

John Lennon had always taken a condescending view of the Rolling Stones because for years the Stones had aped the Beatles. John had also been tight with Mick's hated rival Brian Jones until his mysterious swimming pool death in 1969—a death of which John believed Mick innocent. Perhaps the most revealing moment in John's relationship with Jagger had come during their joint appearance on the *Rock 'n' Roll Circus,* when a stoned John, playing a TV interviewer, had done a satiric turn with Mick as pop star, that concluded with John slipping his hand inside Mick's shirt and feeling him up. John always said that he liked the Stones' "real stuff," like "Satisfaction" and "Honky Tonk Woman," but he could not stomach their "fag stuff."

Jagger and Lennon envied each other in certain ways: Mick was impressed by John's intelligence and John by Mick's image. But there was never any trace of competitiveness in their bearing toward one another in private. They were simply fellow travelers along the Alps of superstardom, disposed now to kick back and survey the scene with the bemused eye of old veterans.

As a hip member of the Stones' organization remarked: "Mick Jagger had a deep reverence or respect for John Lennon which he did not dare display because it could be used against him." What Mick *could* do was defer to John in private, while John, for his part, picked Mick's quick brain. It was a good balance of temperaments. Also, the presence again of Mick in John's life signified that Lennon was groping his way back toward the current rock scene, an impression confirmed by John's participation at this time in studio sessions with Elton John and David Bowie, the rival stars of glitter rock.

In the year 1974 that forever changing figure, John Lennon, the Man Who Could Have Been Anything, was leading the life of a rock patriarch. Every night his flat was full of stars and fans, producers and engineers, hangers-on, and journalists—any and every sort of person who constituted rock society. Some of these men brought their women, and many brought their habits. There was much drinking of wine and snorting of the spices of life. John laughed and talked, reminisced and prognosticated, holding forth on the current state of the world and the rock scene. As the cartons of hot Chinese food were served out on the plates and the jukebox Capitol had provided boomed with the old classics or somebody previewed a hot new tape on the hi-fi, John found himself for the first and only time in his life a clubbable man. Though he complained that all this company was driving him mad, it didn't interfere a bit with his work, which was coming better now than at any time in years. In fact, it was obvious that John Lennon was *hot*. That was why all the new superstars were trying to inveigle him into appearing on their shows or cutting a track on their latest albums.

If all these notes of vitality and self-satisfaction are not sufficient proof that John Lennon, that perpetual Humpty Dumpty, was back together again, a final bit of evidence will cinch the argument: the revival of Lennon's legendary sense of humor. Howard Smith observed: "John Lennon had a self-deprecating sense of humor that Yoko tried to stifle because she thought it was not befitting a great artist." Now that Yoko was off the set, John's wicked humor came bubbling back to the surface of his mind. The last great public demonstration of his wit occurred on a Saturday afternoon in September 1974, when Lennon sat in for disc jockey Dennis Elsis at WNEW-FM.

Unlike his appearances on film or TV, where the lights, cameras, and the voyeuristic focus of the media made him uncomfortable, John's situation in a broadcasting studio—alone, invisible, surrounded by soundproof walls, and in command of a microphone—was ideal for unpacking his mind and playing his favorite word games. Not only could he spin his treasured records from the good old days, but he could discourse upon them in a manner that often blew everybody's mind because he used them to lay bare the hidden processes of plagiarism. And he wasn't shy about demonstrating how inferior the Stones had always been to the Beatles by playing back-to-back their respective versions of "I Wanna Be Your Man," a little ditty that John and Paul had dashed off for the Stones at the beginning of their career, when they were still pebbles.

When the cue came for the commercial, John went straight into the pitch: "'Tonight, at the Joint in the Woods'—guess who's there!—'it's Ladies' Night!'" Then, bethinking himself of his recent consciousness raising, he observed, "They won't like that," and changed the copy to read: "Women's Night." His women's libbing dissolved immediately, however, in his ad-libbing as he read on, playing the ad strictly for sexist laughs: "'Featuring an eight-*piece,* all-female group, Isis' or Is Is, depending where you come from. 'All females admitted at half-price.' Oh, good! Bowie can get in! . . . 'Coming next Wednesday night at the Joint in the Woods'—there's nothing like a joint in the woods!" said he, losing his green card possibilities in one blow! "*'T Rex!'*"

The weather report got the same treatment, with heavy innuendos underscoring the barometer reading: "Sixty-nine inches and *falling!*" The forecast? "Tomorrow will be sunny followed by munny, tunny, wenny." (An echo of British humorist Stanley Unwin's "In my megag medicold there are hypodermy, bandy, tablings and sally volatty!') "Tomorrow will be just the same as today, only different." And so on for two balmy hours.

When all the evidence of John Lennon's state of being during the latter half of 1974 has been assembled, it becomes clear that he was enjoying a unique period of felicity. For though he had known many spasms of joy and triumph in the course of his astonishing career as a pop star and in the early days of his relationship with Yoko Ono, the basic tenor of Lennon's life had always been punitive and unhappy. Now, with May Pang, he appeared to have found just what he had always craved: love and devotion, sexual submission and responsiveness, an indefatigable aide in his work, and, above all, a person who demanded nothing for herself but lived entirely to make John happy.

YOU CAN'T CATCH ME

Two days before Lennon started recording *Walls and Bridges,* in June 1974, Al Coury, Capitol's promotion chief in California, burst in upon John and May at the Record Plant crying, "I've got them! They're here!" After five months of hassling, the Spector tapes had been recovered.

The hard-driving promo man had been inspired to go after the tapes when John Lennon had told him: "You'll never get them back. Nobody will find Phil. Those fuckin' tapes are *gone!*" Coury anticipated that he might not even be able to reach Spector because he had heard the story going around in the business that Spector had been in a terrible car crash that had disfigured his face. (He had not heard the even more bizarre fact that Phil had sent to every man who had participated in the rock 'n' roll album a cassette of out-takes from the Lennon sessions in which John sang dirty lyrics, talked about drugs, and made a drunken fool of himself. In the sentimental "Just Because," John was supposed to deliver one of those old-fashioned "Are You Lonesome Tonight?" recitations, but instead, he went off on a startling tangent, confiding, "I wanna take all them new singers—Carol and the other one, Nipples [Carly Simon]. I wanna take them and hold them tight—all them people James Taylor had. *I wanna suck your nipples, baby!*")

Undismayed, Coury got in touch with Spector's lawyer and confidant, Marty Machete, who had claimed hitherto that there was nothing he could do with Phil. But matters had changed. Capitol had put Warner on notice that they had paid the recording costs for a solo album by John Lennon, who was under exclusive contract to EMI. Warner backed off the project immediately, but now they were demanding reimbursement from Spector. Coury promised Machete that he would receive a check for the full amount the moment he delivered the tapes. A week later, a big truck pulled into the Capitol lot. Out tumbled a mountain of twenty-four-inch master tapes. Coury copied everything overnight and rushed the stuff to the airport, where he saw it loaded into the security hold of the flight he was taking to New York.

Despite his bizarre behavior, Spector demonstrated that he was still a good businessman. He got $90,000 for the tapes plus a 3 percent royalty on every track used, as well as the right to retain two tracks for his own purposes.

For a long time John Lennon refused to listen to what he had done in the studios of L.A. Finally, one night, he jacked up his nerve and played through the nine songs that were his portion of the original eleven, listening to the best and second-best takes. Turning to May, he said: "These are awful!" Not only was he roaring drunk, but the band was not together or in tune. Nor was there any way to mend the tracks. Spector had recorded everything with all twenty-four channels open, which meant there was so much leakage from one channel to another that you couldn't cut out anything completely. Lennon had wanted that "Back to the Fifties" sound—and he'd got it.

John should have bitten the bullet and completed the rock album now because he had made a legal commitment to the music publisher Morris Levy to include three rock standards from Levy's catalog in the next Lennon album released. Since these songs wouldn't fit into the design of *Walls and Bridges,* John couldn't proceed with that album without violating his agreement. Ironically he had gotten himself into this pickle by writing one of his best songs.

Back in 1969 Timothy Leary had asked Lennon to compose a campaign song for the acid guru's race for governor of California. Leary's slogan was: "Come together, join the party." The obvious puns, sexual, convivial, and political, concealed an occult meaning derived from the *I Ching,* one of whose hexagrams is titled "Come Together." John couldn't write the song, but he liked the title so much that he employed it as the refrain of a radically different kind of song: a travesty of the whole funky, boogie, soul groove—pop music's big black sacred cow. Taking off from a favorite Chuck Berry tune, "You Can't Catch Me," whose melody Lennon abstracted to a Johnny-One-Note riff, he welded a fly whisk of vocal hiss to a hypnotic jungle beat over which he chanted the lyrics down a speaking tube. As the listener gradually worked out the meaning, which emerged through constant replays like invisible writing held over a candle flame, what stood forth was a caricature of some great old black cat, like Chuck Berry, with Afro eyeballs, knee-length hair, and a mouth full of portentous but nonsensical black bullshit—a character out of R. Crumb.

"Come Together" was the coolest, hippest song of the decade, but the undeniable similarities in words and melody between Lennon's new song and Berry's old standard could be construed as infringements on the rights of the copyright holder—Morris Levy. When Levy had challenged Lennon with a lawsuit in October 1973, Harold Seider prepared to fight the action, but Yoko had told Seider to settle out of court because she didn't want Lennon coming back to New York. The deal that was eventually hammered out stipulated that in his next album Lennon would include three songs owned by Levy publishing company, Big Seven, including "You Can't Catch Me," and that Lennon would induce Apple to license three Beatles' songs to Big Seven. When *Walls and Bridges* appeared on 16 September 1974 without the stipulated songs, the irate publisher demanded a sit-down with the man who had dared to cross him. At that moment John Lennon met the third evil fairy.

It was highly appropriate that John Lennon should conclude his rock 'n regression by falling into the tentacles of the man *Variety* described once as the "octopus of the music industry" because this tough old operator represented the harsh reality behind the jolly myth of the Rockin' Fifties. Levy was actually one of the first men who made rock 'n' roll a lucrative business.

After starting in the jazz nightclub business, as the owner of the Royal Roost (with its pimp hangout, the Cock Lounge) and, later, one of the operators of Birdland, Levy had gotten in on the ground floor of rock 'n' roll through his partnership with the famous Alan Freed. As soon as the Cleveland DJ arrived in the Apple in 1954, he was teamed up with Levy by Bob Leader, boss of WINS, who wanted a tough, experienced man like Morris to handle the "promotions"—the now-legendary shows at the St. Nicholas Arena and the Paramount Theater that established rock show biz. When Levy reminisces about his crazy partner, always juiced and into kinky stuff like dressing up as a woman, he likes to pull Freed's original contract from his desk. Freed was hired by the station for a mere $15,000 a year, but he was scamming for heavy bread from the minute he hit town. The first warning Levy got that his new partner was crooked came in a call from Leader. "Moish," sighed the station boss, "we got a problem. This guy Freed has been in town for three days, and already he's given away 150 percent of himself!" There was the real Alan Freed.

A sinister Pied Piper, the "Father of Rock 'n' Roll" was the rat as catcher. He grabbed the kids and led them to the great rock candy mountain. He named their music, coined its us-against-them rhetoric, created rock show biz, including the package tour, and beamed his enormously popular radio show—on which he played records while thumping out the beat with his fist on a phone book—from a little pie-shaped building on the north side of Columbus Circle clear around the world and even into towns like Liverpool, via Radio Luxembourg. Yet,

THE LIVES OF JOHN LENNON

though he became one of pop culture's most sentimentalized heroes
and martyrs (viz. *American Hot Wax*), Alan Freed is really one of the
principal exhibits in the Rock 'n' Roll Hall of Ill Fame. Jerry Wexler,
the veteran producer, expressed perfectly how people in the industry
felt about Freed when he called him the "biggest livid prick in the
world!"

Perhaps Jerry was thinking of the time his company, Atlantic Records, installed a swimming pool at Freed's Westport home. No sooner
was the job done than the top jock stopped plugging the label's product. When Levy called to find out what was wrong, Freed declared: "I
had to prove that they didn't own me!" That was typical of Freed, who
was not only a crook but a self-righteous hypocrite. Even Morris Levy
had to concede that the "Father of Rock 'n' Roll" was not a nice man.
Speaking as one Jew to another Jew about a third Jew, Levy said simply: "He could have been another Hitler."

The Freed partnership led Levy to establish Roulette Records, in
which Freed held a 25 percent conflict of interest. Three months after
the company was launched, the mob walked into Levy's office and announced, "We're your partner."

"How come?" barked Levy.

"Alan Freed sold us his piece" was the chilling reply.

Levy had to duck 'n' dodge to slip out of that noose. On the other
hand, Freed turned Levy on to some easy scores.

Take the time Freed was enjoined from calling his show *Moon Dog
Rock 'n' Roll House Party*. (The suit was lodged by Louis Hardin, the
original Moon Dog, a blind street musician, who stood on the corner of
Fifth Avenue and 42nd Street swathed in a khaki blanket, holding a
Wotan spear and wearing a horned Viking helmet.) When the DJ renamed his show *Alan Freed's Rock 'n' Roll Party*, Levy decided to tear a
leaf out of the Moon Dog decision and copyright this new label, "rock
'n' roll," which Freed had pasted on the music back in 1951, when it
was known exclusively as rhythm and blues. Henceforth anybody who
wanted to make commercial use of the most frequently employed
phrase in the vocabulary of popular music had to pay a licensing fee to
Morris Levy. Eventually a court broke Morris's lock on the rock, decreeing that the term had passed into the public domain. But Morris
found lots of other ways to make a buck off the Big Beat.

So it was Welcome to History Night on 8 October 1974, when John
Lennon, the Man Who Loved Rock 'n' Roll, came walking into the Club
Cavallero, on 58th Street between Fifth and Madison, a private bar and
dining room owned by Morris Levy and much frequented by wise guys.
Indeed, it was as if John Lennon were destined to experience now as a
middle-aged superstar just what he might have gone through if he had
been a talented young punk in the days of Frankie Lymon, another of

Morris Levy's properties. Met by the maître d', the Lennon party—John, May, and Harold Seider—were seated at a horseshoe banquette. Up came Phil Kahl, an old-time song plugger, now vice-president of Big Seven Music. Kahl sat down on one of the two outside chairs at the table. Shortly afterward the other chair was filled by the muscular form of Morris Levy.

John Lennon, who harbored all the familiar stereotypes of Jews, probably expected some gray-haired old Hebe with a cigar hanging from his purple lips. Instead, he encountered a hardy-looking man, still in his forties, with the build of an ex-boxer. No sooner were the introductions completed than Levy leaned over to Lennon and growled: "What happened?"

This was Lennon's cue to go into his act. By now he had told the story of his mishaps with Spector so many times that the yarn had assumed the proportions of a comic epic. Lennon also knew that he had to make this one of his better performances. So for nearly an hour he recited the Tale of Phil the Terrible. As the story advanced from the dissolute sprawl of the studio to the gun exploding in the hall to the weird rumors of Spector in casts after laying down his bike on a remote Arizona highway, Levy nodded with sour-mouthed acquiescence, like a man who has heard it all before. Then, when all the stories had been told and all the chuckles chuckled, the mood went right back to where it had been when Lennon walked in.

"That's spilt milk," rasped Levy. "Now, where do we go from here?"

Harold Seider replied jocularly: "Would two hundred thousand dollars heal this breach?"

Levy didn't crack a smile. Instead, he turned to Kahl and said: "Tell him why two hundred thousand *wouldn't* help."

Kahl then went into a long rap about how many thousands of dollars of sheet music and copyright fees and moneys from this and that source the world around would have poured into the coffers of Big Seven if John Lennon had fulfilled his commitment by recording three Levy-owned songs from the 1950s. It wasn't the kind of demonstration that would have impressed anybody from the Harvard School of Business but the point was made: Levy wasn't going to let Lennon off the hook cheaply.

Now the question arose: What could be done with the tapes that had been recovered? Lennon explained that the tapes were not in a state in which they could be released. There were a lot of technical problems. Really, only three tracks could be released immediately—a long way from an album! Lennon had considered putting these three on an EP (a seven-inch LP), but everybody had warned him that this format, popular in economy-minded Britain, would not fly in America. So the basic question was how to resolve the project.

Lennon confessed that he was ashamed to have wasted $90,000 on an undertaking that had come to grief, but investing more effort and money was not appealing because they had missed the ideal moment. Rock 'n' roll nostalgia had peaked the previous year with *American Graffiti*. By bringing out an album of oldies now, they would be launching it on a receding instead of a rising wave. What's more, after all the noise the sessions had made in the industry, every reviewer in the game would pounce on the album and, if it didn't come up to snuff, would give it a terrible lambasting. The whole thing was a shame, Lennon sighed, because the idea had been good and he had even come up with some terrific packaging and marketing ideas. There had been a Seven-Up commercial on TV that had featured an old-time greaser in a leather jacket, who came on and said: "Hi! Remember me?" Lennon wanted to put on his leather jacket, grease back his hair the way he'd worn it as a Teddy Boy, and do that bit. He would stare straight into the camera and say: "You should have been there!"

"We could do a terrific job on that, John," suddenly exclaimed Morris Levy, adding: "Have you ever heard of Adam VIII?" May Pang recognized the name; it was one of those companies that advertise "20 All-Time Hits by Chubby Checker for $4.98" on TV. It was also one of Morris Levy's ten or fifteen current businesses.

Now it was the old pro's turn to do the talking, giving the famous rock star a little lesson in the mail-order record business. How you "run the country," doing intense sales blitzes first in one region, then another, buying your time and then monitoring the cost according to your CPO (cost per order), even going after the people who won't write in by cutting a deal with K Mart or Sears, Roebuck to act as "retail fulfillment centers," where the viewers can go to pick up the albums in special racks. Oh, Levy had done very well with his packages, like the Chubby Checker package, which had raised Chubby's club date price from $300 to $3,000 per week!

What Levy didn't tell Lennon at first was that just two years before, he had done a lot of work on a two-pocket Beatles' package with Allen Klein that was designed to knock out the bootleggers who were pitching albums on local TV programs all around the country. Though that deal had not panned out, it had brought to light an interesting fact: The Beatles had an exception in their contract with Capitol that allowed Apple to put out mail-order packages without receiving permission from the record company. So if Lennon went for Levy's pitch about TV merchandising, there was a legitimate way to market the product.

As the discussion developed, Lennon got more interested in the idea. John was, after all, a TV addict. Nobody appreciated more than he the magic of the medium. Now he recognized that if he were to offer his oldies album exclusively on TV, he would solve a lot of his problems. By going outside the normal release channels, he would by-pass the critics and lay the goods right in the record buyers' hands. Also, he would score an industry first because never before had any major artist offered new instead of repackaged merchandise in this market. Best of all, he would screw EMI, which he felt had always screwed him. The more Lennon thought about the idea, the more exciting it appeared.

Once Levy saw that he had John hooked, hauling him in was easy. Taking out a ballpoint pen and reaching for a paper napkin, Levy began to conjure up enticing figures. By adding to the mail-order sales the merchandise they would move in retail fulfillment centers, by coupling with the album sales the sales of the even more expensive eight-track cassettes, and then by taking the final breathtaking leap from the American market to the *world market,* Levy came up with a grand total of between four and six million units worth approximately *$25 million!*

Lennon was riveted. The only question in his mind was: Is it legal? Turning to Harold Seider, he asked: "Can we do this?" Seider knew Lennon's contracts practically by heart. He had gone over them clause by clause with Allen Klein when they were being drawn up. He warned Lennon that he was under contract to EMI until January 1976. About the American rights, he could not be sure; about the world rights, there was no question they were reserved to EMI. They would have to get a release.

"Who would you talk to at EMI?" asked Levy, eager to personalize his problem.

"I would go to Len Wood," replied Seider, referring to the group head of EMI Records.

Levy smiled and cracked: "When are you leaving for England, Harold?"

Meantime, there was plenty of work they could do right here and now. Lennon could go back in the studio and record the nine songs that would be needed to round out the package. Levy explained that the idea in mail order was to give the customers a helluva bargain: twenty tunes for less money than you would normally pay for ten. Lennon shot back that twenty was out of the question. He made it a fixed rule never to put more than twenty minutes of music on a side because if you put more, you had to reduce the size of the grooves and diminish the amplitude (i.e., volume) of the recording. On the other hand, by shortening the songs and doing a couple of medleys, he could squeeze in fifteen or sixteen songs. As for the price, the royalties, who would pay for what—those were business matters in which John Lennon took no interest. So at this point the meeting split into two parts. Levy and Seider put their heads together over the numbers, while

John, May, and Phil Kahl started compiling lists of songs to be considered for inclusion in the album. Kahl offered himself as facilitator. He would obtain copies of the original 45s, the lead sheets for the musicians, and would contact the publishers for rates and permissions. When Levy heard the word "rates," he barked, "Get 'em cheap!"

When John Lennon left the Club Cavallero that night, he was riding high. Suddenly everything was looking good again. They were going to take a lemon and squeeze it into Lennonade. After a year of hassling, John was about to put out his rock 'n' roll album. By the following Monday night, when John and May turned up again at the Club Cavallero, a great deal of work had been done. John was able to tell Morris Levy that everything was in high gear: Several key musicians were about to fly in from the Coast, the rest of the band had been engaged in New York, the time had been booked at the studio, and progress had been made in obtaining the records and lead sheets. Now the next step was to gather all the musicians together and rehearse them carefully so that when they started to cut, they could go from song to song without wasting time. The only problem was how to keep everybody on the strict schedule John projected. Musicians were like kids; if you didn't keep an eye on them, they could wander off and stall the whole process.

Levy had a solution. Why not bring the musicians up to his farm? They could spend a few days there, rehearsing without distraction. Then they could come back to the city and go straight into the studio. John was not taken by the idea. He explained that there would be problems of transportation because the players were arriving from the Coast at different hours. Levy said he would provide the transportation. John said they would need their amps and drums and other gear. Levy said he would provide a van. John said they would want to record their playing, to get an idea how it sounded. Levy offered to provide the necessary recording gear. So it was decided that on the following weekend everybody would roll up to Ghent, New York, and spend a weekend working in the country.

Dairy farming turned out to be yet another of Morris Levy's multifarious businesses. Arriving at his remodeled and luxurious farmhouse, where the taps on the bathroom sinks were spouting fishes, John and May found everything in readiness. Phil Kahl had positioned the piano correctly, set up the music stands as they would be in a recording studio, and even laid out on each player's stand every lead sheet in alphabetical order.

The weekend went smoothly. They would have a huge breakfast at nine, rehearse till lunch, take a walk in the woods, and rehearse again after supper. When the hour got late, they would play backgammon or shoot craps on the coffee table. John lost $1,500 without even touching

the dice—Morris was showing him the game. The only untoward incident occurred one afternoon during a break. Jesse Ed pulled three
rifles out of the gun rack and, helping himself to some ammo, told the
others: "Let's do a little target shooting." Walking out past the pond in
back of the house, they took their stand on the firing range. When it
came John's turn to shoot, he emptied the entire magazine without so
much as hitting the target. Pissed off by his characteristic ineptness, he
was walking back to the house with the boys when they heard a gurgling sound. Turning around, they saw Morris Levy's rowboat sinking
into the pond!

On Monday the band went into the studio and started cranking out
songs like clockwork. By the end of the week all the recording had
been completed. A week of editing and mixing followed. As always,
Lennon drove everyone hard to finish the task. Then came the great
moment. On the night of 1 November 1974 John and May appeared
once again at the Club Cavallero.

"I've finished with it," John told Morris Levy. "It's grrreat! I don't
want to see it again." Levy asked if he could have a copy. John said that
one was on the way. Soon a messenger arrived from the Record Plant
with two reels of 7½ RPM tape. It was the album in its entirety. The
only thing lacking was a title. John's mind was running on titles like *Old
Hat* or *Gold Hat,* but he wanted to think further. In any case, in less
than three weeks Lennon had done the whole job, thanks to the powerful push he got from Morris Levy.

The natural thing now would be to rush the album into production
for Christmas release. This is what Levy wanted, as he declared when
he met with Harold Seider and Michael Graham, an attorney from
Marshal, Bratter, Greene, Allison & Tucker, the New York law firm
that was representing Lennon in the dissolution of the Beatles' partnership. "What kind of a deal are you proposing?" asked Harold
Seider.

For the first time Levy did a complete breakdown of costs. The figures demonstrated that somebody would have to make a big concession, for to put a $4.98 album on the aisle racks of K Mart or
Woolworth or a big supermarket chain, the store would have to get
$1.50. When $1.25 for the TV advertising was added and then the
standard production costs—40 cents to manufacture the record, 15
cents to make the jacket, 3 percent freight charge to move the merchandise to the stores plus the 2-cent-a-cut royalty to the publisher and
the ½ percent to the American Federation of Musicians—were thrown
in, along with Levy's profit—$1.00 an album—what would be left for
John Lennon and Capitol (which had invested $90,000 in the project)
was 23 cents an album. John's normal royalty would have been 60

cents, to say nothing of what the record company ordinarily received. One look at the figures made the whole deal appear unworkable.

At this point it would have made sense to pack it in, but the best Seider could manage without any mandate from Lennon was a delay. He told Levy that this was not a good time to go after EMI because the Beatles were about to sign their settlement agreement, which had been in the works for years, and nothing should be done that might rock the boat. Levy accepted Seider's excuse, but he continued to act on the assumption that he had a deal, though nobody had said a word about this deal to the other interested party, Capitol.

This failure of communication between Levy and Capitol mirrored the lack of communication between Lennon and Levy that had led to the blowup after the release of *Walls and Bridges*. In both cases, the man who might have been expected to take action was Harold Seider. If he had gotten in touch with Levy before *Walls and Bridges* was released and told him the story of the rock 'n' roll album, he would have shielded his client from the charge of having acted in bad faith. Now with Levy and Capitol running on a similar collision course, Seider appeared to be standing back and allowing another, even more serious incident, to occur. Why?

Harold Seider's behavior has to be understood in terms of the role in which he had cast himself in his dealings with John Lennon, as an adviser who looked to his client to make all the final decisions. This sounds like a reasonable approach, but it was very ill-suited to John Lennon. John had always looked to his manager to tell him what to do in business matters. Asking Lennon to make his own decisions on such issues was asking too much. What made matters worse was Lennon's habit of ducking any issue that he didn't want to confront and his tendency to reverse himself. "If I sign something and later I don't like it," Lennon had warned Seider, "I'll say I was crazy. I'll disavow it." So advising Lennon was no way to solve his problems. You could *manage* him, as Brian Epstein, Allen Klein, and Yoko Ono had done, each in his own way, but you couldn't get anywhere with an approach like Seider's because, as he himself finally conceded, "John wanted to be dominated."

As Christmas 1974 approached, so did the long-awaited dissolution of the Beatles' partnership. The 202-page settlement agreement, product of eighteen months' work by a score of attorneys, embodied carefully considered solutions to all the Beatles' financial and legal problems. The primary problem was how to reconcile the conflicts in interest among the partners. Paul, for example, wanted to be indemnified against any claim Klein might make against the Beatles because Paul had not wanted Klein in the first place and had never signed the management agreement. Ringo's concern arose from the fact that he was the only member of the group who had not developed into a successful songwriter or solo recording star. George had dipped into the Apple till for £320,000 to buy Friar Park, a bizarre Victorian gothic folly, in which he had installed a state-of-the-art recording studio; he didn't want to pay the 90 percent tax on this asset. Lennon, who had taken far more money out of Apple than any of the other partners, had lavished millions on his movies and art projects, as well as pouring $300,000 to $400,000 into Tittenhurst. If he were made to pay taxes on all these expenditures, he would be ruined. On the other hand, it wasn't fair to expect Apple to swallow the expenditures of John, George, and Ringo when Paul had not charged off to the company his projects. So one of the primary purposes of the agreement was achieving *parity* among the partners, both retroactively and prospectively.

In a complex pattern of trade-offs, Paul was given £300,000 in cash, and the Eastmans £170,000 for their work on the Apple-Maclen litigation. George's publishing company, Harrisongs, was granted a loan of £250,000, secured against Friar Park, to defray most of his debt to the company. Ringo was allotted Tittenhurst, and John was obliged to give Apple 50 percent of his films plus some of his independently produced songs, like "Instant Karma," as well as other assets. But he was compensated by being given a controlling veto over the commercial exploitation of his work.

The most important results of the agreement were (1) the release of the Beatles' frozen royalties and (2) the right obtained by each Beatle to receive directly any money he earned from his individual efforts after October 1974. Lennon's share of the impounded funds was about £1.5 million, and he got another £1.5 million (which he could not take out of the U.K.) by selling his ATV stock. Since the pound fluctuated at this time between $2.25 and $2.50, John Lennon's entire fortune after his years with the Beatles could not have exceeded $7.5 million. Thousands of Americans had that kind of money.

The greatest shortcoming of the agreement was its failure to provide for the dissolution of Apple, through which the earnings of the Beatles as a group would continue to flow. When the settlement was signed, however, it was presumed that the dissolution of Apple would soon follow. In fact, the company remains in existence to this day performing basically the same function: the ultimate demonstration of the Beatles' subsequent failure to "come together."

The date for signing the agreement was pegged to George Harrison's concert at Madison Square Garden on 19 December 1974. The signing was envisioned as a festive occasion; a huge suite was booked at the Plaza, with a bar and a buffet. A long table was covered with green baize, and the documents were laid out in the order of signing. By midnight, the appointed hour for the ceremony, the suite was full of men in business suits, talking, eating, drinking, and exuding a great sense of relief. Paul and Linda had brought portable TV gear to record the event for posterity. Only Ringo was absent because he was ducking a subpoena issued by Allen Klein, but he was at the other end of an open line to England, participating by long distance.

As the clock advanced toward 2:00 A.M., Harold Seider began to get uneasy. John was chronically late, so no one had commented on his absence at first, but now he was holding up history. Stepping into a side room, Seider picked up a phone and dialed Sutton Place. When John answered, Seider demanded: "Where are you?"

"I was sleeping," replied Lennon.

"You're supposed to be here to sign the settlement agreement," snapped the astonished lawyer.

"I'm not signing it," responded John.

"Why not?" Seider gasped.

"The stars aren't right," answered John, and hung up.

Seider, who by now knew Lennon too well to be floored by anything he did, turned to the assembled party and announced: "John said he isn't going to sign because the stars aren't right."

Instantly George ran up to Seider and thrust his face into Seider's face, jabbing his finger aggressively as he barked: "*You're* the astrologer, Harold! You just want to renegotiate!"

That was the opinion of everyone but Paul, who turned on John's lawyers and gave them a good tongue-lashing. "Lennon isn't the leader of this band anymore!" snarled Paul. "He's acting like a child!"

As the words came pouring out, Michael Graham recalled: "We didn't say *one* word to Paul because he was 100 percent right!"

The man who was most furious that night was George Harrison, who had just had a rough time at the Garden, where the fans had expressed their displeasure at having to suffer through a long session with Ravi Shankar, only to have a dose of religious medicine thrust down their throats by the Maharrison. George was also burning from an encounter with John a few days earlier, when he had demanded of Lennon: "Where were you when I needed you?" He was alluding to Bangla Desh and all the other times in the past four years when John had copped out on his old mate. "I did *everything* you said," George spat out bitterly, "but you weren't there!"

It was a just rebuke, but what George failed to recognize was that as a totally self-absorbed man, John Lennon expected everybody to do things for him but acknowledged no obligation to reciprocate. Instead of reaching out to George and seeking to appease him, the best John could manage was to say: "You always knew how to reach me."

At that moment George had thrust his head in close to Lennon's face and hissed: "I want to see your eyes. I can't see your eyes." John obligingly removed his sunglasses, replacing them with a pair of clear glasses. "I *still* can't see your eyes!" screamed George, tearing Lennon's glasses off his face and hurling them to the floor. Normally such an act would have made John leap at his attacker like a wild animal. Miraculously he stood there, frozen.

Now on the night of the signing, when George saw that John had copped out on him again, he snatched up a phone and called Lennon. Getting May Pang, he barked: "Just tell him I started this tour on my own and I'll end it on my own!" (He was alluding to a belated offer by John to lend his support to George onstage.) With that, the timid Beatle slammed down the phone. The next night John and George were reconciled socially, but their personal relationship was at an end.

What made John Lennon balk at the last moment? May Pang reported that from the moment the settlement was explained to John, he began to betray his reluctance to sign the pact. "From hints he had dropped since we had been together," she explained, "I had learned that John's departure from the Beatles had essentially been Yoko's idea. Without Yoko to drive him forward, he felt strangely ambivalent about officially ending the Beatles at that moment. By nature, also, he felt inclined to take a position opposite from that of Paul McCartney. Paul desperately wanted that agreement signed. Whether or not it was the best thing for him to do, John, on principle, was inclined not to want to sign it."

When the call came on the afternoon of the signing day, indicating the time and place, John locked himself in the bedroom and refused to come out.

"John, what's the matter?" cried May.

"I'm not goin' to sign the agreement," he said from behind the door.

"What?" she demanded, astonished.

"It's not fair. I've got to pay more taxes than the others. I'm being taxed twice as much."

May, beside herself, called Yoko, who sent John a message by hand containing a warning by her astrologer not to sign.

What was really troubling Lennon is best explained by Harold Seider: "John knew he had gone to the Apple well and dipped in the most, [but] he didn't want to pay any money back [and] he wanted to minimize his taxes. He had dipped into American Apple for approximately a million bucks. There were recording costs, primarily Yoko's, for $180,000; film production costs of about $55,000; custody expenses; the immigration case for another $55,000; the Syracuse museum fiasco for $70,000; various promotion expenses. He bought assets—furnishing his apartment, TVs, guitars—for another $100,000. There were personal things. He had borrowed money from Apple, et cetera. If Apple had said to him, 'Look, John, all the money you dipped is yours, personally,' he would have had to pay taxes on the million. In those days the tax went up to 72 percent. . . . We worked out an arrangement whereby Apple absorbed all but $150,000 minimum to $250,000 [which was offset by a loan of the dollar equivalent of £100,000 from Apple California]. We informed John that no matter what Apple did, there was no way to guarantee that the American government would accept the attribution of these expenses to a Beatles company. He had a potential exposure of a million dollars. . . . Actually, he paid only the minimum."

After a brief holiday in Florida, John signed the papers in New York on 29 December. On 31 December 1974 the High Court of Justice issued an order dissolving the Beatles and Company and dismissing the 1970 action brought by Paul McCartney. Officially that date marks the end of the Beatles.

After the first of the year the issue of the rock 'n' roll album came to a head. Lennon's attorneys sent Morris Levy a letter saying that they were prepared to license the Apple songs stipulated in the agreement of the previous year. Levy fired back a letter saying that this agreement had been superseded by a new deal that gave him world rights to the oldies album. Meantime, Capitol decided to put this same album into regular release.

At a crucial meeting with Lennon, production chief Al Coury explained the facts of life to the star. He warned that Lennon's TV marketing strategy would create serious problems with the rack jobbers and the one-stop operators, as well as with the retail outlets, all of which would feel defrauded. John's own image would suffer from being hawked like cornflakes. Ultimately he might run into serious legal trouble. John was not persuaded by any of these arguments, but he caved in. As he told Judge Thomas P. Griesa the following year, "They [Capitol] talked me out of it. I am still intrigued by the idea. I am not convinced." Yet he had made the sort of decision that should rest on strong conviction.

When Morris Levy discovered that John Lennon had double-crossed him *again,* he was enraged. This time there could be no excuse, no cop-out. Lennon had simply reversed himself without warning and without even having the decency to pick up the phone and explain what had happened. Levy had two alternatives: Either drop the project or go full steam ahead and damn the torpedoes!

On 30 January 1975 Harold Seider arrived at Morris Levy's office, having called the day before to announce that Capitol was releasing the rock 'n' roll album. Seider found Levy talking on the phone. According to Seider's subsequent court testimony:

Mr. Levy got off the phone. . . . He looked at me and he smiled and he said, "I'm coming out with the album. I've been had! You don't need the consent of EMI. The Beatles have fulfilled all their recording obligations."

I told Morris that he was crazy, that it was sheer folly on his part and that I had not lied to him about the necessity to obtain the consent of EMI.

Morris said, amid the profanity, that I was lying. That he had a copy of the contract. He got up from his desk and picked up a sheaf of papers and waved them at me. He says, "I got a copy of the contract!"

I said, "Where did you get that from? Allen Klein?"

He said, no. He got it from the ECM tape case [a record piracy case involving the Beatles].

I said, "You've bought Allen Klein's bullshit!"

He said that his lawyers had read it and that John Lennon was the President of Apple and he didn't need the consent of anyone to make the deal.

He turned around and pressed a tape recorder. [It] played, "You Can't Catch Me." It sounded like John Lennon's voice.

This scene was equivalent to a declaration of war. Immediately both sides in the dispute went into action. Levy drove his people hard, and within ten days of his confrontation with Seider, on 8 February, TV stations in the New York area began pitching a new John Lennon album titled *Roots*. It was a typical mail-order package, with an old picture of Lennon on the jacket and on the back a lot of ads for other albums by Adam VIII. Lennon caught the commercial on the tube, but it wasn't anything like what he had planned to do. After all the time and thought, the money and suffering that had been lavished on this pet project, this was to be its sorry fate!

Capitol demanded that Harold Seider file an injunction to stop Levy from distributing the album. Seider, recognizing how small were the chances of success, demanded that Capitol fight back in the marketplace. Capitol responded by moving up its release date from March to February and using its muscle in the industry to shut down Levy's operation.

A flock of telegrams were sent out to Levy's pressing plants, album manufacturers, advertising agencies, and television stations. The telegrams warned that if these companies did anything to further the production or promotion of this unauthorized album, they risked being sued by Capitol. The threat was highly effective. Overnight Levy's whole operation collapsed. He sold about 1,500 albums and a handful of eight-track cassettes. The "octopus of the music industry" proved easy to catch.

Rock 'n' Roll (the long-sought title was found when an art director lettered the words across the mock-up of the jacket just to round out the design) was released by Capitol on 23 February. It was priced at $5.98, $1 below standard, and offered in the E. J. Korvette stores for only $3.29. Eventually the album sold about 350,000 copies, a disappointing figure not much different from the total for *Mind Games* and *Some Time in New York*. Clearly there were 350,000 people in the United States who would buy any album that bore John Lennon's name.

It took two trials—the first, in 1975, ending in a mistrial, and the second not beginning till January 1976—to straighten out the mess that John Lennon had made of his rock 'n' roll album. Both Lennon and Levy were found guilty of infractions, the former incurring relatively small damages, the latter a whopping penalty of $400,000.

To this day Levy can't get over Lennon's sudden about-face: "I didn't realize he was weak. I didn't make that at all. He appeared strong when he was with May Pang. He could make her jump through a needle."

If Levy is still filled with resentment at Lennon's vacillating character, Harold Seider is only somewhat less chagrined by this embarrassing imbroglio. His final judgment? "I think it would have been better to bring out the album as a TV package."

A CHANGE OF HEART

Shortly after John and May had moved to Sutton Place, Yoko had embarked on a tour of Japan. According to Harold Seider, who was involved in planning the expedition, "She did the tour to get Spinozza. She thought she could get Spinozza alone." Apparently, her idea was to have David find himself living in a world in which he could not ask for a cup of coffee without turning to Yoko.

What was clear to Yoko, however, was just as clear to David. Though he must have liked earning leader price and taking a producer's percentage of Yoko's records (eventually he exchanged his 1.5 percent of retail for cash), he must have recognized that the time had come to cut and run. After giving assurances to everyone he recruited that he would go on the tour, at the last moment he copped out. By that time Yoko was so deeply committed that she could not withdraw. She was obliged to go to Japan, even though her thoughts were fastened firmly on David in New York, whom she sought frantically to reach by phone.

Yoko's first performance that August was at a hippie peace festival in a little town called Koriyama. It had taken years for the hippie movement to spread to Nippon, and even now the vast majority of the local populace loathed the idea of the festival, comparing the 40,000 kids who descended on the town with a cloud of rice-eating locusts. Because there was no place to bed all these visitors, they flopped at the railroad station. One of the clerks reported in the national press: "They pissed everywhere in Koriyama. The dirtiness of the public toilets was disgusting. Excrement was piled as high as a mountain. There was big trouble in cleaning it up. And the shit from these hippies! Well, I don't know what they're eating, but it was as thick as those ropes they use to have mass tug-of-wars."

When Yoko stepped off the train, her eyes widened with fear because her appearance was a signal for hundreds of fans, reporters, and cameramen to rush her. At the critical moment a squad of special riot police intervened and threatened anyone who came closer with a beating. The press was outraged both by the condition of the town and by the savagery of the police. The festival, whose motto was "Let's unite in love and peace," was off to an angry and violent start.

That night the show began two hours late. The ghostly finger of a waggling searchlight probed the sky. Rock music at earsplitting volume blared from twenty onstage speakers. When Yoko finally appeared, she was so disoriented that her first words were "Good afternoon."

Reporters outdid themselves in their efforts to characterize Yoko's performance. "She screams 'Don't Worry, Kyoko,'" wrote one journalist, "and moves about, disheveling her very gray hair and revealing her aging body." Among the images employed to describe her singing were "a drunk throwing up in the gutter" and "the stomach pumping of a suicide attempt." At one point the show was interrupted when a young man jumped out of the crowd naked and screamed in the comical accent of Osaka: "I can't stand it! I want to 'uck Yoko Chan!"

Not only did the press savage Yoko's performances, but they targeted on her exorbitant demands for interview fees. "Yoko has her own strict fee system," wrote one reporter. "It's the Hundred Thousand Yen System—every request is met by a demand for a hundred thousand more than the previous interviewer paid." His conclusion was: "Though in everything else she ignores the established rules of society, being aggressive about 'doing her own thing,' when it comes to money, she appears to have been strongly influenced by Zenjiro Yasuda [i.e., Yoko's billionaire grandfather]."

Midway through the tour Frank Andrews, Yoko's psychic, turned up. He was circling the globe, doubtless at Yoko's behest (and at Lennon's expense) because such a journey was Yoshikawa's ultimate prescription for enhancing anyone's powers—especially someone Yoko was encharging with important duties. Andrews found Yoko transformed by the excitement of being a star. She appeared surer of herself and clearer about her intentions. According to Andrews, her primary intention was to divorce John Lennon as soon as she returned to the United States.

Yoko's new confidence and determination were also apparent in the remarkable series of interviews she gave Masako Togawa, a well-known public personality in Japan, who has been at various times the mistress of a geisha house, a pop singer, and the author of some widely read pornographic novels. Ms. Togawa was, like Yoko, a liberated woman who stood outside the pale of conventional Japanese society. Speaking as one sister to another, she took a very bold and direct line in her interrogations.

Commencing with the issue of women's lib, whose lesbian wing had acclaimed Yoko, Togawa asked whether Yoko had ever had sexual relations with a woman. Yoko replied that she had not, but she had been propositioned by a women's lib lesbian. Turning next to Yoko's new obsession with magic, the interviewer asked: "How do you feel when you are called 'Yoko, the witch'?"

Yoko replied: "It sounds nice. It's a powerful word, isn't it?" One of the most revealing exchanges occurred on the subject of Kyoko. "My feeling towards Kyoko has undergone a tremendous change," Yoko confessed. "If I were to see her now, I would be scared and nervous. It's somewhat similar to seeing the men you used to know. . . . In the past I thought of her as part of myself, but not having seen her for years, I feel otherwise. Once you overcome the congenial feelings towards children, you come to reject them. . . . After all, Kyoko was not that important to me. I still feel an attachment to her but only from the pains of delivering her."

This is the kind of startlingly iconoclastic statement that one expects from John Lennon, not Yoko Ono. Indeed, the whole interview appears to be inspired by John's legendary frankness, which Yoko had suddenly come to embody now that she was back in her hometown.

When Togawa asked how Yoko reconciled marriage and ego, Yoko's reply was couched in the form of a typical progression of events. She explained that she was highly susceptible to love but not in the physical sense; that when she felt love, she was self-sacrificing. What's more, she was eager to perform all the traditional female duties: cooking, washing, cleaning. She was very jealous by nature, though she did not exhibit her jealousy but kept it inside and brooded upon it. But in each of her three marriages she had been the one to initiate the break. In fact, looking back upon them all, she could discern a clear pattern: "I would get bored. . . . After about four years, my burning feeling disappears, although the next year, I continue to think about it. One year is a long time—and then comes the separation."

This remark led inevitably to the issue of greatest interest to the journalist: "The reason you are living separately now is for your work alone?"

YOKO: That is just the ostensible reason. I think my feelings towards him have changed.

TOGAWA: What do you mean by that?

YOKO: Man and woman have a period in their relationship of feeling extremely close together, [a time] when they want to know each other more. I think we are past that period.

TOGAWA: So your relationship now is based on something like inertia?

YOKO: Inertia doesn't give me the feeling that I am alive.

TOGAWA: Then Lennon also regards the separation as you think of it?

YOKO: He might have some reservations about accepting my
view, but when a thing is over, it's over!

By the time Yoko got back to the States in September, her determination to end her marriage had begun to weaken. "The Japan tour broke
her bubble," remarked Harold Seider. "Once Yoko realized that John
was beginning to stand on his own and she was becoming a nobody, she
knew her only salvation would be getting back with John. . . . She knew
that on a divorce all she would get would be money and she would be
off the scene." So Yoko resumed her mind games with John, but she
was shocked to discover that instead of winning almost every hand, she
began to lose. According to May, she would call John at the studio, and
he wouldn't take her call. When she did get through and started threatening divorce, instead of breaking down and begging her to recon-
sider, he barked: "Hurry up and get it over with!" Finally, John
publicly insulted Yoko, inflicting on her a painful loss of face.

On the night of 14 November 1974, John and May attended the
opening of *Sgt. Pepper's Lonely Hearts Club Band on the Road*. John had
extended his invitation to include Yoko, but she had declined. Just before the curtain went up, Harold Seider came down the aisle and said
that Yoko had come with Arlene and was unhappy with her seats at the
back of the house. Instantly May offered to exchange seats with Yoko.
John turned to Seider and snapped: "She'll have to sit in the back!"
When the show ended, John grabbed May by the hand and rushed up
the aisle and out of the theater so rapidly that Yoko could not intercept
him. As the limousine pulled away from the curb, she was left standing
on the pavement, shouting, *"John! John!"*

The moment John arrived at the Hippopotamus, the disco where
the opening-night party was being held, he started belting down drinks
at the bar. Soon he was flirting openly with every girl who caught his
eye. Eventually he was engulfed with women, cramming them in his
face, as in the old days at the Speakeasy. May was furious and fearful
of what would happen when the booze cooked up his brains. She went
home and called Yoko. (John left with two black chicks.) "Was he on
liquor?" asked Yoko. May replied, "Yes."

"Was he on cocaine?"

Again, the answer was yes.

There was a perceptible pause before Yoko spoke again. Then she
said: "You know, May—I'm thinking of taking him back."

But retrieving John was no longer as easy as it would have been just
a few months earlier. He had swung into a new groove and was gaining
fresh impetus every day from the sudden revival of his career. For the
first time since he had left the Beatles, John stood at the top of the
charts. *Walls and Bridges* and its first single, "Whatever Gets You

Through the Night," had both gone to No. 1. (The morning the news broke, Yoko hissed at May Pang on the phone: "Everybody knows it's *hype!*") Neither album nor single was representative of Lennon in his prime; but this was the year 1974, and the level of achievement in rock music had fallen drastically since the late Sixties. Whatever the value of John's success, it was honestly achieved. He had written typically self-revealing lyrics about themes with which his public could identify: love lost; love found; fear of getting old and dying; remorse over past follies. What was lacking was melodies; most of the songs, like his breathless hit, hung from the slightest of hooks.

The two best pieces belonged to familiar Lennon genres; in fact, "Steel and Glass" was simply a remake of "How Do You Sleep." Ironically, its target, Allen Klein, was the very man who had stood at John's side when he had launched his notorious attack on Paul. What had made John shift Klein from the Friendly to the Enemy List? The story is interesting because it provides a perfect illustration of how one day's savior always became the next day's betrayer in the life of John Lennon.

Back in the days when Lennon's official income was but £5,000 a month, Allen Klein had arranged things so that John and Yoko could dip into the funds of Apple for anything they felt they needed in order to maintain their careers and life-style. To sustain the Beatles' high levels of expenditure, Klein deferred collecting the $5 million he claimed in commissions and actually reached into his own pocket to lend John, George, and Ringo a million dollars. Once he had been dismissed and given to understand that the "Beatles" had no intention of paying him any of the money they owed him, he sued them to collect. Even at that point Lennon and Klein remained on such friendly terms that a month before John wrote "Steel and Glass" he spent a weekend at Klein's summer house at Westhampton. Not only were the rights and wrongs of his position with Klein of no consequence to Lennon, but even their personal relationship counted for nothing, for at the same time John was accepting his former manager's hospitality, he was composing this cruel put-down. Striking at Klein's soft spots with the same unerring aim he had shown for Paul's, Lennon alluded callously to Klein's loss of his mother (who had died of cancer when Allen was a baby), to the manager's craving to be indispensable to his clients, and even to his body odor. (If Klein had protested this treatment, Lennon would doubtless have dismissed the song as just a fit of temper, now past, and therefore virtually forgotten and certainly, for that reason, forgivable.)

"#9 Dream" is in the tradition of Lennon compositions about altered states of consciousness. It was also an attempt to make amends to George Harrison for John's failures as a friend. The cosmic sound of the track is highly reminiscent of Harrison, as is the sensitive playing of

Jesse Ed Davis in George's signature style. Buried in the track is the voice of May Pang whispering, "Hare Krishna, George." Speaking of George, for whom John had a love he could never voice, Lennon said: "He [George] has less respect for himself than I have for him." To which Jesse Ed replied: "He's more intent on being a conduit than a musician," a penetrating observation. What makes the song John Lennon's last important composition, however, is not its homage to Harrison but its dreamlike atmosphere, particularly that sense of bewitchment we feel while seeing spectral shapes we cannot bring to focus or hearing words that we cannot understand.

Elton John, who appears on *Walls and Bridges,* was busy courting Lennon at this time, a strange infatuation considering how radically different were their temperaments: the one a man of stinging truth, the other the eternal pop sentimentalist, a regression to the moon and June days of the old Tin Pan Alley, as well as a figure of camp fun and Hollywood theatrics. Yet the two stars, the one at the peak of his fame and the other making a surprising comeback, hit it off immediately, perhaps because Elton had scored precisely the kind of success that Lennon found least threatening. The upshot of their friendship was that Lennon agreed to appear onstage at the Garden on the night of Elton's big Thanksgiving Day concert.

Lennon hadn't appeared before an audience since the *One to One* concert two years before, the equivalent on his time scale of a decade. Naturally he was frightened. He spent the hours before his entrance backstage, getting high on coke and vomiting. When his cue came, however, he was ready. Walking out onstage with a couple of recent hits under his belt, he received an ovation. Just as keen on making up with Paul as he had been with George, he announced to the vast audience: "I thought we'd do a number by an old estranged fiancé of mine called Paul." The fans had no chance to react to John's statement because he launched at once into "I Saw Her Standing There," precisely the sort of right-down-the-middle classic Beatles tune that was least to be expected after all the things John had said about Paul and the Beatles in the past few years. Clearly John Lennon had his mind set upon reconciliation.

Three weeks later Allen Klein called Yoko. It was his birthday, and he was feeling sentimental. Representing the Beatles had been the greatest experience of Klein's life as well as the summit of his professional career. Now that it was over, he felt a great sense of loss. Since he couldn't make overtures to John, he made them to Yoko, who was, like himself, out in the cold. "Why don't you call me?" he cajoled. Yoko responded in a flirtatious manner. Klein felt that she was coming on to him, hoping that he would make a pass so that she could use it to arouse John's jealousy. As Klein put it, "She's the most conniving person I have ever met."

"You never take me to lunch," she teased.

Klein replied that nothing would please him more.

"Will you come alone this time?" she challenged. (Klein always brought his girlfriend, Iris.)

When they met at an Italian restaurant near Times Square, they exchanged gifts. He gave her a chocolate cake, and she presented him with two glasses on whose bottoms were painted girls who appeared to disrobe as the glasses emptied.

Once the social amenities had been concluded and the pair settled down to serious talk, Yoko confessed that she was highly alarmed by John's new attitude. "Harold is telling him to move everything out to California, where there is communal property, and fuck me," she declared. (Actually, Seider had never regarded divorce as a possibility, and even if he had, he would not have offered such absurd advice.) "Will you help me?" she implored.

Klein smiled and answered consolingly: "Yoko, I don't think John is gonna fuck you. But if he does, I'll help you." Two days later Yoko sent Allen Grubman (David Spinozza's lawyer) to review the financial data on Lennon in Klein's possession.

Lennon was starting to make money again. Harold Seider had negotiated a good deal with ATV to recover John's half of the writers' share in Lenmac. (Paul had signed a parallel agreement.) In exchange for a new seven-year contract with Northern Songs that gave him half the publisher's share on everything he wrote, Lennon got a $150,000 advance plus a host of fringe benefits, including an office in the Capitol Building. Lennon reported earnings to the IRS in 1974 of $1,199,295 plus $107,939 for Yoko, which, after federal, state, and city taxes, left the Lennons with a net income of about $951,000. In 1975 John would do much better, owing to his settlement with the Beatles.

Yoko was not relying solely on lawyers to solve her problems with her increasingly distant husband. She had been working day and night with her psychics to regain control of John. Everybody in the John Green circle remembers how his phone was ringing constantly, no matter what the hour. Gabe Grumer, Green's disciple, recollected: "At the time when Yoko was working on getting her husband back, she would call incessantly. She would call in the middle of dinner. Wendy would say, 'Hold on a minute!'—and Green would know who it was. He would read for Yoko for ten minutes and then go back to dinner. It could happen as much as four times in four hours—and often did!" Even more suggestive of the hopes Yoko was building on Green were her visits to Wendy's studio apartment in the Brevoort, on Fifth Avenue, just above Washington Square. Yoko Ono was accustomed to people coming to *her;* for her to descend to the humble abode of a member of her staff bespeaks a matter of considerable urgency.

On Thanksgiving evening, as Wendy and Green were preparing to serve a feast to their friends, the downstairs buzzer rang. Green answered and then announced that they were receiving an unexpected caller—Yoko Ono. She burst into the studio apartment, dressed in black cloak, black boots, black sweater and slacks, all crowned with her long black hair. A uniformed chauffeur followed her, carrying a big hamper filled with bottles of wine and expensive-looking cheeses. The liveried driver looked absurd in this hippie pad, with its "tropical corner," full of potted plants and strung with a hammock, and its two "working altars," displaying garishly painted plaster saints. Yoko said nothing to the young people who had gathered for the dinner. She curled up in a chair and passed an uneasy half hour, flipping nervously through a clutch of magazines. Then she left as abruptly as she arrived, bound for the Elton John concert at the Garden.

When John Green's guests pressed him for details of his relationship with Yoko, he would say only that he had come to exercise a great influence upon her life. Nor was he exaggerating. In the short space of six months Green had progressed from outsider to trusted adviser and confidant. At the same time that his role had deepened in terms of intimacy and importance, it had changed in terms of its goal. Engaged originally as psychic defender, Green was now acting as psychic aggressor.

The first real test of his powers came at Christmas. John, May, and Julian were vacationing at Morris Levy's condominium in West Palm Beach. Levy prided himself upon being a good father; hence, when Lennon complained that he didn't know how he would entertain his eleven-year-old son at Christmas, Levy had the answer on the tip of his tongue. He had offered to take John, May, and Julian to Florida, where he was planning to show his own eleven-year-old, Mark, the wonders of Disney World.

Lennon spent the holiday holed up in a bedroom, watching TV and brooding over the Beatles' dissolution agreement. One day he requested that a copy of the document be sent to him. Yoko got wind of the request and offered to provide as courier Kevin Sullivan, a tall, handsome, powerfully built young friend of John Green's. Sullivan was told that instead of flying into West Palm Beach, he must take a plane to Miami and then go back up the coast so as to approach his destination from the south—one of Yoshikawa's prescriptions. When Sullivan, having run up a $70 cab fare, presented the papers to Lennon, May asked the courier what he was planning to do that evening. He said he was eager to get back to New York because "we're giving a party." At that moment John Lennon turned around and eyed Sullivan, who snapped to the fact that John assumed "we" meant Kevin and Yoko. Now Sullivan understood why he had been chosen to deliver the papers. He felt that Yoko was counting on his virile good looks to provoke her husband's jealousy.

The critical moment in the retrieving-of-John campaign occurred a couple of days later. When the Lennon-Levy party moved up to Disney World at Orlando, nobody bothered to notify Yoko because they were going for only two days. When she discovered that she couldn't reach John by phone, she turned to John Green for help.

Her problem was now his problem. He knew that if he failed her at a moment like this, she would lose faith in him and he would lose his most valuable client. On the other hand, only a fool would think he could find the whereabouts of someone by looking at a spread of cards. So Green told Yoko to obtain from Disney World a list of motels in the vicinity of the fun park. With the list before him, he read over every name. Meantime, probably by dialing the same number she had called, he discovered that the only motel on the grounds of Disney World was the Tiki Polynesian. When he concluded his prolonged study of the problem, he told Yoko that she would find John at the Tiki Polynesian. Lennon would not be registered under his own name, but the hotel employees would have recognized him, and they would deliver her message.

Yoko picked up the phone instantly and put through the call. Getting the hotel, she asked for John Lennon. When the operator replied that no John Lennon was registered, Yoko explained that he was a member of Morris Levy's party. A little more to and fro and she got the word: Morris Levy was registered at the hotel, and if John Lennon was with him, the message would be delivered. May Pang recalls that when they got back to the motel that afternoon, they found a message from Yoko under the door.

When John called the Dakota, his first question was: "How did you find me?" Yoko giggled and explained that she had this amazing card reader named John Green, who could find anyone. John snapped: "You better get rid of him because I don't want anybody like that on my tail."

Thus was born "Charlie Swan," the name that John Green adopted henceforth in his dealings with the Dakota in order to deceive John Lennon. The name has a numerological significance, but its basic meaning is metaphorical. As John Green explained to his friend Jeffrey Hunter, "The swan is a symbol of hypocrisy. Though it appears to be pure white, when you lift up its feathers and examine the skin, you see that underneath it is all black."

A HEAVY COUGH

December 1974 marked the moment of greatest alienation between John and Yoko. Knowing only too well that cutting Yoko's phone line is like cutting her lifeline, John began refusing to take her calls or slamming down the phone in the midst of the conversation. What must have alarmed her even more than these insults were the signs of mounting strength and stability in the enemy's camp, especially the news that John and May were preparing to buy a stone house in Montauk. If John Lennon was buying a home with May Pang, things were getting serious. The time had come for Yoko to make the supreme effort.

Like a skillful general, instead of stepping up her unpromising attack, she withdrew. She stopped calling John and went off to California, where she knew virtually no one. When she got back to New York, about 10 January 1975, she rang up John, according to May Pang, and made a surprising announcement: She had discovered a new and absolutely effective cure for smoking! It was the same claim that Tony Cox had made in Denmark when he had urged John to fly in Don Hamrick; what's more, the method was also the same—hypnosis. If Hamrick had failed, why should another hypnotist succeed?

Lennon didn't raise this question. He was ready to try anything because he was suffering from a hacking cough produced by smoking two packs of Gaulois a day. What made Yoko's offer even more beguiling was the way she now began to play mind games with John, calling him up and announcing that she had made an appointment for him with the smoking therapist, only to call back a few days later to cancel and reschedule his appointment with this mysterious wonder worker. After Yoko had played this game for two weeks, May Pang pointed out to Lennon that he was being teased. John didn't object. He liked being teased.

By the last day of the month, when John's next appointment fell due, May Pang had become very apprehensive about this eagerly anticipated cure. She had lived for so many years on such an intimate footing with John and Yoko that she had developed an uncanny sensitivity to the vibrations that passed back and forth between these strong personalities. What she was getting now from Yoko were very strong vibes, portending something really big. So when the appointed hour arrived on Friday afternoon, 31 January, and there was no call from Yoko canceling the session, May grew alarmed. She tried to dissuade John from going to the Dakota. She said that she had never yet asked for anything from him, but today she *was* asking, nay, *begging* him, not to go!

John made light of the whole business, assuring May that he would be home in time for supper. Then tomorrow, he told her, they would drive out to Montauk and take one last look at the house before they bought it. Two weeks later they were scheduled to go down to New Orleans, where Paul was cutting the album which became *Venus and Mars*. This was the moment for which May had worked so hard. She was sure that once John got into the studio with Paul, the inevitable would happen. As far back as September John had said publicly that he would like to record again with the Beatles. Everything was in readiness now for the long hoped-for reunion. May was virtually holding her breath that winter afternoon as she saw John go out the door.

The first sign May received that something strange was afoot was when she called the Dakota around ten o'clock in the evening and asked to speak to John. Yoko, obviously in the midst of some urgent activity, barked, "I can't talk to you right now! I'll call you later!" and threw down the phone. May sat up all night, waiting for John, but he never came home. At ten o'clock Saturday morning she called again. This time Yoko answered in a hushed and furtive tone. May could tell from long experience that Yoko was lying next to the sleeping John. When May asked to speak to John, Yoko whispered: "You can't. He's exhausted. The cure was very difficult." Then, assuring May that John was all right, Yoko promised to have him call later. May received no call that day or the next.

It was not until Monday afternoon that May finally came face-to-face again with John Lennon.

They had booked successive appointments with a dentist several blocks from their apartment. When May walked out of the dentist's office, she discovered John sitting in the waiting room. One glance, and she knew that something had happened to him. "His eyes were red-rimmed and there were bags under them," she reported. "He looked at me vaguely and seemed dazed. His eyes were dilated and his manner [was] weird." (May's description of Lennon's exhausted appearance and befuddled manner was confirmed the very next day, when the veteran reporter Pete Hamill arrived at the Dakota to conduct an interview with John, pegged to the rock 'n' roll album. Lennon looked to Hamill like "a man recovering from a serious illness." When John opened his mouth, he talked like a patient coming out of an anesthetic. "It's '75 now, isn't it?" he groped, although the date was 4 February, not 4 January. "And on this day you've come here," he said vaguely, "I seem to have moved back in here. By the time this goes out—I don't know?" Hamill got the impression that John was saying: "What do I do now?" What he actually said was: "Could you come back in a few days?" For once the great master of the press interview could not rise to the challenge.)

May waited for John, and when he came back into the reception room, she asked him if he was coming home. He blinked and said, "Uh . . . right . . . OK." May scrutinized him carefully now, struggling to understand what had come over him. He reminded her of those zombielike creatures in *Invasion of the Body Snatchers*. When they got inside the flat, John said: "I guess I should say this to you now. Yoko has allowed me to come home."

"What!" cried May.

John repeated the formula verbatim: "Yoko has allowed me to come home." Then he turned to pack a few things in a bag.

May burst into tears. She had spent an agonized weekend, dreading this very thing. Now the worst had come to pass. She was dumbstruck. But not for long. Stepping into the living room, she dialed Yoko's private number. When she answered, May said icily: "Congratulations, Yoko. You've got John back, and I'm sure you'll be very happy."

Yoko's response startled May. "Happy?" Yoko echoed bitterly. "I don't know if I'll ever be happy."

When May replied, "Isn't this what you wanted?" Yoko made a quick excuse and rang off.

May returned to questioning John and learned that his cure had been reminiscent of primal therapy. May was convinced now that John had been brainwashed, but she couldn't think of any way to undo this weird spell. "When did she tell you you could come home?" she asked.

"I don't know . . . it just happened," mumbled Lennon, like a bad boy caught out. "Nobody wanted it . . . it just came up."

Finally, May got to the real issue. "What about the love we felt for each other?" she demanded. "When did that stop?"

John's reply astonished May no less than had Yoko's answer a moment earlier. "Yoko knows I still love you," said John. "She's allowed me to continue to see you. She said she can be the wife, and you can continue to be the mistress." At this point he jumped up and retrieved his coat, from which he removed two tiny bottles filled with fluids.

"Yoko sent you a present," he explained. "One is for you, and one is for me. I'm supposed to put some on you." With that he opened the bottle and smeared on May a horrible-smelling oil. Then he dabbed himself with the other oil, which smelled like roses. Reeking of these essences, they got into bed and made love.

When it was over, John smoked a cigarette. Then he announced: "I have to go home now." Throwing on his clothes, he ducked out the door, caroling: "Don't worry about a thing. I'll call you tomorrow."

May took her oil to a *botánica,* a shop that sells Santería cult figures and charms. The proprietor sniffed it and explained that it was a mixture of sulfur, arrowroot, and chili powder. "Whoever gave it to you," he warned, "must really hate you."

May Pang never discovered the cause of John Lennon's abrupt about-face. Indeed, it would be hard for anyone to explain such a sudden and motiveless reversal. One minute John had seemed perfectly content in his new life with May. In fact, he was preparing to commit himself to it even more fully by buying them an expensive house. Then, the next minute, John had thrown up everything he had achieved in the past eighteen months and was back where he started with Yoko. Even if one assumes that he would have found his way back to her eventually, normally it would have taken some precipitating cause to turn him around, either a spell of deep depression or a sudden burst of uncontrollable anxiety triggered by some clear and present danger. Because there was nothing of the kind, another reason must be sought.

Perhaps the key to what occurred lies in Lennon's own description of his weekend of "treatment" at the Dakota. "I was throwin' up all the time," he told May. "I kept fallin' asleep, and when I woke up, they would do it to me again." Who is "they" and what is "it"?

The use of the Santería essential oils points clearly to John Green and/or Joey Lukach. Joey is an avowed expert in concocting magical potions and a hypnotist. In 1973 he boasted to one of his disciples, Dorothy DeChristopher, that he had entrée to the Dakota and was fetched to and from the building in a limousine. He was also tight with the owner of the nearby *botánica,* on Amsterdam Avenue and 77th Street.

John Green, for his part, has testified in print that he met John Lennon for the first time on this very weekend. Yoko rang him up and announced breathlessly: "John's home!" Her next words were startling: "I think he's been poisoned."

When Green arrived a half hour later, he was introduced to a John Lennon who gave no signs of being poisoned. All John complained about, according to Green, were problems that actually belonged to a later time, like being ripped off for money or having "lost the muse."

Ultimately, of course, it hardly matters whether John Green or Joey Lukach or John Doe played the smoking therapist. All John Lennon had to get into his head between bouts of vomiting and nodding out was that it was time for him to change his address and to say: "Yoko has allowed me to come home."

LYING IN

"We're pregnant!" Yoko giggled girlishly one day in March, as she skittered into the Black Room, where John was discussing his next album with Bob Mercer of EMI. Just back from an examination by her gynecologist, Yoko was big with news of immense importance for her marriage. John was beside himself with glee. After receiving Mercer's congratulations, he astonished the EMI man by declaring, "Well, Bob, I guess that shelves the work for some time now. I'm going to devote the next nine months to making sure that Yoko has this baby."

John's startling statement betrayed his keen awareness of all the dangers that threatened this belated pregnancy. Yoko had miscarried often in the past. What's more, he knew that once her initial enthusiasm waned, she might not want to sacrifice nine months of her life on the altar of maternity. "When I got pregnant with Sean, I was going to have an abortion," she confessed years later. "But John said, 'We're *not* going to do that.' So I told him, 'OK, I'll carry it, but after that the baby is your responsibility.'" John also knew that it would never do for him to appear to be stealing a march on Yoko by playing the artist while she was constrained to play the mother. Hence, for all these reasons, it made good sense for him to hang up his career and concentrate on the baby.

Yet John might not have been so eager to relinquish his work if he had not been in the grip of a writer's block. Just six weeks earlier, when he left May Pang, he had been arockin' and arollin' like a young man. Only a week before he packed it in at Sutton Place, he had composed two songs, "Popcorn" and "Tennessee," the latter not about the American state but about the famous playwright, the titles of whose works were skillfully woven through the lyric. No sooner was John back at the Dakota, however, than he started having trouble with his writing. Many times a day he would jump up and start chording out a new song at the piano; then he would "lose the muse." By April he was reduced to sitting all day by the kitchen window, playing over old Beatles' songs on his acoustic guitar. Yoko pronounced this activity "pathetic" and worried what the neighbors would think. So the timely announcement of her pregnancy took John off the hook and gave him a fresh purpose in life just when his professional goals were beginning to seem unattainable.

Everything John Lennon ever said about Sean testifies to his vision of this second child as being radically different from his firstborn. Julian was in Lennon's eyes a Saturday night baby born out of a bottle of whiskey, unplanned, unwanted, and a pain in the ass. Sean was a love child, conceived at a moment of reconciliation, prepared for as carefully as wealth, knowledge, and experience could assure and destined to fulfill a great destiny that could make him eventually a new messiah. Taro, the name Yoko contributed, is always given in Japan to the firstborn son. Sean is the Irish form of John. Clearly, in Sean Ono Taro, John Lennon recognized the ultimate opportunity to fulfill his fondest wish: to start all over again. For though John's life had brought him the most awesome success imaginable, he never stopped resenting and bewailing it to his dying day. He would have been happy to take it all back and start again, but failing that, he could at least assure that his son was reared in a totally different manner, being shielded from all the horrors that had plagued his father's childhood and given the comforts, pleasures, and opportunities that John had been denied.

The first unmistakable sign of Lennon's determination to play his marriage da capo was his decision to remarry Yoko on their anniversary. This time he wanted a Druid ceremony that would symbolize his descent from the ancient Celts, for as Yoko was always boasting about her nine-hundred-year-old family, John had to acquire a genealogy of comparable antiquity. What he found in the very sketchy evidence of the Celts in Britain was the cult of the Druids and the legend of Queen Boadicea, an Amazonian matriarch who led her people into battle at the head of an army—in John's version—of women warriors followed by the men and children. John Green, who often led his little band of disciples in exotic festivals on the holidays of the spiritist calendar, got into the spirit of the Druid wedding immediately.

He erected an altar in the White Room and sent John out, like a kid to the grocery store, to purchase white candles, a chalice, and a statue of St. Margaret from an emporium called Blessed Are the Blessed Be. John had so much fun on this mission that later he could do five minutes on it, mimicking the lispy, overserious proprietor and describing the cellophane-wrapped merchandise, heavy on cursing candles in the shapes of naked men and women, as well as the whole pantheon of gaudily robed black-faced Santería saints. On their wedding day bride and groom were supposed to remain out of each other's sight until the moment of the ceremony. When this prohibition proved inconvenient, it was rejected as an improper Christian imposition on what was supposed to be a pure pagan rite. At the conclusion of the wedding John and Yoko slipped on each other's fingers rings of green jade that were later to be consecrated by being dipped in the sea. Soon John was complaining that his ring was too tight to wear.

The John and Yoko of the Druid wedding ceremony were the same kids playing grown-ups who had made *Imagine,* with all its solemn-silly rituals. Their capacity to stimulate each other imaginatively had always been the most enchanting aspect of their relationship. Yet there was far more to John's joy than just the recovery of his favorite playmate. He was manifestly relieved to be back behind the sheltering walls of the Dakota. May Pang has described with great satisfaction how pleasant it was to see John spending evening after evening in the company of the famous rockers, but what May never seems to have realized was how draining and exhausting these evenings were for John, who experienced these social calls not only as invasions of privacy but as temptations to slide back into that self-destructive life-style he had just escaped from on the Coast. As a boy who could never say no, John Lennon longed for a protective presence, a firm negator, who would stand between him and the world, rejecting its demands and accepting the blame for telling all these nice people to go to hell. May Pang offered a protective screen, but it was like rice paper in comparison with the massive granite of Yoko Ono's presence.

Hence, behind John's desertion of the rock scene lay his fear of life in general, his feeling that work and play, love and sex were all very well, but the most important thing was *security.* After all, he had never stood alone nor aspired to be the master of his life. Always he had found some decisive figure, female or male, Mimi or Yoko, Epstein or Klein, who would stand over him and tell him what to do. He might rant and rave against his guardians, threatening to run away or actually walking out on them, but the door that led out of one relationship led directly into another of precisely the same character. Only once during his entire life did John Lennon essay that terrifying terra incognita where there were no protecting mother figures—during the Lost Weekend. No wonder this period haunted him to his dying day, when he was still describing it in terms of the wanderings of Sinbad (!) the Sailor, out on the deep, battling the monsters and barely saving his skin. It was John Lennon's horror of freedom and independence, those virtues so thoughtlessly celebrated in rock song, that drove him back time and again to Yoko—if it can be said that he ever really left her. But, by the same token, once John felt safe again and totally free of any responsibility for his own welfare, the other side of his mother complex began to raise its angry head.

Yoko had allowed John to come home only on certain conditions—which he couldn't disclose to the public. Instead of slipping back inside the marriage bed, he was obliged to spend a probationary period sequestered in the Black Room. Here he dossed down on a mattress laid upon the black carpet and spent his time in solitary pursuits: reading books on magic, composing *Skywriting by Word of Mouth* (utterly inferior to his earlier humor books because no serious themes stir behind its facile puns), ogling the mirror-sided TV, playing records on his jukebox, and struggling, with diminishing success, to write songs at his ebony-finished upright piano. Though he relished the longed-for peace and comfort that came with his return to his monastic existence, as a mature man he could not long tolerate the sexual deprivation that was the lot of a monk.

With May Pang, John had enjoyed sex every day in every way that his horny imagination could suggest. John had a "raging hard-on," according to Jesse Ed Davis, who not only had plenty of opportunities to feel the vibes between this pair but was the recipient of John's ribald confidences. Now Lennon was back with the woman whom he had denounced years before as a "prude." No Druid ceremony alone was going to restore to the Lennons' marriage its lost sexual glamour.

It is an open question what had happened to the sexual passion that had once consumed John and Yoko. She told Marnie Hair that before her marriage she and John had sparks coming off their bodies when they made love, and John celebrated their honeymoon by drawing an extensive series of erotic lithographs that leave nothing to the imagination when it comes to asking what the Lennons did in the sack. When he was asked why so many of the pictures represented him going down on Yoko, he replied: "Because I like it." As soon as the Lennons started living together, however, they became stone junkies, which must have given the quietus to their passion. Subsequently John apparently suffered from impotence. Just two years after the marriage, when John denounced Yoko to Klein, the Lennons' sex life was clearly on the wane. It may not be surprising to learn that in the month of May, only three months after he came home, he responded to an invitation to spend a weekend in Philadelphia, broadcasting on behalf of a local charity, with the words "Great! Yoko and I need some time apart." For by then Yoko had reneged on her promise that John could continue to enjoy May as mistress. Actually, no sooner did Yoko announce her pregnancy than May found herself being given the bum's rush.

Earlier, John had turned up at Sutton Place with one of Yoko's assistants, Jon Hendricks, to remove everything but the bed (tainted by May), the sofa (on which Julian had slept), and the wall mirrors, which John couldn't pry loose. He had even gone so far as to claim any of May's clothes that happened to fit him, compromising only on the T-shirts, which they divided evenly. Meantime, he had continued working every day with May at the studio and the office of Lennon Music in the Capitol Building, where they rounded off their labors on the official version of the rock 'n' roll album (which differs slightly from the Levy version) as well as did the publicity on the album.

When their work was done, they would go back to their stripped-down apartment to make love. No sooner was the fun over, however, than John would be smitten by fear that Yoko would find him out. Leaping out of bed, he would take a quick shower to remove the tell-tale odor of the "other woman" and then would anoint himself with the sweet-smelling, come-hither-love-to-me oil that Yoko had ordered him to apply to his body. May talks of the "two Johns" in her life at this time. Actually, there was but one man oscillating between two states of being: horny and guilty.

When John told May that she would have to vacate the apartment, she was outraged because he had persuaded her to give up her old flat, which she could afford, to move into the penthouse at Sutton Place. Where was she to find the money now to rent a new apartment in house-famished New York? When she complained that she hadn't been paid in eighteen months, Lennon said that he would see what he could do, but he didn't do a thing until Harold Seider, dismayed by May's predicament, raised the issue at a meeting with the Lennons. The moment the word "compensation" was out of his mouth, Yoko delivered her opinion: "I think she should be thrilled that she was able to spend so much time with John. *That* should be her compensation!" Lennon, conceding nothing, asked Seider, warily, what he thought was fair. The lawyer replied that May should at least receive her back salary because she had never stopped working for John and had done a good job of taking care of him. John was not willing to part with a penny, but eventually he did consent to put May back on the payroll for a year at $15,000. Naturally she was expected to report for work every day and behave precisely as she had done before she became John's mistress.

In April, May had been sent off to London to work at Apple. When she returned the following month, she was fired, although she continued to receive her salary for the stipulated period. Every penny of it was sorely needed, for when this highly qualified young woman, who had piled up a stack of impressive credits during her years with the Lennons, went out to seek another job in the record industry, she discovered that she had been blackballed. John Lennon's recording contract with EMI was due to expire on 26 January 1976. Every company in the business was hoping to sign him up. The feeling was that he would never sign with a label that had May Pang on its payroll.

*   *   *

Once John had lost May, his attitude toward Yoko began to change. Instead of feeling the love that is inspired by the sense of being saved, John began to experience the hatred that children evince when they are thwarted of their dearest desires. Indeed, his whole situation at the Dakota was becoming reminiscent of how he had lived as a child with Mimi at Mendips. As the months rolled on and his free contacts with the outer world drastically diminished, John could see that the old techniques of psychological control—isolation, observation, regimentation, even low feeding—were coming into play again. Inevitably they fomented all his old rebelliousness and cruelty.

John would invite Yoko to dine at a restaurant, a gracious gesture that any wife would appreciate. But when they were seated at table, he would order a brandy Alexander. Drinking was forbidden at home, but in a public place Yoko was powerless to stop John from imbibing. As one Milk Shake after another slid down the famous throat, the Lennon tongue would turn sharp and nasty. Pinioned by social convention, Yoko was obliged to submit mutely as John cut her up like cat food. Perhaps he would josh her about her nobly melancholy features, making her samurai dignity the butt of his Liverpool-shogun vulgarity. Or perhaps he would complain of sexual deprivation, demanding that if she didn't want to fuck him, she should at least provide suitable substitutes, like some nice young girls—or boys! When Yoko could no longer tolerate this outrageous behavior, she would jump up from the table and flee the restaurant. That was John's cue to go out on the town.

Hailing a cab, he would roll down Fifth Avenue to 12th Street, where stood Ashley's, the hottest disco in town and the favorite hangout of the music biz crowd. A ground-floor bar-restaurant with a dance hall upstairs, Ashley Pandel's joint was experiencing in the year 1975 its fifteen minutes of fame. When John Lennon walked in, the red carpet would roll out. John could drink without paying, score drugs off virtually every dude in the house, jive with the celebs and DJ, and, when the hour grew late and his courage grew great, walk in the cloakroom and thrust his hand up the hatcheck girl's skirt. One morning he called Yoko at seven and confided: "I'm watching three lesbians make it. I hope they make it with me next!" Another night he went home with two waitresses, expecting to make it a threesome. When the girls refused, he whipped out his cock and began masturbating, growling: "Fuck it! I'll do it meself!"

The only trouble was that when the light began to lance down 12th Street, John might find himself out in front of the club, turning his pockets inside out and discovering that he didn't have a dime to get home! Had he been robbed or given all his money away? Who the hell could remember after such a night? So he might take it into his head to walk a few blocks, trying to get himself together. Then the next thing he knew, he was looking at some asshole who was giving him that "Beatle John!" look that Lennon dreaded worse than the evil eye. Throwing up his hand to cover his face, he would moan: "No! No!" Then, like a vampire caught by the dawn, he would hurl himself into the back seat of a cab. Rolling north through the gathering tide of morning traffic, he would seek the sanctuary of the Dakota, where, thank God!, he could always stumble up the steps to the office and ask old Winnie, the concierge, to give him five dollars for the hack.

Yoko wasn't slow to recognize the dangers posed by this sort of behavior. Just as she had once sought to sate John's lust by procuring him a discreet and trustworthy mistress, so now she arranged with reliable people, like Elliot Mintz or Tony King, to have her husband taken to a whorehouse. (John was too insecure to go by himself, and Yoko wanted a full report on how he behaved.) One of these establishments, a Korean brothel on 23rd Street, still proudly displays Lennon's signed photograph. Here John could indulge his yearning to see women get it on with women, either by going down on each other or by using dildos. He could also have his fill of rubber-firm bodies and nimble-fingered jerk-off artists. Nor was there any danger that these illiterate foreign prostitutes would create a scandal by, as Yoko put it, "writing a book."

When the summer came on and the asphalt turned soft, another solution offered. John could be packed off with one of the servants to Montauk, where Yoko arranged to rent the very same place, the stone house near Gurney's Inn, that Lennon had been planning to buy for himself and May Pang. Getting John out of the city must have been one of Yoko's most fervent wishes because he was driving her crazy with his efforts to protect the unborn baby. Not only did he insist upon supervising Yoko's diet and pushing her about the apartment in a wheelchair, but she found that she couldn't go into the bathroom without finding him on her tail.

The effect of this Mimi-like surveillance was just the opposite of what John intended. While, for the baby's sake, he stopped smoking for the first and only time in his life, Yoko became so nervous that she ran up her consumption of Kools to four packs a day. While John dieted and fasted to a shadow, Yoko developed an insatiable appetite, including a constant craving for chocolate. Every time John Green arrived to do a reading, he would find his client giving the maid orders for food and drink on a scale out of keeping with either her customary diet or what was appropriate to a pregnant and bedridden woman. Soon she was noticeably overweight, and John, obsessed as always with his Fat Elvis phobia, was making Yoko's life miserable. She was obliged to hide her chocolates and other indulgences, enjoying them only on the sly. What she couldn't conceal were the effects of her overeating, which eventually touched off a violent quarrel, in the course of which John kicked Yoko in the belly.

So John was sent off to the shore, where Yoko rarely went because she hated the insects and dreaded the effect of the sun on her skin, fair skin being in all Oriental cultures a sign of high caste. Sending John off without supervision created, however, a whole series of fresh problems because he would go out at night and get drunk, which would lead to mischief with the locals. All the same, Yoko must have been glad to get him out of her hair.

John described Yoko's pregnancy as a "miracle," and when all things are considered, the word does not seem excessive. Many couples would have abandoned the idea of having children by this point, not just because of past failures but on account of the doctors' pessimistic prognoses. For the Lennons' reproduction problems had grown progressively worse over the years. Originally they had been able to initiate pregnancy, but Yoko had been unable to carry the fetus to term. Her first miscarriage had occurred after she began hemorrhaging on 7 November 1968, a few weeks subsequent to the London drug bust. Her next miscarriage began on Lennon's twenty-ninth birthday, 9 October 1969, a curious and perhaps significant coincidence. Her third happened during primal therapy in August 1970, when one of Los Angeles's leading obstetricians put her into Cedars of Lebanon, where she registered under the name of Allen Klein's assistant, Iris Keitel.

For years afterward the Lennons sought in vain to have a child. The cause of their failure was identified in 1972, when a test revealed that John had such a low level of active sperm that he could not impregnate her. Now, without John receiving any kind of treatment or assistance through artificial insemination, Yoko had become pregnant. What made the pregnancy even more miraculous was the fact that it was produced by only a single act of intercourse.

John informed his cousin Dr. Leila Harvey, in a letter written in the summer of 1975, that the baby had been conceived on the night of 7 February. Yoko told John Green that conception occurred on 1 February—the night that John returned to the Dakota for his cure. The reason both husband and wife could point to a single date is that, as Yoko explained, she had had vaginal intercourse with John only once during the first months of their reconciliation.

Another remarkable feature of the pregnancy was the widespread confusion over its anticipated term. John told many people that the baby would be born in November, which, in view of the date of conception, is natural. He cited that month in his letter to Leila and gave May Pang the same date, remarking, "It will be a Scorpio, and I know how to deal with Scorpios" (May's sign). He must have told the same thing to Ringo, who presented the baby on its birth with a ring engraved "November." On the other hand, in a couple of letters of roughly the same date as that to Leila, he announced that the baby would be born in October, presumably at the end of the month, which is the date that was published in the press on 8 October, the day before Sean's birth.

In one of the letters that cite October as the month of birth, John exclaims after the date, "What else!" His aside must have been inspired by the recognition that, as he told Fred Seaman years later, "She's always trying to have babies on my birthday." Yoko's motive was an occult belief that if a child is born upon its father's birthday, it will receive his soul when he dies. Hence, Yoko's goal was to bestow her husband's genius upon her child.

In June *Rolling Stone* published the interview that Pete Hamill had been sent to do three days after John returned to the Dakota in February. The primary reason for the delay was that Hamill had not been invited back to finish the job for about five weeks, the earliest date at which he could have quoted back to John the latter's statement "Our separation was a failure," which appeared in *Newsweek* on 10 March. During that long hiatus John and Yoko had had plenty of time to put their heads together and come up with the latest stanza of the Ballad of John and Yoko.

This new stave turned on an event that never happened: a wordless exchange of meaningful looks backstage at the Elton John concert on Thanksgiving, 1974. John claimed that he didn't know Yoko was in the house because if he had, he would never have been able to go onstage. The truth was that Yoko had spent much of the preceding week raising hell with John about the seats she had been assigned for the concert. When John described to Hamill the great moment at which the alienated but faithful lovers caught sight of each other, he waxed romantic: "There was just that moment when we saw each other and like, it's like in the movies, you know, when time stands still." Later, John added, a "friend" told him: "A friend of mine saw you backstage and thought if ever there were two in love, it's those two." That line was picked up and quoted repeatedly by John and Yoko fans, some of whom announced in the following years that they were patterning their marriages on that of the rock world's most fabled lovers.

What was disquieting about the interview was not the movie footage backstage at the Garden but the way John flogged himself with almost masochistic intensity for his wicked behavior during the Lost Weekend. Instead of explaining his behavior as the product of a failed marriage, he made it appear that he had simply gone crazy. He never mentioned

May Pang, nor did he suggest by so much as a word the crucial fact that his "mad dream" had actually ended *nine months* before he returned to Yoko, when he settled down on Sutton Place to enjoy the most normal existence he had ever known. Asked to account for this travesty of the truth, Harold Seider remarked: "He [John] was under an obligation to perpetuate the myth. Given the fact of Yoko's domination, there was no way he could have said: 'Hey, she wanted to get laid, I wanted to get laid, she wanted to get a divorce.' . . . He had spent his whole marriage making her the martyred person. . . . Unless he was prepared to break with Yoko, he could not tell the truth. . . . He understood diplomacy. He had to say: 'I was the bad boy. She sent me away.'"

Pressed to explain the total contradiction between the reality of Lennon's life and the way he presented himself to the public, Seider observed: "The real Lennon was not the public statements that he made. They were made [that way] because they were *public* statements, and he was looking to make a point. Not that he really believed it, but he wanted to make the point." Didn't Lennon experience guilt about lying? Seider retorted: "He couldn't give a shit because to a certain extent he had contempt for the media because they bought all the crap. . . . He was there to manipulate the media. He enjoyed doing that. . . . He understood how to use the media. You got to give him credit for that, and you got to give *her* credit . . . they would use the media . . . but it was not that they believed it, but that was the image they wanted to present."

Once John had finished making propaganda, however, he offered a final glimpse of himself that cut to the core of his being. Explaining that the root of his problem was his refusal to grow up, John confessed: "I don't want to grow up but I'm sick of not growing up—that way. I'll find a different way of not growing up. There's a better way of doing it . . . [but] I have this great fear of the *normal* thing . . . the ones that settled for the *deal*! That's what I'm trying to avoid. But I'm sick of avoiding it with violence."

The month after John Lennon told the rock public how happy he was to be back with Yoko Ono, he resumed his affair with May Pang. Now, however, their relationship became a clandestine affair. With their penthouse long gone and May living with a girl who worked all day at home, the lovers' greatest problem was finding some place to be alone. If they went to a hotel or motel, John, who never carried money, would be obliged to pay with his American Express card, which would mean a bill that Yoko was certain to see because she opened all the mail, just as she monitored all the calls that went in and out of the apartment. The only solution John could hit upon was to schedule an appointment with his $200-an-hour lawyer, Michael Graham, and then tell the astonished attorney to drive his client and his client's former assistant to Connecticut to examine some property. When they had parked in a secluded place, John told Graham: "OK, Michael, take a walk!"

A little later in the summer Richard Ross, proprietor of Home, a rock musicians' hangout on Second Avenue at 91st Street, went into Mount Sinai Hospital to be treated for Hodgkin's disease. Richard, who adored John and was an old friend of May (who had steered a lot of rockers, including John, to Home), provided another opportunity for the unhoused lovers. After chatting with his visitors, he said: "You two look like you need some time alone." Then he hauled himself out of his sickbed and went to the lounge, while John and May hopped in the sack. After he was discharged, Richard continued to play the role of Pandarus. He would ring up May and tell her that a "friend" wanted to see her. That was May's cue to hustle over to Ross's apartment on 92nd Street near Madison Avenue, where she would rendezvous with John. Two or three times a week John and May met in this fashion until the birth of the baby produced a temporary break in their relations.

In September John got permission from Yoko to spend a week at Cape Cod with Ross, who was now well enough to travel. The two men were both keen on learning to sail, though neither of them knew the first thing about managing a boat. Sailing and the sea were lifetime obsessions with Lennon, who had been taken down to the docks as soon as he could toddle and introduced to the old salts by his sailmaker grandfather. At the age of sixteen John and Pete Shotton had tried to enroll in ship stewards' school so they could get to sea, but Mimi had stopped them in their tracks. The first time John went on a full-blown holiday as a Beatle, he and George, with their wives, had flown to Tahiti and rented a professionally crewed schooner. That was the model for their later cruises on luxury yachts about the isles of Greece. Now that John was no longer writing, he desperately needed some fresh project to keep his mind occupied. That summer at Montauk he had conceived the notion of buying a big sailing boat and voyaging around the world with Richard and their wives. John would be the vessel's captain, and Richard's wife, Cynthia, an airline stewardess with a level head, would study navigation and become their ocean guide. First, however, it was necessary for the men to get a bit of practice in handling small boats in coastal waters.

John and Richard took off for the Cape in the latter's glamorous Maserati, but Lennon, always tight with a buck, insisted that they stay in a cheap, fly-infested room with a kitchenette that smelled of sewage. After a weekend at Martha's Vineyard the two mates went down to the ferry on Monday morning to load their car. There Lennon looked up and saw the face that was to float through his mind for years to come.

Alexa Grace looked at twenty-five like the young Ingrid Bergman of *For Whom the Bell Tolls*. A commercial illustrator and an artist who modeled tiny clay figurines, she had the shy, withdrawn personality of Laura in *The Glass Menagerie*. That day she was in pain because after living for five months with a man with whom she was deeply in love, she was being sent back to the city so that he could enjoy his freedom. The moment Lennon caught sight of the little ceramic figures Alexa was carrying, he was intrigued. He suggested that they take out the little figures and "play." Alexa sat down with John, and instantly they both were in the land of "Imagine."

Lennon gave charming new titles to all the pieces he examined, which aroused Alexa's interest more than the fact that he was famous because she was a jazz fan and a rock star was not her idea of a hero. John appeared so sensitive and so funny that she began to lose her habitual reticence. By the time they arrived at Hyannisport, John was urging Alexa to postpone taking the bus to New York. "We'll take you anywhere," he promised expansively, just as Richard, horrified, saw a loading vehicle back into his costly car and virtually rip off the door.

The accident suddenly crystallized their incipient relationship, and soon the three of them were tooling around the region, eating in a health food restaurant, visiting a crazy old lady who sold tartan kilts, and exploring the countryside. When John made a little pass at Alexa, she turned on him angrily and told him that she was not a groupie! John backed off instantly, recognizing that she was, in fact, a shy and vulnerable artist like himself and that it would be better if they didn't spoil their fun by playing the mating game. Alexa, for her part, felt comfortable about sleeping on a cot while John and Richard occupied their beds. Next day she went sailing with her new friends, and even though she realized that they didn't know what they were doing, she felt perfectly safe aboard the boat, which finally had to be towed back into the dock. Though Alexa felt secure, she observed that John did not. He was perpetually anxious. When she suggested they go horseback riding, he was so intimidated by the size of the animals that he declined to mount one. When Richard would roar around a curve in the road, John would cry out in alarm. When they were about to enter an old barn, John remarked only half-jokingly that he would feel better if he had a hammer in his hand. Alexa noticed also that every time a problem arose John's first impulse was to call Yoko.

The little idyll ended after a day and a night on Alexa's grandmother's farm near Napanoch in the Catskills. After driving down to New York, John and Richard dropped Alexa off at her pad in the East Village. John promised to visit and show her his art. Instead, Alexa began to receive from time to time unsigned postcards with pasteups of her illustrations or odd little drawings, which struck her as the work of an art student who had never developed. Obviously John was thinking of her. He was also checking her out because several times Richard Ross came calling on her, undoubtedly at John's behest. Years elapsed, however, before John and Alexa met again, just as accidentally as they had that day on the ferry slip at Martha's Vineyard.

Early in October, in the thirty-fifth week of pregnancy (according to John's reckoning), Yoko was ordered to enter New York Hospital. At this moment all the plans the Lennons had made for the birth of their child suddenly fell to the ground. For they had planned to have a natural birth at home, with John present throughout, in accordance with the fashionable theories of Lamaze. No sooner was Yoko in the hospital, however, than the doctor declared that a caesarian delivery was obligatory. This decision meant that if Yoko could hold on to the baby until 9 October, Sean would be born on his father's birthday. May Pang predicted that Yoko would succeed.

On 8 October the Lennons received a good augury. Leon Wildes called John at home and told him that a three-judge panel had just ruled in his favor in the government's case to deport him. Such a ruling was tantamount to granting permission for Lennon to become a permanent resident of the United States. "Am I gonna be able to stay here?" exclaimed John, hardly able to believe it. Then he revealed his own big news. "I'm going over to the hospital," he confided. "Yoko is going to be induced tonight. You know, tomorrow's my birthday! Please stay near the phone. I'll call you and you'll explain it to her."

Soon Wildes received a call from Yoko, who said: "Come over with Ruth [Mrs. Wildes], and we'll sit and read the decision." Yoko had gone through every phase of the legal maneuvering with her lawyer; consequently, she was much more interested in learning the details of the judges' decision than was John, who, as always, was more concerned with the product than with the process. The Wildeses arrived that evening and found Yoko resting comfortably in a room with a fine view of the East River, the very same room which Jackie Kennedy had occupied when she gave birth to Caroline. The lawyer and his wife remained at Yoko's bedside until midnight, celebrating their long-sought victory.

After midnight Yoko was wheeled into the delivery room. The baby was born at 2:00 A.M.

At six in the morning Leon Wildes was awakened by the ringing of his phone. Picking up the receiver groggily, he heard a voice say: "It's John!"

"John who?" answered the lawyer, struggling to focus his mind.

"It's a boy!" crowed Lennon, without pausing for explanation. Apparently everything was in order at that hour. But not much later a series of events occurred that haunted John and Yoko for years to come. The most detailed account of this catastrophe was supplied by Yoko to Professor Jon Wiener, who incorporated it in his analysis of John Lennon's political and social beliefs, *Come Together*.

Yoko began by explaining:

> Most people think we scheduled the Cesarian [*sic*] birth to coincide with John's birthday. But that wasn't how it happened. We had prepared for a natural childbirth, Lamaze and all that. Early the morning of October 9, the contractions were starting. We went to the hospital. At that point the doctor decided to take precautions and deliver the baby by Cesarian.
>
> They injected me with a partial anesthetic and then realized they didn't have my blood type, which was rare. So they called around to other hospitals to get it. That threw the timing of the anesthetic off. When the blood arrived, they had to give me a second injection. Then they delivered the baby. Cesarian birth is painful, and usually they give you another injection afterwards. I was in agony, saying, "Please give me something." But they said they couldn't give me anything because I had already had two heavy shots.
>
> The baby was taken to intensive care. John kept checking and reporting back to me, "He's fine, he's fine." But the baby was having problems—muscle spasms. The doctors thought he might have something wrong. John was so choked up, but he was hiding it from me.
>
> They decided to test my urine, and they came and told me and John that they had found evidence of drugs in my urine and that the baby might have been damaged by this. John shouted, "We weren't taking any drugs! We were on a health food diet!" He said, "We're taking our baby and getting out of here!" The doctor said, "If you take the baby, we'll get a search warrant to search your residence, and we could get a court order to take your baby away from you for being unfit parents." We were terrified. But we knew we hadn't taken any drugs.
>
> Our private physician tried to help us, and he did what he could, but once the baby was in intensive care, the intensive care doctor had the power to make decisions.
>
> We had planned that I would nurse the baby, and I kept asking to. But for three days they didn't allow me to see the baby. Finally, they let me go down to intensive care. When I saw our baby for the first time I cried. The baby was all strung up with tubes and wires. Then they told me I couldn't nurse the baby ever, because I hadn't started to nurse him in the first three days and that it was too late. . . .

John said, "I didn't tell you: to test the baby, they took fluid from his spinal cord." It was a very difficult thing for the doctor, and if the needle had been just a little bit off, the baby would have been paralyzed for life. They were doing this just for a test. It turned out there was no reason to do it. But the doctor was proud and excited that he had done it without paralyzing the baby.

Finally, they decided there was nothing wrong with the baby. Just nerves, maybe! Then they admitted that what the urine tests had picked up was the extra anesthetic they had given me because they had had to wait for the right blood. John and I actually ran out of the hospital carrying the baby. A nurse ran after me saying, "We need to do one more blood test and we have to cut his toe and take some blood." John shouted, "Not another test! Poor kid! Have some pity, please!"

When we got home, the baby's spasm was still there. John and I took turns staying up at night and rubbed Chinese herbal medicine on Sean every two hours. We prayed. The spasm stopped after several months of this. [Four months after Sean's birth Jesse Ed Davis took a number of Polaroids of the infant with John and Yoko; in every picture he was surprised to see that the baby was a "blur."] Since then Sean has been a very healthy boy. John was always afraid to tell this story, about the hospital. . . . He was afraid they could still take Sean away from us.

There are several difficulties with this account. For one thing, Yoko was not rushed to the hospital on the morning of 9 October in the midst of a medical crisis. She entered the hospital several days before she gave birth and was resting comfortably in her room just two hours before the baby was delivered. Secondly, when the baby began twitching on the morning following the birth, Yoko herself went into "convulsions." According to John Lennon's interview with *Playboy* in November 1980:

"Somebody had made a transfusion of the wrong blood type into Yoko. I was there when it happened, and she starts to go rigid and then shake from the pain and trauma. I run up to this nurse and say, "Go get the doctor!" I'm holding on tight to Yoko while this guy gets to the hospital room. He walks in, hardly notices that Yoko is going through fucking *convulsions*, goes straight for me, smiles, shakes my hand, and says, "I've always wanted to meet you, Mr. Lennon, I always enjoyed your music." I start screaming: *"My wife's dying and you wanna talk about music!"*

Tremors, twitching, and kicking movements are symptomatic of withdrawal from narcotics. Obviously what the doctors concluded after they conducted the test of Yoko's urine was that she was a drug addict. Before they reached this conclusion, however, they must have thought the problem lay with the baby alone; hence, the spinal tap.

That narcotics were the issue was made clear by Yoko in an interview with Barbara Graustark in *Rolling Stone* of 1 October 1981. Asked about her and John's admitted use of the drug, Yoko responded:

> The trouble we had for being known to take heroin is incredible. For instance, when we had Sean, we had stopped taking drugs for a long, long time, because we really wanted a baby. When I had the baby, because of the Cesarian section, the doctors had to give me sedatives. And when Sean was born, he was shaking a little. It lasted, on and off, for about a month. But instead of thinking that sedatives had this effect, the hospital actually accused John and me of taking drugs during my pregnancy. They not only accused us, they threatened us, saying that they had to detain Sean in the hospital because we were not qualified parents. It was the most frightening moment of our life. They might have disqualified us as parents!

It should be recalled that Yoko had first become pregnant by John during the height of their initial period of heroin addiction. The next time she announced that she was pregnant was just two weeks after they had switched over from heroin to methadone at the London Clinic. Just four months after Sean was born, Yoko ran into Jesse Ed Davis, who had been summoned to New York to testify in the Morris Levy case. He recalls that Yoko rolled up his sleeve, inspected his arm, and then asked: "Know where we can get some?"

Yoko's denial that she had planned to deliver the baby by caesarian section on John's birthday is likewise contradicted by the testimony of her intimates. When Fred Seaman asked Lennon how Yoko had managed to have the baby on his birthday, John looked at his helper as if he were a fool and snapped: "Caesarian section. How do *you* think?" Fred, who was pretty ignorant about matters like pregnancy and childbirth, was still unsure. "At first I thought he was pulling my leg," he writes in his unpublished book, *Living with John.* "He often told outrageous lies with a completely straight face just to get someone going. But later Yoko admitted it, too. Sean was surgically removed from Yoko Ono more than a month prematurely so that when John died he could inherit his [John's] soul . . . both my Aunt Helen and my Uncle Norman confirmed that Yoko had discussed it with them beforehand. They had advised her against it. Helen was horrified, concerned that the child might die, but Yoko had consulted with her psychics, who assured her that the deed could be done without concern. She and John went to the hospital on an emergency basis to overcome the rather delicate question of medical ethics the procedure might raise."

The story of how John and Yoko were allegedly mistreated and abused at New York Hospital is one that Lennon alluded to often in the years to come. Marnie Hair remembered a night in the winter of 1978 when she, John, and Yoko were sitting in the kitchen of the Lennons' next-door neighbors, the well-known New York restaurateur, Warner LeRoy, and his wife, Kate. John, in an exceptionally good humor, gave the familiar yarn a startling new twist.

At the point in the story when the head of obstetrics accused John and Yoko of being drug addicts, Lennon raised his voice in tones of exasperated innocence and cried: "I was absolutely clean!" Then, pausing for effect, like a stand-up comic poised to deliver a throwaway line, he turned suddenly on his wife and asked off the cuff, "You weren't using, were you, Yoko?" The malicious innuendo hardly had a chance to register before John was off on his next bit. When the Lennons took their leave that evening, Marnie and the LeRoys compared notes. The crack about Yoko's "using" had gone by so fast that they had to confirm it to themselves. When they all agreed that he said it, they dismissed the insinuation as being just another example of John's wicked sense of humor.

At Thanksgiving, 1979, Yoko sent the four-year-old Sean to Hale House for Infants with a $10,000 contribution. Hale House is a facility that specializes in the treatment of babies born of drug-addicted mothers.

POSTPARTUM DEPRESSION

When Yoko came home from the hospital, John greeted her with a boyish display of affection. He made a big pile of fan mail for Mother and set beside it a little pile for Daddy. Then he crowned Yoko's stack with several pieces of jewelry. As she walked feebly into the apartment, still shattered by what she called her "brush with death," she was in no mood for third-grade tributes to Mommy. Taking one glance at John's offerings, she seized the jewels, ignored the mail, and tottered into the bedroom, where she got between the sheets with her lifeline, a white Princess phone.

The woman Yoko selected to rear Sean was a middle-aged Japanese nanny named Masako, who was solid as a rock and highly capable. Once Masako recognized that neither Yoko nor John could be relied upon to do anything for the baby, she took complete command and gave Sean the best care possible. Masako got along well with John, but her basic loyalty was to Yoko, outside whose door she would sleep on a tatami mat, unless Yoko was ill or emotionally disturbed. At such times Masako would sleep at the foot of Yoko's bed.

With the household firmly in the grip of the women, who conversed constantly in Japanese, a practice that angered Lennon, whose principal device for controlling reality was language, John found himself redundant in his own home. What's more, he resented Yoko's increasing absorption in everything but his own welfare. Until Sean was born, John had been the focus of the household. In effect, he had been Yoko's baby. Though he often complained that she would not allow him anything of his own, he reveled in the fact that she never left his side. Now the symbolic baby had been replaced by a real infant. So instead of being fulfilled by the birth of his son, John Lennon was profoundly depressed.

When his resentment reached the boiling point, he would take his customary revenge by publicly humiliating Yoko. One night at Ashley's, during supper with Tony King, Elliot Mintz, and Richard Ross, John turned on Yoko and began screaming, *"I want May! I want May! I want May! I don't want you!"* Despite every effort to calm him, he grew increasingly agitated, shouting: *"Get me May! Get me May!"* Then he pointed at Yoko and yelled at the men: *"Take her home! I don't want her! Take her home!"* Tony King helped Yoko out of the restaurant, while Richard Ross and Elliot Mintz took John off in search of May, who turned out to be in Florida on holiday. By January 1976 matters were taking a dangerous turn, when suddenly John discovered the medicine for all his ills.

Hanging out with Jesse Ed Davis one night in Led Zeppelin's lavish suite at the Plaza, John was startled by the sound of loud vomiting from the bathroom. Raising his head like a bird dog, he said: "Maybe he's got something left!" Instantly both men were in the loo, where they discovered the Zeppelin's drummer, John Bonham, down on his knees before the toilet.

When Lennon asked if he could have a hit, Bonham pulled the bag out of his pocket and gasped: "Here! Take it all! I don't want to ever see it again! Ech!"

John and Jesse poured out the fine China White and started horning it. No sooner did John get his nose full than he thrust his head into the toilet bowl next to Bonham, where they started puking in tandem. Jesse Ed, who holds his dope well, sat on the edge of the tub, staring in fascination at the strange spectacle presented by the stars. "They would look at each other and gag and vomit and make these horrible retching sounds." He chuckled. "Then they'd look at each other and laugh! With all this drool dribbling down their faces!" (Actually the joke wasn't all that funny. In 1980 John Bonham strangled to death while vomiting at the home of Jimmy Page, leader of Led Zeppelin.)

During the course of the night Jesse Ed introduced Lennon to the purveyor of all this ultrafine smack, James Wu. Known as the "Chinaman," Wu was a bespectacled little dude who loved rock stars and was generally to be found nodding out in their dressing or hotel rooms. Jesse Ed had first made Wu's acquaintance in New Orleans, while on tour with Rod Stewart and the Faces, which had its share of drug users. "We'd run out and needed a fresh infusion," recalled Jesse. "One of the guys was a stone junkie. He said: 'Well, I'll just call the Chinaman.' James Wu was out on the next plane. We sent the limo out to the airport to pick him up. He showed up with what looked like a loaf of Wonder Bread. There was an exchange of cash that you wouldn't believe! I'm talkin' about briefcases full. . . . Next morning we had to play the gig at the Superdome with Loggins and Messina and Fleetwood Mac. About ten o'clock in the morning I heard this knock on the door. It's James Wu. He's sick. He said [hoarse voice]: 'Listen, can I buy some of that back from you?' Stupid motherfucker! He'd sold it all to us. I said, 'Oh, man, you don't have to spend any money. I'll *give* it to ya.' He poured out a huge hit and slammed it right in front of me! That's the first time I ever saw anyone shoot any heroin. Before that it had always been sniffing and snorting. After that it just degenerated into—well, you can imagine."

John Lennon and James Wu were made for each other. Wu had the jam, and Lennon had the bread. Jesse Ed estimates that John's habit was soon costing him between $600 and $700 a day. What's more, Wu continued as Lennon's connection for years. In November 1978 Wu was living just a few blocks from the Dakota and going down to Chinatown every day to fetch up supplies for his two best customers, one of whom was the drug smuggler with whom he lived and the other, John Lennon.

John resumed his relationship with May Pang in January 1976, but instead of their meeting at Richard Ross's apartment two or three times a week, the frequency of these assignations diminished to once every two or three months. One of the problems was the tightening of Yoko's surveillance of John now that she was free of the distractions of maternity. Another obstacle was Ross's growing reluctance to act as go-between. Yet another reason why Lennon wasn't as keen as before was the sexually dampening effect of heroin. Though May could never figure out what had come over her lover, she observed during the next few years an astonishing change in the man she knew so well.

"The John I encountered in the[se] years seemed totally lacking in ambition," she remarked. "He seemed capable of concentrating for only short periods of time. Sometimes he would just sit there and look at me through glazed eyes. His spirit, his wit, his insight seemed to have disappeared, and he appeared to have no energy at all."

When John wasn't making love to May, he liked to reminisce about their good times together. He rarely said anything about his life with Yoko and Sean, but he always told May how much he missed her. That she was spending month after month looking for work in an industry that had blackballed her because of her relationship with Lennon didn't trouble John in the least. As always, he dismissed from his thoughts anything that might disturb his peace of mind.

There were some things that he could not so easily dismiss. During the first six months of 1976 he was hit by a dismaying sequence of surprising fatalities among his friends and family. The first shock was the news that Mal Evans had been shot to death by the police in Los Angeles. Like everyone who knew Mal, John could not comprehend how such a sweet, gentle, pacific man could come to such a violent end. The story is strange.

In 1975 Mal had received a divorce from Lil. As a result, he felt cut off completely from everything—the Beatles, his family, and England—that had once sustained him. Though he found a few odd jobs in the record industry, in which he enjoyed the courtesy title of producer, he worked only when his old bosses or other British pop stars were in town. When he drank, he would moan that nobody loved him for himself; he was just the Beatles' Mal. He did hold one trump, however, which he was about to play. During his years with the Beatles he had kept a diary, which, judged from the excerpts that appeared in the Beatles' fan mag, would have made interesting reading. Mal was making preparations to publish this valuable record when, on the night of 4 January 1976, he went crazy.

Grabbing a .30 caliber lever-action rifle, he chased Frances Hughes out of the house in which he was living with her and her four-year-old daughter. Terrified, Frances called the police, reporting that Mal had "flipped out" and "gone berserk" from taking pills. What alarmed her most was that he had retreated to an upstairs bedroom with her little girl. When the cops arrived, they hollered up the stairway for Mal to come out with his hands up. *"No!"* he shouted. *"You'll have to blow my head off!"* The officers, who had crept up to the second floor, kicked in the door and confronted their man with guns drawn. Mal was lying on a bed with the rifle in his hands.

"Drop the rifle!" shouted both cops.

Mal responded by taking aim at the cops. Instantly they opened fire. Mal was hit by four bullets that struck the side of his nose, his upper left chest, lower left chest, and lower left leg. When his weapon was examined, it was found to contain four live rounds, one in the firing chamber.

Next day Jesse Ed Davis met Frances Hughes at the house of Harry Nilsson. She was devastated and blamed herself for Mal's death. She said that he had been drinking and remarked despondently, "He probably doesn't even know he's dead, wherever he's at." An autopsy demonstrated that Evans was neither drunk nor drugged. He had a "therapeutic level of Valium" in his blood and an amount of alcohol equivalent to one drink. A burst of self-destructive despair had prompted him to commit suicide by provoking the police to act like a firing squad.

Mal's death was followed swiftly by those of many others in the Lennon circle. Late in March, John learned that his father was dying in a charity ward at Brighton. He called the old man and spoke to him for half an hour. Freddie was virtually speechless with the pain of stomach cancer, but he was comforted by the thought that after six years he and his son had finally been reconciled. Just two weeks before Freddie's demise, Paul's father expired. Then, in May, John learned that his fa-

vorite aunt, Mater, was dead. The effect of all these fatalities was especially profound on a man who had always been obsessed with mortality.

The obsession had certainly found plenty of reinforcement in Lennon's life. He had already lost most of the people who meant the most
to him: his mother, his father, his Uncle George, his stepfather, John
Dykins, his closest friend, Stu Sutcliffe, and his manager and lover,
Brian Epstein. John knew that *The Book of the Dead* teaches that the soul
must be prepared to die: if it is ripped violently from its seat, instead of
journeying securely to a higher karma, it is doomed to wander forlornly in the void. Mal Evans's death drove home to him the danger
posed by the sort of ending that John anticipated for himself—a sudden and violent death at the hands of an assassin. That was why Lennon had laughed so hysterically when he learned that Mal's ashes had
disappeared en route to England. As John saw it, "Mal's soul has
wound up in the dead letter office." Would John end up there, too? He
sought to assuage his mortal fears by embarking on a forty-day fast,
sustaining himself by drinking fruit juice.

All through the year 1976 John was beset with serious legal problems. Depositions and affidavits, office conferences and court appearances burdened his mind. His testimony in the second Morris Levy trial
in January extends to a couple of hundred pages in transcript, including a highly detailed account, that fascinated Judge Thomas P. Griesa,
of how he went about making records. Long and costly as was this
action, it was just a dustup in comparison with the epic battle the Beatles fought with Allen Klein.

When the Beatles dismissed Klein, they owed him a lot of money
because he had lent John, George, and Ringo $1 million out of his own
pocket as well as deferred all his billings, which over the years had
mounted up to $5 million in commissions and fees. When Klein recog-
nized that the three Beatles had no intention of paying even a penny of
what they owed him, he launched a tremendous legal barrage aimed at
the group collectively and individually, including all their companies in
Great Britain and the United States. Eventually forty attorneys were
working on these cases on both sides of the Atlantic, suing and coun-
tersuing. For four years, from 1973 to 1977, the litigation dragged on,
until the Beatles' legal fees reached an estimated $8 million. It paid for
them to hold out, however, because most of the money they spent on
lawyers would have been claimed by the British government in taxes.

Klein's suit against John Lennon was based on the oral contract
made on 27 January 1969, when John and Yoko engaged him to represent them personally, particularly with regard to Lennon's interest in
Northern Songs. Klein claimed more than $900,000 (20 percent of the
redemption value of Lennon's ATV stock) as the reasonable value of
the services he performed that year in the battle to win control of the

publishing company. By May 1976, when the issue was debated in a New York court, it was already becoming clear that the Beatles' strategy of fighting until, as John put it, "Klein will have run out of money," was not going to work. The day was fast approaching when the famous deadbeats would be forced to pay up.

Lennon's luck turned finally on 27 July 1976, when Immigration and Naturalization announced, as a follow-up to the finding of the three-judge panel, that he would be granted permanent resident's status in the United States. John faced the cameras for the first time since Sean's birth, holding up his green card (actually blue) and saying how happy he was to have won his long fight. Actually the only difference the ruling made in the way John lived was that now for the first time since August 1971 he could leave the United States confident that he would be readmitted. This new mobility was seized upon immediately by Yoko.

The rationale for John Lennon's mysterious 'round-the-world trip in October 1976 would be hard to explain to anybody who was not a subscriber to the eccentric system of Takashi Yoshikawa. Basically the directional man's idea is that by circling the globe in a westerly direction, the traveler blows his circuits clear and puts himself back on a new and positive footing with the universe. The result is supposed to be good luck and success in his next undertaking. At one time or another Yoko Ono sent herself and all her key men around the world, particularly when she was about to encharge one of them with some important responsibility. The most rapid of these circumnavigations was that made by John Green—in fifty-five hours! As John Lennon wasn't planning to do anything in particular, it's hard to understand why it was so important for him to girdle the globe. Perhaps Yoko was trying to snap him out of his prolonged depression. If that was her design, she couldn't have chosen a worse method, for John Lennon was a sensitive plant that resented any, even the sightest, change in his environment or routine. He was particularly averse to going anywhere alone; in fact, the last time he had gone anywhere by himself was way back in December 1960, when he had been booted out of Hamburg and come home carrying his amp on his back. Now Yoko dispatched John on a journey clear around the world—all by himself. It is highly unlikely that she could have persuaded him to perform such an unnatural act if she had not found the perfect lure. The reason he went was that she told him he could stop at Bangkok, where he would experience unimaginable pleasures in the famous red-light district.

When John Lennon proffered his gold American Express card to the reservations clerk at the Mandarin Hotel on Hong Kong island, he must have been dying to get up to his suite, where he could stretch out in bed and gaze peacefully at the telly, while listening to the radio and sipping a scotch and Coke. As one drink led to another, however, Lennon began to feel, lying drunk in this exotically decorated hotel suite on the other side of the world, rather like Alice when she stepped through the looking glass. Then he went to pieces.

"I played this game with myself in Hong Kong," Lennon told John Green when the trip was over. "I started taking off different layers of myself as if they were layers of clothing and setting them out about the room. I imagined my different subpersonalities as sort of ghostly forms. I would lie there listening to the radio and wait till one of my other selves came up and took control. Then I would project, see it sitting in a chair or standing by the door and talking to me. There were rules to this little game. Wherever I placed one of these ghosts, that's where he had to stay. Hanging on a hook in the closet, draped over the dresser, wherever. I kept them there for days. It was like creating my own haunted house.

"Every time I had successfully peeled off another layer I would go in and take a bath. After every bath I would take another drink. The baths were to help me relax, but they were also a test. If I found that I couldn't emotionally handle being in the water and had to jump right out of the tub again, then I knew that I hadn't managed to get that last layer off successfully.

"I don't mind telling you there were some very scary moments. Every little sound and shadow seemed twenty times louder and a hundred times larger. I was exposing myself, and I was afraid that someone, that invisible, unknown someone, maybe my long-absent [recently deceased!] father, would come storming into the room and catch me and I would die of fright.

"I played that game for three days before I left my rooms. I would wake up out of half sleeps and look around to see if all my mes were still draped around where they were supposed to be, and they were. My goal was to get them all off and leave them in the room and not come back. I thought I could escape them that way, but of course, it didn't work. They can walk through locked doors, you know. When I finally did go out, it was sunrise. I started down the street with just my passport and credit cards, thinking I had tricked those other mes and got away."

When he left the hotel, he was caught up in the flow of people making their way down to the Star Ferry, which crosses the harbor to the mainland at Kowloon. Once out on the water, he looked off the stern and caught sight of the Victoria Peak, the mountain that dominates the island. Instantly he flashed back to another beautiful morning, twenty years before, when he was visiting Mater in Scotland. He was walking on the heath, gazing at a distant mountain and feeling an extraordinary sense of inspiration.

When John stepped off the ferry at Kowloon, he felt exhilarated. Having freed himself of his spooks, he experienced a unique sensation: for the first time in his life, he was himself—*the real John Lennon!* But at the first turning John found his spooks lying in wait for him. Recognizing that he hadn't shaken them, he abandoned the effort to outrun his other selves. "I went back for my suitcase," he reported, "and said to the rest of my ghosts, 'Come on!' and we all went to Bangkok."

Unlike his visit to Hong Kong, which John discussed subsequently with several people, his stay in Bangkok was concealed from everyone save Yoko. Nevertheless, it's easy to imagine him in the city because the facilities offered the tourist are so familiar and because Lennon's tastes were so fixed. Bangkok, flush from the years when it was the American serviceman's favorite R&R resort, boasted at this time about a thousand massage parlors that were all whorehouses. When John walked out of the world-famous Oriental Hotel on the banks of the Chao Phraya River, he would have been accosted by steerers, who would have presented him with their comically garbled cards, reading, perhaps, "You haven't had your job blown until one of our girls does it."

Stepping into the first parlor that caught his fancy, he would have found a room stacked on one side with bleachers on which were lined up the girls, each one holding in her hands a placard with a big number. When he had picked the best numbers, the girls would check out the job with the mama-san and then lead him to a private room. Here they would disrobe, revealing themselves as tiny, undeveloped creatures with small breasts and virtually no pubic hair, very shy, very soft-spoken, talking almost in whispers, and utterly compliant. Having sex with these girls is the closest thing in the world to legally sanctioned child abuse, which is why Thai whores are the favorites of jaded men.

John's girls would be reluctant to do anything kinky but would be eager to whack him off, blow him, or have intercourse. The cost of the toss was about the price of a movie ticket. John might have also indulged himself with a Thai boy, who enjoys precisely the same reputation among sophisticated homosexuals as do the girls with straight men. Naturally there would be no problem about procuring his favorite marijuana, Thai stick, or in buying high-quality heroin at astonishingly low prices. As John was abroad for at least two weeks, spending only four days in Hong Kong, it is likely that he had a nice long layout in the cathouses of Bangkok. Some men wouldn't have come home.

When John got back to New York, in late October, he spent the last two evenings he would ever share with Pete Shotton. John made it clear to

Pete that the old Lennon was now going to be replaced by a new one, who was intent on cleaning up his act and becoming a model parent. John told Pete that he was off booze and tobacco, on a macrobiotic diet, and studying Japanese in anticipation of visiting Yoko's family in Nippon. He showed such exaggerated concern about waking the baby that he and his guest had to watch TV with the sound virtually inaudible.

Shortly after Pete's visit, John went back to smoking and drugs. He did take a six-week intensive course in Japanese at the Berlitz School, but he never developed the slightest capacity to communicate in that language. The only resolution to which he held fast was his determination to eat no more than 750 macrobiotic calories per diem. Eventually he went down to 120 pounds, lying most of the time in bed, a wealthy victim of malnutrition. His anorexia did prove one thing, however: by denying his body its natural craving for food, John Lennon proved that he was master in his own house.

THE LENNONS BUY A
LENOIR

"I don't want to go and I *won't!*" cried Lennon when John Green suggested his employer attend the annual meeting of Apple in November 1976. As John had paced the kitchen nervously, chain-smoking Gaulois, he spat out his detestation of the whole business scene. "I've stopped going to meetings and pretending to know what's going on, collecting solicitous smiles and pats on the back while they're screwing the shit out of me. No, thanks. *You go!*" When Green replied that John should not be represented by a card reader, Lennon barked, "All right, Yoko can go." Doggedly Green insisted that if Yoko went, John should also attend to lend her credibility. To this proposal John had answered scathingly, "I'll pin a note to her shirt. 'Dad gives permission.' How's that?" When Green came back with the old line "If you don't take care of your business, it won't take care of you," John replied bitterly, "It's taken care of me all right. Business and businessmen have cost me ninety percent of what I've ever made. Well, I've tried doing it myself and I've tried letting other people do it, and the result is the same. I lose money. If Yoko wants to handle it, that's her prerogative or yours, as the case may be. It can't get any worse, so I'm not risking anything, am I?"

Actually, there was no reason why John Lennon should have attended the Apple board meetings; none of the other principals appeared at the meetings because they dealt primarily with the implementation of the settlement agreement and the dissolution of Apple, matters best left in the hands of the lawyers and accountants. What *was* surprising about this tirade was the indifference it revealed in Lennon's mind about who represented him in his business affairs. This was a new and potentially dangerous development. Its onset can be associated with the dismissal of Harold Seider in April 1976. Ostensibly

Seider was fired because somebody had to take the rap for the Morris Levy fiasco, and Seider felt it was his duty to be the fall guy. Privately, however, he ascribed his dismissal to the machinations of Yoko Ono.

Seider had studied Yoko carefully during the three years he had been the Lennons' counselor. It was clear to him that Yoko felt that she should have enjoyed the success that John had attained. "How can that oaf be so successful," she would ask, "when I am so much more talented and educated?" Despite her low opinion of John, however, Yoko had no intention of divorcing him, because, in Seider's view, she saw him as the "bank," and Yoko was so concerned about money that the lawyer believed that if she ever went broke, she might kill herself. Now that she and John had agreed to make no more art, it was clear to Seider that Yoko's primary goal was to gain total control over the "bank," which put her on a collision course with Seider, whose goal it was to prevent anybody from gaining control over his client. Hence, Seider was doomed because Yoko "couldn't allow a moderating influence upon John, with him having an alternate opinion."

Dismissed without warning in March 1976, Seider received nothing by way of explanation except a notice, which read: "We are going to make a change. Hope you will understand. Call me." When Seider called Lennon, he did not get through. Nor was he the only man dismissed. There was a complete purge of all the Lennons' lawyers and accountants, whom Yoko must have viewed with distrust because they all had been hired on Seider's recommendation.

The next manager of the Lennons' affairs was Michael Tannen, Paul Simon's lawyer, a dynamic personality of the sort who gets involved in his client's life. Seider predicted that Tannen's tenure would be brief because the reticent Lennon would not find Tannen's style of management congenial. Tannen lasted, in fact, less than six months. Even so, in Seider's view, he performed a vital service because "Yoko was using him as an intermediate step in order to arrange complete control. She couldn't go from me to herself immediately. She had to get John conditioned to the idea that nobody was capable of doing the job but her." She also had to interject herself into the management of Lennon's business affairs because these were the heart of the "bank." Hitherto Yoko had never been allowed to meddle in Lennon's business because Seider had stood in her way. "Had she intruded herself overtly," he remarked, "both I and the lawyers would have resigned. She was not the client."

Unlike John Lennon, who was always alarmed and enraged at the prospect of confronting a roomful of men in business suits talking a language he could not comprehend, Yoko Ono experienced no qualms at first about plunging in over her head in matters about which she knew nothing. Rather, she appeared highly titillated by the prospect of stepping into her father's shoes. That she lacked the ability, training, and experience requisite for conducting business didn't trouble her in the least because she felt herself to be in possession of a secret weapon.

All her life, Yoko had been in search of a magic man, an *Arabian Nights* genie, who could realize all her dreams through his extraordinary ability and industry. Now she felt that she had such a prodigy in John Green. Nor was she without good reasons for holding Green in such high esteem. After all, when the tarot reader had come into Yoko's life, she had been the estranged middle-aged wife of an erratic pop star past his prime and desperate to regain his youth. Now, just eighteen months later, Yoko had recovered her husband, borne a child against tremendous odds, and stood upon the threshold of achieving total control of the Lennon fortune. That was the real reason Sean's middle name was "Taro[t]."

John Green demonstrated soon that he had an answer for everything. When Yoko panicked on the eve of her debut at the conference table, he told her to demand that the meeting be held in New York, where she would be on home ground. When she went into the conference room, Green was standing by at his phone. Every time Yoko had to make a decision, all she need do was excuse herself and duck into the nearest phone booth. There she could pour out her problems and receive in return the calm and reasonable voice of the "cards." When she complained that Lee Eastman patronized her, Green consoled her by pointing out how each of the "Apples" had taken her aside and dished the others. Knowledge like that, he assured her, was in itself a kind of power.

Power was, as Green knew well, the key term in Yoko's thinking; it was to enhance her power that she had turned to magic, and it was the sensation of powerlessness that drove her into her panic states and produced that blind clutching at straws, which Seider had interpreted as Yoko's faith that "if she tried everything, something would work." So when the meeting concluded, like most Apple meetings, without having achieved a thing, Yoko felt that she had triumphed.

The seal was set on her triumph on 10 January 1977, when Allen Klein, having finally gotten his money out of the Beatles, sought to heal the wounds in his relationship with Lennon by paying Yoko an extravagant compliment. Acknowledging her emotional last-minute appeal for a settlement, Klein told the press that Yoko had displayed "Kissinger-like ability in negotiation." Little did he anticipate that his absurd statement would be seized upon by the media and blown up into the myth of the Japanese banker's daughter with a genius for business—Yoko Millions, listed among the Fortune 500.

*   *   *

Once John Green became the Lennons' secret business adviser, he found himself managing a fortune but receiving the same compensation of $150 a week that he had when his duties were confined to reading over Yoko's diets. Obviously Green had to do something to remedy this injustice, but he knew his client well enough to recognize that she took service as her due and was not the type to reward her lieutenants according to their merits. One day, in the course of a routine reading for a new client, Green discovered the solution to his problem. Oddly, this new client was also named Green—Sam Green, a glamorous jet set art dealer.

Gabe Grumer, John Green's principal disciple, recalled that Green told him in October 1976 that he had just read for an art dealer who had tried repeatedly to reach Yoko Ono but could never break through. John Green had treated this revelation at first with feigned indifference; then he had decided to disclose to the dealer that he was Yoko's card reader. Instantly Sam Green had made a proposal. He had just learned about a Renoir—*"Jeune filles au bord de la mer"* ("Young Girls at the Seaside")—that was going for $200,000. Was there some way that John Green could introduce Sam Green to Yoko so that he could offer her the painting? If Sam made the sale, he would add $300,000 to the price, and they could split the profit down the middle. John Green was both tempted and troubled by the offer. He asked Grumer for his judgment on the ethics of the deal. Grumer replied that it was highly unethical, but faced with the same temptation, he would take the money. After all, Yoko's demands were excessive, and she never paid for what she got. What choice had Green but to reimburse himself as best he could?

Sam Green confirmed this story but said that shortly after concluding his deal with John Green, he bumped into the Lennons outside Bloomingdale's. Yoko recognized Sam from the old days, when he had worked at the Green Gallery for Dick Bellamy, the man who had introduced the Lennons to Jim Haristhis. She greeted Sam enthusiastically, asking him if he had anything special. He snapped open his attaché case and produced the transparencies of the Renoir.

The principal player now became Samuel Adams Green, Jr., suffering at thirty-six from a loss of momentum in what had been until recently a very exciting career. A wild shoot sprung from fine old American stock, Sam embodied his family's social graces as well as its fondness for travel and good taste in art. What he didn't share was its dedication to scholarship. Though his father was a professor of art history and his mother a professor of social psychology, Sam, Jr., was a college dropout who had begun his career as a useful tool in the hands of Andy Warhol. "Sam had society teeth and a beard and he especially liked society ladies who were dying not to be stuffy anymore," recollected Warhol in *POPism*. "He'd say things to them like 'There's this madman named Warhol who brings his entourage into your house and apparently makes an entire movie in an afternoon. You must meet him.' And since Sam knew about drag queens and offbeat things, the ladies thought he was fun. I met a lot of grand gals with Sam when we were out looking for fun." What Warhol was really looking for among the "grand gals" of mainline society was money, which Green helped him acquire by selling Warhol pictures to the ladies and by putting on the first Warhol retrospective when Sam was curator of the Contemporary Institute of the University of Pennsylvania at Philadelphia. Meantime, Sam shifted from wealthy society ladies to much bigger and more elusive game, like Greta Garbo, whom he wooed successfully through her lifelong companion, Cecile Rothschild, devoting enormous amounts of time and energy working on her behalf and even taking serious risks to win her trust and affection.

When Sam showed his transparencies to Yoko, he explained that the famous coloratura soprano Lily Pons had just died and left her niece this Renoir, worth half a million and sure to appreciate in the next decade to twice that amount—a prediction that proved accurate. Yoko promptly asked John Green to read on the painting; he found in the cards a complete confirmation of Sam Green's representations, concluding that the picture was a good investment. The only impediment to the sale was the fact that most of the Lennons' money was tied up in England and could not be taken out of the country. Sam Green solved that problem in a jiffy. He said they could ship the picture to London, where the sale could be consummated, payment being made in impounded pounds. Then, after a cooling-off period, during which the picture would be hung in a museum, a way could be found to smuggle the work back into the United States. Not only would the Lennons have made a potentially profitable investment, but they would have transformed their untransferable money into an American asset. In fact, the deal could be sweetened by arranging a large overpayment, with the seller rebating the money through a Swiss bank, the Lennons to receive their refund in dollars.

Yoko was delighted with the plan, but she didn't want to take Sam Green's evaluation without confirmation. She started calling up art experts, most of them people whom Sam Green suggested. One authority recalled Sam's calling him and saying that he was selling Yoko a Renoir worth $200,000 for $500,000. When Sam begged the expert to endorse the latter figure, the art scholar said that he would do nothing of the kind. Yoko called shortly afterward and announced, "I'm going to buy a painting for an investment, and I would like your opinion about it. It's a Lembrandt."

"Mrs. Lennon," replied the expert, "don't you mean a Lenoir?" When it came time to pronounce on the picture's value, the authority sidestepped the issue, saying, "Oh, Mrs. Lennon, it's so hard to set a value on art."

While Yoko was calling around to make sure that she wasn't buying a lemon, Sam Green was working desperately hard at ironing out all the technical details. The lawyer for the Lily Pons estate kept demanding ironclad guarantees. The Lennons' accountant, Eli Garber, and their lawyer, Tannenbaum, also threw some blocks into the path of the deal. Every day Sam talked for hours not just with these people but with Yoko herself, with whom he began to build up a very close relationship by telephone.

On 9 December 1976 Sam Green flew to London and completed the deal for the Renoir. The Lennons were delighted to have their useless pounds converted into a masterwork, to which they obtained possession within a year, the painting hanging meantime in the Walker Gallery in Liverpool. The two Greens felt that not only had they made a great score but they had laid the foundation for their future fortunes. The only person who was displeased was Wendy Wolosoff, who was shocked and disillusioned by her spiritist lover's abrupt plunge into the depths of mercantile scamming. As soon as the holidays ended, Wendy demanded that John Green get out of her apartment—and her life. Nevertheless, when the first money came through from Switzerland, Sam Green drew Wendy a check for $500 and sent it to her with a covering note dated 9 January 1977. "Dear Wendy," he wrote. "This is only a small expression of my thanks for your friendship and support during the long trial which resulted in our getting rich. I hope you enjoy your part. You deserve it."

Each of the Greens spent his winnings doing what was dearest to his heart. Sam Green's greatest love was for discovering and decorating uniquely desirable residences. He already owned a sixteenth-century palazzo in Cartagena on the coast of Colombia. Now he crowned his real estate acquisitions with a magnificent parlor-floor apartment at 15 East 75th Street, just a few doors off Fifth Avenue. This town house had such an imposing drawing room that Sam decided to decorate it in the splendid style of Louis XIV. The adjacent room he projected as a vaulted picture gallery and the rear of the flat as a duplex bedroom complex. Sam made light of the cost of the renovations. He knew he had struck gold with the Lennons.

John Green was a stranger to money. The previous year he had earned $15,000. Now he had $150,000 in cash! He began throwing his loot around like a sweepstakes winner. He gave one party after another and treated his friends generously. His greatest beneficence was shown toward his disciple Gabe Grumer, who aspired to own a small business. Green gave Grumer $40,000 to open a health food store in Greenwich Village called Gabe's. The health food fad was just beginning in New York, and Green figured on getting in on the ground floor and building up on the boom, until he had not just a store but a restaurant, a company that distributed unpasteurized milk, and a farm that grew organic produce.

John Green also obtained the use of the Lennons' loft at 496 Broome Street, which had been unoccupied since May 1973, when Joko Productions was dissolved. The two-story building consisted of a high-ceilinged ground floor with a long staircase climbing one wall to the mezzanine, which projected forward from the rear wall about half a floor, its center being cut out to allow the dim radiance from a skylight to fall to the ground floor. Beside this light well on the mezzanine, John Green positioned his two indispensable items of furniture: his gigantic bed and his sorcerer's altar. The bed was a platform eleven feet long and eight across. The altar, erected against the back wall, was a three-inch-thick slab of slate, six feet long and two and a half feet wide, resting upon a welded steel frame. Over the altar hung by black chains a wooden chandelier, which illuminated a cross carved from a tree blasted by lightning. Flanking the cross were five plaster saints of goodly size that had been taken out of a decaying Roman Catholic church on West Broadway. (Green delighted in the thought that anybody who saw the altar—like the Irish cop who came around once to investigate the fall of a thirty-pound stone through the skylight—would assume that Green was a devout Catholic.) When Green's subsequent housemate Jeffrey Hunter brought in to clean out the place two laborers who happened to be Brazilian, one man glanced at the altar and grunted to the other, "Macumba."

MAKING MAGIC

On 16 January 1977 Yoko was on the phone to Sam Green: "You can do *anything*! Charlie Swan says you can do anything! You are our *marvel* man! Now you've got to drop everything and focus on this! It's the *most* important thing to John. Now that he's got his green card, he wants to be at the inauguration!"

Sam Green was aghast. This was Sunday. The inaugural festivities would begin Wednesday. It was too late! "Yoko," he gasped, "I've only been to Washington twice in my whole life! I don't know a single politician! I wouldn't know where to begin!" The more Sam squirmed, the harder Yoko pressed him. After he had exhausted himself, he hung limp and silent for a moment.

Yoko seized the opportunity to close the discussion. "You'll manage!" she pronounced emphatically—and hung up.

On Monday morning Sam dialed limousine services only to discover that all the limos had been reserved weeks or even months in advance. He called hotels and found them booked solid. He implored Ports of Call, his travel agent, to make a special effort. It said the airlines were offering only standby. Imagine John and Yoko on standby!

On Tuesday, when Sam arrived at the Ginger Man to have lunch with his friend Janie Lahr (the daughter of the famous comedian Bert Lahr), he was boiling with rage. "Those goddamned Lennons are driving me mad!" he ranted. "Their latest thing is that they want to go to the inaugural tomorrow. There's no way it can be arranged at the last minute!" Then he spilled out the nightmare of the resourceful social connector who can't get his foot in the door.

After he had blown himself out, Janie Lahr said: "You're really upset, aren't you? You know, I may be able to help you! One of my best friends is Robert Lipton, the TV producer. He's producing the inaugural show on CBS. When we finish here, I want you to go straight home and wait for a call. If there is anything I can do, you'll know this afternoon."

Sam was pacing his floors when the phone rang. A calm female voice announced that she was calling from the office of Robert Lipton. All arrangements were being made to fly Sam and the Lennons to Washington to see the show the following night. Hotel accommodations would be provided at the Watergate, and the party would have tickets to the inauguration, Thursday, as well as to the balls that night. A limousine would be awaiting their arrival at the airport in Washington and would remain at their disposal until departure on Friday morning.

"*Magic!* I made magic for them!" cried Sam, when he thought back on the coup. Then he offered the only possible explanation for his last-minute success: "They must have been saving it all for Haile Selassie!"

John Lennon was blissfully stoned when he arrived at JFK to catch National's 4:05 flight to Washington. As he sat in the first-class cabin chuckling at this last-minute triumph, he kept nodding out, his discourse sloping off on some strange inconsequent track as he lost consciousness. Sam Green must have shown his bewilderment because the next time John came out of his stupor, he fed Sam a typical Lennon put-on. "I suppose you're wonderin' why I'm so drowsy," drawled John. "It's because me adrenal glands are all fucked up. It's from drinkin' twenty or thirty cups of espresso a day. I've got to cut it down." Then, lips wreathed in a smile, he nodded out again.

When the party arrived at the Watergate, John said he had to take a nap. He took quite a few naps in the following days, some of them in public.

That night Sam Green and the Lennons got dressed in formal evening attire and repaired to the John F. Kennedy Center for the Performing Arts. Yoko wore a white strapless gown by Bill Blass with massive chains of gold and jewels about her neck and her hair done up, at Sam's urging, in a chignon. John threw over his dress suit a black cape lined with white satin and combed his hair back from his forehead like a Romantic poet. After witnessing a very political variety show, they went backstage with the other VIPs to greet President-elect Carter. Sam was tickled by the fact that he was greeted warmly by so many celebrities, whereas virtually no one said hello to John and Yoko. Lauren Bacall, the Lennons' neighbor at the Dakota, hailed Sam effusively and embraced him affectionately, while tossing the Lennons a breezy "Hi, John and Yoko!" When Lennon was presented to Carter, the dialogue was on the coy side. "Maybe you remember me," said John— "I'm an ex-Beatle." The President remembered—and that was that.

Ironically, the straitlaced Baptist provided the occasion for the first great cokehead inaugural. Wherever the Lennons went, they found flocks of busy bees buzzing over fields of white pollen. The Lennons were very tight-nostriled as they gazed at all the happy tooters. They were not going to jeopardize their newly found respectability by doing drugs in public.

The next afternoon brought the event for which everyone had gathered in Washington, the inaugural ceremony. John and Yoko had no interest in the ritual or in the President's address. They were as resolutely nonpolitical now as formerly they had been gung ho. During the hours when the nation watched the historic event, the Lennons entertained a party of celebrities at the Lion d'Or, Washington's most fashionable French restaurant. The luncheon was Sam Green's idea, and it went off beautifully, receiving the endorsement of notables like Warren Beatty and Jack Nicholson. That night, instead of attending a ball, the Lennons and Green got into their limo and toured the city's monuments, which were illuminated and looked beautiful against the clear night sky.

John returned to New York, exhausted but exhilarated, proud to have been as welcome to the current administration as he was anathema to the previous government. Indeed, he chattered on like a kid just back from the circus. Proudly he displayed his engraved invitation from the White House, with its gold-embossed seal. He even invited the neighbors, Kay and Warner LeRoy, to view a tape of the show, on which John and Yoko were flashed a couple of times. It had all turned out a nice job of public relations.

Yoko arrogated to herself all the credit for the inaugural expedition, but she was impressed by Sam Green's ability to work wonders at her command. About a month later, in the course of their daily phone call, Sam got on the subject of his house at Cartagena. He had stumbled upon this sixteenth-century seaport, once the haven of the Spanish treasure fleet, some years since and become enthralled by its air of undisturbed antiquity. Behind the picturesque walls and towers of the fortified harbor lay dilapidated palaces, plazas, and cathedrals. Sam envisioned the place becoming the latest rallying point for the jet set, a Caribbean St.-Tropez. After a few days' shopping he had bought a noble house, with a ballroom, dungeon, and tower looking out to sea. Fearful of what might happen to the property during his lengthy absences, he decided to enlist the aid of the district's most powerful *bruja,* who turned out to be a formidable old hag named Lena. Standing almost seven feet tall and displaying fingers twice the normal length, with an extra joint at the end, she spoke English with a lilting Jamaican accent because she was a native of Providencia, an island off the coast, long a possession of Great Britain.

Before Sam could proceed further, Yoko burst out: "You know a witch! I must meet her!"

Delighted to be of service, Sam assured Yoko that nothing could be easier. All she had to do was jump aboard one of the thrice-weekly flights on Avianca, and in four hours she could be face-to-face with Lena the Witch. Yoko made light of the journey. What really concerned her, she said, was assuring that the meeting be held under the most favorable auspices. Soon she and Sam were engaged in tedious and interminable calculations, as Yoko struggled, with the aid of her book of magic numbers, to determine the ideal moment for this occult encounter. As it turned out, on the weekend Yoko coveted, the witch was booked. She had to journey into that fearsome region, the Guajira Peninsula (where Indians clad in G-strings and toting machine guns conduct much of Colombia's trade in contraband) to attend a fourteenth-month pregnancy—in other words, a demon birth! When Yoko was informed of this awesome fact, she brushed it carelessly aside. "Why can't she help me and the pregnant woman at the same time?" she demanded. When Sam got a call through to Cartagena, he received a disappointing reply. Lena said that she could not accommodate Yoko because the same spirits would be needed for both clients and the fourteenth-month pregnancy had priority.

The final plan called for Sam to go down to Cartagena first, to be followed on 1 March 1977 by Yoko and her psychic bodyguard, Charlie Swan. So far as Yoko knew, this was to be the first meeting between Sam and Charlie, whose real name, John Green, she now disclosed to Sam, pledging him in the same breath never to reveal this secret to Lennon.

Yoko's primary motive, according to John Green's conversation with Jeffrey Hunter, was to bind John Lennon more closely to her. She feared that his deepening depressions would drive them apart again.

John Green published years later a long and amusing account of this trip, in which he depicts himself as acting with his customary coolness and address. The truth is that he was frightened by the prospect of journeying into the heart of darkness to meet an authentic witch. At four in the morning on the day of his departure, he was closeted with a female astrologer to whom he confessed that he was feeling paranoid. As troubling to him as the witch were the likely effects of social intimacy with Yoko because Green set great store by his air of psychoanalytic detachment. As the predawn consultation proceeded, he rehearsed all the poses he might adopt, the lines he could run, the ploys he could employ. As he performed, his voice assumed the purring tone of Vincent Price, but his anxiety betrayed itself in embarrassing little jokes. He told the astrologer that they must be up, showered, and ready to do business at 9:00 A.M. "Then," he jested, "you can use your riding crop as much as you want. Don't worry about the marks— I'll say I'm a monk."

When Yoko Ono and John Green walked out of customs at Cartagena airport that afternoon, they expected to be picked up in a limousine and whisked off to Sam Green's house. Imagine their shock when they were mobbed by about fifty shouting, gesticulating camerawielding reporters and photographers! They had run head-on into the annual film festival, whose press corps recognized Yoko instantly and assumed the giant man beside her was John Lennon! Though the sponsors of the festival knew better, they decided to capitalize on the press's misconception. No sooner had Yoko and Green disappeared through the gate of Sam's house than a crowd began to form outside. The reporters demanded to know when John and Yoko were going to hold a press conference. When no date was announced, the papers voiced their indignation in headlines: JOHN AND YOKO DO NOT APPEAR AT OPENING OF FILM FESTIVAL . . . JOHN AND YOKO DO NOT ATTEND MAYOR'S RECEPTION. The situation was becoming alarming. Yoko had assumed her magic journey would be cloaked in impenetrable secrecy. Now she had the whole South American press corps yapping at her heels. Finally, Sam Green announced that a press conference would be held the next day. When the press showed up, he explained that the conference would have to be postponed yet another day because Yoko's hairdresser had failed to arrive—an excuse that would easily be honored south of the border.

Though Sam was willing to handle the press, he wanted no part of the sessions with Lena. John Green, for his part, had been mastering his fears as he prepared to confront Lena. He had determined to adopt a pose that would combine the proper respect for the witch with unmistakable signs that he himself was no novice in the black arts. Bedecking his chest like Joseph Lukach with beads and amulets and drawing himself up to his full height, the massive Green strode forth to encounter the black sorceress. When she appeared, he was astonished to see that she was a head taller than he, and her costume consisted only of a brightly patterned rag about her head with more of the same gaudy stuff wrapped around her chest and riding up her narrow hips like a miniskirt. Instead of greeting Green with ceremonial mumbo jumbo, Lena caroled, "Hello, gentleman!" The ponderous Green extended his arms and presented the witch with the gift of a statue of St. Lazarus, the keeper of the gates. When Lena saw the cheap plaster saint proffered in a shoebox, she turned up her nose in obvious contempt for the offering.

"How many magics do you know with a toad?" she challenged.

"Seven," Green ventured.

"*I* know seventy-five!" shot back the witch.

It was clear from the jump who was going to dominate this situation.

The meeting of Lena and Yoko could be a model for all professional-client relationships. Without wasting a moment, both parties declared themselves frankly. Lena said: "What do you want Lena to do for you, child?"

Yoko answered just as directly: "Everything!" Just to show what that entailed, she dug into her costly alligator bag and pulled out a list, which she ran down like a character in a Gilbert and Sullivan patter song. "I have a lot of enemies," she began, "and they are always trying to hurt me and curse me, so I'll need some protection from that. Maybe it would be better if you protected the whole family because it's a very dangerous situation for all of us. And you should be sure to protect me from my husband as well as my enemies because sometimes he can be dangerous, too, and I need to be protected from him. Then there's health. Our baby has terrible health, and there is nothing the doctors can do, so they try to tell me nothing is wrong; but he does get sick sometimes, and it would be good if that didn't happen. Can you do that? Good. And the other thing is career. I think you should do something for my career and my husband's career separately, and then something for our career together, but not for his career with anyone else. And also, my friends here in the house, Sam Green and Charlie, are so important to me. I don't know what I would do without them. Sam has so many other friends; maybe I won't be able to get him to do things for me when I need him. Could you make him somehow a sort of slave of mine during his lifetime so I can rely on him? Can you please do that? And also Charlie—could you arrange it so that he works for me and only me? And the other thing is this thing inside me that I want you to get out [an IUD]. The doctor put it there; but it's foreign, and it causes me pain all the time. No one believes me that it hurts; but it does, and I want you to stick your hand inside me and take it out!"

Lena had gone along with all of Yoko's requests up to this point. Now she displayed a serious reservation. Glancing down at her huge hand, with its extra joints, and then up at little Yoko, Lena repeated incredulously: "You want me to stick my hand in you and grab hold on this thing you have in there and pull it out?"

"Yes," urged Yoko. "Exactly! To heal me, you understand?"

"Well, child," replied the witch, "I can stick my hand into you all right, but I don't think that's going to heal you. I think that's going to *kill* you!" Even Yoko had to take no for an answer.

During the days that followed, the old witch displayed the full resources of her art. She poured jars of consecrated water over Yoko while she stood in a tin tub. Then she pranced about her client, her big splayed feet slapping the tiles of the inner courtyard as she uttered the piercing cries of jungle birds and animals. Giving Yoko unpalatable potions to drink and unintelligible spells to recite, Lena also operated upon the combs and underwear that belonged to John and Sean. (The witch failed to divine that John never wore underwear.) Finally it was time to consummate all these spells by making a living sacrifice and signing a pact with the devil. For Lena was not a "white" witch. She was the real thing—a practitioner of black magic. There was no knowing what she planned to do to seal the bond with Lucifer. All she would say was that a witch's moon was nigh, and they had to make ready for the sacrifice.

"What sacrifice?" Yoko kept demanding.

To which the old witch would reply: "Don't be silly, girl. We've got to make a sacrifice with the blood of an innocent to the one who has the power."

"I thought *you* had the power," answered Yoko in her most innocent little-girl manner.

"Magic isn't something anybody *has*," answered the witch wisely. "Magic is what passes through."

By the last night in Cartagena Yoko and John Green had gotten involved in a serious dispute. When she had confessed that she was terrified of taking the final step, he had advised her not to take it. But it turned out that she was just as frightened of not doing what she was told because she feared that if she copped out at the last minute, the witch's curse might boomerang on Yoko. Money was also a consideration, for if Yoko didn't complete the ritual, how would she justify its expense to her husband? As Green struggled to solve these problems, he was astonished to hear Yoko's own solution. "If I did the ritual but I changed some little part of it," she suggested, "that wouldn't be like doing it, would it?" In other words, Yoko Ono wanted to cheat the devil.

When John Green saw where this argument was leading, he read Yoko the Occult Riot Act. If she had no faith in what she was doing, he lectured, she should abandon the whole business and, if need be, lay the blame for the fiasco on him. In fact, Yoko was already starting to blame Green for getting her into this predicament, but the lure of the witch's promise to get Yoko everything on her list of wishes proved irresistible. When the waning moon reached its final phase, sacred to Hecate, Yoko agreed to complete the ritual.

That night Lena and John Green had a good talk as they waited for the moon to signal the moment of magical consummation. When Green brought up Yoko's apprehensiveness, Lena ascribed it to a spirit that possessed Yoko. "She has a little devil in her," explained the witch, "a little devil who is always hungry, always greedy for more and more, and the more you give him, the hungrier he gets. That's a wicked little devil to have inside you." When Green demanded to know how the witch would deal with the little devil, Lena replied: "I give that devil all he wants and more. I think that I can make him swell up so much he will burst and die . . . I'll kill him with kindness, which is a very good way to kill a devil."

Yoko approached the witch's altar, clutching John Green's arm. As the smiling Lena beckoned and cooed, "Closer, child, come closer," the terrified Yoko edged forward, impelled to the last by the hope of having all her desires fulfilled. The final step, however, was sinister. Green wrote:

> Yoko reached the edge of the little pile of debris that Nora [as John Green disguised "Lena"] had chosen for her stage. "Now, child, it is time to sign." Her eyes directed Yoko's to the altar and a fettered dove that lay beside the sputtering flame. The old witch slipped her long powerful fingers into a pocket and removed a folded piece of paper, the contract. This she opened with deliberate care and placed on the altar as if for the dove to read. Its surface was covered with a crazy-quilt pattern of writing that I recognized as a witch's alphabet, the sort used in Elizabethan times. Again the bony fingers dipped into a pocket, this time retrieving what appeared to be a small sharpened stick. One long arm reached out and swept up the dove. Powerful fingers held back the wings and forced its tiny head downward. Nora rolled back her eyes and prayed her prayers of sacrifice. Suddenly, deftly, the hand with the stick moved and did its work. The dove had no warning and made no outcry as the instrument pierced the back of its neck and erased its brain. Slowly Nora removed the point and held the victim outward. "Sign, child, sign now."
>
> "I want Charlie to do it."
>
> "Sign, child!" The tone was more demanding.
>
> "But . . ." Yoko was clearly panicking. Suddenly, she turned to me. "Charlie, do it! Please, Charlie, I'll take care of you, John and I will! Just do this for me. Sign it."

John Green took the proffered pen and signed the document in blood. When he was done, Lena smiled with satisfaction and dismissed her clients. As Green and Yoko returned to their quarters, Yoko sought to reassure her proxy that no harm would befall him. "You have lots of protections," she insisted. "That was very brave signing your name like that."

"My name?" responded Green. "Why Yoko, I didn't sign *my* name!"

"But you must have!" burst out Yoko. "You had to! Otherwise, I won't get the things I wished for! . . . Whose name was it? Charlie, you didn't. Not *my* name! Not mine!"

As Yoko cried out in terror, John Green turned off into the shadows so she couldn't see his smile. "I decided," he confided, "that I would wait awhile before I answered that particular question."

The following morning Yoko and John Green set off on their return journey. No sooner had they departed than Lena was banging at Sam Green's door, shouting, "Where's my money?" When Sam asked what price had been agreed upon, Lena told him it was "sixty thousand." What she had meant originally was sixty thousand pesos, but Yoko had misconstrued this demand and committed herself to paying sixty thousand *dollars*. On the other hand, Lena had promised to give Yoko a "money bush," a plant that produced banknotes like leaves. When she laid this unpromising bit of vegetation on Sam, he discreetly dumped it and bought Yoko a more interesting-looking plant when he returned to New York. On his next trip to Colombia, Sam was toting a huge stack of hundred-dollar bills. Receiving her fee coolly, Lena asked, "When is my baby, Yoko, coming back?"

Yoko and John Green should have been back in New York four hours after they took off from Cartagena, but this short hop was transformed into a long and embarrassing ordeal because Yoshikawa, that master of indirection, had warned Yoko that the route from Cartagena to New York posed serious dangers. The only way to offset this taboo was to return to New York from the opposite direction—that is, from the north instead of the south—and to spend twice as long at the northern point of departure as she had at the southern point of arrival. Translated into practical terms, this prescription meant that Yoko had to take a flight to Bogotá and from there to Los Angeles and on to Anchorage, Alaska. Once she had reached the far north, she was obliged to remain there for two full weeks before she could fly home.

When Yoko and John Green got off the plane at Bogotá, one of the world's greatest drug-trafficking centers, they were detained by tough Colombian customs officials, who had read all about this famous couple's suspicious behavior at the Cartagena Film Festival and were aware of John Lennon's troubles with the American authorities because of his drug conviction. The Colombians were no fools. They knew what famous gringos like this pair were usually doing in their country. They ordered Yoko and Green to step into separate rooms for questioning. Yoko was not prepared with a plausible story to account for her presence in Colombia. Obviously she could not tell these scowling officials that she had just signed a pact with the devil. Nor could she explain why she hadn't attended the film festival. Customs ordered a strip search. Yoko was compelled to disrobe in the presence of a female agent, who then slipped a vinyl glove on her hand, coated it with K-Y jelly, and thrust it into Yoko's orifices. What Lena the Witch feared to do, Colombian customs did without hesitation.

After this shocking episode Yoko and John Green proceeded on their good-luck journey to Anchorage. When they arrived, they holed up in a dreary motel, where Yoko spent half her time on the phone and the other half listening to Green read on the conversation she had just concluded. As Yoko rarely slept for more than two hours at a time, the relentless routine of calls and readings was sustained almost twenty-four hours a day. By the time they got back to New York, John Green was gaga. Sam Green, whom Yoko rang up immediately to pour out her woes, could barely contain his laughter.

SAVING FACE

After a lifetime of being a black sheep in Japan, Yoko Ono decided in 1977 to become a snow-white ewe. Her plan was to return to the homeland and reclaim her place in society on the strength of her restabilized marriage, her new son, and her recent commitment to business. As was often the case when she undertook to fulfill her personal designs, she cloaked her intentions in the self-sacrificing language of duty. She told John that he would be seriously remiss as a father if he did not give Sean an opportunity to lay claim to his "heritage." After all, the boy was as much Japanese as he was English. (Actually he was being reared exclusively as an American.) If he were not taken at an early age to his mother's country, he would not acquire the necessary acculturation. Even more important, he would not be acknowledged as a full-fledged member of the Ono clan, which would mean that he could not inherit his share of the family's jewels and real estate. To avert these grave dangers, it was necessary that the Lennons make preparations immediately to spend five months in the Orient, living in the highest style, which would cost, of course, a vast amount of money. Fortunately all the cost could be written off as a business expense.

Though John usually followed Yoko's lead without argument, he was very skeptical about this Japanese expedition. Basically he didn't want to go, and if he went, he didn't want to remain there nearly half a year. John's six-week course at Berlitz wouldn't enable him to speak Japanese, and the trip would deprive him of summer at the shore. What's more, even though he was not a student of Japanese civilization, he could see that a lot of Yoko's arguments were poppycock. Two-year-olds don't require acculturation, and even if Sean were older, how could he possibly pass for Japanese when he lived in New York with his English father and his totally Westernized mother? No matter what John thought, however, he could not hold out long against Yoko. So with deep misgivings he prepared himself for this latest leap into the unknown.

Actually, as John discerned, the real issue lay not with Sean but with Yoko. What had gotten into her, he demanded, that she should suddenly want to show off in front of the very people whom she had regarded all her life with scorn and contempt? The answer was twofold: On the one hand, Yoko was determined, now that her marriage was back together again and she was the mother of a male child, to assert herself against her mother, who had always patronized her and disparaged her as a maverick. On the other hand, Yoko was in the process of altering her identity, as she exchanged the role of the artist for that of the businesswoman. Business was traditional in her family, and now, for the first time in her life, she would be defining herself in her family's terms. So on both grounds what she was seeking in Japan was not so much Sean's as her own heritage.

Yoko spent the whole spring making preparations for her summer campaign. Some measures, like adjusting the family's diet, were sensible, if unnecessary. Most of her activity, however, was based on how she anticipated they would be received. She expected that every time she and John appeared in public, they would be besieged by reporters and photographers, just as they had been years before. As they would be constantly onstage, it was necessary that they prepare themselves like movie stars on a personal promotion tour. The first requirement was a fresh costume every day because nothing would look worse than being seen twice in the same clothes. Five months of daily changes for three people translates into a Fujiyama of rags. Yoko insisted on buying everything in New York, but no matter how much she purchased she could never get enough. Finally, as she saw her time running out, she commissioned John Green to finish the shopping and then hold himself ready to dispatch reinforcements for the Lennons' wardrobe as required.

After wardrobe, the next most important consideration was accommodations. Yoko insisted that the family be lodged in Tokyo's finest guest quarters, either the Imperial or the Presidential Suite of the Hotel Okura. The only difficulty with this costly decision (these suites with their attendant rooms rented for about a thousand dollars a day) was that such prize accommodations were sought by many wealthy people and companies, which sometimes booked years in advance. Yoko's challenge, therefore, was to arrange her visit so that every time the family was obliged to vacate their suite, she could make it appear that they were leaving voluntarily because they had other plans. As for what the family was going to *do* in Japan for five months, Yoko hardly gave the matter a thought. She knew what *she* was going to do.

Needless to say, every step in these elaborate preparations was checked by Yoko's psychics. A tarot hot line was installed in the kitchen of Apartment 72, where John Green slept every night that summer on a sofa so that he would not miss Yoko's midafternoon call, which came through in New York at about three in the morning. Toshikawa calculated that the moment most favorable for the departure of John, Sean, Masako, and Nishi Fumiya Saimaru, John's gofer, would be at the end of the first week in May, with Yoko to leave five days later. He ordered them to make their final approach to Tokyo from the south, which meant that they would have to pass through their destination, going on to Hong Kong, where they would all gather and then fly back to Tokyo together.

John endured the long, tedious journey to the Orient well. Nishi's photos of Lennon in Hong Kong show him looking youthful and happy as he leads his dolled-up toddler through the grotesqueries of the Tiger Balm Garden. But when the whole family arrived at Tokyo, there was a slipup at the Okura, and the Lennons had to spend their first days in less desirable accommodations. Aghast at this bad omen, Yoko soon discovered that much worse things lay in store for her.

She had arranged a big press conference without troubling to inform John. When she broke the news to him, he refused to meet the press. A desperate volley of messages flew back and forth on the tarot hot line, with John Green clamoring to know what she had planned to tell the press. Yoko had promised the reporters a big scoop, which turned out to be a pipe dream about the Lennons writing a Broadway musical. After much unpleasantness John was persuaded to tell the press that at some future date he *might* write a show. The Japanese press was very disappointed and gave the Lennons a distinctly cool reception.

No matter. The issue would be joined the first time Yoko spoke to her mother. Yoko was counting on receiving this call rather than making it herself. But as she waited for this gratifying moment, days went by. Finally, growing apprehensive, Yoko consulted with Green. He advised her to make the first advance. Reluctantly she agreed. The mother, who had always been a match for Yoko, was well prepared. When asked why she had not phoned, the old lady replied that she had no idea that Yoko had arrived; in fact, she had assumed when she didn't hear from her daughter that the trip had been postponed. As the season was already well advanced, she had decided that she could no longer delay in responding to the numerous invitations she had received from friends requesting her to be their guests in the country. Consequently, she was going out of town that very day and would not be able to see John and Yoko till August.

Yoko countered by saying how dreadful it was that they should have come all the way to Japan just to see Mrs. Ono and now must wait two months to accomplish their purpose. Did she not realize what an inconvenience this would cause John, who was such a busy man? The mother replied that she assumed John was so rich that he didn't have to work and that Yoko could travel back and forth from America to Japan as easily as her sister and her husband. There was a solution to their problem, however. Just to show John that the family was not indifferent to his arrival, Mrs. Ono would send to Tokyo Reiko, Akiko, and Takako, the young daughters of Yoko's brother Keisuke. The girls could play with Sean and entertain John until the whole family could be united in August.

Thus, at one blow, the old lady overthrew all of Yoko's plans, while burdening her with three little girls, aged eight, ten, and twelve, who were suitable neither as playmates for Sean nor as companions to Uncle John. What's more, the cost of boarding these children at the Okura was enormous, as was their insatiable appetite for expensive toys and clothes. Soon John would be making bitter puns about his "Japan-nieces."

Next, Lennon turned sullen and refused to participate in any outings. Day after day he sulked in his vast suite. Morosely he eyed Japanese TV, which offers one channel for tourists, showing travelogues. Then, one night, he allowed himself to be coaxed into going out to supper at one of Tokyo's most prestigious restaurants.

No sooner were John and Yoko seated than John cast an appraising look about the room, filled with wealthy and elegant patrons. "Ya know, what they say about the Japanese is right!" he exclaimed in a loud, strident tone, like the worst white-devil foreigner. "They all *do* look alike!"

Yoko was horrified. She knew that virtually everybody in the room was capable of understanding John. Whispering frantically, she begged him to lower his voice and hold his tongue. John's only response was to continue speaking in the same loud, provocative tone, inquiring, "Which is the preferred term for these people—'nip' or 'gook'?" That did it! Yoko jumped to her feet and dragged John out of the restaurant.

When Yoko poured out her problems to the groggy John Green, he told her that John was suffering from imprisonment. Why not give him a little freedom? "Buy him a bike," counseled the oracle.

A couple of nights later Green got a call from John. "What have you been smoking?" John demanded. Then he recounted how Yoko had outfitted the whole family with bikes. Now, when John went down the street, he was accompanied by Yoko on her bike, the three Japanese nieces on their bikes, and a hotel employee on a bike with a sidecar in which rode Sean. "We're a fuckin' parade!" barked John.

By 1 July, after only a month in Japan, Yoko was at her wits' end. She felt so humiliated by her mother that she rang up Sam Green in New York and told him to get in touch immediately with Lena the

Witch. "Remind her," said Yoko, speaking in a very clear, cool, businesslike manner, "that she told me that she would save my face to the world. And also—about the money! It is not so much for money but for saving face. It is a very urgent thing and has to be done in twenty-four hours. Urgent. It is a very strong save-face situation that came about. Just tell her roughly: all she has to do is emphasize the work that she did."

Sam Green fell over himself to be of help. "I'm going to really emphasize," he swore, "that she ought to get every spiritual power that she has and that she's got to work all day and all night. Somehow I'll get the message to her. This is a very important crisis, and she's got to make it turn out all right."

When the day arrived on which the Lennons were obliged to leave their precious suite, John refused to budge. He said that if the hotel wanted them out, it would have to evict them. At this point Yoko's mother came up with another of her helpful suggestions. She pointed out that while Yoko's brother Keisuke and his wife were on holiday, the ancestral home at Karuizawa was unoccupied. Why shouldn't John and Yoko go to the famous resort town? This sounded like a good idea because it would take the Lennons out of the concrete labyrinth of Tokyo and put them into a verdant mountain district. Once John and Yoko had committed themselves to the move, however, Mrs. Ono pointed out that the house was no longer hers to dispose of as she pleased. They would be obliged to rent it from Keisuke. She mentioned a figure that was outrageously high. Yoko, determined to show herself indifferent to expense, consented to pay the exorbitant price.

If John Lennon thought he was going to pass now from modern Westernized Japan to the ancient Japan of the countryside, he was in for a rude shock. Though the area around Karuizawa contains some well-preserved mountain greenery, the town, founded by Yankee missionaries, looks like a bad imitation of Bar Harbor, Maine, and is filled with tourists who are looking to eat pancakes with maple syrup. The "ancestral home" for which John was paying through the nose—and being urged to buy—turned out to be an ordinary American split-level house, with the kind of sliding doors you buy at Sears, Roebuck. The neighbors were all wealthy society people, but they behaved exactly like American suburbanites. As John observed with astonishment, all they did was ride bikes, play tennis, and have backyard barbecues, at which the women wore Pucci dresses. In the evening Yoko would drag John from one old classmate's house to another, where they would sit in front of the glass-topped coffee table, surrounded by an expanse of wall-to-wall carpeting, trying to ingratiate themselves with the locals. John would wear a tan linen suit and act quite charming—when he could find someone who dared converse in English. Yoko talked a mile a minute in Japanese, but everyone looked at her and John with detached amusement.

By early August the strain of living in such a totally alien environment, the exasperation produced by being treated like a hapless child (Yoko had taken to doing things "for John's good," like hiding his cigarettes), and the anxiety generated by seeing hundreds of thousands of dollars being pissed away on nonsense combined to produce in John Lennon a profound depression. One night John Green was awakened by an SOS. "Charlie!" Yoko burst out. "I think John's gone crazy!" When Green objected that Yoko was always calling John crazy, Yoko gave him a description of John's behavior that would have given pause to the most skeptical observer of Lennon's moods and conditions.

"He doesn't talk to anyone," Yoko gasped. "He doesn't seem to hear anyone talking to him. Sometimes he just stands in the corner and moans. It's terrible. I knew he didn't like it here. I knew he wanted to get out, but I kept hoping that if we just waited a little longer, he would get used to things here. I think the pressure was too much for him. He doesn't have a very strong mind, you know. I think he's snapped!"

A few nights later, Green got a call from Lennon. When Green asked John what he had been up to, Lennon replied, "I've been dead, Charles." Then he went on to explain what had killed him: "Yoko killed me; this place killed me; the damned Japan-nieces killed me."

Green concluded from this conversation that John was just "playing dead"—as a means of punishing Yoko. This interpretation was not so much wrong as it was inadequate to explain the state to which Lennon had been reduced. At a later date Lennon described for Green in far greater detail what had happened in Japan.

"I'd lie in bed all day, not talk, not eat, just withdraw. And a funny thing happened. I began to see all these different parts of me. I felt like a hollow temple filled with many spirits, each one passing through me, each inhabiting me for a little time and then leaving to be replaced by another. I realized then what the problem is that I have to solve. I have to be *all* of those people. But I can't be all those people all the time. And in the past, whenever I became one of them, I became that thing, that person so totally that I forgot the others. I don't know how to stop. I have no device, no magic, to keep an easy flow from one part of my personality to another. I need that because, Charles, the secret, *the* secret, is *changing*."

Some wives would have abandoned their travel plans if they had discovered that these arrangements were driving their husbands into semipsychotic states of mind. Not Yoko Ono. She decided that what John needed was distraction. First, she called up Sam Green and ordered him to fly around the world in a westerly direction, leaving on

16, 18, or 21 August. She told him that such a trip would improve his abilities and bring him luck. When Sam arrived at Karuizawa, he found himself being treated like royalty. Yoko took him around to all the split-levels, introducing him as a distinguished guest. There was much bowing and smiling, especially by Sam, who found the whole scene irresistibly funny. "It was the Southampton Bath and Tennis Club." He chuckled as he recollected the lengths to which the Japanese went to ape the manners of a WASPy American summer colony.

Sam's tone changed to one of deep respect, however, when he talked about the balance of his stay in Japan. For after he left Karuizawa, he went to Kyoto (after trying in Tokyo to sell for $400,000 a piece that belonged to the Gimbels), where Yoko had arranged for him to stay at her expense at the famous Tawaraya Inn, where she knew he would be waited on hand and foot, while he savored all the exquisite delights of the purest Japanese taste and the most refined sensibility. Yoko exhibited a princely generosity on this occasion, remarking simply, "You should experience these things when you are in Japan."

Sam Green was just a momentary distraction; what John needed after three months in the alien world of Japan was a male companion who could help him through the remaining two months without creating any fresh problems. Yoko decided that the ideal man for the job would be Elliot Mintz, but when she summoned him to her aid, he complained that he was having a lot of trouble with his hilltop house, which was starting to slide down the hill. Yoko cut him short by offering $30,000 if he would jump on the first plane to Japan. Mintz was soon on his way to Karuizawa.

On the night of 24 August, after putting a welcoming gift of flowers and walnut sweet rice in Mintz's room at the Mampei Hotel, John Lennon sat down to his typewriter and began to tap out a letter to himself in the style of a diary. Over the course of the next thirteen days, which covered the end of his stay at Karuizawa and his return to the Okura in Tokyo, he made a couple of other entries, so that the writing he mailed to New York amounted to three single-spaced pages, containing a finely cut histological slice of his mind.

The moment you start reading these entries, you sense yourself to be inside a private mental space that is oddly familiar in its quiet, intimate, self-absorbed atmosphere. It is the other side of the looking glass that normally reflected John Lennon, the inner process from which he scooped up from time to time the ideas and imagery of his songs. The first clue to the real character of this mental process is the visual appearance of the manuscript: single-spaced between the sentences as well as between the lines with minimal margins and no capitals, save for emphasis—in fine, a clot of words. The mental impression is likewise congested. Although there are lots of striking phrases, because John had a great faculty for striking off laconic aperçus, it is hard to find these bits after reading beyond them because things seem to fall into the cracks and disappear. These cracks are produced by another trick of Lennon's mind, his flea skips from one idea to another, often far away, the same faculty that made John an instinctive surrealist.

Once into the writing, you can watch his mind function like a Venus flytrap. Myopic and short-spanned, it seizes on anything that comes within its limited range, but after every bite it turns back to contemplate its true object, itself, which it continually examines, scolds, ridicules, exhorts, or rolls back to some earlier time, like the protagonist of *Krapp's Last Tape* with his memory machine.

The sound of Yoko vomiting in the bathroom sets John's mind running with thoughts about her being pregnant again. After a further stream of associations, he comes around to how he feels about being marooned in Japan. Reflecting that he's been alone all his life and likes to be alone, he remarks ironically on how he is always trying to "JOIN SOMETHING," even though "basically i don't like people." He feels "guilty and alienated," but he recognizes this tendency is just a neurotic symptom because "nothing worth knowing ever came out of a mob." So it's not so bad being in Japan because every place is the same to a solipsist and life is "DEJA VU," the same old thing every time, the only difference being that as you grow older, the pace slackens to "SLOW MOTION."

The other theme that exercises him intensely is the failure of his talent. Oddly he notes that he has plenty of tunes but no words worth singing. His consolation is that in the Eighties he will flourish again because, though he doesn't say so, the psychics have predicted that early in the decade his numbers will be right. The letter concludes with a few wry remarks on the death of Elvis, who John was wont to say had died when he went into the army: a sage observation. On this note he signs off, giving no sign of emotional disturbance, at most appearing a little blue, which is probably how he usually felt when he was not high on drugs or excitement.

Before leaving Japan, the Lennons held another press conference at the Okura on 11 October. The only Western paper present was the faithful *Melody Maker*, which reported that Yoko did most of the talking. John was dressed as if for an immigration hearing: in a black suit, white shirt, and pearl gray tie, with his hair cut in the conventional manner. The only statement about himself that he offered during the forty-five-minute session was the official party line: "We've basically decided to devote our time to be with our baby as much as we can until we feel we can take the time off to indulge ourselves in creating things outside the family." When the reporter for *Melody Maker*, who had been forbidden to ask direct questions, approached Lennon after the conference concluded, John told him the truth: "We really have nothing to say."

Just as John had departed for the Orient five days before Yoko, now Yoko left for New York ahead of John, flying in an easterly direction along the shortest route. Lennon, left behind at the Okura with Sean, Mintz, and Nishi, sat around in his huge suite, awaiting the signal to depart, which could be given only after Yoko had consulted with Yoshikawa. Days elapsed without orders to move, and John became depressed, as he always did when Mother took off. "I would just like to be in my own bed with my Scott amp next to me and my books," he complained to his baby-sitter. Meantime, in New York, Yoko was raging against John to Marnie Hair.

Yoko was furious because after all her efforts that summer to improve her social standing, John had caused her to lose face in the most painful manner. She had been thrilled to receive an invitation to a banquet given by people of the highest class, who wished to honor the Lennons. What made the invitation especially valuable in Yoko's eyes was the fact that women are rarely invited to such feasts because the entertainment is provided by geisha girls. But when Yoko had announced her great coup to John, instead of showing appreciation for his wife's efforts, he had refused to attend the affair, claiming that his Japanese was not adequate for such an occasion. Yoko had retaliated by leaving the Okura for her mother's house, prior to flying back to New York. When she got home, she locked herself up in the apartment for days. As she told her troubles to Marnie, she looked gaunt and shrunken, her skin yellow and her hair lank. "I'll get him for this!" she swore. "I'll get him!"

When Yoko gave John his travel orders, she told him that the directional man had decreed that he and his party must fly home in a *westerly* direction, which meant a twenty-five-hour journey via Hong Kong, Singapore, Dubai, and Frankfurt, where they would be obliged to remain overnight. Appalled as John was by this prospect, he didn't have the courage to fly in the face of Mother's magic. He lived by faith, the faith he had expressed to Elliot Mintz when he arrived, exhorting him: "Trust her! Just trust her!"

OLD MacLENNON'S FARM

About six weeks after the Lennons returned to New York, they got a terrible fright. Around ten o'clock one night in November the phone rang, and Yoko took the call in the kitchen. A man with a Puerto Rican accent asked for Yoko Ono. She replied as if she were the maid, saying, "So sorry. They not here."

Instantly the guy jumped through the phone like a mugger. "I know it's you!" he barked. "Now shut up and listen!" As Yoko stood there, transfixed, the voice menace started laying down his demands. "We want a hundred thousand dollars or we'll snatch your son! We won't hurt him, you understand? But we'll grab him!"

Finally, recovering her wits, Yoko cried, "Who is this? Who is it on the phone, please?"

The answer was calculated to fill her with fear. "We are a group of professional terrorists," explained the voice. "Do not call the police or the FBI. We will know if you do! Many famous people have already been contacted by our group and paid the money. The police can only protect you for so long—a week, two weeks, maybe a month. Then they go away. We will watch, and we will wait. And we can wait for a year or *two* years. Then we will be back!"

By the time the guy hung up—after saying that he would call again the next day—Yoko had turned to stone. For a while she didn't dare open her mouth. Then she told the story to Masako because they could talk in Japanese. (Yoko was convinced the apartment was bugged and they were all under surveillance.) Finally, she worked up the nerve to walk up the long hallway to the bedroom and tell John. He was dumbstruck, too. Instead of snatching up the phone and punching out 911, he discussed the threat with Yoko in whispers.

The self-proclaimed terrorists could not have chosen better victims. John and Yoko were so paranoid that it took only one call to bring them to their knees. If they had had immediate access to $100,000, they would have handed over the money to save their lives. As it was, they were too broke to pay blackmail. Finally, over Yoko's objections, John called John Green.

Green reacted as would any normal person, hollering, "Call the cops!" But John insisted that before they do anything, Green must read the tarot cards to assess the seriousness of the threat. When the answer came back that they were in trouble, John finally broke down and did what he should have done immediately. No sooner did he inform the police than they alerted the FBI.

Businesslike men in suits and short haircuts arrived immediately from the bureau's office on East 69th Street. The Lennons were advised to sit tight while the agents sought to entrap the mysterious Latin caller. A tap was put on the phones. A group of feds disguised as Con Ed men went to work at the Dakota. Armed guards from a private security agency were posted at the apartment's front and back doors. More calls were received, and arrangements were made to pay the $100,000. On the big day a parcel wrapped in newspaper was left at the desk downstairs. The police followed one suspicious-looking man but lost him. Soon it became clear that the extortionist would not take the bait. At that point there was nothing left to do but continue living—carefully.

Now when Sean went out to play under Masako's supervision, he did not go to the playground across the street from the Dakota but to one on the far side of the park next to the Metropolitan Museum or down near Central Park South. The child was always attended by an armed bodyguard, or if he was taken somewhere in a car—for example, to his favorite place, Great Adventure, the wild animal preserve in New Jersey—the chauffeur would be an armed security man. A number of further threats were received, but eventually Lennon came to view his molester not as a spokesman for a Puerto Rican revolutionary group but merely as the "Latin crazy."

No sooner had the threat of kidnapping begun to subside than the Lennons suffered a fresh grief, inflicted on them by the target of their own kidnapping attempt, Tony Cox. One day in November Yoko received out of the blue a call from Kyoko. The fourteen-year-old daughter whom Yoko had not seen in almost five years would not disclose where she was living, but she did make it clear that she was about to pay Yoko a visit. Then Tony got on the phone and began to bargain over the issue in his usual manner. He wanted assurances that John and Yoko would not play any tricks on him, and he proposed to send over his brother, Larry, with a legal paper for the Lennons to sign. Yoko was willing to do anything at this point to see her child again. For the next month she lived in anticipation of the visit, shopping for fresh bed linens to prepare the room in which Kyoko would stay and chattering nervously about this great event. When the night of the visit arrived, just before Christmas, the nerves of both John and Yoko were stretched taut with anticipation. Then nothing happened. They waited and waited, until finally it became clear that Tony had copped out again. John raged, and Yoko wept. Their dream was over.

By December the Lennons had another serious problem on their hands that would distress them for years to come. They were in trouble with the IRS. The trouble had begun when they got back from Japan and the accountants added up the bills for the trip. The total was a staggering $700,000. Yoko said airily that the whole sum should be charged off as a business expense. The accountants replied that virtually none of the money was tax-deductible. The Lennons had taken a five-month pleasure trip and spent a fortune. Much of this money would be taxable as personal income at the top rate of 72 percent, and the bill would be payable on 15 April 1978. If the money were paid, the Lennons could not afford to go on living as before; if the money were not paid, the interest and penalties would add another huge dollop of debt to their tax burden, launching them on one of those fatal spins that have destroyed so many wealthy but improvident people.

Yoko's only suggestion was to start selling product endorsements or to appear with John on TV commercials. Sam Green suggested that she make a donation of some of her recently acquired artworks to a museum in exchange for a big tax deduction. Sam, highly experienced in this sort of negotiation, could wheel and deal until he got an evaluation that would price the work far beyond what the Lennons had paid. To this reasonable proposal, Yoko turned a deaf ear. She would never part with her possessions.

Finally, someone thought of John's Flower Power Rolls-Royce. The tea caddy car had been sold to a collector in the States back in 1970, but the deal had fallen through, and the limo had come back to the Lennons. Dusty and forgotten, it stood in a Manhattan garage, yet it was "a famous symbol of a glorious era and therefore a priceless historic artifact," as Sam Green pitched it to the bemused officials of the Cooper-Hewitt Museum on Fifth Avenue, a recently established institution dedicated to the decorative arts. After the usual Arab-market haggling that goes on constantly behind the imposing facades of the great cultural institutions, the Lennons got a $225,000 tax credit for their old car, although its market value at the time was less than $100,000. In 1985 the museum auctioned off the car at Sotheby's for a cool $2,299,000.

Such quick fixes offered only temporary relief for the Lennons' chronic tax problems. What they really needed was a long-term tax shelter. Once again, Sam Green proved his worth by coming up with a lawyer named George Teichner, who ran an outfit called Dreamstreet that offered investments in farms and dairy herds in Delaware County, New York, the area that supplies the city with milk. Every dollar spent on a legitimate farming enterprise entitled the investor to four dollars in tax forgiveness. What's more, a skillfully operated dairy farm could be run as a highly profitable enterprise, particularly if its livestock were prize breeding cattle whose stud services and embryo-transfer calvings were scientifically managed, as were those of Dreamstreet Holstein, the farm management branch of the business.

John Green was very keen on this investment. In fact, the more he pondered the project, the more ideas for exploiting the land popped into his fertile brain. Eventually he was able to lay such a list of profitable ventures in Yoko's hands that she was persuaded that by putting a few hundred thousand dollars in cash into this business she would be *on* Dreamstreet. But when she presented her plan to the conservative accountancy firm of Oppenheim, Appel, Dixon & Company, they warned her that she was asking for trouble with the IRS, which took a dim view of such schemes. John Green's judgment prevailed, however; soon the whole deal was wrapped up in a neat little package, ready for signing in time to beat the tax deadline. At the last minute Lennon threw up a roadblock that nearly wrecked the hay wagon. "Farms! What the fuck do I know about farms?" he ranted. "What are they good for? Milk and cheese! All they produce is mucus!"

When Yoko failed to persuade John, she sought the help of John Green. Instead of arguing the value of the investment from a business angle—he knew the very word "business" would get a roar out of Lennon—the wily card reader offered the plan as the fulfillment of Lennon's oft-expressed longing to get out of the city and into nature. But Lennon kept insisting that business and money were evil things and that it was better to give the money to the government.

Too clever to be out-talked by the likes of John Lennon, Green pointed out that what the government did with the money was use it to buy armaments. Lennon the peacenik was actually contributing millions of dollars for the purchase of bombs and guns and other lethal devices. This thought gave John pause. While he pondered the problem, Green persuaded Lennon at least to give the farms a look. Reluctantly John consented.

One morning in November a convoy of two black stretch limousines pulled away from the entrance to the Dakota and headed for upstate New York. In the lead car were John, Yoko, and Sam Green. In the car following were Sean and Helen Seaman, who had been segregated from the rest of the party so that Sean's hollering and crying would not disturb John on this critical occasion. Once the cars had started cruising through the lovely district of the cattle farms, John's mood began to change. After all, his uncle George had been a dairy farmer. Some of John's earliest memories were of going about in a brown float loaded with silver churns and making deliveries of milk that was ladled out and poured into pitchers with much good cheer and pleasant chat.

As the big, cushioned limo purred along the empty roads of upstate New York, John began to gaze fondly at the gently rolling countryside. Soon he expressed a desire to get out of the car and walk about on the land. When Sam spotted a hilltop that promised a fine view of this beautiful district, he stopped the car. While Yoko sat inside, puffing on her cigarette, John and Sam set out to climb the hill. John was so out of condition that he was swiftly winded. Though the slope was not steep, he had to stop frequently, like a man with a bad heart. It cost him an effort to reach the top of that hill, but when he stood upon the crest and gazed out across the countryside, so similar in appearance to his native Lancashire, his imagination came to life.

He sat down and started sketching out the house he would build on this spot: the fireplace here, the sundeck there—soon he was summoning up the image of them all having coffee out of doors and watching the sunrise. "John was a true homebody," remarked Sam. "There was nothing he liked better than creating new homes. His basic dream was to build a castle on a hill that nobody could reach but which offered him a commanding view of the world."

When the limos turned back to New York that afternoon, John was over the moon about "Old MacLennon's Farm." He wound up buying three defunct and one working farm for $740,000 plus $100,000 worth of used equipment. A hundred and twenty-two cows cost him $1.5 million, and ten bulls $350,000. On the whole $2.7 million deal the Lennons put down only $375,000, giving notes for the balance. The following year they sought to reap the harvest on their investment by claiming losses of $716,129 plus a $195,000 investment tax credit, $306,129 in depreciation on the cattle and equipment, and $410,000 in other expenses. To their chagrin, the IRS disallowed a large portion of these claims, charging that the farms and cattle had not been bought as profit-making enterprises but rather as tax dodges, entailing no real risk. The revenuers also disallowed a deduction of $143,920 in limousine expenses for the trip to Japan and $127,000 in charitable deductions. Instead of granting the $225,000 allowance for the historic limo, they cut the figure in half. Ten years later the matter was still at issue in tax court, with the IRS claiming an additional $876,141 for the year 1977.

On 3 May 1978, just as the Lennons were about to take possession of their property, a fire leveled a barn, garage, and toolshed on one of the Lennons' farms in Franklin. Richard Lorhman, an experienced investigator, reported that the blaze had been set by an arsonist. Subsequently there were many more fires on Dreamstreet Farms, including another conflagration on a Lennon property. These alarming incidents cast a pall over the cheery idea of Old MacLennon's Farm. Yoko put a caretaker named Penny King on one farm but had nothing more to do with the properties. The cattle were another matter; they were managed successfully by Dreamstreet Holsteins.

The grave financial crisis with which the year 1977 concluded served to bring out sharply the contrasting characters of John and Yoko. She worked and worried ceaselessly as she struggled to find a solution to the family's problems. He refused to concern himself or assume any share of the responsibility for escaping their predicament. The most he would do was offer a prayer for Yoko's success. In fact, to protect himself once and for all from all the disturbing demands of business, Lennon took a drastic step that he had long contemplated. He bestowed on Yoko a power of attorney that gave her complete control over his fortune. Henceforth she could write checks, sign contracts, and comport herself in matters of business as if she were John Lennon.

ROCK BOTTOM

By 1978 John Lennon had ceased to resemble himself. Wasted by dieting, fasting and self-induced vomiting, he weighed only 130 pounds. Totally enervated by lack of purpose and exercise, he rarely left his bed. Drugged all day on Thai stick, magic mushrooms, or heroin, he slept much of the time and spent his waking hours in a kind of trance. Though he kept up the pretense of running the house and taking care of Sean, he was so zonked out that his presence in the apartment was hardly noticed. People who worked for the family would say, "Is there a real John Lennon?"

What had happened to John? The same thing that happened to Howard Hughes and many another wealthy, self-indulgent recluse. Lennon had simply refused to pay the price for staying alive, the toll levied in terms of involvement, responsibility, and effort. Finding in Yoko Ono someone who was willing, in fact eager, to lift off his shoulders all the burdens of existence, John had drifted far away from reality. He had taken up residence in the fantastic realm of "Imagine," where nothing that *is* matters at all and where everything one fancies can be achieved effortlessly through magic. The results of this irrational translation were profoundly ironic.

Instead of finding peace and comfort in his protective bubble, John was tormented constantly by scores of petty discomforts that came pouring out in his notes to his gofers. There was always something wrong with the TV, the morning paper had failed to arrive, or the soap in the kitchen was not organic. John's health, which he thought he was guarding with his self-denying regimen, was actually being undermined. He complained of colds and fevers, chronic indigestion and constipation, headaches and toothaches, dizzy spells and tachycardia. Once he exposed his gums to Marnie and showed her an eruption that had him quite worried.

Though Lennon was a hypochondriac, alarmed by every ache and pain, he never sought professional help, doubtless because he knew that any legitimate doctor would demand that his patient give up illegal drugs. Preferring to doctor himself, John was forever tinkering with his diet by calculating his balance of yin and yang. Nor was his emotional health any better than his physical condition. Indeed, the only difference that his boy-in-the-bubble existence had made in his irritable temper was that instead of directing his rage at worthy targets, he now discharged it on petty vexations produced by children and animals. Screaming with fury, he would seize one of his beloved cats by the tail and pitch it down the hall or would suddenly erupt in rage over something that Sean had done and give him a kick in his Pampered ass.

Perhaps the cruelest irony of Lennon's self-destructive life-style was the way it had reduced him to the hapless condition of Elvis during his final years. Though John wasn't fat, he had brought himself through starvation to the same state of befuddled torpor. There was one great difference, however. No matter how low Elvis sank, he had to rouse himself periodically to make a living, whereas John was free to sink to the very bottom.

One of Lennon's principal complaints was that he no longer had access to sun and sea. So in the spring of 1978 Yoko, guided doubtless by Yoshikawa, took the whole family to the Caribbean Club on Grand Cayman Island, a very offbeat choice because at that time nobody thought of the Caymans as a resort area, their reputation being exclusively that of the greatest center for offshore banking in the Western Hemisphere. After arriving in a Learjet from Miami, the Lennons settled in a private cottage on the beach, where they enjoyed a sunny vacation until it was time to fly to Japan for their summer vacation.

After the terrible experiences of the previous year Yoko had to be much more cautious about making demands on John. The length of the stay was considerably curtailed and the routine at the Okura became that of a sanatorium. Every day John swam in the hotel's splendid pool, often with Sean; in the afternoon John received expert shiatsu massage, a therapy to which he had been introduced the year before by Yoko. As the blind masseurs probed for those nerve centers diagrammed on acupuncture charts or the little masseuses trampled his back, John must have felt all his pain being rubbed out. For the rest he doubtless enjoyed his daily naps and his health food meals, which alternated with visits to fine restaurants, where he sampled the delicacies of Japanese cuisine, including Kobe beef, which was one of John's favorite dishes in Japan. Always fond of shopping, he would go to Tokyo's "Electronic Village," where he would stock up on state-of-the-art equipment like his favorite thirty-inch color TV receiver. He also bought a lot of clothes, including silk kimonos, Japanese footwear, and other items of Oriental apparel, which he mixed tastefully with his Western costumes.

Though this regimen was restful and restorative, it was also notable for its lack of intellectual or imaginative substance. As in New York, Lennon was completely out of touch with the life about him and oblivious of the cultural treasures heaped up nearby. He does not appear to have attended the Kabuki theater or spent time in the museums or taken any interest in Japan's remarkable crafts. He went to the classical capital of Kyoto, but its temples, palaces, and wondrous gardens left no mark on his mind, if indeed he even saw them. Nor was John any less indifferent to the garish pop culture of Japan, the "floating world" of geisha girls, the porn shows, or the Japanese mob. Lennon lived like a turtle.

When the Lennons returned from Japan in September 1978, they were not accompanied by the highly capable Masako. Sean's nanny had decided to remain behind in the service of Yoko's mother, who soon retired this able servant. Masako's defection was inspired by her constant quarreling with Yoko, for whom she had lost respect. Like most of her compatriots, she could not tolerate Yoko's behavior. In fact, she would tell Marnie Hair that Yoko was not a true Japanese, pointing to the wave in her hair, which she said was the sign of an affair which Yoko's grandmother had had with a Russian violinist.

Losing a retainer was nothing new for Yoko Ono, but "Nana," as Sean called her, was different because she had been the boy's surrogate mother since infancy. When he discovered that she had abandoned him, he must have been terribly hurt. In fact, he must have suffered much the same trauma as his father had experienced at a similar age. What was even worse was the fact that little Sean was destined to experience this baffling loss of a parental figure time and again throughout his childhood, just as John had experienced it repeatedly. For each of Sean's subsequent nannies also broke off abruptly with Yoko and vanished into thin air so far as the boy could see. Thus, the fate of the Lennons, symbolized by Strawberry Fields, was destined to persist into yet another generation.

John's own attitude toward Sean had crystallized by this time into the form it retained to the end of his life. "Beautiful" was the word that always sprang to Lennon's lips when he thought about his infant son, whom he showered with gifts and sought to pamper and protect in every conceivable manner. Yet at the same time that he was spoiling the boy, John was depriving his son of his father's presence most of the day and refusing to teach him even the most elementary lessons in self-control. Perhaps the most striking feature of John's behavior was its inconsistency. Up until the fall of 1978 John had sworn that Sean would never be sent to school to suffer as John had suffered. Then, when he was barely three, Sean was enrolled in nursery school. Asked by John Green to explain this remarkable turnabout, Lennon replied that Sean got so little attention from his mother and such bad vibes from his father that it was better for him to be out of the house. But this conviction proved no firmer than its predecessor. The moment Sean complained about the school, he was removed.

John Lennon tried hard to fulfill the idealized role of father, but he could never sustain the part. Invariably something would go wrong, and John would throw a fit. Then he would suffer from guilt and self-hatred until it was time to start all over again. His efforts were not wholly unsuccessful, however, because Sean did love his father and constantly sought his presence.

Although John became in his last years a kind of invalid, pale, wasted, generally confined to his sickroom, his underlying character never altered. If Yoko left him alone or sent him off somewhere for a few days, he reverted to type. That's what happened in late September 1978, when she dispatched him to the Hawaiian Islands.

Odd journeys to distant and unlikely places became a feature of Lennon's life in his last years, as Yoko sought to make him (or herself!) feel better by posting him in promising directions. Why she chose Hawaii is as much a mystery as why she later picked Cape Town. It may have had something to do with the fact that the Ono family enjoyed a special status in the Islands.

Before Pearl Harbor, when Eisuke Ono was an official of the Yokohama Species Bank in San Francisco, he had performed great services on behalf of the Hawaiian Japanese, who were desperately seeking to protect their fortunes in the event of war. So successful was Eisuke that he earned the enduring gratitude of many of these families. Hence Yoko was sending John to a place where she had good connections. But if any of those hardworking, highly successful Japanese-Americans caught sight of John Lennon during this visit, they must have been terribly embarrassed. For no sooner did John check into the Sheraton Hotel at Waikiki Beach than he took off on a tremendous binge of drinking and drugging that soon made him look like a bum.

One day, as he was staggering along the Alawai Canal, unshaven, shaded, beat-looking, he was suddenly hailed by Jesse Ed Davis. John's old pal was just back from the East Coast, where he had spent the summer on Andy Warhol's estate at Montauk, working for Tom Sullivan, the once-celebrated "Cowboy" of Studio 54, a flamboyant redneck drug smuggler keen on passing as an aspiring rock star. Sullivan had spent a fortune that summer making a dreadful movie titled *Cocaine Cowboys*, starring himself and Jack Palance with a cameo appearance by Andy Warhol. The smuggling scenes were so realistic that right in the middle of the shooting the set was raided by thirty men from the Drug Enforcement Agency, FBI, and local police. The bust turned out to be a bust when the parties squared off in court, but the subsequent heat so alarmed the Cowboy that he galloped off to Hawaii with Jesse Ed, who had lived in the Islands for years. This pair of hard players was hanging around the Western Union office, waiting for some bread from New York, when they spied the great John Lennon staggering up the street.

"Motherfucker!" cried Jesse Ed when he recognized John. "What are *you* doing here?"

John gave Jesse and Tommy a quick squint through his shades. Then, in a raspy, drunken voice, he snapped, "Come in here!" They ducked into the lobby of the Hyatt Hotel. When Lennon felt he was safely out of sight and hearing, he confessed that he was "running away from Yoko."

"What happened?" exclaimed Jesse Ed.

"I don't want to talk about it!" rasped John, casting an eye at the Cowboy in his towering ten-gallon hat, skintight jeans, cobraskin boots, and glove-encased left hand, deformed by the flames of a burning plane. "You know where we can get somethin'?"

Jesse Ed said he had the connection—did Lennon have the loot? John said he had $300. That was all it took to get the boys into a cab and over to Uwe Beach, where they found a dealer built like a refrigerator, named Timmy. The transaction was swiftly concluded, and the gang took off for home. When Jesse Ed asked John where he was staying, Lennon said he didn't know but he had the key to the room.

Once back at the hotel, the action accelerated like the jerky frames of an old movie. Lennon, was the buyer, so he had the first crack at the smack.

"John knew just what to do," recalled Jesse. "He didn't even need a tourniquet." Lennon had "good ropes." After John got off, Jesse and Cowboy followed. Then they all kicked back to enjoy the high. Ordering up a quart of Smirnoff and a couple of containers of orange juice, they tuned the TV to *Star Trek.*

When the alcohol had mingled nicely with the heroin, John asked if there was someplace they could go and play. Jesse Ed said that there was a real bust-out joint not far away that would welcome a little entertainment. Grabbing a couple of guitars that John was carrying, the boys made their way to the John Barleycorn in Pearl City.

When the management recognized the guest star of the night, they raised no objection to the band. Jesse Ed recalled that the three of them played and sang three rock 'n' roll standards: "Roll Over, Beethoven," "Peggy Sue," and another song of like vintage. When their little set was done, they passed the hat and collected a total of twenty bucks. Thrilled at their success, they jumped in a cab and made for a

72-foot ketch in the harbor, on which two French playboys, scions of the Cointreau and Pernod families, were partying with a crew of pretty girls.

Next day John Lennon took off for New York.

When John got back to the Dakota, he found everyone preparing for what now became an annual event: the double birthday party for John and Sean at Tavern on the Green. The celebration was Marnie's idea, and the restaurant was doubly convenient because it was owned by the Lennons' neighbor Warner LeRoy and was situated only five blocks south of the Dakota. A rich kid's party, with fancy decor and professional entertainers, like the inevitable magician, the event was held in a glittering room facing the park, walled with glass and hung with crystal chandeliers. John togged out for the occasion like a nice young suburban daddy, wearing a conservative corduroy jacket and his old striped rep tie from Quarry Bank. When the party ended, the kids were taken to the LeRoys' duplex, which has a screening room.

After twenty minutes of watching *Dumbo*, John murmured, "I can't stand this, Marnie. Let's go down to the kitchen and have a cup of coffee." When they had settled down in the Lennons' kitchen, Marnie observed that John was unusually nervous. "He was jumpy," she recalled. "I thought it was just jet lag. He was drinking coffee and scratching around the earpieces of his glasses, scratching the nosepieces of his glasses, scratching along his cheeks, scratching—he was making me very nervous doing that. I said, 'Why don't you scratch your teeth?' He said, 'I would if I could!' Finally, Yoko came down and sat in a chair and went to sleep. . . . Yoko scratched plenty, too, but I thought this was due to her wool allergies and cat allergies."

One of the nice things about Marnie Hair was that she didn't know the first thing about drugs.

After the birthday party John withdrew to his room and remained in seclusion. Every day, when Marnie would come to pick up or deliver the kids, she would find him incommunicado. After he had been hibernating for weeks, Marnie remarked: "If he doesn't come out of that room, he's going to turn to mold!"

"Listen," snapped Yoko, "we're gonna treat him like the fungus he is—keep him in the dark and feed him horseshit!"

As a rich junkie John Lennon could obtain unlimited quantities of China White, the very pure heroin that comes into the States from Southeast Asia. Rarely did his connection fail. But nobody operates with 100 percent efficiency in the drug game. There were days when the runner came back from Chinatown with a long story and an empty hand. When that happened, someone else had to take the responsibility for getting John his medicine.

One day Marnie was mildly puzzled when Yoko called her and said with a sense of urgency in her voice: "Meet me downstairs at the entrance to your building!" Expecting to be picked up, as always, by a stretch limo with a tiny woman in the back seat, Marnie was astonished to see Yoko scurrying down the block, trying to look inconspicuous. When the doorman of Marnie's building lunged forward to assist Yoko, who had stuck out her hand to flag a cab, she shrank back from the curb and whispered to her friend: "Do you think he recognized me?" Then Yoko dismissed the doorman and asked Marnie to go out on the street and hail the taxi.

Once the women were on their way downtown, Yoko began chattering nervously about everything under the sun. Marnie knew better than to ask any questions. After a long and circuitous drive they reached Alphabetsville, the most forbidding part of the Lower East Side, where the avenues bear letters as names, like A, B, C. Cruising past vacant lots, boarded-up stores, and dilapidated tenements, the driver came to a stop in front of a scabrous old wreck of a building that appeared completely abandoned. Sheets of galvanized iron had been nailed over the doors and windows.

Yoko told the hackie to wait and then ducked out of the cab. Up the dirty steps, littered with broken bottles and discarded beer cans, she scampered until she got to the door. At that moment a hand reached out and pushed open a rent between the sheet metal and the doorjamb. Yoko ducked inside.

Marnie was alarmed. Entering a building like this was a very dangerous act for anyone, much less a little woman like Yoko, whose purse was always stuffed with $100 bills. As the meter ticked on, minute after minute, Marnie's anxiety mounted. She was just beginning to think how she might rescue her friend when the sheet metal over the door bowed out again and Yoko emerged, like a cat slipping out of the house. Jumping into the back of the cab, she shouted: "57th Street and Sixth Avenue!"—the address of the Zen Tea Room. Then, with a sigh, she leaned back and smiled at Marnie.

Early in December Yoko flew to London to attend an Apple board meeting. Though John was smacked out, he couldn't resist the temptation to go catting. No sooner was Yoko out the door, than he called up May Pang. The first time she answered, he was so anxious that he automatically hung up. The next time he began an embarrassed conversation that concluded with her agreeing to call in sick to her new employer. When John arrived an hour later at May's apartment in the

East 60s, he looked half dead. It was raining and he'd had trouble getting a cab. He was so breathless that he was wheezing. When he sat down, he held May's hand against his heart, which was racing madly. May recognized what courage it had taken John to slip out of the house. Gradually she drew him out. When she asked him if he still wanted to record, he replied: "Of course I do! I never stopped wantin' to make music." At the same time he said he loved having Yoko act as his manager, pointing out that Billy Joel was managed by his wife, Elizabeth. When May countered that Billy Joel was very active both on the stage and in the studio, John changed the subject.

All that afternoon John and May spent in bed. Time and again they played "Reminiscing" by the Little River Band, a sentimental song that reminded John of his time with May. Finally, he began to get nervous, explaining that he had shut the door to his room to make it appear that he was still at home. May was saddened to see John fading away before her eyes, but she summoned a smile and told him how much she loved him. "I love you, too," he replied. Then he was out the door, down the hall, and into the elevator. May blew him a kiss good-bye. It was the last time she saw him.

When Christmas rolled around, a season that John found emotionally troublesome, the mood at the Dakota was glum. John Green was urging Yoko to take John to a doctor; Yoko was resisting, contending that a doctor might want to institutionalize John, and then he wouldn't be able to get all the things to which he was accustomed at home. Yoko's own spirits were so low that Green was beginning to fear that she would lose her battle with the other Apples. Hence, it was just as important that she do something for herself as that she help John. On Christmas Eve the patient gave herself a massive dose of her favorite medicine, shopping. The story of her treatment is well told by Jack Cohen, star salesman of Bergdorf Goodman's fur department:

"One snowy, icy Christmas Eve Yoko Ono telephoned to say that she and John would like to look at some furs in their apartment at the Dakota. Faster than I can tell you, a security man and I were on our way there with three trunks full, thirty-seven pieces in all. We put the trunks in the kitchen because Yoko and John wanted to look at them there, alone [it was the only room with a good light and a full-length mirror]. We waited in the living room. After what seemed forever, John came in and said how nice we were to have come over on such a terrible afternoon and would we have a glass of wine with them. I was sure this was a polite effort to apologize for buying nothing. But when we got to the kitchen, John said, 'We'll take it.' 'Which one?' I asked, hoping that at least it was an expensive piece. 'All of it,' said John, 'the collection.' That was a sale of almost $300,000."

*   *   *

The Lennons continued their cure in March 1979 by renting an immense oceanfront mansion in Palm Beach. When Julian joined them during his spring holiday, John took the opportunity to make a fresh start with the boy. When Julian was twelve, John had offered him a joint. Now he began to teach Julian the guitar, father and son playing together after dinner. John was sensible of how badly he had neglected Julian in the past and guilty about having substituted expensive gifts for real love. He proposed to reverse this pattern, but when he started explaining his intentions, he bungled the job so badly that he only succeeded in alarming the youngster. Painfully, stammeringly, Julian struggled to explain how hard it was to be the son of a superstar. Though he and his mother had very little, his schoolmates insisted that Julian's house was papered with ten-pound notes. The only way he could placate these brutal boys was by sharing the goodies that his father provided. If John were not going to give Julian any more expensive presents, he would be in serious trouble. What's more, Julian had brought John a gift. Or was all this talk of gifts some game John was playing?

Reacting to Julian's timid little speech as if it were a slap in the face, John jumped back a yard. Instead of talking to his son and making their minds meet, Lennon threw up his hands and announced that he had made a terrible mistake. Everything was going back to where it had stood before. Henceforth Julian would get his gifts—and be damned!

While John was reflecting sorrowfully on the pains of parenthood, Yoko was agonizing over the Lennons' latest financial disaster. Counting on a big dividend from Apple at year's end, she had balanced her budget with money that had not yet come to hand. The shrewd Lee Eastman had inferred from her persistent demands for a big slice of Apple pie that she was in financial trouble. He persuaded the other Apples to refuse to declare a dividend, with the intention of starving Yoko out and compelling her to make concessions that would profit her partners. Caught flat-footed, she panicked. Alarm bells rang in New York. A team of accountants flew down to Florida to deal with the emergency.

After going over the Lennons' affairs, the accountants could offer no real solution. They told Yoko that her only recourse was to go to whatever banks would extend her credit and borrow money at whatever rate was demanded. This verdict alarmed Yoko anew because when she relayed it to John, he might blow up and strip her of her all-important power of attorney.

Yoko need not have worried. John Lennon was not about to challenge her management of his affairs. John had built up a myth about Yoko's business prowess. The myth was essential to his life-style because it enabled him to slough off all his business responsibilities. If he had started examining this fantasy critically, it would have fallen apart in a minute. But, then, where would that have left John Lennon? Back with the men in the business suits!

So it is not surprising that even at this moment of crisis, when he was coming under the kind of pressure that could have cost him permanent assets, Lennon refused to take the slightest notice of what was transpiring. As Yoko rushed about frantically, trying to avoid a confrontation, John holed up in his room, chain-smoking Thai stick, drinking wine, and snorting cocaine and heroin.

Week after week that grim winter, John Lennon lay in his crib under the spell of his mother's milk. Much of the time he was asleep. Many hours were spent in blissful swooning or daydreaming. Totally prostrate, John couldn't even raise his head to look at the TV screen; instead, he employed a pair of trick glasses with prism lenses that enabled him to watch while lying flat on his back. In that strange, periscopic attitude, John Lennon passed the winter.

When Lennon was lucid, he did a lot of reading, especially about magic and the supernatural. He was particularly fascinated by charismatic religious relics, like St. Guadalupe's Rebozo and the Shroud of Turin. Even more characteristic of Lennon's mind was an obsession with ancient civilizations, the Egyptians, Celts, and Vikings, all peoples whom he believed to have possessed invaluable knowledge lost to modern man. The Vikings fascinated him in particular because they were Europe's first great pirates, and John was drawn still to anything that smacked of the sea and nautical adventure; in fact, his two greatest book heroes were men of the sea: Thor Heyerdahl and Sir Francis Chichester.

The triumphant journey of the young, bearded, half-naked men on the raft *Kon Tiki* must have rung a peal of victory bells in Lennon's mind because it confirmed so many of his treasured convictions: his faith in the powers of ancient civilizations, his defiance of received opinion, and, above all, his profound conviction, based on experience, that a handful of young men possessed by an idea can work miracles.

Chichester, the great solo sailor, was another story. He embodied to a supreme degree precisely those virtues in which John Lennon was most lacking: self-reliance and self-sufficiency. A one-man crew, by turns master and mate, navigator and radio operator, mechanic and swabbie, cook and steward, Sir Francis was everything that Lennon could never be. Above all, Chichester was a man of supernal courage who had been a daring long-distance flier before he became Britain's last great sailor. It is a sign of John's imaginative identification with

Chichester that he borrowed from him the title by which Lennon was known in his last interviews: "househusband."

The book that meant the most to John at this time was Jean Liedloff's *The Continuum Concept.* A woman who had suffered in youth from a bad relationship with her mother, Liedloff was deeply impressed by how Venezuelan Indian women carry their children everywhere strapped to their bodies. Reflecting upon the effect of this practice, she came up with a novel idea.

What children require most after birth, she argued, is a smooth and secure transition from the environment of the womb to the drastically different atmosphere of the outer world. Continuous physical contact with the mother facilitates this transition, which, in turn, enables the children to take their first steps in life confidently. By contrast, physical separation from the mother at birth breaks the continuum and undercuts the child's self-assurance just when it is forming its first impressions of the reality upon which its entire life must be built.

Lennon was deeply impressed by this argument, which spoke to his condition in the same radical terms as had, years before, Arthur Janov's *The Primal Scream.* What really hit John was an excursus toward the end of the book on the apparently unrelated topic of heroin addiction. Reflecting on the ambiguous word "fix," usually understood in the sense of "fixing up" the junkie after he has become "sick" from drug deprivation, Jean Liedloff worked around to another aspect of the term, the idea of "fixity" or stability. She wrote, in a passage that must have made Lennon's glasses jiggle:

> Psychiatrists who have made long studies of addicts say that most of them are extremely narcissistic and that their intense preoccupation with heroin is a surface manifestation of a more profound preoccupation with themselves. . . . The dominant emotional characteristic of the addict is said to be his enormous compulsion to abdicate responsibility for his own life. . . . It appears that, in some very essential way, the feeling heroin gives is like the feeling the infant has in arms. The long directionless search for a vague something is ended when the heroin user experiences the lost feeling. . . . The personality of the addict, centered upon the drug, discards any semblance of maturity it had managed to attain and settles at the infantile level where the continuum was interrupted.

Her words struck Lennon as home truths. Better yet, they pointed to a positive outcome. Junkies who survive to a certain age usually relinquish the drug spontaneously, Liedloff contended, because they have sated their desperate hunger for the maternal embrace.

THE GOLDEN LADY

In January 1979 Sam Green took off for Egypt on the maddest caper of his entire career. His mission? To discover the whereabouts of a gang of grave robbers and their secret dig in the desert. Sam was desperate to locate these thieves because their operations offered him the greatest opportunity yet in the scam he had been running with John Green ever since the Lennons bought the Lenoir.

Sam and John Green had recognized as soon as they got their first remittance from Switzerland that selling European masters to John and Yoko was not the right way to play the game. All famous painters have an easily ascertained book value. If you inflate that value by 100 percent or more, someone is bound to come along and tell your client that he's taking a screwing. During the negotiations over the Lenoir, for example, Yoko had rung up Tom Hoving, the former director of the Metropolitan Museum of Art. He had said the picture was overpriced. Now who wants to sing through that static? So the Greens had put their nimble wits to work figuring out a way to get off the big board and into some kind of art that had no clearly established market value. One day, with a jolt that nearly knocked out his lights, Sam Green found the answer—in the mysterious sands of Egypt!

Sam had been crazy about everything Egyptian since 1969, when he read Peter Tomkins's *The Secret of the Great Pyramids*. After taking off for Cairo, he had spent days brooding over the great stone facets. Time and again he returned to the Nile, drawn by the same magic. Naturally he picked up a lot of knowledge about the country. One of his most interesting discoveries was that the book prices of Egyptian artworks were completely out of date because this exotic stuff was rarely traded. An item that had been sold last in 1918 might be worth ten times more today, but nobody appeared to appreciate that fact. Consequently, a dealer in Egyptian art could quote any price he pleased.

The big drawback was that very little Egyptian stuff came on the market and 90 percent of what was offered was fake. That problem could be solved by buying the stuff from an expert reputable dealer, like Lucien Viola of L'Ibis Gallery on East 67th Street. But the difficulties didn't end there because authentic pieces were often far from beautiful. They belonged in the halls of a museum, not upon the walls of a Manhattan luxury apartment. Then Sam had another brainstorm.

Why not tell Yoko that these hoary relics, unearthed from tombs and temples, possessed *magical* properties? The Lennons already had pyramids in their pad. They put plants under them, like the Money Bush, or used them for meditation. So they were presold on Pyramid Power. Now all it would take would be some weird pieces that could be pitched as having the *power*—mummies, sarcophagi, chthonic deities, stuff like that—and Yoko would snap them up. Magic would excite her a lot more than tax write-offs. So magic was the name of the game.

The Egyptian gambit started off modestly enough with the purchase of an alabaster portrait of a woman that was dirt cheap—about $12,000. The Lennons put it on the mantel in the White Room—and loved it! Next, they bought a couple of pieces from an excavation; one was a boat with oarsmen and a cute little stern pavilion. Then they got more ambitious and bought a three-foot basalt bust of a scribe with hieroglyphics on his back. Finally, they took the plunge, acquiring a massive museological specimen.

Sekhmet is an enthroned lion-headed goddess that stands almost seven feet high and weighs two tons. Eighty years it lay in a warehouse in Switzerland, until Yoko hauled it across the Atlantic. Sam's idea was to acquire the piece for $300,000, then give it to the Fairmont Park Art Association in Philadelphia in exchange for an evaluation of $1 million that would become a tax deduction when it was declared a charitable contribution. Yoko would not hear of surrendering the piece, though it was not a unique figure—there are as many as 730 Sekhmets—and though it was damaged—a great part of the nose chipped away, the ears and the disk top missing. Yoko was fascinated by the idea of a two-ton woman with a head like a lion. But the statue was not even uncrated. It was taken off the ship and stashed in the Morgan Manhattan Warehouse, where it lay until 1986, when it was auctioned at Sotheby's in New York for $742,500. Yoko didn't have to see Sekhmet. Her satisfaction lay in the thrill of acquisition, the pride of possession.

The Golden Lady was quite another story. This gold-leafed sarcophagus studded with semiprecious stones—a piece from the twenty-sixth dynasty (about 3,000 years ago)—contained under unbroken seal the mummy of a woman. The hieroglyphic inscription identified the woman only as being "from the East." The moment Yoko heard that mysterious phrase, she was convinced that this mysterious woman was actually herself in a previous incarnation.

She had John Green read on the mummy immediately. He found the cards favored the purchase of the piece, offered at three-quarters of a million dollars. He could not confirm, however, that the woman "from the East" was Yoko Ono back in the days when she was a queen in Egypt. Nevertheless, the bargaining for the Golden Lady was driven along at a furious pace because Yoko told Sam Green that it was far more important to lay hands on this invaluable piece than it was to save money.

The problems of acquisition did not end with the purchase of the sarcophagus. For one thing, there is a law against bringing a dead body into the United States without the proper documents from the embalmer. For another, it is contrary to customs regulations—indeed, nothing could be more suspicious!—to enter with a big box that cannot be opened for inspection. Sam Green, always so adroit at threading bureaucratic mazes, was taxed to the limits by the Golden Lady. For days on end he called first one, then another official, pulling strings. Finally, the path was cleared. The magic lady could be removed from the bank vault in which she had been impounded by customs and conveyed to the Pyramid Room of Apartment 72 at the Dakota.

On 29 January 1978, about one o'clock in the afternoon, the art movers tramped into the apartment, bearing their precious burden. Two wooden sawhorses had been set up to receive the sarcophagus. Once the crate was securely in position, it was pried open and the inner wrappings were removed. But when the gold-gleaming sarcophagus was exposed, Yoko was horrified by the face carved on the lid of the burial box. The mysterious woman from the East was an ugly little creature who didn't bear the slightest resemblance to Yoko Ono!

A couple of days later, when John Green came up to the Dakota for his weekly consultation, he found Yoko in a highly agitated condition. She commanded him to look at the sarcophagus. "Is there something special I should be looking for?" he inquired blandly.

"Yes, the face! Look at that face! If that's what the woman inside looked like, then I don't think it could be me."

"Why not?" asked Green, playing it dumb.

"Because she's not Japanese."

"No one ever said that she was, Yoko," Green replied calmly. "She was 'from the East,' and from the look of it, she was Persian."

Yoko was furious. "So you're saying that I was wrong about this being one of my previous incarnations, and that probably amuses you, doesn't it?" she hissed. "I've spent a lot of money on this, and I wanted the power that it was supposed to hold. I think that I have wasted my money."

Green had an answer for her. "Fortunately," he replied, "it's worth more in dollars than you paid for it, even if it isn't worth it to *you*."

Yoko was not assuaged by this argument. She marched around the coffin, giving it contemptuous looks.

"If you don't like it we could always sell it," said Green helpfully.

"No, that's no good," snapped Yoko. "I told John that I had to have it because it was me, and now I'm stuck with it!"

Being an Egyptian princess was just one of Yoko's fantasies. She and John were also thrilled by the idea that they were reincarnations of Josephine and Napoleon. As they read the story of the famous lovers, Josephine, eight years older than Napoleon, was a witch from an island, who gave the general the power that enabled him to rule. Her great ambition was to make him invade Egypt so that she could gain the ultimate supernatural power, which was locked up in its ancient tombs and temples. When Napoleon spent a night in the Great Pyramid, he emerged a changed man. Clearly John had to follow in the emperor's footsteps and attain the same illumination. Such notions made John adore Yoko. Once, in Sam Green's presence, Lennon burst out: "Look at that woman [pointing at Yoko]! Isn't she exotic? I had a dream when I was really young. I wanted to marry a foreign princess. I thought I was gonna get an Indian. But I got somethin' that's just as exotic-lookin'! She's a princess in her country."

Eventually the need to keep working the Egyptian vein led Sam Green out of his depth and made him the victim of an even keener shark. It all began one day when he was talking to a Boston dealer who revealed that the source of the best merchandise was an Egyptian who had discovered a buried temple and was seeking the money to complete its excavation. Sam arranged to meet the Egyptian and hear his proposition. The digger said that all he needed to commence operations was $46,000. There were problems, of course. The biggest difficulty lay in concealing the excavation from the prying eyes of the Egyptian authorities, who were always cruising over the archaeological sites in observation planes.

When Sam Green recounted the story to John Green, that canny country boy came up with two solutions to the surveillance problem. One was to establish a chicken farm in the desert, under whose Quonset huts the digging could proceed while the dirt was camouflaged as chicken shit. The other, more plausible, device was to establish a factory for manufacturing bandages of Egyptian cotton; the site could be concealed with long strips of white cloth, supposedly bandaging material drying in the sun.

Having solved this problem, Sam Green took the scheme to Yoko, who put up the money in a flash. The Egyptian took the cash but offered nothing in return but promises. When he opened a gallery in another city and began selling the same sort of material, Sam realized that they had been gypped. But he didn't give up hope. He decided to go to Egypt and discover for himself the whereabouts of the illegal excavation. To Yoko he said only that he was going to the dig.

On 19 January 1979, Sam flew first to London, where he stopped to party with some friends. No sooner did he start having fun with the society people than he got an emergency call from Yoko. She told him that Charlie Swan had discovered through reading the cards that the only solution to the Egyptian problem was for Yoko to go to the secret dig *herself.* (Most likely, Yoko decided to go herself and then shifted the responsibility to the cards.)

As if this startling declaration were not bad enough, Yoko announced next that she intended to bring along Lennon! After rattling off some nonsense about their numbers being in harmony for once, she ordered Sam to obtain suitable accommodations for the royal couple in Cairo and then make all necessary preparations for a journey into the desert.

When Sam put down the phone, he knew his only hope lay in delay, in somehow forestalling this fatal development. Ringing up the Lennons' travel agent in New York, he begged her to say that there were no open flights to Egypt. She checked her computer and came back with the alarming news that John and Yoko had already booked their flight and would be arriving soon in Cairo.

When Green got to the swarming city on the Nile, he found the tourist season at its height. Only by offering a hefty bribe to the concierge of the Hilton Nile was he able to procure the Lennons a suitable suite. Fortunately he had confirmed his own reservation from New York. Now his game was to hold Yoko in check with one hand, while with the other he bribed the people who knew the whereabouts of the dig. But the moment Sam Green confronted Yoko in the arrival lounge, he knew he was in trouble.

Bursting with energy, she announced that she was going to accompany Sam to the dig. He warned that her presence would attract so much attention that the whole scheme would be exposed. He was planning to go in disguise, he explained, swathed in robes and burnoose like a Bedouin. "If you can go in disguise, so can I!" snapped Yoko, thrilled by the idea of masquerade. In a flash she conjured up a picture of herself costumed as a Middle Eastern princess, accompanied by John, who would be identified as her bodyguard.

Now Sam threw up a whole series of roadblocks. He said that by rushing to Cairo to meet Yoko, he had upset his original schedule and missed his contact man, who had gone to New York to meet Sam. But as fast as he came up with a lie, just as fast she batted it down. Eventually poor Sam felt himself becoming hopelessly disoriented. "It's hard to remember so many stories!" he wailed. Clearly this was a case for John Green. If Sam could reach his partner in New York, there might be some way to make the tarot oracle curb Yoko's pressure. Now the problem became the phone service, which had broken down under the heavy usage of the peak season.

To kill time, Sam decided to take the Lennons on a sight-seeing expedition to the famous step pyramids at Saqqarah. Arriving at sunset, they bribed a guide to take them about after closing time. The experience was thrilling. "We were all tingling with excitement," recalled Sam. "John kept saying: 'This is a magical place, a magical time. I've been here before!'" In the photograph of the party taken inside the tombs, a weird aura emanates from every face. John, inspired to behave as he had in youth, broke off a tooth from a mummy's mouth and popped it in his pocket. By the time he got back to the hotel, he was so uneasy about having taken something that might be tainted with a curse that he discarded the tooth immediately.

No amount of tomb hopping could wear out Yoko. Sam was amazed at her energy. "She has the stamina of a bat!" he emoted. "She can whiz around all night long! She is a driven person!" At night Yoko would wait till John nodded off; then she would slip over to Sam's room to continue their plotting. The more Sam procrastinated, the more Yoko fought to overcome his resistance. Just as he was lying about the difficulties of the situation, she started lying about the ease of the solution. She claimed that she was receiving instructions from her distant psychics through mental telepathy and even by possession. "Sam!" she cried. "This is not *me* talking; this is the *supernatural*! And the supernatural has always been right. *This* is the way we're going to do it!" Then she rattled off a scenario in which they bribed their way past a military checkpoint and went plunging into the wasteland guided by her voices.

Meantime, Sam would duck out of the hotel to meet with the head of the secret police, who, he was convinced, knew the whereabouts of the mysterious dig. He also kept hammering away at the telephone operators in the basement of the hotel, trying to get a line to New York as well as bugging his local travel agent to obtain flights to the States. Often he bumped into Yoko in the telephone room.

She wasn't doing any better than Sam with her overseas calls. No amount of bribing, threatening, or cajoling could put her in touch with Charlie Swan. What was frustrating their frantic endeavors were the 'round-the-clock preparations being made to receive Secretary of State Cyrus Vance, who was about to descend upon the hotel with an enormous retinue. Vance was scheduled to occupy the very suite in which John and Yoko were quartered. When that moment came, Sam knew that he would have to give his clients his room and sleep in the closet. In fact, he could already hear John teasing him about being a "closet queen"! Oh, it was a tight little corner into which this con artist had painted himself.

Yoko's biggest problem was keeping John from going stir crazy. She often delegated her baby-watching chores to Sam, who would sit for hours on end in a velvet-upholstered banquette in the preposterously overdecorated hotel restaurant, talking with the apathetic Lennon. "The little woman has it all planned," John assured the fuming Sam Green. "There's no point in not going along with her. I tried, and it doesn't work—believe me! And she's more often than not right. So I just sit back and wait for what the oracle says next." That was Lennon's basic rationalization. He could apply it to particular moments, like the present, or he could extend it to cover his whole life. "The big plan is that I do nothing for the next four years," John told Sam one afternoon. "Yoko says that everything I do is doomed to failure until the year 1982. That year, according to the numbers, I'll conquer the world again. Before that, if I try anything, I'll just fall on me face."

When Sam Green sought to uncover the reasoning behind this strange sentence, he was astonished at how little understanding Lennon exhibited of the occult formulas that determined his life. "The way I understand it," Lennon explained lamely, "one and nine makes a ten. Two and eight makes a ten. A ten is a one, and a one is the best place to start. Follow me? So Yoko and I will both be ones in 1982, and that's the best time to start up the old career again. Till then I just cool me heels, smoke me ganja, watch the telly, and let her do all the fussing with the business."

For days John and Sam sat in their banquette, John drinking endless cups of coffee while Sam sipped cocktails. Meanwhile, Yoko kept watch by the phone in her room, sitting for hours on end with the dead instrument in her hand, as she burned the split ends of her hair with the tip of a cigarette. Sam sought time and again to distract John by offering to show him around the city. He pictured the delights of horseback riding near the pyramids, an exploratory walk through the ancient necropolis or a visit to the Great Museum, which stood just across the street. Lennon would have nothing to do with anything that demanded the slightest physical exertion. He was a prisoner of apathy. In fact, he was a bound prisoner. One of his habitual mannerisms was binding his wrists with a bit of string, a rubber band, a robe tie, whatever lay at hand. He also wore a pin whose design was a butterfly caught in a spider's web.

The only thing John would do is talk, in the manner of a monologist, rambling on from one theme to another, often reaching back to the years with the Beatles. One day he drifted into his recollections of

Brian Epstein. He conceded that he had loved Brian "more than he could love a woman." John was intent, however, on making clear that he had never been sexually intimate with Brian. He admitted that he had almost wanted to try it, but he just couldn't—and didn't. Sam—whom John regarded as gay—got the impression that John wanted to put on record that he was no fag.

Sam Green was finally rescued by the surprising appearance of Tom Hoving. The borzoi-faced Hoving fastened upon the Lennons, who were alarmed to be seen by him because they were supposed to be on a secret and dangerous mission. In a flash, Sam Green saw how he could turn this chance encounter to his advantage. Getting through finally to John Green in New York, Sam barked, "For chrissake, find something in the cards that demands their immediate return!"

Green called Yoko and began a heavy reading, in the course of which he identified a dangerous presence in her vicinity. "There is someone near you who will obstruct your purpose and betray your intentions," he intoned as if he were the voice of the cards.

"Tom Hoving!" gasped Yoko.

Immediately Green read on Hoving. Yes, it was clear now. Hoving was on assignment for the Egyptian government. He would detect them and denounce them to the Egyptian police. They were in grave danger. They must flee—immediately!

The ordeal was over—but not quite! Arriving at Rome on 18 February, John, Yoko, and Sam had to wait three hours for a Pan Am jumbo jet. When the movie was announced in the first-class cabin, it turned out to be *Sgt. Pepper's Lonely Hearts Club Band*. It was agony for John and Yoko to watch it. Then all the "steerage" passengers began sending up requests for autographs, a real drag! As the plane approached New York, it ran into a terrible blizzard. They circled the city for hours. Finally, the plane ran out of food and liquor. To distract the passengers, there was a *second* showing of the Beatles' film. At last they landed—in Boston! There they waited for hours for a flight to New York. When they arrived at Kennedy, they were eighteen hours late.

With sixteen pieces of luggage, they couldn't fit into a cab. Sam Green summoned up his last strength and found them a limo. As soon as the Lennons were assured that all their bags were aboard, they slammed the door and left poor Sam standing on the curb.

CREATURE OF HABIT

When John and Yoko got back from their third annual holiday in Japan,* they made a pact to give up heroin. Yoko discussed her drug problem with John Green. Instead of coming up with a magical solution, Green warned her that heroin was ruled by a demonic spirit. The only solution, he insisted, was to abandon the drug forthwith. So powerful was his persuasion that he actually convinced Yoko a couple of times to flush her stash down the toilet. But afterward she complained about the cost and discomfort of these sacrifices. Finally she turned away from John Green to seek the aid of Sam Green, who proved much more sympathetic.

Sam took the position that since Yoko could not be dissuaded from using the drug, it was best to accept her addiction until she could be persuaded to seek help from a doctor.

Meanwhile, Kit Carter was making his deliveries every morning. Sometimes he would bump into John Lennon in the outer office. Kit had been instructed by Yoko that if anyone was present, he was to go into the bathroom and put the packet in a tampon box beneath the sink. That is what he did. Months later, when Kit was finally introduced to John by Yoko, she said: "John, you remember Kit."

This trip lasted only a month, from 23 July to 28 August 1979. The portion of it spent at Karuizawa was witnessed by Hideo Nagura, the teenage son of Yoko's cousin and lifelong friend Reiko. Hideo's recollections are of interest not just because they come from the Japanese side of the fence but because they show how obvious was John Lennon's plight. "We could never figure out who was John," he reported, explaining that every day Lennon would appear in a fresh costume, complete with hat and wearing a variety of hairstyles, including sometimes a beard. He appeared in search of an identity, hoping that some accidental occurrence would give him a clue. Isolated and bored, John read a lot but never listened to music. The Japanese would say that he should make some music because it was important for Sean to see that his father worked. The only thing John did was buy clothes for himself and for the child, who was always dressed like a doll. Yoko appeared to enjoy her visits to her family's home, but she had few friends. The oddest thing about her, Hideo recalled, is that she had predicted John's death and sought to avert it.

John replied with a meaningful intonation: "Yes, I remember Kit quite well."

It was clear to Kit that John knew what was going on. Indeed, how could he not know when by December Yoko was presenting a clinically perfect picture of a heroin addict. Yet every time she received a delivery, she would warn, "John must never know!"

Unlike Yoko, Lennon had developed such a loathing for himself, according to John Green, that he applied his enormous powers of determination to getting off horse—and he succeeded. To keep himself from relapsing, John began employing a sensory deprivation tank located in the attic of the house he had recently purchased on Long Island. Lennon would climb inside this big cedarwood box, resembling a coffin, and close the lid. Floating for up to half an hour in the dark, buoyed by the warm saline solution, he experienced a sensation that reminded him of getting high.

While John was spacing out, Yoko was, as usual, gunning her engine. Her latest obsessions were the Broadway theater and the real estate market. Her interest in the stage had surfaced first when she announced in Japan that she and John were going to write a musical, but what had focused this fantasy was Lee Eastman's recent success in investing in Broadway shows. Yoko's idea was to write a musical titled *The Ballad of John and Yoko* that would be set at the Dakota and would rehash all the familiar episodes in the rock world's favorite fairy tale. When John Green warned her that the cost of such an enterprise would be enormous, Yoko countered that the cost would be virtually nothing because they could dress the set with furniture from Apartment 72 and employ their own wardrobe. When Green objected further that Lennon could not compose a full theater score, Yoko replied that *she* would write the score and give the credit to John.

Yoko's preoccupation with buying property grew out of Green's efforts to persuade her to make a large investment that would generate a hefty tax loss. The moment the fateful words "real estate" were out of his mouth, Yoko caught the bug. "Real estate!" she echoed. "I'm very good at real estate." Then she explained how she had bought Apartment 72 in 1973 for $105,000 and seen it rise in just seven years to its current evaluation of $400,000. (What she didn't say was that the decision to buy the flat had been made by Harold Seider.) Now Yoko took off on what became her greatest shopping spree.

Her first move was to research the entire East Coast real estate market. Studio One was soon littered with hundreds of prospectuses, magazines, and brokers' sheets that Yoko read relentlessly and then dropped on the floor. As she considered each property, Green read up on it. Meantime, he begged her to avoid the ostentatious and concentrate on the B-grade stuff that, with a little paint and paper, could be transformed readily into income property. But Yoko would hear nothing of such degrading proposals; she wanted fine old houses and estates that she would be proud to own. When she started dickering for these costly places, instead of employing intermediaries to conceal her identity, she announced herself immediately to the brokers, who responded by upping their prices. Even worse was her usual refusal to stir outside the office to examine the properties she was buying. She picked out mansions and farms like a suburban matron shopping for clothes from a mail-order catalog.

Her property-buying blitz got off to an impressive start on 18 December 1979, when she signed the papers for El Salano, one of those immense Mediterranean villas that lie along South Ocean Boulevard in Palm Beach, Florida. A twenty-two-room monument to conspicuous consumption, designed by society architect Addison Mizner, this soon-to-be-landmarked white elephant boasted fifty yards of private beach, morning and afternoon pools (one filled with salt water, the other with sweet water), and a grand ballroom whose towering Palladian windows rose to a cypress ceiling carved in intricate Moorish patterns. The his-and-her bedroom-and-bath suites were so large that they occupied almost an entire floor.

The Lennons had happened on this property the previous winter, when they turned up one night while the owner, the well-known society hostess Brownie McLean (whose family had owned the Hope Diamond) was giving a dinner party. Mrs. McLean gave John and Yoko a quick tour of the block, and John said, "We'll take it," meaning they would rent the house for three weeks. Then Yoko had decided that it was foolish to rent for a month what you could buy and leave empty for eleven months. So despite the fact that upkeep on the house was close to $100,000 per annum and the building so dilapidated that it would take a couple of million dollars in skilled labor to restore it to its original grandeur, the Lennons bought the mansion for $750,000. There was only one stipulation: Yoko insisted that Brownie McLean, who had been in possession of El Salano for a lifetime, must be off the property with all her things in forty-eight hours. The locals recall a mad scramble, with trucks loading in the middle of the night, as if in anticipation of a hurricane from the Gulf.

Yoko's next acquisition was inspired by a prophecy of Edgar Cayce, who had predicted that when the deluge came, causing Manhattan to sink beneath its rivers, only a few regions in the entire country would survive the inundation. One of these was tidewater Virginia, where Yoko purchased two colonial farms, one of 22 and one of 128 acres, along the Potomac. The houses on these farms were known to Sam Green's father, a historian of American architecture, who explained that one orchard had been laid out two hundred years before by Thomas Jefferson. Assured by Sam that these were "two of the finest estates anywhere," Yoko popped for $400,000—a small price to pay for survival.

Another place that was psychically guaranteed to be secure from disasters was Iron Gate, an ordinary house near Livingston Manor, an ugly little town in the Catskills. The house's only good feature was the surrounding wood of ninety acres, extended by subsequent purchases to four hundred acres. It is doubtful that John Lennon ever laid eyes on this property, which was staffed by a friend of John Green, a sculptor named Joe Attardo, who had renovated Studio One.

The actual selection of these survival shelters was the work of Yoko's latest clairvoyant, Marlene Wiener, an obese woman, known at the Dakota as the Chocolate Psychic because she was always presented with a box of candy when she appeared. Yoko would often send Marlene pictures of houses that she judged by putting her hand over her eyes and going into a trance.

In addition to their many distant properties, the Lennons owned five apartments at the Dakota, but only two of these flats, Apartments 71 and 72, were full-scale residences; the others were Studio One, Apartment 4 (the Seamans' room-and-a-half over the gate), and Apartment 911, a garret storage space. Yoko became interested in Apartment 71 when its occupants, Allen and Etheline Staley, went away for a year in 1977. To safeguard the Lennons' privacy, Yoko sublet the flat and kept it empty. When Ethelene Staley got home, her Dominican maid, Rosa (who also worked for the Lennons), pulled the sheets off the bed and displayed the mattress covers, which bore inch-long Santería conjuring symbols. The Staleys sold their six-room flat to Yoko in the fall of 1978. She used it subsequently for storage.

The only house that the Lennons visited frequently was Cannon Hill, a weathered oak-shingle three-story structure situated at the foot of a hill overlooking Cold Spring Harbor, on the north shore of Long Island. Purchased in the spring of 1979 for about $400,000, this old place was built on a scale totally out of keeping with the family's needs. There were fourteen bedrooms, a whole floor of social rooms, and, above the kitchen wing, seven rooms for maids and governesses, with but a single bath. The house did enjoy, however, a superb view across the water to the wooded shore of Connecticut.

The man entrusted with the lucrative job of renovating Cannon Hill was a young shop clerk, recently turned decorator, named Samuel G. Havadtoy, whom the Lennons had met by chance in the fall of 1978. Shopping along Lexington Avenue, they had passed an antiques store at 70th Street, in whose window stood an Egyptian revival desk that struck Yoko as perfect for herself. Entering the shop, the Lennons discovered that the proprietor, Stuart Greet, a decorator, was absent, but his assistant, a skinny young man in glasses, was eager to serve them. He ingratiated himself so successfully with Yoko that she not only bought the desk but invited him to offer his suggestions for the decoration of Studio One, which was still not complete though the flat had been purchased in 1976 and renovated the following year.

Samuel Havadtoy's personal history is mysterious. Born in Transylvania in 1951, he was taken at an early age to Budapest. His mother— the principal figure in his life—was a Jew, a survivor of the Holocaust. Recognizing that her son, a bright boy who had won a prize from the local Komsomol, would have no future in Hungary, Mrs. Havadtoy had arranged to smuggle him out of the country to Paris, where he lived for a time with relatives. Then he went to England, where a rich old matron put him up at her country house. One night at a club in London, young Sam met a big, fat, red-haired Englishman, who looked rather like Goldfinger. Shortly thereafter, Samuel Havadtoy left for New York under the aegis of Stuart Greet.

Havadtoy's arrival in 1972 at the age of twenty-one, with nothing but the clothes in his suitcase, was witnessed by Bart Gorin, who was then Greet's chauffeur. Havadtoy moved in with his patron and remained with him for the next seven years. Finally, Greet established his protégé in a co-op in the East 80s and bought him a little house in Hampton Bays.

When Havadtoy struck out on his own in November 1978, shortly after meeting the Lennons, he sought to emulate his former employer in every way. The Samuel Havadtoy Gallery was an echo of the Stuart Greet Gallery, offering antiques as well as Havadtoy's services as interior decorator; the brownstone that he purchased at 192 East 82nd Street, just west of Lexington Avenue, was the counterpart of the building that Greet owned farther down the same avenue; and just as Greet had lived with Sam and employed him as a shop assistant so Havadtoy began living with his new lover and helper, Luciano Sparacino.

Luciano was a high-strung, hawkishly handsome boy from Brooklyn, with aquiline features and thick dark hair styled in the latest coif. His most striking trait was his extreme nervousness, suggestive of the blurred wings and darting movements of a hummingbird. A brilliant hairstylist and makeup artist, he was living by himself and doing well when he met Havadtoy. They spent their first hour together at the Right Bank, a subsidewalk French restaurant on Madison Avenue, a few blocks from Greet's shop. Luciano proposed to the cool and taciturn Havadtoy that they play checkers on the red-checked tablecloth.

Moving a penny impulsively toward his opponent, he exclaimed: "There! Now it's your turn."

As Luciano explained, "I thought he was going to jump me or jump two and take two. What he did was take *all* the pennies off the cloth. I laughed and said, 'Boy! Do you know more than I do!'"

Havadtoy replied: "That's the only way I live."

Luciano found Havadtoy's audacity attractive. He would have gone off with him that night but for a jealous companion. The very next night, however, the young men met again, at a party. Sam was feeling so ill that he didn't try to seduce Luciano. He simply said to him in an imploring tone: "I want to see you!"

Before Luciano could respond, his jealous companion screeched: "I'm watching you two! No papers exchanged!"

Luciano whispered: "I'll call you at Stuart Greet's."

A couple of days later they dined at the Russian Tea Room and went to see *Stardust Ballroom*. "He fell in love," remarked Luciano matter-of-factly. "He told me that I would never stay with him. People like me never stay with him because he's not attractive enough. But he was so attracted to me that he would never leave me."

What Havadtoy did, in fact, was persuade Luciano to set up housekeeping with him in his recently purchased brownstone and become his assistant in the ground-floor gallery. It was here in 1979 that Havadtoy and Luciano began working for Yoko, buying pieces for her homes and eventually undertaking the renovation of Apartment 72 as well as the house at Cold Spring Harbor.

While Yoko was absorbed in real estate, John Lennon began to show signs in the spring of 1980 that he was coming out of his prolonged period of hibernation. Actually he had first begun to stir about in his den the preceding spring, when he had bought a Sardonyx, the "space guitar," which, when attached to the Harmonizer, makes the guitar sound like all the instruments of the orchestra. With a Compurhythm 88 providing the beat, John could sit atop his bed and play like a one-man band. He had also sketched out the plan of a tour, making use of the new technology developed during the Seventies for stadium concerts. He envisioned video cameras in cherry pickers stationed before the stage so the audience could see the band on giant screens. All these activities antedate by more than a year his actual return to composition and recording. They attest unmistakably to his longing to go back to making music. They also raise the important question: Why did Lennon do no writing between the years 1975 and 1980?

It is clear from John's diary letter of 1977 that he was resigned by that time to spending the balance of the decade in an unproductive state, his moment of rebirth being set for the year 1980. In the spring of 1977 John told a young fan named Mario Casciano that he and Yoko had decided to cut the "umbilical cord to the past" by closing down the Lennon Music office in the Capitol Building. John said he was hanging up his guitar because "music was also part of his past."

The spring of 1977 corresponds with the moment when Yoko took complete control of the family business and proclaimed herself a businesswoman. Hence, it is possible that in exchanging the role of artist for that of businessperson, she may have felt that it would be unjust for John to pursue his artistic career when she had relinquished hers. On the other hand, John's letter from Japan makes it clear that he was not inspired at this time and that he had nothing to say, which is not surprising in view of the way he was living. John Lennon's songs had always arisen spontaneously from his life, particularly at moments of crisis or deep emotional involvement. He sometimes compared himself to a diarist and could have echoed Goethe's famous remark "All my poems are occasional verses." To function as a journalist, a writer must feel that he has something new to report. The only dispatch Lennon could file was that he was "Watching the Wheels Go Round."

All the same, as John told May, he never lost the desire to make music; in fact, he suffered so much from this baffled yearning that to keep it from being continually aroused and then frustrated, he adopted the practice of listening only to Muzak or classical music stations. Otherwise, as he explained in one of his last interviews, "If I heard anything bad [on a rock station], I'd want to fix it and if I heard anything good, I'd wonder why I hadn't thought of it." In fact, he *was* thinking of it, constantly, but he concealed his thoughts, as he had learned to do as a boy when he was living with Mimi.

Once John got off heroin, his natural strength began to revive, and with it his yearning to get back to work. Yet Yoko would not lift the ban on making music. No matter how restless he became, she kept warning him that if he tried to work against the stars, he would fall flat on his face and suffer a humiliating failure. Hence, his long silence.

When Fred Seaman reported for work on the morning of 15 January 1980, he was dying to ask John about a call that had come through the office the day before from Paul McCartney. Paul had rung up from the Stanhope Hotel, where he was staying with Linda and the kids prior to taking off for a tour of Japan with Wings. Yoko had taken the call, and Paul had told her that he had scored some "dynamite grass," offering to bring some to John. When Yoko blocked this move, Paul retaliated instinctively by boasting that he and Linda were going to occupy the Presidential Suite of the Hotel Okura—the Lennons' official residence in Tokyo.

This jab had a shattering effect on Yoko. She told Sam Green that she felt that Paul and Linda were invading her home. Immediately she informed John, who became just as upset as she. He was still upset, his head turtled into a bowl of shredded wheat, when Fred entered the kitchen that morning. Inquiring with feigned casualness about Paul's call, Fred met with a blank response at first. But the thing lay so heavily on John's mind that he couldn't remain silent for long. Bit by bit he disclosed the story, revealing finally what most troubled him. "He's going to spoil our hotel karma," complained John. "We've had really excellent hotel karma so far, and I'd hate to see them contaminate it for us. If Paul and Linda sleep there, we'll never have peace when we go back in that room." Fortunately all was not lost. "I already talked to Mother," said John. "She and Charlie Swan are working it out." Indeed, they were!

All day long Yoko and John Green remained closeted in Studio One. On no condition were they to be disturbed, Richie DePalma told Fred Seaman. Meantime John was burning with impatience to learn the result of their confabulation. Again and again that afternoon he buzzed Studio One to find out what was happening. When Fred went home that night, he thought the Lennons had gone mad.

Next morning, while watching the seven-o'clock news, Fred was startled to hear that Paul McCartney had been busted in Tokyo for drugs! Rushing to the Dakota, he was greeted by Richie, who smiled sarcastically and said: "Isn't it funny the way Paul got busted in Japan today? Especially since he called yesterday asking if he should bring over some smoke?" As the day wore on, hourly reports were received from Japan on the McCartney case.

They disclosed that when Paul, Linda, and the children had passed through customs at Narita Airport, they were asked to open their luggage. The grass was discovered in Linda's makeup bag, which contained twenty joints in a plastic Baggie. ("Linda always used to get paranoid if she was down to her last three ounces of smoke. That's why she took supplies with her to Japan," explained Jo-Jo Laine, wife of Denny Laine, lead guitarist of Wings, adding, "She thought she was above the law.") The moment the drugs were discovered, Paul stepped forward and took full responsibility for them. The police were summoned, and he was led away in handcuffs.

At police headquarters, Paul was subjected to a five-hour interrogation, the first in a series of grillings that continued for the next ten days. When he wasn't being taken step by step over his entire life by ever-fresh teams of police officials, he was confined to his cell, where he was denied the right to bathe, change his clothes, play his guitar, or use writing materials. When the British vice-consul appeared, instead of cheering Paul up, he said ominously, "Well, it could be eight years, you know." After ten days Paul was taken in handcuffs to the airport and put aboard a plane for England. His eleven-concert tour was canceled, and 100,000 ticket buyers had to be given refunds.

On the afternoon of the bust a holiday mood prevailed in the Land of Lennono. John told Fred Seaman to get every paper he could lay his hands on, particularly the British papers. He was determined to relish every crumb of Paul's misfortune. When Yoko's informants reported that Paul's jailhouse guards were making him sing "Yesterday" over and over again, Lennon's joy knew no bounds. Slapping his thigh with glee, he burst into song himself, howling the line about how Paul's troubles had seemed so distant. John boasted to Fred: "We could get him off like that!" snapping his fingers. "Mother's got all these connections. . . . But of course, he'd never call to ask for help. It would be beneath him." (Paul had asked for and received Yoko's help in Japan when his original application for a visa had been twice rejected on the grounds of prior drug offenses. Yoko had urged her cousin Hideaki Kase, son of Japan's first representative to the United Nations, to use his influence. Paul got his visa.)

The day after the bust Fred drove John and Yoko to Suffern, New York, to inspect yet another house. John loaded a pipe with Thai stick and crowed: "This is dynamite weed!" Then, smoking contentedly in the back of the station wagon, he uttered his last word on the subject of Paul's arrest: "You know, it's Paul's arrogance towards the Japanese that screwed him. I just know it."

Yoko chimed in: "That's right!"

A year later John Green told Jeffrey Hunter: "She claimed to have made the arrangements by telephone, telling undisclosed Japanese authorities that McCartney had a low opinion of the Japanese."

Sam Green corroborated this statement, adding: "She had a cousin over there who runs customs. One call from Yoko and Paul was finished."

YOKO IN LOVE

While Yoko was having Paul busted for drugs in Japan, she was sinking herself into the terminal phase of heroin addiction. Her skin was green, her cheeks were hollow, her speech was slurred, and her hips and legs were black and blue from bumping into things. She would wear the same clothes for days and never bathe. When Sean would go to her for a kiss, he would recoil and cry: "Mommy! You stink!" Sam Green was now very concerned about Yoko. He asked constantly: "Where will this end?" It was obvious that matters could not long continue upon such a disastrous course. Yet nothing changed until the first week in April 1980, when Yoko finally summoned up the courage to confront her addiction.

At that moment the Lennons were at Palm Beach. They had arrived with Julian on the day before Yoko's birthday, 18 February. John had celebrated the occasion in a highly ambiguous manner. He had sent Fred out to purchase hundreds of white gardenias. When Yoko awoke and saw the flowers, she was horror-stricken. In Japan gardenias are the flowers of death. They are always banked around the corpse at funerals. Presumably John had acted without knowledge of this fact, but it is also possible that he had learned it and forgotten it and was subconsciously rebuking Yoko for sinking into the living death of heroin addiction.

The holiday in the sun, which entailed such pastimes as a boat cruise and much lolling about in El Salano's two swimming pools, came to an end just before Julian's birthday. John took the boy back to New York to see *Beatlemania* on Broadway and gave him an expensive Rolex watch, which Julian promptly lost, quaking with terror at the thought of his father's wrath. On the day of his birthday, 8 April, he was put aboard a plane to England. Now, her immediate responsibilities discharged, Yoko faced the sour music of detoxification.

Though Yoko had persuaded herself—against all reason—that John did not suspect her of being addicted, she was not so foolish as to think that she could go through the Sturm und Drang of heroin withdrawal without revealing her secret. Clearly her first move had to be getting John Lennon out of the house. She instructed John Green to give Lennon a tarot reading and then send him off to some distant place, promising him that he would be vouchsafed great spiritual revelations. Green refused to cooperate. He told Yoko that she should confront John with the fact that she was hooked and work out a solution with his cooperation. Yoko took matters into her own hands and told John that he must leave immediately for the house at Cold Spring Harbor because she was about to be initiated into a secret society and the rites demanded absolute privacy. Gullible as ever, Lennon allowed himself to be bundled off on 9 April with Fred, Sean, and the indispensable housekeeper (and informant), Uda-San.

Getting John out of the house was not the last of Yoko's problems, for that very week her mother had arrived and was planning to remain in New York for a month. Desperate to start her cure, Yoko treated the aristocratic old woman with astonishing rudeness, ordering her about like a servant and screaming at her, "Don't talk!" When she persisted, Yoko hurled a fork at her. Another of Yoko's devices for humiliating her mother was the use of obscene language, which went through the old lady like a knife. When all else failed, Yoko resorted to pure invective, shouting in English, "You're the most stupid, frivolous person! Do something about your hair!"

On the morning after John's departure for Long Island, Yoko had her customary rendezvous with Kit at 7:00 A.M. Instead of conducting her tea bag ceremony, she said: "Pardon the expression, but this is getting to be a fucking drag!"

"Yes, it is," replied Kit politely. "What do you want to do?"

Yoko told Kit he must fly to London that very night to buy morphine. "This is the way John and I did it before," she explained as she tore open her bag and began pulling out handfuls of hundred-dollar bills. When she had tossed scores of hundreds on the desk, she signaled Kit to take the cash and gave him the names of some people in London who would help him in his quest.

As Kit contemplated this sudden and dangerous mission, he asked, quite reasonably: "Can't we buy morphine in New York?" Yoko had no patience with such a question. She was now in the grip of one of her manic obsessions. In her mind nothing stood between her current affliction and complete relief except this little purchase in London. She shooed Kit out of the office.

Sam Green seized the opportunity presented by Kit's absence to persuade Yoko to see a doctor. Finally, she agreed. On the morning of 22 April Sam took her to the office of Dr. Robert Freymann.

Many New York musicians employed the services of Dr. Freymann, who had been the attending physician at the death of Charlie Parker. In fact, on any morning outside the doctor's office, just off Fifth Avenue in the East 80s, a crowd of beat-looking, sickly men would be seen hanging around the door, awaiting the physician's arrival. As the hour of seven struck, he would pull up in an immaculate Mercedes. Emerging from the car with his coat draped across his shoulders, the picture of health himself—pink skin, full head of white hair, handsome Germanic features—the good doctor would greet his tattered flock cheerfully by raising two fingers of his right hand, wiggling the digits in the toodle-oo gesture, and lisping, "Goot morning, junkies! Follow me!"

On the morning that Sam arrived with Yoko, who disguised herself with a wig, dark glasses, and a man's overcoat, matters were not proceeding so smoothly at 1010 Fifth Avenue. In fact, no sooner had Sam and Yoko seated themselves in the waiting room than a nurse came running out, screaming, "The doctor's had a heart attack! I think he's dead!" Instantly all the patients scrambled for the door. Sam grabbed Yoko and split. A week later Green enlisted the aid of a capable medical man, Dr. Rodney B. Ryan, who agreed to come to the Dakota and treat this famous patient.

Withdrawal from heroin is no worse than a bad case of the flu, but junkies are notoriously incapable of suffering, which is one of the reasons why they become junkies in the first place. Yoko proved a very bad patient. She was terrified of the pains of withdrawal, loath to discipline herself, and full of ideas for eluding the treatment. She developed all the familiar symptoms, from shakes and shivers to the illusion that spiders were crawling beneath her skin. When she started threatening suicide, Sam moved into the Dakota and stayed with her night and day for the next two weeks.

Detoxification produced a paradoxical effect on Yoko. Instead of sinking into a sickbed, she dashed about the Dakota, babbling incoherently in what one of the servants identified as archaic Japanese. Her demands, always peremptory, now became utterly bizarre. One night poor Sam was sent out at eleven o'clock to a Korean greengrocer to buy five crates of parsley. When he got back with his load of herbs, he and Yoko ground up the stuff, and she immersed herself in a parsley bath—one of John Green's prescriptions. Sam slept at the foot of Yoko's bed, like the faithful Masako, but he got so little sleep that finally he broke down and wept. In desperation he summoned Dr. Ryan, who spent five hours with the patient. Dr. Ryan offered Sam a very valuable piece of advice that Sam wasn't wise enough to heed. "Sam, be careful," the doctor warned. "One addiction is always replaced by another addiction."

John Green's behavior during the crisis stood in sharp contrast with that of his partner. Yoko's principal adviser refused to see her. He justified his delinquency by maintaining that direct involvement with his client at such a moment would impair or destroy their working relationship. Actually, nothing could have damaged the relationship more than his refusal to come to Yoko's aid. Sam Green, by contrast, was rewarded with a check for $100,000.

John Lennon had no idea what was going on at the Dakota during this period because he could not make a telephone call. Just before she had begun her cure, Yoko had gone out to Cold Spring Harbor and persuaded John to take a ten-day vow of silence. For a compulsive talker like Lennon, this was a terrible ordeal. Soon John became so irascible that people at the house spent their days figuring out how to avoid him. He sustained himself by reading Gordon Liddy's best seller, *Will*, whose theme is how to triumph over adversity through the exercise of willpower. Lennon identified deeply with Liddy, particularly in the most dramatic episodes, as when Liddy tied himself to the top of a tree during a lightning storm or when he awed the black prisoners in jail by holding a burning match under his outstretched palm. Every time John would run into Fred, Lennon would mime the act of striking a match, holding it under his hand, and writhing in pain.

One day, when the worst phase of Yoko's detoxification was over, Sam Green decided to take his patient out to lunch. Dressing Yoko up in leather hot pants, he led her a few blocks from his house to Mortimer's, a chic East Side restaurant, always crowded with jet set types fresh from shopping on Madison Avenue. This was not the sort of place where Yoko should have appeared in her ruinous condition. Hot pants revealed all the bruises and blemishes on her legs from the shots she had been taking and from banging into furniture. When she walked unsteadily into the restaurant, clutching Sam's arm, her striking costume, dark glasses, and unmistakable long black hair created a sensation.

Sam was not exactly unknown to this crowd. Inevitably the buzz began that something was going on with "those two." The titillation produced by the surprising coupling would have counted for little, however, if Yoko had not suddenly made a scene. Spotting Bianca Jagger at a neighboring table, Yoko rose from her chair and stumbled over to the dusky beauty. "Woman to woman," said Yoko, "I know what you're going through!" (Bianca had recently divorced Mick.) No sooner did Yoko utter those words than a palpable frisson ran through the crowded room. Rock star couple! Divorce! New man! Instantly Sam and Yoko were an "item," duly reported in *The News of the World*, which John Lennon read assiduously.

Once Yoko was totally free of drugs, she began to cry the blues. Sam

Green, who had drifted by now into the role of male nurse, pleaded with her to put forth her real strength. "You say your life is a mess, your marriage is terrible. There is one thing you can do," he exhorted. "You're a talented artist—do your art!"

Almost immediately Yoko started batting out songs. Among the first was "Walking on Thin Ice," one of whose couplets alludes to Yoko's gift to Sam of a samurai sword as a token of her gratitude to him for rescuing her from drug addiction. In a week's time Yoko tossed off most of the songs that appeared later on *Double Fantasy* and *Milk and Honey*. She would call Sam at four in the morning and read him the lyrics. Then she would insist that he come over the next day and help her improve her hasty words. Sam failed to recognize the full implications of this collaboration.

While Yoko was undergoing the momentous experience that would conclude with her announcing to an astonished John Green, "No more business—I'm an artist again!" John and Fred were living placidly at the shore. They were also getting to know each other after a yearlong relationship that had been conducted through endless lists of chores, curt phone calls, and an occasional soul-baring monologue by John that left Fred speechless. Not that the twenty-five-year-old Seaman was lacking in knowledge or sophistication. Quite the contrary, he had seen quite a bit of the world. Born in Germany and reared in a castle on Majorca, he had lived alternately in Europe and the United States, and had just been graduated from the City College of New York with honors in journalism. Though highly attuned to music, he had never been a Beatles fan or a Lennon idolator, a fact that stood him in good stead with John, who wanted neither. What shocked and bewildered Seaman was simply the eccentricity of the Lennon household and the total disparity between the Lennons' real life and the image they presented to the world.

Though Fred had been told when he first reported for duty in February 1979 that he would be expected to help John "cook brown rice," he soon discovered that his real job was to drive around most of the day in a green Mercedes station wagon with a pocket crammed full of cash for buying all the toys and delicacies Lennon craved. Every Monday Fred would go to the Bank Leumi on Broadway and 66th Street and withdraw $3,000 for his errands and $1,000 each for John and Yoko. By the end of the week his money would be gone, but John often squirreled his away for some really big blowout, like taking Sean to F. A. O. Schwarz, New York's most lavish toy store.

When John and Fred went off to play on Long Island, Yoko warned the "boys" not to wander from home. But once John got free from Mother, he began to do a little exploring. Ensconced in his big diesel station wagon with Fred at the wheel and Fats Waller jiving from the speakers, John would cruise the neighboring towns of Cold Spring Harbor and Huntington. Crawling down the main stem at ten miles per hour, he would spot girls like a fighter pilot, warning, "Fox at four o'clock!" If they passed a clothing store that had something groovy in the window, he would order Fred to go into the shop and purchase the garment. But never once, in all their meanderings, did they make any contact with the local people. So concerned was John about protecting his privacy that he wouldn't even allow couriers from the Dakota to come to the house. They were directed to a little police station, whose accommodating sergeant would allow the messengers to call Cannon Hill to summon Fred.

Another precaution John adopted was imposing on Fred an absolute ban on picking up local girls. Apologetically but firmly Lennon demanded that Fred find a steady girl and then swear her to secrecy.

John's sexual needs were satisfied in another fashion. According to an interview with John Green, in the London *Sun:*

> Yoko would call to say that John was "getting restless" and that he seemed to be fond of a particular woman. She wanted to know if she could expect trouble and how much she should offer. . . . When Lennon was living on Long Island, a masseuse who also worked for Yoko was driven out for him. "John had made comments regarding the fact that he thought she was attractive and that he was interested," says Green. "Yoko took that hint and took the lead from there." The masseuse was sacked after several meetings. Yoko felt she was "a little too much interested in power and playing a power game."

When Marnie Hair took the kids out to Cold Spring Harbor by limousine in May, she noticed that another limo followed them from the Dakota. When they arrived, a small, attractive Oriental woman emerged from the second car. She proved to be a masseuse from Manhattan. She moved into a room adjacent to Lennon's and took care of him all week, preparing his meals and taking them up to his room, which she would visit at other set times as well.

Proximity to salt water always inspired John with fantasies of running off to sea. One day he told Fred to go into town and buy them a little boat. Once John got the hang of cruising about the harbor in a dinghy with a two-horsepower engine, he got a great deal of satisfaction out of this pastime. He insisted on taking the tiller and even learned how to yank the motor to life with a lanyard, a mechanical feat that made him swell with pride. When the engine would fail to start, John would seize an oar and hand another one to Fred, crying, "Stroke!"

John would seize an oar and hand another one to Fred, crying, "Stroke!"

On May Day Fred was dispatched by John to buy a small sailboat, which he named *Isis*. The name knotted together the cow-headed Egyptian goddess and Yoko, who was always talking about the cow auctions of Dreamstreet. The man from whom Fred bought the boat was the young owner of the local marina, Tyler Coneys. He taught John and Fred how to sail. Once John got into the wind, he began to crave the real thing. He told Fred it would be wonderful to cross the Atlantic and sail right up the Thames to London, instead of taking the limo in from Heathrow. This idea of sailing back to England soon hardened into an obsession, which John communicated to Yoko. Normally she would have been alarmed at such a notion, but now she welcomed it— to John's surprise.

John's desire to go sailing fell in happily with Yoko's desire to push him as far away as possible so that she could enjoy her new life. Allowing him to go clear across the ocean, however, was obviously out of the question. So after a lot of hocus pocus, John was dispatched at the behest of Yoshikawa to Cape Town to put him in the ideal psychic alignment for undertaking a journey that entailed some risk. After spending several days being driven about the African metropolis by a black chauffeur, who took Lennon to a funky massage parlor, John prepared to come home. First, though, he called May Pang and told her that she must come out and visit him at Cold Spring Harbor. It was the last time they spoke.

When Lennon got back to New York early in June, he was given the oracle's finding. John was free to embark on an ocean voyage, but the only direction in which he could sail with safety was southeast. That meant that his destination had to be Bermuda. Though this decision harmonized both John's and Yoko's desires, it demands to be pondered. For years Yoko had told John that he had to be protected from himself, that if he were allowed to go free, something dreadful would befall him. Now she was suddenly cutting him loose to sail for days across the Atlantic Ocean, past stormy Cape Hatteras and into the Bermuda Triangle, in a small vessel manned by an unknown crew. What's more, instead of exercising her customary control over every detail, she allowed all the arrangements to be made by Tyler Coneys, of whom she knew nothing.

On the morning of 4 June 1980 John Lennon left Cannon Hill, bound for Newport, Rhode Island. He took off in a Cessna with Tyler Coneys and his cousins, Ellen and Kevin, who were the other members of the crew. Coneys had chartered a forty-three-foot schooner, the *Megan*

Jayne, whose captain, a burly, bearded man known as Cap'n Hank, was prepared to sail the next day. The plan was that once John reached Bermuda, he would send for Fred, who would fly down with Sean and Uda-San. As little Sean stood upon the runway waving good-bye, John Lennon set off upon his great adventure.

Not since he had climbed aboard Allan Williams's crowded mini-van and gone off to Hamburg had Lennon taken such a thrilling leap into the unknown. Alone among strangers, far out on the sea, he was taking the sort of risk that he had spent his whole life avoiding. What's more, he was fulfilling one of his most cherished childhood fantasies: the great dream of going off to sea, like his father and grandfather. Since he didn't know the first thing about ocean sailing, his duty station was the ship's galley, but what did it matter so long as he went to sea?

Inevitably the ship ran into a tempest, which incapacitated the crew, one after another. Finally, the captain told the cook to get behind the big knurled wheel and hold her steady. Suddenly John found himself standing on the rolling deck in his yellow waterproof, lashed to the rail, like Gordon Liddy up in his storm-tossed tree. He was terrified at first by the sight of the sea heaving with awesome weight and force. Driving the ship into the waves made the spray fly back from the prow, stinging John's tender face and streaming down his glasses. But as the minutes stretched into a quarter, a half, a full hour, Lennon began to feel his courage rising. It was just like going onstage. At first you panicked and you were ready to throw up your guts, but once you got out there and started doing your stuff, you forgot your fears and got high on your performance. Now, as the sea rose ominously before him, Lennon shouted back at it. He even sang! Chanteys, sailor songs, old ballads he'd heard as a boy in Liverpool, came pouring out of his throat. Soon he was picturing himself as an ancient Viking in a long shield-slung ship making for Greenland or Labrador or Vineland. For five hours Sailor John stood his watch and stood his ground. When, at last, he was relieved, he went below a different man. In fact, for the first time in his life he felt himself fully a man.

The night that John embarked on the *Megan Jayne,* Yoko and Sam Green entertained John Cage and Merce Cunningham at supper. Sam was startled when Yoko presented herself and Sam as a couple. At the end of the evening, Yoko asked Sam to come to Cannon Hill the following day to offer suggestions for renovating the house. Sam said that he was going to his place on Fire Island, but he would stop along the way—if he could leave in time to make the last ferry. When he reached the house the following afternoon, he ordered the limousine driver to wait. No sooner was he engrossed in his examination of the property than Yoko sent word to the driver to go back to New York.

When Sam realized that he was stuck at the house, he began to get apprehensive—even more so when it came time to retire, and Yoko started coming on strong. Sam sought to avoid a showdown. They argued back and forth for hours. "She harangued me," Sam recalled. "'Why not?' she said. '"We're friends.'"

Sam recoiled. "No, it's too complicated," he insisted. "I don't want to do it. I love you—but not that way! And I don't want to get involved with you."

No matter what he said, she had an answer. "This went on till four o'clock in the morning," Sam recollected, adding ruefully, "By that time my resistance was nil."

When they got into bed, there was a lot of kissing and fondling. Sam felt that Yoko did not desire vaginal intercourse. "She actually fears penetration," he explained.

The next morning, after having breakfast with Yoko and Sean, Sam escaped from the house and went off to his retreat on Fire Island, where he brooded upon this alarming development for the whole weekend. Yoko Ono did not represent the first time that he had gotten deeply involved with a powerful and bizarrely eccentric woman. There had also been his affair with the late Barbara Baekeland, the flamboyant international society matron, ex-wife of the Bakelite heir.

Sam had met this woman in the Sixties on a cruise of the Mediterranean aboard the yacht of Cecile Rothschild, the lifelong companion of Greta Garbo. Soon he found himself caught up in a terrifying triangle with this aging red-haired beauty and her Dorian Gray son, who were incestuously involved with each other and intent on seducing Sam. The psychotic son murdered his mother eventually, and after his discharge from a mental hospital he came straight to New York, intent on finding Sam. Fortunately Bart Gorin, who had become Sam's personal assistant, had been given instructions about what to do in the event this crazy came calling. Instead of murdering Sam Green, the young man went to his grandmother's house and stabbed the old lady eight times.

Now here was Sam, only a year later, getting involved again with a tigress in heat, who had a husband capable of murderous violence. It was a perilous situation, and if Sam had been wise—or less addicted to danger—he would have taken his seduction as the signal for a quick retreat. Instead, on Monday morning he took the train back to the city and had lunch with Yoko at Tavern on the Green, where she insisted on holding hands with him in public. That afternoon they took a plane to Tampa, where they had a consultation with a well-known psychic, Leonard Zemke. Yoko told Zemke that she and Sam were destined to spend the rest of their lives together. When they got back to New York, they drove out to Cannon Hill, where Fred Seaman witnessed with amusement their game of cat and mouse. "The two of them disappeared upstairs for some time," recalled Fred, "and then Sam Green came panting down the stairs, his normally neat clothing in disarray, gasping something about the Black Widow trying to trap him." Sam remained at Cannon Hill for three days and then fled to the solitude of Oakleyville.

The next week Sam had a guest at his home, a young actor named Bob Herman. One night Herman got up about four in the morning to take a leak. As he stepped out on the porch facing the bay, he spotted a skiff anchored only about twenty feet offshore. A man was sitting in the boat, smoking a cigarette. Herman ducked under cover and observed the man for an hour. It was obvious that he was on stakeout. When Sam learned about the incident the next morning, he associated it with other suspicious events that had occurred recently near this totally isolated cluster of houses. Green began to worry that John Lennon had put him under surveillance.

Once Sam and Yoko became sexually intimate, the character of their relationship changed radically. Yoko determined to remake Sam so that he would be her ideal consort. She told him that she was going to remove his mercantile taint and enable him to become the sort of person he should have been from birth. "I am going to support you," she announced, "until you are in a career that will make you richer than anybody." At that point she assumed responsibility for Sam's major expense, the renovation of his lavish East Side apartment. One evening late in June she told him that as a step toward his elevation he must go that very night to see a marvelous psychic whose name was Joseph Lukach. He would make a study of Sam and give him potions that would strengthen him spiritually.

Sam was taken by limousine to Yonkers, where Joey was living with his companion, Hunter, in a suburban bungalow with a backyard and garage. Sam saw Lukach as a "butterball in caftans of Indian linen, with garlands around his neck [the insignia of the Yoruba priest] and wearing lipstick with pink nails." Lukach was very mannered but appeared very sharp. He read Sam's cards and his palm. His character analysis was succinct but penetrating: "You are drawn to powerful women and bring romance into their lives."

Joey drew up a twelve-page report on Sam that was dispatched to Yoko. When the long night's work concluded at dawn, Sam was given three flasks of clear fluids. These potions were supposed to free him of past karma and assure him of future success. Joey also provided a couple of decanters filled with potions that were to be imbibed jointly by Sam and Yoko. They were, he explained, love philters.

HEAT WAVE

Gaunt-faced and long-haired, bone thin and bare-legged—an Indian holy man perched like a lotus atop a Danish modern sofa with an Ovation guitar in his hands—that was the image of John Lennon that Fred Seaman knurled to focus in his camera on his first night in Bermuda. Intent on doing a little home cooking for the crew of the *Megan Jayne,* John had tried out his voice in a bluesy holler and then bent myopically over the fretboard as he groped for the chords of his first song. Suddenly he began frailing the strings with a fast, hard, urgent beat, the same beat he had spent his youth churning out as the rhythm guitar of the Beatles. Lifting up his long, lean face, flushed with fresh color, he opened his mouth, and out flew the voice of a gruff, tough Liverpool sailor. Biting off each word and spitting it out, Lennon improvised a wicked parody of Bob Dylan's born-again tract "You Gotta Serve Somebody." John called his send-up "Serve Yerself!"

Sizing up the sort of young freak he had sarcastically addressed in "Revolution," John congratulated the earnest seeker after enlightenment upon his discovery of Jesus, Buddha, Muhammad, and Krishna. *But,* warned Long John, the most important sail was missing in the lad's rigging. Aye, and which one is that? *Mother!* You're damned right! Mother is every bit as important as the great sages—and any lad who doesn't recognize the debt he owes the woman that bore him is a damn fool! Then, dispatching his disciple with a couple of musical kicks in the ass, Lennon broke off his chantey amid the laughter and applause of the healthy, handsome young sailors lying about at his feet. These new comrades assumed that this was the way the great star carried on all the time. Only Fred Seaman recognized what an extraordinary change the last two weeks had wrought in John Lennon.

No sooner did Lennon get a minute alone with Fred than he revealed the amazing fact that his adventure aboard the yacht had revived his creative powers. He had actually composed two songs during the cruise and now was hot to write some more. What he needed was privacy and good working conditions. Fred was to get rid of the boat people immediately and then rent John a fine waterside villa. Money was no consideration. When Fred remarked that Tyler Coneys would be hurt by such an abrupt dismissal because he regarded himself now as a friend, John snapped: "I don't have any friends. Friendship is a romantic illusion."

Fairylands Undercliff, the yellow seaside villa in Hamilton Terrace that Lennon occupied with Fred, Sean, Uda-San, and, later, Helen Seaman, is a secluded retreat at the end of a neck of land, situated below the road at the water's edge. Sitting out on the patio one night shortly after his arrival, John was listening to Bob Marley's soulful album *Burnin'* when suddenly he was inspired. Explaining excitedly to Fred that one of the tracks, "Hallelujah Time," had been going around in his mind for years, John said that he had just realized why this tune had always obsessed him. It was the line about not having long to live. That was precisely how John felt—so that should be his first song! Instantly he started improvising on the line from the Marley album, which became "Living on Borrowed Time." Signaling Fred to fetch the recording gear, John sang and strummed, while Fred beat on a guitar case, until Lennon was satisfied he had gotten down what was in his head. Then, lighting up a joint, he kicked back contentedly and began to paint in rapt tones his vision of his great comeback album.

It would be an album soaked from end to end with the soft, sensuous sounds of the Caribbean. Bermuda was in the Caribbean, wasn't it? It wasn't! Well, fuck it! What difference did that make? It was an ocean isle, tropical and sexy, full of the sounds and moves of rhythm and blues. In fact, if they really wanted to get the right sound, they should go to Jamaica! Go to the same studio that Bob Marley used! Get down with the Rasta men and smoke ganja in big spliffs or hash in chillums. Then they could get that deep-down, superfunky bass-box sound that comes straight from Trenchtown. You couldn't get that sound in New York. No way!

As John went on that evening, projecting his dreams upon the overarching night sky, Fred Seaman was thrilled. After more than a year of watching his hero live like a man in the grip of a wasting disease, Fred was witnessing the rebirth of the real John Lennon—the greatest songwriter of modern times.

But the rocket flight of Lennon's imagination was disrupted the very next morning when he picked up his phone and poured out his vision to Yoko. Alarmed by this unforeseen development, she scrambled to get him back under control, according to Sam Green, who became henceforth a reluctant observer of Yoko's efforts to steer her husband onto a course that accorded better with her designs. The stages in this turnaround were many and the process long; in fact, the most decisive step was taken after the album was out of John's hands, which was appropriate in view of the fact that the record originated not with John Lennon's creative revival in June but with Yoko Ono's in May.

Once Yoko had a stack of new songs, she had to figure out some way to turn them into a hit album. Long experience had taught her that solo albums were of no avail. What's more, if she cut an album on her own, John would demand the same right; then the fans would leave her record on the shelf while they bought Lennon's. So it was vital to Yoko's success not only that she yoke John to her album but that some way be devised so that the fans could not listen to his songs without also hearing her songs.

Since Lennon had taken off on what he assumed would be a solo album, Yoko's first challenge was to find some way to cut in on him. Her solution to this problem was the concept of the "heart play," a dialogue between married lovers. In presenting Lennon with this idea, she put him in a bind because if he rejected the concept, he would incur the guilt of rejecting the myth of John and Yoko, to which they both had dedicated their lives. If, on the other hand, John embraced Yoko's proposal, he would have to reverse the whole orientation of his projected album by substituting an anniversary waltz for a swan song. It took scores of long-winded long-distance phone calls and, later, some highly explosive face-to-face exchanges in New York before Yoko prevailed. Eventually, however, Lennon was persuaded to abandon his vision of a reggae album with a tango attitude in favor of a record on which two people employing discordant musical idioms sing alternately, but never together, at cross purposes.

The ultimate irony of *Double Fantasy* was that Yoko came off sounding better than John. For while he, deprived of his original inspiration, fell back timidly on the clichés of his earlier work, she was clever enough to jump on the bandwagon and exploit the style of the late Seventies. What made the irony even more exquisite was the fact that it was Lennon who launched Yoko on the New Wave.

One night in a disco at Hamilton he had heard the B-52s' "Rock Lobster." Instantly he recognized that its sound had been influenced by Yoko's squalks and shrieks. Next day he told her that her style was the latest thing. When Yoko reported this news to John Green, he took the idea a giant step forward.

Green was managing a New Wave performer named Mande Dahl; consequently he was hip to all the current trends in the music business. He advised Yoko to cut a record in the techno-puppet style. "You know," he said, "like 'Kiss, kiss, kiss . . . Take, take, take me . . . Hold, hold, hold me . . . in your arms." Yoko laughed at the idea—but went to work on it at once. "Kiss Kiss Kiss" became—after it was released as the flip side of John's single from *Double Fantasy,* "Starting Over"—the first Yoko Ono track that ever got any play in the clubs.

By adopting as her new style the robotic rhetoric of the new wave, Yoko presented John with the further problem of harmonizing her sound with his. He wanted to make his music wash in and out with the sensuous but melancholy sound of the surf at Negril, but now instead of cutting in Kingston with flesh and soul, he would have to cut in New York with flash and filigree.

During his creative ordeal John craved, as always, moral support. In the old days at Kenwood, Pete Shotton would sit for hours a few paces from Lennon while he worked at his songs, sustaining his friend by his presence. That was the sort of help that John wanted now from Mother, but she kept postponing her promised visit, pleading the pressures of business.

Though Yoko was not at John's side, she was always at his ear. "All those songs were done over the phone from Bermuda to her on my screen porch," recalled Sam Green. "He would call her. He was pursuing her. She said that [my house] was the only place she could work. They were spending five or six hours a day on the phone. Asked, "What can they do for five hours at a time?" Sam replied, "She can encourage him to write love songs to her so they can put them on her album. She had to encourage every one of those songs and make sure they were good for her."

The real reason Yoko was always to be found that summer at Sam Green's secluded house on Fire Island was that she and Sam were in the midst of a very hot love affair. By the middle of June Yoko had sucked Sam into that you-are-me-and-I-am-you-and-we-can't-be-apart-for-a-moment symbiosis that is her only idea of love. Sam Green, a hit-and-run personality—the sort of man who makes dazzling appearances, then, suddenly, ducks into his hole—was driven mad by Yoko's smothering possessiveness. Every chance he got, he would make a dash for his hideout. Yoko would pursue him relentlessly by phone. Just to make sure that he couldn't plead the line was busy, she installed a phone under her own name, which also made it look better when John called, island to island.

One Sunday morning Sam clocked forty-one calls from Yoko. What was the emergency? She felt a cold coming on and was frantic to get a shot of vitamin C before the infection reached her throat and spoiled her voice. These telephone marathons began to take their toll on Sam. Bob Herman recalled that every evening after supper Yoko had Sam on the phone for two hours straight. (She must have rung up Sam the moment she had finished talking to John.) Bob would come around every half hour to recharge Sam's glass with vodka. One night, after putting down the phone with a sigh of relief, Sam got up from his chair—and fell face forward on the deck.

If Yoko Ono made enormous demands on her lover, insisting that he share every one of her thoughts and impulses, she was also extremely generous to him. Just as she had showered gifts on David Spinozza at the outset of their relationship, so now she bound Sam Green to her by the prodigality of her presents. Any day she couldn't fly to his island hideaway, she would take a limo to the seaplane dock on the East River and load a flying boat with all the foods without which Sam could not be expected to survive: kilos of caviar, pounds of Scotch salmon, piles of French cheeses, all bought from nearby Zabar's. Or if she were going out to the island herself, she would send Myoko over to Tanaka's, the Japanese food store on Amsterdam Avenue, for the dried seaweed, brown rice, fresh ginger, and sesame seeds that she required for the little repast she would prepare with her own hands and feed to Sam with chopsticks. One day, when the telephone tensions got too high, Sam did something unprecedented: He hung up on Yoko! That was a danger signal. Yoko realized she had gone too far. Next day Bart Gorin was summoned to the Dakota and ordered to courier to Sam by seaplane a peace offering. When Sam, sweaty and sandy from the beach, opened the package, he stared at its contents in silent amazement. Yoko's gift was a 4.5 karat yellow diamond, worth about $4,000. Sam had it made into a stickpin.

On the night of 26 June Yoko took Sam to the Hit Factory, where she had arranged to demo her songs with a seven-piece band. She wanted him present because he had inspired these love songs and she wished to sing them directly to her lover, exactly as John had sung to May Pang in the studios of L.A. "I'm Your Angel" describes perfectly Yoko's attitude and behavior toward Sam, the birthday greeting in the last stanza having been inspired by Sam's birthday on 20 May, the approximate date of the song's composition.

On the day after this all-night session Yoko finally broke down and flew to Bermuda, her reluctance to leave New York being manifest in the way she kept postponing her departure all day, until finally she was down to the last flight, due to arrive in St. George's at 9:30 P.M.

When John and Fred left the house for the airport, they had so much time ahead of them that they dismissed their driver and had a beer in a tavern near the field. The prospect of seeing Mother turned John on high. He got into a long rap about how, until he met Yoko, he had always seen sex essentially as rape. The conversation would have gone on much longer if Fred had not glanced at his watch. With a groan, he announced that it was already 9:30! Dashing out of the bar, they hailed a cab and drove to the airport. When they arrived, the building was deserted, save for an old man sweeping up. The porter told them that a little Japanese woman had gotten off the last plane. She had wandered around for a few minutes and then burst into tears. John was transfixed with guilt. Jumping back in the cab, he told Fred that when they got home, he would have to bear all the blame for their tardiness. Yoko would threaten to fire him, but John would be his champion.

That night John was on his best behavior with Yoko. He brought her into the sun-room and serenaded her. Then he played the tape of his first new songs in five years. Yoko, squatting on her feet, said nothing and exhibited no emotion. When John started importuning her to go with him for a day to Jamaica to check out the studios, Yoko said that it was impossible because she had to return to New York on Sunday. That news so shocked and angered John that he suddenly turned on Yoko and began berating her for her neglect of both him and Sean. He warned Yoko solemnly that she would pay in the future for neglecting the boy. He told her, too, that her excuse—that she lacked the maternal instinct—was just a cop-out for not doing her job. Finally, winding up on a peak of contemporary rhetoric, he denounced her for being "macho."

Yoko was not concerned. She told John that as soon as the album was finished, she would buy him a house in Bermuda and the whole family would be able to relax. Even though he was hurt, frustrated, and offended by Yoko's behavior, he allowed himself to be consoled by this empty promise.

After Yoko left Bermuda, John began to worry about her behavior in New York. He told Fred that Mother was spending a lot of time with Sam Green and Sam Havadtoy. He even made some references to drugs at the Dakota. One day in early July, after days of failing to get Yoko on the phone, John went into his room and wrote in a couple of hours the best piece on *Double Fantasy*, "I'm Losing You." The song acted like a catharsis. The moment it was complete, he became calmer and stopped trying to reach Yoko. He was determined, all the same, to find out what was happening at home. He told Fred to fly up to New York, an act that Yoko sought to block. When Fred was ready to depart, John gave him a cedarwood box in which John had put a lock of his hair wrapped in a fresh handkerchief. The idea was to work a little of Yoko's magic on Yoko herself.

When Fred arrived at the Dakota on 4 July, Yoko was spending the four-day holiday with Sam Green on Fire Island. The sight that greeted Fred's eyes when he walked into Studio One spoke volumes about the sort of life Yoko had been leading in John's absence. "Her office," he recalled, "was strewn with papers, her dirty clothes were all over the floor, and there were half-eaten plates of sushi in advanced states of decay on her table." Upstairs he found many bottles of scotch and vodka, Sam Green's favorite drinks. When Fred tried to pump Myoko, all he could learn was that Sam Havadtoy and Luciano were bringing Yoko "envelopes." (Luciano said that he and Sam would sometimes deliver a package of cocaine as big as a fat paperback book.) What really rocked Fred was the rumor that Yoko was planning to divorce John and move all his belongings into Apartment 71. Then she was going to marry "Sam." Fred assumed this meant Sam Havadtoy. Naturally none of this gossip was reported to John because Fred did not want to start a war.

One of the most amusing staves in the Ballad of Sam and Yoko is that entitled "The Hottest Day of the Year." For 21 July 1980 was a day of infernal heat. In New York the temperature rose to 102 degrees. Yoko was bored with Fire Island and eager to find a fresh diversion. "John is rich," she told Sam Green. "Why don't we rent a plane and fly somewhere?"

Sam was bored with flying and riding in limousines. He suggested that they rent a convertible and take off on the open road. In no time they were motoring up the Merritt Parkway, an attractive old highway that leads into Connecticut. "Why don't we visit your folks?" said Yoko out of the blue. The mere idea sent a chill down Sam's spine. After a few ineffectual efforts to dissuade her, he drove off the highway near Middlebury and gave the house a call.

"I just happen to be driving by, Mom," Sam drawled. "It's eight o'clock, and I'm with somebody. What are you all doing?"

Mrs. Green replied in hushed tones, "This is a very special night for your sister. The boy she's been living with for a year—we think they've made a special dinner for us because they are going to announce their *marriage*. We have a special candlelit thing with hurricane lanterns out in the backyard. Your father is barbecuing, and your sister has gotten all these things, and so I hope you don't upset all their plans. But of course, we'd love to see you."

Sam replied, "Yeah, but I'm *bringing somebody*."

Tensing, his mother asked, "Who are you bringing?"

"Yoko Ono. You know who that is?"

Mrs. Green must have been relieved that it was not someone even more bizarre because Sammy had really upset the tureen a few times in the past, especially on that never-to-be-forgotten night when he turned up at a formal dinner party with Candy Darling, that blond floozy—who turned out to be a *man*! And Sam was *living with her*! What was Yoko Ono compared to an Irish street hustler from Queens who thought he was Marilyn Monroe?

What happened when the couple arrived at the barbecue is best told by Sam Green: "It was a lovely dinner and Yoko assumed that it was all being put on for her. She behaved as if this were her family, her future in-laws, saying things like: 'I can see Sam and me sitting here when our hair turns gray.' What she didn't realize was that my sister was sitting there with white knuckles, thinking: Why the fuck has this little gook come and stolen the most important night of my life! And you know what? They never *did* announce their marriage, and they never got married! What happened was that everybody—my mother, my sister, and definitely my father—got the impression, which Yoko gave them, that Yoko was there because she was going to be part of the family. I tried to keep up appearances, saying, 'She should have the nice guest bedroom.' She never slept in that bed. She snuck down while everybody was still awake, creaking up and down the hallways, coming to my room, which was three-quarters of a mile away. [The old manse has forty-four rooms.] She didn't even go and mess up her bed in the morning the way you're supposed to. She was making sure that everybody knew!"

Sam Green says that when they came back from Connecticut, they began doing legal research to determine precisely what portion of John's wealth Yoko could obtain by divorce. Needless to say, this was not a simple question, owing to the fact that John's finances were entangled in the affairs of Apple. John had been forced to redraw his will recently when it began to appear that in the event of his death, Apple might be able to retain part of his future income. A further complication was the Equitable Distribution Law, which had gone into effect on 19 June 1980, introducing into New York divorce law the concept of a fifty-fifty division of communal property. As for Sam Green's feelings about marriage to Yoko, he didn't welcome the prospect, but he was prepared to become her husband and enjoy her wealth.

Researching and planning the divorce were not enough to satisfy Yoko. She wanted to enjoy her new status immediately. Just as John put Cynthia out of his life without troubling to notify her, now Yoko did the same thing to John. She ordered Luciano to take all of John's possessions—his clothes, guitars, hi-fi gear, books, etc.—and remove them to Apartment 71. Yoko explained that when John returned, he wanted to have total privacy, even from his own family. The orders were carried out, but when Sam Green learned of the move, he was appalled at its cruelty. "You can't do it!" he protested. "You simply can't do it!" After a heated exchange John's things were brought back and restored to their normal places.

This attempt to push John out of the apartment raised the question of what was to become of Lennon when Yoko divorced him. After years of infantile dependency, John was little more than a child. Abandoning him would be like abandoning a little boy. At the age of forty he would experience again precisely what he had suffered at the age of five.

WELCOME HOME

Yoko anticipated John's return with an anxiety bordering on hysteria. He had been away for nearly five months, while she enjoyed total freedom.

Yoko prepared herself for the coming encounter with the aid of Luciano, whom she enlisted to style her hair and advise her on makeup and costume. When he arrived on the big day, she had yet another task for him to perform. That night, while she and John were sitting at a table under a big umbrella in the back garden of Barbetta, a restaurant in the theater district, Luciano popped out from behind the fountain, where naked putti poured water from jars on their shoulders, and took several flashlit snapshots. "What are you doing?" demanded the astonished maître d'.

"I'm doing fine!" huffed the mad-looking hairdresser as he dashed out the door and jumped into a waiting car. When he got home, his phone was ringing. It was Yoko. She was thrilled at how well her sneak attack had worked.

Luciano couldn't see the point of the stunt until the next day, when he read Liz Smith's column. She wrote that the night before a "Mafia-style" photographer had harassed the Lennons while they were having a quiet dinner in a restaurant. Luciano was enlightened: "That was my introduction to the art of creating incidents in one's private life to promote one's business interests."

The day after John's return, Yoko was scheduled to do some glamour shots with photographer Brad Martin. Luciano was styling her hair when John walked into the room. Impressed by his wife's appearance, he quipped: "How much do you charge?" Yoko identified Luciano as the mystery photographer. John's mood changed abruptly. "Why didn't I see you?" he demanded sullenly.

Luciano, furious at being put in a false position, shot back: "Why didn't you know about it in the first place?"

By the following day Lennon's anger had subsided. When Luciano

651

entered the kitchen of Apartment 72, having been sent up by Yoko to fetch a pair of boots, he found John lounging on a sofa in the nude. "So, it's you!" cried Lennon humorously.

"Yes, it is!" snapped Luciano testily. "But you can't break my camera now."

John laughed and then fetched a long sigh, saying, "Oh, well, I guess Yoko has been up to her old tricks again."

At that moment Luciano noticed that one of the young gay men who were employed as workers about the flat was in the room. This set Luciano to thinking about, and later investigating, John's sexual preferences. He concluded: "John was quite frankly bisexual. His tastes were for hookers and young men about seventeen or eighteen."

Soon Luciano was enjoying the confessional intimacies of a hairdresser with his client. Yoko complained of John's weakness and apathy. She lamented her lack of fulfillment as a woman. Once when Luciano was going on about how Sam Havadtoy never finished anything he started, Yoko told Luciano that he should be doubly happy: first, because he had an active sex life; second, because his lover was *not* a famous man. She went on to say that her sex life with John had all but ended. "Let's face it," she remarked resignedly, "after eleven years of marriage the fire dies." Yoko also told Luciano that she and John were at odds over the issue of having more children. John wanted a daughter, but Yoko was opposed to the idea. Though pregnancy test kits were strewn all over her office and the Lennons indulged in superstitions, like putting scissors or eggs under the bed, Yoko's obstetrician had written to tell her that she was beyond the age for bearing children. What was most interesting to Luciano was the discovery that Yoko had made up her mind to divorce John as soon as work on the new album was completed. She told him: "I need to free myself of the Lennon name."

No sooner had John started rehearsals for the album than Yoko dragged him out to Sam Green's house on Fire Island. John must have been astonished when he entered this simple beach house and found it equipped with a piano and a Yamaha electric piano, like a recording studio. Sam had spent three years getting a phone installed, yet Yoko had wafted these instruments over the Great South Bay in just the last few days.

The plan was for John to work while Yoko and Sam played. It failed within its first hour of execution, for no sooner did John and Yoko wade ashore from the seaplane than they learned Sam was on the ocean side of the narrow barrier island with Sean. When John came striding down to the beach and saw this man whom he regarded as "one of Yoko's fags" with his son, he displayed his extreme displeasure.*

Next morning he appeared despondent. He went out on the porch and sat motionless with his head in his hands. "Something wrong?" inquired Sam.

"Yeah," answered Lennon, "I gotta get back to work. I have to get out of here."

"Call a seaplane," snapped Sam. "It'll get you out of here."

That day the Lennons left and never returned. Yoko told Sam that John had been upset to find in the toilet some dirty comic books. Sam divined a deeper cause for John's dejection.

Two weeks later Sam spent the weekend with the Lennons at Cold Spring Harbor. John had just completed his first week in the studio. He was very unhappy because he had no confidence in himself or his material. It was at this delicate moment that Yoko started unveiling her demands for 50 percent of the album. John exploded with rage. "If that's what you want," he shouted, "there's not gonna *be* an album!" With that, he marched out of the room and stomped up to his bedroom, where he slammed the door. He remained in seclusion for the balance of the weekend, communicating only by slipping messages under the door.

It was characteristic of Lennon that even while suffering a crisis of confidence, he could still behave publicly with supreme self-assurance. From his first day at the Hit Factory, he was in complete command. His producer, Jack Douglas, who shared the title with Yoko, was both an excellent technician and a former rock musician. He had worked on virtually all of the Lennons' albums since *Imagine,* first as an assistant to Roy Cicala, then as chief engineer. Unlike Cicala, however, who would turn to Lennon every time Yoko gave an order and say, "Is that OK, John?" Jack was highly responsive to Yoko's demands. When he had been summoned to Cold Spring Harbor in June to discuss John's long-awaited comeback album, Yoko had told him, "I want to put a few things on the record." Then she had given him a whole stack of tapes, some of them going back thirteen years.

"How many songs are you planning to put on the album?" Jack had asked.

---

*Lennon's reaction was perfectly in character, but it raises a difficult question. The previous November John had redrawn his will, naming Sam Green as Sean's guardian in the event of Yoko's death or her refusal to assume responsibility for the child. Why had Lennon appointed as Sean's potential guardian a man whom he couldn't even bear to see playing innocently with his son on the beach? Granted, Lennon was notoriously indifferent to legal matters and had grown accustomed to acting as a rubber stamp for Mother. But it is still astonishing, even if it was her idea, that he left his child in the care of someone he disliked.

Yoko replied: "As many as I can." Then she warned him to say nothing about her songs when he called John in Bermuda.

Lennon ordered Douglas to hire a brand new band, explaining later, "I spent too many hours, days, months, and years in the studios with the guys [his former sidemen]. When we would record, it would be an excuse to get out of our heads on everything. It would take us eight hours and we would get one track if we were lucky. . . . I was too tight with Jim [Keltner] and all the others to ever get on their backs and say, 'No, I don't like it.' . . . Now I can come in and from day one be the boss."

That was precisely how Lennon behaved on the first day, when he went into the booth to check out the band. "OK, drummer," said John to Andy Newman, "let's hear your drums. Everybody else, shut up! Give me your bass drum. OK, give me your snare drum. . . ." When the sound had been balanced, John examined the patterns Newman was playing. He reacted candidly: "I don't like it. Here's what you're going to play. I want this on the foot. I want this on the snare. When you do a fill, I don't want it to be any busier than 'dat, 'dat, 'dat, 'dat.' No 'diddle, diddle, dum.' Now, in the chorus, you double up on the snare drum." In five minutes John had his drum part just the way he wanted it.

Equally impressive to the players was the straight-ahead style in which John worked. As Newman remarked, "His idea of making a record was: 'Look, here's a song. It's real simple. You guys know how to play your instruments. Forget about all the frills. Just accompany me.' You knew that in twenty minutes he was going to start taking the thing and in an hour he wanted it done. It changed your whole approach to the recording because you knew you didn't have three hours to fuss around. . . . It made you go for a gut performance. If he had to sing it more than five or six times, he'd get fed up and say, 'Right, forget it. That's enough. We'll do it another time. Let's try a new one.'"

Though Lennon acted confident, he was very unsure of himself after five years of exile from the studio. His anxiety was most apparent in the ways he sought to mask his voice. As he told Fred: "The more insecure I am, the more instruments I put on a track." With *Double Fantasy*, Lennon's anxiety reached unprecedented heights, which meant that so many additional sounds had to be piled onto the tracks that eventually Jack Douglas ran out of space. At that point, all recording stopped for a couple of days while the producer and his engineer exercised their utmost ingenuity in attaching to their twenty-four-track tape console another twenty-four-track machine.

When it came to recording Yoko, a far greater effort had to be made. John had made it clear to Jack Douglas from the start that the goal of the album was to make Yoko a star. That meant that the musicians had to exercise all their creativity in the development of her songs and the engineer had to employ the most advanced techniques in the recording of her voice. Douglas knew from long experience that Yoko's problems were that she had no voice and could not sing on key. His solution was to record her at such high gain that if she swallowed, it would practically blow the monitors off the wall and to reserve ten of his twenty-four tracks for her vocal on the assumption that "she couldn't possibly go flat in the same place every time." Then, when everybody went home, Jack would stay up till dawn, selecting the best note from each take and assembling these scraps by hand, one syllable at a time, into phrases. To assure himself that he got that one good note on every syllable, he would make Yoko repeat her songs endlessly. Finally, she would get it right, and he would announce: "That's a print!"

Even Jack could not dissuade Yoko from doing things that were foolish. When she demonstrated "I'm Your Angel," everybody objected that the song was an obvious steal from Eddie Cantor's old hit "Makin' Whoopee." "It's a good thing it's in 3/4," Jack had told Yoko, "because if it was in 4/4, you'd be in trouble." But when it came time to cut the track, Yoko insisted that they do it in 4/4. When Jack protested, Yoko told him that she was acting on the advice of her psychic. What's more, she assured him, she had never heard the Cantor song. When *Double Fantasy* was released, the copyright holders of "Makin' Whoopee" brought a million-dollar action against Yoko that was settled out of court in February 1984 for an undisclosed sum.

When Yoko was not at the Hit Factory, she was at Studio One, taking care of business. The item that stood at the top of her agenda was publicity. Veteran of many a media saturation campaign, she stood now on the threshold of her greatest PR blitz. *Double Fantasy* was not just a comeback album; it was a news event. It marked the return to public awareness of one of the most idealized pop heroes of modern times. A press agent's dream, the album offered endless opportunities for exploitation. The only question was: Who should get the job?

Most people would have reached out for one of the giants of the PR game, one of those hip New York advertising agencies or a great image maker like David Garth. Not Yoko Ono. She engaged an obscure flack who had come to her attention purely by accident. While monitoring John Green's performance as manager of pop singer Mande Dahl (preliminary to asking Green to manage the Lennons, an offer he turned down, fearing it would destroy his long-standing relationship with Yoko), she had noted how much publicity the young singer had received during a disco date in Boston. When she learned that Dahl's publicity had been handled by a local man, Charles Cohen, she summoned him to New York, where she put him through the drill for prospective employee: preliminary interview, casting of horoscope, etc. In just two days Yoko made her decision, engaging Cohen for a full year at what he described as a "fabulous fee."

The out-of-town press agent was immediately impressed by Yoko Ono's grasp of the machinery of self-promotion. She knew exactly what she wanted and how to get it. Opening her voluminous files, which contained every notice she had received since her career began in 1961, she read out passage after passage of caustic criticism or downright ridicule. All that must change, she demanded. *Double Fantasy* was going to be Yoko's ticket not to fame, which she possessed already, but to honor and esteem. The line to be taken, she explained, was that the album was a "world music event," completely free of commercial overtones and dedicated to establishing Yoko Ono as a "legitimate artist and a good person, concerned with her relationship with her son and John and the serenity of the universe."

No sooner was Cohen engaged than he received a rush assignment. He was ordered to leak to the press the news that Yoko had auctioned a Holstein cow at the New York State Fair at Syracuse for a record-breaking price of $265,000. (Actually, the cow had been sold by Dreamstreet Holsteins.) Yoko explained to Cohen that "she wanted to emphasize the fact in her new image-building campaign that she loved animals and that they raised animals for milk and not for slaughter." The story was picked up immediately by hundreds of papers all around the world.

Next, Yoko conceived an idea for copping a lot of publicity on John's and Sean's joint birthday. A skywriting plane would fly over Central Park, spelling out in puffs of smoke: HAPPY BIRTHDAY JOHN & SEAN. LOVE YOKO. "We got tons of press," Cohen recalled enthusiastically. (John Lennon, who refused to go up on the roof of the Dakota to watch the plane, wrote across the bill for the puff job: "Never again.")

Cohen's most important task was arranging the countless interviews with press, radio, and TV that would soon saturate the media. Again, Yoko dictated the procedure that was to be followed in setting up the interviews. She demanded to know in advance:

1. The size of the publication's circulation
2. The other celebrities it had recently covered
3. The photographer who would be given the assignment
4. The interviewer's astrological data

Though John was averse to giving endless interviews because he had to do virtually all the work, Yoko knew that once he was faced with the press, he would rise to the occasion. Yet she wasn't relying simply on John's wit and eloquence to push the album—Yoko had a lot of tricks up her sleeve. As Cohen observed, "She's very, very shrewd," so shrewd, in fact, that he told her that if she ever wanted to go into the PR business, he would be delighted to make her a partner in his firm. As an illustration of Yoko's shrewdness, Cohen offered her technique in leaking information. "She never wanted to be quoted directly," he recalled. "If an item had to go to Suzy or Lisa Robinson or one of those people, it always had to say: 'A source close to the Lennons.'" The reason for this indirect ascription was that "Yoko never wanted to look as if she was shoving and triggering off all this PR." Likewise, she was clever at inventing beguiling rumors. Cohen might be instructed to tell the gossip columnists: "A mystery person is sending white roses every day to the Hit Factory." The "mystery person" was, of course, Yoko Ono, but it made no difference in its effect on the public. Cohen was amazed at how the hungry media gobbled up all this malarkey. "I was getting thirty or forty calls a day for five months," he said. "I had to hire an extra man just to take the Lennon calls."

Two moments in this prolonged and costly campaign stand out in Charles Cohen's memory. One was the way in which the initial announcement was snatched up by the wire services; the other was how the most important single interview was arranged. On 10 August Yoko ordered Cohen to prepare a press release announcing that she and John were coming out of retirement and were working at the Hit Factory. On 12 August he read the copy to her on the phone. "That's excellent, Charles," she responded. "Go with that!" At 3:00 P.M. that day Cohen called John Mullins, the AP Chief in Boston. When he announced the news, Mullins put two reporters on the phone immediately. That night the electronic media flashed the story around the world.

The big interview was with *Playboy*, which normally works six months ahead on its major features but which agreed to squeeze in a full-length conversation with John and Yoko in the January number, which would be on the stands in December, soon after the album's release. What made this interview such a great coup from the public relations standpoint was the publisher's agreement to surrender his normal right of editorial control to Yoko Ono. "Yoko granted the interview on one condition," Cohen stressed, "that she had prior approval [i.e., nothing could be printed unless she approved it]. They went for it. She was very, very adamant about prior approval."

The interviews, designed to hype *Double Fantasy*, proved to be far more important than the album because it was they, not the album, that actually projected the Lennons' theme—the interplay between John's and Yoko's imagined selves. The interviews also provided the last great demonstration of John Lennon's unrivaled ability to make even his most preposterous notions sound completely plausible.

The game of gulling the public began on 9 September, the day
Playboy's interviewer, a naïve young man—actually a typical fan, obsessed with the possible reunion of the Beatles—sat down with John
and Yoko in the kitchen of Apartment 72. "John leaned back in his
chair, his hands clasped tightly around the cup of tea," wrote David
Sheff, all agog because he felt that he and his Sony were about to record a historic moment. "He watched the steam float upward," Sheff
reported.

Then Lennon delivered. "I've been baking bread."

"Bread!" exclaimed the astonished interviewer.

Without turning a hair, John continued calmly: "And looking after
the baby." Having launched his account of his hidden life on this startling note, John went on to develop with obvious relish the theme of
himself as "housemother" or "housewife." Sometimes he got so carried
away by this fantasy that the whole story teetered on the edge of the
risible. There was a clear note of self-parody in his account of how he
would receive Yoko in the evening, simpering, "Did you have a hard
day at the office? Would you like a little cocktail?" That was laying it on
pretty thick, but Lennon wasn't daunted because he had learned from
a lifetime of experience that there is no lie easier to swallow than the
"big lie," the whopper so fantastic that nobody could possibly invent
it—or forget it!

Every time John paused for breath, Yoko took up the yarn and spun
out her complementary fantasy. Just as he caricatured himself as a suburban housewife measuring out his day in terms of his domestic routine, getting up to feed the baby, planning his lunch menu, and then
settling down to the cooking and baking, so she presented herself as
being "more macho than most guys" but suffering in her early years
from a feeling of being "emasculated" or "castrated." Denying that
there was such a thing as penis envy, Yoko insisted that there was a
condition in men that she called "womb envy." She insisted that it had
been good for John to indulge his yearning to be a woman, just as Yoko
had fulfilled herself by adopting the male role as head of the family
business. Her task had been rendered terribly difficult, however, by the
incomprehensible antagonism that she constantly encountered, clearly
a product of male chauvinism. John joined her in savaging the business
representatives and lawyers at the Apple meetings, ridiculing them as
"big and fat, vodka-lunch, shouting males, like trained dogs, trained to
attack." Men were basically animals in John Lennon's view, but Yoko
was equal to the worst of them, being a born animal trainer.

But when Sheff raised the question of whether Yoko might also be
controlling John, the idea made him explode in rage. "If you think," he
barked, "I'm being controlled like a dog on a leash because I do things

with her, then screw you! Because—*fuck you brother and sister, you don't know what's happening!*"

As Lennon's monologue continued through the next nineteen days, extending eventually to a 193-page book, it soon became clear that though ten years had elapsed since John last revealed himself to the public, virtually nothing had happened during all this time. Most of his rap, apart from the sex-reversal routine, concerned the distant past, whose most celebrated episodes, like his meeting with Yoko, had grown threadbare through constant retelling. What John was really intent upon in his final interviews was not revealing himself but making propaganda for his wife. "She's the teacher and I'm the pupil," he insisted, adding shrilly, "She's taught me everything I fucking know . . . she was *there* . . . when I was the *Nowhere Man.*"

At the same moment that Yoko was promulgating the idea that she and John were beyond concern for money, she was struggling to cut a new deal with a record company that would put millions of dollars in their hands. When Bruce Lundvall, president of Columbia Records, called the studio one day, John remarked: "I wouldn't take a penny less than Paul got—or the other son of a bitch [i.e., Mick Jagger]."

Yoko seconded John vigorously, vowing, "I'm going to destroy Paul! I'm going to get more than him." (Paul received, reportedly, $22.5 million.) When Yoko sat down with Lundvall and explained that the album would be half John's songs and half her songs, he said such an arrangement was completely out of the question. He was willing to offer Lennon a big advance, but it would be contingent on his delivering a Lennon album, not a John and Yoko medley.

As week after week elapsed without a contract, Lennon began to get nervous. "We're almost finished, and I don't have a record deal!" he would complain to Jack Douglas. Jack suggested that Yoko consult with his very capable manager, Stan Vincent, who had offered his expertise free of charge. Vincent sketched out a deal that would have given Lennon five to seven million dollars on signing. Yoko had her lawyer, David Warmflash, go over the figures; then she picked a quarrel with Vincent that alienated him forever. When Ahmet Ertegun, the famous boss of Atlantic/Warner, came up to the sixth floor of the Hit Factory one evening, Yoko scolded him for intruding and made him get back on the elevator immediately. To everyone's amazement, she appeared more intent upon driving off than drawing in the big labels. Then, on the night of 19 September, David Geffen appeared at the studio.

Geffen had been out of the record business for years. Now he was starting up his own company, but he had hired only one artist: Donna Summer. Jack Douglas was dismayed by the appearance of a man whom he regarded as a "sharpie," but Lennon was relieved; as Douglas observed, "John was just glad he had a deal and the album would come out." People in the know, however, were surprised by the paltriness of the advance, a mere million, and the inclusion in the deal of 50 percent of Lennon's publishing income from the new songs. Yoko had thrown in these rights, despite their enormous value. As a result, David Geffen made a double fortune out of *Double Fantasy*.

What had inspired Yoko to go with little David instead of one of the goliaths of the industry? According to his own account, when Yoko told him how Columbia had rejected the idea of splitting the album fifty-fifty between herself and John, Geffen had smiled benignly and said: "I wouldn't have it any other way."

If publicity stood at the top of Yoko's agenda, the matter that stood at its bottom was security. Back in February 1980, Yoko had begun to employ an ex-FBI man, Douglas MacDougall, to advise her on how to protect Sean and secure the houses she was purchasing. As MacDougall came and went at the Dakota, reporting on his progress in protecting homes that John rarely, if ever, visited, he observed that his client's principal residence had virtually no security. Yoko would answer the door if the desk announced a delivery, and there had been occasions when fans had gotten not only into the building but even into Apartment 72. In one instance they walked into John's bedroom! What made the security man blow his stack, however, was not these familiar dangers but the special risks to which the Lennons were exposing themselves by their enormous press campaign for *Double Fantasy*.

One morning MacDougall picked up the *Daily News* and read an interview with Yoko in which she gave the name of the studio where they were working and even the approximate hours of their departure and return. Snatching up the phone, he got through to Yoko and gave her an ultimatum. "Yoko," he began, "I don't really care if you want to get yourself killed . . . but I really don't want you killed. . . . And also, it's gonna hurt my reputation if you're killed. Because people know that though I'm not handling *your* security, I'm involved with it in some way. I quit!"

Yoko replied: "I know what you're saying is right, but I have to sell records!"

On 25 September MacDougall was summoned to Studio One to offer his suggestions for protecting the Lennons. When he arrived, he discovered that Yoko had preempted the time alloted to him for a business discussion with two representatives of Geffen/Warner. The best she could offer the security adviser was five minutes in the bathroom. His recommendation was that she hire an armed bodyguard to ride to and from the studio in the limousine. When the Lennons arrived at either destination, the bodyguard would get out of the front of the car, check out the situation, then, after satisfying himself there was no danger, open up the back door of the limo and cover his clients while they entered the building. Yoko said that she would run the idea by John. The next time MacDougall spoke with her, she said that John had rejected the notion of a bodyguard. MacDougall assumed that Lennon felt his masculinity had been challenged, but John Green told Jeffrey Hunter the real reason was that the Lennons were embarrassed to do drugs in front of ex-cops. MacDougall was still not dissuaded. He said that if they didn't want a bodyguard riding with them in the car, they could hire two security men and station one at the Dakota and the other at the studio. Again Yoko turned him down flat.

That evening John Lennon was talking on the phone to Jesse Ed Davis. "I just fired my bodyguard," Lennon reported.

"Why?" demanded Davis.

"It's my rationale," replied John, "that if they're gonna get ya, they're gonna get you anyway. First, they kill the bodyguard."

CUTTING

Once the recording process started, Yoko began to withdraw emotionally from Sam Green. Instead of regarding him as her manager, producer, or consort, she began to treat him as her flunky. Looking for some way to make herself more comfortable during the endless hours at the Hit Factory, where she planned to stand guard every moment over Lennon, Yoko ordered that a room at the studio be reserved for her private use. Sam was commanded to furnish this room overnight with a piano, sofa, pictures, and bric-a-brac. As there was no time to shop, he had to take things from his own apartment. Yoko also took to summoning Sam to spur-of-the-moment rendezvous in hotel rooms near the studio. She would tell John at lunchtime that she had to attend a meeting with the Apple representatives at the Plaza; then she would duck over to another hotel on Central Park South, like the Park Lane or Essex House.

Sam's intimates recall this slip-away period with great amusement. He would be holding forth enthusiastically in his magnificent Louis Quatorze salon on East 75th Street when the phone would ring. After a quick, cryptic exchange his face would register extreme disgust. Next, he would bustle about the apartment, gathering up his sunglasses, cigarettes, and keys. "Sam!" some teasing friend would carol. "Where are you going?"

Sam would offer an obscene reply as he walked out the door.

The rooms for these assignations were booked by Yoko's new tarot card reader, Desiah Restab, a blousy Englishwoman in her mid-forties, who employed the alias "Desiah Kane" when she made the arrangements. Sam's diary shows that in September he met Yoko on the third, fourth, fifth, thirteenth, fourteenth, and seventeenth days of the month. When he would arrive at the suite, he'd find Desiah completing her task by ordering from room service the lavish refreshments that Yoko considered appropriate for a chic hotel tryst. A kilo of beluga caviar on ice, a bucket of French champagne, and a chilled bottle of

Russian vodka would be laid out ceremoniously under Desiah's watchful eye. Then she would follow the waiter out the door.

Yoko would arrive breathless with tension, smoking one Nat Sherman after another while babbling about the album and her problems with John. Her attitude toward Sam was that he had been bought and paid for so it hardly mattered how little time they had together or what was the mood of their hasty encounter. She would have her moment of passion, then go back to the studio.

Sam would return home full of self-revulsion. "At that point I knew I was being used as a gigolo," he confessed. "I knew she was using the money to do it because she had no caring for me at all. She was no longer addicted to me." Sam was still addicted to costly decorating schemes. In fact, his lavish East Side apartment had burned up every dollar he possessed, and he was desperately overextended. Hence, he had no choice but to do Yoko's bidding.

John Lennon liked to cut records fast, but he never surpassed the pace he set in August 1980. In two weeks of virtually 'round-the-clock effort, he laid down twenty-two tracks, almost enough material for two albums. Jack Douglas contributed a lot of good ideas, but many were aborted by Yoko. Thus, Jack wanted to fly with John to Japan for a week's work with the synthesizer wizard who had made *Sonic Seasonings,* an album that fascinated Lennon. Yoko vetoed the plan because she feared the Japanese musician would try to cut into the act. Jack also brought to the studio two keymen from the highly successful Beatle-oriented band Cheap Trick, a group he had discovered and recorded. The guitarist Rick Nielsen and the drummer Bun E. Carlos jammed with Tony Levin on bass and George Small on keys in a memorable session that realized beyond anything Lennon had imagined the potential of his last good song, "I'm Losing You." Yet when the musicians returned the following day, Yoko turned them away, insisting that they were out to exploit John. But Douglas preserved the remarkable mood of their playing by running the jam through the headphones of the studio musicians who actually cut the track.

Midway through the sessions Yoko recognized that John was bonding with the men in the studio. Although she stood guard every night in the booth, she often fell asleep on the sofa with her head on a white satin pillow and her body covered by a white satin quilt. (John blew up a photo of her in this condition which he taped over the console as a symbol of Yoko's contribution to the album.) The moment the cat's eyes would close, the mice would start to play. John would reach inside a hollow standing ashtray for a bottle of Jack Daniel's. After a couple of good snorts he would excuse himself and go into the machine room, where he would gobble down a pizza or a Whopper, which he relished after years of being compelled to eat "shaved fish." Sometimes Yoko would go home, leaving John behind. Then he would send out for some coke, and everybody would get high and happy.

Naturally, word of the recording sessions got around. One night Goldie Hawn showed up with Sylvester Stallone. Yoko's informers reported the incident immediately. Next day, when Jack picked up his phone, he heard a hysterical Yoko screaming, *"It's not good for his health! He's going to go wild again!"* Jack couldn't see any signs of disturbance in Lennon. John was behaving like any rock star after a session.

Most of the work on *Double Fantasy* had been completed by the time of John and Sean's double birthday party, held this year on 13 October to coincide with the release next day of the album's first single, "Starting Over." John got a wonderful present that morning at the studio when Jack rolled out a table stacked with more than two hundred cassettes containing every word that Lennon had spoken since the second day of work. John had ordered that a tape be kept running in the studio at all times to preserve his chatter, but when at the end of the first session he had leaned back in the booth and uncorked a two-hour monologue on his history as a musician, Jack decided to install four mikes on that side of the glass to capture these precious reminiscences. His foresight was rewarded by a continuous flow of discourse in the months following as Lennon, starved for a chance to talk and unburden his mind after years of silence in his bedroom, reviewed his entire life, improvising an oral autobiography. This tape record was supplemented by a journal that John had authorized Fred Seaman to keep the preceding spring and that Jack Douglas regarded as Fred's principal task. Lennon, possessed by the conviction that his life was about to end, decided to make a final effort to set his story down once and for all.

At the party that afternoon John Lennon looked as if he had been reborn. Cutting the album had done him more good than any treatment could have achieved. Jack Douglas and his woman, Christine Desautels, recall that the more the album advanced, the stronger John became. Though Lennon complained to Jack that he had never once gotten laid during the whole course of the sessions, one of his favorite lines being "Has anyone seen my wife?" he was now starting to betray an interest in other women, asking Christine, for example, "Do you think women would find me attractive?" He was especially taken with the striking-looking Swedish movie actress Maud Adams. Christine, who knew Adams was tight with Ringo's ex-fiancée, Nancy Andrews, called her and learned that the Swedish beauty was between boyfriends. "Tell her," said Christine, "that John Lennon is very interested in meeting her." Maud Adams was soon on her way to New York—but not soon enough.

Along with Lennon's mounting self-confidence came his natural sense of humor. Peter Boyle, whom Yoko had permitted to develop a relationship with John because his wife, Loraine Alterman, stood high on Yoko's "Friendly Journalist" list, was taking pictures of the party. He called out to Marnie Hair, telling her that he would give her ten dollars if she would kiss John. Lennon turned to Boyle and said archly: "Here's a picture that's worth a lot more!" With that, he planted a kiss firmly on Fred Seaman's mouth.

As soon as *Double Fantasy* was completed, Yoko unleashed a series of surprise attacks on her closest associates. Her first victim was Sam Green. On 23 October Sam was obliged to repay a $100,000 loan from his bank. Yoko had assured him that she would cover the note. "It's a gift," she had said, "but we have to hide it from John and the office." Now she changed her tune. On the afternoon of the party, Sam received a visit from Yoko's lawyer, David Warmflash, who asked a lot of questions about the loan and Sam's financial condition. On the day before the loan fell due, Sam called Yoko and said in his most honeyed tones: "Tomorrow is loan day at the bank. You said you would cover it." Yoko replied that she would cover it, but first she wanted Sam to go down to Yoshikawa's flat and get a reading.

At three in the afternoon Sam arrived at 42 West 13th Street. The directional man asked his customary questions and made his usual calculations. Then he called up Yoko and, while Sam stood by, spoke to her in Japanese for twenty minutes. When the conversation concluded, Yoshikawa handed the phone to Green.

"Your apartment is in the wrong place," began Yoko. "Directional man says you should be living further east. Get another apartment in the 50s near the river. I will pay for it. Meantime, drop your keys to your apartment tonight at the Dakota." Then she proceeded to lay down a series of similar commands, no less devastating. Sam was ordered to fire his assistant, Bart Gorin, immediately. He was to report daily to Studio One to work in a secretarial capacity. In short, he was to be stripped of his property and demoted in status to the rank of a minor employee—a symbolic castration.

As Green listened to this astounding sentence unfold, his gorge rose. Finally, he burst out: "What's gotten into your gourd? You know I'm not going to do those things!"

Yoko replied ominously: "You will be destroyed."

"Oh, yeah!" Sam shot back. "We'll see!" With that he slammed down the phone.

Said Bart Gorin: "It was their one real conversation."

Next day, when Bart reported for work, Sam told him that they were going out for breakfast, an unprecedented act. When they sat down in the local luncheonette, Sam said: "We don't know Yoko." Bart could not believe that a relationship of such length and intensity could end with a single phone call. He protested that something would happen to relieve the situation. Sam assured Bart grimly that everything was over. He was dead right. Sam Green and Yoko Ono never spoke again.

What, in fact, ended the relationship? Bart maintained that it was Sam's collusion with John Green. Yoko had long suspected that the two Greens were defrauding her. She would invite Bart into her presence, set him at ease, then suddenly ask him if he knew John Green or Charlie Swan. Bart would feign ignorance. Allen Dahl, a hippie carpenter who did a lot of work for Sam, remembered that before Sam Green was axed, he got a call from Yoko in which she said: "I know you've been a very bad boy. Maybe we can work something out." What she wanted at that point, said Dahl, was for Green to sell everything and give her the money. Luciano attributed Sam Green's downfall to Sam Havadtoy, who showed Yoko a catalog in which a pre-Columbian goblet that Sam had offered Yoko for $30,000 was advertised for $8,000.

Yoko's resentment at being bilked might have been a factor in her decision to destroy Sam Green, but this was an ancient abuse that Yoko had long suspected, consistently overlooked, and, in effect, condoned. Though she sent David Warmflash after Sam, no attempt was made to prosecute him when he claimed the sums he had received were gifts. It is characteristic of many rich people to conspire with their retainers to be cheated rather than to confront their true indebtedness to these invaluable people by paying them what they deserve.

Sam Green rejected all these explanations of his downfall. He said simply: "She wanted to get rid of the witnesses."

John Green, the other major witness to Yoko's private life, had been seeing the door close in his face since May. In August the latch snapped. The oracle refused to recognize his ouster until October and did not have his final showdown with Yoko until six weeks after Lennon's death, but his fate was sealed long before. He, too, was faced with financial ruin, for though he boasted to Jeffrey Hunter that he had managed his finances so astutely that he had not been obliged to pay a penny in state or federal taxes on the million dollars he had earned during the past four years (living all the while rent-free at Broome Street), he had made some disastrous business and personal commitments that had cost him a lot of money.

In contrast with her treatment of Sam Green, whom she had cut off with a single blow, Yoko adopted with John Green the technique of the slow freeze. "Around August," reported Hunter, "Yoko began to refuse John Green's telephone calls. For years they had a standing appointment every Friday of the week. John Green would first call and then go up to the Dakota for these meetings. In addition to the Friday meetings, she normally called daily, often ten times over a four-hour evening period, or they would stay on the phone together for several hours over one call. In August, when he called to confirm the Friday meetings, they were invariably postponed. For the first two months of noncommunication, Green was nonchalant, pointing out that this had happened in the past. By October he was clearly worried that something had gone very wrong in his relationship with Yoko.

"He did not hear from Yoko until January 1981," continued Hunter, "and this was from Richie DePalma, who called to say that the removal men would be coming over in forty-five minutes to empty the building. In fact, they appeared at the door almost as soon as the phone was put down. When DePalma called, he said that Yoko might be with them, which added considerable tension to the event. The following Friday Green made his usual call to the Dakota and was granted an appointment by Yoko. She all but said he was fired but reserved her final decision to February, at the Chinese New Year. Green asked for his money, but Yoko refused to pay him. Green was paid quarterly in arrears, and it was clearly understood that the money was a retainer. [His salary was $2,500 a week.] Yoko refused to pay him on the grounds that she had not used his services. John Green pointed out that it was a retainer and the use or nonuse of his services was irrelevant. She still refused to pay." Subsequently Yoko sent a man down to Broome Street to lock Green out, but through an error he locked Green inside the building. Green took Yoko to court and collected $70,000.

The next man Yoko might have been expected to fire was Sam Havadtoy. She had nearly gone to war with him the previous May, when she threatened a court action to collect a $100,000 loan secured against his brownstone at 132 East 82nd Street. Havadtoy had reacted violently, threatening a countersuit or a tell-all book. He also got his money out of the building fast by selling for $100,000 a half interest to his principal tenant, Anne Falafi, wife of the Moroccan ambassador to the UN. Instead of suing him, Yoko allowed the crisis to subside, but the incident left a bad taste in Havadtoy's mouth. Donna Stillwell, a clerk in Havadtoy's gallery, recalled: "Sam was always angry at Yoko. He would say: 'Let's proclaim this "Nab a Nip Day!"' He would talk to her on the phone and say: 'Oh, I saw your picture in the *SoHo News*. You looked so beautiful! Like you were twenty!' Then he'd hang up and say: 'She looks *fifty*, if she looks a day!'" But Yoko made an exception of Havadtoy in her purge.

The man Yoko most wanted to put in his place at this moment was her husband. The combination of his steadily mounting self-confidence and his increasing consumption of food, booze, and drugs was making him impossible to manage. Marnie Hair remembered a night when she and Yoko were sitting in Studio One eating chocolates. Yoko was having a fit. "She was screaming and hurling invective," recalled Marnie. "She was going to do something about him. He was 'delusional.' She was going to get back at him and show him who was the boss. He had started thinking that he was going to start taking some things over again. She said she'd 'fix him.' . . . It may have been his not wanting to have her around because of her effect on the fans and the press. She saw herself as the man behind the throne—and I use that word advisedly. She had the balls. He cottoned on to that, but at the same time he resented it. He resented a lot of stuff—the running interference for him that she always did. But it was so tangled, that relationship. Such a hate thing going on. . . . It was no secret that sooner or later there was going to be a divorce."

A day or two after the birthday party Yoko informed Jack Douglas that John was going to Palm Beach and would not be back for six months. Actually, Yoko had arranged to send John back to Bermuda. She had given $10,000 in cash to Fred Seaman and dispatched him to the island, with orders to rent Fairylands again, equipping it with all the electronic gear that John needed to work. Throughout the latter half of October Fred received a steady stream of instructions from the Dakota, every call concluding with the assurance that "John and Yoko are going to come down in a couple of days." They never came. Finally, Fred was ordered to close up the house and return to New York. He arrived on Halloween.

KILLER NERD

In mid-October 1980 Mark David Chapman, a fat, bespectacled, baby-faced security guard at a vacation condo at Waikiki Beach, read an article in *Esquire* titled "John Lennon, Where Are You?" The piece was slugged: "In Search of the Beatle Who Spent Two Decades Seeking True Love and Cranial Bliss Only to Discover Cows, Daytime Television, and Palm Beach Real Estate." The iconoclastic author, Laurence Shames, had been assigned the impossible task of unearthing the greatest show biz recluse since Greta Garbo. Shut out by the Lennons' Maginot Line, Shames had outflanked the star's defenses by canvassing his farms, cattle, mansions, business reps—in a word, his estate. The effect of sizing up Lennon from this financial perspective was startling. The man whom millions viewed as the "conscience of his generation" emerged as a typical Seventies type—"a forty-year-old businessman, who's got $150 million . . . good lawyers to squeeze him through tax loopholes . . . who's stopped making errors and stopped making music.'"

Shames was actually describing Yoko Ono rather than John Lennon, but John had invited this sort of attack by turning his life over to Yoko. Now he was to pay for this confusion of images, for Mark David Chapman had been seeking a famous victim. After he read that piece in *Esquire,* he knew whom he must kill.

A classic example of the "killer nerd," the dwarf ego who will pay any price for fame, Chapman was no sooner incarcerated on murderers' row at Attica (along with other killer nerds, like the Son of Sam) than he began cutting deals for books, films, and articles. He wanted to be played by Timothy Hutton on the screen and to be published by Rupert Murdoch.

The most remarkable thing about Chapman was not his personality but how well he had kept it hidden to the age of twenty-five. According to the standard battery of psychological tests, his profile was one of extreme hostility, yet up till the year he assassinated Lennon, there was virtually no evidence of the rage that had seethed inside him since he was a kid.

"Mark was a boy who didn't know the meaning of 'hate,'" recalled one of his former bosses in the YMCA, at whose camps Chapman worked for years as a highly popular counselor. Not just a dedicated guardian of youth, Mark was a fervent born-again Christian, who had renounced his hippie life-style (including the use of amphetamines, barbiturates, marijuana, and LSD) at the age of seventeen after Jesus manifested Himself, coming into the room where Mark was sitting and standing at his left knee, which he felt "tingling from the tip of the toe to the top of my head." Overnight Mark transformed himself into a model young Christian, dressed in black slacks, white shirt, and tie, with hair cut short and neatly combed, and around his neck a big wooden cross. For a year he went everywhere toting a Bible and trying to make converts. At his Pentecostal church Mark played the guitar, spoke in tongues, and danced in the spirit. Eventually he started dreaming of going off to distant lands as a missionary. In fact, he did go with a Y group to Beirut but was obliged to return immediately when war broke out. No wonder Chapman's friends, colleagues, and family were stunned by the news of his crime. How could little Mark have committed the terrible sin of murder?

After Chapman had been examined by no fewer than nine psychiatrists and psychologists, the consensus was that he was suffering from pathological narcissism, characterized by a "grandiose sense of self-importance, fantasies of success, power, and ideal love, indifference to the feelings of others, a need for constant attention and admiration, feelings of rage, shame, humiliation and inferiority in response to criticism and entitlement to special favors" plus "a proneness to manipulative suicidal gestures."

Although the primary motive for the murder was instant fame, this ambition does not exhaust the inventory of Chapman's incentives. Another highly important factor in the process of selecting, stalking, and killing Lennon was Chapman's profound identification with the character of Holden Caulfield in J. D. Salinger's *The Catcher in the Rye*. The moment Chapman killed Lennon, he put down his gun and picked up *Catcher*. Standing quietly in the gateway of the Dakota conning the book, Chapman presented the picture of a Bible-reading young missionary serenely awaiting martyrdom in the cannibal's kettle. Just as Thomas à Kempis titled his famous work of devotion *The Imitation of Christ*, so Mark David Chapman might have titled his autobiography *In Imitation of Catcher*, for from the age of eighteen, when he discovered this famous rendering of modern youth, Chapman had discovered one similarity after another between his life and that of Holden Caulfield.

At first glance the parallels between the fictitious preppy from a classy WASP family in Manhattan's Silk Stocking District and the suburban-mall boy sprung from the marriage of an ex-army sergeant and a former nurse in the New South are far from obvious. But if you scrape off the surface and focus on their core personalities and the cardinal episodes of their lives, you soon see why this book became Chapman's private bible. Holden and Mark David are one at the critical poles of *love* (for children and the idea of childhood) and *hate* (against the whole adult world, especially all those big shots and hotshots that Holden loves to blow away with his killer word, "Phony!") It was in fulfillment of a "mission of ultimate significance" that Chapman, who had come to see himself as the "Catcher in the Rye of this generation" decided to kill John Lennon as a symbol of the phonies of this world and to promote the reading of *Catcher*, "this extraordinary book that holds many answers."

The final ingredient in the witch's brew that constituted Mark David Chapman's mind was his primitive Manichaean conviction that the world is a battleground for the forces of light and darkness, a belief that had a terrifying vividness for him because he felt that his brain was a radio receiver that constantly brought in the actual voices of God and the devil issuing their commands. *Command hallucinations* figured prominently both in Chapman's killing of Lennon ("my mind kept saying, 'Do it! Do it!'") and in his decision to plead guilty to the crime ("God visited me in my cell, [He spoke] in a very small male voice, [He] told me to plead guilty"). By the same token, Chapman knew that he would never have the strength to carry out his mission alone, so on the eve of the crime, he prayed to Satan, who steadied his hand and enabled him to kill Antichrist.

Chapman's life can be divided into two parts, "before" and "after" his nervous breakdown when he was twenty-one. Before his crackup Mark David was a boy with a bright future, the darling of the YMCA camp bosses, the boyfriend of a charming girl named Jessica Blankenship, and the favorite counselor of scores of kids, who called him Captain Nemo. Then he went off to Convent College in Tennessee with Jessica, intent on qualifying himself to take a permanent post in the Y, which would enable him to work abroad. But Chapman could not tolerate the pressures of school. Within a single semester he had broken down and left the college—and his girl!—denouncing the place as a nest of phonies.

He got cold comfort from his family, from whom he had been emotionally alienated since childhood. The only person who offered Mark David any constructive help was his good-ole-boy buddy Dana Reeves, who was commencing a career in the police. He advised Chapman to become a security guard, a job which entailed no more than a short course and a bit of training on the pistol range, where Chapman

proved a good hand with a gun. Packing a pistol proved a poor substitute for protecting innocent children, the basic task of the Catcher in
the Rye, so Chapman decided to take one last crack at college. Again
he failed. This time he was so humiliated that he found his consolation
only in the thought of suicide. Before he died, however, he craved one
final pleasure. He wanted to visit Hawaii, which he had been told was a
paradisial land.

After six months in the Islands, in June 1977, Chapman attached a
hose to the exhaust pipe of his car and tried to asphyxiate himself. He
failed at self-murder just as he had failed at many other things. He
wound up at Castle Memorial Hospital, where he was kept for two
weeks while being treated for "severe neurotic depressive reaction."
Discharged as an outpatient, he clung to the institution by getting a job
in the hospital's housekeeping department and doing voluntary work
in the psychiatric unit. Then, suddenly, he decided to take a trip
around the world.

Aided by a Japanese girl, Gloria Abe, who worked at Waters World
Travel, Mark spent four months carefully planning his journey. On 6
July 1978 he took off, traveling in a westerly direction, his first stop,
Tokyo, where his arrival coincided roughly with that of John and Yoko.
When he returned on 20 August—about a month before Lennon's arrival at Honolulu—he impressed everyone as being a different man:
upbeat, relaxed, and planning a new career in social work. He had sent
Gloria a number of cards and letters; now they began to date. They
were an odd couple: He was four years her junior, a southern American Jesus freak; she was the daughter of a prosperous Japanese baker,
a Buddhist and a devotee of tarot, astrology, and the occult. After they
were married in June, Chapman began to exhibit a new personality.
The once-obsequious hospital worker became now a bossy and bellig-
erent character, who saddled his wife with absurd demands and restric-
tions, while spending her money freely on his latest obsession,
collecting art.

Chapman coveted a $5,000 gold wall plaque of Salvador Dali's "Lin-
coln in Dalivision," which represents the assassination of Abraham Lincoln superimposed on the crucifixion of Jesus Christ. The dealer who
displayed the piece, which Mark planned to purchase with money
given to him by his father-in-law, reported that Chapman was constantly in the gallery blithering about assassination and crucifixion,
these themes having become as closely entwined in his head as they
were in the mind of John Lennon.

In December 1979 Mark left his job in the hospital's printshop after
failing to get a promotion, and went to work again as a security guard,
albeit one who did not carry a gun. This backward step was accompanied by an outburst of uncharacteristic behavior. One acquaintance

described Chapman at this time as "a creep, a negative, cold, ugly person." An official of the Church of Scientology, located across the street from the condominium where Chapman worked, characterized the young guard as a "classic case of covert hostility. He used to walk back and forth in front of our building, kicking pebbles and muttering threats. For three months we got as many as forty threatening phone calls every day. A voice would whisper, 'Bang! Bang! You're dead!'" Chapman confessed subsequently to making these calls.

On 17 October, after reading the *Esquire* piece on John Lennon, Chapman went on to the library and borrowed a copy of Anthony Fawcett's *John Lennon: One Day at a Time*. He would read a little of the book and then get angry, complaining that Lennon was a phony, always preaching about peace and love while living like a millionaire. Mark also started making tapes of Beatles' records that he would alter by changing the speed of the tape. When he played these tapes for Gloria, she thought the voices sounded like those of elves. Mark liked best to listen to the tapes in a darkened room, sitting nude in the lotus position and chanting, *"John Lennon, I'm going to kill you, you phony bastard!"*

Chapman signed out from work for the last time on 23 October. Instead of writing his own name, he scrawled "John Lennon," then crossed it out, with short, stabbing strokes. Back in August he had written a letter to an acquaintance in Italy, giving the Dakota as his return address. The letter had said that Chapman was planning on going soon to New York upon a mission. So it is possible that Chapman was already thinking of killing Lennon even before he read the *Esquire* article, which simply served to confirm his resolve because it provided him with an even stronger motive for ridding the world of this Antichrist, who symbolized to him all the big phonies. The announcement of the forthcoming release of *Double Fantasy* must have contributed a further inducement because it signaled that the corrupter of the youth was once again about to lead the children astray, just as he had done in the past when he had proclaimed the Beatles more popular than Jesus.

Though Chapman had considered killing many other celebrities, including Ronald Reagan, Jacqueline Onassis, Elizabeth Taylor, George C. Scott, Johnny Carson, David Bowie, and Eddie Albert, as well as his own father, once he got John Lennon into his sights, Mark moved with dispatch.

Four days after quitting his job, Chapman walked into J and S Sales in downtown Honolulu, a shop whose motto is: "Buy a gun and get a bang out of life." From a salesclerk named Ono, he bought a Charter Arms .38-caliber Special, a snub-nosed five-shot revolver used by detectives because it is easily concealed. He also purchased a pair of handle grips to improve his aim. When he received a call from an employment agency asking if he were interested in a new job, he replied: "No, I already have a job to do."

On 27 October, he purchased with a Visa card a one-way ticket to Newark. On the twenty-ninth, he bade Gloria good-bye, saying only: "I'm going to New York to make it all different." On the thirtieth, he arrived in the city, and spent a night at the Waldorf Astoria (like Holden) before checking into the Vanderbilt Branch of the YMCA at 224 East 47th Street. No sooner was he unpacked than he began retracing Holden Caulfield's Via Dolorosa.

Chapman visited the "lagoon" at the foot of Central Park, whose disappearing ducks had so puzzled Holden. He watched the children riding the carousel and climbing atop the statue of Alice in Wonderland. Making his way north and west across the park, he found the Museum of Natural History, where Holden had met his adored sister, Phoebe.

The Museum lies just five blocks north of the Dakota, where Chapman now began to hang about, reading a history of the building, which he found fascinating. To get closer to his target, he moved into the Olcott Hotel, just half a block from the Dakota.

One day he picked up a girl named Anne who worked at the Dairy in the Park. He said he was looking for company and suggested that they see David Bowie in *The Elephant Man*. Next day he met her at the Arsenal and presented her with a bouquet of flowers. They took a ride in a hansom, saw the show, and went up to the observation deck of the Empire State Building. Later, coming back through Times Square, Chapman denounced the area as a hotbed of "faggots," drug peddlers, and prostitutes. On the other hand, he showed great sympathy toward freaks, discussing the movie of that title. He also denounced the New York City gun law.

What inspired this attack was the discovery that he could not buy bullets for his weapon without a hard-to-obtain gun permit. To remedy this deficiency, he flew down to Atlanta on 8 November and hooked up again with Dana Reeves, who was working as a deputy sheriff in the redneck town of Decatur. The peace officer saw that Mark got his load: five hollow-nosed rounds that fly to pieces on contact, tearing their target to bits.

When Chapman got back to New York on 9 November, he was poised to strike. He had completed his preparations, staked out his quarry, and was armed to kill. Then the angels of God suddenly found voice and drowned out the devils of hell. On 11 November Mark called Gloria and announced that coming to New York had been a mistake. For the first time he revealed to her that he had come to the city to shoot John Lennon, adding that only his love for her had stopped him. "I have won a great victory," he declared. "I'm coming home."

On 10 November John Lennon called up Jack Douglas. The producer, who had not heard from Lennon in twenty days, was surprised and delighted by the call. Not only was John in town, instead of being in Palm Beach, but he was burning with eagerness to get back into the studio. "We've got tons of work," he exclaimed. "I was just startin' to get a full head of steam. I'm not gonna stop now!" Douglas was already committed to another job, but by switching it to the late shift, he cleared the time from 1:00 P.M. to 7:00 P.M. daily to work with Lennon.

What made Douglas especially eager to continue his collaboration was his recognition that John was coming into his own again. "John was totally satisfied with himself mentally and physically," declared Douglas. "He was starting to make a break. It had to do with his fortieth birthday. He told me: 'I'm happy to be forty years old. I'm in the best shape I've ever been in my life and I feel the best I ever felt.' . . . He was starting to become independent, lookin' to get out of that situation [his marriage] in the worst way."

Another sign of John's revival was the flood of fresh plans cresting in his mind. He wanted to fly out to the West Coast with Jack right after New Year's and start work on an album with Ringo. He earmarked three songs from his Bermuda collection for his old mate, asserting on the tape of "Nobody Told Me There'd Be Days Like This": "This song is for Richard Starkey, formerly of the Beatles." (Yoko issued it subsequently as the first single from *Milk and Honey*.) John was also eager to establish a commercial recording studio on Riverside Drive. The house was to be set up so that a band could sleep there while recording. "Can you imagine," John said, "how many people would book into a studio if my name were on it? All we have to do is make sure that we have one room for ourselves where we can always work." Another of Lennon's projects was the rerecording of his standards, from "Help!" through "Strawberry Fields" to "I Am the Walrus." John felt that all these tracks could be improved both compositionally and acoustically. He denounced the old arrangements, particularly George Martin's famous splice on "Strawberry Fields," which Lennon castigated as a "stupid mistake."

One day when John and Jack were stuck in traffic on 57th Street, John composed in the car "Street of Dreams" (a song that subsequently disappeared) by inventing a chorus and adding a bridge left over from the heyday of the Beatles, circa 1965. For years John had been searching for the right place into which to snap this bit of music. As soon as he arrived at the studio, he seated himself at the piano and cried, "Listen!" Then, as he banged out the chords, he sang the song into the

Sony Walkman that he carried now like a memo pad. When he finished, he popped the tape out of the machine and slipped it into his pocket, crowing, "That's for *my* record!"

The record he had in mind was the album that would follow *Double Fantasy*. Often in the last weeks of his life, especially when he was sitting with Jack after work, having a drink and smoking a joint, John would say, "You and me and Lee [DeCarlo, Jack's assistant] will lock ourselves in a room and make a no-bullshit John Lennon album. No women will be allowed—not even Chris [Jack's woman]!"

When "Starting Over," the first single from *Double Fantasy*, was released in mid-October, it performed as desired, soaring to the top of the chart. A contrived and campy throwback to a style of long ago, the song was merely a bit of fluff, but it provided the thrill of hearing a new John Lennon record. When the album was released in mid-November, the reaction was very different. Though it got an enormous amount of airplay, its chart performance was very sluggish. It never rose higher than eleven while John was living. John was deeply disappointed by the album's weak sales and bad reviews, especially the sneering put-downs from Britain, where the triumph of punk had made Lennon old hat. John was also taken aback by Bruce Springsteen's *The River* (particularly "Hungry Heart"), which made him think that he should have included some of his heavier songs, like "Serve Yerself!" on his album.

Lennon was suffering at this time from doing too much coke. His ravaged appearance in his final days—the big blue bags under his eyes and the death's-head boniness of his face—was underscored by the hole he had burned through his septum, which he was scheduled to have repaired (by grafting tissue from the roof of his mouth to the damaged divider) the week following his death.

What made John's lot even harder was Yoko's demand that he fashion a hot new solo single for her that could be released at Christmas. One day, when the battle over this record was at its height, Fred Seaman walked in upon his employers. He heard John say: "When I wanted to put out a solo album, you wouldn't let me because it always had to be 'John and Yoko'! Now you want to do a Yoko Ono thing. And if you do one, *I* want to do one!"

Yoko had a ready answer to that childish argument. "OK," she said, "you can do one later. But for now I just want to get this single out." Thus was born "Walking on Thin Ice," a six-minute disco mix of a song recorded earlier but laid aside for further work. John Lennon would spend the last two weeks of his life laboring day in, day out to make this track a big hit for Yoko.

* * *

On 26 November Yoko sprang a surprise on John. That afternoon, she told him, they were going to shoot a video of *Double Fantasy*. (The project had been in the works for the past three weeks, but Yoko had warned her staff to say nothing of the matter to Lennon.) The filming commenced with the couple strolling through Central Park. Then the scene shifted to the Sperone Gallery at 142 Green Street in SoHo, where Fred Seaman arrived at 6:00 P.M., just before the shooting began. The big white loft was buzzing as a sizable film crew trained their attentions on the set: a large mattress covered in white set on a white platform in a white room illuminated by floodlights simulating sunlight pouring through a bedroom window. When Ethan Russell, the British photographer in charge of the project, gave the signal to roll, John and Yoko, dressed in Japanese kimonos, he in black, she pale blue adorned with flowers, approached the bed and circled it slowly. Suddenly Yoko removed her kimono, standing naked before the camera. John stared at her in amazement. Then he raised his finger and pointed at her large, pendulous breasts, quipping, "Tits!"

"Come on, my dear, you, too!" Yoko urged John, who had not been told that he was going to work in the raw. Reluctantly he removed his wrap, appearing highly embarrassed. The strip-off scene was repeated four times, until Russell was satisfied. Then it was time to shoot John and Yoko making love.

Glumly John lay down on the bed naked, embracing Yoko from the side. Unsatisfied, Russell instructed Lennon to mount Yoko, a position he was obliged to hold for the next half hour, while the director conferred with Yoko about camera angles. Meantime, the still photographer, Allen Tannebaum, circled the scene restlessly, taking scores of shots. A transistor radio on a stool near the bed obligingly played, among other songs, "Woman" and "Starting Over."

After a dinner break at 9:00 P.M. Fred cued in "Kiss Kiss Kiss," which played loudly as John feigned intercourse with Yoko for thirty minutes. At each break in the shooting Jerry Caron, Sam Havadtoy's gofer, would hold a mirror before Yoko's face, while her servant, Toshi, would wipe the sweat from her forehead with a cloth dipped in a bucket of ice water. Another member of the crew stood by with a bucket of fuming incense. Finally, nothing remained but to get some close-ups of Yoko feigning orgasm, while lip-syncing the words of the song, concluding with its erotic cry in Japanese: *"Mote! Mote! Mote! [More! More! More!]"*

BANG! BANG! YOU'RE DEAD!

When Mark David Chapman got back to Hawaii, he showed Gloria his gun and even insisted that she pull the trigger. He was intent on making her understand that he was in a position to take John Lennon's life. At the same time he insisted that the whole episode had been a bad dream and that he would never have gone through with the murder, even if offered the chance. For the next three weeks he did nothing but watch television. During this period he had two hallucinations, which he interpreted as divine messages. Walking past a plaque on his wall listing the Ten Commandments, Mark saw the Sixth Commandment, "Thou shalt not kill," leap forward. Another day, while watching a cartoon, he suddenly spied the same phrase on the screen.

By late November Mark was telling Gloria that it was time he grew up. He was a married man now and ought to be able to support a family. What he needed to do first, however, was go off by himself for a while, to think things over. He had decided to return to New York. She needn't fear that he would do anything wrong. He had thrown the gun and the bullets into the ocean.

At this same time he called the Waikiki Counseling Clinic, where he had gone before when he felt suicidal. He made an appointment with a psychologist, but he didn't keep it. Instead, on Friday, 5 December, he left Hawaii, arriving in New York on Saturday afternoon. After renting a room at the YMCA on 63rd Street between Broadway and Central Park West, he checked out the nearby Dakota. Then he went out on the town. A cabdriver named Mark Snyder (a moonlighting law student) picked up Chapman that evening at Eighth Avenue and 55th Street.

The driver recalled that Chapman was carrying a heavy satchel and appeared "very agitated." He offered the cabbie $5 and some cocaine if he would make a couple of short stops. The first address was the Century, an ornate Art Deco apartment house, on Central Park West, whose side entrance confronts the main entrance to the 63rd Street Y. Chapman entered the building through this door, which is guarded by a doorman. Five minutes later he emerged and hopped into the cab, giving an address across town at East 65th Street and Second Avenue.

Chapman was in and out of his second stop in two minutes. When he got back into the cab, he gushed: "I just have to blurt this out. I just dropped off the tapes of an album John Lennon and Paul McCartney made today. I was the engineer, and they played for three hours straight." The driver recalled that Chapman "started shaking his head in a mad frenzy, smiling to himself, like he had some inner thoughts that were sending him into outer space." By the time they reached their last stop, Bleecker Street and Sixth Avenue, an area with a large number of well-known record stores, Chapman's mood had changed. He exploded in a "jealous rage at people who were successful, like rock stars."

While Chapman was railing against rock stars, the target of his hatred was erupting in a towering rage. Early Saturday evening John Lennon had the last of his terrible rages, which he now called "fugues." Marnie Hair, who witnessed this fit, reported that in all the years she had known John, she had never seen him so angry. It was the children who drove John crazy. "Sean and my daughter didn't know where they wanted to spend the night," explained Marnie. "He just broke out in a rage. He picked Sean up. Threw him in bed! Picked up my daughter, threw her at me! He was screaming and hollering and yelling. I said, 'Fuck you! I'm leaving!' . . . The kids were tired. They were whining, they were bitching, they were obnoxious—but they were kids! Babies! But he couldn't stand that. He had been alone with them for an hour, an hour and a half. That was about all John could take. . . . Yoko was down in the studio. She didn't want any part of this stuff. So she sent Helen up, and Sean was crying and screaming and cowering—because John could put the fear of God into you! Helen said it got so bad that she had to take Sean out of the city to her place in Pennsylvania."

That night John and Yoko gave a long and tedious interview to Andy Peebles of BBC Radio that started at the studio and wound up after midnight at Mr. Chow, the Lennons' favorite restaurant. Peebles insisted on dragging John and Yoko through the entire history of their recording career, prompting them from notes, like an oral examiner: "1970—as we move through—in February, 'Instant Karma.'" John answered gamely, but the only things of value to emerge from this session came at the very end, when the notes were put aside. Then John spoke candidly about his current life. Peebles responded by asking as his final question: "What about . . . your own sense of security these days?"

John's answer explained why it was so easy to kill him: "She [Yoko] told me that, 'Yes, you can walk on the street.' . . . But I would be walking around tense, like waiting for somebody to say something or jump on me. And it took me two years to unwind. I can go right out this door now and go into a restaurant. You want to know how great that is?"

By ten-thirty the following morning, Pearl Harbor Day, Mark David Chapman was standing outside the Dakota, waiting for John Lennon to come out the door. Chapman was restless, however, so after offering to get the doorman coffee, he left at lunchtime and didn't come back. Instead, he spent that Sunday afternoon moving his things from the Y into the Sheraton Centre at Seventh Avenue and 52nd Street. He had decided to move because his room at the Y was small and also because he had been alarmed by the sight a homosexual, who reminded him of the "flit" who had molested Holden Caulfield. After booking Room 2730 for seven days at $82 a night, paying with a Visa card, Chapman unpacked his bag, laying out his clothes, Bible, passport, and tapes of the Beatles and Todd Rundgren. He ate supper in the hotel restaurant and then began the enactment of the most dramatic episode in *Catcher* by summoning to his room a prostitute.

Chapman behaved toward the woman exactly as did his hero in the book, engaging her in conversation (plus giving and receiving a massage) but not engaging in sexual intercourse. When she left his room at three in the morning, Mark stood on the threshold of the most memorable moment in the entire book: Holden's confrontation with the sleazy elevator operator who provides a whore and then demands twice the agreed-upon price. When Holden finally comes across with the cash, the elevator man flicks the boy contemptuously across his penis. Holden lashes out in rage but gets the worst of the fight. Then, slipping into a revenge fantasy, he pictures himself like a Hollywood gangster, wounded but holding a gun, crawling down the stairs to the floor below, where he rings for the elevator. When the operator opens the door, Holden says, "he'd see me with the automatic in my hand and he'd start screaming at me, in this very high-pitched, yellow-belly voice, to leave him alone. But I'd plug him anyway. Six shots right through his fat hairy belly. Then I'd throw my automatic down the elevator shaft. . . ."

The elevator operator scene could not be performed now. It would have to wait until the following night.

On Monday morning, around eleven o'clock, Chapman awoke and dressed himself warmly, pulling on long johns and layering himself with a shirt, sweater, and jacket, before donning his scarf, coat, and fake fur hat. Before he left his room, he took all the things he treasured and arranged them on a table in what he called a "display." He laid out a picture of Dorothy from *The Wizard of Oz*, an eight-track tape of Todd Rundgren, a copy of the New Testament (in which he had written "Holden Caulfield" and added to the words "Gospel According to John" the name "Lennon"), his expired passport, a letter of recommendation from an official of the Y, and pictures of himself taken when he worked at Fort Chaffee. Before leaving, he walked into the room a couple of times to test the effect of his arrangement. After making a few last improvements, he went downstairs and bought a copy of *Catcher*. On the title page he wrote: "This is my statement." (His plan was to remain silent after the murder, making the book his spokesman.) Carrying the red paperback and the copy of *Double Fantasy* that he had purchased Saturday night, he walked up to the Dakota and asked the doorman if John Lennon had been seen that morning. Then he offered to stand treat for lunch for Jude Stein and another woman, fans who were always at the gate. Over a hamburger and two beers at the Dakota Coffee Shop, he described his long flight to Tokyo and his journey 'round the world.

Back at his post after lunch Chapman struck up a conversation with Paul Goresh, an amateur photographer from New Jersey, known in the Lennon circle as Fat Dave. Goresh observed that Chapman was not a knowledgeable Beatles' fan because when Allen Klein entered the Dakota, shielding his face with his hand, Chapman failed to recognize the famous manager.* Goresh demonstrated his familiarity with the Lennon family by greeting Helen Seaman and Sean when they stepped out of a blue Chevrolet station wagon. He even introduced Chapman to them, explaining that Mark was a fan who had come "all the way from Hawaii." Chapman was thrilled and called Sean "the cutest little boy I have ever seen."

Inside the Dakota, John Lennon was having a banner day. In the morning, anticipating a photo session with the top rock photographer Annie Leibovitz, who had been commissioned to shoot a cover for *Rolling Stone,* Lennon had slipped over to Veez A Veez on West 72nd Street to have his hair styled short in front, almost like bangs, and long in the back. Leibovitz, who likes to lay her celebrities bare, had heard that John and Yoko had been filmed feigning coitus. She had come with a drawing of them entwined in the nude. When John saw what

---

*Allen Klein was out on bail, awaiting the result of his appeal of a conviction for failing to declare certain income for the year 1970. On 9 August 1979 he had been sentenced to two years in prison, suspended on condition that he spend two months in a jail or treatment facility. The complaint against him had grown out of an investigation of the most famous promotion man in the record business, Pete Bennett. The promo man's job was to jockey Apple's new releases to the top of the charts by laying on the most important wholesalers, rack jobbers, and distributors the 5,000 unmarked copies of each new release that Capitol provided at cost, 23 cents a copy. It was a cheap way of increasing sales, but it became a crime when, after the records were sold for a profit, the money was not reported as income to the IRS. When Klein's appeal was denied, he served two months in a Manhattan jail in 1981.

was wanted, he snapped: "Fine, no problem" and stripped down immediately. Yoko refused to go beyond removing her black top. Leibovitz told her to keep her shirt on because she preferred the contrast of a completely clothed and a totally naked figure. Then John got down on top of Yoko, who was lying on her back with her hands behind her head and a faraway look in her eyes, as if she didn't even notice the mad-looking nude man who had curled up on her in the fetal position and was pressing a passionate, closed-eye kiss against her unresponsive cheek. When the photographer showed Lennon the Polaroid, he responded: "That's great! That's really our relationship. Promise it will be on the cover." When it ran the following week, it blew everybody's mind because it reduced the marriage of the rock world's most celebrated lovers to the image of an impassive bitch and her blindly sucking whelp.

At 1:00 P.M. John gave his last interview. Dressed in a red T-shirt with a blue sweater and his black leather "ruffian" jacket, he talked to Dave Sholin, a San Francisco DJ, in Studio One. Lennon sounded coked up as he ran out the familiar party line for the last time, his enthusiasm so forced at moments that he became strident. He was still in full cry at 5:00 P.M., when he recognized that it was time to leave for the Record Plant. Since the Lennons' car had not arrived, Sholin offered John and Yoko a lift in his limo. When they stepped out on the sidewalk in front of the building, Paul Goresh rushed over with Mark Chapman in tow.

The fat fan in the horn-rims held out his album mutely for the great star to sign. John bent over it earnestly, inscribing "John Lennon 1980." As John wrote, Goresh zoomed in on the famous profile, catching the moony face of Chapman in the background, smiling stuporously.

"Here, is this what you want?" asked John, returning the album.

Chapman, struck dumb by Lennon's presence, turned a moment later to the radio engineer and asked: "Did you guys do an interview with Lennon?"

When the car pulled away, Chapman asked Goresh: "Did I have my hat on or off in the picture? I wanted my hat off." Then, reflecting for a moment, he exclaimed: "They'll never believe this in Hawaii!"

As darkness fell, the fans left, but Chapman and Goresh remained in front of the building, talking. When Fred Seaman came walking briskly out of the archway, bearing a box of outtakes from Yoko's 1974 sessions with Spinozza, Goresh stopped Fred and said: "This is Dave Chapman. He really scored!" Chapman, grinning, held up his album.

"Congratulations, man!" Fred smiled as he hurried off to the garage under the adjacent Mayfair apartment building.

When Fred arrived at the building that housed the Record Plant, he found David Geffen waiting for the elevator. He said that he had been summoned by Yoko. As they rode up to the tenth floor, he remarked, thinking out loud: "She's a tough customer. You never know what's really on her mind." What was on her mind that night became clear the moment Geffen walked into the studio. Lennon gave a thumbs-up signal to Jack Douglas in the booth, and out of the monitors came blasting "Walking on Thin Ice." As the room vibrated to the disco beat, John's groaning guitar alternating with Yoko's batlike squeaks, Lennon the salesman went to work on Geffen the customer. "It's fantastic! A smash!" enthused John. "It's better than *anything* we did on *Double Fantasy*," he added, honestly. Then he delivered his punch line: "Let's put it out before Christmas!"

Geffen smiled and replied: "Well, let's put it out *after* Christmas and really do the thing right. Take out an ad."

"An *ad*!" echoed Lennon with mock amazement. "Listen to this, Mother, you're gonna get an *ad*!"

Geffen deftly changed the subject, announcing that *Double Fantasy*, which stood at twelve with a bullet, had just gone gold in England. As he made the statement, he observed Yoko giving him a look that to him meant: "It better be number one in England because John wants it so badly." (Yoko was planning to send Sam Havadtoy to London to buy $100,000 worth of records to guarantee a chart topper. Ironically, that is precisely what Brian Epstein had done with "Love Me Do." John Lennon was literally "starting over.")

Before the session ended, during a period when Yoko was out of the studio, John leaned back against the tape machine, where he had delivered so many monologues during the past four months, and said to Jack: "Don't repeat to Yoko what I'm going to tell you." Then he went into the same rap that he had laid on Fred that night he conceived the album in Bermuda. John said that his days were numbered and that he was living on borrowed time. He didn't allude to assassination, but he appeared completely resigned to dying. He even discussed what would happen to his legend after his death, boasting that he would become much more famous than Elvis. Jack had heard Lennon speak of death before—but never with the sense of its imminence that he conveyed that night.

When Yoko reappeared and the Lennons began to discuss their supper plans, John's mood reverted to normal. Announcing they were going over to the Stage Deli to grab a bite, John assured Jack that he would be at the studio at nine o'clock the following morning to master the new single. Normally Jack would have ridden home with the Lennons, but this night he had to remain behind to work on another record. He walked John to the elevator, where they said good-night. His last recollection of Lennon is a smile, a wave, and a cheery "See you tomorrow morning, bright and early!"

The limousine took the Lennons directly home, rolling up Eighth Avenue to Columbus Circle and then continuing north along Central Park West to 72nd Street, where it made a sharp left turn and pulled up in front of the Dakota.

Mark David Chapman was still in front of the building, standing close to the sentry box. Until 8:30 he had enjoyed the company of Paul Goresh; then the photographer had announced that he was going home. Chapman urged him to remain. "You never know," he warned. "Something might happen, you know. He might go to Spain or something tonight—and you might never see him again!"

After Goresh left, Chapman had struck up a conversation with the doorman, José Perdomo, a genial, red-faced, white-haired Cuban. They had talked of Cuba, the Bay of Pigs, the Kennedy assassination. At one point a derelict came up, panhandling. Chapman gave the bum $10. Later he laid $50 on the doorman. Perdomo found Chapman calm and rational. After the killing he told Fred Seaman: "Chapman was not crazy."

When the limousine stopped in front of the building, the hour was 10:50. Yoko hopped out first, followed by John, who was carrying a tape recorder and some cassettes. As she passed Chapman, he said, "Hello." When John walked by, he gave Chapman a hard look. As Chapman said later: "He printed me."

All that night Chapman had been praying alternately to God and to the devil—the one to lead him out of temptation and the other to give him the strength to complete his mission. Now, at the critical moment, he heard a voice in his head saying: "Do it . . . do it . . . do it!"

Taking two steps into the carriageway, he pulled the snub-nosed pistol from his pocket and dropped into the combat stance, knees flexed with one hand holding the gun for sighting while the other supported the shooting hand at the wrist. He spoke no word. His gun spoke.

The first two shots caught Lennon in the back and spun him around. Two of the next three shots hit him in the shoulder. One bullet went astray. The sound of regular firing was echoed by that of shattering glass as the bullets passed through Lennon's body and smashed into the wood and glass windbreak. When Chapman had emptied his gun, he stared at the driveway, expecting to see John Lennon's body lying there. He saw nothing.

Chapman was so out of it as he shot Lennon that he failed to see his man open the door of the windbreak and stagger up the five steps to the office, where he fell flat on his face. Jay Hastings, the young, long-haired night man, was reading a magazine when he heard sounds of breaking glass followed by footsteps. "John Lennon stumbled in, a horrible, confused look on his face," recollected Hastings. Yoko followed, screaming, *"John's been shot!"* For one crazy moment Hastings thought the whole scene was a gag. Then he saw Lennon collapse, the tape recorder and cassettes in his hands clattering across the stone floor.

Hastings pressed an alarm button under the desk, summoning the police from the nearby 20th Precinct station house. Then he rushed to John's side to remove his shattered glasses, which were gouging into his nose, and to cover him with his uniform jacket. When Hastings pulled off his tie to apply it as a tourniquet, he recognized for the first time how desperate were John's wounds. Blood was pouring out of his mouth and chest. "His eyes were open but unfocused," reported Hastings. "He gurgled once, vomiting blood and fleshly material." Yoko was screaming now for a doctor. Hastings jumped up and punched out 911. Returning to Lennon's side, he murmured: "It's OK, John, you'll be all right!"

José Perdomo had been stunned by what he had witnessed. As the tears streamed down his face, he cried out at Chapman: "You shoot a man like that!"

Mark, dropping instinctively into the attitude of the defensive adolescent, answered: "Don't worry, José."

Suddenly the thought crossed the doorman's mind that Chapman might be crazy. "You know what you do?" he demanded.

"Don't worry!" Chapman repeated. Then, like Holden Caulfield, he dropped his empty weapon.

José promptly kicked the gun out of reach and implored Chapman: "Please! Go away!"

Mark looked at the doorman despondently. "José, I'm sorry!" he said softly. "Where would I go?"

At that moment he turned around and beheld a girl standing in the driveway. Nina Rosen had walked past John and Yoko when they had gotten out of their limousine; then she had heard shots and doubled back to discover what had happened. When she asked Chapman what was going on, he told her: "If I were you, I'd get out of here!" After he repeated that warning a couple of times, Nina left. The only other witnesses to the shooting, a pair of men in a cab that had pulled up behind the limousine as it was discharging its passengers, had ducked back into the cab, which made a screeching U-turn on 72nd Street as it took off down Central Park West. By that time José Perdomo had ducked into the office to report that the killer had put down his gun. Jay Hastings went out immediately to keep his eye on the murderer. He found a pudgy young man, bareheaded and without a coat, standing under the glaring gate lantern, reading a paperback book.

By that time 72nd Street was full of sirens. Two blue and white squad cars came racing up to the building with their roof lights flashing white and red. Chapman had removed his coat and hat to show that he was not carrying a concealed weapon. Now he put his hands atop his head with the elbows forming a shield for his eyes. Summoned by a terse dispatch, "Shots fired. 1 West 72nd Street," Officer Tony Palma and his partner, Herb Frauenberger, arrived at the Dakota at the same moment as Officer Steve Spiro with his partner, Pete Cullen. Scrambling out of their cars, the patrolmen were directed by the doorman, who shouted, "He's the one who did the shooting!"—pointing at Chapman, who was standing in the shadows by the gate.

Spiro drew his revolver and shouted, "Don't move! Put your hands on the wall!" He repeated his orders until he could collar the 200-pound Chapman with his left arm and swing him around to act as a human shield in case there was another gunman lurking nearby.

The moment Chapman was seized, he began bleating: "Please don't hurt me! Please!" As Spiro glanced over his right shoulder at the door to the building, he saw three bullet holes in the glass panes of the windbreak. At that point the doorman cried out that Chapman was alone. Spiro threw Chapman back against the wall of the archway. Instantly the murderer started to cry, sobbing, "I acted alone! Please don't hurt me!"

Jay Hastings stuck his head out of the windbreak at this moment, and Tony Palma shouted: "Is someone shot in there?" Instantly Palma was up the steps followed by Frauenberger. Discovering a man lying face down in the office with a small Oriental woman standing over him crying, Palma, who had no idea of the victim's identity, turned the man over and saw that he was badly wounded. "All I saw was red," recalled Palma. He looked up at his partner and said: "Grab his legs and let's get him out of here!" Instantly they lofted Lennon onto their shoulders and made their way out of the office.

Jay Hastings tagged along, trying to lend a hand. He recalled that he could hear John's bones creaking. As the officers laid Lennon in the back of a third squad car, which had just pulled up, Hastings observed that Lennon was completely unstrung, his limbs lying akimbo.

Palma told Officer James Moran in the third car: "Rush him to the hospital!"

As the car took off, Moran turned in the front seat and yelled at Lennon, "Do you know who you are?" John could not speak. "He moaned and nodded his head, as if to say, 'Yes.'" Moran switched on his siren as his driver, Officer William Gamble, raced through a red light at Columbus Avenue, and tore across town and down Ninth Avenue to 58th Street, where they swung into the emergency entrance of

Roosevelt Hospital. The hospital's major trauma team had been alerted already by a radio call from Tony Palma.

Meantime, Steve Spiro had pushed the handcuffed Mark Chapman into the back seat of his car. Getting behind the wheel, the officer erupted in exasperation, shouting at Chapman: *"Do you know what you did? Do you?"*

Chapman replied earnestly: "Listen, I'm sorry. I didn't know he was a friend of yours."

Instantly Spiro flashed, "Wacko!" He retracted that opinion as soon as he got Chapman to the 20th Precinct station. Spiro was particularly impressed by the businesslike tone Mark adopted when he spoke with Gloria in Honolulu. The call (recorded by the police) sounds like that of any husband getting in touch with his wife after an alarming experience from whose unpleasant consequences he wishes to shield her, while dismissing his own danger as a trifle.

MARK: Hi!

GLORIA: Hi, Mark. I love you.

MARK: I know. I love you, too. Well, the police were there?

GLORIA: No, first call I got was the reporter.

MARK: Oh, no! Are you at home?

GLORIA: Yes, your mom and dad are here.

MARK: OK. Well, I don't want to talk to anybody else.

GLORIA: I know.

MARK: But I don't want you crying 'cause I want you to hear me.

After hammering away for a couple of minutes with characteristic obsessiveness about the importance of summoning the police to protect herself against the press, Mark was suddenly stopped in his tracks when the timid Gloria managed to ask: "Has it hit you yet what you've really done?"

Instantly Mark replied: "Oh, I have to go."

When Lennon was brought into the emergency room, he had virtually no pulse. The two bullets that had hit him in the back had pierced the lung and passed out through the chest. (One of them was discovered in his black leather jacket.) A third bullet had shattered his left shoulder bone and exited. A fourth bullet had hit the same shoulder but ricocheted inside his chest, where it severed the aorta and cut his windpipe.

A team of seven medical men labored to save Lennon with every device and technique. "It wasn't possible to resuscitate him by any means," reported Dr. Stephen Lynn, the hospital's director of emergency services. "He had three holes in his chest, two in his back, and two in his left shoulder. He'd lost three quarts of blood from the gun wounds, about 80 percent of his blood volume."

The official cause of death was shock produced by massive hemorrhaging. Off the record, some of the staff said it might have been better if Lennon had been left undisturbed and the resuscitation attempt had been made by the ambulance crew. They also expressed astonishment at Lennon's wretched physical condition.

Yoko had been brought to the hospital by Tony Palma, who discovered now that the man he had found bleeding to death was John Lennon. Palma recalled taking Yoko to a little room where she could use the phone. She called David Geffen, who appeared shortly thereafter. When he saw her, he picked her up like a child.

"Someone's shot John!" she babbled. "Can you believe it? Someone shot him!"

At that point Dr. Lynn entered the room.

Yoko demanded: "Where is my husband? I want to be with my husband. He would want me to be with him. Where is he?"

Lynn braced himself and announced: "We have very bad news. Unfortunately in spite of massive efforts, your husband is dead. There was no suffering at the end."

Yoko replied: "Are you saying he is sleeping?"

Officers Palma and Frauenberger took Yoko back to the Dakota, stopping first at the Hotel Pierre, where Geffen was staying. When they returned to the Dakota, they slipped into the building by the back door. The moment Yoko got home, she picked up her phone and started making calls. She claimed subsequently to have called the "three people John would have wanted to know: Julian, Aunt Mimi, and Paul McCartney." There is no evidence that any of them received such a call.

SEASON OF THE WITCH

The night John Lennon was shot, Sam Havadtoy and Luciano Sparacino were resting in their bedroom. Sam was asleep, and Luciano was watching *Quincy*. The phone rang. Luciano could barely distinguish the voice of Danny, one of the workmen at the Dakota, who was shouting, "Did you hear? John's been shot! Turn on Channel Five now!" Luciano pressed the selector—and there was the coverage. Immediately he shook Sam awake.

At eleven-fifteen the official announcement was made: John Lennon was dead. A moment of stunned silence followed. "Poor Yoko! Poor Yoko!" exclaimed Havadtoy as he picked up the phone.

When he discovered that all the lines were busy, Luciano urged him: "Go over there! You'll get in!"

Sam never really came home again.

Fred Seaman was coming out of the St. Mark's Theater when he noticed a hippie holding up the *SoHo News,* which bore on its front page a photo of Yoko over a review slugged YOKO ONLY. Tears were streaming down the man's face. "What's the matter?" asked Fred.

"Isn't it ironic?" said the hippie, pointing to the cover. "I mean, since John was shot."

"Shot!" echoed Fred. "What do you mean, 'shot'?"

When he heard the answer, he ducked into a phone booth. After failing to get through, he rang up Richie DePalma's house in Queens and learned from his wife that John was dead. Hopping a cab, Fred took off for the Dakota.

Outside the gate he found a crowd of mourners listening to portable radios and wailing "Give Peace a Chance." In Studio One Richie was taking calls while Havadtoy paced the floor restlessly, complaining that Yoko would not receive him upstairs.

Soon Fred was summoned to Apartment 72. When he entered the kitchen, he found Yoko in a pink silk nightgown seated on a sofa with her head in her hands. She was flanked by David Geffen and Inspector Richard J. Nicastro, the Manhattan borough commander. The police official was trying to interrogate Yoko, but the only response she would make was to moan: "The shock is too great! I can't, I can't do this now!" Finally, she looked at Fred and told him to send up Havadtoy. When he received Yoko's summons, he practically ran to the service elevator.

After the departure of Inspector Nicastro, Yoko retired to her bedroom with Geffen and Havadtoy to focus upon her immediate problems. The first and most urgent task was making the funeral arrangements. John Lennon had anticipated receiving the customary rites, making provision for them in the first item of his will; yet only a few hours after his death, Yoko announced through Geffen that there would be no funeral—only a silent vigil to be held at a time set later.

Her next concern was the prompt execution of the will. After a night spent mostly making phone calls, she was up and about at seven o'clock, ready to meet with her lawyers and financial advisers. After she had conferred with them for some hours in Studio One, the will was sent down to the court district for probate that very afternoon. The will itself was a simple four-page document that had been drafted by David Warmflash and signed by Lennon about a year before he died, on 12 November 1979. It deeded to Yoko 50 percent of the estate, valued in excess of $30 million, and put the other 50 percent into a trust whose provisions did not have to be publicly declared. The trust makes some provision for John's children and perhaps even Kyoko, whom Yoko had always urged John to adopt, but what amounts the children were to receive and how the balance of the estate was allotted are matters only of rumor.* The only provision of the will that appears odd is the appointment of Sam Green—who was not even consulted about the matter—as Sean's guardian in the event that Yoko chose not to serve in this capacity.

If the public provisions of the will provided no cause for surprise, the disposition of John Lennon's body certainly did. Lennon had a horror of cremation, a practice that he inveighed against and that he once proposed to protest in a song. Despite his aversion, his widow arranged to have his body burned. She assigned the task to Douglas MacDougall, who had reported for duty within hours of the murder. The ex-FBI man employed a ruse reminiscent of the way the Beatles used to escape from concerts. After the body had been delivered in a station wagon to the Frank J. Campbell funeral chapel, where the stars

*Under American law, if a writer dies before the expiration of a twenty-eight-year copyright, the renewal right passes outside his will to certain stipulated heirs. Either the wife and the children share equally, or the wife receives 50 percent and the children divide the remainder in equal portions.

are usually laid out, MacDougall got a cremation certificate from the mortician. Then he sent an empty casket out to be loaded aboard a hearse. When the vehicle departed, all the reporters who had been hanging around the premises took off in pursuit. At that moment Mac-Dougall had the body loaded into another hearse, which sped north out of the city to the Ferncliff Mortuary in Hartsdale.

It was not until this time, on the afternoon of Wednesday, 10 December, that Helen Seaman finally broke the news of his father's death to Sean, Yoko having found it impossible to face this painful task. The five-year-old was highly disturbed by this barely comprehensible news. Instinctively he demanded to see his father one more time. When Helen relayed the child's request to Yoko, she buzzed Fred in the office and told him to ring up the crematorium and order them to hold off on the cremation until Sean could arrive. The call came too late.

That night MacDougall walked into Studio One, carrying a package about a foot high disguised by gay gift wrappings to fool those hanging around the Dakota. "What's that?" asked Fred Seaman.

"That," replied the security expert, "was the greatest rock musician in the world."

Fred felt a wave of nausea but said nothing. Next moment he buzzed Yoko.

"Bring the ashes upstairs," she ordered. Because Fred wouldn't touch the package, the delivery was made by Warmflash. Shortly afterward Fred was summoned to the bedroom, where he found Yoko on the phone.

When she signaled him to put the ashes under her bed, he broke into her conversation and announced: "I want a leave of absence."

Yoko, holding the phone under her chin, replied: "OK. I can see you're under a lot of strain. Take a little break, but don't do anything reckless."

While the world mourned, the Dakota hummed with fresh activity. Delegating to her staff and friends the responsibility for her child and other personal matters, Yoko dedicated herself night and day to her career. Virtually with his dying breath, John had given his wife the thing she most craved in the world: a shot at the top of the charts. Now it was up to her to make sure the shot told.

On Tuesday evening, less than twenty-four hours after Lennon was killed, Yoko slipped out of the Dakota to have supper with David Geffen, who brought along Calvin Klein and Steve Rubell, formerly manager of Studio 54, recently discharged from prison for income tax evasion. Seeking to avoid notice, they went, reportedly, to Harlem's Little Italy, dining at the Blue Book on East 116th Street. Geffen was in an exultant mood that night, as his behavior later at the Dakota demonstrated, when he boasted openly of the enormous amount of money he was making for Yoko. He had cause for rejoicing because Lennon's murder had transformed an album that dealers were already returning for credit into a sensational blockbuster that sold more than six million copies. And Geffen had insured John Lennon's life for a large sum of money when he signed him up.

Yoko had already come up with an audacious idea for hyping her new record to the top of the chart, but it all turned on the cooperation of Jack Douglas.

On Wednesday, when Douglas picked up his phone, on guard against a prankster, he had asked suspiciously, "Who's this?"

"It's Yoko" came the answer. "Go to the studio tonight. I've booked time. We're working."

"OK," intoned Jack resignedly. "I don't know what you have in mind, but I'll be there."

When he arrived, Yoko presented him with two reels of Lennon's conversation and another tape of David Spinozza playing classical guitar. She ordered Jack to cut up Lennon's speech and insert certain phrases into the flow of the music. Jack worked ten hours straight that night with the chain-smoking Yoko at his side. So deeply troubled was he that the tears sometimes coursed down his cheeks. The other people at the studio were so freaked out by the sound of Lennon's voice that they sealed off the tenth floor. Only Yoko appeared unaffected. As the work progressed, she would order, "Give it more of this!" or, "Give it that!" Douglas assumed that the tape was to be used during John's funeral service. In fact, it was destined to be the flip side of "Walking on Thin Ice." Yoko planned to give her record an extra boost by coupling it with a sentimental souvenir of the dead star.

That afternoon she had called up Spinozza for the first time in years. When he came on the line, the first thing he heard was Yoko saying, "Can you believe that! Can you believe that shit!"

Shocked by her tone, Spinozza had gasped: "Yoko! Are you OK?"

"I'm OK! I'm OK!" she snapped. A few days later they met to talk business. She offered him $100,000 for the track on which he played guitar, probably the highest fee ever earned by a studio musician.

During the night, while Jack was laboring over his editing console, Bob Ezra, producer of Pink Floyd, came into the booth. He asked Jack to meet him in the tape library. When they were alone, Ezra said: "Jack, get away from this woman. Believe me . . . she's gonna hurt you—or do something to you. She's using you all over the place." Next night, when Jack and Yoko resumed their work, Ezra told Douglas that there was a plane awaiting him at Butler Aviation, the private facility the rock stars use at La Guardia. All Jack had to do was get aboard and the plane would take him to a resort in Canada. Jack insisted on completing his task because he thought he was still serving Lennon.

Ezra proved a true prophet. In the spring Douglas discovered that Yoko was not going to pay him his royalties as coproducer of *Double Fantasy* (for which he and Yoko won a producer's Grammy) and most of the tracks on its sequel, *Milk and Honey*. When Douglas took her to court to obtain the $3.5 million to which he was entitled under the contract, Yoko testified that he had switched contracts on her and thereby gotten a far greater percentage than they had agreed upon. The jury refused to believe her testimony, awarding to Jack Douglas the full sum. But when Yoko threatened to drag out the case, which had been in process for years already, by filing an appeal, Douglas settled for a half million less.

Though Yoko, with her extraordinary fixity of purpose, was able to keep her mind firmly on her goals throughout the turbulent period following upon John's death, many of the other people at the Dakota fell prey to paranoid suspicions and fears that were heightened by sinister rumors, crazy threats, and the continual presence of armed bodyguards, for after ignoring Douglas MacDougall's advice before the killing, Yoko now went to the opposite extreme, demanding more protection than it made sense to have. In fact, the next time MacDougall was dismissed, the reason was that he had scoffed at Yoko's demand that Sean be surrounded by no fewer than four armed men every time he stepped out the door. Naturally, in such a negatively charged atmosphere, there was constant speculation about Lennon's murder, most of it turning on the possibility that Chapman might have been, as in *The Manchurian Candidate,* a brain-washed automaton in the employ of either some government agency or a personal enemy of Lennon.

The only thing that could have dispelled these fears and fantasies would have been a full-length report by the New York Police Department. The materials for such a report were actually compiled in the course of a lengthy investigation conducted in anticipation of Chapman's trial. Indeed, a particularly strong effort was made to clear up every doubt about the Lennon murder because according to former Detective Ron Hoffman, who spent six months on the case, the NYPD anticipated becoming the target for the same kind of criticism that had rained down on the police departments of Dallas and Memphis after the assassinations of John F. Kennedy and Martin Luther King, Jr. "We *knew* that when this case went to trial, no matter what happened, we were gonna be criticized for *years,* for *generations* to come," reported Hoffman. "We did our best. There was nothing too insignificant to go into. Nothing!"

Hoffman laid particular emphasis on the fact that the police did not confine themselves to investigating the murderer but sought to exhaust every conspiracy theory as well, for from the moment the murderer was identified, people began pointing to those aspects of his behavior or background that they found suspicious. Thus, it was noted that Chapman, married to the daughter of a native Japanese, had planned to kill Lennon on Pearl Harbor Day; that for an ill-paid security guard, he had a lot of money in his possession; and that his reported movements about the city before the crime suggested that he had connections in a place where, presumably, he knew no one. "Half the case was disproving the conspiracy theories," explained Hoffman, citing as prime targets of investigation: "Yoko's family, the Japanese angle, the Pearl Harbor theory."

Nothing was found to substantiate these suspicions. Even so, every long-distance call and credit card purchase by the Dakota was checked, and investigations were made of John Lennon's private life, including his sex habits and, presumably, his use of drugs. Nor was the work confined to New York. Detectives were dispatched to Atlanta and Honolulu to work up Chapman's history. Eventually two file drawers were stuffed with reports. In the light of this industry it seems odd that during the six years of intense research that formed the foundation for this book, virtually no one was found whom the police had interrogated closely, even among John Lennon's closest associates.

On 22 June 1981 Chapman, acting against the advice of his court-appointed attorney, suddenly pleaded guilty to murdering John Lennon. The surprise plea (it had been confidently expected that he would plead insanity) aborted the trial; there was simply a hearing and a sentencing, on 24 August, when the murderer was condemned to twenty years to life and incarcerated at Attica.

Thus the most notorious murder case in the recent history of New York City was buried in the files of the police department, where it remains to this day, inaccessible to Freedom of Information Act inquiries.

On Sunday, 14 December 1980, the world paid its final respects to John Winston Ono Lennon. A ten-minute vigil was held around the globe, commencing at 2:00 P.M. New York time. 100,000 people assembled in Central Park at the Bandshell on the Mall. As all normal radio and television broadcasting was suspended, millions of people watched this crowd thrusting splayed fingers into the air as "Give Peace a Chance" played through public-address speakers. Then an announcer exhorted the assembled thousands to pay strict heed to the request for ten minutes of silent meditation. But the vigil in the chill air was marred by the ominous droning of helicopters overhead, crammed with TV newsmen and binocular-wielding police spotters. The end of the ground silence was signaled by music of Bach. John would have preferred "Whiter Shade of Pale."

All through the weeks following John Lennon's assassination, the person who made himself most helpful to Yoko Ono was Sam Havadtoy. He virtually moved into the Dakota from the first night and remained there until the first of the year, working indefatigably on Yoko's behalf. When, for example, Julian Lennon arrived, Yoko assigned to Havadtoy the care of the boy, who later complained bitterly that Yoko had no time for him. Havadtoy was also useful in countless other ways, even going so far as to bring over from Budapest his mother, who cooked Yoko's Christmas dinner. In view of this dedicated service, it is odd that by the first of the year, when Fred Seaman reported back for duty, Havadtoy's name should have stood high on the "Enemy List."

The ostensible cause for his fall from grace was a bill he had presented to Yoko for $100,000. The size of the sum is explained by the extent of Havadtoy's services in months past, for not only was he still engaged in the renovation and decoration of Cannon Hill as well as Iron Gate, but all through the preceding summer and fall he had been supervising the renovation and redecoration of parts of Apartments 72 and 71. In any case, Yoko had challenged a number of items in the bill, and Havadtoy had threatened a lawsuit, which prompted Yoko to cut him off. This must have put him in a serious position financially, for virtually all his income was derived from the Lennons. In fact, on the day after John's death Havadtoy had shut down his gallery and dismissed the staff, explaining that with Lennon dead, there would not be enough money to continue operating as before. Yet at the same time that he was preparing himself for a financial squeeze, he purchased on 15 January 1981, according to New York City real estate records, two buildings at 1190 and 1192 Lexington Avenue around the corner from his brownstone. (Today a fourteen-story "splinter" building stands on the site, whose owner of record is Yoko Ono.) What makes this purchase all the more surprising is that it coincided with his banishment from the Dakota.

Havadtoy was dismayed by Yoko's behavior, but he kept imploring her to give him a hearing. Finally, on 2 February, he was granted an appointment. When he arrived at Studio One, he told Fred Seaman and Richie DePalma that he was disillusioned and depressed, vowing that he would never work for Yoko again, though he might consider acting as her escort, as he had been doing before he was ejected. When Fred took Sam upstairs to Apartment 72, Yoko greeted the decorator with a scolding. Somehow he appeased her, for when she phoned Richie DePalma at the conclusion of the meeting, she announced that

Havadtoy had been forgiven. The good news was received by the staff as the signal for a celebration, with everyone toasting Sam's "rehabilitation" in champagne.

Yoko's primary motive in taking Havadtoy back into the fold can be descried in the account in Seaman's journal of a meeting she conducted earlier that same day. As her people sat on the floor at her feet, Yoko had gone into a long rap, comparing John Lennon's death with that of John F. Kennedy. "In many ways John was more powerful than Kennedy," Yoko had explained, because "music is more pervasive than politics . . . it goes into people's living rooms, bedrooms, toilets." Yoko had gone on to compare herself with Jackie Kennedy, remarking that "Jackie at least had the Kennedy family to fall back upon for support, and later Onassis, but I have nobody. . . . I can still barely manage . . . the shock of John's death has made me very weak." Hence, it made good sense for Yoko to take back Havadtoy at this moment because after the dismissal of all her key men she desperately needed help.

That spring Havadtoy's position was enhanced further by Yoko's falling out with the man upon whom she had been building her hopes for a great career, David Geffen. After "Walking on Thin Ice" did better than any solo record in her entire career, Yoko had recorded and rushed into production a solo album titled *Season of Glass* that offered on its cover a photograph of Lennon's shattered and bloodstained glasses. She exhorted Geffen to hype the album to the top of the charts by any and every means. When he failed to do all she demanded, she filled the air of Studio One with denunciations of him, accusing the producer of making millions in "blood money" and then refusing to repay the favor she had shown him.

Once Geffen was out of the picture, Havadtoy became Yoko's principal lieutenant. Soon she was treating him just as she had done Tony Cox and Sam Green in years past. The relationship developed with characteristic rapidity, and in April, at Cold Spring Harbor, according to Luciano, Yoko and Sam became lovers. On 16 June they slipped out of New York, bound for Budapest. Ostensibly the purpose of this carefully concealed trip was to pay a visit to Sam's mother, but according to a source in the Hungarian press corps, Yoko and Sam were wed in Hungary. When the couple returned to New York, Sam Havadtoy moved into Apartment 72 and has resided there ever since.

On the day Havadtoy returned from Hungary, he appeared at Luciano's flat at 55th Street and Lexington, an apartment that had been rented for Luciano in May by Sam and Yoko. Looking his former lover squarely in the eye, Sam announced: "Luciano, do you realize that I am now a man?"

Outraged by the aspersion implied by this remark, Luciano snapped: "What were you before—*Tinker Bell*?"

Sam left, but as soon as he got back to the Dakota, he called Luciano to press home his point. "Luciano, you don't realize," he insisted. "This is the *natural* thing to do."

Luciano did not concur; he attributed Havadtoy's sudden involvement with Yoko not to nature but to financial expediency, musing bitterly: "What better solution than to help a very, very wealthy widow to whom he also owed money?"

For a long time Yoko concealed from the press the fact that she was living with Havadtoy, but then a discreet acknowledgment was made that Havadtoy was her "companion," a fact that could hardly be concealed as photographs of the couple walking in the park or attending public events multiplied in the press. For Yoko and Sam became as inseparable as Yoko and Tony or Yoko and John had been. Yet to this day the only references to marriage by either Sam or Yoko have been denials, Havadtoy going so far as to say that he has a document from the Hungarian government that proves he and Yoko were *not* married in that country. Obviously it was a very sensitive issue, for as gossip columnist Liz Smith remarked when confronted by the widespread rumor that Yoko and Sam were married, "It would be disastrous for her image."

Behind the thick walls of the Dakota, however, there was from the moment of Yoko's return from Budapest an abundance of evidence to the depth of her involvement with her new "companion." The first time Marnie saw her friend after that trip, Yoko displayed Sam's baby pictures, which she had received from his mother. Acting like a young bride, she declared that she was going to learn Hungarian and even master the native cuisine. Little Sean also observed unmistakable signs of the new intimacy. One day he told Marnie, "I have a new daddy." Marnie assured the boy that he was mistaken; his father was dead. "No, Marnie," Sean insisted, "Sam is sleeping with Mommy. I have a new daddy."

Sam Havadtoy, for his part, had a new image. Yoko had Sam dress up in John's clothes and wear his hair long like Lennon, an impersonation that shocked and embarrassed Yoko's neighbors at the Dakota, like Rudolf Nureyev, who exclaimed: "What is he wearing John's clothes for?" Yet, at the same time that Sam was becoming a Lennon clone, Yoko was treating him exactly as she had her most dedicated assistant, Tony Cox, whom Sam actually resembles from a distance. In fact, the effect of seeing Yoko on the street or in the park clutching Sam's arm as if she were in danger of falling, was like that of a weird double exposure—the image of Yoko and Sam superimposed on the image of Yoko and Tony.

Yet there was one area in which Sam imposed his will on Yoko: the decorating and management of their home, which changed radically once he was in residence. Instead of the affluent squalor so characteristic of New York's Upper Bohemia, the flat exhibited now the meticulous taste of an interior decorator. The floors were spotless, the dishes stacked neatly in the kitchen, a formal dining room was installed in what had been the Playroom, and the children were confined to their quarters. The most important change was in the sleeping arrangements. Now, instead of lying down for a couple of hours before dawn in her office or in Sean's room, Yoko could enjoy for the first time in a decade a luxurious bedroom.

By knocking together the Nursery and Library, Havadtoy contrived a thirty-foot chamber that appeared to have been covered by a fresh snowfall. The long-haired white fur rug echoed the white walls, white furniture, and white king-size bed raised on a platform with a futon. The large adjoining bathroom offered a color contrast, its walls being of dark blue smoked glass embellished with wisps of cloud, its furnishings, including a quadrangular tub big enough for three and a toilet on a dais, all in gold and amethyst.

Though Yoko enjoyed no further success as a recording artist after "Walking on Thin Ice," which was nominated for a Grammy (a belated tribute to Lennon's prowess as a producer), she succeeded much better at the more congenial task of promulgating her new image as a celebrity widow. Every month for years after John's death, an item would appear in the press or on a TV or radio show that informed the public of Yoko's current condition: her lasting grief, her withdrawn and lonely life, her widow's rituals, like cutting off a thirty-inch lock of hair, and her close and affectionate relationship with her son. Credited with being a master of public relations, Yoko owed much in this area to the labor of her dedicated and capable public spokesman, Elliot Mintz.

Mintz had arrived at the Dakota early on the morning after John's death, having jumped aboard the first flight out of L.A. the moment he heard the news. Like Havadtoy, he devoted himself night and day to Yoko's service, until finally he settled down to become her media jockey, a role for which he was ideally suited by virtue of both experience and temperament. He had already demonstrated his skills after the death of his friend Sal Mineo, when he intervened in what could have become an ugly and salacious postmortem of the star's reputation to clear the air by calling a press conference and making a series of media appearances that restored the Mineo image. Now he put the same abilities to work on behalf of Yoko, always being on deck—a bright, engaging little man, beautifully turned out—to lead the inquiring reporter through the staves of the Ballad of John and Yoko.

Testifying from his long and intimate acquaintance with the Lennons, Mintz would regale the press with tales of the deep and tender love that John and Yoko bore for each other and how they had led a life of calm contentment while John brought himself to the most perfect condition of mind and body during his years of retirement. When the themes of grief and bereavement began to wear thin, Yoko and Mintz modulated to the sad history of betrayal and treachery on the part of Yoko's most trusted employees and friends, an account that was written out at great length and endorsed by David Sheff in *Playboy*. Eventually the resourceful Mintz was called upon to counter the effects of the devastating disclosures made by May Pang and John Green in their book-length accounts of life with the Lennons.

Finally, Yoko assumed the role that she had always coveted: as a public benefactor. She donated funds to worthy causes and institutions, like Strawberry Fields, and undertook to relandscape the portion of Central Park nearest the Dakota, receiving in exchange for a donation of $1 million the honor of having this tract named Strawberry Fields. The dedication on 9 October 1985 was marked by a ceremony in which Yoko appeared side by side with Mayor Edward I. Koch and other city officials.

Though such moments of public glory must have been profoundly gratifying to a woman who had suffered so long and so acutely from a bad press, it was not the sole measure of Yoko's triumph. Equally important was the fact that the woman who doubted she would ever be happy now appeared to have found happiness. Sam Havadtoy was attentive to Yoko's slightest wish, indefatigable in executing her designs, good with Sean, and entirely content to remain in the background, even going so far as to get off a plane well behind Yoko so that he would not appear with her in photographs. When the couple were seen in the streets of New York, Yoko was always clutching Sam's arm, and when they were recognized in the stores, Yoko would be observed snapping her fingers and pointing to the item she wanted as Sam hastened to do her bidding.

Marnie Hair was one of the first to recognize that Yoko had finally found what she was seeking. Invited a year after John's death to a little midnight supper on Christmas Eve as Yoko and Sam's only guest, Marnie found her friend a different person. Yoko behaved with all the graciousness and charm of a woman of high breeding, preparing the feast with her own hands and feeding it to her guests with chopsticks. Sam presented Yoko with a beautiful pre-Columbian necklace that Yoko removed at one point in the evening and hung about Marnie's neck so that she, too, could share in the pleasure. "They were like puppies," Marnie enthuses. "They fondled each other. That was the happiest I had ever seen her. She was genuinely happy. She was joyous and young and tension-free. She wasn't taking anything either. She looked marvelous!"

SOURCES

The primary source for the life of John Lennon is the enormous amount of information he provided about his own character and history in the course of almost twenty years of continual scrutiny by the media. Out of this welter of tape and print, four major statements stand forth: a lengthy interview with the author of this book in December 1970, published in *Charlie*, June and July,1971; the interview of December 1970 conducted by Jann Wenner for *Rolling Stone*, published subsequently as *Lennon Remembers* (New York: Fawcett, 1972); the interview of August 1971 by Peter McCabe and Robert D. Schonfeld, published as *John Lennon: For the Record* (New York: Bantam, 1984); and the interviews conducted in the fall of 1980 by David Sheff, published as *The Playboy Interviews with John Lennon & Yoko Ono*, edited by G. Barry Golson (New York: Playboy, 1982).

The present biography was the product of six years of intense research conducted all around the world. As the goal was to recover everything that could be learned about three distinct themes, John Lennon, the Beatles, and Yoko Ono, the work had to be shared with a staff of research assistants, who conducted scores of interviews on the author's behalf, took photographs of local people and places, and rummaged through the available documents, particularly the national press of England, the United States, and Japan. Approximately 1,200 interviews were conductd in total, some subjects being interviewed over the years as many as thirty or forty times.

Second in importance to the interviews but indispensable for any writer are the previously published biographies, particularly the authorized version of the Beatles' lives and career, *The Beatles*, by Hunter Davies (New York: McGraw-Hill, 1968). This book was reviewed not just by the Beatles and their manager but also by their relatives, which resulted in the deletion of countless matters of interest and importance. Of lesser value is the two-volume account by Ray Coleman, *John Winston Lennon* and *John Ono Lennon* (London: Sidgwick & Jackson, 1984), which may be regarded as a semiofficial biography because it was written in cooperation with Lennon's two widows and reflects their points of view on matters of concern to them. Many of the crucial matters slighted in the official lives were put into the record by Peter Brown and his writer, Steven Gaines, in *The Love You Make* (New York: McGraw-Hill, 1983), which offers a full and fascinating account of Brian Epstein.

The most vivid and compelling accounts of Lennon as a personality are to be found in the memoirs of Pete Shotton, *John Lennon in My Life,* written with Nicholas Schaffner (New York: Stein & Day, 1983), and of May Pang, *Loving John,* written with Henry Edwards (New York: Warner Books, 1983). Both books suffer from their authors' infatuation with their subject, which forbids them to find fault with the man they love; but the abundance of intimate detail more than compensates for their special pleading. For the early history of the Beatles, two books are indispensable: Allan Williams's *The Man Who Gave the Beatles Away,* written with William Marshall (London: Hamish Hamilton, 1975), a delightfully pungent account of the Merseyside beat scene at its beginning, and Pete Best's *Beatle!,* written with Patrick Doncaster (London: Plexus, 1985), a sober, straightforward account that does not flinch when the going gets tough. The best treatment of the Beatles' recording career is George Martin with Jeremy Hornsby's *All You Need Is Ears* (New York: St. Martin's Press, 1980). The most thorough and thoughtful study of the Beatles' music is Wilfrid Meller's *Twilight of the Gods* (New York: Schirmer Books, 1973). The only reliable history of the group's career is provided by the exhaustively researched *The Beatles Live!* by Mark Lewisohn (London: Michael Joseph, 1986). The missing years at the end of Lennon's life are illuminated fitfully but amusingly in John Green's *Dakota Days* (New York: St. Martin's Press, 1983).

As it would be burdensome to the reader to cite the source for every statement not tagged in the text, the notes below are confined to identifying the principal sources used in the book, the names indicating, when not otherwise identified, tape-recorded interviews. Many of these people contributed information to more than one section of this book, but are listed only once to avoid needless repetition.

Childhood and Youth:

All the surviving members of the Stanley family were interviewed, including Lennon's aunts, Mrs. Mimi Smith and Mrs. Anne Cadwallader; his half-sisters, Mrs. Julia Bird and Jacqui Dykins; his first cousins, Stanley Parkes, Leila Harvey, M.D., Michael Cadwallader, and David Birch, and his uncle by marriage (to Harriet Stanley), Norman Birch. Further details were obtained from friends and neighbors, schoolmates and teachers. Mrs. Pauline Stone, formerly Mrs. Alfred Lennon, provided an abundance of information concerning her late husband's life drawn from her unpublished biography of Freddie, which is based in turn on his 125,000-word manuscript autobiography: this account was supplemented by Freddie's brother, Charles Lennon. Other sources include John Dykins's brother and sister-in-law, Leonard and Evelyn Dykins; his second wife, Mrs. Veronica (Rona) Parry; Meg Dogherty; Barbara Baker, and William Pobjoy. Several of the original Quarry Men—Rod Davies, Colin Hanton, Len Garry, and Nigel Whalley—plus Charles Roberts described the group's early days. Art college was the theme of interviews with Ann Mason, Helen Anderson, Ian Sharp, June Furlong, Arthur Ballard, Rod Murray. Thelma Pickles, Veronica Murphy, Adrian Henri, Mike Kenny, Sam Walsh, and Mike Evans. Cynthia Lennon declined to be interviewed, but she has recounted the history of her relationship with Lennon three times in print: in *A Twist of Lennon* (London: W. H. Allen, 1978) and in the books of Peter Brown and Ray Coleman.

The Early Beatles and Beatlemania:
The Mersey scene was the subject of interviews with Ted "Kingsize" Taylor, David May, Graham Nash, Morris Goldberg, Johnny Gentle, Tom Keyes, Pete Best, Barry Wormersley, Alec Payton, Ron Ellis, and Spencer Leigh. The Hamburg tenderloin is thoroughly described in F. H., Miller's *St. Pauli und die Reeperbahn*, (Hamburg, 1960); the city's daily life is best studied in the pages of the *Hamburger Abendblatt*. Other sources include Jürgen Vollmer, Dirk Vellenga. Tony Waine, Paddy Delaney, John Morris, Jim Gretty, Rosemary Evans, Brian O'Hara, Ida Holly, Rex Makin, Dick Rowe, Ron White, Dick James, Alan Davidson, Joe Flannery, Ricky Brooks, Maxine Brooks, Ron King, Walter Hofer, Keith Howell, Geoffrey Ellis, Brian Sommerville, Dezo Hoffmann, Wendy Hanson, Nicky Byrnes, Vivian Moynihan, Vic Lewis, Alun Owen, Walter Shenson, Unity Hall, Tommy Hanley, Sid Bernstein, Ed Leffler, Norman Weiss, Roy Gerber, Brian Morris, Les Anthony, Dot Jarlett, Ken Partridge, Geraldine Smith, Jenny Kee, Victor Lownes, Timothy Leary. For a fuller account of the Beatles' meeting with Elvis, see *Elvis* by Albert Goldman (New York: McGraw-Hill, 1982). For Lennon's relationship with Bob Dylan, see *Dylan* by Robert Spitz (New York: McGraw-Hill, 1988).

Yoko Ono:
As with Lennon, a principal source for Yoko's life is the large body of interviews that she has given to the press and electronic media in the United States, Europe, and Japan over a period of nearly thirty years, extending from the end of the Fifties down to the present day. The fullest and most satisfactory account of her childhook, however, is that of her mother, Isoko Ono, who was interviewed at length in 1981 by Donald Kirk, aided by Emiko Hayashi, who published their account in *The Ballad of John and Yoko* (Garden City, N.Y.: Doubleday, 1982). Another important source is *The Butterfly* by Michael Rumaker (New York: Charles Scribner, 1962). For Sarah Lawrence: Betty Rollin, Joanna Simon, Richard Rabkin, M.D., Meyer Kupperman. For the New York avant-garde of the late Fifties: John Cage, Merce Cunningham, La Monte Young, Diane Wakoski, David Tudor, Jackson Mac Low, Yvonne Rainer, Simone Forti, Ray Johnson, Henry Flynt, Carolee Schneeman, Charlotte Moorman, Hilda Morley Wolpe, Erica Abeel, Martin Garbus, and Shusaku Arakawa. Yoko's account of her return to Japan in 1962 was published in Japanese in the newspaper *Bungei Shunju* in Tokyo in 1974; Tony Cox's complementary narrative appeared in *Radix* (Berkeley, March/April 1981) and was supplemented by an interview with the author in 1984. Further sources for Tony Cox: his brother, Larry Cox; his aunt, Mrs. Blanche Greenberg; his cousin, Mrs. Frances Westerman-Collins; his closest friend, Al Wunderlich; Tony's girlfriend before Yoko, Linda Vivona; his mentor, La Monte Young; plus John Cage, Sam Wagstaff, and Russell Smith. The most exhaustive account of the early psychedelic underground of New York is Peter Stafford's unpublished collection of interviews with all the LSD pioneers, *Psychedelics 101*. Michael Hollingshead recounted his own career in *The Man Who Turned On the World* (London: Blond & Briggs, 1973). Further sources for Tony and Yoko: Mrs. Rutger Smith, Kate Millett, Jeff Perkins, Tanaka Kozo, Nam Jun Paik, Dan Richter, Ivan Karp, Paul Morrisey, Al Carmines, Bennett Sims, Ann McMillan, Mario Amaya, Whitey Caizza,

Yayoi Kusama, Jon Hendricks, David Bourdon, Jill Johnston, Adrian Morris, Peter Blake, Maggie Postelwaite, Michael White, and Kiki Kollekek.

Last Years of the Beatles, First Years of John and Yoko:
For *Sgt. Pepper* and the Summer of Love: Barry Miles, John Dunbar, Robert Fraser, Peter Blake. Medical data presented at the Brian Epstein inquest was evaluated for this book by Jay Meltzer, M.D., Mark Taff, M.D. (formerly of the Nassau County Medical Examiner's Office) and Jesse Bidanset, M.D., professor of forensic toxology at St. John's University Medical School. For the final phase of the Coxes' marriage: Bill Jacklin, Jodie Fridiani, Nicholas Logsdail, Victor Herbert, Ornette Coleman, Mrs. Pauline Stone, née Jones, Linda Moore, Jeff Buck. Lennon's encounter with Brigitte Bardot is described in *Bardot: Eternal Sex Goddess* by Peter Evans (Drake Publishers, 1972); additional details in *Fifty Years Adrift in an Open-Necked Suit* by Derek Taylor and George Harrison (Surrey, U.K.: Genesis Publications, 1985). For the Beatles' financial battles: interviews with Allen Klein and Harold Seider; the Northern Songs embroglio is recounted in great detail by financial reporter Stella Shamoon in *Apple to the Core* by Peter McCabe and Robert D. Schonfeld (London: Martin Brian & O'Keeffe, 1977).

John and Yoko in America, The Early Years:
John Brower, Howard Smith, Sarah Kernochan, Steve Gebhardt, Tom Basalari. Arthur Janov's history, personality, and therapeutic technique were described at length by Dr. George DeLeon, who evaluated *The Primal Scream* for publication and brought one of his own patients to Janov's clinic to study the effects of the treatment; further information was provided by Susan Braudy, formerly of *Newsweek,* who interviewed Janov and wrote about him with the aid of Martin Kasindorf's background reporting; Bobby Durst provided the point of view of a fellow patient, with Allen Klein and Harold Seider adding further details. For the first phase in New York: David Peel, Amalie Rothschild, Jonas Mekas, Lindsay Maricotta, Henry Edwards, Saul Swimmer, Al Steckler, Jill Johnston, May Pang, Iain Macmillan, Rosalyn and Sherman Drexler, Noah Slutsky, Alan Douglas, Ross Firestone. For the Everson show: Jim Haristhis, David Ross, Richard Bellamy, Alex Holstein, Philip Corner. For George Macuinas: Nijole Vailitis, Almus and Peter Salcius, Kevin Harrison. For the radical phase: Jerry Rubin (whose interview was supplemented with information from his *Growing (Up) at Thirty-Seven* [New York: M. Evans, 1976], A. J. Webberman, Stew Albert, John Sinclair, Craig Pyes, Ken Kelley, Leon Wildes, Adam Ippolito.

The Lost Weekend:
David Spinozza, Carole Realini, Arlene Reckson, Jesse Ed Davis, Ronnie Bennett, Larry Sloman, Judith Malina, Mack Rebbeneck, Frank Andrews and "Lil," one of the two people interviewed who requested that their identity not be disclosed (the other being "Kit Carter"). Most of John Green's circle was interviewed, including Wendy Wolosoff, Gabe Grumer, Kevin Sullivan, Joe Attardo, Felice Nathans, and Jeffrey Hunter. Dorothy DeChristopher provided information on Joey Lukach. Takashi Yoshikawa refused to be interviewed, but he has circulated the manuscript of a book, *How to Control Your Life by Understand-*

ing Ki-ology, that explains his system. Other sources for this period: Morris Levy, Alexa Grace, Cynthia Ross Desfugerido.

The Final Years:

Marnie Hair, Sam Green, John Green, Bob Herman, Fred Seaman, Ethelene Staley, Tom Sullivan, James Wu, Luciano Sparacino, Jack Douglas, Christine Desautels, Bart Gorin, Anthony Gronowicz, Donna Stilwell, Elliot Postel, Charles Cohen, Douglas MacDougall, Paul Goresh, Tony Palma, Ron Hoffman. Mark David Chapman was the subject of two biographers: Gregg Unger, an editor at *New York,* and Jim Gaines, an editor of *People.* Both published articles on Chapman at the time of his anticipated trial, and both interviewed him at length in prison, as well as investigating his family background, marriage, friends, and so forth. Unger abandoned his efforts to turn his material into a film and shared it with the author of this book; Gaines published his findings in *People* in 1987. Through a Freedom of Information inquiry, the author of this book was able to obtain most of the material in the file of the New York District Attorney.

INDEX